Kitab al Irshad
The Book of Spiritual Guidance

SHAYKH NURJAN MIRAHMADI

PUBLISHED BY THE
SUFI MEDITATION CENTER SOCIETY

Rising Sun of the West

Copyright © 2019

by Shaykh Nurjan Mirahmadi

ISBN: 978-1-989602-00-3

All rights reserved.

No part of this book may be used or

reproduced in any manner whatsoever

without written permission.

Published and Distributed by:

Sufi Meditation Center Society
3660 East Hastings
Vancouver, BC V5K 2A9 Canada
Tel: (604) 558-4455

nurmuhammad.com

Special thanks to the Publishing Team for making these books possible

Mrs. Amina K. ❧ Ms. Wida M. ❧ Mrs. Nadia H. ❧ Ms. Aumbrine K.
Mrs. Hafsa M. ❧ Mrs. Saira K.

First Edition: September 2019

TABLE OF CONTENTS

About the Author i
Universally Recognized Symbols vii

Reality of the Sun – Prophetic Light (Nur Muhammadi ﷺ) 1

   Peace and Heavenly Power Flow Through Fajr (Morning Prayer) 3

   Sun is the Source of Light; Be Like a Moon and
   Reflect the Light..29

   The Universe Within – The Sun (Heart), The Moon (Face),
   and 11 Planets (Essential Organs)...57

   Open the Sun Within Your Heart, Allah ﷻ Will Fill It With
   Heavenly Power 81

Reality of Stars – Sahabi (Holy Companions) 109

   The Star of Prophet Muhammad ﷺ...................................... 111

   Secrets of the Star and Guidance to Enlightenment....................... 143

   The Heart is the Sun, The Face is the Moon 157

   3 Points of Upper Star – Islam, Iman, Ihsan
   Opening Your Vision... 181

   3 Points of Lower Star 666 Dajjal – Material Desires 197

   Six Powers of the Heart and Reality of Star................................. 215

   How a Star is Born – Perfection Through Powers of the Heart ... 241

   Two Faces of the Moon and the Sun of Creation
   Reality of Hijrah and The Cave 267

Reality of the Moon – Ulul Amr (Saints) 301

   Who Are the Moons of the Nation?
   Rashideen, Mahdiyeen, Kamileen 303

Full Moons – Qamarun – Rashideen, Mahdiyeen, Kamileen 325

Follow the Perfected Muhammadan Guides,
Rashideen, Mahdiyeen, Kamileen 353

The Light of the Sun Burns All Impurities 375

The Face of the Shaykh Has Authority and Power 395

The Moon Doesn't Overtake the Sun (YaSeen 36:40) 415

Illuminate the Eternal Light Within the Heart, Not the Light
of the Brain (YaSeen 36:68 & 16:70) 441

Follow the Full Moons 461

Be the Moon and Follow the Sun –
Even If You Are Nabi Musa ﷺ 463

Seek Out the Full Moons of Guidance –
Secret of Juzba (Magnetism) 487

How to Accompany 'Ibadullah – Whom Allah ﷻ Has Taught 511

Fulfill Your Trust (Amanat), Covenant ('Ahd), and
Your Allegiance (Bayah) 535

Empty Your Cup, "I Wish I Was a Thing Forgotten"
(Holy Qur'an, 19:23) 557

ABOUT THE AUTHOR

PROFILE

For the past two decades, Shaykh Nurjan Mirahmadi has worked hard to spread the true Islamic teachings of love, acceptance, respect and peace throughout the world and opposes extremism in all its forms. An expert on Islamic spirituality, he has studied with some of the world's leading Islamic scholars of our time.

Shaykh Mirahmadi has also founded numerous educational and charitable organizations. He has travelled extensively throughout the world learning and teaching Islamic meditation and healing, understanding the channeling of Divine energy, discipline of the self, and the process of self-realization. He teaches these spiritual arts to groups around the world, regardless of religious denomination.

BACKGROUND

Shaykh Nurjan Mirahmadi studied Business Management at the University of Southern California. He then established and managed a successful healthcare company and imaging centers throughout Southern California. Having achieved business success at a remarkably young age, Shaykh Nurjan Mirahmadi shifted his focus from the private sector to the world of spirituality. In 1994 he pursued his religious studies and devoted himself to be of service to those in need. He combined his personal drive and financial talents to work for the less fortunate and founded an international relief organization, a spiritual healing center, and a religious social group for at risk youth.

In 1995, he became a protégé of Mawlana Shaykh Hisham Kabbani for in-depth studies in Islamic spirituality known as Sufism. He studied and accompanied Shaykh Kabbani on many tours and learned about Sufi practices around the world. Together with Shaykh Kabbani, he has established a number of other Islamic educational organizations and relief programs throughout the world.

Shaykh Nurjan Mirahmadi has received written *ijazas* (authorization) to be a Spiritual guide, from two of the World Leaders of the Naqshbandi Sufi Order; Sultan al-Awliya Shaykh Muhammad Nazim al-Haqqani ق and Mawlana Shaykh Muhammad Hisham Kabbani. He is authorized to teach, guide, and counsel religious students around the world to Islamic Spirituality.

IJAZAS (AUTHORIZATION)

Shaykh Nurjan Mirahmadi has taught and travelled extensively throughout the world from Uzbekistan to Singapore, Thailand, Indonesia, Cyprus, Argentina, Peru, and North America. He teaches the spiritual sciences of Classical Islam, including meditation *(tafakkur)*, subtle energy points *(lataif)*, Islamic healing, the secrets of letters and numbers *(ilm huroof)*, disciplining the self *(tarbiya)*, and the process of self-realization *(ma'rifah)*. He teaches the Muslim communities the prophetic ways of being kind, respectful and live in harmony with people. He emphasizes on good manners and respect, and often reminds his students that the spiritual journey begins from within and "You can't give what you don't have."

ACCOMPLISHMENTS

One of Shaykh Nurjan's greatest accomplishments has been the worldwide dissemination of the spiritual teachings of Classical Islam through his books and online presence. The Prophet Muhammad ﷺ has told us, "Speak to people according to their levels." In an era of social media, Shaykh Nurjan's ability to reach a new generation of spiritual seekers through the Internet has been remarkable. His *NurMuhammad.com* website alone has over 1,500 unique visitors each day, and since its inception has seen more than 200,000 downloads of the book *"Dailal Khairat"*, 1.5 Million free downloads of *Naqshbandi Muraqabah*, and another 700,000 downloads of the *Naqshbandi Book of Devotions (Awrad)*, as well as many more articles. His Facebook pages "Shaykh Nurjan Mirahmadi" and "Nur Muhammad" combined have over 1.1 million followers. Furthermore, his YouTube Channel, "The Muhammadan Way" has 3.5 million views, and his Google page, "Shaykh Sayed Nurjan Mirahmadi" has over 2.7 million views.

Shaykh Nurjan Mirahmadi focuses on the worldwide social media presence working on ways to bring knowledge to all seekers around the world. In 2015 he launched an Online University, called "SimplyIman.org", to spread these traditional Spiritual Islamic teachings even further and make it accessible to all seekers around the world.

For over 20 years Shaykh Nurjan has dedicated his life to spreading the true Islamic teachings of love, acceptance, respect and peace. He has established several non-profit organizations since the early 1990s and, over the past decade, he has founded numerous educational and charitable organizations. In the Greater Vancouver region alone, he has established the following:

Divine Love: Hub-E-Rasul TV Series – launched in May 2017, this weekly half-hour Islamic television show covers a wide range of topics, focusing on spreading Prophet Muhammad's ﷺ message that Islam is a religion based on peace, love, and acceptance.

The show airs every Saturday at 1:30 pm (PST) on Joytv, reaching 7 million viewers Canada-wide. It reaches the online community through social media and through its website **huberasul.net**. For a full channel listing please visit **www.huberasul.net/schedule**.

Muhummadan Way App (Over 20,000 Users Worldwide) – a comprehensive resource of Islamic information for all mobile devices. Created for both Muslims and non-Muslims, it provides users with a wealth of knowledge including access to books, supplications, prayer times, month-specific practices, a media library of audio and video files, an events calendar, and much more.

Ahle Sunnah wal Jama of BC – this organization is a resource for authentic content, books, and articles from the Qur'an & Sunnah from around the world. It works in collaboration with the well-known international organizations, Al Azhar University of Cairo, Dar al Ifta of Egypt and Islamic Supreme Council of North America.

Hub-E-Rasul ﷺ Conference – monthly Mawlid & Mehfil-e-Dhikr events are organized and held throughout the Lower Mainland. The aim is to revive the teachings of the Qur'an and *Sunnah* by celebrating holy events in true Islamic spirit *(Isra wal Mi'raj, Lailatul Bara'h, Lailatul Qadr, Mawlid an-Nabi* etc.)

Naqshbandi Islamic Center of Vancouver – this Center is a place for people of all faiths and beliefs to attend weekly *zikr* programs (circles of remembrance) three times a week (Thursdays, Fridays, and Saturdays). Shaykh Nurjan teaches above and beyond the principles of Islam including the deep realities of *maqam al-iman* (belief) and *maqam al-ihsan* (excellence of character).

SMC – an outreach organization that spreads teachings to the Western audience including concepts such as meditation and charity. It reaches out to other faiths to increase peace, love, and acceptance in the interfaith environment.

Simply Iman Cloud University – an international online platform allowing people from around the world to pursue studies in various aspects of faith and spirituality from a classical Islamic perspective. Students have the opportunity to learn at their own pace and engage in an open dialogue with a teacher in real-time.

Fatima Zahra Helping Hand – this charity organization runs a food program every two weeks which feeds more than 500 less fortunate people in the downtown eastside of Vancouver. It also collects clothing and non-perishable food items for the BC Muslim Food Bank and the Burnaby Homeless Shelter.

Shaykh Nurjan's Published Books – these titles are available at all major retailers and online.

- YASEEN – Prophet ﷺ is the Walking Qur'an
- Divinely Praising Upon the Pearl of Creation
- In Pursuit of Angelic Power
- Levels of the Heart – Lataif al Qalb
- Secret Realities of Hajj
- The Healing Power of Sufi Meditation

Shaykh Nurjan has established an international presence through many social media outlets including:

- FaceBook **(Shaykh Nurjan Mirahmadi)** with over 1.1 million followers
- YouTube Channels
  - **The Muhummadan Way** – 3.5 million views with over 800 videos
  - **Divine Love: Hub-E-Rasul** – based on the acclaimed TV series with over 27,000 views and 173 videos
  - **Shaykh Talks** – video series of short, powerful talks focusing on Spiritual Reminders and Motivational Topics
- **NurMuhammad.com,** a comprehensive website containing many resources covering the deep realities of classical Islam.

Shaykh Nurjan's sincere mission is to spread the love of Sayyidina Muhammad ﷺ throughout the city for our families and children. If you would like to be a shareholder in all these blessings, we invite you to support our Center by any means possible. We hope to strengthen our efforts by joining our hands in raising the Honourable Flag of Sayyidina Muhammad ﷺ.

UNIVERSALLY RECOGNIZED SYMBOLS

The following Arabic and English symbols connote sacredness and are universally recognized by Muslims:

The symbol ﷻ represents *Azza wa Jal*, a high form of praise reserved for God alone, which is customarily recited after reading or pronouncing the common name Allah, and any of the ninety-nine Islamic Holy Names of God.

The symbol ﷺ represents *sall Allahu 'alayhi wa salaam* (Short Form: *saws*) (God's blessings and greetings of peace be upon the Prophet), which is customarily recited after reading or pronouncing the holy name of the Prophet Muhammad ﷺ. It commonly appears as *pbuh* (peace be upon him) in English translations.

The symbol ؑ represents *'alayhi 's-salam* (peace be upon him/her), which is customarily recited after reading or pronouncing the sanctified names of prophets, Prophet Muhammad's ﷺ family members, and the angels.

The symbol ؓ represents *radi-allahu 'anh/ 'anha* (may God be pleased with him/her), which is customarily recited after reading or pronouncing the holy names of Prophet Muhammad's ﷺ Companions.

The symbol ق represents *qaddas-allahu sirrah* (may God sanctify his or her secret), which is customarily recited after reading or pronouncing the name of a saint.

REALITY of the SUN

PROPHETIC LIGHT
NUR MUHAMMADI ﷺ

ALLAH'S APOSTLE SAID, "THE HOUR WILL NOT BE ESTABLISHED UNTIL THE SUN RISES FROM THE WEST AND WHEN THE PEOPLE SEE IT, THEN WHOEVER WILL BE LIVING ON THE SURFACE OF THE EARTH WILL HAVE FAITH, AND THAT IS (THE TIME) WHEN NO GOOD WILL IT DO TO A SOUL TO BELIEVE THEN, IF IT BELIEVED NOT BEFORE."

— AL BUKHARI (4535) AL MUSLIM (157)

Peace and Heavenly Power Flow Through Fajr (Morning Prayer)
'Salaamun Hiya' (97:5)

سَلَامٌ هِيَ حَتَّىٰ مَطْلَعِ الْفَجْرِ ﴿٥﴾

97:5 – *"Salaamun hiya hattaa mat la'il fajr."* (Surat Al-Qadr)

"Peace it is until the emergence of dawn." (The Power, 97:5)

Muhammadan Guides Have Heavenly Authority

A'udhu billahi minash shairanir Rajeem, Bismillahir Rahmanir Raheem, "Atiullaha wa atiur Rasula wa Ulil amre minkum..." (Obey Allah, Obey the Messenger, and those in authority among you).

...أَطِيعُوا اللَّهَ وَأَطِيعُوا الرَّسُولَ وَأُولِي الْأَمْرِ مِنْكُمْ... ﴿٥٩﴾

4:59 – *"...Atiullaha wa atiur Rasula wa Ulil amre minkum..."* (Surat An-Nisa)

"... Obey Allah, Obey the Messenger, and those in authority among you..." (The Women, 4:59)

Alhamdulillah, from their knowledges and from their hearts; that Allah ﷻ sends to the reality of Prophet ﷺ and Prophet ﷺ sends to the *ulul amr* (saints). The *ulul amr* whom are real and sincere, whom Allah ﷻ has granted what Allah ﷻ wants to grant. Their authority is from the Heavens. There are *ulul amr* (those in authority) of *dunya*

(material world) who are authorized by *dunya* people and they authorize each other. And there are those who are authorized by the Heavens. And *alhamdulillah*, that Allah ﷻ granted us a tremendous *ni'mat* (blessing) to be from them, to be following them, Sultan al-Awliya Mawlana ق. Allah ﷻ sanctify their secret and raise their *darajats* (stations) infinitely higher.

Our Journey Starts With Shari'ah (Divine Law, Natural Law of Creation)

In these days of difficulty and hardship that we ask that Allah ﷻ dress us. A reminder for us is from Surat Al-Qadr (Chapter 97, Holy Qur'an), where Allah ﷻ is granting from the oceans of Divinely Power. In everything there are levels of knowledge. They have the level of *shari'ah* (Islamic Jurisprudence), and cause and effect that governs the physical world, the world of form.

Tariqah (Spiritual Path) is the Way to Reach Divinely Realities

Ilm at-Tariqah (spiritual path) that Allah ﷻ grants to those who are taking a path. They are on *"tawasaw bil haqqi wa tawasaw bi sabr."*

إِنَّ الْإِنسَانَ لَفِي خُسْرٍ ﴿٢﴾ إِلَّا الَّذِينَ آمَنُوا وَعَمِلُوا الصَّالِحَاتِ وَتَوَاصَوْا بِالْحَقِّ وَتَوَاصَوْا بِالصَّبْرِ ﴿٣﴾

103:2-3 – "Innal insaana lafee khusr (2) Illal ladheena aamano wa 'amilos saalihaati, wa tawasaw bil haqqi wa tawasaw bis Sabr. (3)" (Surat Al-Asr)

"Verily, Mankind is in loss. (2) Except for those who have believed and done righteous deeds and advised each other to truth and advised each other to patience. (3)" (The Declining Day, 103:2-3)

They are on a path of *haqq* (truth) to reach towards realities. They are making an ascension. When Allah ﷻ is saying that the people of *tafakkur* (contemplation) know (Holy Qur'an, 45:13), the people of the door, *ulul baab* know (Holy Qur'an, 2:269), the people of understanding know, that have you ascended and made your ascension? It means those who struggle and strive against themselves and against their bad character, Allah ﷻ grants them a level deeper than the *shari'ah* (Divine Law), which is based off the *shari'ah*. Then it's the knowledge of *tariqah* (spiritual path).

يُؤْتِي الْحِكْمَةَ مَن يَشَاءُ ۚ وَمَن يُؤْتَ الْحِكْمَةَ فَقَدْ أُوتِيَ خَيْرًا كَثِيرًا ۗ وَمَا يَذَّكَّرُ إِلَّا أُولُو الْأَلْبَابِ ﴿٢٦٩﴾

2:269 – "Yu'til Hikmata mai yasha o; wa mai yutal Hikmata faqad otiya khairan kaseeraa; wa maa yazzakkaru illaa ulul albaab." (Surat Al-Baqarah)

"He gives wisdom to whom He wills, and whoever has been given wisdom has certainly been given abundant goodness. And none will remember except the People of the door." (The Cow, 2:269)

The Levels of Knowledge in the Reality of a Circle

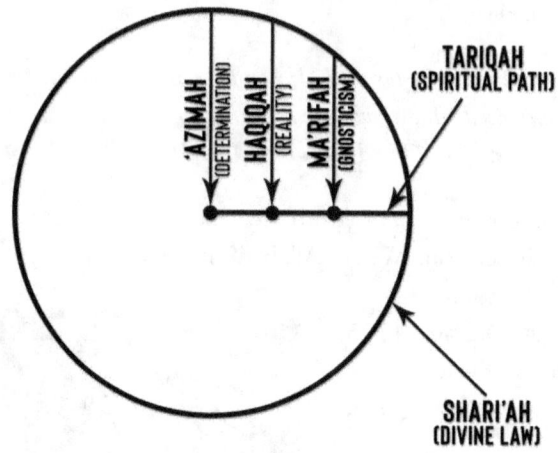

1. Shari'ah (Divine Law)

From the knowledge of the *tariq* (way) and the way towards the *ma'rifah* (gnosticism) of Allah, it becomes like the circle, which is *shari'ah* (Divine Law) that governs everything.

2. Tariqah (Spiritual Path)

There is the radius from every point of the circumference to the center, which is the center of power. The nucleus is the center of power that emanates through all the circumference. Every *'izzat*, every reality, once we understand just one circle, then every reality will begin to unfold. That the knowledge of *shari'ah*, *tariqah*, and *ma'rifah*.

3. Ma'rifah (Gnosticism)

Those who are taking a path on each step of that *tariq* (path) can go deeper into the oceans of *ma'rifah* (gnosticism). Those who are gnostics in the way of Allah, it means they have been dressed by *shari'ah* (Divine Law). Then Allah is granting them the knowledge of *tariqah* (spiritual path). Then from the knowledge of *tariqah* granting them the knowledges of *ma'rifah* (gnosticism).

4. Haqiqah (Reality)

From the knowledges of *ma'rifah* (gnosticism), they are now granting as they are drawing closer to the realities. They are now granting them *haqiqah;* the *haqqaiq,* the truth of that reality, like the essence of that reality.

5. 'Azimah (Determination)

Then the knowledge of *'Azimah*; that they are so close to the center of the Divinely Presence, the Divinely Kingdom, that Allah ﷻ is granting them the knowledge of *'Azimah* and its magnificence and munificence.

Surat al Lailatul Qadr (Night of Power)

From the understandings of difficulty that is coming onto *dunya* (material world), that is a tremendous power in Surat al-Qadr (Power).

إِنَّا أَنزَلْنَاهُ فِي لَيْلَةِ الْقَدْرِ ﴿١﴾ وَمَا أَدْرَاكَ مَا لَيْلَةُ الْقَدْرِ ﴿٢﴾ لَيْلَةُ الْقَدْرِ خَيْرٌ مِّنْ أَلْفِ شَهْرٍ ﴿٣﴾ تَنَزَّلُ الْمَلَائِكَةُ وَالرُّوحُ فِيهَا بِإِذْنِ رَبِّهِم مِّن كُلِّ أَمْرٍ ﴿٤﴾ سَلَامٌ هِيَ حَتَّىٰ مَطْلَعِ الْفَجْرِ ﴿٥﴾

97:1-5 – "Innaa anzalnaahu fee lailatil qadr. (1) Wa maa adraaka ma lailatul qadr (2) Lailatul qadri khairum min alfee shahr. (3) Tanaz zalul malaa-ikatu war roohu feeha bi izni-rab bihim min kulli amr. (4) Salaamun hiya hattaa mat la'il fajr. (5)" (Surat Al-Qadr)

"We have brought it down on the night of power. (1) And what will explain to you what the night of power is? (2) The Night of Decree is better than a thousand months. (3) The angels and the Spirit descend therein by permission of their Lord for every Command/affair. (4) Peace it is until the emergence of dawn. (5)" (The Power, 97:1-5)

Allah ﷻ is describing that the *Lailatul Qadr* (Night of Power), 'We indeed revealed this Message on a Night of Power. What will explain to thee what is the night of Power? The night of Power is better than a thousand months. Therein come down the angels and the Spirit by Allah's ﷻ permission, on every order coming by that authority and reality. And there is peace until the rising of the morning.' "*Salaamun hiya hatta matla il-Fajr*" (Holy Qur'an, 97:5).

The Power of the Sun

This diagram is going to give us an understanding of the *shams* (sun) and the power Allah ﷻ is granting to a sun. So, you look at the sun. For us just to understand, because realities are difficult to convey without some sort of visual, that they want us to perceive. To be dressed by a *qadr* (power), to be dressed by Allah's ﷻ *Rida* (satisfaction), to be dressed by protection in days of difficulty, more protection is needed; more understanding is needed.

We start with "*kulli amr*", that every "*malaikati war ruhfiha bi idhni rabbihim*" (The angels and the Spirit descend therein by permission of their Lord, Holy Qur'an, 97:4).

تَنَزَّلُ الْمَلَائِكَةُ وَالرُّوحُ فِيهَا بِإِذْنِ رَبِّهِم مِّن كُلِّ أَمْرٍ ﴿٤﴾

97:4 – *"Tanazzalul malaikaatu war Roh, fiha beizne Rabbihim min kulle amr."* (*Surat Al-Qadr*)

"The angels and the Spirit descend therein by permission of their Lord for every Command/affair." (The Power 97:4)

The Sun is a Sign of Eternity

If you make the circle of the sun as an example, because the sun for us is a reality of eternity. The sun for our understanding because Allah ﷻ teaches, 'I will show you upon the horizon and then upon yourself.'

سَنُرِيهِمْ آيَاتِنَا فِي الْآفَاقِ وَفِي أَنفُسِهِمْ حَتَّىٰ يَتَبَيَّنَ لَهُمْ أَنَّهُ الْحَقُّ... ﴿٥٣﴾

41:53 – *"Sanureehim Aayaatinaa fil aafaaqi wa feee anfusihim hattaa yatabaiyana lahum annahul haqq…"* (*Surat Al-Fussilat*)

"Soon will We show them our Signs in the (furthest) regions (of the earth), and in their own souls, until it becomes manifest to them that this is the Truth…" (Explained in Detail, 41:53)

The signs upon yourself is going to be much more complicated. To understand the horizon, that which is eternal around us is the sun. It has been there from the time of Sayyidina Adam ﷺ. Every prophet has seen that sun. So, for us to understand eternity, it is the *shams* (sun). That is why we say *Shams al-Arifeen* (the Sun of all Knowers). *Shams an-Nabiyin* ﷺ means the sun of all the prophets. S-U-N, not S-O-N. It means the eternal authority, power and *qudra* of that reality.

Then Allah ﷻ is describing every angel and the *ruh* (soul), with the permission of Allah ﷻ is descending upon you with every *amr* (command). Every *amr* has to do with every order, every command. For us to understand now just the *Shari'ah* level of the sun.

$$ تَنَزَّلُ الْمَلَائِكَةُ وَالرُّوحُ فِيهَا بِإِذْنِ رَبِّهِم مِّن كُلِّ أَمْرٍ ﴿٤﴾ $$

97:4 – "Tanazzalul malaikatu war Roh, fiha beizne Rabbihim min kulle amr." (Surat Al-Qadr)

"The angels and the Spirit descend therein by permission of their Lord for every Command/affair."
(The Power 97:4)

We Can Live on Earth Because of Our Proximity to the Sun

The power that Allah is dressing is a symbol of Allah's *Qadr*. So, He says, in My *Qadr* (Power), in that sun, every order is moving through that sun because you still probably don't know the importance of the sun in your existence. But once we study just a little bit about the sun, you breathe from the sun and you can see from the sun. You have warmth and life on this planet, because of our proximity to the sun. If Allah puts you on the moon you would be frozen, or you would have been cooked at 250 degrees. So, the Earth is precisely positioned for a life and an existence on this Earth and it is nourished by the power of that sun.

'Kulli Amr' (All Divinely Commands) Move Through the Sun of Realities

What they found that you put in that Sun *"kulli amr"* is that every *amr*, every order of Allah, is emanating through that sun, if you look at this diagram. That order and the *ruh* has to do with the secret of Sayyidina Muhammad's ﷺ light. Everything is from Prophet's ﷺ light. The *malaika* (angels) carry the orders from the Divinely Presence as the purified lights, the purified souls. They don't make up, they don't deviate, they don't go left, they don't go right.

So, Allah's ﷻ *'Izzat*, Allah's ﷻ Command, *atiullah*, comes to Prophet ﷺ, the *ati ar Rasul*. From Prophet ﷺ to *ulul amr*, they are amongst the *ulul amr* – the people of the *amr*, of the conveyance, of the orders. Every order of Allah ﷻ is moving through that sun.

﴿...يَاأَيُّهَا الَّذِينَ آمَنُوا أَطِيعُواللَّهَ وَأَطِيعُوالرَّسُولَ وَأُولِي الْأَمْرِ مِنكُمْ...﴾ ٥٩

4:59 – "...*Ya ayyu hal latheena amanoo Atiullaha wa atiur Rasula wa Ulil amre minkum...*" (Surat An-Nisa)

"...*O You who have believed, Obey Allah, Obey the Messenger, and those in authority among you...*" (The Women, 4:59)

Photons of the Sun are Malaika Reaching the Farthest Planet in the Galaxy

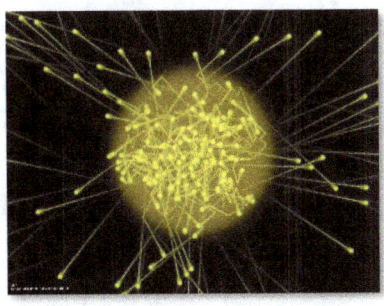

It means then on the *shari'ah* (Divine Law) level, they begin to teach us that everything that is coming from that sun are *malaika* (angels) with authorities from Allah ﷻ. So, when they began to study the sun, they saw that there was a photon inside the sun. There is a light inside the sun that penetrates everything. They went deep into the Earth, fifty miles underground and they said there was a photon there. They went out to the outer planets with satellites and they said the photons of our sun for this galaxy reaches the farthest levels of the planets. *Kulli amr* (all commands), Allah says that My Power, My *'Izzat* with *malaika* (angels) and the authority of the *ruh*, means there is a reality from Prophet giving command to those *malaika* (angels) that deliver Allah's order.

تَنَزَّلُ الْمَلَائِكَةُ وَالرُّوحُ فِيهَا بِإِذْنِ رَبِّهِم مِّن كُلِّ أَمْرٍ ﴿٤﴾

97:4 – *"Tanazzalul malaikatu war Roh, fiha beizne Rabbihim min kulle amr." (Surat Al-Qadr)*

"The angels and the Spirit descend therein by permission of their Lord for every Command/affair." (The Power 97:4)

Malaika (Angels) Carry the Amr and Nourish All Galaxies

They found that all your nourishment, what is coming to you of your sight, your breath, the plants; everything is in need of the photon. It

means in need of Allah's *malaika*. These angels are carrying every command all the way to the farthest planet of that galaxy and each sun is filled with its angels with an authority from the *ruh*. It's nourishing the galaxy that Allah has put under its command. It means every angel is being dispersed, that the flower on this Earth it requires your ray, and the angel will reach to that flower exactly the way Allah wants it.

Everything is nourished and everything is in the best of *hisaab* (account). It can't be random. There is no randomness. That Allah ﷻ gives a command and that angel's ray is responsible to hit that flower, to hit that human, to hit that mountain, wherever it is supposed to go and to nourish what Allah ﷻ wants it to nourish. It moves precisely.

لِيَعْلَمَ أَن قَدْ أَبْلَغُوا رِسَالَاتِ رَبِّهِمْ وَأَحَاطَ بِمَا لَدَيْهِمْ وَأَحْصَىٰ كُلَّ شَيْءٍ عَدَدًا ﴿٢٨﴾

72:28 – *"Liya'lama an qad ablaghoo risalati rabbihim wa ahata bima ladayhim wa ahsa kulla shay in 'adada."* (Surat Al-Jinn)

"That He may know that they have conveyed the messages of their Lord; and He has encompassed whatever is with them and has enumerated all things in number." (The Jinn, 72:28)

Salatul Fajr (Morning Prayer) is Full of Allah's ﷻ Peace and Mercy

Malaika bring *salaamun* (peace). At *Shari'ah* level of *salaamun*, it brings *salaamun*, brings peace to everything. This is Allah's ﷻ *ni'mat* (blessing). It brings peace. It brings reality and tranquility. It brings the secret of *hayat* and eternity, life and oceans of ever-living and ever-existing coming from these rays with the *salaamun*.

Peace and Heavenly Power Flow Through Fajr (Morning Prayer)

$$ سَلَامٌ هِيَ حَتَّىٰ مَطْلَعِ الْفَجْرِ ﴿٥﴾ $$

97:5 – *"Salamun, hiya hatta matla'il Fajr."* (Surat Al-Qadr)

"Peace it is until the emergence of dawn." (The Power, 97:5)

That *salaamun* dresses everything. So then, there are so many poetries and *nasheeds* (praisings) about the morning dew. How Allah ﷻ feeds everything in that morning. At night, it looks like it is dying. Everything is frightened. As soon as the *Fajr* (morning prayer) is rising, there is water, there are drops on flowers. There is a condensation taking place as Allah ﷻ is sending *salaams*. Allah ﷻ is sending a *rahmah* (mercy) upon this Creation that it has and produces a dew, a water, a life-force that nourishes it, until the  rays begin to come and dress it and bless it. Even if you don't see the sun, its rays are penetrating everything.

Shari'ah (Divine Law) Shows That Allah ﷻ Governs the World

So then that *salaam* (peace) is coming, the *"hiya"* is in reference to the power that Allah ﷻ is bringing upon the Earth. So, the *Shari'ah* level is for us to understand that,  *'Ya Rabbi*, this power, this *"izzat* that You have dressed everywhere in the world of form is under Your *Shari'ah.'* *Shari'ah* (Divine Law) is that what governs in the world of form. That sun can't go anywhere; it is directly and precisely where Allah ﷻ wants it. It's governed by Allah's ﷻ *'Izzat* (Might).

الشَّمْسُ وَالْقَمَرُ بِحُسْبَانٍ ﴿٥﴾

55:5 – "Ash Shamsu wal Qamaru bihusban."
(Surat Ar-Rahman)

"The sun and the moon [move] on their fixed courses by precise calculation." (The Beneficent, 55:5)

So, the world of form is showing and Allah ﷻ is showing that from this world of form, I have given this power and this authority to what it represents. Within the rays of that sun, why it nourishes and why it penetrates everything is because I am telling you that the angels and the *ruh* are coming with all My *Amr*. It is a station of Allah's ﷻ *Amr* (command). For us to understand, they are coming with every command upon that Creation and nourishing and performing everything that I am asking of it, precise.

تَنَزَّلُ الْمَلَائِكَةُ وَالرُّوحُ فِيهَا بِإِذْنِ رَبِّهِم مِّن كُلِّ أَمْرٍ ﴿٤﴾

97:4 – "Tanazzalul malaikatu war Roh, fiha beizne Rabbihim min kulle amr." (Surat Al-Qadr)

"The angels and the Spirit descend therein by permission of their Lord for every Command/affair." (The Power 97:4)

Tariqah (Spiritual Path), Ma'rifah (Gnosticism), and Haqiqah (Reality) Teach Humans Are the Honoured Creation

Then the knowledges of *tariqah* (spiritual path), the knowledges of  *ma'rifah* (gnosticism) and the knowledges of *haqiqah* (reality) begin to come and say, *"Wa laqad karamna bani Adam"* (I have honoured the children of Adam). Their honour, their reality, is much higher. They are the custodians of all My Grace and all My Realities.

﴿وَلَقَدْ كَرَّمْنَا بَنِي آدَمَ...﴾ ﴿٧٠﴾

17:70 – *"Wa laqad karramna bani adama..."* (Surat Al-Isra)

"And We have certainly honored the children of Adam..."
(The Night Journey, 17:70)

They (saints) begin to teach that this sun and this reality that is going to bring an *'izzat* to us, this carries the *amr* (command) of Allah ﷻ. These realities that are coming down, the world of form is only interested in the photon. It is only interested in the form.

All Amr (Commands) Come From the Heart of Prophet Muhammad ﷺ

The people of *haqqaiq* (realities) are asking to reach to Allah's ﷻ *Qadr* (power), *'Ya Rabbi*, we want to reach Your *Qudra* and Your Power.' The realities that are dressing Your Holy Qur'an, *"Qaf wal Qur'an al majeed."*

ق ۚ وَالْقُرْآنِ الْمَجِيدِ ﴿١﴾

50:1 – "Qaf, wal Quranil Majeed." (Surat Qaf)

"Qaf. By the honored Qur'an." (The Letter Qaf, 50:1)

Every power Allah ﷻ is sending through the Holy Qur'an. It means that every *amr*, every order, every authority is symbolically moving through these rays. That if you want to catch the reality of this *amr* (command), from what the *malaika* (angels) are coming, bringing of *isharat* and orders from the heart of Sayyidina Muhammad ﷺ.

The Ruh Carries a Secret That Governs Malaika (Angels)

The *ruh* is the authorized Muhammadan *wali* (saint) who is in charge of that reality because the *ruh* is carrying a secret from Prophet ﷺ. That secret is what governs the *malaika* (angels) on that station. Allah ﷻ is describing, 'All My Commands for that planet are coming from there.'

Every *amr*, every order, every command is coming to you from a source of power. We still don't know the *haqqaiq* (realities) yet, but for us to be symbolic. That Allah ﷻ is showing there is a source of power and it is reaching to you; the angels are reaching to you.

Peace and Heavenly Power Flow Through Fajr (Morning Prayer)

'Salaam' is Loaded With Power and Knowledge

You want to be granted from this *salaam*? *Ahl al-haqqaiq* (people of the reality) come and begin to teach, this *salaam* is a loaded reality. "*Salaamun*" means it is coming with this *seen* of *salaam*. What is Allah ﷻ going to be dressing you? Because the people who are accepting Qur'an, they pray *Salat al-Fajr* (morning prayer), so then there must be a *haqqaiq* in the reality of that sun. The *haqqaiq* will show itself to be much more powerful than the sun.

It means Allah ﷻ is saying that, 'You want to reach My *Amr*, My orders that are carried by the *malaika* (angels) and the *ruh* for you to understand the most purified realities of Prophet ﷺ?' You say, 'Yes, we want, *ya Rabbi*, this *salaam*.'

Decoding the Salaam (Peace)

They come and teach this *salaam* is carrying this *sir*, it is carrying *nur al anwaar wa seerat al asrar*. It is carrying the 'secret of light, the light of all secrets'. It is carrying upon its tongue and its orders, this *laam*, is the conveyance of knowledge, *lisanul haq* (holy Tongue of Truth). It carries upon it an *'izzat*, there is an *alif* here. It carries upon it an *'izzat* from Allah ﷻ of that *sir*. And it comes through this *meem*.

SIR (SECRET)

سلام			
Salaam			
م	ا	ل	س
Meem	Alif	Laam	Seen
محمد ﷺ	عِزَّتُ الله	لسان الحق	سر
Muhammad ﷺ (Muhammadan Reality)	'Izzatullah (Allah's Might)	Lisanul Haq (The Tongue of Truth)	Sir (Secret)

Note: Please read English from right to left to coincide with Arabic.

Meem of Salaam – Pray Tahajjud to Enter Maqam al Mahmud

Where Allah tells you to pray *tahajjud* (voluntary prayer) because you can enter into *Maqam al-Mahmud*.

وَمِنَ اللَّيْلِ فَتَهَجَّدْ بِهِ نَافِلَةً لَّكَ عَسَىٰ أَن يَبْعَثَكَ رَبُّكَ مَقَامًا مَّحْمُودًا ﴿٧٩﴾

17:79 – *"Wa minal layli fatahajjad bihi, nafilatal laka 'asaa an yab'athaka Rabbuka Maqaman Mahmooda."* (Surat Al-Isra)

"And pray in the small watches of the morning: (it would be) an additional prayer (or spiritual profit) for thee: soon will your Lord raise you to a Station of Praise and Glory! [Maqam al Mahmood]"
(The Night Journey, 17:79)

This is from Prophet ﷺ. This *"salaamun"* that *awliyaullah* (saints) are inspiring for us to reach. That you want to be dressed by this *sir* (secret), you want this conveyance? Because the *malaika* (angels) are going to be conveying to your heart these realities. This *meem* is the Muhammadan dress. *Maqam al-Mahmud* means

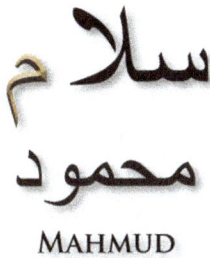

MAHMUD

it is coming from Prophet ﷺ. Sayyidina Muhammad ﷺ on Earth, Sayyidina Mahmud ﷺ within the Heavens.

Pray Salatul Fajr, Allah ﷻ Dresses You With Qadr (Power)

This means from *Salat at-Tahajjud* to *Salat al-Fajr*, all these dresses are coming, this *salaam* is coming. So, in the level of *tariqah* (spiritual path), they are teaching that keep your *Salat al-Fajr* (morning prayer).

Keep your *Salat al-Fajr*, Allah ﷻ will dress you with *qadr* (power). If you are missing your *Salat al-Fajr* you are missing a tremendous dress of *qadr* (power). To pray it by missing (pray later), that is one reality. Ask for *istighfaar* (forgiveness) and pray. But how pious people become pious is because they are becoming *"fuluk ul mashhoon"*. They are becoming loaded souls, loaded with tremendous amounts of power.

وَآيَةٌ لَهُمْ أَنَّا حَمَلْنَا ذُرِّيَّتَهُمْ فِي الْفُلْكِ الْمَشْحُونِ ﴿٤١﴾

36:41 – *"Wa ayatul lahum anna hamalna dhurriyyatahum fil fulkil mashhooni."* (Surat YaSeen)

"And a sign for them is that we have carried their atoms/forefathers in the loaded ship." (YaSeen, 36:41)

Praying Salatul Fajr is the Remedy for All Problems

There is an energy that is dressing their soul, dressing their soul, why? Because they are at *Salat al-Fajr* (morning prayer), Allah ﷻ promised *"Salaamun hiya hatta matlal Fajr"*. Later we go to the higher levels of *"hiya"*, but for this understanding and the difficulties that sickness and many difficulties begin to come and it's *najat* and its safety, is in *Salat al-Fajr*.

سَلَامٌ هِيَ حَتَّىٰ مَطْلَعِ الْفَجْرِ ﴿٥﴾

97:5 – "Salamun, hiya hatta matla'il Fajr." (Surat Al-Qadr)

"Peace it is until the emergence of dawn." (The Power, 97:5)

They are warning that what is coming upon the Earth of negativity is something that can't be imagined. It is not something that you just sort of say, 'Okay, I know this person is going to go away.' No, he is not going away. 'My husband is a good person, he prays. I don't need to pray.' Your husband may have a nice grave, you may be in a different condition. Or vice versa.

So, they are warning for us that you want Allah's ﷻ *Qadr*? You want Allah's ﷻ Power? He ﷻ is promising, from Holy Qur'an, 'I am going to be sending you a *salaam*, I am going to be sending you *salaam*.'

Salaam Has a Sirr (Secret) of Maqam al-Mahmud

Awliyaullah (saints) come and are telling you from the level of just *tariqah* (spiritual way), telling you that *salaam* you should be really striving for because it has a *sirr*, a secret, within it. There is a *lisan* (tongue) and angels who are going to begin to teach in your *Fajr* and this is a tremendous reality from Sayyidina Muhammad ﷺ. It is an immense reward because *Maqam al-Mahmud* is that Prophet's ﷺ energy and lights will come lower at the time of *Fajr* to receive people. It means it opens the *ni'mat* (blessings) from Allah ﷻ that Prophet's ﷺ light to reach closer to people, to bring them closer back into that reality and begin to dress them.

سلام			
Salaam			
م	ا	ل	س
Meem	Alif	Laam	Seen
محمد ﷺ	عزّت الله	لسان الحق	سر
Muhammad ﷺ (Muhammadan Reality)	'Izzatullah (Allah's ﷻ Might)	Lisanul Haq (The Tongue of Truth)	Sir (Secret)

*Note: Please read English from right to left to coincide with Arabic.

Everything in Creation is Waiting For Fajr Because It's Faraj (Salvation)

It means the *awrads* (spiritual practices), the *zikr* (remembrance), and every *amal* (action) that we are doing, its energy and power is coming, and they are warning for us is keep the *Salat al Fajr*. If you are sick, keep your *Salat al Fajr*; it is the best of medicine and best of remedies.

If misguided and faith is low and doubt is entering, pray *Salat al Fajr*. Allah's ﷻ *salaamat* is coming, Allah's ﷻ *najat* (salvation) is coming. Allah's ﷻ angels and the authority of the *ruh* will be dressing as He is dressing His leaves and flowers and nature and everything in Creation is waiting for *Fajr*.

Every bird begins to sing because now the *faraj* has come, the salvation

has come; they see the lights, they see the energies. There are so many creatures who go out just to lick that water, the first drop of water that is coming on the leaves. How many creatures come out just to drink that, come out just to take that, because they know Allah's ﷻ *ni'mat* (blessings) and mercy is upon that light and that energy. So, they are warning for us in the days of difficulty, don't lose your *Fajr*. Keep your *Fajr* prayers. Allah's ﷻ *salaams* (greeting of peace) is going to be dressing. Allah's ﷻ lights and energy are going to be dressing.

Seen Has 'Ilm al-Yaqeen, Ayn al-Yaqeen, and Haqq al-Yaqeen (Knowledge, Vision, and Truth of Certainty)

Then they begin to go into the levels of the *haqqaiq*, the levels of reality, that this is coming, this *salaam*. What makes it so immense for our Creation is that this again has *'ilm al-yaqeen*, *ayn al-yaqeen*, and *haqq al-yaqeen* (Knowledge of Certainty, Vision of Certainty, Truth of Certainty). So, think then what Allah ﷻ is going to be dressing this *sirr* (secret). This *'ilm al-yaqeen*, *ayn al-yaqeen*, *haqq al-yaqeen* is

going to be coming down on a tongue. The tongue of the Muhammadan reality is now coming towards the believer.

Don't Miss Your Awrad – It's Your Daily Connection to Saints

Those of *Ahl al-Turuq* (People of spiritual path) in which the *turuqs* are  teaching them, giving them *wazifas* and *awrads* (spiritual practices). Don't lose those *awrads*, don't drop those *wazifas*. Everyday there is a *wazifa* that needs to be done. Anyone who doesn't do it enters into thirty days of darkness. There is no way to stop it for one day. When you do the *wazifa* and *awrad* (spiritual practice), it is like a 'dial-up', a login into a computer. That you are dialing-up into one of those authorities, from one of these *ulul amr* (saints).

That Prophet ﷺ gave them that reality, give them these recitations. If they adhere to that recitation they are connecting into that reality. It means from their authority, of their *amr* (command) what Allah ﷻ dressed to them, they are going to be dressing you from *'ilm al-yaqeen, ayn al-yaqeen, haqq al-yaqeen* (knowledge of certainty, vision of certainty, and truth of certainty), through a tongue of reality which is a Muhammadan *haqqaiq* (realities). So, by keeping all of that, it begins to dress, dress, dress you.

'Hiya' is All the Power and Knowledge That Allah ﷻ Sends to Earth

Then they begin to teach what realities Allah ﷻ is going to open? This *hiya* is in reference to *qadr*, Allah's ﷻ *'izzat* and power. It's *Qadr, qadr, qadr, hiya*. *Hiya* is in reference to Allah's ﷻ Power. *Awliyaullah* (saints) come and teach that *hiya* is every *uloom* (knowledges), *uloom al-awaleen wal-akhireen* (knowledges of the beginning to the end).

Ya of Hiya Represents All Knowledges from Alif to Ya

Every *kalam* (word), every knowledge is from the *alif* all the way to the last letter *ya*. Every knowledge is from letters. As you write these letters, these are knowledges being conveyed, realities are being conveyed. Then they teach that everything is an eternal circle of realities. That once you reach to the *ya*, the *ya* actually goes back and begins with the *alif*, the *ya* connects to the *alif*. This means every knowledge from *alif*, all the *huroof* (Arabic letters) to *ya* is coming to  that servant. Every reality that Allah (ﷻ) is going to teach is through these letters. If Allah (ﷻ) compacts and condenses the letters and sends you a *ya*, He is sending you a *yaqeen*. He is sending you a knowledge.

Ha of Hiya is for Hidayat – Guidance and Love

Every type of reality is coming in that *Salat al-Fajr* and Allah (ﷻ) granted  its *hidayat*. This *ha* is for *hidayat*. You want guidance, you want all of these realities; *hiya* is coming loaded. So, *"salaamun hiya"* (Holy Qur'an, 97:5). Allah (ﷻ) is saying, 'This *salamat* that is now coming towards you with *'ilm al-yaqeen, ayn al-yaqeen, haqq al-yaqeen* (knowledge of certainty, vision of certainty, and truth of certainty) as a Muhammadan reality.

سَلَامٌ هِيَ حَتَّىٰ مَطْلَعِ الْفَجْرِ ﴿٥﴾

Peace and Heavenly Power Flow Through Fajr (Morning Prayer)

97:5 – *"Salamun, hiya hatta matla'il Fajr." (Surat Al-Qadr)*

"Peace it is until the emergence of dawn." (The Power, 97:5)

It means then they are going to begin and at higher levels, the servant is going to begin to understand the lights are presented to him in *Fajr*. There will be angels and *awliya* (saints) at their *Fajr* and every knowledge is being conveyed into their heart from the secret of *hiya*. Allah ﷻ condenses, that every *kalam* (word) I have from *alif, baa, taa, thaa*; everything that is making My Knowledges, all the Holy Qur'an are in those letters. He said, 'I am going to package them all in a *ya* for you and I am going to send it accompanied by *hidayat* and guidance.'

HA

If you look at the *ha*, it has a *waw*. It's a *waw* inside a cave. The people of true guidance they have a *waw* within their heart. It means everything they do is based on love. These are the people of immense love that Allah ﷻ is going to send a *hiya* to them that every knowledge, every reality is going to be conveyed to you.

هي	
Hiya	
ي	ه
Ya	**Ha**
Alif to Ya (All Letters Alif to Ya Contain All Knowledge)	**Hadi** (Guide)
يقين	هداية
Yaqeen (Certainty)	**Hidayat** (Guidance)

*Note: Please read English from right to left to coincide with Arabic.

Every Knowledge is Conveyed at Fajr

So why then pious people and those who follow *awliyaullah* (saints) they never miss, unless they are sick or have difficulty, they never miss their *Fajr*? Because that is the time of their schooling. That is time in which Allah (swt) is dressing them and blessing them. Allah (swt) is conveying every *salaam*; it means every *mushkilat*, every difficulty is taken away at *Fajr* time. Every knowledge is conveyed at *Fajr* time. Every association and blessing and *barakah* is granted at *Fajr* time.

That is why the *Fajr* is actually *Faraj*, that you move around the letters

and it's *faraj*, salvation. Allah (swt) is granting the nation of Sayyidina Muhammad ﷺ a tremendous salvation to be free from difficulty. Then in all the levels of *haqqaiq* (realities) because you are first coming to the commands of Allah (swt) to pray the Fajr. Then they begin to describe the *haqqaiq* of that reality, that it takes away every difficulty, takes away every *mushkilat*. Every *du'a* (supplication) that is going to be accepted is most accepted at *Salat al-Fajr*.

Spend Tahajjud in Contemplation

Then for *Ahl al-Ma'rifah* (people of gnosticism) who are going and asking for knowledges that all the knowledge they heard, and they studied, as soon as they enter into *Salat at-Tahajjud* (voluntary worship) and they begin to contemplate that what did the Shaykh just talk about? Then that night when you are meditating and reading the articles or reading that understanding or listening again  to it. Or even just meditating to Surat YaSeen at *Fajr*, at *Tahajjud* time, connecting your heart with Mawlana Shaykh Nazim ق and listening to

Peace and Heavenly Power Flow Through Fajr (Morning Prayer)

Surat YaSeen, which is the heart of Prophet ﷺ. YaSeen is the heart of Holy Qur'an. Then Allah ﷻ says, 'When Qur'an is recited, stop. Sit, contemplate, meditate so that Allah's ﷻ Mercy can dress you.' *"Salaam"* can dress. It means every reality will be opened at that time.

وَإِذَا قُرِئَ الْقُرْآنُ فَاسْتَمِعُوا لَهُ وَأَنْصِتُوا لَعَلَّكُمْ تُرْحَمُونَ ﴿٢٠٤﴾

7:204 – "Wa idhaa quria al Qur'an fastami'u lahu, wa anseetu la'alakum turhamon." (Surat Al-A'raf)

"So when the Qur'an is recited, then listen to it, remain silent and pay attention, that you may receive mercy." (The Heights, 7:204)

We pray that in those days of difficulty Allah ﷻ grant us a *himmah*, a strength not to leave. *Shaytan* (Satan) only wants difficulty for us and *Shaytan* makes everything to be difficult, 'Don't do that. Don't, don't, don't listen to him. Don't pray your *Fajr*. Don't do like that. Don't do your *award* (daily practices). Don't do like that. Don't come here'. Why? To put hardship upon the believer until they turn into difficulty and immense hardship. We pray that Allah ﷻ give us a *himmah* and strength to follow whatever Allah ﷻ wanted for us and to be dressed by Allah's ﷻ infinite *rahmah*, immense *rahmah* (mercy) that can't even be imagined.

Subhana rabbika rabbal 'izzati 'amma yasifoon, wa salaamun 'alal mursaleen, walhamdulillahi rabbil 'aalameen. Bi hurmati Muhammad al-Mustafa wa bi siri Surat al-Fatiha.

Sun is the Source of Light;
Be Like a Moon and Reflect the Light

The Sun of Knowledge Will Rise From the West

Alhamdulillah, that in the understanding of *tafakkur* (contemplation) and the ways of *ma'rifah* (gnosticism) and from the *arifeen* (knowers) and from the teachers of reality; alhamdulillah, Prophet ﷺ described that 'the sun would rise from the west.'

عن أبي هُرَيْرَةَ رَضِيَ اللهُ عَنْهُ قَالَ : قَالَ رَسُولُ اللهِ صَلَّى اللهُ عَلَيْهِ وَسَلَّمَ : (لَا تَقُومُ السَّاعَةُ حَتَّى تَطْلُعَ الشَّمْسُ مِنْ مَغْرِبِهَا ، فَإِذَا رَآهَا النَّاسُ آمَنَ مَنْ عَلَيْهَا ، فَذَاكَ حِينَ لَا يَنْفَعُ نَفْسًا إِيمَانُهَا لَمْ تَكُنْ آمَنَتْ مِنْ قَبْلُ). روى البخاري (4635) ومسلم (157)

Qala Rasulullah ﷺ: "*La Taqomu Sa'atu hatta tatlu'a ash Shamsu min Maghribeha, fa idha ra aahan Nasu Aamana man 'alayha, fadhaka heena la yanfa'o nafsan Imanuha lam takun aamanat min qablu.*"

Narrated Abu Huraira: Allah's Apostle said, "The Hour will not be established until the sun rises from the West: and when the people see it, then whoever will be living on the surface of the earth will have faith, and that is (the time) when no good will it do to a soul to believe then, if it believed not before." Al Bukhari (4535) Al Muslim (157)

That the *ishraaq*, we don't have east and west in Islam, we have *ishraaq* which is the rising of the sun, the rising of reality, and the *maghrib* which is the setting, and the closing of realities, the setting which brings in

Sun is the Source of Light;
Be Like a Moon and Reflect the Light

darkness. This means where the sun used to rise in the east. The Eastern world now is in a darkness, whether they are cutting people's heads or buying gold and consuming beyond imagination that there's no more spirituality. And that that reality is now shifting to where this (the west) used to be *maghrib* (sunset); where inshaAllah, Allah ﷻ and Prophet's ﷺ words to be true, that the *ishraaq* and the knowledges and the rising sun of realities will be shining.

Just from a level of science, that who is studying light and the physics of light and the reality of light? All of that is *malakut* (heavenly). Light is that which is eternal. Who's studying that which is eternal? It is the west. All their physics and all their projects are all based on understanding light. While the rest of the nation, Allah ﷻ knows what they're in search of; how many A's in the pronunciation of Allah ﷻ and say *'Allah, Allaaah'*, they put five A's. This is the highlight of their *maqhz* (brain) and their

understanding. Their pursuit became very material, their understanding became very material. And there is no longer the pursuit of realities and light and that which is eternal.

Allah's ﷻ Signs Upon the Horizon Are in Perfection

The first thing that *awliyaullah* (saints) come into our lives and want us to contemplate is that when Allah ﷻ describes, 'I show you the signs upon the horizon and I show you within yourself these realities,'

Shaykh Nurjan Mirahmadi

﴿سَنُرِيهِمْ آيَاتِنَا فِي الْآفَاقِ وَفِي أَنفُسِهِمْ حَتَّىٰ يَتَبَيَّنَ لَهُمْ أَنَّهُ الْحَقُّ ۗ ... ﴿٥٣﴾

41:53 – "Sanureehim ayatina fil afaqi wa fee anfusihim hatta yatabayyana lahum annahu alhaqqu…" (Surat Al-Isra)

"We will show them Our signs in the horizons and within themselves until it becomes clear to them that it is the truth…"
(The Night Journey, 41:53)

The signs upon the horizon, why? Because they are in perfection. One, there is no created *shirk* (partnership with Allah). There is no way Allah would create a partnership. So, anything you look in nature must be perfect; there's no *shirk* in it, there's no *bid'a*, there's no innovation. That's from our ego when we invent these things.

So why did Allah direct us first to, 'Look to My Creation, because I manage this creation. It's perfect. If you take an *ajir*, if you take an example in life of how I want My creation to operate, you can govern your lives accordingly.' That's why when people start typing and comment that, 'Oh this is *shirk*, this is *shirk*,' you're crazy! Allah doesn't create *shirk* (partnership with Allah).

The Sun's Photons Go Through the Entire Galaxy

Allah creates a sun filled with power. To show how small we are and how much we are in need, because we have to understand outside these realities, and then we begin to really understand the direction in which to move inside. When we look outside at what they're asking us to look in the relationship between the sun and the moon. We said before that the photons of this sun penetrate our entire galaxy. They have not built anything that can stop them. The photon goes straight through the planet, no matter walls and iron. And no matter what you create, those photons go straight

Sun is the Source of Light;
Be Like a Moon and Reflect the Light

through, all the way to the end of the galaxy. It means we are nourished by that *shams* (sun).

You have breath by that *shams* (sun). How could that be *shirk* (partnership with Allah)? Allah ﷻ created it that way. Allah ﷻ is the power behind that. That cause and effect, that Allah ﷻ wants us to know that you can't breathe without that sun, you can't eat without that sun, you can't live on this earth and have warmth without that sun, and it creates all the energy fields in your life.

If the sun has an eruption, this whole earth is upside down. The electromagnetic field that comes from that sun on minor eruptions disrupts everything on earth, makes people to have agitated hearts, agitated beings because we are energy beings. They said a category five eruption on the sun can 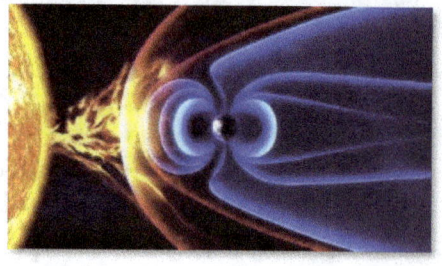 destroy everything on earth. It will create an electromagnetic pulse, in which the energy that shoots from the sun begins to move towards the earth, penetrates the layers of the earth and knocks everything out.

Allah ﷻ is great! And Allah ﷻ wants to show, 'Look, this is just My little creation, how much you are in danger from it.' How much you are in need of it. How much you should understand, because worship is for Allah ﷻ; but to understand Allah's ﷻ creation is a part of *deen* (religion) and belief. That, '*Ya Rabbi*, Your '*Azimah* and Your Magnificence and Munificence, this creation that You created, and what power and what importance you gave to it.'

اِنَّ فِي خَلْقِ السَّمَاوَاتِ وَالْأَرْضِ وَاخْتِلَافِ اللَّيْلِ وَالنَّهَارِ لَآيَاتٍ لِأُولِي الْأَلْبَابِ ﴿١٩٠﴾ الَّذِينَ يَذْكُرُونَ اللَّـهَ قِيَامًا وَقُعُودًا وَعَلَىٰ جُنُوبِهِمْ وَيَتَفَكَّرُونَ فِي خَلْقِ السَّمَاوَاتِ وَالْأَرْضِ رَبَّنَا مَا خَلَقْتَ هَـٰذَا بَاطِلًا سُبْحَانَكَ فَقِنَا عَذَابَ النَّارِ ﴿١٩١﴾

3:190-191 – *"Inna fee khalqis Samawati wal ardi wakhtilafil layli wan nahari, la ayatin li Olel albab. (190) Alladheena yadhkurona Allaha qiyaman wa qu'odan wa 'ala junobihim, wa yatafakkarona fee khalqis Samawati wal ardi, Rabbana ma khalaqta hadha batilan subhanaka faqina 'adhaban nar. (191)" (Surat 'Ali 'Imran)*

"Indeed, in the creation of the heavens and the earth and the alternation of the night and the day are signs for those People of understanding (People of the Door of Knowledge). (190) Who remember Allah while standing or sitting or [lying] on their sides and contemplate the creation in the heavens and the earth, [saying], Our Lord, You did not create this aimlessly/in vain; exalted are You [above such a thing]; then protect us from the punishment of the Fire. (191)" (Family of Imran, 3:190-191)

The Sun and the Moon are 'Fulukul Mashhoon' (Loaded Ships)

Then Allah ﷻ says, 'Look at the moon, how the moon completely follows the sun, completely in obedience.' We said before from *Surat YaSeen*, starting from 38th verse to the 41st verse, that Allah ﷻ describes the *shams wal qamar*.

وَالشَّمْسُ تَجْرِي لِمُسْتَقَرٍّ لَهَا ۚ ذَٰلِكَ تَقْدِيرُ الْعَزِيزِ الْعَلِيمِ ﴿٣٨﴾ وَالْقَمَرَ قَدَّرْنَاهُ مَنَازِلَ حَتَّىٰ عَادَ كَالْعُرْجُونِ الْقَدِيمِ ﴿٣٩﴾ لَا الشَّمْسُ يَنبَغِي لَهَا أَن تُدْرِكَ الْقَمَرَ وَلَا اللَّيْلُ سَابِقُ النَّهَارِ ۚ وَكُلٌّ فِي فَلَكٍ يَسْبَحُونَ ﴿٤٠﴾ وَآيَةٌ لَّهُمْ أَنَّا حَمَلْنَا ذُرِّيَّتَهُمْ فِي الْفُلْكِ الْمَشْحُونِ ﴿٤١﴾

36:38-41 – "Wash Shamsu tajree limustaqarril lahaa; zaalika taqdeerul 'Azizil 'Aleem. (38) Wal Qamara qaddarnaahu manaazila hattaa 'aada kal 'urjoonil qadeem. (39) Lash shamsu yambaghee lahaaa an tudrikal qamara, wa lal lailu saabiqun nahaar; wa kullun fee falaki yasbahoon. (40) Wa ayatul lahum anna hamalna dhurriyyatahum fil fulkil mashhooni. (41)" (Surat YaSeen)

"And the sun runs his course for a period determined for him: that is the decree of (Him), the Exalted in Might, the All Knowing. (38) And the

Sun is the Source of Light;
Be Like a Moon and Reflect the Light

Moon, We have measured for her phases/mansions (to traverse) till she returns (appearing) like the old (and withered) lower part of a date-stalk. (39) It is not permitted to the Sun to catch up the Moon, nor can the Night outstrip/overtake the Day: Each (just) swims along in (its own) orbit (according to Law). (40) And a sign for them is that we have carried their atoms/forefathers in the loaded ship." (YaSeen, 36:38-41)

That they are like a *fuluk* (loaded ships). *Fuluk – fa, lam, kaf –* that it is a ship, which means it denotes that it's carrying something. It's carrying realities, *fulukul mashhoon*, that these are loaded ships. Why Allah ﷻ uses that word in the description of the sun and the moon? That they are ships and they are moving in an orbit. This means these are in the realities of light.

Then we begin to look at the understanding of the sun because we want to go into magnetism, about the importance of building spiritual magnetism which is an energy. But if we don't understand the world of light and the world around us, there's no way to understand and truly comprehend what they want us to mimic within our inner reality. That when you look at that sun, then they begin to show you, you can Google 'size of the universe', and planets and stars within the universe.

You Can't Approach the Sun, How Can You Approach Allah ﷻ?

There is a sun; there's now a sun a hundred times larger than our sun; there is a sun a thousand times larger than our sun; there's a sun one billion times larger than our sun. And our earth like a dot to this little sun. Imagine those huge realities that Allah ﷻ, and all of it

is an example of our approach to Allah ﷻ. Allah ﷻ says, *"Ateeullah, atee ar-rasul wa ulul amrin minkum."*

أَطِيعُوا اللَّهَ وَأَطِيعُوا الرَّسُولَ وَأُولِي الْأَمْرِ مِنْكُمْ... ﴿٥٩﴾

4:59 – *"...Atiullaha wa atiur Rasula wa Ulil amre minkum..."* (Surat An-Nisa)

"... Obey Allah, Obey the Messenger, and those in authority among you..." (The Women, 4:59)

Ateeullah is the inner power of the entire universe. Allah ﷻ says that, 'Oh you foolish mankind. You can't approach from where you are to that little sun. How is it that you are coming to Me?' As if you can penetrate the heavens, you need a *sultan* (king), you need a permission!

يَا مَعْشَرَ الْجِنِّ وَالْإِنْسِ إِنِ اسْتَطَعْتُمْ أَن تَنفُذُوا مِنْ أَقْطَارِ السَّمَاوَاتِ وَالْأَرْضِ فَانفُذُوا ۚ لَا تَنفُذُونَ إِلَّا بِسُلْطَانٍ ﴿٣٣﴾

55:33 – *"Ya ma'ashara al jinni wal insi inistata'tum an tanfudho min aqtari asSamawati wal Ardi fanfudho, La tanfudhona illa bi Sultan."* (Surat Ar-Rahman)

"O gathering/assembly of jinn and mankind, if you are able to penetrate through the atmosphere and pass beyond the zones of the Heavens and Earth, then Penetrate. You will never be able to pass, Except with a King, you need a sultan." (The Beneficient, 55:33)

The Sun Will Burn You and Annihilate You

Can you move from this earth in the direction of the sun? You'll be burned, you'll be annihilated. Even you look and gaze at the sun, it takes away your eyesight; it'll burn all your retina. It doesn't even want to be looked at. You can't sit and observe it. In heliophysics they don't allow you to directly observe it; it will burn all of your eyesight.

Azimatullah (Greatness of Allah), Allah ﷻ is describing, 'Look, look, how you think you are coming to Me?' Allah ﷻ is teaching that we need a means in which to approach. We have to look at the greatness. When you say, *"Allahu Akbar,"* Allah ﷻ says, *"Ana Akbar";* I'm even greater than what you can perceive.' But the problem is that people perceive very small in their understanding of Allah ﷻ. To think that in the way of *ma'rifah* (gnosticism) you are going directly with your soul into Allah's ﷻ presence. He says, 'First you direct yourself to the sun. See if you could go into the sun's presence. It will burn you, annihilate you. And that sun is a drop in the dot of that other sun that is one billion times its size.'

The Greatness of Sayyidina Muhammad's ﷺ Light

This means that you're in need of an approach. You are in need of building your dress and building your light and approaching through this whole chain of realities in your way of *ma'rifah* (gnosticism). Because the physical has to match the spiritual. That if you can't traverse from here and  go directly into the light of the sun, how you think you can reach to the reality of Sayyidina Muhammad ﷺ? All the *naat shareef* and all the *salawats* (praisings) is that sunlight is only a drop from the light of Sayyidina Muhammad ﷺ.

تیرے لبوں کی لا لی سحر میں   ہے نور تیرا شمس و قمر میں
سارے نبی تیرے در کے سوالی   پھولوں نے تیری خوشبو چُرا لی

Hai noor Tera Shams o Qamar may   *Tere labo ki laali sahar may*
Phoolo ne Teri Khushbu chura li   *Saare Nabi tere dar ke sawali*

Your light is in the Sun and the Moon,
The dawn has the redness of your holy lips

All flowers have stolen your fragrance,
All prophets are at your door seeking help

Allah ﷻ took from *Nurul Muhammadi* ﷺ (Light of Prophet Muhammad ﷺ), put it into the sun and that's a drop of the sun that you're seeing. And the greater sun has more *Nurul Muhammadi* ﷺ; the greater sun has more *Nurul Muhammadi* ﷺ, all the way to the biggest sun which they call the pistol star, which is the centre of the entire created universe. That is then the centre of *Nurul Muhammadi* ﷺ, where Allah ﷻ describes in *Surat At-Tariq*, which is The Piercing Star.

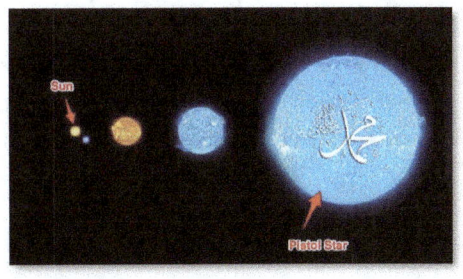

وَالسَّمَاءِ وَالطَّارِقِ ﴿١﴾ وَمَا أَدْرَاكَ مَا الطَّارِقُ ﴿٢﴾ النَّجْمُ الثَّاقِبُ ﴿٣﴾ إِن كُلُّ نَفْسٍ لَّمَّا عَلَيْهَا حَافِظٌ ﴿٤﴾

86:1-4 – "Was Sama e wat Tariq. (1) Wa ma adraka mat tariq? (2) AnNajmu ath thaqib. (3) In kullu nafsin lamma 'alayha hafiz. (4)" (Surat At-Tariq)

"By the Sky and the Night-Visitant (therein). (1) And what will explain to thee what the Night-Visitant is? (2) (It is) the Star of piercing brightness [Pistol star]. (3) There is no soul but has a protector over it. (4)" (The Nightcomer, 86:1-4)

Sun is the Source of Light;
Be Like a Moon and Reflect the Light

We Are So Insignificant in Allah's Light

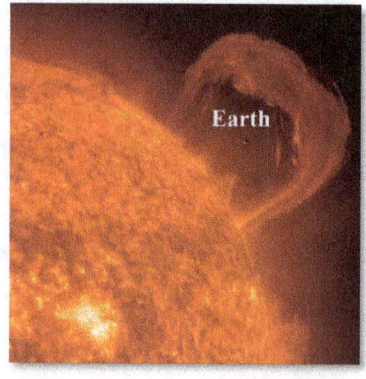

This means Allah wants us to understand that this light we are talking about is so powerful. In your physical realm, you cannot approach them. In your physical realm, you're so insignificant and small and so unseen – you are what they call an epsilon in their formula – that the earth itself, to this sun, is a dot. Imagine to the sun that's a billion times the size of the Earth is not even visible. And imagine you upon the Earth – completely invisible, not even recognized. So, with that little piece of being you are, you think so highly of yourself, that you have such an ability to approach. Approach then this *dunya* (material world). But Allah says, 'There is a means in which to reach that; but you have to go through a *sultan* (king).'

يَا مَعْشَرَ الْجِنِّ وَالْإِنسِ إِنِ اسْتَطَعْتُمْ أَن تَنفُذُوا مِنْ أَقْطَارِ السَّمَاوَاتِ وَالْأَرْضِ فَانفُذُوا ۚ لَا تَنفُذُونَ إِلَّا بِسُلْطَانٍ ﴿٣٣﴾

55:33 – *"Ya ma'ashara al jinni wal insi inistata'tum an tanfudho min aqtari asSamawati wal Ardi fanfudho, La tanfudhona illa bi Sultan."* (Surat Ar-Rahman)

"O gathering/ assembly of jin and mankind, if you are able to penetrate through the atmosphere and pass beyond the zones of the Heavens and Earth, then Penetrate. You will never be able to pass, Except with a King, you need a sultan." (The Beneficient, 55:33)

It means it has to be a permission through the level and the understanding of the heart, that the soul has that ability.

The Shams (Sun) is an Imitation From Nurul Muhammadi ﷺ

The soul can reach towards these lights and the reality of these lights.

That *shams* (sun) is an imitation from *Nurul Muhammadi* ﷺ. So, it means they approach towards the reality of Prophet ﷺ far more powerful, far more *hayba*, far more difficult. And they are in *darajats* (levels). That Prophet ﷺ being the *imam* (leader) of all lights and then all the *anbiya* (prophets), all the *rasuls* (messengers) are the stars that are taking from the *imam*, taking from Prophet ﷺ.

يَا إِمَامَ الرُّسْلِ يَا سَنَدِيْ
فَبِدُنْيَايَ وَ آخِرَتِيْ

أَنْتَ بَابُ اللهِ مُعْتَمَدِيْ
يَا رَسُولَ اللهِ خُذْ بِيَدِيْ

Ya imamar Rusli ya sanadi
Fabi dunyaya wa akhirate

Anta babullahi mu'tamadi
Ya Rasulallahi khud biyadi

O' Leader of the messengers, O' my support, you are Allah's door, upon whom I rely,

O' Messenger of Allah! Hold my hand in the material world and in my hereafter

*Sun is the Source of Light;
Be Like a Moon and Reflect the Light*

All the *Ashab an-Nabi* ﷺ and *Ahlul Bayt an-Nabi* ﷺ (family of Prophet ﷺ) are taking and inheriting from the prophets and from the *anbiya* (prophets). Another set of stars; and that's why Prophet ﷺ described, 'My Companions, they are like *najm* (star). Any one of these stars you follow, you will be guided', because they are ships. When you follow that light, that light dresses you and blesses you and carries you; and  that's why Allah ﷻ describes them, 'They are ships.' You'll be dressed by their light, not the imitated light but the real light.

أَصْحَابِي كَالنُّجُـــومْ بِأَيِّهِمْ اَقْتَدَيْتُمْ اَهْتَدَيْتُمْ

"*Ashabi kan Nujoom, bi ayyihim aqta daytum ahta daytum.*"

"*My companions are like stars. Follow any one of them and you will be guided.*" (Prophet Muhammad (pbuh))

Importance of the Moon in Our Growth

 Then when we want to understand *tafakkur* (contemplation) and the importance of *tafakkur*, it means magnetism. The understanding of magnetism is that Allah ﷻ gave us an energy in our being and to energize our being more than the energy that we have. There's no way to go directly to the sun. If you try to connect directly to Allah ﷻ, you will be annihilated. If you even try to connect directly to Prophet ﷺ, you'll be annihilated. So, what Allah ﷻ gave for us, "*ateeullah atee ur Rasul wa ulul amrin minkum.*"

Shaykh Nurjan Mirahmadi

...أَطِيعُواْ اللَّهَ وَأَطِيعُواْ ٱلرَّسُولَ وَأُوْلِي ٱلْأَمْرِ مِنكُمْ... ﴿٥٩﴾

4:59 – "…*Atiullaha wa atiur Rasula wa Ulil amre minkum…*" (*Surat An-Nisa*)

"…*Obey Allah, Obey the Messenger, and those in authority among you…*" (The Women, 4:59)

The *ulul amr* (saints) and the concept of the moon begins to open up. The moon sends us a light in which we can grow. All growth, all development is through the moonlight. It sends enough of the sun's light that allows us to absorb that light and nourish our self and build our self. And the sun shines enough energy to sweeten the self. So, it means all growth is by the moonlight.

Understanding Juzba (Magnetism) and Purifying Your Iron

The understanding of magnetism is that, '*Ya Rabbi*, I'm nothing, I'm nothing, I'm nothing but dress me from these lights, bless me from these lights.' They begin to teach that you have within you iron. The iron within your body has to be purified. We take a path towards eating good, drinking good, praying and acting good which begins to purify that iron. That iron within the body, when it becomes pure, energy sticks onto that iron. The energy that you are building by reflection, begins to stick onto that iron and you're building your inner reality. You're building the energy and the *qudra* (power).

This means then they teach through the way of *tafakkur* (contemplation) that you want to reach towards the light of Prophet ﷺ, then stare at the reflection of Sayyidina Muhammad ﷺ. Imitate! Allah's ﷻ imitating, look, look, how you can't stare at the sun directly, not yet, not who you are. But look to the moon. It means all night long you can stare at the moonlight and there's no burning your eyes. And it builds for you that reality.

Full Moon Affects People's Energy and Mood

The moon, when you begin to research, it has an effect on earth. That's why people go crazy and they call them lunatic. It's based on the lunar phase of the month. When the month is in full, which means it's  reflecting fully the light of the sun upon the earth and many people go crazy. Because that light of *Nurul Muhammadi* ﷺ (Light of Prophet Muhammad ﷺ), it begins to touch people and if they're not able to contain that energy, they become crazy; they become agitated, crime escalates, and all sorts of difficulties come. Because the amount of light coming on a dark, dark world. Any time you shine a heavenly light on a dark, unheavenly area, it becomes agitated because the two don't mix.

The *haq* (truth) and the false never mix. By virtue of the *haq* (truth), when it comes, it begins, *zahuqan*. Allah ﷻ describes, 'It shatters and obliterates every falsehood.' They don't mix; they don't hang out together. When the moonlight begins to shine, every evilness is running for shelter, running for cover; hence they become agitated and aggravated.

وَ قُلْ جَاءَالْحَقُّ وَزَهَقَ الْبَاطِلُ، إِنَّ الْبَاطِلَ كَانَ زَهُوقًا ﴿٨١﴾

17:81 – "Wa qul jaa alhaqqu wa zahaqal baatil, innal batila kana zahoqa." (Surat Al-Isra)

"And say, Truth has come, and falsehood has perished. Indeed falsehood, [by its nature], is ever perishing/bound to perish."
(The Night Journey, 17:81)

Sayyidina Adam عليه السلام Was Told to Fast on 3 White Days of the Full Moon

But believers, they're waiting for the full moon; that the full moon, Prophet ﷺ described, 'Fast on those three days to receive the dress of that light.'

قَالَ قُدَامَةُ بْنِ مِلْحَانِ رَضِيَ اللهُ عَنْهُ:(كَانَ رَسُولُ اللهِ صَلَّى اللهُ عَلَيْهِ وَسَلَّمَ يَأْمُرنا بِ صِيَامِ أَيَّامِ الْبِيضِ ثَلَاثَ عُشْرَ وَأَرْبَعَ عُشْرَ وَخُمْسَ عَشَرَ قَالَ وَقَالَ: هُوَ كَهَيْئَةِ الدَّهْر

Qala Quddamatu bin Melhaane (ra): Kana Rasullulahi (saws): "Yamurna bisSyami ayyamil baytin salasa 'ushura, wa arba'a 'ushura, wa khumusa 'ashara qala wa qala: Huwa kahay-ated dahre."

The Companion of the Prophet (pbuh) said, "The Prophet of Allah (pbuh) advised us to fast on the white days (full moon days) on the thirteen, fourteen and fifteen, and he said: it accounts for the whole eternity."

That light of the full moon was so powerful it had taken away the darkness that had dressed upon Sayyidina Adam عليه السلام from his sin. When they came and told Sayyidina Adam عليه السلام that, 'You had been darkened by your sin.' That if you fast these three days, the light or what they call the white days, that the light is so powerful, it will dress you and bless you and correct you of all imperfections.

Sun is the Source of Light;
Be Like a Moon and Reflect the Light

عَنِ ابْنِ مَسْعُودٍ عَنِ النَّبِيِّ صَلَّى اللهُ عَلَيْهِ وَسَلَّمَ قَالَ:"اِنَّ آدَمَ لَمَّا اِكَلَ مِنَالشَّجَرَةِ أَوْحَى اللهُ إِلَيْهِ: أَهْبُطْ مِنْ جِوَارِيِّ، وَعَزَّتِي لَايُجَاوِرُنِي مَنْ عَصَانِي.

فَهَبَطَ إِلَى الْأَرْضِ مسودا، فَبَكَتِ الْأَرْضُ وَضَجَّتْ.

فَأَوْحَى اللهُ: يَا آدَمَ صُمَّ لِي الْيَوْمَ يَوْمَ ثَلَاثَةَ عَشَرَ، فَصَامَهُ فَأَصْبَحَ ثُلُثُهُ أَبْيَضٌ.

ثُمَّ أَوْحَى اللهُ إِلَيْهِ:صُمَّ لِي هَذَا الْيَوْمَ يَوْمَ أَرْبَعَةَ عَشَرَ،فَصَامَهُ فَأَصْبَحَ ثُلُثَاهُ أَبْيَضٌ، ثُمَّ٧أَوْحَى اللهُ إِلَيْهِ:صُمَّ لِي هَذَا الْيَوْمَ يَوْمَ خَمْسَةَ عَشَرَ، فَصَامَهُ فَأَصْبَحَ كُلُّهُ أَبْيَضٌ، فَسَمَّيْتُ أَيَّامَ الْبِيْضِ.

'An ibn Mas'udin 'anin Nabi (saws) Qala: "Anna Adama lamma ikla minash shajarati awhAllahu ilayhi: 'Uhbut min jiwariyi, wa 'izzati la yujawiruni min 'asani. Fahabata ilal ardi maswada, fabakatil ardu wa dajjat." Fa awha Allahu: "Ya Adami Sumun lil yawmu yawma thalathata 'ashshara, fasamahu fa asbaha thuluthu abuydun." Thuma awhAllahu ilayhi: "Sumun li hazal yawmu yawma arba'at 'ashshara, fasamahu fa azbaha thuluthahu abuydun, thuma awhAllahu ilayhi: "Sumun li hazal yawmu yawma khamsata 'ashshara, fasamahu fa asbaha kulluhu abaytu, fasammaytu ayyamal buydi."

The prophet of Allah, Muhammad (pbuh) said, "When Adam ate from the tree, Allah (AJ) revealed to him, 'You are removed from My Closeness, by the mean of My Might. My proximity is not granted for the one who disobeys Me'." Adam (as) went to the earth blackened. The earth cried and wailed.

So, Allah (AJ) revealed to him, Adam (as), "Fast the thirteenth day (of the month) for me." Adam fasted, and a third of him whitened. Then Allah (AJ) revealed to him, "Fast the fourteenth day for me". Adam (as) fasted and his two third whitened. Then Allah (AJ) revealed to him, "Fast the fifteenth day for me." Adam (as) fasted and his whole body whitened, so they call it the white days." [Narrated by Ibn Mass'od (ra)]

This is the history of Islam, is where all the realities of Islam. But they left everything and went into very material understandings. The understanding and the physics of light, the physics of this reflection. How all of this is based on our life on this earth, the relationship between the sun and the moon; everything to do with our life on earth.

The Ulul Amr/Awliya (Saints) Are the Perfected Moons

Then with our magnetism they are teaching us that this energy that you have is not sufficient for you. When you begin to take a way, a purification and cleansing of the self, then you begin to learn. 'I have to learn how to make *tafakkur* (contemplation) and *muraqaba* (meditation).' That these *ulul amr* (saints), these *awliyaullah* (saints) on earth, they are like moons, each more powerful than the other. When I focus upon that moon, I am able to bring enough light in my life and begin to dress myself from that light. It's not worshipness, just like when you're looking at the moon in the sky and you're breathing from the sunlight. Allah (swt) doesn't create *shirk* (partnership with Allah). We're in need of it; we're breathing from it.

Allah (swt) is then describing, 'If you need that, imagine what you need spiritually.' It means we are being nourished by the light of Prophet (saws). This is an imitated sun. Without the light of Prophet (saws), you can't eat. Without the light of Prophet (saws), you can't breathe. Without the *Ashab an-Nabi* (saws), *Ahlul Bayt an-Nabi* (saws) and the *ulul amr*, that reflection would not be coming to us. So, then Allah (swt) says, *"Wa laqad karamna Bani Adam,"* that, 'We have given you such an honour,' to be dressed from these realities, blessed from these realities.

Sun is the Source of Light;
Be Like a Moon and Reflect the Light

﴿٧٠﴾...وَلَقَدْ كَرَّمْنَا بَنِي آدَمَ

17:70 – *"Wa laqad karramna bani adama…"* (Surat Al-Isra)

"And We have certainly honored the children of Adam…"
(The Night Journey, 17:70)

The Moon Only Focuses on the Sun, on the Reality of Sayyidina Muhammad ﷺ

Then our whole way of understanding to reach towards these realities is that, '*Ya Rabbi*, let me to be in the presence of these full moons,' that their whole life is the way of Prophet ﷺ. That's when you understand the moon, the moon's only focus is the *shams* (sun). The moon's only focus is on Sayyidina Muhammad ﷺ.

Even you see how they speak will be different. When someone is not a moon, they talk too much about the owner of this entire creation. It's like the little planet that shot all the way to the front and talking about something that's way beyond their capacity. But can the moon talk about anything other than the sun?

That's why Allah says, 'They don't overtake each other. The day doesn't outstrip the night and the night doesn't outstrip the day,'

لَا الشَّمْسُ يَنبَغِي لَهَا أَن تُدْرِكَ الْقَمَرَ وَلَا اللَّيْلُ سَابِقُ النَّهَارِ ۚ وَكُلٌّ فِي فَلَكٍ يَسْبَحُونَ ﴿٤٠﴾

36:40 – *"Lash shamsu yambaghee laha an tudrikal qamara wa la allaylu sabiqun nahari, wa kullun fee falakin yasbahoon."*
(Surat YaSeen)

"It is not permitted to the Sun to catch up the Moon, nor can the Night outstrip the Day: Each (just) swims/floats along in (its own) orbit." (YaSeen, 36:40)

It means its entire focus; its entire job is to follow the sun. You take the reflection of the sun because these are all by analogies and allegories, that the reality is Prophet ﷺ. If you are following Sayyidina Muhammad ﷺ, loving Sayyidina Muhammad ﷺ, trying to do your best to please Sayyidina Muhammad ﷺ, that is the light of Allah ﷻ within the heart of Prophet ﷺ.

Awliya (Saints) Are the Loaded Ships Carrying the Souls

That sun of reality will begin to dress you and those are the full moons. Those are the *awliyaullah* (saints) and the *saliheen* (righteous); their whole life is to follow Prophet ﷺ. They are on the *qadm as-Siddiq*, they are on the footsteps of the *siddiqs* (truthful) and those *siddiqs* (truthful) on the footsteps of Sayyidina Muhammad ﷺ. And Allah ﷻ describes them, 'They are like a ship. They are like ships.'

وَآيَةٌ لَّهُمْ أَنَّا حَمَلْنَا ذُرِّيَّتَهُمْ فِي الْفُلْكِ الْمَشْحُونِ ﴿٤١﴾

36:41 – *"Wa ayatul lahum anna hamalna dhurriyyatahum fil fulkil mashhooni." (Surat YaSeen)*

"And a sign for them is that we have carried their atoms/forefathers in the loaded ship." (YaSeen, 36:41)

Sun is the Source of Light;
Be Like a Moon and Reflect the Light

This means that when you focus on them, there's no worshipping. You focus on them like you're sunbathing, like you're going out onto the beach and looking at the sun. When you focus on them in your *tafakkur* (meditation) and say, '*Ya Rabbi*, let me to always be in the presence of your full moons; let me to be dressed by their light, blessed by their light,' their energy begins to dress our energy. Their reflection begins to dress our  reflection. As much as we can carry that light and to be dressed by that light, the light begins to dress our entire being. Where that light is going to clean is in the iron of the body. That *nazma* and that energy that begins to reflect upon us, just like it's reflecting on the outside [we have to explain it in detail because people are going to watch on the video and then they start to make all sorts of comments]. But when they don't understand the perfection which Allah ﷻ created this universe and this galaxy, that you are taking its reflection and living on this earth. Now for your spiritual pursuit, why would it be something different?

Follow the Path of the Saintly Moons (Ulul Amr)

The energy you have is not sufficient to reach the station that you want. Then connect with the moon. And that's why they took *bayah* (allegiance). When they took *bayah*, they connected with these moons, with these *ulul amr* (saints). And they took a path in which, where Allah ﷻ describes an *ayat* (verse) for you: "*Wa hamalna dhurriyatahum fee fulookul mash'hoon.*"

وَآيَةٌ لَّهُمْ أَنَّا حَمَلْنَا ذُرِّيَّتَهُمْ فِي الْفُلْكِ الْمَشْحُونِ ﴿٤١﴾ وَخَلَقْنَا لَهُم مِّن مِّثْلِهِ مَا يَرْكَبُونَ ﴿٤٢﴾

36:41-42 – "Wa ayatul lahum anna hamalna dhurriyyatahum fil fulkil mashhooni. (41) Wa khalaqna lahum mim mithlihi ma yarkabon. (42)" (Surat YaSeen)

"And a sign for them is that we have carried their atoms/forefathers in the loaded ship. (41) And We have created for them similar (vessels) on which they ride. (42)" (YaSeen, 36:41-42)

'A sign for you is that we carried you in the loaded ship.' Those are the souls that are traversing these realities and, 'We created *mislihim*, and those that are like them,' which means the students and the *muqaddams* (lead/advanced follower) that are trying to follow the path of their moons. They took a life of annihilating themselves; I'm nothing, I'm nothing, I'm nothing, and my whole *nazar* (gaze) is on you, and your *nazar* on your Shaykh and your *nazar* on your Shaykh  and that Shaykh's *nazar* (gaze) completely on Prophet ﷺ.

That gives you the entire government of the spiritual realm because their face always to the face that they receive power from. Their moon is always attached to that sun and that sun dressing them completely, from where? From Allah ﷻ. Because the power of the sun is from where? It is from Allah ﷻ. It means the Prophet's ﷺ light is dressing them.

Sun is the Source of Light;
Be Like a Moon and Reflect the Light

Zikr Purifies the Iron in the Blood Which Purifies the Heart

Then our whole life is to follow that reality. I'm nothing, dress me from 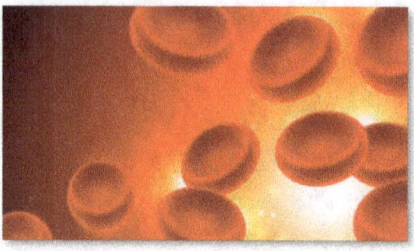 that light. That light begins to dress the iron within the body. As much as we can purify that iron with *zikr* (remembrance), with good food, with drink, everything to be healthy within the body, that iron is being purified. As soon as you bring this energy onto the body, keep it onto the iron, that iron goes into the heart. Because when you understand the cells and the blood cells of the body, the red from the blood is the iron within it. This means that *nazma* and that energy attaches to that iron; that iron moves into the heart.

As soon as your life is based on *zikrullah* (remembrance of Allah ﷻ) and following the reality; every time you say '*Allah*', it stamps that iron, it electrifies and energizes that iron. Then the body will send it throughout the rest of the body. It means the breath comes in, these energies come in, they stamp upon the iron, the iron moves into the heart, stamped by the *zikr* (remembrance), moved out onto the organs of the body and the entire being is 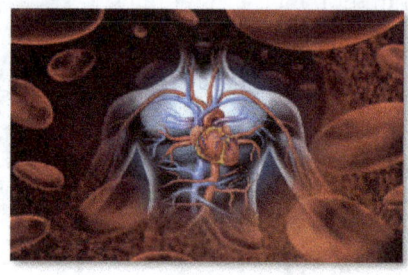 being purified because our heart is the sun.

Allah ﷻ is beginning then the opening of our understanding that, 'If you want to copy My galaxy, My universe, then mimic what I'm doing upon My creation.' So as soon as we focus on the moon, focus upon that light because it is the reflection of the sunlight, we annihilate our self, purify our self.

Reality of Magnetism, Haqiqat ul-Juzba on Spiritual Connection

They begin to teach the iron within you is going to carry that energy and then your breath brings that energy in and stamps that iron and moves it into the heart. From the heart, it is stamped and moved to all the organs of the body and now your *juzba* is building. That is from *haqiqat ul-juzba*, that you can't have no *juzba* (magnetism) and you won't have any magnetism if you are not in the *tafakkur* (contemplation) of one of these *ulul amr* 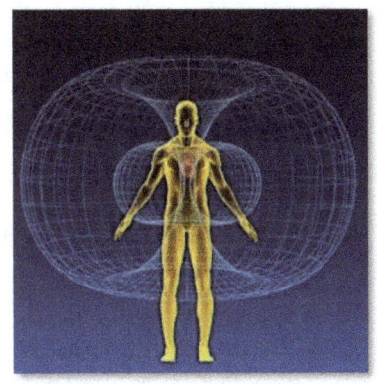 (saints), because Allah ﷻ dresses nobody directly.

"*Ateeullah*", because nobody can reach the station of *ateeullah* – It's impossible. This is a station for the prophets. "*Ateeur-rasul wa Ulul amrin minkum.*" So, Allah ﷻ made our life to be easy, be connected to these *ulul amr* (people of the Command). By being connected to the *ulul amr* (saints), they dress us and bless us from these realities.

...أَطِيعُواللّٰه وَأَطِيعُواْالرَّسُولَ وَأُوْلِي الْأَمْرِ مِنْكُمْ... ﴿٥٩﴾

4:59 – "*...Atiullaha wa atiur Rasula wa Ulil amre minkum...*" (Surat An-Nisa)

"... Obey Allah, Obey the Messenger, and those in authority among you..." (The Women, 4:59)

Spiritually Connect With Your Shaykh (Guide)

This means *haqiqat ul-juzba* is based on our grasping of *tafakkur* and contemplation, that as much as I negate myself in life and I'm nothing, I'm nothing; *ya Rabbi*, let me to be dressed by these lights, blessed by these lights. Then Allah ﷻ says, 'Okay, then be like a moon. Take the

Sun is the Source of Light;
Be Like a Moon and Reflect the Light

course of one of them. Follow them. Make your whole *nazar* (gaze) upon them, that your gaze be upon them,' which means follow their path.

And when you're not with them physically, you keep with them spiritually. It means in *tafakkur* when you are sitting and contemplating, you don't need to always be with them (Shaykhs) physically. You train yourself that spiritually when you connect, that let my moon to always be present with me, *ya Rabbi*, that my guide and my *murshid* (teacher) is always  present with me. That I'm nothing and that my spiritual vision begins to see and sense them.

You use the imitated, which is the body, to reach towards the reality which is the soul. The time that you spend with your physical body with these moons and these realities, with these guides was so that you would

 open the reality of your soul with them. You spent time, you looked at them, you understood them, you understand the *surat*, you're following their path, you have a love for them. As soon as you sit and contemplate that, 'I don't want to ever be alone *ya Rabbi*, let me to always be like your planets. Let me always to be in the presence of that moon which is always in the presence of that sun which is always reflecting your light.'

The Presence of the Shaykh Dresses You With Juzba (Magnetism)

You train yourself all the time to be in that presence. Every time you're sitting and contemplating, you're taking that dress of that presence. When you sit in the *majlis* (association) of the *zikr* (remembrance), you annihilate yourself and keep in the presence of that reality. You do it constantly, why? Because Allah ﷻ describes the moon and the sun, they never leave an  orbit, there's no timeout. The moon doesn't say, 'Oh, okay, no I'm not going to do this now.' It's continuously in an orbit, moving, moving, moving, moving. It means our life is continuously on that reality, that at

 every moment, I'm asking to be in that dress, to be blessed by that dress, that I'm nothing, I'm nothing; let me to reflect that dress. And it begins to send, as much as we can contain, as much as we build ourselves with good practices; as much as that light begins to stay. As much as that light begins to stay and that becomes *haqiqat ul-juzba*. The *juzba* (magnetism) becomes so strong that people are attracted to them, why? Because it's like moonlight

Sun is the Source of Light;
Be Like a Moon and Reflect the Light

The Moons of Reality Take Away Your Difficulties

The *jazba* (magnetism) of the moon, it can move the tide of the entire ocean. So, when we say that this doesn't make sense, then Allah's ﷻ teaching that, 'Look on the outside. The moon on the outside controls so many emotions and energies, it controls the tide of the oceans.

Then imagine what the moon that you focus on can do – what type of energies it can bring, what type of emotions it can cleanse, what type of difficulties it takes away.' All the lunacy that we have is our disconnect from this reality. All the difficulties we have is the disconnect from that reality.

As soon as you go back into the way of *tafakkur* and contemplation, you are reconnecting with the life that Allah ﷻ wanted us to always be connected with, so that you are fulfilling *ateeullah, ateeur Rasul wa ulul amrin minkum*.

أَطِيعُواللَّهَ وَأَطِيعُواْالرَّسُولَ وَأُوْلِي الْأَمْرِ مِنْكُمْ... ﴿٥٩﴾

4:59 – "...*Atiullaha wa atiur Rasula wa Ulil amre minkum*..." (Surat An-Nisa)

"... Obey Allah, Obey the Messenger, and those in authority among you..." (The Women, 4:59)

That chain of light is reaching to us and it takes away insanity, it takes away sickness, it takes away difficulty. It takes everything away and dresses us, blesses us. And if it affects an ocean, imagine that the 70% of water within our body, how it's affected by that light.

We pray that Allah ﷻ grant us more and more understanding from what's outside and around us to the reality that's actually within us and that we can copy that reality and move towards Allah's ﷻ Satisfaction, *inshaAllah*.

Subhana rabbika rabbal 'izzati 'amma yasifoon, wa salaamun 'alal mursaleen, walhamdulillahi rabbil 'aalameen. Bi hurmati Muhammad al-Mustafa wa bi siri Surat al-Fatiha.

The Universe Within
The Sun (Heart), The Moon (Face), and 11 Planets (Essential Organs)

In the holy month of Dhul Hijja and the holy *Hajj* (pilgrimage), these are the blessed days. These are the days in which Allah ﷻ wants to gift to the servant the lights of Divine Realities. That all of the Heavens are open from *malakut* (heavenly realm) to *mulk* (earthly realm); everything is opened to begin to dress the souls of servants. Those who are ascending through their *Islam* (submission), through their *iman* (faith), and through their *Maqam al-Ihsan* (Station of Moral Excellence). It means these are the holy nights in which Allah ﷻ is blessing and dressing them.

Hajj (Pilgrimage) is the Pay Day – Reward of 12 Months Journey

Those who took a path of every year starting in Muharram to imitate the way of *awliyaullah* (saints), where they understood there are twelve *hijabs* (veils), and their life is a constant *hijrah* (migration) into the Divinely Presence. They take a path and follow *Ahl al-Haqqaiq*, the People of Realities.

إِنَّ عِدَّةَ الشُّهُورِ عِندَ اللَّهِ اثْنَا عَشَرَ شَهْرًا فِي كِتَابِ اللَّهِ يَوْمَ خَلَقَ السَّمَاوَاتِ وَالْأَرْضَ مِنْهَا أَرْبَعَةٌ حُرُمٌ ۚ

9:36 – *"Inna 'iddatash shuhoori 'indal laahis naa 'ashara shahran fee Kitaabil laahi yawma khalaqas samaawaati wal arda minhaaa arba'atun hurum." (Surat At-Tawbah)*

The Universe Within – The Sun (Heart), The Moon (Face), and 11 Planets (Essential Organs)

The number of months with Allah is twelve [lunar] (in a year) – so ordained by Allah the day He created the heavens and the earth; of them, four are sacred." (The Repentance, 9:36)

Alhamdulillah, this is the pay day. This month of Dhul Hijja, and these  first ten days, are the days in which Allah ﷻ dresses that servant who has been traveling through the deserts of *dunya* (material world) and coming on to their twelfth month through all their testings and everything throughout the year. This is the time in which Allah ﷻ and the *rahmah* (mercy) of Sayyidina Muhammad ﷺ begins to dress. The *barakah* (blessings) of *awliyaullah* (saints) begins to dress and bless these souls. We pray that Allah ﷻ includes us amongst them.

We are coming only by means of our love for Allah ﷻ, love for Sayyidina Muhammad ﷺ, love for *awliyaullah* (saints), and pious people. We claim nothing, and our actions are nothing and we pray Allah ﷻ be *Ghaforur Raheem* (All Forgiving, Most Merciful) and forgive us where we are coming short. Allah's ﷻ Greatness and *Azimah* is something that can't be imagined. My smallness is so small that I am astonished if Allah ﷻ even notices me. It means He can wipe out sins in an instant. All we have to do is ask and Allah ﷻ grants, *inshaAllah*.

Know the Arbab (Lords) That Govern You

In these holy months, it's a reminder for ourselves that the reality of *Hajj* (pilgrimage) is infinite in its understanding. For *Ahlul Tazkiya*, and the people who are trying to clean and purify themselves, that from holy *Hadith* of Prophet ﷺ, 'Who knows himself will know His Lord.' Who does not know himself will not know his Lord.

مَنْ عَرَفَ نَفْسَهُ فَقَدْ عَرَفَ رَبَّهُ

"Man 'arafa nafsa hu faqad 'arafa Rabba hu."

"Who knows himself, knows his Lord." (Prophet Muhammad (pbuh))

So, we took a path in which we are trying to know our self. That way of knowing the self means you are going to find all the *rabs* (lords) and all the *arbab* (lords) that are governing *insan* (humankind). So, there is not only one *rab*, Allah ﷻ. Allah ﷻ is the Creator! But there are many lords upon this heart that are governing this body not to submit, not to pray, not to fast, not to give in charity. Had we conquered these *rabs* and destroyed the false lords that govern this body, we could be walking on water. We would be seeing the Seven Heavens and hearing the *zikr* (chanting) of *malaika* (angels).

It means if we didn't achieve that, then they are reminding us there are many lords upon your heart. These were the idols in which Prophet ﷺ was fighting – 360 idols in Makkah. Makkah is the state of the heart. 360 idols that were blocking and encompassing Makkah because it is significant for the heart. It means that we have 360 *lataif* (subtle energy points) on the body. Each one of them has an idol on its place that is trying to block us from submission to Allah ﷻ.

12 Surats (Chapters) of Holy Qur'an in 12 Lunar Months

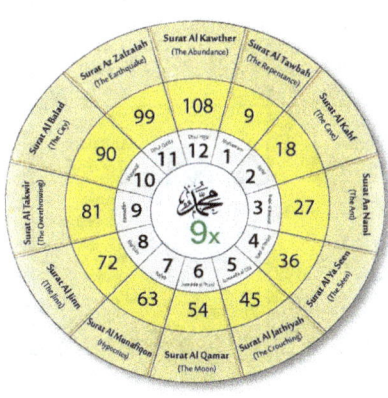

And what we talked about before is that Sayyidina Yusuf عليه السلام, the 12th Surat (Joseph – 12th chapter of Holy Qur'an) is for the common people. Because this reality will go all the way up till 9x12, which is Surat Kawthar (The Abundance – 108th chapter of Holy Qur'an). *Ahli Kawthar* (People of the Kawthar) means the people of *ma'rifah*

The Universe Within — The Sun (Heart), The Moon (Face), and 11 Planets (Essential Organs)

(gnostics) are moving from base 9. They move through the Surat Tawbah (9th chapter of Holy Qur'an) all the way to the 12th *hijab* (veil) which is Surat Al Kawthar (108th).

12 Lunar Months		Common People		Awliyaullah (Saints) Power of 9	
Month	Name of Month	Chapter of Holy Qur'an	Name of Surat	Chapter of Holy Qur'an	Name of Surat
1	Muharram	1	Surat Al Fatiha (The Opener)	9 9x1=9	Surat At Tawbah (The Repentance)
2	Safar	2	Surat Al Baqarah (The Cow)	18 9x2=18	Surat Al Kahf (The Cave)
3	Rabi'ul Awwal	3	Surat 'Ali 'Imran (Family of Imran)	27 9x3=27	Surat An Naml (The Ant)
4	Rabi'ul Thani	4	Surat An Nisa (The Women)	36 9x4=36	Surat YaSeen (YaSeen)
5	Jumadal Awwal	5	Surat Al Ma'idah (The Table Spread)	45 9x5=45	Surat Al Jathiyah (The Crouching)
6	Jumadal Thani	6	Surat Al An'am (The Cattle)	54 9x6=54	Surat Al Qamar (The Moon)
7	Rajab	7	Surat Al A'raf (The Heights)	63 9x7=63	Surat Al Munafiqoon (The Hypocrites)
8	Sha'ban	8	Surat Al Anfal (The Spoils of War)	72 9x8=72	Surat Al Jinn (The Jinn)
9	Ramadan	9	Surat At Tawbah (The Repentance)	81 9x9=81	Surat At Takwir (The Overthrowing)
10	Shawwal	10	Surat Yunus (Jonah)	90 9x10=90	Surat Al Balad (The City)
11	Dhul Qi'dah	11	Surat Hud (Hud)	99 9x11=99	Surat Az Zalzalah (The Earthquake)
12	Dhul Hijja	12	Surat Yusuf (Joseph)	108 9x12=108	Surat Al Kawthar (The Abundance)

For us common people, we are on the 12th Surat of Holy Qur'an as an example for us in this holy 12th month, the month of completion. Where Sayyidina Yusuf عليه السلام is inspiring within ourselves that, 'You are going to be thrown into a hole, into a well and you are going to be isolated,' and then all our life is about fixing that self.

Obey Allah ﷻ, Obey the Messenger ﷺ, and Those in Authority (Saints)

That before that *Hajj* (pilgrimage) and from *Bismillahir Rahmaanir Raheem, Atiullah ati ar Rasula wa ulul amri minkum*, (Obey Allah, Obey the Messenger, and those in authority among you.)

...أَطِيعُواللَّهَ وَأَطِيعُواْ ٱلرَّسُولَ وَأُوْلِي ٱلْأَمْرِ مِنْكُمْ... ﴿٥٩﴾

4:59 – "...*Atiullaha wa atiur Rasula wa Ulil amre minkum...*" (Surat An-Nisa)

"... Obey Allah, Obey the Messenger, and those in authority among you..." (The Women, 4:59)

Islam (submission), *iman* (faith) *wal Maqam al-Ihsan* (Station of Moral Excellence). These are three that are governing our entire life. *Maqam al-Ihsan* (Station of Moral Excellence) from *atiullah* (obedience to Allah ﷻ). *Maqam al-Iman* (Station of Faith) from the obedience to Prophet ﷺ where Prophet ﷺ describes that, 'You have to love me more than yourself.' Then you have the *Maqam* of *Iman* (Station of Faith).

لَا يُؤْمِنُ أَحَدُكُمْ حَتَّى أَكُونَ أَحَبَّ إِلَيْهِ مِنْ وَالِدِهِ وَوَلَدِهِ وَالنَّاسِ أَجْمَعِينَ

The Universe Within – The Sun (Heart), The Moon (Face), and 11 Planets (Essential Organs)

"La yuminu ahadukum hatta akona ahabba ilayhi min walidihi wa waladihi wan Nasi ajma'yeen."

"None of you will have faith till he loves me more than his father, his children and all mankind." (Prophet Muhammad (pbuh))

Then *Ulul amri minkum* (people of the command amongst you) means to follow the *ulul amr* (saints) in our lives. That is the way to achieve our *Islam* (submission).

- ***Maqam al Ihsan*** – from *ati ullah* – Obedience to Allah
- ***Maqam al Iman*** – from the obedience to Prophet – To love Prophet more than yourself
- ***Maqam al Islam*** – from *Ulul amri minkum* – To follow the *ulul amr* (saints) to achieve *Islam* (submission)

Islam is Not a Label, It's the Action of Submitting

Islam is not a noun that you wear upon yourself and say, 'I am a Muslim.' You are not a Muslim until you reach submission. Once you have reached submission, Allah declares the title, 'Now you are a Muslim. You are somebody who is submitting.' If you are not somebody who is submitting, then you are merely wearing Islam like it is a Versace or Polo. It is just a noun. It is not really an action for you.

First Make Inner Hajj (Pilgrimage) to Your Heart

We took a path of action that Allah inspired us. Allah took us and threw us onto that path. On that path, these *ulul amr* (saints) inspire that before that (physical) *Hajj* (pilgrimage), make the *hajj* (pilgrimage) within yourself. When Allah talks about His Holy House, He is talking about your heart. That you have a Ka'bah within yourself and that  make your heart My House. It means bring Me into your heart. The heart that is occupied with everything of this material world. It's occupied by its desires, its *hawa*, it is occupied by its wants. It is occupied by what it wants to eat and see and do. Those are all *rab*, these are all the *arbab* (lords) of *dunya* (material world) that block the body and say, 'Don't submit to *Rabbi al 'Aala*, don't submit to the Lord Most High. Submit to our desires.'

So, our *hajj* (pilgrimage) is not only the $15,000 package in Saudi Arabia, but the first *hajj* (pilgrimage) is within ourselves. It is so easy, so, nobody can say, '*Ya Rabbi*, I didn't have the means to make it.' No, you slept with that being everyday. That *hajj* (pilgrimage) is you. That way is within us. There is no ticket required, you see him or her every night. What they want from us is then the House, your heart, is the Holy Ka'bah of Allah ﷻ. Busy yourself going into your heart. Busy yourself with all your being.

قَلْبَ الْمُؤْمِنْ بَيْتُ الرَّبْ

"*Qalb al mu'min baytur rabb.*"

"*The heart of the believer is the House of the Lord.*" (Hadith Qudsi)

Alif, Laam, Ra – The Reality of Rabaniyoon

Sayyidina Yusuf ﷺ reminds us because it is a big reality. *Alif, Laam, Ra*, because this is the reality of the *Rabaniyoon*.

الر ۚ تِلْكَ آيَاتُ الْكِتَابِ الْمُبِينِ ﴿١﴾

12:1 – "*Alif-Lam-Ra; tilka Aayaatul Kitaabil Mubeen.*"
(*Surat Yusuf*)

"*Alif, Lam, Ra. These are the verses of the clear Book.*" (Joseph, 12:1)

The Universe Within — The Sun (Heart), The Moon (Face), and 11 Planets (Essential Organs)

'Izzatullah bi lisan al Haqq into the *Laam* of Sayyidina Muhammad ﷺ, and the *Ra*; these are the stories, the *qisas* of the *arbab* (lords). These are the souls, the lordly souls. These are not the houses of the commoners but the house of lords. It means Allah ﷻ has gifted to souls lofty titles.

الر		
ر	ل	ا
Ra	Laam	Alif
Rabaniyoon (Lordly Souls)	Lisan ul Haq (Tongue of Truth)	'Izzatullah (Allah's ﷻ Might)
Ulul Amr (Saints)	RasulAllah ﷺ	Allah ﷻ

Note: Please read English from right to left to coincide with Arabic.

If we keep ourselves to be from commoners, it means we are not trying to reach towards the Heavens. We are trying to be people of the barnyard who eat, drink, and go to the bathroom. Allah ﷻ said that is why I sent you down because you ate, and you weren't supposed to go to the bathroom in Paradise. It means that is not our reality. Our reality is the lofty titles. The lofty soul which Allah ﷻ wants from us, "Be *Rabaniyoon*." It is in Surat 'Ali 'Imran, Verse 79.

... وَلَـٰكِن كُونُوا رَبَّانِيِّينَ بِمَا كُنتُمْ تُعَلِّمُونَ الْكِتَابَ وَبِمَا كُنتُمْ تَدْرُسُونَ ﴿٧٩﴾

3:79 – "…*wa lakin kono rabbaniyena bima kuntum tu`allimoonal kitaba wabima kuntum tadrusoon.*" *(Surat 'Ali 'Imran)*

"…*Be Lordly Souls/faithful servants/worshippers of Him, Because (of what) you have taught the Book and you have studied it earnestly."* *(Family of Imran, 3:79)*

Be *Rabaniyoon*. You learned the *kitab* (book) and you taught the *kitab* and your whole life is to be from that reality.

The Sun, the Moon, and 11 Stars Bowing to Awliyaullah (Saints)

Prophet Yusuf (Joseph) ﷷ comes into our life and teaches, that he said to his father, '*Ya Baba*, I am having a dream that the 11 planets are bowing to me and the Sun and the Moon are bowing to me.'

إِذْ قَالَ يُوسُفُ لِأَبِيهِ يَا أَبَتِ إِنِّي رَأَيْتُ أَحَدَ عَشَرَ كَوْكَبًا وَالشَّمْسَ وَالْقَمَرَ رَأَيْتُهُمْ لِي سَاجِدِينَ

12:4 – "Idh qala Yosufu li abeehi ya abati innee raaytu ahada Ashara kawkaban wash Shamsa wal Qamara raaytuhum le sajideen." (Surat Yusuf)

"[Of these stories mention] when Joseph said to his father, "O my father, indeed I have seen [in a dream] eleven stars and the sun and the moon; I saw them prostrating to me." (Joseph, 12:4)

Awliyaullah (saints) come into our life and teach, 'That that is the reality of *awliyaullah* (saints).' What did Prophet ﷺ describe from the prophets of *Bani Israel*? My *ulama* (scholars) inherit the realities and the stations of *Bani Israel* and the prophets of *Bani Israel*.

عُلَمَاءِ وَرِثَةُ الْأَنْبِيَاء

"*Ulama e warithatul anbiya.*"

"*The scholars are the inheritors of the prophets.*"

The Universe Within – The Sun (Heart), The Moon (Face), and 11 Planets (Essential Organs)

Allah ﷻ doesn't care for *dunya* (material world), He cares for the *malakut* (heavens) and the World of Light. When Allah ﷻ gives *awliyaullah*, gives pious people, He doesn't give them cash; He doesn't give them an accounting license, He gives from His Heavens. He ﷻ says, this Heaven is under your control, these stars are under your control, this Moon is under your control, and this Sun is under your control.

وَسَخَّرَ لَكُم مَّا فِي السَّمَاوَاتِ وَمَا فِي الْأَرْضِ جَمِيعاً مِّنْهُ إِنَّ فِي ذَلِكَ لَآيَاتٍ لَقَوْمٍ يَتَفَكَّرُونَ

45:13 – *"Wa sakhkhara lakum ma fis Samawati wa ma fil Ardi jamee'an minhu, inna fee dhalika la ayatin liqawmin yatafakkaron."* (Surat Al-Jathiya)

"And He has subjected/gave the authority to you, as from Him, all that is in the heavens and on earth: Behold, in that are Signs indeed for those who do Tafakkur, reflect/Contemplate [Meditate]." (The Crouching, 45:13)

How many galaxies do we have within this universe? Billions! So, Allah ﷻ is not running out. He says, I can bring a galaxy in an instant and you will be placed under control of it. That is what I want to give to you from the *mulk* of the Heavens, the *mulk* of *dunya* and then from the *malakut*, Heavens, which is *kulli shay* (all encompassing). Glory be to the hand that encompasses the *malakut* (heavens). That one holds everything.

فَسُبْحَانَ الَّذِي بِيَدِهِ مَلَكُوتُ كُلِّ شَيْءٍ وَإِلَيْهِ تُرْجَعُونَ ﴿٨٣﴾

36:83 – *"Fasubhanal ladhee biyadihi Malakutu kulli shay in wa ilayhi turja'oon." (Surat YaSeen)*

"Therefore, Glory be to Him in Whose hand is the [heavenly] dominion/ kingdom of all things, and to Him you will be returned." (YaSeen, 36:83)

Don't think that it is something small, that Allah ﷻ says, *"Wa laqad karamna bani Adam"* (Holy Qur'an, 17:70). He says, I want to give you what you can't imagine. What *awliyaullah* are in charge of, I want to give that to you. I want these 11 planets and the Sun and the Moon to be at your feet, under your command but you must govern yourself accordingly.

The Universe Within

Sun (Heart), Moon (Face), and 11 Stars (Essential Organs)

What they begin to inspire, when you look within yourself and contemplate and meditate within yourself, that you have eleven essential organs. You have a heart which is your *shams* (sun), and you have a head, your brain, your face, which is your *qamar* (moon). So, Allah ﷻ, just as every father says, if you can manage the small, I will give you the big one to manage. But if you can't manage yourself, how am I going to give you the Heavens to be under your control?

Then our whole *tazkiya* (purification) is about understanding myself. What is the reality of my organs, what is the reality of my sun, and my heart? What is the reality of the moon that is my face?

The Universe Within – The Sun (Heart), The Moon (Face), and 11 Planets (Essential Organs)

The Condition of the Heart Affects the Whole Body

So then other people and other religions busy themselves in trying to open their energy and play with other planets because they work on a different system. *Awliyaullah* (saints) from Prophet ﷺ say, there is one focus for you, it is the heart. 'There is one piece of the flesh that if it is good, all of you is good; if it is bad, all of you is bad.'

أَلَا وَإِنَّ فِى الْجَسَدِ مُضْغَةً إِذَا صَلَحَتْ صَلَحَ الْجَسَدُ كُلُّهُ، وَإِذَا فَسَدَتْ فَسَدَ الْجَسَدُ كُلُّهُ، أَلَا وَهِى الْقَلْبُ

"Ala wa inna fil Jasadi mudghatan idha salahat salahal jasadu kulluho, wa idha fasadat fasadal jasadu kulluho, ala wa heyal Qalb."

"There is a piece of flesh in the body, if it becomes good (reformed) the whole body becomes good but if it gets spoiled the whole body gets spoiled and that is the heart." (Prophet Muhammad (pbuh))

Prophet ﷺ taught them, taught the companions, taught the *Ahlul Bayt* (his Family), and taught *awliyaullah* (saints). You want to inherit from the Heavens? You want to inherit from the Heavens go into the heart; don't waste your time on anything else. This is not about the brain, this is not about the endocrine system, this is not about the liver; this is only 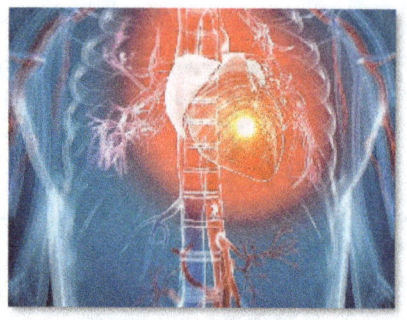 about the heart. Conquer the heart; who governs the heart governs the entire body!

Our Way is Waquf al Qalb – Vigilance of the Heart

Then the way of *ma'rifah* (gnosticism) they begin to contemplate and look into the heart and they begin to observe all the desires of the heart. Be vigilant upon the heart that every word the *ulul amr* (saints) speak and teach, how is it affecting my heart? If my heart is palpitating and becoming nervous, something is wrong. It means *waquf*, vigilance of the heart; your whole life is about being vigilant with your heart. Every reality they are teaching, is it causing distress in the heart and why? Then there is something there, there is an issue. Is there a desire that governs the heart that is in conflict with what they are teaching of these realities?

It means our way is based then on complete vigilance over the heart. We are observing the heart and the desires and wants that are coming into the heart. It means how then to protect the heart and how then to bless and clean the heart? Where Allah ﷻ describes, this is My house. Clean it, wash it, bless it and circumambulate around it.

... أَن طَهِّرَا بَيْتِيَ لِلطَّائِفِينَ وَالْعَاكِفِينَ وَالرُّكَّعِ السُّجُودِ ﴿١٢٥﴾

2:125 – "...An Tahhir baytee liTayifeena, wal 'Aakifeena, wa ruka'is sujood." (Surat Al-Baqarah)

"...Purify/Sanctify My House for those who perform Tawaf (circamambulation) and those who seclude themselves for devotion and bow and prostrate [in prayer]." (The Cow, 2:125)

Be Cautious When You Don't Want Zikrullah (Remembrance of Allah ﷻ)

This is the heart. I wash my heart *bi zikrullah*, I am going to wash my

heart with praising upon Prophet ﷺ, with *majlis* (association) of *zikr* (remembrance). Only the *zikr* and *awrad* (daily practices) has an energy that begins to purify the heart. It is not something easy. And if you are not capable of doing the *zikr* and making the *salawat* (praisings on Prophet ﷺ), don't attribute it to yourself and say, 'Yeah, you know, I couldn't do it.' No, there is an even scarier thought that Allah ﷻ is not permitting you to

The Universe Within —The Sun (Heart), The Moon (Face), and 11 Planets (Essential Organs)

mention His Name on your tongue or on your heart! That, you should be very scared of.

Allah Gives Permission For His Holy Name to Be Mentioned

Allah describes in Surat An-Nur, We allow Our Name to be mentioned in their homes.

فِي بُيُوتٍ أَذِنَ اللَّـهُ أَن تُرْفَعَ وَيُذْكَرَ فِيهَا اسْمُهُ يُسَبِّحُ لَهُ فِيهَا بِالْغُدُوِّ وَالْآصَالِ ﴿٣٦﴾

24:36 – "Fee buyotin adhina Allahu an turfa'a wa yudhkara feeha ismuhu yusabbihu lahu feeha bilghuduwwi wal asal." (Surat An-Nur)

"(Lit is such a Light) in houses, which Allah has permitted to be raised to honour; and that His name be mentioned therein: In them He is glorified in the mornings and in the evenings, (again and again)." (The Light, 24:36)

Allah says, We allow Our Name to be mentioned within their homes. Your home is your heart. If Allah does not give permission, there is no way you will mention His Name upon your tongue or your heart. That is scary.

That is when you begin to cry, '*Ya Rabbi*, please inspire me to do my *awrad*, please inspire me to constantly make *darood shareef* and praise upon Sayyidina Muhammad.' My house is my heart; it's the only house that matters. Every other house may go in a tidal wave, may go in a *tufan*, or tornado, but what I am taking into this grave is this house. And Allah says then, 'We have to allow Our Name to be mentioned within your heart.' It means then my whole vigilance is, '*Ya Rabbi*, please make me to have firmness in my *zikr* (remembrance). Make me to have firmness in the *salawat* (praisings) upon Prophet ﷺ.'

Protect Your Heart More Than Your Wealth

Ya Rabbi, let me be vigilant upon my heart and what is trying to come to my heart and what is trying to attack my heart. Your heart becomes more precious than your home.

You can see people and what they prioritize in life. If your home has twenty carats of diamonds and I drove by your house, I bet everything will have solid metal and be locked. All night long you will be thinking, 'Someone is going to come and break through the window and steal everything. Where am I going to hide it (diamonds)? I will dig it in the ground.' Dig, dig, dig, and then I will also make all the doors and windows with steel.

Allah ﷻ says, this is for *dunya* (material world); imagine what I am putting and bestowing of reality into your heart. Why are you so quick to put it everywhere so that it can be stolen? It means then pious people

are vigilant of their heart. They don't go anywhere where it is not necessary to go. They don't open their heart where it is not necessary to open because they know that Allah ﷻ is depositing a treasure within the heart, and *Shaytan* (Satan) knows it and wants to just pick at it, and pick at it until you have *shak,* doubt, in your belief. If doubt begins to enter into the belief, know that *Shaytan* is mining your heart. He is pulling it out, he has got all the treasures and it is a full-on raid on your heart.

The Universe Within – The Sun (Heart), The Moon (Face), and 11 Planets (Essential Organs)

Be Careful Where You Go – Do They Take Your Light or Give You Light?

So, they teach us, 'Be vigilant of the heart. If you want these treasures to be placed upon the heart you have to have *istiqaamah* and have firmness in your belief, firmness in the practices, firmness in the *zikr*, and firmness in the love of Prophet ﷺ.' *Ya Rabbi*, my path is to love Sayyidina Muhammad ﷺ more than I love myself.

أَمْ حَسِبْتُمْ أَن تَدْخُلُوا الْجَنَّةَ وَلَمَّا يَعْلَمِ اللَّهُ الَّذِينَ جَاهَدُوا مِنكُمْ وَيَعْلَمَ الصَّابِرِينَ ﴿١٤٢﴾

3:142 – "*Am hasibtum an tadkhulo alJannata wa lamma ya'lami Allahu alladheena jahado minkum wa ya'lama asSabireen.*" (Surat 'Ali 'Imran)

"Or do you think that you will enter Paradise while Allah has not yet made evident those of you who fight in His cause and made evident those who are steadfast/Patient?" (Family of Imran, 3:142)

All I want are the shining suns that represent the love of Sayyidina Muhammad ﷺ. I am not interested in sitting with anyone else because anyone else will take the jewels from my heart.

Some people go everywhere like it is a free *bazaar* (marketplace). You don't know who is putting jewels into your heart or who is taking the jewels from your heart, because within two or three words of what they say you find yourself having doubt and darkness comes. So, you don't just go anywhere, you don't just pray anywhere. You want to make sure that is a shining sun and those are the lovers of Sayyidina Muhammad ﷺ. They are going to deposit the love of Sayyidina

Muhammad ﷺ into my heart. If it is not, and they are not shining that light, they are going to send darkness into my heart. They are going to come against the *Sunnah* (way of Prophet ﷺ), they are going to come against the *Hadith* (traditions of Prophet).

We said before, in your heart and in your mind don't ever say, 'This is a weak *Hadith*.' There is only a weak believer who is filled with *shak* and doubt. All they want now is to attack the *Sunnah* of Prophet ﷺ, attack the greatness of Sayyidina Muhammad ﷺ by constantly putting doubt, constantly putting doubt and they say, they are only *Ahlul Qur'an*. This is *hizbush Shaytan* (party of Satan).

Qur'an does not open without the love of Sayyidina Muhammad ﷺ. We  are not the people who have any doubt. If you don't understand that it came from Prophet ﷺ then you should be making *tafakkur*, contemplation, and connecting your heart with the heart of Sayyidina Muhammad ﷺ. He ﷺ will confirm within your heart exactly what it is and its reality!

The Heart is the Real Sun

It means we took a path of how to open the heart and as soon as we open the heart, we realize the organs and their importance. Allah is saying, if you don't have a Sun your galaxy is already dead; how are you going to manage My galaxy? So, we go and say to the Shaykh, 'I wonder if this person was enlightened? He  is watching TV and levitating off the ground, is he enlightened? Does

The Universe Within – The Sun (Heart), The Moon (Face), and 11 Planets (Essential Organs)

he have spiritual power?' That is very easy for us, if the person's heart is lit, and lit with faith, that will dress all the organs. From the *Hadith* of Prophet ﷺ, if one piece is good, all of that person is good; if the heart is bad, all of it is bad.

أَلا وَإِنَّ فِى الْجَسَدِ مُضْغَةً إِذَا صَلَحَتْ صَلَحَ الْجَسَدُ كُلُّهُ، وَإِذَا فَسَدَتْ فَسَدَ الْجَسَدُ كُلُّهُ، أَلا وَهِىَ الْقَلْب

"Ala wa inna fil Jasadi mudghatan idha salahat salahal jasadu kulluho, wa idha fasadat fasadal jasadu kulluho, ala wa heyal Qalb."

"There is a piece of flesh in the body, if it becomes good (reformed) the whole body becomes good but if it gets spoiled the whole body gets spoiled Heart emanating light and that is the heart."
(Prophet Muhammad (pbuh))

This means if the heart is lit, their galaxy has a Sun. Whatever practices they are doing, their heart is becoming stronger and stronger and stronger and what is the most favoured time for Islam? It's the full moon, the time of perfection, because the Moon is capturing all the light of the Sun.

So then they begin to teach, 'If your heart is lit, and you lit the heart with *awliyaullah*, lit it with *zikr* (remembrance), lit it with the *salawat* (praising) for Prophet ﷺ, and lit it with *Islam* (submission), and you are now entering the realities with *Iman* (faith), that heart is burning like a sun and your face is like a moon.'

Life Depends on the Imitated Sun, Imagine the Power Allah ﷻ Gave to Awliya

People of *tafakkur* (contemplation) stop there and make *tafakkur*. What power does the Sun have on Creation? If that is an imitated Sun and *awliyaullah*, and pious people, if their hearts become a real Sun, that Allah ﷻ gives them *Nurul anwaar wa siratul asraar* (The light of every secret and the Secret of every light). If that *nur* (light) really opens within their heart what type of power does that light have? Don't you take your vision from the Sun? Don't you take your breath from the Sun? Isn't all the vegetation you are eating from the *shams* (sun)?

What then are you getting from the *awliya* (saints) if their souls are more powerful than the Sun? Sayyidina Yusuf عليه السلام said, 'They are all bowing down to me,' which means 'my station is above their station'. What are you then taking from their souls if their heart is emanating and dressing?

What do you take from the Moon? How it raises vegetation, how it brings the tides up and down; it means everything on this *dunya* (worldly life) is affected by that Moon. So, it is not something small. It is so huge that *Shaytan's* (Satan's) only interest is to make sure nobody reaches that reality. If you should reach that reality you are more powerful than a thousand men on this *dunya*.

The Universe Within – The Sun (Heart), The Moon (Face), and 11 Planets (Essential Organs)

If your heart becomes a sun, it is a sun in which eyes can see. We talked about the Sun in the Heavens. How is it shining (continuously), then it has *lail* (night), then when it enters the Earth it is *nahar* (daylight). The Sun is always shining but we don't have the eyes to see its light. Only when it enters *dunya* we can only see that line of it, that electromagnetic pulsar. What it enters into *dunya* Allah ﷻ gave us the ability to see. So what light is Allah ﷻ sending upon the souls of *awliya* (saints) and the realities of these souls? They open their heart and their heads become like a full Moon  and every organ of their body is governed in its reality.

Your Breath is the Power of Your Heart, Your Sun

Then they come into your life (and teach) that within yourself is the Tree of Life, which are your lungs. And *nafas ar-Rahmah* (breath of mercy) is going to be the power and *qudra* for your entire galaxy because you want to inherit. '*Ya Rabbi*, I want to inherit Your Heavens, I want to inherit Your Heavens.' So, then what are you doing smoking? You see some people saying, 'Oh this is a big Shaykh and he is puffing on a cigarette.' His *sidratul muntaha* (tree of life) is on fire. What are you 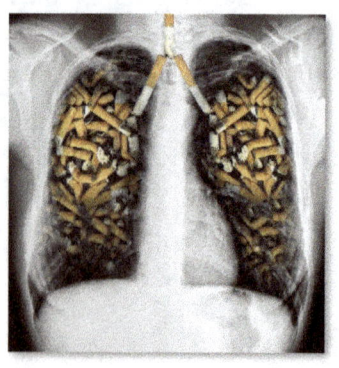 talking about? How is he a big Shaykh? You think he is from *awliyaullah*, that Allah ﷻ gave him to inherit from the Heavens, yet his Tree of Life is on fire? It's impossible.

Everything within our body is of importance. You are breathing in (for) this galaxy that Allah ﷻ gave to you, every breath of *nafas ar-Rahmah* that comes in. Our way is based on the power of that breath. That *nafas* (breath) is the power of your sun. It comes into the lungs and dresses from Allah's ﷻ *zikr* (remembrance) and lights and *rahmah* (mercy). From that the blood takes it and goes into the heart.

If your breath is bad your heart is destroyed, not the fragrance, but the quality of the breath. It means if the breath is not coming in pure and 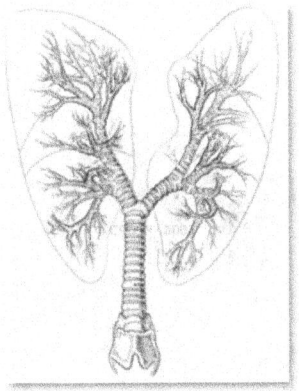 clean, the heart is destroyed. That pure and clean breath is what gives energy to the heart, gives the power to the heart. Then the lungs you see them as an upside-down tree, why? Because this is the Tree of Life. Every life, every reality of yours, is coming through that breath. If you don't govern the breath and understand that breath, that it is a treasure from Allah ﷻ. *Awliyaullah* tell us there are 24,000 treasures in one day, 24,000 realities in one day. Every breath is with a *shukr* and thankfulness to Allah ﷻ.

Shaytan Wants to Destroy the Defense of Your Galaxy

It means then also guard your liver and kidneys. You understand that you have to govern your breath and no doubt *Shaytan* wants to come into my being, and how is he going to come into people's livers? By inspiring them to drink that which is not *halal* (permissible). When they drink something questionable or outright forbidden it is entering into the blood system, it is like *shayateen* (devils) that are attacking the body.

Shayateen want to destroy the defense of that galaxy. They know that if you become a powerful galaxy you are going to wreak havoc on the *shayateen* and their plans for *dunya*, but if you empower yourself it is a difficulty (for them). They know that to destroy the liver, inspire him to drink that which is not acceptable, allowing the *shayateen* inside the body and into the liver. The *shayateen* are coming within the blood and attacking the heart.

The Universe Within – The Sun (Heart), The Moon (Face), and 11 Planets (Essential Organs)

Shaytan Brought E-Cigarette and Sheesha to Kill You Faster

It means in every movement they are attacking the body, and they (*awliya*) begin to inspire and teach us, 'Be careful of your breath, govern your breath that with the *Qudra* (power) of Allah ﷻ dressing you, you don't want anything forbidden within it.'

Shaytan is so obsessed with destroying *insan* (human being) that he makes him to smoke now from a cold smoke, because he couldn't kill him enough with a warm smoke. You can only breathe so deep with fire. Have you been to a sauna and you take a deep breath and it starts to burn after that? So *Shaytan* asks, 'How am I going to get my *dhuriya*, progeny, deeper into that *insan*? I'll make him smoke something cold.' The e-cigarette is a cold vapour to take the *shayateen* (devils) deeper into the body. The *sheesha* has 100 cigarettes in every puff, to completely kill and destroy the lungs so that you destroy the heart and the blood of that *insan* (human being).

First Make Hajj to Your Heart

Allah ﷻ wants that to purify ourselves, purify your being. Make your first *Hajj* (pilgrimage) within your heart. Govern all your organs so that they are perfected and purified and that *Shaytan* is repelled from your being. Only at that time, Allah ﷻ grants sincerity and the heart is lit and the moon is shining, which means their galaxy is lit with energy. Any deficiency within their

organs, their sun will clean it, the sun within their heart; the energy that Allah ﷻ is depositing will begin to clean all the organs and everything of their being. At that time Allah ﷻ begins to grant the inheritance of the Heavens. Then the *Hajj* (pilgrimage) of *Iman* (faith) is towards the reality of Prophet ﷺ.

Subhana rabbika rabbal 'izzati 'amma yasifoon, wa salaamun 'alal mursaleen, walhamdulillahi rabbil 'aalameen. Bi hurmati Muhammad al-Mustafa wa bi siri Surat al-Fatiha.

Open the Sun Within Your Heart, Allah ﷻ Will Fill It With Heavenly Power

Atiullah wa Atiur Rasul wa Ulul Amri minkum.

...أَطِيعُواْ ٱللَّهَ وَأَطِيعُواْ ٱلرَّسُولَ وَأُوْلِي ٱلْأَمْرِ مِنكُمْ... ﴿٥٩﴾

4:59 – "*...Atiullaha wa atiur Rasula wa Ulil amre minkum...*" (Surat An-Nisa)

"... Obey Allah, Obey the Messenger, and those in authority among you..." (The Women, 4:59)

Alhmadulillah, always a reminder for myself that, *ana abdukal Ajeez, wa dayeef, wa miskin, wa zhalim, wa jahl*, and we exist by the Grace of Allah ﷻ, that Allah's ﷻ *Rahmah* (mercy) be upon us and that we live by that *rahmah* (mercy).

Even Children Know That Everything is From Allah ﷻ

Always a reminder when trying to understand *haqqaiq* (realities), Allah ﷻ owns everything. Allah ﷻ is the Creator, Allah ﷻ the Sustainer, Allah ﷻ gives life and takes death – all of that, everybody understands is from Allah ﷻ. *Ma'rifah* (gnosticism) is not that you  simply say Allah ﷻ owns that. That my kindergarten children can say that. Go to the kindergarten, ask the children, 'Who made the sun?'

*Open the Sun Within Your Heart,
Allah ﷻ Will Fill It With Heavenly Power*

'God.' That's not *ma'rifah* (gnosticism). Just to simplify it say, 'God made the sun.'

'How do you breathe?'

'God makes you to breathe.'

Okay, but this is not what they're talking about. When Allah ﷻ wants the servant to understand a reality, it means they bring the servant into the inner working of that reality. That they begin to teach the servant in the *ma'rifah* (gnosticism), *la sharik*, make no partner with Allah ﷻ. What you're about to see, understand that there is no partnership with Allah ﷻ, *la shabih*, there's nothing like unto Allah ﷻ.

So, it means the child says everything from Allah ﷻ. But *ma'rifah* (gnosticism), Allah ﷻ wants to clarify that, 'Yes, I'm the Power of the

sun, I created the sun, but I'm not the sun. I'm everywhere and yet I'm nowhere, for you to see. I'm everywhere.' So *ma'rifah* (gnosticism), Allah ﷻ when He wants to bring the servant towards *arifeen* (knowers), to be the knowers; the reason *ma'rifah* has a *meem* is that Allah's ﷻ going to show that, 'I created all this creation out of the reality of Sayyidina Muhammad ﷺ. And when I love you, I'm going to bring you into My Love and My Love is *yusalluna 'alan-Nabi* ﷺ. My whole Love is for Prophet ﷺ.'

إِنَّ اللَّهَ وَمَلَائِكَتَهُ يُصَلُّونَ عَلَى النَّبِيِّ يَا أَيُّهَا الَّذِينَ آمَنُوا صَلُّوا عَلَيْهِ وَسَلِّمُوا تَسْلِيمًا ﴿٥٦﴾

*33:56 – "InnAllaha wa malayikatahu yusalluna 'alan Nabiyi yaa ayyuhal ladhina aamanu sallu 'alayhi wa sallimu taslima."
(Surat Al-Ahzab)*

"Allah and His angels send blessings upon the Prophet [Muhammad (pbuh)]: O you that believe! Send your blessings upon him, and salute him with all respect." (The Combined Forces, 33:56)

Sayyidina Muhammad ﷺ Was a Chosen Messenger in the World of Light and Malakut (Heavenly Realm)

Allah ﷻ says, 'I created this creation for the love of Prophet ﷺ, for that light and that beauty to be known.' Because you think from the world of form, that Allah ﷻ came up, chose somebody and said, 'You're going to be the proof, and I'm going to give you a message.' But this is *qadim*, this is ancient from the world of light. It was all created for that light, for that reality. It's not from the world of form, it's from the world of light that  everything has already been created; everything has been partitioned, and the world of form merely manifests Allah's ﷻ Will. It's not happening here, Allah's ﷻ not choosing, 'You're the messenger, you're going to be a pious person.' No, you're going to be; it's already been written from *malakut* (heavenly realm)!

When Allah ﷻ created that creation and wanted to be known, He named that light that it's coming from *Muhammadun RasulAllah* ﷺ, 'and I am *La ilaha illallah*' (there is no God but Allah). Allah ﷻ distinguished and said, 'I am *la ilaha illallah* and there's nothing like unto me. But I'm yet the Power of everything. I see and I hear everything, but you can't see Me and you can't hear Me. You see My Signs. You'll see My Signs everywhere.' And the greatest of signs of Allah ﷻ is Sayyidina Muhammad ﷺ, not only the physicality. The greatest sign of Allah ﷻ, *nur al anwar wa sirrat al asrar* (the secret of all light and the light of every secret) is known as *Muhammadun RasulAllah* ﷺ. So, Allah ﷻ is the Creator, but when Allah ﷻ wants the servant to understand, He's going to bring them in to the *haqqaiqs* (realities) and how I made this.

Nucleus is the Sun of Every Atom and Power of Your Manifestation

When we are talking about, *'Ya Rabbi,* show us something from eternity,' Allah (swt) describes the  sun, 'You see the sun and all its power and all its might. I show you another sun, very small within yourself, and it's your atoms and the nucleus that lies within your atom is a sun, is a power, is an energy that is unimaginable.' And that nucleus is the power of your entire manifestation. The energy that's coming to your nucleus is the energy that makes all your electrons to move. As a result of their movement, you're like a hologram that's appearing. Then Allah (swt) says, 'I show you again another sun and that's your heart.'

The reason for these teachings is one that Allah's (swt) Magnificent Creation that, 'You don't know the complexity in which I've created the heavens and the earth. You don't know the complexity in which I created your entire being, that you have three to four trillion cells within your being.' What is the power of every one of those cells, and what authority that cell has for its movement, and how that cell knows to die or to continue living. Everything within *insan* (humankind), from the physicality to  their molecules and atoms, and then all the universes and all the trillions and trillions and trillions of creation upon them; and the creation itself.

It means then the seeker, when Allah ﷻ says, 'I'm going to show you the signs upon the horizon and within yourself, My Signs, so that you understand My Magnificence.' You understand that when you say *"Allahu akbar"*, Allah's ﷻ reply, *'Ana Al-Akbar,* I'm even more greater than you could ever imagine.' The complexity in which Allah ﷻ manages all this creation.

سَنُرِيهِمْ آيَاتِنَا فِي الْآفَاقِ وَفِي أَنفُسِهِمْ حَتَّىٰ يَتَبَيَّنَ لَهُمْ أَنَّهُ الْحَقُّ... ﴿٥٣﴾

41:53 – "Sanureehim ayatina fil afaqi wa fee anfusihim hatta yatabayyana lahum annahu alhaqqu..." (Surat Al-Isra)

"We will show them Our signs in the horizons and within themselves until it becomes clear to them that it is the truth..."
(The Night Journey, 41:53)

Obedience to Allah ﷻ, To the Messenger ﷺ and People of Divinely Command

It means then that *qadir* and that power that Allah ﷻ is creating, He says, 'Look to that sun. Do you see My Power and my *'Izzat* in that sun?' *"Izzatullahi wa Rasuli wal mu'minin"* (Holy Qur'an, 63:8). *"Atiullah wa Atiur Rasul wa Ulul Amri minkum"* (Obey Allah, Obey the Messenger, and those in authority among you).

وَلِلَّهِ الْعِزَّةُ وَلِرَسُولِهِ وَلِلْمُؤْمِنِينَ... ﴿٨﴾

63:8 – "...Wa Lillahil 'izzatu wa li Rasooli hi wa lil Mumineen..." (Surat Al-Munafiqoon)

"...And to Allah belongs [all] honor, and to His messenger, and to the believers..." (The Hypocrites, 63:8)

*Open the Sun Within Your Heart,
Allah ﷻ Will Fill It With Heavenly Power*

And

...أَطِيعُواللهَ وَأَطِيعُواْلرَّسُولَ وَأُوْلِي الْأَمْرِ مِنْكُمْ ﴿٥٩﴾

4:59 – "...*Atiullaha wa atiur Rasula wa Ulil amre minkum...*"
(Surat An-Nisa)

"... Obey Allah, Obey the Messenger, and those in authority among you..." (The Women, 4:59)

Everything in our life, its secret will be on these three. Obedience to Allah ﷻ is only Sayyidina Muhammad ﷺ, complete and *kamil* (perfected); obedience to Prophet ﷺ is obedience to Allah ﷻ and those who understood and they *itibah* (follow) and they followed, they became the *ulul amr*, those whom Allah ﷻ granted His Divinely *Amr*, His Divinely Orders, because they are the people of obedience. They obey and they follow the order of Allah ﷻ.

Sayyidina Ibrahim's ﷺ Quest to Find Allah ﷻ

1. He Saw Station of Stars – (6:76)
Diwan e Awliya (Spiritual Gathering of Saints)

This means then we study the lovers of Allah ﷻ that, what power that sun has – so powerful that people began to worship it? It's not something small, it has an immense power. And Sayyidina Ibrahim ﷺ in Holy Qur'an in the *ma'rifah* (gnosticism) of Sayyidina Ibrahim ﷺ, there's an *ayat* (verse) of the Qur'an where Sayyidina Ibrahim ﷺ is describing in his *ma'rifah* (gnosticism), 'I came across the stars, and I said this must be Allah ﷻ.'

فَلَمَّا جَنَّ عَلَيْهِ اللَّيْلُ رَأَىٰ كَوْكَبًا ۖ قَالَ هَٰذَا رَبِّي ۖ فَلَمَّا أَفَلَ قَالَ لَا أُحِبُّ الْآفِلِينَ ﴿٧٦﴾

6:76 – *"Falamma janna 'alayhil laylu raa kawkaban, qala hadha Rabbi, falamma afala qala la uhibbul afileen."* (Surat Al-An'am)

"So when the night covered him [with darkness], he saw a star. He said, "This is my lord." But when it set, he said, I like not those that disappear." (The Cattle, 6:76)

Then he realized, no, the stars, they set. It means now he's directing us to the heavens that, 'In my *ma'rifah* (gnosticism) and in my love of Allah (swt), I look to what's superior in creation. I came across the stars and wanted to understand how these stars operated.' And through his *tafakkur* and contemplation, Allah (swt) began to show that these stars and the power of these suns, because these stars are light. He understood a reality from these lights.

And Allah (swt) described that, 'No, no, I'm even better than that. These also have a time in which they go down,' and then Sayyidina Ibrahim (as) clarifies, 'I went to the moon,' because these are all stations. The stars are the *diwan e awliya* because Prophet ﷺ said, 'Follow my Companions, any of my Companions, they are like a *najm* (star).'

أَصْحَابِيْ كَالنُّجُومْ بِأَيِّهِمْ اَقْتَدَيْتُمْ اَهْتَدَيْتُمْ

"Ashabi kan Nujoom, bi ayyihim aqta daytum ahta daytum."

"My companions are like stars. Follow any one of them and you will be guided." (Prophet Muhammad (pbuh))

What could be the set of the stars, they're the *Sahabi*! They're representing Prophet ﷺ who said, 'Follow any of my Companions, they

*Open the Sun Within Your Heart,
Allah ﷻ Will Fill It With Heavenly Power*

are like stars on a dark night,' because they represent eternal light and to denote to us that the sky is dark, but they shine with my light, they shine with the light that Allah ﷻ put upon their heart. And Sayyidina Ibrahim عليه السلام reached to those associations and was astonished by their light and for a moment maybe thought that this is Allah ﷻ.

2. He Saw Station of the Moon (6:77)
Maqam Fardani, the Ghawth (Highest Station of a Saint)

Allah ﷻ *la sharik*, there is no partner with Allah ﷻ, and he went to the moon.

فَلَمَّا رَأَى الْقَمَرَ بَازِغًا قَالَ هَٰذَا رَبِّي ۖ فَلَمَّا أَفَلَ قَالَ لَئِن لَّمْ يَهْدِنِي رَبِّي لَأَكُونَنَّ مِنَ الْقَوْمِ الضَّالِّينَ ﴿٧٧﴾

6:77 – "Falamma raa alQamara bazighan qala hadha Rabbi, falamma afala qala la in lam yahdinee rabbi laakonanna minal qawmid dalleen." (Surat Al-An'am)

"And when he saw the moon rising, he said, "This is my lord." But when it set, he said, Unless my Lord guides me, I will surely be among the people gone astray." (The Cattle, 6:77)

And the reality of the moon is *maqam al fardani*; which means it is the

maqam (station) of the *ghawth*, of the highest of *awliyaullah* (saints). And he reached and he thought maybe this is Allah ﷻ. Why? Because of the light and the realities that Allah's ﷻ dressing upon that soul, that in the way of *ma'rifah* (gnosticism) and the way of moving towards these realities of what Allah ﷻ dressed upon these lights, because you will never know Allah ﷻ. There is no place in which you occupy a space with God; you breathe a space with God, you have even a proximity with Allah ﷻ because Allah ﷻ is outside of the Oceans of *Hayat* (living). We are a created creation – how you can imagine that you have a breath with God, *astaghfirullah*! That's why Allah ﷻ says, '*La sharik*. You know yourself.' And Prophet ﷺ said, 'He who knows himself will know his Lord, his *Rabb*.' He didn't say you're going to know Allah ﷻ; you're going to only know the signs of Allah ﷻ because it draws into our own understanding, so you begin to look at all this magnificence.

مَنْ عَرَفَ نَفْسَهُ فَقَدْ عَرَفَ رَبَّهُ

"*Man 'arafa nafsahu faqad 'arafa Rabbahu.*"

"*Who knows himself, knows his Lord.*" (Prophet Muhammad (pbuh))

3. He Saw Station of the Sun (6:78)
Ayat al Akbar (Great Sign of Eternity)

Then Sayyidina Ibrahim عليه السلام, when he left the moon and understood this is not Allah ﷻ, He puts in Qur'an, Allah ﷻ uses the words in Qur'an to describe this *ma'rifah* (gnosticism) of Sayyidina Ibrahim عليه السلام, that  he came across *Ayat al Akbar* (a Great Sign). *Ayat al Akbar* is in reference to the sun, that one of Allah's ﷻ great, great signs of creation is the *shams*, is the sun.

فَلَمَّا رَأَى الشَّمْسَ بَازِغَةً قَالَ هَٰذَا رَبِّي هَٰذَا أَكْبَرُ ۖ فَلَمَّا أَفَلَتْ قَالَ يَا قَوْمِ إِنِّي بَرِيءٌ مِّمَّا تُشْرِكُونَ ﴿٧٨﴾

6:78 – "*Falamma raa ash Shamsa bazighatan qala hadha Rabbi hadha Akbaru, falamma afalat qala ya qawmi inni baree oon mimma tushrikoon.*" (*Surat Al-An'am*)

*Open the Sun Within Your Heart,
Allah's Will Fill It With Heavenly Power*

"And when he saw the sun rising, he said, "This is my Lord; this is the greatest (of all)." But when the sun set, he said: O my people! I am indeed free from what you partner with Allah." (The Cattle, 6:78)

Then immediately it directs all pious people that, 'What is the power, *ya Rabbi, Ayat al Akbar,* that you're making us to look at the understanding? With our eyes, we are seeing eternity.' Nothing else has eternity; every tree you've seen, it has died; every person you've known, they've come and gone. With your physical eyes you can look at eternity, it has always been. And it's staying until Allah wants it to leave.

Allah's Qudra and Power Moves in the Sun

You begin to understand Allah's eternity and then they begin to teach you, there's a power. The greatest power that you can understand, don't say, 'Only Allah, oh Allah's the power.' We know that! But in the way of *ma'rifah* (gnosticism), Allah wants you as a creation, 'I want you to see My Power. Where you're going to see the greatest of My Power is in the sun, in the *qudra* (power) of the *shams* (sun),' of what

type of light is shining from that? What type of force is shining from that sun? What type of effect that light has on your existence? You breathe by that sunlight, you eat by that sunlight, you have existence and warmth by that sunlight; if Allah moved that sun, our existence is dead, you're not living on this earth. When you say, "Allah", Allah's not going to send you a light in which you exist by yourself.

It's by cause and effect that, 'This is My Sign, this is my *Ayat al Akbar.* My *Qudra* and Power is moving in that, and you don't dare say it's Me,' because *la sharik, la shabi*, there's nothing like Allah ﷻ. But you say this is a light from Allah's ﷻ lights and creation.

Lail (Night) Represents the Binary Code of Zero – Be Nothing

Awliya (saints) come into our life and begin to describe these are the lights of Prophet ﷺ, these are the realities of Prophet ﷺ, *"Inna anzal nahu fi Lailat al Qadr."*

إِنَّا أَنزَلْنَاهُ فِي لَيْلَةِ الْقَدْرِ ﴿١﴾

97:1 – *"Inna anzalnaahu fee laylatil-qadr."* (Surat Al-Qadr)

"We have brought it down on the night of power." (The Power, 97:1)

Lailatul Qadr (Night of Power) means that *awliyaullah* (saints) understood these lights and these realities they want to reach that, '*Ya Rabbi*, let our soul and our being to reach to Your *Haqqaiq*.' Then follow that creation and its understanding, that as soon as you're going to move to that *Lailatul Qadr* (Night of Power), it means take a life in which *lail* represents the binary code of being nothing. Be a zero and a *nuqt* (dot); the day is when you manifest, the night is when you are nothing. Only in your state of nothingness you can approach and be dressed by that *qadr*, 'Because I'll show you the sign outside until you will begin to understand the sign inside.'

Open the Sun Within Your Heart, Allah ﷻ Will Fill It With Heavenly Power

$$\text{سَنُرِيهِمْ آيَاتِنَا فِي الْآفَاقِ وَفِي أَنفُسِهِمْ حَتَّىٰ يَتَبَيَّنَ لَهُمْ أَنَّهُ الْحَقُّ ... ﴿٥٣﴾}$$

41:53 – *"Sanureehim ayatina fil afaqi wa fee anfusihim hatta yatabayyana lahum annahu alhaqqu..."* (Surat Al-Isra)

"We will show them Our signs in the horizons and within themselves until it becomes clear to them that it is the truth..."
(The Night Journey, 41:53)

So, they took a life in which they negate themself, negate themself, negate themself to reach towards Allah's ﷻ *Qadir*.

The Ruh (Soul) is From the Ocean of Oneness

"Tanazalul mala'ika..." I'll skip to the *ayat* (verse) that's important for us to understand, all of them are important, *"Tanazalul mala'ikati wa ruh fiha beizne Rabbihim min kulle amr"* (The angels and the Spirit descend therein by permission of their Lord for every Command/affair.)

$$\text{تَنَزَّلُ الْمَلَائِكَةُ وَالرُّوحُ فِيهَا بِإِذْنِ رَبِّهِم مِّن كُلِّ أَمْرٍ ﴿٤﴾}$$

97:4 – *"Tanazzalul malaikatu war Roh, fiha beizne Rabbihim min kulle amr."* (Surat Al-Qadr)

"The angels and the Spirit descend therein by permission of their Lord for every Command/affair." (The Power 97:4)

It means upon that sun, how it's governing, because *awliyaullah* (saints), these *awliya* that we are all connected to, they are in that reality. And they want to understand the inner works of how Allah ﷻ is operating that sun. It means every photon that's reaching to every creation in its galaxy, it's responsible for that galaxy. So, Allah's ﷻ *Qudra* (power) is coming, *"bi izni rabbihim"* (by permission of their Lord), the *ruh* (soul) and *mala'ika* (angels).

The *ruh* (soul) is always from the Ocean of Oneness, *Ar-Ruh*, the One. If you take your soul and another soul, and another soul, and another soul, and return it back into the ocean of souls, how many souls do you have? One. Only the world of form has form. If I take three cups, how many cups I have? Three cups. But if I take a soul like a drop of light and throw it into the ocean, and take another soul and take it into the ocean, throw it into the ocean, take another soul, throw it into the ocean, it's but one ocean, because it's under *tawhid*; *La ilaha illallah Muhammadun RasulAllah* ﷺ (There is no God but Allah, Prophet Muhammad (pbuh) is the Messenger of Allah).

Only the world of form manifests and separates itself and Allah ﷻ is the One whom crushes all manifestation and says, 'Be nothing like *lail* (night). Annihilate yourself to be nothing. Come back into that ocean of power.'

The Ruh Gives the Amr (Command) to the Angels

That sun for us only to understand is an ocean of power and emanating. And they know that the science and *haqqaiq* (realities); the *haqqaiq* can describe the science of it, that that photon is reaching and nourishing everything in the galaxy; in our galaxy all 11 planets are nourished by this sun. It means that there must be an angel on every photon and going exactly where Allah ﷻ wants it, by the command of the *Ruh* (Divine light), because, *"Atiullah wa Atiur Rasul wa Ulul Amri minkum."*

*Open the Sun Within Your Heart,
Allah ﷻ Will Fill It With Heavenly Power*

...أَطِيعُواْ ٱللَّهَ وَأَطِيعُواْ ٱلرَّسُولَ وَأُوْلِي ٱلْأَمْرِ مِنكُمْ... ﴿٥٩﴾

4:59 – "…*Atiullaha wa atiur Rasula wa Ulil amre minkum…*" (Surat An-Nisa)

"… Obey Allah, Obey the Messenger, and those in authority among you…" (The Women, 4:59)

This means there is a Muhammadan representative on that station and that station is in charge of giving the *amr* (command) to the angels.

Because the angels are from *ulul amr* (saints). It means the angels are taking from Allah ﷻ, going to Prophet ﷺ, from Prophet ﷺ to the highest station of *awliya* (saints), the highest station of their souls, the highest station of perfection. And giving every *amr* and every order is being sent out throughout this galaxy; and everything is being nourished by it.

وَيَسْأَلُونَكَ عَنِ ٱلرُّوحِ ۖ قُلِ ٱلرُّوحُ مِنْ أَمْرِ رَبِّي وَمَا أُوتِيتُم مِّنَ ٱلْعِلْمِ إِلَّا قَلِيلًا ﴿٨٥﴾

17:85 – "*Wa yas'aloonaka 'anirrooh; qulir roohu min amri rabbee wa maaa ooteetum minal 'ilmi illaa qaleelaa.*" (Surat Al-Isra)

"And they ask you, [O Muhammad], about the Ruh (soul). Say, "The soul (comes) by the command (Amr) of my Lord. And mankind have not been given of knowledge except a little." (The Night Journey, 17:85)

Allah ﷻ describes then that power, 'That reality is better than 1000 months', which is 83 years, which is a lifetime for us.

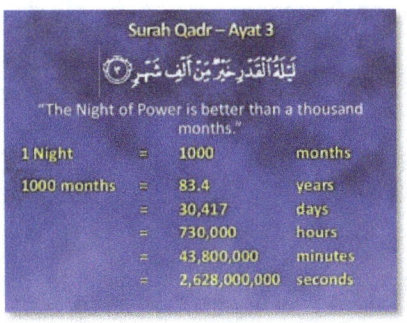

لَيْلَةُ الْقَدْرِ خَيْرٌ مِنْ أَلْفِ شَهْرٍ ﴿٣﴾

97:3 – "Laylatul Qadre khairum min alfe shahr." (Surat Al-Qadr)

"The Night of Decree is better than a thousand months." (The Power, 97:3)

'Unless you are understanding My Creation, you are wasting your life.' Everything else that you are running for, is from the material world; that's why all the *salawats* (praisings) – *Shams al Arifeen, Al Qamar* – all of these realities because Allah's ﷻ Creation is perfected. *Insan* (mankind) is imperfected because *insan* has a will. The planet has no will, the sun has no will; it has surrendered every will to Allah ﷻ. So always you see the signs of Allah ﷻ in complete obedience.

The Direction of Salat (Prayer) is to Face the Rising of the Sun

So then follow that sun like the *qamar* (moon). And the *qamar's* whole  life is just to follow the direction of the sun. It is interesting because the direction of all *salat* (prayer) should be facing the sun and the rising of the sun. The *qibla* (direction of prayer) of *dunya* (material world) is to face Ka'bah; but how to find the direction of Ka'bah is that you should be facing the light, 'Rabbul mashariq wal maqarib.'

$$رَبُّ الْمَشْرِقَيْنِ وَرَبُّ الْمَغْرِبَيْنِ ﴿١٧﴾$$

55:17 – "Rabbul mashriqayni wa Rabbul maghribayn."
(Surat Ar-Rahman)

"[He is] Lord of the two sunrises and Lord of the two sunsets."
(The Beneficent, 55:17)

Who came up with north and east, north and south? Allah ﷻ makes no mention of north and south; it's, 'I am the Lord of the rising and the

setting,' because there's no east and west. It's falsely translated as east; *mashariq* because *ishraq*, which means the rising. Allah ﷻ says, 'I am the Lord of everything that rises,' and *maqarib* because you have a death, not Allah ﷻ. There's a rising and there's a death. More important, 'There's a sun and there's a moon, and you should be taking the same path as My Creation.'

$$رَبُّ الْمَشْرِقَيْنِ وَرَبُّ الْمَغْرِبَيْنِ ﴿١٧﴾$$

55:17 – "Rabbul mashriqayni wa Rabbul maghribayn."
(Surat Ar-Rahman)

"[He is] Lord of the two sunrises and Lord of the two sunsets."
(The Beneficent, 55:17)

The Planets and Our Entire Being are Circumambulating the Light

So now the astronauts went up in space and they don't know where to pray because their understanding is incorrect. Their understanding is only from *had dunya* (limit of material world), so they keep trying to figure out where is the Ka'bah? They're now debating on, all the big *ulema* (scholars) talk to bring *futawat*, because their understanding is *had dunya*. So, the *dunya* (material world) left, they say, 'Where do you pray now, we don't see any *dunya*!' But if they had the *uloom* (knowledge) of *malakut* (heavenly realms), they would direct themselves to where the sun is rising, Because Allah ﷻ is describing, 'Your entire being faces light. Your cells of your electron, they circumambulate the light of your nucleus.' The entire 11 planets, they circumambulate the sun and we call it a solar system.

Allah ﷻ doesn't create *shirk* (idolatry); Allah ﷻ doesn't create anything incorrect. It's Allah's ﷻ creation that is actually supposed to be teaching us. It means then when we understood the power of the sun, that all *malaika* (angels) are coming out with all of the *isharats* (signs) and *"kulli amr"*, why Allah ﷻ added the adjective of *"kul"*, in case some other *madhab* (school of thought) comes and says, 'Okay, *amr*, I'll accept, Shaykh, but not all the *amrs*. Maybe the *amr* that comes to *insan* is not in that.'

تَنَزَّلُ الْمَلَائِكَةُ وَالرُّوحُ فِيهَا بِإِذْنِ رَبِّهِم مِّن كُلِّ أَمْرٍ ﴿٤﴾

97:4 – "Tanazzalul malaikatu war Roh, fiha beizne Rabbihim min kulle amr." (Surat Al-Qadr)

Open the Sun Within Your Heart,
Allah ﷻ Will Fill It With Heavenly Power

"*The angels and the Spirit descend therein by permission of their Lord for every Command/affair.*" (The Power, 97:4)

Allah ﷻ says, 'No, no. We added a *"kul"*, like a contract so that it can't be debated.' Says *"kulli amr"* – every *amr*, every order is coming. This means every order from Allah ﷻ is coming on that power and it's coming to a *ruh*, and from a *ruh* to the angels and being distributed throughout creation.

Heart of Sayyidina Muhammad ﷺ is the House of Kulli Amr (All Divinely Commands)

Then Allah ﷻ said, 'If you understand that power and you understand that *'izzat*, I gave you a sun within your heart. Your heart is the sun, your heart is My House, your heart is the source of every reality,' because why? Who's Allah's ﷻ Beloved? Sayyidina Muhammad ﷺ!

قَلْبَ الْمُؤْمِنْ بَيْتُ الرَّبْ

"*Qalb al mu'min baytur rabb.*"

"*The heart of the believer is the House of the Lord.*" (Hadith Qudsi)

Where was Prophet's ﷺ *Lailatul Qadr* (Night of Power)? In his heart. Where was Qur'an emanating from – from the heart of Prophet ﷺ. Where is Qur'an continually emanating from in *malakut* (heavenly realm) and in the world of light – from the heart of Prophet ﷺ. So, Allah's ﷻ describing, in the heart of Prophet ﷺ is the oceans of real

power. In that ocean of power, Allah ﷻ is describing that, 'Every order of Mine is coming into the heart of Prophet ﷺ,' and standing guard is a *ruh* (Divine light), and all the angels, all the purified and *kamil* (perfected) souls that take the command from Allah ﷻ, they bring the command to Prophet ﷺ, from Prophet ﷺ comes down to all the *ulul amr* (saints) and everything within the heavens is moving. That's the real ocean of *qadr* (Divine power), symbolized in the understanding of the sun.

Sanctify Your Heart and Make It the House of Allah ﷻ

Then Allah ﷻ is describing, 'Your cells understand that. Your nucleus has that and now for you to understand, your heart has that. If you submit your heart, I'm going to make it like a *shams* (sun); you're going to be from *shams al arifeen*. You're going to have a heart that's like a sun that's going to shine brighter than all of these suns.' This is all an imitated sun. But you have a conflict with your head because your head is trying

to be the sun and you don't yet know your physiology, that what Allah ﷻ created us?

Shaytan comes and teaches that you should do all your thinking from your head. Allah ﷻ, *Ar-Rahman*, comes and teaches, 'Leave your head, it's worth nothing, all your thinking should be from your heart. All your

*Open the Sun Within Your Heart,
Allah Will Fill It With Heavenly Power*

concentration should be from your heart, that your heart is My House, not your head. Purify and sanctify your heart and make it My Home.'

...أَن طَهِّرَا بَيْتِيَ لِلطَّائِفِينَ وَالْعَاكِفِينَ وَالرُّكَّعِ السُّجُودِ ﴿١٢٥﴾

2:125 – *"...An Tahhir baytee liTayifeena, wal 'Aakifeena, wa ruka'is sujood."* (Surat Al-Baqarah)

"...Purify/Sanctify My House for those who perform Tawaf (circamambulation) and those who seclude themselves for devotion and bow and prostrate [in prayer]." (The Cow, 2:125)

If you make it My Home it will be, it will be where My Lights are locating; it will be a *masjid* for you, it will be a Ka'bah for you. And every emanation will be coming from your heart. I'll send a *ruh*, I'll send an authorized light to govern and to be a *sultan* upon your heart. And with that *ruh* and every authority of that *ruh*, it will come with all the *amr*, all the orders of Allah because they are *ulul amr* (People of the Command). They are the people of the *amr*. And the angels stand guard upon their heart for whatever command is coming, they know that heart is, *"qalb al mu'min baytullah"*.

قَلْبُ الْمُؤْمِنْ بَيْتُ الرَّبْ

"Qalb al mu'min baytur rabb."

"The heart of the believer is the House of the Lord." (Hadith Qudsi)

They know that this heart is the heart of the *mu'min* in which Allah has sent a representative of that *ruh* and all the angels stand command upon that heart to carry out the order of Allah. But the heart has to be in submission, *itibah* (follow). The only way is to turn everything off and submit.

The Head is Our Biggest Enemy That Doubts and Questions Everything

But the conflict that everybody has is between their head and their heart. Everything that they debate is from their head. Every question they have is from their head. Every doubt that they have is from their head. *Ahl al tafakkur* (people of contemplation), because they want to explain the reality to see the grandeur of this reality, what Allah ﷻ has a gift in store, that don't waste your life for nothing. That seek these realities.

Then they begin to teach, this is the secret of your binary code, shut your head off and open your heart, and your whole path is based on that struggle. That is the great fight. That is the great *jihad* that Prophet's ﷺ

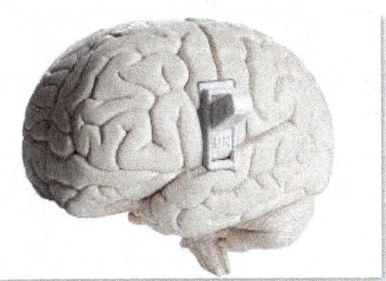

describing, that how to battle against yourself, how to put within your heart that I have to reach to these realities, and that everything about me has to be shut off, especially my head because the head doubts and questions everything. And yet the head knows nothing.

You were trained in school to use your head and to ignore your heart. You trained in school to have the worst of manners and to have doubt and continuously question everyone, as if that was a sign of good character, which was not of good character. Everything about the reality is the way of *tafakkur* and contemplation, that I have to sit with myself.

I have to struggle against myself. I have to understand these realities and this light that's coming into my heart, and that my biggest enemy is going to be my head. And as soon as you hear yourself whispering against the Shaykh, against the teaching, against the way, against the centre, then you know *shaytan* is already battling against you.

Shaytan Attacks the Head First Through Your Ears

The heart is something that can be fortified with *zikr* (remembrance), with lights, with practices because the angels are standing guard to protect it. So *shaytan* (satan) is not going to come first for your heart,

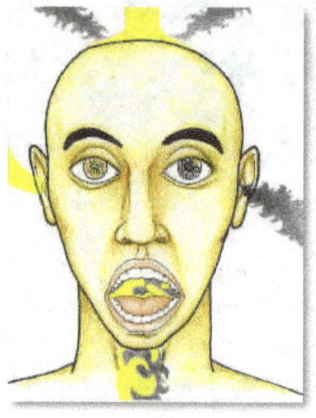

he easily comes straight at your head because your head is open and not something guarded. Allah put too many orifices, too many openings upon the head. You have two big ears that, eeh, just loving to hear everything, what what what what, what, what, what, nosy people, look, look, look, look, look, what, what? Your business is not to look anywhere, look at your shoes, look at your feet. Try to understand with the ears that this *shaytan* (satan) is going on all these ears. The warning is in dangerous days of difficulty and darkness, there are so many *shayateen* (devils), so many *shayateen* everywhere that the believer is under tremendous difficulty because as soon as they move, there are thousands of them just whispering, whispering.

If you're going to take your life by your head and entertain every whisper that's coming and think, 'This, oh I'm so clever today. Yeah, I found what they're doing wrong, I found what he's doing wrong, I found what his teaching is wrong,' *Shaytan* (Satan) is playing with you. And he understood now he has a position of an *imam* (spiritual leader) with you because he says, 'Hey, this guy listens to me and he doesn't even have to be in the bathroom!' Because we said before, he gives the biggest *khutba* (discourse) in the toilet. *Tariqah* (spiritual path) knows that. On this internet they come back and say, 'Shaykh, I never heard this before,' because this is the abode that Allah ﷻ put for *Shaytan* (Satan). His house is the toilet. As soon as you enter into the bathroom, don't you realize he's giving you a *khutba*, teaching you Qur'an, teaching you *hadith*, teaching you *haqqaiq* – from

where? *Amabad*, he sits up there, in the corner, 'Oh servant of mine, and let me start teaching you.'

Be Vigilant of Your Eyes and Ears, They Are Windows and Doors to Your Soul

This means that the head is completely under *shaytanic* (satanic) attack. So then, our whole way is to be vigilant; when *waswas* (whispering) comes, block it. The minute it comes block it, make *salawat* (praisings) on Prophet ﷺ, spit and make *istighfar* that you are under a satanic attack. Don't lend your ears and keep letting it go and go and go and become filled with *shak* and doubt. It means everything about the believer is under difficulty.

If he didn't get you by your ears, he's going to bring you by your eyes, because when these eyes see what they're not supposed to see, you're going to have difficulty within your heart because your layers of protection moved and they're able now to fire all their arrows into the heart.

It means the believer is vigilant with what he hears. He doesn't talk to people who continuously want to say negative and bad things about them, about their way, about their life, about their path, about their choices. This is not a free door for everybody to come through. These ears are doors to your soul. These eyes are the windows to your soul. These were not for public consumption, it's not a place you go to the mall and tell everybody, 'Tell me all your bad stuff.' You would be dead under this attack.

So, it means then the believer is vigilant against *shaytanic* attack and is guarding themselves, they have a vigilance against everything that my ears,

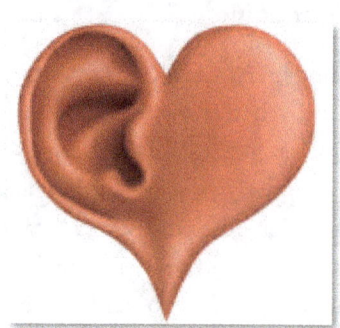

I have to be careful about what they're hearing, especially those whom know you best. They have a secret door to you. They have access to you, they come right into your space and they begin to say things into your ear to bring a darkness into the heart, to bring a *shak*, and to bring doubt into the heart.

Learn from Holy Companions to Hear and Obey (Sami'na wa Ata'na)

It means this path is about understanding the head but fortifying the heart, that Allah's ﷻ light is going to come into the heart. Only when the believer can enter into a state that Prophet ﷺ brought his Companions to *"sami'na wa ata'na"*, we heard *ya RasulAllah* ﷺ and we obey.

$$...\text{سَمِعْنَا وَأَطَعْنَا غُفْرَانَكَ رَبَّنَا وَإِلَيْكَ الْمَصِيرُ} \{٢٨٥\}$$

2:285 – "…Sam'ina wa ata'na, ghufranaka Rabbana wa ilaykal masir." (Surat Al-Baqarah)

"…We hear, and we obey: (We seek) Your forgiveness, our Lord, and to you is the end of all journeys." (The Cow, 2:285)

Why Prophet ﷺ was always stretching that limit, doing things that were beyond belief, to go back and see the Companions. And what Sayyidina Abu Bakr as-Siddiq said, 'Ya Sayyidi, ya RasulAllah ﷺ, if Prophet ﷺ said it, that's it. It's complete for us. We are the people who we heard, and we obeyed,' which means *itibah* (follow). And they learned such a level of love and respect and reverence for Prophet ﷺ they sealed their ears from every negativity and their ears were only for Allah and his Rasul ﷺ. With their training they understood that these eyes are but a deception and they took a path of *"nazar bar qadam,"* that they kept their eyes on their feet. Don't be busy with left or right or what someone else is doing or has or whatever. You just worry about where your feet are taking you in this life.

*Open the Sun Within Your Heart,
Allah's Will Fill It With Heavenly Power*

You Have a Limited Number of Breaths, Use Them in Worship

If they're able to train their ears and their eyes, then they begin to realize their whole life is based on breath. Now some nice Chinese doctor comes, and they described, 'Oh these people are running, do you think this is good for your health, running, running, running, running?' They said, 'Look, I believe you only have so many breaths and only so many beats Allah has destined for your heart. Where are you running to? You're not going to get more beats and you're not going to get more breaths. But you are exhausting your breaths very fast.

There were no *awliyaullah* who were jogging. There were no pious people who were running around the block, doing all sorts of ridiculous things. They understood, they have only a certain amount of breaths; you better conserve them. They were able to hold their breath in their *zikr* and they understood that the heart only has so many beats, it's an engine that only has a certain amount of life that Allah has given to it. Use it in *ibadah* and worshipness, use it to achieve your proximity with Allah.

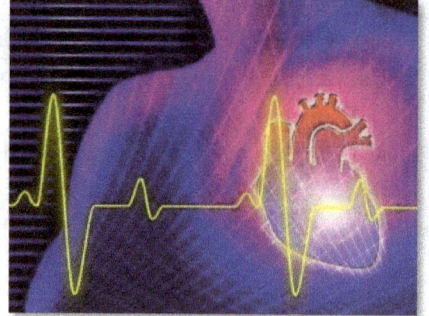

When they understood that breath, then all the *tariqahs* (spiritual paths) are based on the breath, the vigilance of the breath, that as this breath is coming in, *ya Rabbi*, in worshipness, and as the breath is going out in worshipness. If Allah ﷻ grants from your ears, from your eyes, and from your breath, then he begins to inspire upon your tongue.

Subhana rabbika rabbal 'izzati 'amma yasifoon, wa salaamun 'alal mursaleen, walhamdulillahi rabbil 'aalameen. Bi hurmati Muhammad al-Mustafa wa bi siri Surat al-Fatiha.

REALITY of STARS

HOLY COMPANIONS
SAHABI

"MY COMPANIONS ARE LIKE STARS. FOLLOW ANY ONE OF THEM AND YOU WILL BE GUIDED."
—PROPHET MUHAMMAD ﷺ

The Star of Prophet Muhammad ﷺ

*I*nshaAllah, to share first for ourselves always a reminder, if anyone takes benefit and understanding, *alhamdulillah*.

Prophet Muhammad ﷺ is the Imam (Leader) of All Messengers

In the understanding of the self, 'who knows himself will know his Lord.' From many teachings of Prophet ﷺ, spiritual teachings of Prophet ﷺ, many *hadith* (traditions) of Prophet ﷺ, and through the heart of pious people. The opening and expansion of the heart, the expansion of understanding, and Allah's ﷻ infinite Oceans of Knowledge that there is no limitation. That Allah ﷻ is infinitely expanding the Oceans of Knowledge. And at every moment there must be new knowledge.

مَنْ عَرَفَ نَفْسَهُ فَقَدْ عَرَفَ رَبَّهُ

"Man 'arafa nafsahu faqad 'arafa Rabbahu."

"Who knows himself, knows his Lord." (Prophet Muhammad (pbuh))

From ancient understandings and realities that one basic concept is, that everything is owned by Sayyidina Muhammad ﷺ, that Allah ﷻ asked all the prophets that, 'If he *(alaihis salaatus salaam)* comes in your time, you must follow him. He is the *Imam* (Leader) of all *risalat* (messengership).'

All *risalat* is in the messengership of Prophet ﷺ. There's only one messenger, he is Sayyidina Muhammad ﷺ. They were given a certain amount of light, certain amount of information, enough for their people, but from the ocean of Sayyidina Muhammad ﷺ. So that's why he is the *Imam* of all messengers *(Imam al Mursaleen)*.

يَا إِمَامَ الرُّسْلِ يَا سَنَدِيْ   أَنْتَ بَابُ اللهِ مُعْتَمَدِيْ
فَبِدُنْيَايَ وَ آخِرَتِيْ   يَا رَسُولَ اللهِ خُذْ بِيَدِيْ

Ya imamar Rusli ya sanadi   *Anta babullahi mu'tamadi*
Fabi dunyaya wa akhirate   *Ya Rasulallahi khud biyadi*

O' Leader of the messengers, O' my support,
you are Allah's door, on whom I rely

O' Messenger of Allah! Hold my hand,
In my life and in hereafter.

It means that, and all messengers accepted to be Muslim. Nabi Musa (Moses) ﷺ asked to see Allah ﷻ. As a result of what he saw he said, *"Anna awal ul Muslimeen."* Sayyidina Ibrahim ﷺ said, *"Anna awal Muslimeen."*

قُلْ إِنَّ صَلَاتِي وَنُسُكِي وَمَحْيَايَ وَمَمَاتِي لِلَّـهِ رَبِّ الْعَالَمِينَ ﴿١٦٢﴾ لَا شَرِيكَ لَهُ ۖ وَبِذَٰلِكَ أُمِرْتُ وَأَنَا أَوَّلُ الْمُسْلِمِينَ ﴿١٦٣﴾

6:162-163 – *"Qul inna salati wa nusuki wa mahyaya wa mamati lillahi Rabbil 'Aalamin (162). La sharika lahu wa bidhalika omirtu wa ana awalul Muslimin. (163)" (Surat Al-An'am)*

Say, *"Indeed, my prayer, my rites of sacrifice, my living and my dying are for Allah, Lord of the worlds. (162) No partner has He; and this I have*

been commanded, and I am the first of those who submit. (163)"
(The Cattle, 6:162-163)

Prophet Muhammad ﷺ is the Owner of the Reality of the Star

This means that all reality for us to understand these realities is owned by Sayyidina Muhammad ﷺ because he owns the *kalima; La ilaha illAllah* (Allah ﷻ) *Muhammadun Rasulallah* ﷺ. Everything is coming from the ocean of *Muhammadun Rasulallah* ﷺ.

لَا إِلَهَ إِلاَّ اللهُ مُحَمَّدًا رَسُولُ الله

"*La ilaha illallahu Muhammadun Rasulallah.*"

"There is no diety but Allah, Prophet Muhammad is the messenger of Allah."

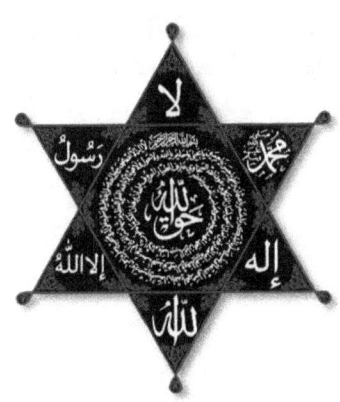

It means that our cousins and our nephews and our friends, they don't own this star; this is owned by Allah ﷻ. And the owner that Allah ﷻ is giving possession of all creation to is Sayyidina Muhammad ﷺ.

The Sun is a Star, Star is Light, and Light is Eternal

With that understanding, we have to move forward in the understanding of the self, that what Allah ﷻ wants is that you are a form and your form is a temporary existence. And that in you which is real, and eternal, is your light. The analogy of Allah ﷻ is that, 'I show you My sign on the horizon and within yourself.'

﴿٥٣﴾ ... سَنُرِيهِمْ آيَاتِنَا فِي الْآفَاقِ وَفِي أَنفُسِهِمْ حَتَّىٰ يَتَبَيَّنَ لَهُمْ أَنَّهُ الْحَقُّ ۗ

41:53 – "*Sanureehim ayatina fil afaqi wa fee anfusihim hatta yatabayyana lahum annahu alhaqqu...*" (Surat Al-Isra)

The Star of Prophet Muhammad ﷺ

"We will show them Our signs in the horizons and within themselves until it becomes clear to them that it is the truth..."
(The Night Journey, 41:53)

The signs on the horizon are the planets and they are from the world of form. And the stars, they are light from the world of light. Allah ﷻ is showing that which is superior is the light. The light is eternal. Planets may come and go but the light stays. Everything on this *dunya* (material world) has perished. What has stayed from the beginning of 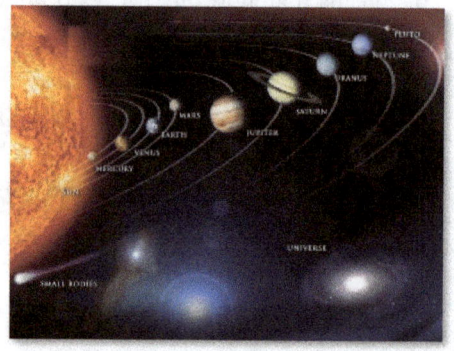 our time until Allah ﷻ calls the end of our time is *shams*, the sun. Nabi Musa ﷺ saw the same sun, Sayyidina Sulayman (Prophet Solomon) ﷺ, saw the same sun. Everyone sees the same sun because Allah ﷻ wants us to take an understanding. All their bodies have died and have been thrown into the dirt. What was eternal was their soul, their light.

Seek the light. Understand the light. Understand your reality. Understand yourself. If you know yourself, you'll know the rules that Allah ﷻ is giving, what's governing us, and as a result of knowing that we begin to know our Lord. It means in every reality is in the reality of self.

مَنْ عَرَفَ نَفْسَهُ فَقَدْ عَرَفَ رَبَّهُ

"Man 'arafa nafsahu faqad 'arafa Rabbahu."

"Who knows himself, knows his Lord." (Prophet Muhammad (pbuh))

Then Surat ul-Najm (Star), 53rd surat – 53 in *huroof* (Arabic letters) equals *Ahmad* (Alif, Ha, Meem, Dal – 1+8+40+4 = 53). It's a description of the reality of Sayyidina Ahmad ﷺ. That he is *"Wahy al*

Qur'an" (Revelation of Qur'an), that he ﷺ is the perfected of Allah ﷻ, that he doesn't even speak out of his desire, that everything he speaks is from Allah ﷻ, describing this is the majesty of the soul.

أحمد ﷺ			
Ahmad ﷺ			
د	م	ح	ا
Daal	Meem	Haa	Alif
4	40	8	1
4+40+8+1 = 53			

*Note: Please read English from right to left to coincide with Arabic.

وَالنَّجْمِ إِذَا هَوَىٰ ﴿١﴾ مَا ضَلَّ صَاحِبُكُمْ وَمَا غَوَىٰ ﴿٢﴾ وَمَا يَنطِقُ عَنِ الْهَوَىٰ ﴿٣﴾ إِنْ هُوَ إِلَّا وَحْيٌ يُوحَىٰ ﴿٤﴾ عَلَّمَهُ شَدِيدُ الْقُوَىٰ ﴿٥﴾

53:1-5 – "Wan Najmi idha hawa. (1) Ma dalla sahibukum wa ma ghawa. (2) Wa ma yantiqu 'anil hawa. (3) In huwa illa wahyun yooha. (4) 'Allamahu shadeedul Quwa. (5)" (Surat An-Najm)

"By the star when it descends. (1) Your companion [Muhammad] has not strayed, nor has he erred. (2) Nor does he speak from [his own] desire. (3) It/He is not but a revelation revealed. (4) Taught to him by one intense in strength. (5)" (The Star, 53:1-5)

Reality of the Soul is 'La ilaha illAllah' – Upward Triangle

In understanding ourselves, then Allah is describing, because it will begin to open many different signs. That you must understand you have a reality of your soul. And the reality and the *tajalli* (manifestation) of the soul and the opening of that reality, the paradise of that reality, is *la ilaha illAllah* (there is no God but Allah). On this diagram, it's that

we're all looking in this direction, so then the left side is your heart. So when I flip it, it will be on my side.

La – In the Forehead – Deny the Head

The first *zikr* (chanting) that all *tariqahs* (spiritual paths) give is to say

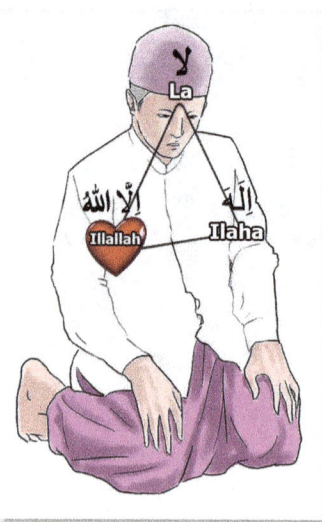

"*La ilaha illAllah*". This means bring the *qudra* (power) of your breath in, then *La* to your forehead, *ilaha* – there's a reality now at the point of the chest of *ilaha*, then *illAllah*.

It means that *nur* (light) and that breath that you're bringing in, you take to the head to void your head, stop thinking with your head. Our way is not the way of the head, but the way of the heart. Your head is never going to know Allah, never going to know the soul. Your head knows accounting, business, math, work, and *dunya* (material world) issues.

It means that *la ilaha illAllah, la ilaha illAllah*; then there's an upward reality, because there is no up and there is no down. Just for us to understand, Allah ﷻ is not up and Allah ﷻ is not down but the reality of the soul in the concept of this triangle, because everything for us is three, recite in three; *"Ateeullah, atee ur Rasul wa ulil amre minkum."*

﴿٥٩﴾ ...أَطِيعُواللَّهَ وَأَطِيعُواْ ٱلرَّسُولَ وَأُوْلِي ٱلْأَمْرِ مِنكُمْ...

4:59 – *"...Atiu Allaha wa atiur Rasula wa Ulil amre minkum..."* (Surat An-Nisa)

"...Obey Allah, Obey the Messenger, and those in authority among you..." (The Women, 4:59)

Prophet ﷺ said, 'Repeat everything three times, we say *shahada* (testimony of faith) three times.' *"Ashhadu an la ilaha illallah, wa ashhadu anna Muhammadan 'abduhu wa Rasulu,* three times." There is a tremendous reality in that understanding. Then in the understanding of the soul – *la ilaha illAllah*. So, when we're all looking at it, *la ilaha illAllah*, this is the heart. It means the upward reality and the soul reality, its power is in *la ilaha illAllah, la ilaha illAllah, la ilaha illAllah*.

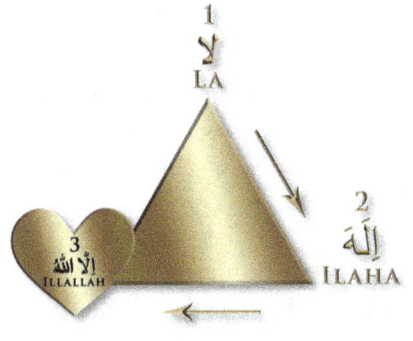

أَشْهَدُ أَنْ لَا إِلَهَ إِلاَّ اللهُ وَأَشْهَدُ أَنَّ مُحَمَّدًا عَبْدُهُ وَرَسُولُهُ

"Ashhadu an la ilaha illallah, wa ashhadu anna Muhammadan 'abduhu wa Rasulu."

"I bear witness that there is no god but Allah, and I bear witness that Muhammad is the messenger of Allah."

Reality of Physicality is 'Muhammad Rasul Allah' – Downward Triangle

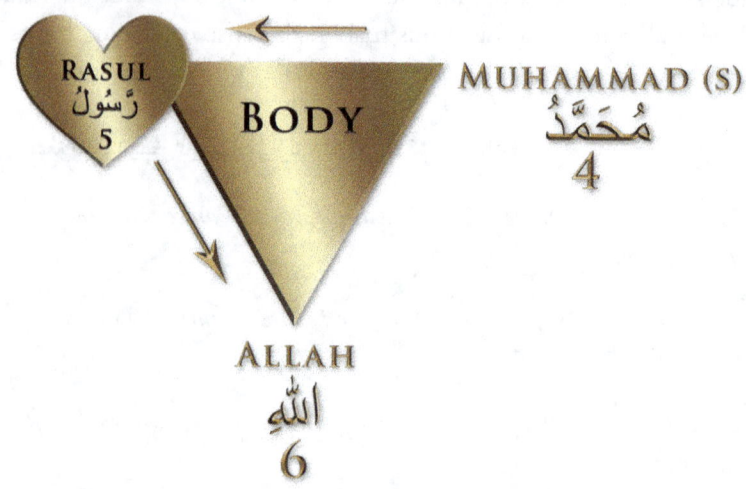

But the downward triangle and its understanding is the physicality. That everybody is struggling with their spirituality, to give energy to their soul. And what is struggling with them? Their desires for *dunya* (material world).

This means then we have these two fights, the upward desire, which is based on the soul; the upward part of the body which is based on your heart, your *lataif* (subtle energy points) of the heart. The energy of the heart comes through your soul. So, the importance of your belly, Prophet ﷺ described that, 'All difficulty is in the belly.'

اَلْمِعْدَةُ بَيْتُ الدَّاءِ وَالْحِمْيَةُ رَأْسُ اَلدَّوَاء

"*Al mi'datu baytud daaye, wal Himyatu rasu addawaa.*"

"The stomach is the house of disease and abstinence is the head of every remedy." (Prophet Muhammad (pbuh))

The belly is like an equator, why? Because the clash of what your soul wants and the *lataifs* (subtle energy points) that are taken on the upper part of the body to empower the heart. And *"Qalb al-mu'min baytullah"* – the heart is the seat of that Divinely Presence.

قَلْبَ الْمُؤْمِنْ بَيْتُ الرَّبْ

"Qalb al mu'min baytur rabb."

"The heart of the believer is the House of the Lord." (Hadith Qudsi)

Prophet Adam's ﷺ Descension and Prophet Muhammad's ﷺ Ascension

The *tajalli* (manifestation) and the reality of Sayyidina Adam ﷺ, because Allah ﷻ has no time, the Adamic *tajalli* (manifestation) is that Adam and the *Bani Adam*, the children of Adam, they are always coming down. They're always being sent from heavenly realities to come down. And the reality of Sayyidina Muhammad ﷺ is always rising up, from *Isra wal-Mi'raj* (The Night Journey and Ascension).

ذُو مِرَّةٍ فَاسْتَوَىٰ ﴿٦﴾ وَهُوَ بِالْأُفُقِ الْأَعْلَىٰ ﴿٧﴾ ثُمَّ دَنَا فَتَدَلَّىٰ ﴿٨﴾ فَكَانَ قَابَ قَوْسَيْنِ أَوْ أَدْنَىٰ ﴿٩﴾

53:6-9 – *"Dhoo mirratin fastawa. (6) Wa huwa bil Ufuqil a'la. (7) Thumma dana fatadalla. (8) Fakana qaba qawsayni aw adna. (9)"* (Surat An-Najm)

The Star of Prophet Muhammad ﷺ

"One of soundness. And he rose to [his] true form. (6) While he was in the higher [part of the] horizon. (7) Then he approached and descended. (8) And was at a distance of two bow lengths or nearer. (9)"
(The Star, 53:6-9)

Then Allah ﷻ wants us to understand your Adamic reality is that always a *tajalli* (manifestation) is coming down and that you must rise up to grab it. But the *tajalli* (manifestation) of *dunya* (material world) is going to take us down. So then understanding the body, Allah ﷻ sends the perfection of creation to come to tame the body desires. So, *Muhammad Rasul Allah, Muhammad Rasul Allah*, that Allah ﷻ sends the reality that if you want to tame your being as all prophets did, and the master of all prophecy and the master of all reality is then in the prophecy of Sayyidina Muhammad ﷺ. That Prophet ﷺ comes to teach us that *Muhammad Rasul Allah*, that *Muhammad Rasul Allah*.

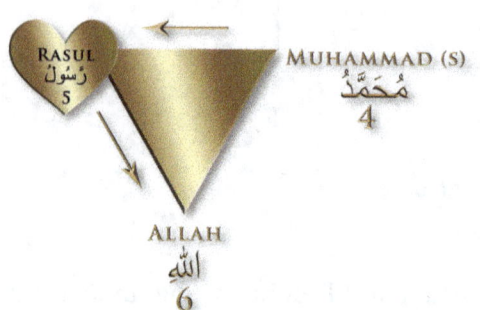

Reality of Surat Ikhlas (Sincerity) and 6 Points of the Heart

So, *La ilaha illAllah, la ilaha illAllah*, then at the same, (you start from right side of the chest) *Muhammad Rasul Allah, Muhammad Rasul Allah.* Because Allah ﷻ sends the reality of Prophet ﷺ to tame the physicality, 'Teach them about My Oneness.' Teach them that Allah ﷻ is *Ahad*

(one). Teach them that Allah ﷻ, Allah ﷻ.

Then teach them from *Dar ul-Ihsan*, *"Hu"*. *"Qul HuwAllahu Ahad."* (Say Allah is One). *Hu* being the highest reality, then *Ahle Allah*, the People of the Book who accept the Lordship of Allah ﷻ. Then the *budparast* and polytheists that Prophet ﷺ was sent to teach them Oneness, that Allah ﷻ is *Ahad* and One.

﴾قُلْ هُوَ اللَّـهُ أَحَدٌ ۝١﴿

112:1 – "Qul HuwAllahu Ahad.."
(Surat Al-Ikhlas)

"Say, He is Allah, [who is] One."
(The Sincerity, 112:1)

Prophet ﷺ Taught Us the Zikr of Allah ﷻ

It means then the reality of the perfection of physicality is in the understanding of *Muhammad Rasul Allah, Muhammad Rasul Allah*. That's why Prophet ﷺ came to *dunya* (material world) to teach us *'Allah'*. Prophet ﷺ came and taught us that, 'Say *'Allah'*, say *'Allah, Allah',* to extinguish all difficulty, all fires, to come to the Oneness of Allah ﷻ. And the key for your paradise is to say, *"la ilaha illAllah, la ilaha illAllah"* (there is no God but Allah).

مَنْ قَالَ لَا إِلَهَ إِلَّا اللهُ دَخَلَ الْجَنَّةَ

"Man qaala La ilaha illAllah, dakhalal Jannah."

"Whoever says 'La ilaha illAllah' (There is no God but Allah), enters Paradise." (Prophet Muhammad (pbuh))

The Star of Prophet Muhammad ﷺ

Zikr of Allah ﷻ is Upon Prophet Muhammad ﷺ

Then Allah ﷻ, they begin to teach us that the *zikr* of *'Allah'* is from Sayyidina Muhammad ﷺ. The *zikr* (remembrance) of Allah ﷻ is,

"InnAllaha wa mala'ikatahu yusalluna 'alan Nabi ﷺ." This means the *zikr* (remembrance) of Allah ﷻ and His *malaika* (angels) is on praising and praying upon the reality of Prophet ﷺ. Then the understanding of these two realities is the perfection of *Insan al Kamil* (Perfected human being).

$$\text{إِنَّ اللَّـهَ وَمَلَائِكَتَهُ يُصَلُّونَ عَلَى النَّبِيِّ ﴿٥٦﴾}$$

33:56 – "InnAllaha wa Malaaikatahu yusalluna 'alan Nabiyi..." (Surat Al-Ahzab)

"Allah and His angels send blessings upon the Prophet (pbuh)..." (The Combined Forces, 33:56)

Tame Your Physicality to Unlock Your Star

That, to understand the soul, and the soul and the energy that it wants – it wants to be in the ocean of *la ilaha illAllah*. But all the desires stop it from coming to *zikr* (remembrance). All the desires stop it from praying, all the desires stop it from fasting, all the desires stop it from *zakat* (charity). All the desires stop it from *Hajj* (pilgrimage). All the desires of the physicality come and overwhelm the body and begin to dress it with bad characteristics.

So then, Allah ﷻ is not going to leave us to ourselves, saying that, 'I know that you have a reality from My paradise. Your soul comes and your energy of your soul comes from My paradise, but you must understand your physicality, tame your physicality,' and at that time you can unlock your star. Unlock the symbol of your soul. Your soul is like a star.

Seek and Accompany the Guides Who Are the Stars on Earth

So, what Prophet ﷺ described from his *Sahabi* (Companions)? 'Follow my Companions, any of them. They are like stars on a dark night.'

أَصْحَابِيْ كَالنُّجُــومْ بِأَيْهِمْ اَقْتَدَيْتِمْ اَهْتَدَيْتِمْ

"Ashabi kan Nujoom, bi ayyihim aqta daytum ahta daytum."

"My companions are like stars. Follow any one of them and you will be guided." (Prophet Muhammad (pbuh))

This means open the reality of the light. The light is eternal. When people say, 'I don't understand what light is. Is it this light bulb?' Then

Allah ﷻ, that's why the analogy of the star. No, that which is eternal, that which you use for guidance, that throughout our lives, they would look to the heavens, look to the stars and they found their guidance. Based on the coordinates of the stars they knew where they were. They traveled by stars. Now we have GPS and it's lost. But the understanding is that if you look to the heavens, you could find your coordinates.

The Star of Prophet Muhammad ﷺ

وَهُوَ الَّذِي جَعَلَ لَكُمُ النُّجُومَ لِتَهْتَدُوا بِهَا فِي ظُلُمَاتِ الْبَرِّ وَالْبَحْرِ ۗ قَدْ فَصَّلْنَا الْآيَاتِ لِقَوْمٍ يَعْلَمُونَ ﴿٩٧﴾

6:97 – *"Wa huwal ladhee ja'ala lakumun nujooma litahtado biha fee Zhulumati albarri wal bahri, qad fasSalnal ayati liqawmin ya'lamoon."* (Surat Al-An'am)

"And it is He who placed for you the stars that you may be guided by them through the darknesses of the land and sea. We have detailed the signs for people who know." (The Cattle, 6:97)

Then Allah ﷻ is saying, 'Look to *dunya* (material world). The people whose realities they are stars, and they are stars on a dark night. By looking at them, accompanying them, being with them, you should find the reality that you are seeking of the Divinely Presence.

عَنْ أَنَسِ بْنِ مَالِكٍ رَضِيَ اللهُ عَنْهُ ، قَالَ : قَالَ رَسُولُ اللهِ صَلَّى اللهُ عَلَيْهِ وَسَلَّمَ : « أَنَّ مِثْلَ الْعُلَمَاءِ فِي الْأَرْضِ كَمَثَلِ النُّجُومِ ، يُهْتَدَى بِهَا فِي ظُلُمَاتِ الْبَرِّ وَالْبَحْرِ ، فَإِذَا انْطَمَسَتِ النُّجُومُ أَوْشَكَ أَنْ تَضِلَّ الْهُدَاةُ » رَوَاهُ أَحْمَدُ.

'An Anasin bin Malikin (ra) Qala, Qala Rasulullahi Sallallahu 'alayhi wa sallam: "Anna mithlal 'ulamayi fil ardi kamathalan Nujomi yuhtada beha fi zulumatil barri wal bahri. Fa iza antamasati anujomi aw shaka an tadillal huda.

Narrated by Anas Bin Malik (ra) that the Messenger of Allah (pbuh) said: " The religious scholars on Earth are like the stars in the sky, they guide people through the darkness of the land and sea. When those stars fade, the guidance will be lost". [Based on Imam Ahmad]

Accept Prophet Muhammad ﷺ to Perfect Your Star

Then the perfection of that, when the body needs to be tamed. How this comes together is when the body needs to be tamed and Allah ﷻ says, 'Tame that body,' which means, 'go and accept Muhammadun Rasulallah ﷺ.' As soon as you accept and say *"Ashhadu an la ilaha illAllah wa ashhadu anna Muhammadan 'Abduhu wa Habibuhu wa Rasuluhu* ﷺ" (There is no God but Allah, and Prophet Muhammad (saws) is His Servent, His Beloved, and His Messenger).

Then what Prophet ﷺ begins to inspire, *la ilaha illAllah*, make your *zikr* (chanting) of Allah ﷻ, read Holy Qur'an. All of that is the power of the soul. Then they begin to show us that for the physicality to be tamed and the reality of your soul to come out, that is the perfection of your star.

The Interaction of the Two Triangles in the Star

Then each, when you begin to look at it, because the people of *tafakkur* (contemplation), they have to contemplate. If *la ilaha illAllah*, if *la ilaha illAllah* is my soul reality and *Muhammad Rasulallah* is then taming of my physicality, then look at both and how they are interacting, *Muhammadun Ilaha*.

Rasul and *illAllah*: Then for your heart to have *illAllah*, it must be with *Rasul* ﷺ. So, Allah's ﷻ saying, 'No way your heart is going to have *illAllah* but Allah ﷻ unless it's with the *tajalli* of My Rasul *(alaihis salaatus salaam)*.

The Reality of 'Allah' is in the Secret of Lam Alif

The only way to open the reality of Allah ﷻ, the real reality, and why Allah ﷻ is in the body and the physical understanding is that in this *dunya* (material world), the power of Allah ﷻ has to come to conquer the physicality. At that time, they begin to teach that to open the real reality of Allah ﷻ is in the secret of *lam alif*. And the people of *silaat* and Islamic martial arts, they call *lam jalala*, that to understand and move now in the Ocean of *Ma'rifah* (Gnosticism) is *lam alif*.

So where do you see *lam alif*? In *Zulfiqar*, the sword of Sayyidina 'Ali ؑ is *Zulfiqar*. The hand is the circle and the two heads are the point. The owner of that reality, where Prophet ﷺ said, *"Ana madinatul 'ilm wa 'Ali baabe Hu."*

أَنَا مَدِيْنَةُ الْعِلْمِ وَ عَلِيٌّ بَابُهَا

"Ana madinatul 'ilmin wa 'Aliyyun baabuha."

"I am the city of knowledge and 'Ali (as) is its door/gatekeeper." (Prophet Muhammad (pbuh))

Bab-hu means he is the door for that reality *(alaihis salaam)* and all the *Sahabi* (Companions), bless them, they are all inside that reality. But where we see that *lam alif* is *Zulfiqar*, in the sword of Sayyidina 'Ali ؑ. Then the reality of *lam alif* and the teaching, but that's not for tonight. This is the understanding of how to tame the reality, how to open the star and the importance of the star.

Now if other people are using it, because they know the secret of it, and all the people of reality know the secret of it, but Muslims have left everything. And why Muslims have no victory in anything they do? Because they left reality, they left the love of Sayyidina Muhammad ﷺ.

You Can't Conquer Anything If You Can't Conquer Yourself

If you cannot have victory over yourself, you have victory over nothing. You can conquer nothing if you can't conquer yourself. Prophet ﷺ is teaching, and teaching *Ummat un-Nabi* ﷺ that, 'How you're going to have victory in anything you do if you don't have victory within yourself?'

And the victory of the self is to know oneself. We get to know ourself that this body can only be tamed by *Muhammad Rasul Allah*. *Muhammad Rasul – Rasul* must be in my heart for *illAllah* to come. It's up, right, left (because it's written like that for you in the diagram). *La ilaha illAllah*, then again from right to left, *Muhammad Rasul Allah, Muhammad Rasul Allah*.

Triangle of Islam, Iman, Ihsan – Upward Triangle

Then to understand you have *Islam* (submission). In your heart you must have *iman* (faith). And to open up the reality of your soul *dar ul-ihsan* (station of moral excellence), so it is the upward triangle.

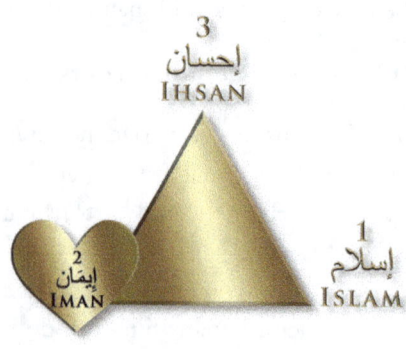

This is all in the understanding of how to open the reality of the *kalima* and this is in the *fiqh* (jurisprudence) of *tawhid* (oneness of Allah), and this is in the *fiqh* of 'don't make *shirk*'. What Prophet ﷺ feared most was for *shirk* (polytheism). It was not the *shirk* of idols (worshipping). He says, 'I fear most is the hidden *shirk* for my community.'

And the hidden *shirk* is *"ananiyah"*, is that when we put ourself in everything. When we begin to worship and pray to ourselves. When we begin to feel our self is important. It means this is all based on *fiqh*, this is the *fiqh* of *tawhid* (oneness of Allah). That *La ilaha illAllah Muhammad Rasulallah*, the only way to reach *la ilaha illAllah* is through the reality of *Muhammadun Rasulallah* ﷺ.

If Iman (Faith) is in the Heart, the Face Shines Like a Moon

Then they begin to show us in *dunya* (material world) that if you want the reality of the soul, *Islam, iman wal ihsan, Islam*, your right side. What hits your heart? *Iman*. If *iman* is in your heart, *Islam* is your foundation, it's firm, *dar ul-ihsan* will show through your face. So, they described Prophet ﷺ as the shining moon. Why the moon? Because his heart is the sun. If the heart is shining and the body is submitting, your face will shine from the light of your heart.

مِنْ ثَنِيَّاتِ الْوَدَاعِ   طَلَعَ الْبَدْرُ عَلَيْنَا

مَا دَعَا لِلَّهِ دَاعٍ   وَجَبَ الشُّكْرُ عَلَيْنَا

Tala'al badru 'alayna   Min thaniyatil wada'a
Wa jabash shukuru 'alayna   Ma da'aa lillahi da'a

O' the full moon rose above us, From the valley of Wada'a,
Gratitude is our obligation, as long as any caller calls to Allah

But most people's faces are darkened by their egos because they are trying to put out something from their head that doesn't exist within their heart. It's a facade. The reality is that there must be *Islam*, there must be submission. Somebody comes and says, 'Oh I can do this, I can do that, I can heal,' oh don't say anything. You are a magician and a liar. You have to be submitting. If you are submitting and your physicality, your donkey is what we consider it; if the donkey is tamed, maybe *iman* (faith) has entered into the heart. If your donkey is wild and crazy, there is no *iman* (faith) in your heart. If there's no *iman* (faith) in your heart nothing is going to be shining through your face. You can put all the mirage you want but there's no light coming through.

Then this is the knowledge of the self; this is the knowledge, 'He who knows himself knows his Lord.' So, all of that is from one *hadith* of Prophet ﷺ and begins to open an ocean.

$$\text{مَنْ عَرَفَ نَفْسَهُ فَقَدْ عَرَفَ رَبَّهُ}$$

"Man 'arafa nafsahu faqad 'arafa Rabbahu."

"Who knows himself, knows his Lord." (Prophet Muhammad (pbuh))

Get to know yourself and your reality, that foundation of your soul must be *Islam*. The foundation of that *Islam* will open *(Iman)*.

Prophet ﷺ Explained Religion as Islam, Iman, Ihsan

These are the three from the *hadith* of Sayyidina Jibreel ؑ that asked Prophet ﷺ, 'Explain this *deen* (religion) to us.' And a man came from the desert all in white and beautiful hair and said, *"Islam, iman wal ihsan."* What is the abode of *ihsan*? He ﷺ says, 'Pray as if you see Allah ﷻ and if you don't see Allah ﷻ know He sees you.'

$$\text{قَالَ: فَأَخْبِرْنِي عَنِ الْإِحْسَانِ، قَالَ: أَنْ تَعْبُدَ اللَّهَ كَأَنَّكَ تَرَاهُ، فَإِنْ لَمْ تَكُنْ تَرَاهُ فَإِنَّهُ يَرَاكَ}$$

"Qala Fa akhberni 'an al Ihsan."
Qala: "An Ta'bud Allaha, Ka annaka tarahu, fa in lam takun tarahu fa innahu yarak."

"Now, tell me about spiritual excellence (ihsan)."
The Prophet (pbuh) replied, "It is to serve/worship Allah as though you behold/see Him; and if you don't behold/see him, (know that) He surely sees you." Prophet Muhammad (pbuh))

It means all of these are in *hadith* (traditions) of Prophet ﷺ given to us as a symbol of a triangle. Later the symbol of the triangle you'll see it in everything in our lives. This triangle has nothing to do with the *fir'auns* (pharaohs); they copied everything because they are from a *dajjal* system. They copy the reality. The darkness always mimics the light. They know there is a secret in it, and they copy it, and they think by copying it they can make their schemes and things to happen. Impossible! because *'Izzatullah*, Allah ﷻ has to open the reality. So always you'll see the parallel of a reality copied by the world of darkness. But then the world of darkness advertises it, and everybody says, 'Ooh, this is something like this!' That's not correct. If it had no power, they wouldn't be using it, but they use it for their darkness.

Anger, Ignorance, and Fire – Downward Triangle

The understanding of that, *Islam, iman wal ihsan*, then Allah ﷻ is describing that your body, that anger, ignorance and fire. So, it goes, ignorance, anger, fire, ignorance (right side), anger (left side), and fire (downward). Without the perfection of your soul, your *Islam* conquers what? Ignorance, because this will go over on this side, and the two will begin to work on each other.

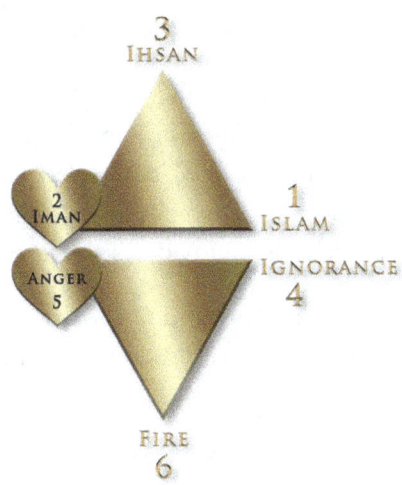

Ignorance is Opposite of Islam (Submission)

How to, this is your body desires before submission. The body is ruled by ignorance. People who are ignorant are angry, because they don't know anything and they're sitting in the dark. And if you turn the lights off here and the person hits their head a couple of times, they become very angry. They say, 'What is this? I don't understand this!' So then to turn the light on, to open the light of the soul, Allah ﷻ begins to release the reality of

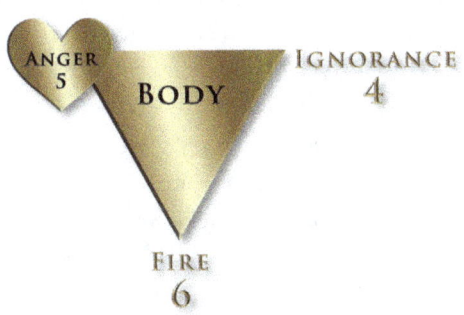

Islam (submission) to all the prophets. They brought *"Innad deena, indallah ul-Islam"* (The religion with God is Islam).

$$\{19\} \ldots \ ۚ \ \text{إِنَّ الدِّينَ عِندَ اللَّـهِ الْإِسْلَامُ}$$

3:19 – *"Innad deena 'indAllahil Islam…"* (Surat 'Ali 'Imran)

"The religion with God is Islam…" (Family of Imran, 3:19)

That every prophet brought *Islam* to submit to the level of their community. The completion of *Islam* (submission) is through Sayyidina Muhammad ﷺ. The *ma'rifah* (gnosticism) and the reality of Prophet's ﷺ *Isra wal-Mi'raj* (Night of Ascension) gave permission now for all creation to understand its reality.

Anger is Kufr and Opposite of Iman (Faith) – Then Wash and Ask Forgiveness

Then how to conquer ignorance must be through *Islam*, but if you are ignorant you have a tremendous amount of anger in the heart. And what Prophet ﷺ described of anger as *kufr* (disbelief). Anger is *kufr* (disbelief). As soon as you became angry, you came out of *Islam*. That's why you have to go make *wudu* (ablution), make your *shahada* (testimony of faith) and pray *istighfar* (forgiveness). Pray two *rakat* (cycle of prayer) asking forgiveness every time you become angry. Every time you become suspicious, every time you are backbiting, every time you enter the ocean of bad character, you have to wash and pray two *rakat* and ask for forgiveness.

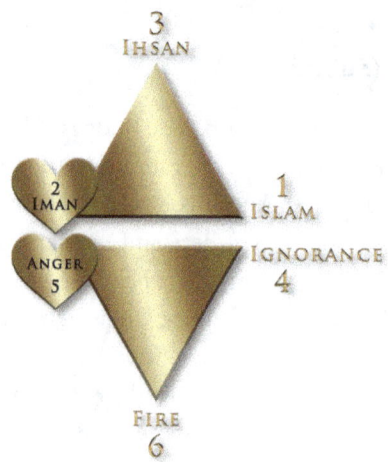

عَنْ عَطِيَّةَ بْنِ عُرْوَةَ السَّعْدِيْ رَضِيَ اللهُ، عَنَ النَّبِيُّ صَلَّى اللهُ عَلَيْهِ وَسَلَّمَ قَالَ

إِنَّ الْغَضَبَ مِنَ الشَّيْطَانِ وَإِنَّ الشَّيْطَانَ خُلِقَ مِنَ النَّارِ وَإِنَّمَا تُطْفَأُ النَّارُ بِالْمَاءِ فَإِذَا غَضِبَ أَحَدُكُمْ فَلْيَتَوَضَّأْ. روى الإمام أحمد في "المسند" (29/505) وأبو داود (4784)

'An 'Atiyat bin 'Urwatul Sa'di (ra) 'Anan Nabi (saws) Qal:

"Annal ghadaba minash shaitani wa innash shaitana khuliqa minan 'Naar, wa innama tutfa annaaru bil Maayi fa iza ghadeba ahadakum falyatawadda." [Rawayil Imam Ahmad fil Musanad wa Abu Dawud]

Atiyah Bin Orwah Alsaadi (ra) said, that the messenger of Allah (pbuh) said: "Anger is from Satan, and Satan was created from fire, and in which fire is extinguished by water. So if one of you got angry he should make Wudu (ablution)." [Narrated by Imam Ahmad in his Musnad (29/505, and Imam Abu Dawood (4784)]

Who Occupies Your Heart – Is it Throne Ar Rahman or Shaytan?

At that time, they begin to teach that if you really had *iman* (faith) in your heart, how could you have anger, *ghadab*? One time Sayyidina Abu Bakr as-Siddiq ﷺ got angry, Prophet ﷺ got up and walked away. Prophet ﷺ presents Divinely Presence. It was a teaching for us that as soon as anger comes into your heart, *qul ja al haqq wa zahaqal batil*.

وَ قُلْ جَاءَالْحَقُّ وَزَهَقَ الْبَطِلُ، إِنَّ الْبَطِلَ كَانَ زَهُوقًا ﴿٨١﴾

17:81 – *"Wa qul jaa alhaqqu wa zahaqal baatil, innal batila kana zahooqa."* (Surat Al-Isra)

"And say, Truth has come, and falsehood has departed. Indeed is falsehood, [by nature], ever bound to depart."
(The Night Journey, 17:81)

That Allah is saying, 'I am the *Haq* (truth) and that *shaytanic* (satanic) anger is falsehood. The two of us are not going to sit in your heart.' Who is going to be occupying your heart? Is it *Arsh ar-Rahman* (The Throne of the Divinely Presence) or is it the throne of *shaytan*? So, it is a deep understanding of our self, that, '*Ya Rabbi*, I'm overtaken by ignorance. I don't know anything and I don't know anything about myself. As a result of not knowing

anything I'm constantly angry, suspicious, jealous, *hasad* – jealous of everything, jealous of everyone, jealous of everything everybody has.' All of the root of that character creates a fire. Every bad characteristic creates a fire within the heart. That fire becomes so strong that it's your ticket to *jahannam* (hellfire). Allah says, 'I don't have to do anything. You have so much fire in your being it is of a fiery nature. By its nature, it will move towards the fire.' And this is the fire of *azab* (difficulty).

Extinguish the Fire of Anger and Turn it to Love

If we don't extinguish that fire and turn it into the ocean of *muhabbat*, love. Love is faith. More *hadith*, that Sayyidina Umar came to Prophet and brought half his wealth. And Sayyidina Abu Bakr as-Siddiq came and brought all his life to the threshold of the Prophet. It is a long *hadith* and Prophet asked, '*Ya* Umar, you have to love me more than you love yourself.'

لاَ يُؤْمِنُ أَحَدُكُمْ حَتَّى أَكُونَ أَحَبَّ إِلَيْهِ مِنْ وَالِدِهِ وَوَلَدِهِ وَالنَّاسِ أَجْمَعِينَ

"La yuminu ahadukum hatta akona ahabba ilayhi min walidihi wa waladihi wan Nasi ajma'yeen."

"None of you will have faith till he loves me more than his father, his children and all mankind." (Prophet Muhammad (pbuh))

Love is the Symbol of Iman (Faith)

Then love was the symbol of *iman* (faith), that you will not have faith within your heart without love, and love for who? Love for Sayyidina Muhammad ﷺ, more than you love yourself.

The *ashiqeen* (lovers of Prophet ﷺ), they love Prophet ﷺ more than themselves. They sacrificed themselves for Prophet ﷺ, every day asking Allah ﷻ, 'How can I be of service to the light of Prophet ﷺ so that Prophet ﷺ be happy?' If Prophet ﷺ is happy, Allah ﷻ is happy.

Reality of 666 – System of Dajjal

So, they begin to teach us that, that body desire, if we don't know this ignorance, don't know this anger and don't understand why we have fire. Where will you have fire? In your genitals. If you're ignorant and you're angry, you can't control your genitals and they are on fire. Either there's abundant amounts of sex or violence, and both of them are now rampant in this world. Both of them, they kill and do anything they want to anything and anyone. And these are all a sign of the lower desire.

Then if you just try to understand that these pyramids, these triangles are 60 degrees. 60 degrees, we don't have a zero in this one, we have *nuqt* (dot), so that becomes 666. The understanding of *dajjal* in their book, it's not in our book, they don't know their book. In their book, 666 was a symbol of the antichrist. Antichrist, anti-Christ teaching because everything about them is *hub ud dunya* (love of material world). Everything about them is the love of *dunya* (material world). They like to be ignorant and they want people to be ignorant. They like anger and they thrive, and  they breed and produce anger, and as a result they love the fire. Everything is about sex and killing now. Turn the TV on now and everybody's killing everybody or having sex with everybody. And this is the system of *dajjal* (antichrist).

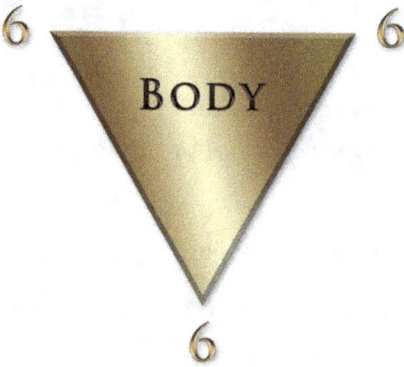

And this is the reality of only three 6's which is 18, which is *hayat* (living). Allah says, 'I've given you *hayat*, I've given you a life but if your life is purely for your physicality you are in a *dajjal* system. You are in satan's hands and if the master of satan appears in your lifetime, you will be following him.' So, Prophet ﷺ came and said, 'Prepare. You never know when the master, the leader of satan appears.'

Complete the Star with Heavenly Reality 18
Six 6s is 36 – Surat YaSeen – Heart of Qur'an

Prophet ﷺ said that, 'Don't let yourself to be from *hayat* of *dunya*,' that, 'counter the *hayat* of *dunya* with the *hayat* of *akhirah*, with 3 more 6's.' The combination of six 6s will come to us now. Six 6s is 36. 36 – "*YaSeen. Wal-Qur'an al-hakim*". (Chapter 36 of Holy Qur'an)

يس ﴿١﴾ وَالْقُرْآنِ الْحَكِيمِ ﴿٢﴾

36:1-2 – "*Ya-Seen. (1) Wal Qur'anal Hakeem. (2)*" (Surat YaSeen)

"*Ya-Seen. (1) By the Qur'an, full of Wisdom.*" (YaSeen, 36:1-2)

Allah ﷻ says, 'The heart of my Qur'an is Surat YaSeen.' Surat YaSeen is Sayyidina YaSeen *(alaihis salaatus salaam)*, is right here. That Allah ﷻ says, 'If you're fearful of this reality (666) and you want my heavenly reality you must be with the six 6s,' not just the people of *hayat al-dunya*, just they are only chasing after *dunya* (material world), but the people whose souls are alive, their hearts are alive and they're able to bring these realities. Only the 6s of the heaven, the 18 of the heaven, they are the *Ahl ul-Hayy, wal-kiram al-Hayy* (people of The Ever-living). They are from the Oceans of *Hayyat*. Their *zikr* is "*Hayy, Hayy, Hayy, Hayy*", from the ocean of the soul; they don't hear anybody from the *dajjal* saying "*Hayy*".

Victory and Allah's ﷻ Mighty Support – Nasran 'Aziza

Only at that time, the people of that reality, they can come to the people of *dunya* (material world) desires and begin to teach them, you say *Muhammadun Rasul Allah* and that the love of Sayyidina Muhammad ﷺ will overtake your body. And the *zikr* (chanting) of *la ilaha illAllah* (there is only one God) will open the soul and the perfection of Prophet ﷺ will come, and becomes what, Suratul Fath, 'The Victory' (Chapter 48 of Holy Qur'an).

The only victory that is a sure victory is if this reality begins to open. If the love of Prophet ﷺ overtakes the physicality and keeps asking, 'Ya Rabbi, open my soul,' Allah ﷻ says, 'Then love Prophet ﷺ. If you want My victory, a manifest victory, *"Inna fatahna laka 'fathan mubinah. Li yaghfira laka-Llah ma taqaddam min dhambika wa ma ta'akhar..."*,

إِنَّا فَتَحْنَا لَكَ فَتْحًا مُبِينًا ﴿١﴾ لِيَغْفِرَ لَكَ اللَّـهُ مَا تَقَدَّمَ مِن ذَنبِكَ وَمَا تَأَخَّرَ وَيُتِمَّ نِعْمَتَهُ عَلَيْكَ وَيَهْدِيَكَ صِرَاطًا مُّسْتَقِيمًا ﴿٢﴾

48:1-2 – *"Innaa fatahna laka fatham mubina. (1) liyaghfira lakaallaahu maa taqaddama min dhanbika wa maa taakhkhara wa yutimma ni'matahu 'alayka wa yahdiyaka siraathan mustaqima. (2)"* (Surat Al-Fath)

"Indeed, We granted you, [O Muhammad], a manifest Victory. (1) That Allah may forgive you your faults of the past and those to follow; and fulfil His favor upon you and guide you to a straight path. (2)" (The Victory, 48:1-2)

I'm going to forgive you all your sins, from the past and future. And I'm going to grant you forgiveness, *"Wa yansuru kallahu nasran 'aziza."*

وَيَنصُرَكَ اللَّهُ نَصْرًا عَزِيزًا ﴿٣﴾

48:3 – *"Wa yansurakAllahu nasran 'aziza."* (Surat Al-Fath)

"And [that] Allah may help you with a mighty victory."
(The Victory, 48:3)

What's Allah's ﷻ *"nasran aziza"*? Allah ﷻ is saying, 'I'm going to grant you a mighty support.' Allah's ﷻ saying, 'I'm going to grant you a mighty support. I'm going to grant your heart a victory, I'm going to grant your heart these realities more,' because he's not granting it to me and you. But if your body is in love with Sayyidina Muhammad ﷺ and the love of *la ilaha illAllah, la ilaha illAllah, la ilaha illAllah,* that victory already is given to Prophet ﷺ. That Mawlana is teaching that Prophet ﷺ *feekum,* that he is already in you.

كَمَا أَرْسَلْنَا فِيكُمْ رَسُولًا مِّنكُمْ يَتْلُو عَلَيْكُمْ آيَاتِنَا وَيُزَكِّيكُمْ وَيُعَلِّمُكُمُ الْكِتَابَ وَالْحِكْمَةَ وَيُعَلِّمُكُم مَّا لَمْ تَكُونُوا تَعْلَمُونَ ﴿١٥١﴾

2:151 – *"Kama arsalna feekum Rasulam minkum yatlo 'Alaykum ayatina wa yuzakkeekum wa yu'Allimukumul kitaba walhikmata wa yu'Allimukum ma lam takono ta'Alamon."* (Surat Al-Baqarah)

"Just as We have sent (within) you a messenger from yourselves reciting to you Our verses, and purifying you, and teaching you the Book and wisdom and teaching you that which you did not know."
(The Cow, 2:151)

The Star of Prophet Muhammad ﷺ

That light is already in you. If you are nourishing that light, the victory is already there. You just have to bring that light and that love out. Prophet ﷺ will bring the victory to the body. He's already victorious to the soul, it's just the physical body has to submit.

When it submits, the *Nur Muhammad* ﷺ begins to come. The *Nur Muhammadun Rasul Allah* – only through *Muhammadun Rasul* on the tongue, is Allah ﷻ. At that time with the love of Sayyidina Muhammad ﷺ, he begins to inspire us; now you say *"Allah, Allah, Allah"* – not Allah ﷻ from outside, but Allah ﷻ from inside'. This means that inside the love of Prophet ﷺ. When they say *"Allah"* ﷻ they say it real. They say it real because it's in the heart of Prophet ﷺ.

We pray that in these holy 10 days of *ma'rifah* (gnosticism) and moving towards the Holy Ka'bah, the symbol of the Holy Ka'bah is that, *"Qalb al-mu'min bayt-Allah."*

قَلْبَ الْمُؤْمِنْ بَيْتُ الرَّبّ

"Qalb al mu'min baytur rabb."

"The heart of the believer is the House of the Lord." (Hadith Qudsi)

Allah's ﷻ saying, 'The heart of My believer is My house,' that, 'the Ka'bah that you built, you built with your hands. My *Tajalli*, My Blessing is on that Ka'bah, but what I built with My two Hands and I blew from my spirit into it is the heart of the believer.' And what believer Allah's ﷻ talking about is the reality of *Muhammadun Rasulallah* ﷺ.

Upper and Lower Triangles Are an Analogy

Everything again is always an analogy; there are no triangles. It's just an analogy – up and down, upper reality, lower reality. What they know now from *dunya* (material world) and how you have your DNA is called a double helix. If you look at the double helix, it's just a series of *lam alif, lam alif, lam alif, lam alif*. And everything is in the DNA, which means everything is in the reality of *lam alif*. DNA is what, *dunya*, DNA. Allah ﷻ says, 'You don't have to guess so hard. Most of these things are right in front of you.'

Subhana rabbika rabbal 'izzati 'amma yasifoon, wa salaamun 'alal mursaleen, walhamdulillahi rabbil 'aalameen. Bi hurmati Muhammad al-Mustafa wa bi siri Surat al-Fatiha.

Secrets of the Star and Guidance to Enlightenment

Stars Are Symbols of Guidance

Understanding our creation is Sufism, is *tariqah* (spiritual path). It is not a particular religion that sets you apart and to be proud of that religion, to be born into a religion. But a religion is a discipline upon the physicality. It means going towards the Star of David ﷺ. It is not exclusive to Jewish people. It is a Star! The prophetic teaching is that follow any of my *Sahabis* (companions), they are like stars on a dark night. Stars are guidance, are saints.

Secrets of the Star and Guidance to Enlightenment

أَصْحَابِيْ كَالنُّجُومْ بِأَيِّهِمْ اَقْتَدَيْتُمْ اَهْتَدَيْتُمْ

"Ashabi kan Nujoom, bi ayyihim aqtadaytum ahtadaytum."

"My companions are like stars. Follow any one of them and you will be guided." (Prophet Muhammad (pbuh))

All prophets came and taught law for the general public and taught spiritual realities for the very few elite who were willing to take a spiritual path and to seek.

The Process of Enlightenment is to Become a Star and a Guide

The process of enlightenment is to become a star. It means that once you become enlightened, you are filled with light. So, when you are filled with light, you are a star. You will guide in this world, in your physicality, because light is glowing from you. And you'll guide in the hereafter because you are a star in the heavens. We take guidance for granted nowadays. But before, when people were sailing on ships, they relied completely on the heavens. They had to look at the sky to determine where they were, because there was no GPS, there was no MapQuest. It means all guidance was coming from that analogy.

The Divine is showing that anyone seeking enlightenment, the reality of that enlightenment is to become a shining star. So *Najm Dawood* (Star of David) was not Dawood's ﷺ, it was Sayyidina Muhammad's ﷺ. It was the Divine Kingdom. It was a gift from the Divine Almighty that anyone applying this law is going to unlock the power of heavenly kingdoms. Understanding that star is towards the station of self realization.

Star is Made Up of Two Triangles

Religion is the First Base of the Upper Triangle

That star is made up of two triangles; one triangle that points towards the Heavens, and one triangle that points towards the earth. The triangle that points towards the heavens represents faith. This means it goes up, down to the right and then the left. The lower base of triangle is your religion, then the next is faith. Religion, faith, then perfection and moral excellence. It means when we split the star and to understand the star, the base of this star is religion. That's why the Divine sends you *deen* and *deen* in Arabic is religion. Whatever the religion is, it's meant to tame your physicality. Not to be lost in its name and to fight over its title but was to tame your physicality. What to feed this body, what not to feed this body. What to give to this body and what not to give to this body. How to treat myself, how to treat my family, how to treat my loved ones, how to treat my community. Religion is for physical taming and for taming our physicality.

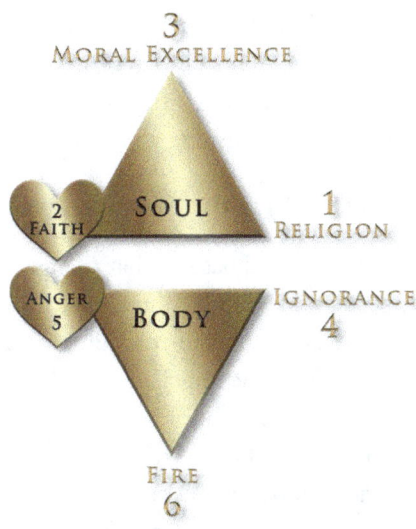

Once we understood that and the upper triangle has to do with power of the soul and reaching the heavenly kingdom. It means once you understood religion and applied a religious faith that works for you, that applies a discipline to your physicality, applies a discipline to your family and your community because it is not the law of the jungle. Because we weren't created as apes; it means we were created in the creation of Sayyidina Adam عليه السلام which was the most noble creation.

Secrets of the Star and Guidance to Enlightenment

{٧٠}... وَلَقَدْ كَرَّمْنَا بَنِي آدَمَ

17:70 – *"Wa laqad karramna bani adama..." (Surat Al-Isra)*

"And We have certainly honored the children of Adam..."
(The Night Journey, 17:70)

The law of the jungle is to take and harm and do as you like and think nothing of it. But the law of the Divine Kingdom has nothing to do with the jungle. It's all based on discipline and not going beyond your bounds, not harming other people, not harming your family, your loved ones, not even harming yourself.

Iman (Faith) is the Second Base of Upper Triangle

Then the second base of that triangle opens up which is *iman* and faith. It means once you have religion, it doesn't necessarily mean you have faith. Because you can pray all day long but not believe in the Divine, not believe in the angels, not believe in holy books, not believe in the day of judgment, and not believe in destiny. It's very apparent. As soon as you talk about angels, people say, 'Oh, don't give us that hocus-pocus.' This means you start talking

about the unseen, they don't want to talk about that. Well, then that's faith. Faith has nothing to do with what you see, touch and feel. It has to do with your heart. It's like love. How do you describe love? It's nothing that you can see, it's not something that you can hold. It's something that you can feel, and everyone feels it. It means that the second pillar of this belief is that you apply the physical discipline, but now the power that is coming into the heart, the power that is coming into the mind is that you have to develop faith.

Close Your Eyes to Build Your Faith

This means then you apply your physical discipline, but you have to spend all your time with your eyes closed. Because faith is built by eyes  closed. Why? Because it has nothing to do with the seen. If your religion is just with your eyes open and everything is based on what you see, you have not yet received faith. It's simple because all you are doing is saying I accept only what I see and what I can touch. But the station of faith and bringing down the material desire has all to do with keeping the eyes closed. It means then you apply your disciplines and you are comfortable with yourself. You are comfortable contemplating, meditating, reciting, chanting, listening to the recitations. And asking, 'O my lord, what I am seeking is not going to be found here in the physical dimensions. I am not going to find it a movie theatre. I'm not going to find it in a grocery store. I'm not going to find it in a nightclub. I am not going to find that faith anywhere but in the heart of the believer.'

قَلْبَ الْمُؤْمِنْ بَيْتُ الرَّبْ

"Qalb al mu'min baytur rabb."

"The heart of the believer is the House of the Lord."
(Hadith Qudsi)

Meditate and Close Your Eyes to Open a Khashf (Spiritual Vision)

It means as soon as you close your eyes and contemplate and meditate, a power in the soul opens up and vision through the soul opens up. Because you are using the faculty of seeing through the eyes but there is another power seeing through the soul. As soon as you close your eyes

and spend your time and a great deal of that time with your eyes closed, the power of spiritual vision opens up. The spiritual vision, which we call *khashf*. All of a sudden you may have like a shot of lightning that shows you something from the Divine, something heavenly, something not from this dimension made to build that faith. That, keep coming, keep coming – what you are seeking is not in this seen dimension but, it's in the unseen dimension.

That builds faith and *taqwa*, fear of the Divine. It means that builds that love that you don't want to do anything wrong because the Divine is opening all these endless mercies for you. You are feeling the angels come. You feel energies come. You feel Divine visions start to open. It means that is the nectar that makes us run towards that Divine Presence. Now I am going to open to you what no eyes have seen, what no ears have heard, and what no  lips can speak because each one has his own gift and her own gift from the Divine Presence.

Mixture of Religion and Faith Builds Station of Moral Excellence (Ihsan)

Then the station of faith. You apply the physical discipline. You apply the spiritual belief and spiritual practices. All of the sciences of that spirituality which is in Sufism, and most faiths have all of these sciences, these two, the religion and faith when they mix, the chemical reaction of your discipline and your faith builds the station of moral perfection. We say the Station of *Ihsan* (moral excellence). It means once you are using that discipline to build your faith, what's being built is this pyramid and the pinnacle of this pyramid has to do with the perfection of your character. That yes, you pray. Yes, you fast. And yes, you do all of these things based on your religion, but you do it because of faith and by love. You do it because of complete sincerity. Based on that, of course you are going to have moral excellence. You are not going to cheat. You are not going to steal. Where Divine says in Holy Qur'an, 'If you give that person one coin, they give it back to you.' But there are people that you give a bag of coins, and you will see nothing back from it.

وَمِنْ أَهْلِ الْكِتَابِ مَنْ إِن تَأْمَنْهُ بِقِنطَارٍ يُؤَدِّهِ إِلَيْكَ وَمِنْهُم مَّنْ إِن تَأْمَنْهُ بِدِينَارٍ لَّا يُؤَدِّهِ إِلَيْكَ إِلَّا مَا دُمْتَ عَلَيْهِ قَائِمًا...﴿٧٥﴾

3:75 – "Wa min Ahlil Kitaabi man in taamanhu biqintaariny yu'addihee ilaika wa minhum man in taamanhu bideenaaril laa yu'addiheee ilaika illaa maa dumta 'alaihi qaaa' imaa…"
(Surat 'Ali 'Imran)

"And among the People of the Scripture is he who, if you entrust him with a great amount [of wealth], he will return it to you. And among them is he who, if you entrust him with a [single] silver coin, he will not return it to you unless you are constantly standing over him [demanding it]…" (Family of Imran, 3:75)

It means that is station of perfection and faith. Divine is showing you that when we can unlock these powers and start building this upper strength of the soul, it means then we truly have the ability to fight against our desires. It means we can fight against that hole towards evilness.

When the Lataif (Subtle Energy Points) Opens, the Power of Soul Opens

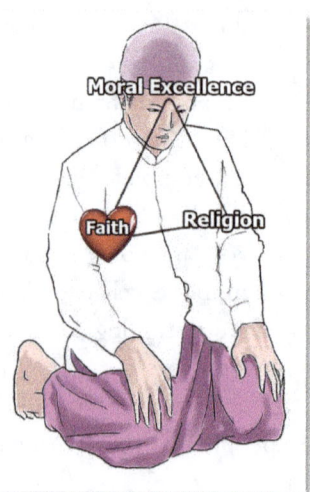

There are two triangles because one is of the Divine and one is the lower triangle; that's why the human creation is split with these two triangles. Upper has to do with heavens. This means the upper dimension, all the way up to your head has to do with the power of your soul and ascending towards the heavens. That's why all the chakras and the *lataif* (subtle energy points) of the heart and the *lataif* of the forehead – all of these when they open, they open the power towards the soul and towards the heavens.

Satan Wants to Keep Us Ignorant

The lower triangle has to do with *dunya* or material desires. It means once we can unlock this understanding, then what is the lower triangle?

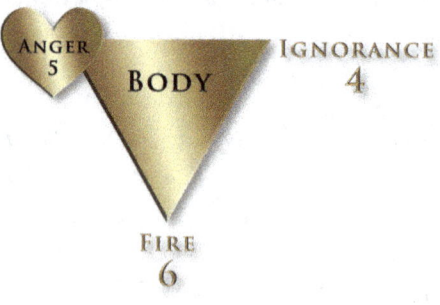

Ignorance. It means when we talk about the concepts of *Iblis* (Devil's name), satan and the devil, evilness or lending ourselves to its wickedness. How is that government governed? It's governed by ignorance, by keeping people in ignorance. Ignorance lends itself towards anger. Ignorant people are very angry. Why? Because they have no idea what's going on. If you're in a room and it's dark and you keep falling over the furniture, you get angry. You say, 'Who put this couch here? Who put this here?' Because you can't see anything in the room because you're ignorant, *jahal*.

So how to come against ignorance? You come against anger. Ignorance is the devil who keeps us to be ignorant – never seeking knowledge, never seeking realities. By keeping us ignorant, he's breeding anger. It means anger starts to develop, 'Who are these people? Who are those people? I don't know this. I don't know that'. That's because of unfamiliarity because we're ignorant of each other. We don't understand and love and have compassion for each other. So, this ignorance brings anger. When ignorance and anger come together, the chemical reaction is fire. That's why the devil is of a fiery nature. It means when we live our life in ignorance and live our life with that anger, that ignorance and anger builds a fire in the lower chakras, the lower *lataif* (subtle energy points). That's why material desire is so based on lower desires. It means they govern their life from the waist down. Whatever from the waist down is appropriate, is where their life has to go.

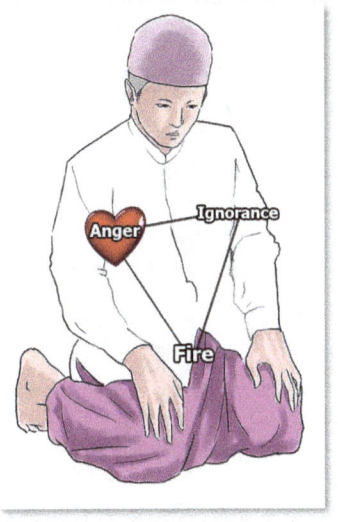

Religion is to Seek Knowledge and Defeat Ignorance

So, commanding that self and understanding that self is that when you apply these disciplines of the star, it means you have a religion. You develop all the sciences of faith. These two develop the station of perfection.

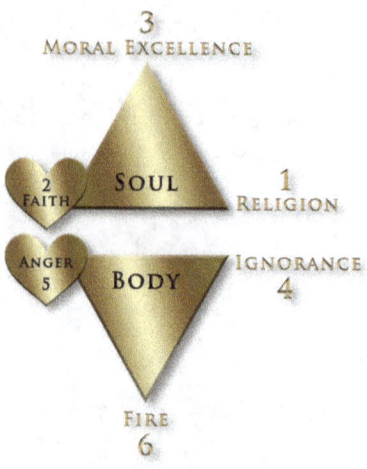

When that power comes from the upper level of the star, it starts to take control of the lower level. Why? Because that religion dispels ignorance. It means if your religion is tolerant, your religion is to seek knowledge even if you have to go to China; it means constantly seeking, constantly looking for that Divine. This religion burns out ignorance. It means it's like water onto the fire.

أُطْلُبُوا الْعِلْمَ وَلَوْ فِي الصِّيْنِ

"Uthlubul 'ilma walaw fis Seen."

"Seek knowledge even (if it is) in China." (Prophet Muhammad (pbuh))

Science Explains That Everything is Light and Energy

It means that the Divine is teaching us, 'If you can unleash these secrets and bring these disciplines upon yourself, entire universes are going to be open to you!' You are going to understand the secrets of creation. You are going to understand the secrets of light.

وَسَخَّرَ لَكُم مَّا فِي السَّمَاوَاتِ وَمَا فِي الْأَرْضِ جَمِيعاً مِّنْهُ إِنَّ فِي ذَلِكَ لَآيَاتٍ لَقَوْمٍ يَتَفَكَّرُونَ ﴿١٣﴾

45:13 – "Wa sakhkhara lakum ma fis Samawati wa ma fil Ardi jamee'an minhu, inna fee dhalika la ayatin liqawmin yatafakkaron." (Surat Al-Jathiya)

"And He has subjected/gave the authority to you [Sayyidina Mahmood (pbuh)], as from Him, all that is in the heavens and on earth: Behold, in that are Signs indeed for those who reflect/Contemplate [Meditate]." (The Crouching, 45:13)

When you say to be an enlightened individual, what is the Divine teaching us? A thousand years ago, if someone came to you and said, 'It's time to be enlightened,' you would say, 'What are you talking about, enlightened?!' But now it doesn't even require faith because science is telling you. Science is telling you that from form, you have  molecular structure. From molecular structure, you have atomic structure. From atomic structure, you have subatomic structure, and below all of that you have quantum light. Quantum physics!

Enlightenment Means to Become Light and Understand Light

It means now we have reached a point in our lives that the Divine is  saying, 'Ok, faith or no faith, it is all going to be laid out for you.' Everything has to do with light. Everything around you is created from light. This floor has a form. Its molecular structure has atoms, the subatomic understanding of this is then it starts to go into light and the understanding of light. It means everything around us is light. So, when you are enlightened, it means you understand everything. Everything has a knowledge. All light is hearing, is seeing, is tasting, is breathing because light is angelic.

And degrees of light – you may open just one level of understanding of light and that is the energy level. But then you may go deeper into the understanding of light which becomes the angelic level of understanding where the angels teach you the reality of each atom of light and how that light is seeing, hearing, smelling, tasting. It means it's all filled within this room. Every atom in this room hears, sees, smells, tastes everything. It means then the pursuit of realities is the pursuit of light – to enlighten oneself, to become light and then understanding all light.

Enlightened Individuals Move at the Speed of Light

It means that's what saints had achieved. That was Einstein's theory. If you became light, then time stopped for you. Why? Because time is relevant to our lives on this Earth. Based on the sun, the moon and Earth. Enlightened individuals are not bound by time anymore. They're moving at the speed of light. It means their soul is understanding everything at the speed of light. That's the importance of what quantum physics is coming to teach all of mankind. I don't know what you're understanding – I don't know anything about physics, but this is what Mawlana Shaykh is teaching.

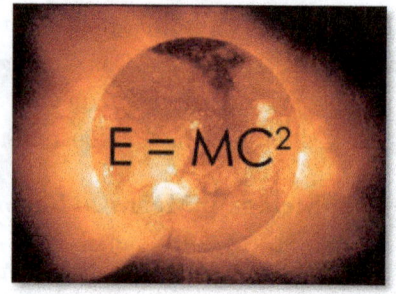

All Parts of Light Communicate With Each Other

They have entire experiments on light where they take one particle of light and they shoot it through a device, and they split that particle of light. They found out that all that light – its source hit and the two points that split, all three of these pieces are communicating with each other at the speed of light.

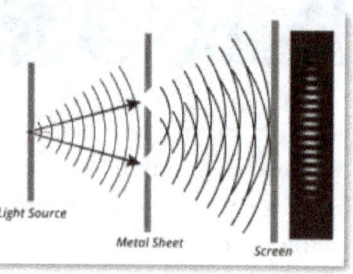

It means the Divine is showing you that you're all from one source of light put into different vehicles of your form. But when you receive and  attain a station of enlightenment, you will communicate with all light throughout this galaxy, throughout this universe. Wherever there is creation, that creation is in light and you'll be able to communicate and understand based on your level of security clearance. It means based on your level of attainment, there are degrees. You'll be given access to more and more of that heavenly knowledge which is the knowledge of light.

May God Almighty bless us, forgive us, take away our difficulties and open for us a way through the saints and through the prophets to reach to that understanding and to unlock our potential. It means with that greatness of what He has bestowed upon us for us to actually pursue that and taste from that. That's the true blessing of this way.

Subhana rabbika rabbal 'izzati 'amma yasifoon, wa salaamun 'alal mursaleen, walhamdulillahi rabbil 'aalameen. Bi hurmati Muhammad al-Mustafa wa bi siri Surat al-Fatiha.

The Heart is the Sun, The Face is the Moon

...أَطِيعُوا اللَّهَ وَأَطِيعُوا الرَّسُولَ وَأُولِي الْأَمْرِ مِنكُمْ... ﴿٥٩﴾

4:59 – "...*Atiullaha wa atiur Rasula wa Ulil amre minkum*..." (Surat An-Nisa)

"... Obey Allah, Obey the Messenger, and those in authority among you..." (The Women, 4:59)

Prophet's ﷺ Companions are Stars / Suns

Throughout the Holy Qur'an, many *surats* (chapters) reference to stars, the *buruj*, the galaxies. *At-Tariq* is a star that they call a piercing star and there is also a piercing star within our entire created universe, where the entire universe has a star billions and

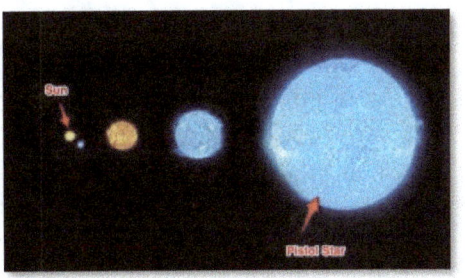

billions the size of the star that we have now as the sun.

وَالسَّمَاءِ وَالطَّارِقِ ﴿١﴾ وَمَا أَدْرَاكَ مَا الطَّارِقُ ﴿٢﴾ النَّجْمُ الثَّاقِبُ ﴿٣﴾

86:1-3 – "*Was Sama e wat Tariq. (1) Wa ma adraka mat tariq? (2) AnNajmu ath thaqib. (3)*" (Surat At-Tariq)

"By the Sky and the Night-Visitant (therein). (1) And what will explain to thee what the Night-Visitant is? (2) (It is) the Star of piercing brightness [Pistol star]. (3)" (The Nightcomer, 86:1-3)

Prophet's ﷺ teaching, 'Follow any of my Companions, they are like stars on a dark night.' It means everywhere we look, they're guiding us to the reality of a *najm*, of a star, and to be a star; that take the reality which God has given and reach its eternal reality.

أَصْحَابِي كَالنُّجُـــومْ بِأَيِّهِمْ اَقْتَدَيْتُمْ اَهْتَدَيْتُمْ

"Ashabi kan Nujoom, bi ayyihim aqta daytum ahta daytum."

"My companions are like stars. Follow any one of them and you will be guided." (Prophet Muhammad (pbuh))

The Reality of the Star and Two Triangles On Our Body

The guides come to teach us about our self, and we have two important triangles upon our self; one related to the soul and one related to the physicality. That you have for your soul from your two chests, from one, two, three. And these are the upper *lataifs* (subtle energy points) or chakras that are important for the power that are coming upon the soul. And you have from four, five, six, to the belly button that are responsible for the energies that are coming to the physicality.

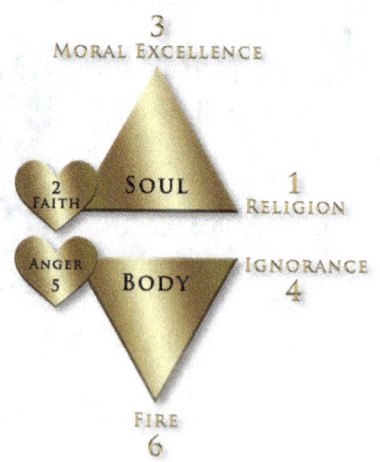

Our life is based on that understanding, that how are you going to govern your reality? How are you going to energize your soul and bring the power of the soul? How are you going to discipline the physicality? If the system is not in check and the physicality is not disciplined, these two will never come to be locked.

The Material World is Operating on the Lower Triangle

The whole material world is operating on the lower, the lower pyramid, which means the plane of the physicality. They're operating at the level of the physicality. What is important in that is that comes ignorance, anger, ignorance, anger under the heart and then a fire within the desires. Now the heart is on the left side. So, this means this upper triangle of my soul on how to open up the reality of my soul, how to discipline the physicality; so, from my right, left, and up to the forehead. Then from the right, left, and down to the navel.

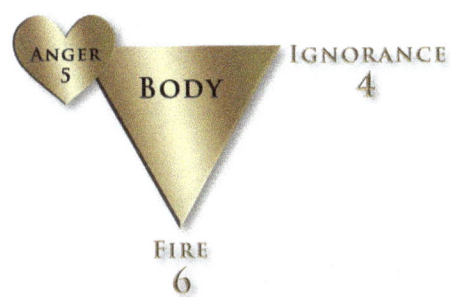

When operating from the physicality, everything is based on ignorance. The 'anger' is into the heart and fire into the belly. So as much as they give to the physical, they're going to increase the level of ignorance. By that ignorance, they increase; by its nature, ignorance will increase anger because ignorant people are very angry people. Why? Because they're in the dark. So, if I turn the lights off, it's a symbolic gesture of ignorance. As soon as you turn the lights off, you'll start to hit everything. As a result of hitting everything, you become angry because you don't know. So, what Prophet ﷺ wanted for the seeker is seek out knowledges and realities.

Then the life of the material world is based on ignorance; that ignorance breeds anger. That is where it's coming into the heart. If you're operating from ignorance and anger, you've developed now a fire within the belly. That fire is the root of all sickness; that fire increases all the lower

The Heart is the Sun, The Face is the Moon

---

desires, all the bad desires, all the bad appetites because the body is on fire.

Seek a Path to Open the Realities of Your Star

What they want from us, is to open the reality of the soul, that you have *Islam, iman wal maqam al ihsan*. It means that the higher level of the soul is that the *Islam, iman, wal maqam al ihsan*. That *Islam* is a word of submission, that I have to live my life, because you have to take the Arabic to understand in whatever language you're 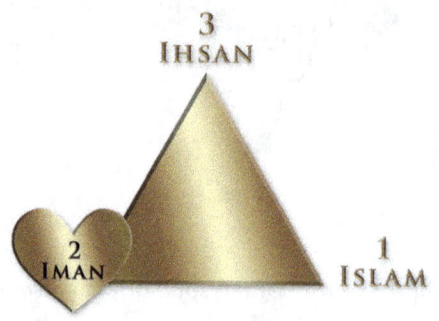 studying the reality. It's not about only the Arabic language, but it's the understanding. What Allah ﷻ wants is not that you follow only the Arabic language, but you follow the understanding, and could be any of Allah's ﷻ creations, that submit your life, submit your life, 'Thy kingdom come, Thy Will be done on earth as it is in heavens.'

"...Thy kingdom come. Thy will be done, on earth as it is in heaven. Give us this day our daily bread; and forgive us our trespasses, as we forgive those who trespass against us; and lead us not into temptation, but deliver us from evil." (The Lord's Prayer)

That is a *du'a* (supplication) for the heart and this is the symbol of the  heart. This is the reality of creation and the opening of creation; and that the heart has to be a star because this is the *lataif* (subtle energy points) of the *qalb* (heart). This is just the opening of the *lataif* (subtle energy points) of the *qalb* (heart). The *lataif* of the *qalb* is based on a star, based on the sun. It means that you have to seek a path in which you are trying to open the realities of a star and say that, '*Ya Rabbi*, I want my soul to be eternal, I want to reach its eternity and its realities.'

Religious Practices Will Bring Down Ignorance

Then Allah ﷻ, says, 'If you want My Heavenly Kingdom, then upon your kingdom and your physicality, submit.' So, our life is about submitting. Only that submission will bring down this ignorance. So, these two triangles are overlocking. It means that what's going to conquer ignorance in the world? It is your *Islam*, your

submission. Take a path in which you submit your will to the Will of the Divine. So, it means your religious and spiritual practices are your submission. When you increase your spiritual practices, it takes away the ignorance. What *shaytan* (satan) wants is don't do anything spiritual; don't do anything that would require you to submit, so that we can operate from ignorance. This means that once we begin to open that reality, which means you're opening that reality of submission, it begins to conquer the ignorance. And you have dominion over the ignorance and begin to wash away that ignorance.

The Light of Faith Will Take Away the Anger

From *Islam* and the process of submission will open the reality of *maqam al iman* (station of faith), because *iman* now enters into the heart, faith enters into the heart. If you are submitting and putting down ignorance, naturally you are building faith; by building faith you take away the fire of ignorance, the anger. The anger that is coming into the heart takes a person from disbelief, takes a person away from belief towards the oceans of disbelief.

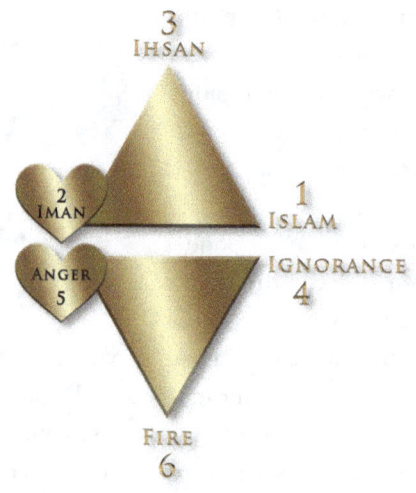

It means then we see how ignorance and anger and fire, it's like a formula of disaster. As soon as you begin to submit your will and seek a spiritual path and seek spiritual understandings, these lights begin to diminish that ignorance. The light of faith, because the practices should become stronger and stronger, the light of faith will take away the anger within the heart.

Anger Takes Away Iman (Faith)

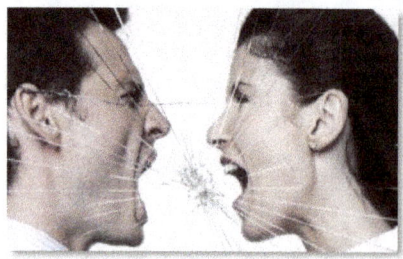

That's why Prophet ﷺ is teaching that *ghadab* (anger) is *kufr* (disbelief), that anybody operating from anger is continuously entering into disbelief.

The danger of anger is so significant that you can do anything in a moment of rage, and it will be nothing based on belief; you can harm people. So, it means your life can't be based on your heart having anger. There is no way! Anybody angry is devoid of faith. That's why the process of spirituality, the process of, 'Who knows himself will know his Lord,' these are all the *hadith* (traditions) of Prophet ﷺ.

مَنْ عَرَفَ نَفْسَهُ فَقَدْ عَرَفَ رَبَّهُ

"*Man 'arafa nafsahu faqad 'arafa Rabbahu.*"

"*Who knows himself, knows his Lord.*" (Prophet Muhammad (pbuh))

Follow in the Footsteps of the Pious Souls: Nabiyeen (Prophets), Siddiqeen (Truthful), Shuhada (Martyrs), wa Saliheen (Righteous)

As soon as I want to get to know myself, what do I want to be? I want to be in the footsteps of the Companions, and the *Nabiyeen* (prophets), *Siddiqeen* (truthful), *Shuhada* (martyrs), *wa Saliheen* (righteous), and they are all with Allah ﷻ and all of them are stars on a dark night. They reached the reality of a star in which they conquered their ignorance and they set an example for us.

وَمَن يُطِعِ اللَّهَ وَالرَّسُولَ فَأُولَٰئِكَ مَعَ الَّذِينَ أَنْعَمَ اللَّهُ عَلَيْهِم مِّنَ النَّبِيِّينَ وَالصِّدِّيقِينَ وَالشُّهَدَاءِ وَالصَّالِحِينَ ۚ وَحَسُنَ أُولَٰئِكَ رَفِيقًا ﴿٦٩﴾

4:69 – "*Wa man yuti' Allaha war Rasula faolayeka ma'al ladheena an'ama Allahu 'alayhim minan Nabiyeena, was Siddiqeena, wash Shuhadai, was Saliheena wa hasuna olayeka rafeeqan.*" (Surat An-Nisa)

"And whoever obeys Allah and the Messenger (pbuh) are in the company of those on whom Allah has bestowed His Favours/Blessings – of the prophets, the sincere Truthful, the witnesses (who testify), and the Righteous, and excellent are those as companions." (The Women, 4:69)

Use Spiritual Practices to Conquer the Anger

Then all their life was about conquering their anger that, '*Ya Rabbi*, how can I have anger in my heart? I have to seek a path in which I am

continuously entering into my heart. And understand that you are going to be testing me at every moment. I have to be able to hold that and not let the anger to come, be able to understand the tools that were given to me to wash, to meditate, to contemplate and to ask God to relieve me of this anger. Don't let that anger to enter into my heart so that the beatific lights of faith enter into the heart,' because faith, *"qul jaa alhaqqu wa zahaqal baatil"*. It means the truth and falsehood, they never come together.

وَ قُلْ جَآءَالْحَقُّ وَزَهَقَ الْبَطِلُ، إِنَّ الْبَطِلَ كَانَ زَهُوقًا ﴿٨١﴾

17:81 – "Wa qul jaa alhaqqu wa zahaqal baatil, innal batila kana zahoqa." (Surat Al-Isra)

"And say, Truth has come, and falsehood has perished. Indeed falsehood, [by its nature], is ever perishing/ bound to perish."
(The Night Journey, 17:81)

Then God is telling us, 'My Kingdom is coming. You want My Will, then conquer your own will, but My Light never sits with falsehood.' This means the angel and the demon, they don't sit in the heart; they don't sit together and just, 'Okay you can talk now and then I'll talk later, you talk now,' no! It's either you're going to operate the heart through demonic, through fire, through rage and anger, or you're going to take a path in which to bring that anger down and continuously take the anger away. And these are all the tools that Prophet ﷺ gave to us.

Use Water to Put Down the Fire of Anger

The greatest tool is water. Water, it fights *shayateen* (devils). *Zikrullah* and the remembrance, the chanting, the praising upon the prophetic reality; all of that brings a light within the heart that burns the *shayateen* and the lights and the fires. It means the heavenly light burns away the rage and the fire. By doing the *zikr* (remembrance), by doing the praisings, by understanding the power of water and washing when we

become angry and taking away all these bad characteristics, then we begin to realize 70% of my inside is water.

عَنْ عَطِيَّةَ بْنِ عُرْوَةَ الْسَعْدِيْ رَضِيَ اللَّهِ, عَنَ النَّبِيُّ صَلَّى اللهُ عَلَيْهِ وَسَلَّمَ قَالَ

إِنَّ الْغَضَبَ مِنَ الشَّيْطَانِ وَإِنَّ الشَّيْطَانَ خُلِقَ مِنَ النَّارِ وَإِنَّمَا تُطْفَأُ النَّارُ بِالْمَاءِ فَإِذَا غَضِبَ أَحَدُكُمْ فَلْيَتَوَضَّأْ. روى الإمام أحمد في "المسند" (29/505) وأبو داود (4784)

'An 'Atiyat bin 'Urwatul Sa'di (ra) 'Anan Nabi (saws) Qal:

"'Annal ghadaba minash shaitani wa innash shaitana khuliqa minan 'Naar, wa innama tutfa annaaru bil Maayi fa iza ghadeba ahadakum falyatawadda." [Rawayil Imam Ahmad fil Musanad wa Abu Dawud]

Atiyah Bin Orwah Alsaadi (ra) said, that the messenger of Allah (pbuh) said: "Anger is from Satan, and Satan was created from fire, and in which fire is extinguished by water. So if one of you got angry he should make Wudu (ablution)." [Narrated by Imam Ahmad in his Musnad (29/505, and Imam Abu Dawood (4784)]

The Heart is the Sun, The Face is the Moon

What You Eat and Drink Affects Your Inner Demons

How then to purify now my inside? If I understood the power of physical water, where I can use the water to take away anger, take away  all sorts of difficulties, then they begin to teach again from Prophet ﷺ that your inner water also has to be purified. What are you eating? Is it clean? Is it pure? Is it in God's name? What are you drinking? Is it clean and is it pure? Don't drink spirits because they're telling you they're spirits! It means don't drink things that are going to bring the satanic influence and the demonic influence within the body. They're going to come and operate in you.

Prophet ﷺ was teaching the *shaytan* (satan) moves through the blood. So, this means he wants to enter into the system and operate. What you feed him is going to be depending upon his strength. That's why don't eat with your left hand. The left hand is for cleaning the body when you've gone to the bathroom. Prophet ﷺ taught that if you eat with your right hand, it cuts the provision of *shaytan* (satan).  Anybody that eats with their left hand, as if he's feeding his *shaytan* (satan).

قَالَ رَسُولُ اللهِ صَلَّى اللهُ عَلَيْهِ وَسَلَّمَ:

إِذَا أَكَلَ أَحَدُكُمْ فَلْيَأْكُلْ بِيَمِينِهِ ، وَإِذَا شَرِبَ فَلْيَشْرَبْ بِيَمِينِهِ فَإِنَّ الشَّيْطَانَ يَأْكُلُ بِشَمَالِهِ وَيَشْرَبُ بِشَمَالِهِ [رَوَاهُ مُسْلِمٌ]

Qala Rasullallah ﷺ: iza akulla ahadikum falayakalu beyaminihi, wa iza shurbin falayushribu biyaminihi. Fa innash shaitana yakalu beshamalihi wa yushribu beshamalihi. [Rawahu Muslimun]

The Prophet (pbuh) said: "Eat with your right hand and drink with your right hand, as Satan eats with his left hand and drinks with his left hand." [Narrated by Imam Muslim]

They say somebody went to a *khashf* (spiritual state/vision) and witnessed that he saw a person and his *shaytan* (satan) was very fat. He saw another person and his *shaytan* was very skinny and starving. He said, 'What happened? Why this *shaytan* is fat and this *shaytan* is very skinny?' They were describing to him, 'This one eats with his left hand and every provision Allah ﷻ gives to him is taken by that *shaytan*. And this other one whom eats with his right hand, his provision goes for him and he's starving that *shaytan*.'

Purify the Real House of Allah ﷻ in Your Heart

This means all of what Prophet ﷺ brought was for energy, the realization of energy, how to perfect the energy, how to wash, how to eat what is holy and what has been sacrificed in God's name, that it be sanctified and purified. What I drink into this body, this is my *masjid* (mosque). This is my temple, this is my place of worshipness. What I do with it, when Allah ﷻ says wash it, purify it, circumambulate, He's talking about the *masjid* (mosque) that is the heart. Not only the *masjid* we build for outside, for worshipness; but the greatest *masjid* (mosque) of Allah ﷻ, the greatest temple or church of Allah ﷻ is the heart of the believer.

The Heart is the Sun, The Face is the Moon

...أَن طَهِّرَا بَيْتِيَ لِلطَّائِفِينَ وَالْعَاكِفِينَ وَالرُّكَّعِ السُّجُودِ ﴿١٢٥﴾

2:125 – "...An Tahhir baytee liTayifeena, wal 'Aakifeena, wa ruka'is sujood." (Surat Al-Baqarah)

"...Purify/Sanctify My House for those who perform Tawaf (circamambulation) and those who seclude themselves for devotion and bow and prostrate [in prayer]." (The Cow, 2:125)

It means then everything we eat and drink, how to purify that blood, that builds the light of faith.

Station of Moral Excellence

When that begins to conquer that anger, the fire of anger is going down, the fires of ignorance are going down and this fire of rage is now from the light of *maqam of ihsan* (Station of Moral Excellence), and is now diminishing that

anger, that fire. Only at that time that the light of perfection begins to open what they call their 'third eye', but this is *maqam al ihsan* (Station of Moral Excellence). It means from their *Islam* and submission, *Islam, iman wa maqam al ihsan*. As soon as they entered into submission, they took the practices of submitting and everything about them is to submit. That even in our prayer, when you put your head to the ground, you're

telling your Lord that, 'This body of mine is a mere donkey, and You are Supreme.' And as soon as the donkey puts its head to the ground, the soul is actually the rider. It's showing God that, 'My donkey is under my control, My Lord, and what you gave from Your Lights is my soul. My soul is supreme, my donkey is under control.'

Don't Let Your Donkey Ride You!

The reverse is the material world, where everyone is carrying their donkey and their soul is oppressed; and that's what angers God, 'As that soul comes from My Paradise. That body of yours, ashes to ashes and dust to dust, that body is going back! Why are you giving the supremacy to the body and not to that which is eternal?' So this means even in the prayer, most in the prayer, is a gesture in which, 'My head and the crown of my creation and all that you want to bestow upon me, my Lord, I submit it into Your Presence, and it's but nothing, and it's subjugate itself entirely to the Divinely Presence.'

And with that majesty, Allah ﷻ is happy and pleased. Allah ﷻ says, 'As much as I bestow onto you, you be nothing in My Presence,' because this is the binary code; God is on and I am off. If I want to be on, then God is distant, saying that, 'Okay, if you want to be the whole show, then that's you.' But take a path in which you're nothing, nothing, nothing, that this binary code, its reality can begin to dress the servant. That becomes *maqam al ihsan* (Station of Moral Excellence).

When the Heart Becomes a Sun, the Face Shines Like a Moon

When their *Islam* (submission), *iman* (faith) and *maqam al ihsan* (station of Moral Excellence) is now shining. The light of *maqam al ihsan* (Station of Moral Excellence) means that the light that's operating through their heart is now beginning to

The Heart is the Sun, The Face is the Moon

dress upon their face. We said this is the *maqam* (station) of the *qalb* (heart), this is the *lataif* (subtle energy points) of the *qalb* (heart) because the heart becomes a sun.

If the heart becomes a sun, your face becomes the moon, becomes the full moon in which it's dressed by the light of your heart. It means if a person has light upon their face, it's because they have light upon their heart. The heart is reflecting to the face. But now everybody wants to put makeup onto their face to beautify their face but that's not what's important. What's important is to beautify the heart.

When the heart is beatific, Divinely lights will reflect upon the face.

That's what Allah is teaching that if you are going to take a path of a star, you have a galaxy. You have 11 essential organs, all of them must be lit up by the power of your sun. You see how I run my galaxy and my universes? Because Allah says, 'I show you the sign upon the horizon and within yourself.'

سَنُرِيهِمْ آيَاتِنَا فِي الْآفَاقِ وَفِي أَنفُسِهِمْ حَتَّىٰ يَتَبَيَّنَ لَهُمْ أَنَّهُ الْحَقُّ ۗ ... ﴿٥٣﴾

41:53 – *"Sanureehim ayatina fil afaqi wa fee anfusihim hatta yatabayyana lahum annahu alhaqqu..." (Surat Al-Isra)*

"We will show them Our signs in the horizons and within themselves until it becomes clear to them that it is the truth..."
(The Night Journey, 41:53)

We Cannot Reach Higher Kingdoms If We Cannot Rule Our Own Body

We say, '*Ya Rabbi*, I want to reach towards Your Kingdom and the control of Your Kingdom to be given.' He says, 'But how can I give you control of My Kingdom when you have no control over your own?' And that's why who knows himself knows his Lord that, '*Ya Rabbi*, I'm going to light my sun. If I don't have a sun, all is destroyed, is worthless'; all your planets have nothing, have no sun.

Prophet ﷺ described if there's one part of you good, all of you is good; if that one part of you is bad, all of you is bad and that's the heart of the person.

أَلَا وَإِنَّ فِى الْجَسَدِ مُضْغَةً إِذَا صَلَحَتْ صَلَحَ الْجَسَدُ كُلُّهُ، وَإِذَا فَسَدَتْ فَسَدَ الْجَسَدُ كُلُّهُ، أَلَا وَهِىَ الْقَلْبُ

"*Ala wa inna fil Jasadi mudghatan idha salahat salahal jasadu kulluho, wa idha fasadat fasadal jasadu kulluho, ala wa heyal Qalb.*"

"*There is a piece of flesh in the body, if it becomes good (reformed) the whole body becomes good but if it gets spoiled the whole body gets spoiled and that is the heart.*" *(Prophet Muhammad (pbuh))*

If the heart is good everything is shining; if your heart is bad, what is the benefit for anything else the person is doing? It is *zulumat* and oppression which means the way of *ma'rifah* (gnosticism) is how to open that reality. That's in *Islam, iman wal maqam al ihsan,* to conquer all the lower characteristics.

Upper Triangle of Kalima – La, Ilaha, IllAllah

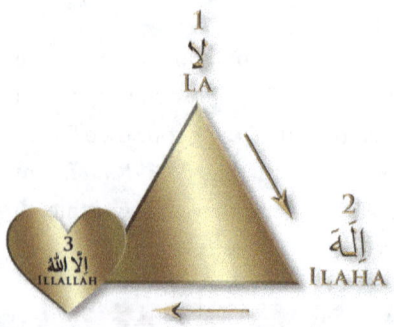

That reality of the soul for now those who understand *Islam* is *La ilaha illAllah Muhammadun RasulAllah* (There is no God but Allah ﷻ and Muhammad ﷺ is His Messenger). It means that in the realities of the soul and the first *zikrs* (chanting) of *tariqah* (spiritual path), is *La*. So, *lam alif* and the secret of that door and that *baab* (door) is the *Zulfiqar* (two-spiked sword). That's why the first *zikr* (chanting) of all *tariqah* (spiritual path).

Imam 'Ali is the Gate Keeper with Zulfiqar – Lam Alif

It's the first *zikr* of *tariqah* (spiritual path) because they are inheriting from what Allah ﷻ and Prophet ﷺ described that, 'I am the city of knowledge and Imam 'Ali ؏ is its *baab*,' is the gatekeeper of that reality.

قَالَ رَسُولَ اللَّهِ صلى الله عليه وسلم "انا مدينة العلم و علي بابها

Qala RasulAllah ﷺ – "*Ana madinatul-ilmin wa `Aliyun baabuha.*"

"I am city of knowledge and 'Ali is the door."
(Prophet Muhammad (pbuh))

It means that gatekeeper stands guard with a *lam jalala*, because the *Zulfiqar* is the *lam jalala*, it's a sword that comes up with two spikes. And that sword is significant for the head can't enter into this reality.

This means the reality of the *la*, is that the first *zikr* (chanting) is *La* (upper point), *ilaha* to the right, *illAllah* into the heart. It means the power of the soul, and later *awliyaullah* (saints), they can do many things based on that *zikr* (chanting) because everything is based on *La ilaha illAllah Muhammadun RasulAllah* ﷺ.

This is where Nabi Musa عليه السلام said, 'Ya Rabbi, I want to go where the two rivers meet,' which means I want the *sirrat al lam jalala*.

وَإِذْ قَالَ مُوسَىٰ لِفَتَاهُ لَا أَبْرَحُ حَتَّىٰ أَبْلُغَ مَجْمَعَ الْبَحْرَيْنِ أَوْ أَمْضِيَ حُقُبًا ﴿٦٠﴾

18:60 – "Wa idh qala Mosa lefatahu laa abrahu hatta ablugha majma'a albahrayni aw amdiya huquba." (Surat Al-Kahf)

"Behold, Moses said to his attendant, I will not give up until I reach the junction of the two seas or (until) I spend years and years in travel." (The Cave, 18:60)

This is the highest of your secrets, the highest of your realities, whose gatekeeper is Imam 'Ali عليه السلام. When Prophet ﷺ said, 'I am the city and he is the gatekeeper, the door of that reality.'

Elevate Yourself With Your Heart, Not Your Head

This means that that *la* is on the forehead. *"La"* in Arabic means 'no'. So, this means that you want the reality, it's not going to be by your head. It means you're not going to sit and read a book and analyze, 'Oh my God, where's like, it's here, it's like that. Okay maybe I can find the door like this and I'll get through the door' – no, no, no!

This head is like what we played on Matrix when they said, 'Is this not real, is this not real!' And then he said, 'What is real? A series of electronic pulses that is sent to your brain?' That just based on your touch and your feel is your understanding of real, from this piece of a flesh locked within a skull? None of that is real. What's real exists within the heart and what the soul sees of what's real, not this, it's an illusion.

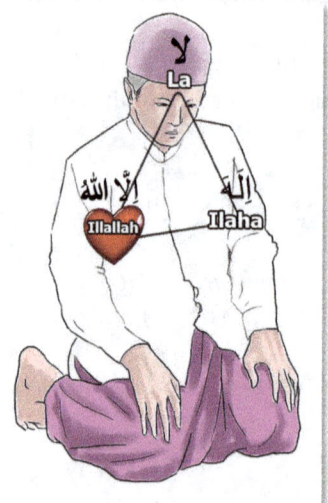

It means that *La ilaha illAllah* is telling us that you bring the energy of your breath in, and it comes up, because the seventh point is here in forehead. Bring your breath and your energy in and comes to the head, *La*. This means all the energy comes to your head, that negate your head, negate your thinking; this path is not going to be based on what your head is understanding. Nothing, negate, nothing, and then divinity; *ilaha, ilaha*, into the right corner, *illAllah* – nothing but Allah into the heart, *illAllah, illAllah*. So, it means the first *zikr* (chanting) continuously, even by holding the breath, they hold the breath, *La, ilaha, illAllah*, and don't take your breath out; and they practice that throughout the day continuously.

Then Mawlana Shaykh Abdul Khaliq al-Ghujdawani ق preferred to do that *zikr* under water so that satanic influence of the *jinn* (unseen beings) wouldn't affect his *tafakkur* and his contemplation. It means they begin to practice *La, ilaha, illAllah*, and begin to feel the movement of that energy and that light is coming to *la* and negate my head, and that is the *Zulfiqar* (two-spiked sword); *ilaha illAllah* and feel the movement of that light within the heart.

Put Out Your Negative Fire With Muhammadan RasulAllah ﷺ

Then to understand that is the power of the soul and that Allah ﷻ sent *Muhammadun RasulAllah* ﷺ as the law-giver to discipline all the physicality. So then on the *zikr* (chanting) of Prophet ﷺ is *Muhammadun RasulAllah* ﷺ, *Muhammadun RasulAllah* ﷺ, *Muhammadun RasulAllah* ﷺ. And that reality brings all that fire down, that opens the reality that Prophet ﷺ, that when this *najm* (star) connects, that Muhammadan lock the physicality. Prophet ﷺ brings the discipline and the light, the majestic lights to discipline the physicality and take it away from its ignorance, from its anger and from its fire. If *Muhammadun RasulAllah* ﷺ ignites the physicality, discipline the physicality, Allah ﷻ releases the reality of *La ilaha illAllah*. That's why the *kalima* is *La ilaha illAllah Muhammadun RasulAllah* ﷺ. So, it means in its perfection, it's *La ilaha illAllah*, and then the light of Prophet ﷺ, *Muhammadun RasulAllah* ﷺ.

And tremendous realities that in Allah ﷻ, in this reality of *Zulfiqar* (two-spiked sword), the gate in the *dunya* (material world) is known to you as Allah ﷻ; that Allah ﷻ, *Ism Jalala* is the Supreme Name that encompasses the attributes of Allah ﷻ. This means it brings the majesty and discipline upon the physicality. But Allah ﷻ is a hidden treasure wanting to be known, wanting to be known by *maqam al ihsan* (Station of Moral Excellence); that, 'You want to know Me, come to *La ilaha illAllah, Muhammadun*

The Heart is the Sun, The Face is the Moon

RasulAllah ﷺ. Come to the *lam alif*, come to the *Zulfiqar* (two-spiked sword), come to where Nabi Musa ؑ wanted of those realities. Come to that *Zulfiqar* (two-spiked sword) of *La ilaha illAllah Muhammadun RasulAllah* ﷺ.

Reality of 313 in the Star

3 Points of the Soul, 3 Points of the Body, and 1 Sultan in the Heart

We pray that Allah ﷻ open more and more understanding for us of its reality. It goes one, two, three, upper triangle, and four, five, six, the lower triangle and seven is right at the centre, is the throne of *Arsh Ar-Rahman*. The Throne of the Divinely Presence is the seven and the secret of the seven, that Allah ﷻ described, 'I created creation in six and rested upon the seventh.'

إِنَّ رَبَّكُمُ اللَّـهُ الَّذِي خَلَقَ السَّمَاوَاتِ وَالْأَرْضَ فِي سِتَّةِ أَيَّامٍ ثُمَّ اسْتَوَىٰ عَلَى الْعَرْشِ يُغْشِي اللَّيْلَ النَّهَارَ يَطْلُبُهُ حَثِيثًا وَالشَّمْسَ وَالْقَمَرَ وَالنُّجُومَ مُسَخَّرَاتٍ بِأَمْرِهِ ۗ أَلَا لَهُ الْخَلْقُ وَالْأَمْرُ ۗ تَبَارَكَ اللَّـهُ رَبُّ الْعَالَمِينَ ﴿٥٤﴾

7:54 – "*Inna Rabbakkumul laahul lazee khalaqas sammaawaati wal arda fee sittati qiyaamin summmas tawaa 'alal 'arshi yughshil lailan nahaara yatlu buhoo haseesanw washshamsa walqamara wannujooma musakhkharaatim bi amrih; alaa lahul khalqu wal-amr; tabaarakal laahu Rabbul 'aalameen.*" (Surat Al-A'raf)

"*Your Guardian-Lord is Allah, Who created the heavens and the earth in six days, and is firmly established on the throne (of authority): He draweth the night as a veil o'er the day, each seeking the other in rapid succession: He created the sun, the moon, and the stars, (all) governed by*

laws under His command. Is it not His to create and to govern? Blessed be Allah, the Cherisher and Sustainer of the worlds!"
(The Heights, 7:54)

This means that all of creation is but one *nuqt* (dot), like a star, and infinite amount of stars are coming into existence, infinite amounts of *nuqts* (dots) are coming. That reality is the reality of the beginning.

The Six Powers of the Heart

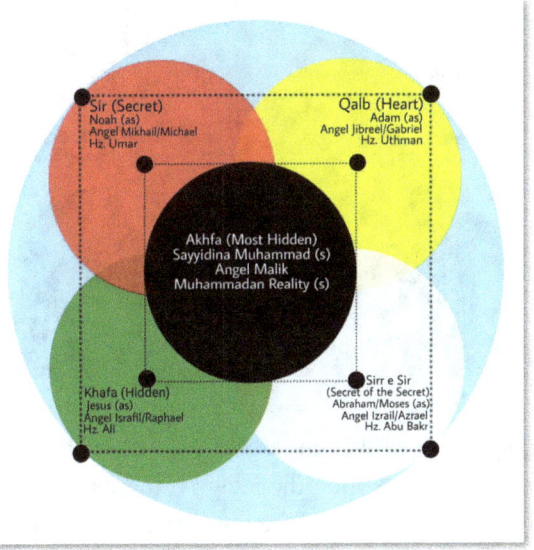

It means that understanding that these are the six powers of the heart held by the seventh, is the crown of creation. This means that when Allah ﷻ opens that reality for the servant and when they open these six points, these are the six powers of the heart. Where Allah ﷻ gives *awliyaullah* (saints) the power over their heart, the power of *juzba* (attraction), the power of *fa'iz* (downpouring), the power of *tawassal* (intercession), the power of their *nazar* (gaze), the power of *tai* (scrolling), the power of *irshad* and guidance. That they are of the seven because Allah ﷻ dressed them from the reality of seven in which their seven faculties are dressed by seven divinely essences of Allah ﷻ.

The Heart is the Sun, The Face is the Moon

7 Attributes That Dress the 7 Holy Openings of the Face

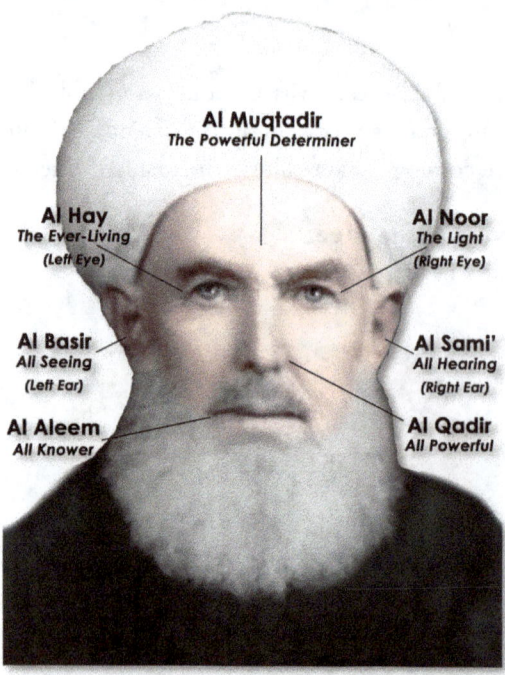

Where John saw in the Bible, in the Book of Revelations, 'I saw seven divinely essences dressed upon the King.' It means in every book, they understood that *WajhAllah* and the Divinely Face you're talking about. When this star opens and the power of that star opens, they become from those who carry the seven. What's seven? It is that they open the two attributes of the ears, they open the two attributes of the eyes, they open the two attributes of the breath and Allah ﷻ gave them power upon their tongue. And Allah ﷻ says, 'Everything perishes but their holy face.' And this is the face in which Allah ﷻ dressed upon Prophet ﷺ, Prophet ﷺ dressed back upon *awliyaullah* (saints).

وَلَا تَدْعُ مَعَ اللَّهِ إِلَٰهًا آخَرَ لَا إِلَٰهَ إِلَّا هُوَ كُلُّ شَيْءٍ هَالِكٌ إِلَّا وَجْهَهُ لَهُ الْحُكْمُ وَإِلَيْهِ تُرْجَعُونَ ﴿٨٨﴾

28:88 – *"Wala tad'uo ma'Allahi ilahan aakhara la ilaha illa huwa kullu shayin halikun illa wajha hu la hul hukmu wa ilayhi turja'oon."*
(Surat Al-Qasas)

"And call not, besides Allah, on another god. There is no god but He. Everything (that exists) will perish except His Holy Face. To Him belongs the Command, and to Him you will be returned."
(The Stories, 28:88)

Subhana rabbika rabbal 'izzati 'amma yasifoon, wa salaamun 'alal mursaleen, walhamdulillahi rabbil 'aalameen. Bi hurmati Muhammad al-Mustafa wa bi siri Surat al-Fatiha.

3 Points of Upper Star – Islam, Iman, Ihsan
Opening Your Vision

Follow the Companions of Prophet Muhammad ﷺ, They Are Stars

Every reality that Prophet ﷺ is bringing for the people of *haqqaiq* (realities) is to improve themselves and for people to understand the way of realities. That Prophet ﷺ was teaching that my companions are like stars in a dark night.

أَصْحَابِيْ كَالنُّجُومْ بِأَيْهِمْ اَقْتَدَيْتِمْ اَهْتَدَيْتِمْ

"*Ashabi kan Nujoom, bi ayyihim aqta daytum ahta daytum.*"

"*My companions are like stars. Follow any one of them and you will be guided.*" (Prophet Muhammad (pbuh))

Anyone of them that you follow, that you take as a guide, because the stars are in reference to guidance not for looking at in amusement. But Prophet ﷺ was giving an *isharat* (sign), that in the event that I am not present with you, that my companions are like guides. And Prophet's ﷺ words are eternal realities. That Prophet's ﷺ *Ahbab an Nabi* ﷺ, lovers of Sayyidina Muhammad ﷺ, are inheriting from that holy *hadith* (Prophetic ﷺ tradition).

Ahbab an-Nabi ﷺ Are Modern Day Reality of Companions

That Prophet ﷺ is not leaving this nation to be unattended. That in this nation *Ahbab an Nabi* ﷺ, they are the modern-day reality of the companionship. They accompany by love and Prophet ﷺ said that you'll be with whom you love.

عَنْ أَنَسِ بْنِ مَالِكٍ رَضِيَ اللهُ عَنْهُ ، قَالَ : قَالَ رَسُولُ اللهِ صَلَّى اللهُ عَلَيْهِ وَسَلَّمَ : « أَنَّ مِثْلَ الْعُلَمَاءِ فِي الْأَرْضِ كَمَثَلِ النُّجُومِ ، يُهْتَدَى بِهَا فِي ظُلُمَاتِ الْبَرِّ وَالْبَحْرِ ، فَإِذَا انْطَمَسَتِ النُّجُومُ أَوْشَكَ أَنْ تَضِلَّ الْهُدَاةُ » رَوَاهُ أَحْمَدُ .

'An Anasin bin Malikin (ra) Qala, Qala Rasulullahi Sallallahu 'alayhi wa sallam: "Anna mithlal 'ulamayi fil ardi kamathalan Nujomi yuhtada beha fi zulumatil barri wal bahri. Fa iza antamasati anujomi aw shaka an tadillal huda."

Narrated by Anas Bin Malik (ra) that the Messenger of Allah (pbuh) said: "The religious scholars on Earth are like the stars in the sky, they guide people through the darkness of the land and sea. When those stars fade, the guidance will be lost." [Based on Imam Ahmad]

الْمَرْءُ مَعَ مَنْ أَحَبَّ

Qala Rasulullah ﷺ: "Almar o, ma'a man ahab."

Prophet Muhammad (pbuh) said: "One is with those whom he loves."

It means that the accompanying, as *Sahabi* (companions) were given the ranks which cannot be compared, but just for the sake of understanding, they were granted that rank by following Prophet ﷺ.

Ahbab and the lovers of Sayyidina Muhammad ﷺ are given a rank of guidance by their love. Because of their love, because of how they followed, because Allah ﷻ dressed them from sincerity – they become *Ahbab*, lovers.

And Prophet's ﷺ words are true that you will be with whom you love. If you are loving Prophet ﷺ, those lovers are in a continuous association with Sayyidina Muhammad ﷺ. That's their proof, that's who they are. That's their *ijaza*, that's their permission. When someone talks about permission, they are in the continuous presence of Prophet ﷺ. They don't move, they don't do anything without the permission  because they're in that reality of love. As a result, Prophet ﷺ dresses them. As a similar understanding that anyone of my *ahbab* you follow, you'll be guided.

﴿يَا أَيُّهَا الَّذِينَ آمَنُوا اتَّقُوا اللَّهَ وَكُونُوا مَعَ الصَّادِقِينَ ١١٩﴾

9:119 – "Ya ayyuhal ladheena amanoo ittaqollaha wa kono ma'as sadiqeen." (Surat At-Tawbah)

"O you who have believed, have consciousness of Allah and be with those who are truthful/ Pious / sincere (in words and deed)."
(The Repentance, 9:119)

The Star of David ﷺ, Solomon ﷺ and Prophet Muhammad ﷺ

Now the reality of guidance is a *najm*, is a star. So, this reality of the star is what Allah ﷻ gave to us. So that in this *insan* (human being), there are two triangles. There's a triangle pointing up that takes from the forehead to the right chest and to the left chest. So, you make a triangle moving from your forehead to the right chest and over, this is your upward. So, three 60-degree angles, this is the Star of David ﷺ, star of Sulayman (Solomon) ﷺ; it's all the star of Sayyidina Muhammad ﷺ.

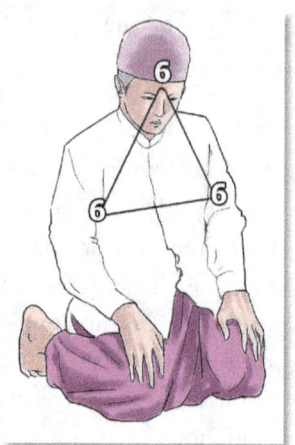

The Lower Triangle – '666' is a Sign of Dajjal

So, three points up. There's also a triangle with three points down from the same point of the chest, the two points of the chest, and it moves to the genitals. There's a triangle pointing down, 60-degree angles, 60 degrees, 60 degrees, 60 degrees. '666' because we don't have a zero (in Arabic), the 6 with the dot (٦ ٠). And 6-6-6 up.

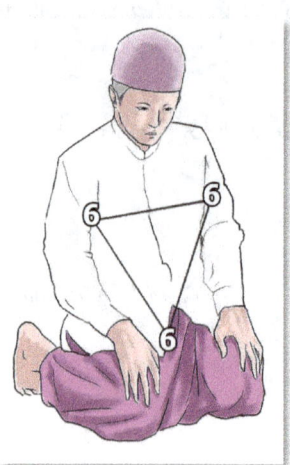

Why these people understand '666' and they say this is the *Dajjal* (anti-Messiah)? A sign from *Dajjal*? It's because the downward triangle is their body. The upward triangle is their soul. If the body and the soul are not locked in the harmony and in the guidance that Allah ﷻ had intended.

Sayyidina YaSeen ﷺ Perfects the Star and Turns Us Into 36

"Wa laqad karamna bani Adam." (We have honoured this creation of Adam and Eve).

وَلَقَدْ كَرَّمْنَا بَنِي آدَمَ...﴿٧٠﴾

17:70 – "Wa laqad karramna bani adama..." (Surat Al-Isra)

"And We have certainly honored the children of Adam..."
(The Night Journey, 17:70)

If it does not reach its perfection, which would be six 6s = 36, which is YaSeen (36th chapter of Holy Qur'an). This is the month of Surat YaSeen, this is the reality. Why? Because the star is an inheritance from Prophet ﷺ. When Prophet ﷺ describes you'll be with whom you love, he says, 'I'm going to turn you into a 36. I'm going to perfect your 6 points up; '666', and I'm going to perfect your six points down.' Your three sixes down, three sixes up become six 6s; 36. Right!

If Star is Not Perfected, '666' Becomes Reality of Dajjal

If you're not perfected up which is now 99.9% of *dunya* (material world), they only have the '666' of the lower desires. And that's why they say the *Dajjal* and the anti-Messiah is bringing people towards that reality. Because the majority of people are operating from their *dunya* (material world) desires. So '666'; it's a sixty degree.

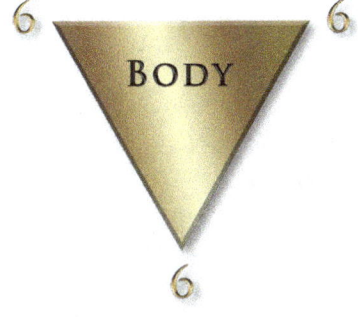

3 Points of Upper Star – Islam, Iman, Ihsan – Opening Your Vision

It's a triangle with 60-degree angles – three of them. 6-6-6 down, 6-6-6 up. If in perfection, it's 36. If it's not in perfection, it's just the lower desires.

Soul's Perfection is in Islam, Iman, Ihsan

So, this means that in this way of reality, the right, the bottom base of the upward reality of the soul: *Islam, Iman, wal Maqam-ul-Ihsan*. The soul's perfection is in the right – Islam. So, your right chest (because you're looking at me it's the reverse) your right chest is Islam; left – into your heart is *iman*. So, remember, *iman* is in the heart. *Maqam ul-Ihsan* (Station of Moral Excellence) is on your forehead or they call it the third eye.

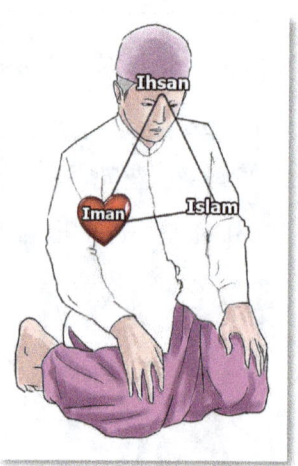

This is an eye of intuition. It means the *Ahlul Basirah* (people of spiritual vision), they see, not from like an eye being up here on their forehead, but the power of their heart makes them to see from their reality, which they see from *Maqam ul-Ihsan* (Station of Moral Excellence). That's why *Maqam ul-Ihsan* is that to know Allah ﷻ Sees you. Because this is now in reference to the *ayn* and the vision of spirituality.

"An Ta'bud Allaha, Ka annaka tarahu, fa in lam takun tarahu fa innahu yarak."

"It (Ihsan – Station of Excellence) is to serve Allah as though you behold [See] Him; and if you don't behold [See] him, (know that) He surely sees you." (Prophet Muhammad (pbuh))

Perfect the Soul Through Islam (Submission)

It means that the upward reality of the soul that Prophet ﷺ is bringing, that if you want to perfect your soul, the soul's reality is based on *Islam*. How good, how clean, how perfected your *taslim* (submission) is. Because let's bring everything back into the English, we are not here to make people Arabs. The Islam, where people are submitting, but they don't know what Islam is. They're submitting themselves to the will of God. And that's what Prophet ﷺ wants. That's what Allah (AJ) wants. Allah (AJ) created all religions, created all His creation, created all that creation with love. What He wants is He wants; 'My will to come, My kingdom to come, My will must be done'.

"Your kingdom come, your will be done, on earth as it is in heaven... And lead us not into temptation but deliver us from evil."
(The Lord's Prayer)

That, Islam is to *taslim*, to submit, 'I submit my will to the will of my creator. At least, I'll take a path in which I attempt to submit my will to the will of my creator.' That becomes the base and the foundation of that soul reality. This is now to unlock the power of your soul.

Perfected Shaykhs Are Stars in the Darkness of an Ignorant World

These are only by the perfected Shaykhs (spiritual guides) in which Allah (AJ) made them to be stars. If you're not a star, how can you explain a star? Prophet ﷺ is teaching that, 'They are my stars on this darkness of *jahal*, of ignorance of *dunya*. They're meant to be guides to bring you back to that reality.'

So, the Islam that they teach you, not the one that you pick up from other books and other places and mix 50 different teachers and most of them aggressive, most of them angry. We were talking  today that if you read a book and you give a lecture and you read *hadith* (Prophetic ﷺ tradition) and you give a lecture, you give a lecture, you give a lecture, people may be astonished at the *hadith* of Prophet ﷺ. But between you and me, it doesn't mean that you read it a thousand times and it changed you. Islam is an action. That I've to make myself to submit, I have to be broken down, I have to efface myself. I can read all I want. But many people are astonished that these scholars go out and read knowledges to people, but their character is very bad. Because what they read and what they did, didn't affect them. This is not the way of reality and they don't become stars.

Awliya Guide Through Testing to Discipline You

Those who accompany guides, the process of their guidance is to grind, to grind, to grind. So that at every moment they're grinding you down, so that it's not your will, not your mind, not what you want to do but what Allah ﷻ wants to do. They inspire you that listen to your heart, listen to your heart. Don't talk too much, listen more! Put difficulty against yourself! Do things that are difficult against yourself! Instead of treating yourself, treat the mosque. Treat your faith. Treat all these different responsibilities that you have! So continuous bombardment against the self and what happens? Their Islam becomes real.

True Iman (Faith) Comes from Your Love of Sayyidina Muhammad ﷺ

Then the Shaykh begins to teach bring faith into your heart – the soul's reality. And then they ask, 'What's the faith? What's real faith?' The love of Sayyidina Muhammad ﷺ is your *iman*. That, love Prophet ﷺ more than you love yourself, is then now the work of the heart.

لاَ يُؤْمِنُ أَحَدُكُمْ حَتَّى أَكُونَ أَحَبَّ إِلَيْهِ مِنْ وَالِدِهِ وَوَلَدِهِ وَالنَّاسِ أَجْمَعِينَ

"La yuminu ahadukum hatta akona ahabba ilayhi min walidihi wa waladihi wan Nasi ajma'yeen."

"None of you will have faith till he loves me more than his father, his children and all mankind." (Prophet Muhammad (pbuh))

Build Your Own Realities Through Silence and Submission

Then, their real submission is working. Not that they read to somebody's something, somebody else's realities and then you begin to believe it's yours. No! You've to make in life your own realities. So, you can build somebody else's dream or you make your own dream. It means that is somebody else's realities, you've to build your own through your own submission, through your own effacing.

If that process is truly crushing and you're secluding yourself, secluding yourself and the first way of *tariqah* (spiritual path) was *samt*, was silence. You're not allowed to speak for seven years in your training. If Sayyidina Abu Bakr as-Siddiq ؓ had a rock in his mouth, and this is the great *Siddiq-al-Mutlaq*, then the seven thousand years of rock

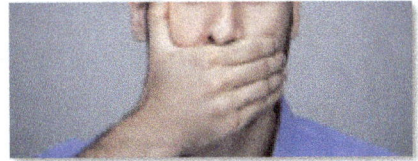

won't be enough for us. There's no permission to talk. You stay silent, stay silent so that you're grinding, grinding, and crushing so that nothing false comes from your mouth.

Real Shaykhs Hide Themselves Until They Have Permission to Speak

So how many years they were hidden? You never saw them. They were always with their Shaykh. You never even saw them in a picture; they weren't standing next to the Shaykh in every picture opportunity. They were hidden. They say, 'Where were you in the conference (in LA)?' They were hidden. 'Where were you when they were talking?' They were hidden. They were mainly in seclusion and isolating themselves.

When *ijaza* and permission came to speak, then you saw their face everywhere. Because it's a dark night and Prophet ﷺ says, 'You're one of my stars. Go out.' If they're not a star, you don't see them. You don't see. If it's not a star, you don't see. It just stays mixed into the darkness of the background. So, they perfected their Islam to be nothing.

Give What You Have For the Love of Sayyidina Muhammad ﷺ, He is Watching

Then as a result their Shaykhs taught them love Prophet ﷺ more than you love yourself! Do everything for that love and for the attention of Prophet ﷺ! Then they say, I'm going to get on a plane. For who? For love of Prophet ﷺ. I'm going to give what I don't even have, for the love of Prophet ﷺ. I'm going to go for the *Mawlid* for the love of Prophet ﷺ. I'm going to go even I don't have anything. I'm going to go buy myself a beautiful suit for the love of Prophet ﷺ. You don't think Prophet ﷺ is watching? This is very sweet.

Not the one who has everything and brings like one baklava. A person may have hundreds of thousands and brings one baklava. Everybody, according to what they have, Prophet ﷺ is watching. There are people who have virtually not that much, but they do everything and it's sincere. It's not the amount that matters. It's relative to who you are, what you have, what you are doing for Prophet ﷺ. If you have all the time in the world and you give all your time to Prophet ﷺ, it's amazing! He is watching, he is loving, he is astonished by this love. In this crazy *dunya* (worldly life), you're doing all this stuff. Now this is the *nazar* (gaze) of Prophet ﷺ.

If you have everything and you give to everyone everything, when it comes to your *deen*, you throw a few pennies and say be happy with these pennies. Prophet ﷺ says, 'Okay! We'll show you what to be happy with.' Everything is relative. So, when you want the attention, they give all their love. That's why it meant to love Prophet ﷺ more than you love yourself.

لَا يُؤْمِنُ أَحَدُكُمْ حَتَّى أَكُونَ أَحَبَّ إِلَيْهِ مِنْ وَالِدِهِ وَوَلَدِهِ وَالنَّاسِ أَجْمَعِينَ

"La yuminu ahadukum hatta akona ahabba ilayhi min walidihi wa waladihi wan Nasi ajma'yeen."

"None of you will have faith till he loves me more than his father, his children and all mankind." (Prophet Muhammad (pbuh))

Take Every Difficulty For the Love of Sayyidina Muhammad ﷺ

All your hard choices are based on that love. When they say move into an area, you move! When they say go to that place, you go to that place! When they say do that *zikr* (remembrance), you do that *zikr*! Everything you're doing is for the love. Just gaze at me, look at me, with your eye of happiness, and I'll be happy. Even if the whole world throws me into fire, but you're happy. Your *rida*  (satisfaction) with me, I'm happy. And they say in the fields of *Karbala*, all people saw was the fire of the enemy and what Imam Hussain ؑ saw, was the open arms of Prophet ﷺ. 'Just run to me. Ignore all these sufferings and sadness, just run to me!' This is the *Sayyidu Shuhada* – the masters of those who see, they teach us.

And that we're weak. We don't want, you know, the horrific difficulty. But through every hardship, let me see the sweetness of Your Holy face, and I'll walk on glass and thorns to reach to You. Prophet ﷺ says, 'If you do that, then you're sincere. Of course, you're my *Ahbab*. You love  me and I love you.' And *Sahabi* (Companions) ؑ were jealous of that title. They said, 'I thought we were the lovers!' He said, 'No, you are my *Sahabi*. You are with me. Of course, you're going to love me.' Because how much the fragrance and beauty of Prophet ﷺ they've seen. But these people have never seen me. They'll give everything for one glimpse of me.

عَنْ أَنَسِ بْنِ مَالِكٍ، قَالَ: قَالَ رَسُولُ اللهِ صَلَّى اللهُ عَلَيْهِ وَسَلَّمَ: ((مَتَى أَلْقَى أَحْبَابِي ؟ فَقَالَ أَصْحَابُهُ: بِأَبِينَا أَنْتَ وَأُمَّنَا، أَوْ لَسْنَا أَحْبَابَكَ ؟ فَقَالَ: أَنْتُمْ أَصْحَابِي، أَحْبَابِي: قَوْمٌ لَمْ يَرَوْنِي، وَآمَنُوا بِي، وَأَنَا إِلَيْهِمْ بِالْأَشْوَاقِ أَكْثَرُ)).
(مُسْنَدُ الْفِرْدَوْسِ- ٤ / ١٤٨)

'An Ansi bin Malik Qala, Qala Rasulullahi (saws):
"Mata alqa ahbabiyu?
Faqala Ashabuhu: bi abina anta wa amnan, aw lasna ahbabuk?
Faqala: Antum Ashabiyun, ahbabiyun: qawmun lam yarweni, wa aamano bi, wa ana ilayhim bil ashwaqi aksara."

Based on Anas Ibn Malik, the messenger of Allah said:
"When would I meet my beloveds?
The companions said: O' by our fathers and mothers, aren't we your beloveds?
The Prophet (pbuh) said: you are my companions. My beloveds are those who had never seen me, and believed in me, and I have a deep longings for them". [Narrated in Musnad Alferdaus (4/148)]

Seek the Holy Nazar (Gaze) of Sayyidina Muhammad ﷺ

And they spent their nights crying that am I worse than Abu Lahab?

That Abu Lahab saw you and bothered you and I haven't done anything bad. Let me see you! Don't make me to feel that I'm worse than Abu Lahab. They cry. They have a dialogue with Prophet ﷺ, 'Please! Abu Lahab saw you. I can't be that bad that I can't see you. Grant me a vision of you! Grant me to gaze at you! Even I'm not worthy of seeing your face!'

عَنْ أَبِي هُرَيْرَةَ رَضِيَ اللهُ عَنْهُ أَنَّ رَسُولَ اللهِ صَلَّى اللهُ عَلَيْهِ وَسَلَّمَ قَالَ:" مِنْ أَشَدِّ أُمَّتِي لِي حُبًّا، نَاسٌ يَكُونُونَ بَعْدِيّ، يَوَدُّ أَحَدُهُمْ لَوْ رَآنِي بِأَهْلِهِ وَمَالِهِ" [رَوَاهُ مُسْلِمْ]

3 Points of Upper Star – Islam, Iman, Ihsan – Opening Your Vision

'An Abi Hurayra (ra), 'Anhu 'anna Rasulallahu ﷺ qala: "Min ashaddi ummati li hubba, nasun yakunona bi'iddiyi yawdi ahadihim law raani bi ahlihi wa malihi." [Rawahu Muslim]

Based on Abu Hurira (ra), the messenger of Allah (pbuh) said: "The most loving of my nation are those who comes after me, and wish if they could sacrifice their money and family for a glimpse/gaze of me." [Narrated by Imam Muslim]

But they asked that everyday let me just see your feet. And visualize the Sandal, the beautiful Sandal and the foot of Prophet ﷺ. And just say let me just to keep my lips on your feet, my head on your feet and I'll be safe. I'll be safe with your love. And your love to dress me and bless me and take away all my difficulties. Until the day that Prophet ﷺ says, 'Gaze at me!' Not asking to gaze at Prophet ﷺ because I don't find myself worthy of that.  But say, '*Ya Rabbi*, let me to see His beloved feet!' Everybody can imagine a foot. You imagine a beautiful sandal, a beautiful fragrant foot and that, '*Ya Rabbi*, just my lips to His Feet, my head to His Feet!' This is an *ihtiram* and a respect. Let me to be fragranced from this station! Then Allah ﷻ, *inshaAllah*, opens the stations of *iman* (faith). Their Islam becomes real, their struggle against themselves become real. They're hidden, hidden, hidden.

All Beauty of This World is to Honour Prophet Muhammad ﷺ

Their *iman* (faith) begins to grow. They begin to love Prophet ﷺ and see that love in everything, everything beatific. Like the *naat* (praising) that we've been reading, the flowers are not here beautiful for me and you.

تیرے لیے ہی، دنیا بنی ہے
نیلے فلک کی، چادر تنی ہے
تو اگر نہ ہوتا   دنیا تھی خالی
سارے نبی تیرے در کے سوالی

Terey liyea hee, Dunya bani hay
Neelay falak ki, Chadar tani hay
Tu agar na hota   Dunya thi khali
Saare nabi tere dar ke sawali

The universe is created for you, the blue sheet of the sky is spread out for you. If you were not in existence, the world would have been empty, All prophets are at your door seeking help

Although sometimes our ego thinks, 'You're so vain. You probably think this song is about you, don't you?' [Laughing]. Vanity! You think  that everything is beautiful because I'm walking in it. No! Allah says, 'No! My beloved Sayyidina Muhammad, he was walking in it! I made all these beautiful flowers for his honour. I made the sun to shine warm for his honour. I made every fragrance to come for his honour.' Then they say this is the station of *iman* and love.

ہے نور تیرا شمس و قمر میں
تیرے لبوں کی لا لی سحر میں
پھولوں نے تیری   خوشبو چرا لی
سارے نبی تیرے در کے سوالی

Hay Noor tera shams o qamar may
Tere labo ki, Laali sahar may
Poolo ne Teri   Khushbu chura li
Saare Nabi tere dar ke sawali

3 Points of Upper Star – Islam, Iman, Ihsan – Opening Your Vision

Your light is in the Sun and the Moon, The dawn has the redness of your holy lips, All flowers have stolen your fragrance, All prophets are at your door seeking help

When Islam and Iman Are Real, then Maqam ul-Ihsan (Station of Moral Excellence) Opens

With the *Islam* (submission) and *iman* (faith) is real then the light of *ihsan*, *Maqam ul-Ihsan* (station of Moral Excellence) is opening into that  servant. When that light, when these efforts are being made and being made and they spend their time in seclusion. They are secluding themselves in their rooms, and sitting on their chairs and on their couches, on their *sijadah* (prayer carpet), in their *sujoods* (prostrations) and putting a candle in their room in darkness. They say this is my grave, I'm not leaving, I'm not leaving, I'm not leaving, and Allah begins to open their heart and they see their lord. They see the lordship of what Allah wants them to see. Because *Maqam ul-Ihsan* (Station of Moral Excellence) is the *maqam* of *Ahlul Basirah* (people of spiritual vision). Their heart begins to open; their reality begins to open. So, this is a brief reality of the upward triangle.

Subhana rabbika rabbal 'izzati 'amma yasifoon, wa salaamun 'alal mursaleen, walhamdulillahi rabbil 'aalameen. Bi hurmati Muhammad al-Mustafa wa bi siri Surat al-Fatiha.

3 Points of Lower Star
666 Dajjal – Material Desires

Ignorance is Opposite to Islam (Submission)

The lower triangle is ignorance, anger, and fire. So, the opposite of Islam is going to be ignorance. Islam is enlightenment and knowledge; knowledge of the soul, knowledge of the realities. The opposite of Islam on the right chest, right below that point is ignorance. So, your right down, right there if not in Islam, you're in ignorance. Islam being submission; whatever the world religion, doesn't matter. If you are submitting your will to the Will of God, seeking out the knowledges of God, seeking out the knowledges of the soul, then you're leaving ignorance.

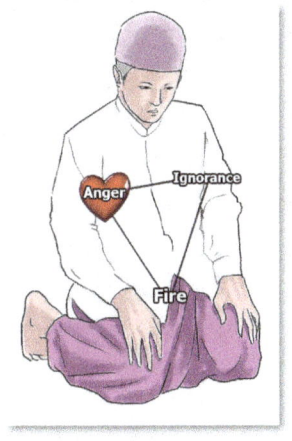

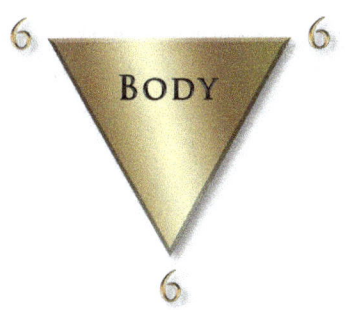

But the devil comes to fool people and says don't worry about the soul – live in a '666' environment! In the lower triangle. Don't think about the soul. Live only for your body! Then that person is what? They're living a life of ignorance, so then their *lataif* (subtle energy points) of the ignorance is opening very powerful, very powerful. It becomes so powerful, it takes away any idea of even submitting.

Anger is Opposite to Iman (Faith)

If the ignorance is building, then the point below the left side of the

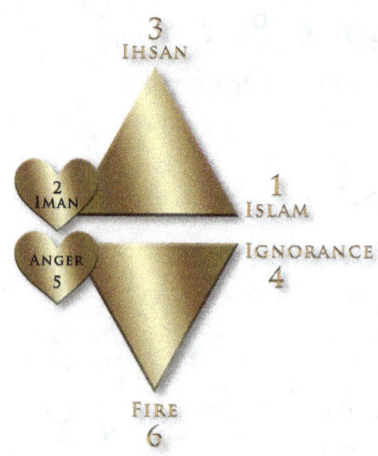

heart where faith should have been growing from the soul, it becomes anger. So opposite, you put in Islam, opposite of Islam is ignorance. For *iman* (faith) your left point of your chest where your heart and the house of Allah ﷻ, there should be *iman* (faith). And inside the house of Allah ﷻ should be only the love of Prophet ﷺ. Because *iman* is to love Prophet ﷺ more than you love yourself.

لاَ يُؤْمِنُ أَحَدُكُمْ حَتَّى أَكُونَ أَحَبَّ إِلَيْهِ مِنْ وَالِدِهِ وَوَلَدِهِ وَالنَّاسِ أَجْمَعِينَ

"*La yuminu ahadukum hatta akona ahabba ilayhi min walidihi wa waladihi wan Nasi ajma'yeen.*"

"None of you will have faith till he loves me more than his father, his children and all mankind." (Prophet Muhammad (pbuh))

Only Love of Prophet ﷺ Should Be in the Heart, in Baytullah

Your self shouldn't be in the heart. Allah ﷻ is even teaching, 'In the house, I don't want you in my house'. Because *"qalabil momin baytullah"*.

قَلْبَ الْمُؤْمِنْ بَيْتُ الرَّبْ

"Qalb al mu'min baytur rabb."

"The heart of the believer is the House of the Lord." (Hadith Qudsi)

Prophet ﷺ is teaching, 'In *baytullah* (house of Allah ﷻ), you shouldn't have yourself in there. Your love should only be for me.' Because Allah ﷻ doesn't want to see me and you in the heart; what I want and my desires. Allah ﷻ wants to see the love of Prophet ﷺ in the heart. If that *Maqamul Iman* (Station of Faith) is not there, what happens with ignorance? Ignorance builds anger.

Anger Dims the Light of Iman (Faith) and Increases Disbelief

Anger is *kufr* (disbelief). Anger is the opposite of faith. So then on your heart at the *lataif* (subtle energy points) of the heart, when there is *iman* (faith), is the top; should be powerful. If there is no *iman* (faith) and the

iman is not growing, it's *ghadab* and anger. So now you begin to understand the reality of the self. If I'm overwhelmed with anger, I actually have no *iman* (faith). Because every time the anger comes, it flushes out the light of faith. That's why Prophet ﷺ described, 'I cannot sit with anger.'

The Holy Messenger (pbuh) has said: "Anger is a smouldering ember (God of war) that is kindled by Satan." (Biharul Anwar: Volume 73, Page 265)

As soon as anger comes to the servant, they enter into disbelief. That, right there is then a tremendous reality. My life is about, 'Is my anger overtaking or is my faith coming?' This is a great yin and yang moment in our lives that I'm trying to build faith. I have beautiful actions. I have good intentions. I'm trying to bring this light and this light and this light. But in a moment of rage, the anger actually then overtakes the faith and burns everything. And that's why it's such an essential part.

Take Away Anger With Wudu and Washing

That's why then Prophet ﷺ gave many, many different realities on how to take out the anger. One is *wudu*, one is the washing.

عَنْ عَطِيَّةُ بْنِ عُرْوَةَ السَّعْدِيْ رَضِيَ اللهُ, عَنَ النَّبِيُّ صَلَّى اللهُ عَلَيْهِ وَسَلَّمَ قَالَ:

إِنَّ الْغَضَبَ مِنَ الشَّيْطَانِ وَإِنَّ الشَّيْطَانَ خُلِقَ مِنَ النَّارِ وَإِنَّمَا تُطْفَأُ النَّارُ بِالْمَاءِ فَإِذَا غَضِبَ أَحَدُكُمْ فَلْيَتَوَضَّأْ.

[روى الإمام أحمد في "المسند" (505/29) وأبو داود (4784)

'An 'Atiyat bin 'Urwatul Sa'di (ra) 'Anan Nabi (saws) Qal:

"'Annal ghadaba minash shaitani wa innash shaitana khuliqa minan Naar, wa innama tutfa annaaru bil Maayi fa iza ghadeba ahadakum falyatawadda." [Rawayil Imam Ahmad fil Musanad wa Abu Dawud]

Atiyah Bin Orwah Alsaadi (ra) said, that the messenger of Allah (pbuh) said: "Anger is from Satan, and Satan was created from fire, *and in which fire is extinguished by water,. So if one of you got angry he should make Wudu (ablution)." [Narrated by Imam Ahmad in his Musnad (29/505, and Imam Abu Dawood (4784)]*

Have an External Reminder to Fight an Internal Sickness

One is the outside action, outside marking of yourself for an internal sickness. If you are serious about fighting a difficulty, then take something as a reminder. Wrap a bow around your hand; a yellow bow, any color bow. Put something on your hand a rubber band, anything and say, 'Ya Rabbi, that I'm going to work on my *ghadab*, my anger.' You have to have an external reminder because *shaytan* (satan) makes you to forget every moment about what you're working on. Say, '*Ya Rabbi*, I want all my good actions and my *iman* (faith) to blossom. But this fire of anger comes and burns this beautiful garden in just but a moment.'

As soon as they put an outside reminder, and for 40 days, they are going to work on not having anger. As soon as they feel anger is coming, they see the reminder. They see, 'Oh my God, I'm working on this. I'm going to go wash.' As soon as they put water onto fire then the *"qulna ya naaru kuni bardan wa salaman"* (Say O to the fire to be cool and peaceful). As soon as they wash, they are training themselves.

قُلْنَا يَا نَارُ كُونِي بَرْدًا وَسَلَامًا عَلَى إِبْرَاهِيمَ ﴿٦٩﴾

21:69 – "Qulna ya Naaru, kuni Bardan wa Salaman 'ala Ibrahim." (Surat Al-Anbiya)

"We said, O fire, be cool and Peaceful upon Abraham."
(The Prophets, 21:69)

If they can't control their mouth, put a lollipop – modern day version of a rock. Because we don't want the liability of somebody saying they choked on a rock, but a nice big tootsie pop with a stick on it and keep it in your mouth. Literally, keep them all the time. If you have a mouth that you can't control, undo the wrapper and put the lollipop into your mouth and you don't talk. For 40 days say, '*Ya Rabbi*, I'm going to try my best to bring down my anger. I'm not going to respond. I'm not going to get angry.'

The Devil Deceives the World to Operate From Lower Desires of '666'

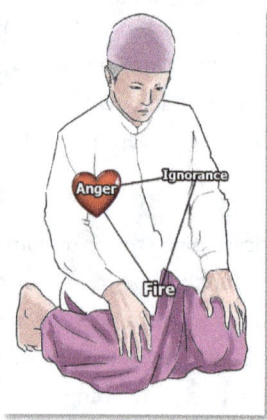

If this fire of anger, for the downward triangle understanding, they live a life of no knowledge, ignorant of the realities of the soul. Then the fire of their ignorance begins to overtake them. As a result of this anger and lack of knowledge, they entered into a darkness in which the fire and rage is in their genital area. The lower desire begins to overtake them and everything about their lower desire is of a fiery nature. So, ignorance and anger make fire.

Then the whole of this dunya (material world) now is operating, and these are the concepts of '666'. If you want to know where is '666', where is '666'. Everyone on earth now is based on that '666', based on that *Dajjal*, the man of deception, the people of deception. And all his deception is about keeping people ignorant; make them to be stupid, make

them to be dumbed down, make them to have no understanding of anything significant and no basis of any knowledge that glorifies Allah ﷻ.

Make the Intention of Studying to Glorify Allah ﷻ, Not Shaytan

Anyone who studies a science and goes through modern university; if what you study its intention is not to glorify Allah ﷻ, it is then glorifying Satan. It's a very simple line. If I study advanced physics, mathematics and sciences with the intention to glorify my lord and when I study I say, '*SubhanAllah! Ya Rabbi*, how you made all this amazing creation!' That knowledge is based on the glorification of Allah ﷻ. If I study it to disprove Allah ﷻ and to think that we came from a baboon, you're in the school of *shaytan* (satan) and *shaytan* is taking away all light and has knowledge that's not based on anything from the heavens.

Immense Ignorance is Entering the World

So, then ignorance and anger make fire. As a result of that, these people are raging. As a result of their raging, they're angry and all they want to do is increase ignorance, increase their anger, and increase the fire upon earth until they burn each other everywhere. So now

what has entered into this earth and is increasing day by day, day by day is of that. Immense ignorance is entering. Immense angers are proliferating everywhere. And then as a result everything begins to burn.

Knowledge is Taken Away With the Passing of Awliya (Saints)

That's why in these days you are seeing so many of *awliyaullah* (saints) being taken. When Allah ﷻ lifts, and Prophet ﷺ described, 'In last days they would take away knowledge from the earth.' And companions were scared that would Qur'an be taken? He said, 'No! But the knowledges will be taken.'

عَنْ عَبْدِ اللَّهِ بْنِ عَمْرِو بْنِ الْعَاصِ، قَالَ سَمِعْتُ رَسُولَ اللَّهِ صَلَّى اللَّهُ عَلَيْهِ وَسَلَّمَ يَقُولُ:

" إِنَّ اللَّهَ لاَ يَقْبِضُ الْعِلْمَ انْتِزَاعًا، يَنْتَزِعُهُ مِنَ الْعِبَادِ، وَلَكِنْ يَقْبِضُ الْعِلْمَ بِقَبْضِ الْعُلَمَاءِ، حَتَّى إِذَا لَمْ يُبْقِ عَالِمًا، اتَّخَذَ النَّاسُ رُءُوسًا جُهَّالاً فَسُئِلُوا، فَأَفْتَوْا بِغَيْرِ عِلْمٍ، فَضَلُّوا وَأَضَلُّوا.

'An Abdullah bin Umari wa binil 'aas, qala sami'tu Rasulallah (saws) yaqolo:

"InnAllaha la yaqbedul 'ilman tiza'an, yantazi'uhu minal 'ibadi, wa lakin yaqbedul 'ilma bi qabdil 'ulamaye, hatta izha lam yabqi 'aliman. Attaghazan nasu ru osan juhhalan fasuyilo, fa aftaw bighairi 'ilmin, fadallo wa adallo.

Amr bin Al-As narrated: I heard Allah's Messenger (pbuh) saying, "Allah does not take away the knowledge, by taking it away from (the hearts of) the people, but takes it away by the death of the religious Scholars till when none of the religious scholar remains, people will take as their leaders ignorant persons who when consulted will give their verdict without knowledge. So they will go astray and will lead the people astray." [Bukhari, Vol. 1, Book 3, Hadith 100]

Love Holds Everything Together – If True Lovers Are Taken Away, the World Will Collapse

Knowledges, because the true stars, the people of *ahbab* and love; their love produces immense oceans of reality. If Allah (swt) takes the lovers away from the earth, what remains is hatred. And everything of this earth from what you cannot see, every building, every molecule, everything around us, its glue is held by love and *muhabbat*.

If Allah (swt) pulls the love, everything begins to turn to dust. The love is pulled and when the love pulls, everything begins to collapse and becomes dust. It means everything begins to burn, begins to collapse. Everything begins to be destroyed. The love is being pulled. The true lovers are all leaving.

Be Present With the Shaykh to Receive His Blessings

That's why we posted that Imam 'Ali (as) said, 'Ask me while I'm here.' There's not a day that's going to be forever.

قَالَ أَمِيرُ الْمُؤْمِنِينَ إِمَامْ عَلِيْ بْنْ أَبِىْ طَالِبْ (عَلَيْهِ السَّلَامَ): (أَيُّهَا النَّاسَ، سَلُونِي قَبْلَ أَنْ تَفْقِدُونَي)

Qala amirul mumineen, Imam 'Ali bin Abi Talib (as):
"Ayyu hannas, salloni qabla an tafqidoni."

The leader of the believers, Imam 'Ali said:
"O people, ask me before you lose me."

When there's a Shaykh, you have to be there present with them. They are there to dress you, to bless you with whatever Allah (swt) put upon their heart to be conveyed to you. *Fitna* (confusion) and incorrect understanding is only the party of *shaytan* that want the people to be in ignorance. Prophet ﷺ would never want that. What Prophet ﷺ wants is the dissemination of *Islam* (submission), *iman* (faith) and *Maqam ul-Ihsan* (Station of Moral Excellence).

$$\text{يَا أَيُّهَا الَّذِينَ آمَنُوا اتَّقُوا اللَّهَ وَكُونُوا مَعَ الصَّادِقِينَ ﴿١١٩﴾}$$

9:119 – *"Ya ayyuhal ladheena amanoo ittaqollaha wa kono ma'as sadiqeen." (Surat At-Tawbah)*

"O you who have believed, have consciousness of Allah and be with those who are truthful/ Pious / sincere (in words and deed)." (The Repentance, 9:119)

Everything You Watch Propagates Anger

Shaytan (Satan) wants no dissemination of knowledge. That's why when you understand the people of '666', (the lower triangle) they don't want knowledge anywhere. They don't put it on their satellites. They don't put it on anything. They want only people to be in ignorance.

They only have the way to propagate a way of anger. Even both television shows propagate anger. Nobody is propagating love. So, they just increase anger. One who says he's for him, shows the anger, and the one against him talks in anger so all they are really doing is propagating anger, anger, anger. Then the people become fiery. They care nothing for this world, they care nothing for people. There's no value. Every television show is about how horribly they want to do to each other and to do it to humanity. Then we understand, the lower triangle based on this reality.

How Awliyaullah (Saints) Become Guiding Stars

The only thing, when Prophet ﷺ describes, 'My companions are like stars' and all these *awliyaullah* (saints), they are inheriting from the holy companions. Why they became a star? Because with that reality of the ignorance, Prophet ﷺ opened for them their true Islam.

عَنْ أَنَسِ بْنِ مَالِكٍ رَضِيَ اللَّهُ عَنْهُ ، قَال : قَالَ رَسُولُ اللَّهِ صَلَّى اللَّهُ عَلَيْهِ وَسَلَّمَ : « أَنَّ مِثْلَ الْعُلَمَاءِ فِي الْأَرْضِ كَمَثَلِ النُّجُومِ ، يُهْتَدَى بِهَا فِي ظُلُمَاتِ الْبَرِّ وَالْبَحْرِ ، فَإِذَا انْطَمَسَتِ النُّجُومُ أَوْشَكَ أَنْ تَضِلَّ الْهُدَاةُ » رَوَاهُ أَحْمَ

'An Anasin bin Malikin (ra) Qala, Qala Rasulullahi Sallallahu 'alayhi wa sallam: " Anna mithlal 'ulamayi fil ardi kamathalan Nujomi yuhtada beha fi zulumatil barri wal bahri. Fa iza antamasati anujomi aw shaka an tadillal huda.

Narrated by Anas Bin Malik (ra) that the Messenger of Allah (pbuh) said: "The religious scholars on Earth are like the stars in the sky, they guide people through the darkness of the land and sea. When those stars fade, the guidance will be lost." [Based on Imam Ahmad]

Awliya's Soul Takes Away Ignorance and Brings the Reality of Islam

That these *awliya* (saints) chose the Islam of realities. That Islam, the power of their soul comes and locks the point of ignorance (at the right side of the chest). It takes away ignorance and brings the reality of their Islam (submission). As a result, it takes out the fire of the downward triangle. The point that would have been ignorance is enlightened by the reality of their Islam. The true Islam of love, of actions, of submitting, of being trained and how to be nothing, to be humble. Not to read about humble and tell people to be humble! But to be humbled yourself, to be brought down and humiliate and humiliate yourself continuously. That brings that down and that light begins to encompass that reality.

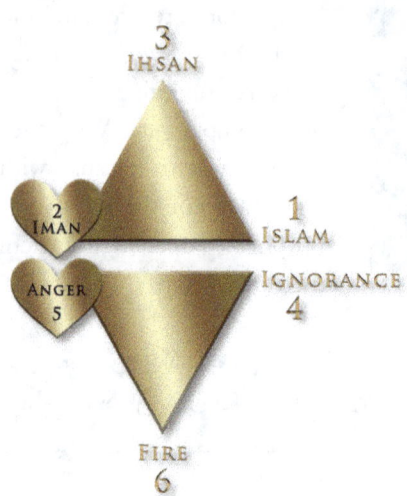

Awliya's Nur Iman (Light of Faith) Brings Down the Anger

Awliya's (saints') anger is brought down by the light of their faith. As soon as they make praising, as soon as they make *salawats* (praising upon Prophet Muhammad ﷺ), the light emanating from their heart immediately extinguishes the fire. Because it's much more powerful, their faith is so powerful. Immediately, they extinguish the anger and then the soul grabs those two points and illuminates them. That's

how the star is now transforming. Instead of having two triangles one up and one down, their triangle, their soul is actually coming out and overtaking their body; where everybody else is reverse. The inside triangle for everyone else, the upper soul triangle is of no power, so their lower body reality overtakes them and they become just a body person.

In this reality, when Allah ﷻ opens the upward reality their soul actually starts to come out and they're operating from their soul. Their soul's Islam puts and takes away ignorance and gives them knowledges. They can speak from what other people can't even understand; that's why we said the knowledges will be lifted from the earth.

عَنْ عَبْدِ اللَّهِ بْنِ عَمْرِو بْنِ الْعَاصِ، قَالَ سَمِعْتُ رَسُولَ اللَّهِ صَلَّى اللهُ عَلَيْهِ وَسَلَّمَ يَقُولُ:

" إِنَّ اللَّهَ لاَ يَقْبِضُ الْعِلْمَ انْتِزَاعًا، يَنْتَزِعُهُ مِنَ الْعِبَادِ، وَلَكِنْ يَقْبِضُ الْعِلْمَ بِقَبْضِ الْعُلَمَاءِ، حَتَّى إِذَا لَمْ يُبْقِ عَالِمًا. اتَّخَذَ النَّاسُ رُءُوسًا جُهَّالاً فَسُئِلُوا، فَأَفْتَوْا بِغَيْرِ عِلْمٍ، فَضَلُّوا وَأَضَلُّوا.

'An Abdullah bin Umari wa binil 'aas, qala sami'tu Rasulallah (saws) yaqolo:

"InnAllaha la yaqbedul 'ilman tiza'an, yantazi'uhu minal 'ibadi, wa lakin yaqbedul 'ilma bi qabdil 'ulamaye, hatta izha lam yabqi 'aliman. Attaghazan nasu ru osan juhhalan fasuyilo, fa aftaw bighairi 'ilmin, fadallo wa adallo.

Amr bin Al-As narrated: I heard Allah's Messenger (pbuh) saying, "Allah does not take away the knowledge, by taking it away from (the hearts of) the people, but takes it away by the death of the religious Scholars till when none of the religious scholar remains, people will take as their leaders ignorant persons who when consulted will give their verdict without knowledge. So they will go astray and will lead the people astray." [Bukhari, Vol. 1, Book 3, Hadith 100]

Awliya Are the Real Stars on Earth and More Powerful Than Red Giants

These *awliya* (saints) are real lovers. These are real stars on this earth.

The knowledges that are coming not only wipe away ignorance but bring all the *haqqaiqs* (realities) of the heavens. The *iman* (faith) that they have is so powerful. It takes away anger and takes away anger of anyone in their presence. Because of the level of *iman*, the light that is coming from that star, their star is bigger than the sun.

The sun is the smallest version. Their sun, their star is bigger than that reality. That's an imitated reality just to show us the reality of a *shams* (sun). Imagine that all this Earth is a speck in the presence of the sun. This Earth, with its seven billion people is like an epsilon in the presence of the sun. Their suns are a billion times larger than that sun. Even a red giant, may be hundred times bigger than that. There are *awliya* (saints) of a different category and different powers of their sun reality. That,

ten thousand earths are like a dot in their presence.

What Allah ﷻ gave to the power of soul can't even be imagined. So, their Islam, it wipes out and their *iman* (faith) wipes out every disbelief, every badness, every sin. Everything is washed and burned in their presence. Every dead comes to life with the reality of their Islam and their *iman* (faith).

Awliya Reached Maqam ul-Ihsan, They See Allah's ﷻ Light in Everything

As a result of their power of their soul, their *Maqam ul-Ihsan* (Station of Moral Excellence), in their light of perfection, it took away the fire of bad desires. This light of *Maqam ul-Ihsan* (Station of Moral Excellence), where to see Allah ﷻ and if you can't see Allah ﷻ know that Allah ﷻ sees you.

أَنْ تَعْبُدَ اللَّهَ كَأَنَّكَ تَرَاهُ، فَإِنْ لَمْ تَكُنْ تَرَاهُ فَإِنَّهُ يَرَاكَ

"An Ta'bud Allaha, Ka annaka tarahu, fa in lam takun tarahu fa innahu yarak."

"It (Ihsan – Station of Excellence) is to serve Allah as though you behold [See] Him; and if you don't behold [See] him, (know that) He surely sees you." (Prophet Muhammad (pbuh))

They have the whole of that reality. Not only they see what Allah ﷻ wants them to see, but they see Allah ﷻ in everything. They see Allah's ﷻ Lights in everything. Every love and every interaction is Allah ﷻ dealing with them. When they sit and see the flower and the fragrance of the flower, it's as if Allah's ﷻ fragrances and love is coming towards them. Because they see the Divine reality in everything.

Divinely Fire of Awliya Burns Our Sins and Gives Us Nur

So, both was a reality, one that they began to see the Divine reality because Allah opened their vision, their *ayn*. Once they began to see the reality, they went so deep into that reality that they found Allah in all of it looking at them and calling them into that love, calling them into that love. As a result, it wiped out that fire. And they're not of a fire anymore that burns and harms people, but the fire of the reality, it illuminates people. Their fire eats the sins of people and gives in exchange to them light and

nur. That's why Prophet described that my companions, my *ahbab* (lovers), because you can add *ahbab* (lovers) because they're the companions of the companions. *Wajibul taqleed* (obligatory following), they followed the way, they became the companions of the companions. Anyone of them you follow, they are like stars on a dark night.

عَنْ أَنَسِ بْنِ مَالِكٍ رَضِيَ اللهُ عَنْهُ ، قَالَ : قَالَ رَسُولُ اللهِ صَلَّى اللهُ عَلَيْهِ وَسَلَّمَ : « أَنَّ مِثْلَ الْعُلَمَاءِ فِي الْأَرْضِ كَمَثَلِ النُّجُومِ ، يُهْتَدَى بِهَا فِي ظُلُمَاتِ الْبَرِّ وَالْبَحْرِ ، فَإِذَا انْطَمَسَتِ النُّجُومُ أَوْشَكَ أَنْ تَضِلَّ الْهُدَاةُ » رَوَاهُ أَحْمَدُ

'An Anasin bin Malikin (ra) Qala, Qala Rasulullahi Sallallahu 'alayhi wa sallam: "Anna mithlal 'ulamayi fil ardi kamathalan Nujomi yuhtada beha fi zulumatil barri wal bahri. Fa iza antamasati anujomi aw shaka an tadillal huda.

Narrated by Anas Bin Malik (ra) that the Messenger of Allah (pbuh) said: "The religious scholars on Earth are like the stars in the sky, they guide people through the darkness of the land and sea. When those stars fade, the guidance will be lost." [Based on Imam Ahmad]

Imagine the one who can explain what the star is. The other one, they at least say they're that, but they don't have understanding of the *haqqaiq* and the reality of it. It's not something you pick and choose to be or not to be in that presence. Those are deep realities to who we are. That Allah ﷻ sent, Prophet ﷺ sent, sent us to achieve that reality.

Six Powers of the Heart Have Opened Upon Awliya

When you accompany them, all of that is going to be perfected upon you. All of the body desires are going to be destroyed upon you until your upward triangle will overtake. Come out of your physicality! That's the Surat Zalzalah; what's hidden in you Allah ﷻ will make it to come out.

إِذَا زُلْزِلَتِ الْأَرْضُ زِلْزَالَهَا ﴿١﴾ وَأَخْرَجَتِ الْأَرْضُ أَثْقَالَهَا ﴿٢﴾

99:1-2 – "Izaa zul zilatil ardu zil zaalaha. (1) Wa akh rajatil ardu athqaalaha. (2)" (Surat Az-Zalzalah)

"When the earth is shaken with her (final) earthquake. (1) And the earth discharges its burdens (from within). (2)"
(The Earthquake, 99:1-2)

The reality comes out, grabs the lower triangle, and brings it up. As a result, Allah ﷻ opens their six points. These are the six *lataifs* (subtle energy points) of the heart and the six powers of the heart are opened upon them. The seventh point is where Allah ﷻ rests upon the throne of their being. Because *qalbil momin baytullah*.

قَلْبَ الْمُؤْمِنْ بَيْتُ الرَّبْ

"*Qalb al mu'min baytur rabb.*"

"*The heart of the believer is the House of the Lord.*" (Hadith Qudsi)

At that time Allah ﷻ establishes his heart on their reality and the kingdom of Allah ﷻ is to be found within them. They are the walking kingdom of Allah ﷻ.

Subhana rabbika rabbal 'izzati 'amma yasifoon, wa salaamun 'alal mursaleen, walhamdulillahi rabbil 'aalameen. Bi hurmati Muhammad al-Mustafa wa bi siri Surat al-Fatiha.

Six Powers of the Heart and Reality of Star

To Reach Your Eternal Reality is to Be a Najm (Star)

Alhamdulillah, Allah's ﷻ guidance to Sayyidina Muhammad ﷺ and Prophet's ﷺ guidance to *ulul amr* (saints). And they come into our lives to teach us about ourselves, that who knows himself will know his Lord.

مَنْ عَرَفَ نَفْسَهُ فَقَدْ عَرَفَ رَبَّهُ

"*Man 'arafa nafsahu faqad 'arafa Rabbahu.*"

"*Who knows himself, knows his Lord.*" (Prophet Muhammad (pbuh))

We are of a certain design, and that when Allah ﷻ wants the servant to rise to a reality, that reality is to be a star, that to reach your eternal reality, to be a *najm* (star). Where Allah ﷻ and Prophet ﷺ described that, that process Prophet ﷺ completed upon his Companions, that, 'My Companions are like stars on a dark night. Any one of them that you follow, you will be guided.'

أَصْحَابِيْ كَالنُّجُومْ بِأَيِّهِمْ اَقْتَدَيْتُمْ اَهْتَدَيْتُمْ

"*Ashabi kan Nujoom, bi ayyihim aqta daytum ahta daytum.*"

"My companions are like stars. Follow any one of them and you will be guided." (Prophet Muhammad (pbuh))

If the Companions are stars, imagine what Sayyidina Muhammad ﷺ must be.

As the Planets Circumambulate Around the Sun, So Are Our Atoms Around the Nucleus

For us to look, Allah ﷻ says, 'I show you the signs upon yourself and upon the horizon.'

سَنُرِيهِمْ آيَاتِنَا فِي الْآفَاقِ وَفِي أَنفُسِهِمْ حَتَّىٰ يَتَبَيَّنَ لَهُمْ أَنَّهُ الْحَقُّ ۗ ... ﴿٥٣﴾

41:53 – "Sanureehim ayatina fil afaqi wa fee anfusihim hatta yatabayyana lahum annahu alhaqqu..." (Surat Al-Isra)

"We will show them Our signs in the horizons and within themselves until it becomes clear to them that it is the truth..."
(The Night Journey, 41:53)

Upon the self is those who want to contemplate and meditate, they try to go into themselves to understand these realities with a guide. And these *kamil* (perfected) guides, they inspire within the heart these

realities. So, what you see on the outside must be occurring on the inside. And we see that the supreme creation on the outside of this *dunya* (material world) are the stars and the suns, what we call a solar system, in which everything circumambulates the star, the sun, the light.

Even Allah ﷻ gives that example within our atoms. All your electrons circumambulate the nucleus, the nucleus is a sun. It is a source of energy, that is the power that Allah ﷻ put a power within that reality. And to reach to that understanding is of the highest of ways.

Naqshbandi Shaykhs Only Speak From Their Own Realities

Alhamdulillah, from Naqshbandi teaching that they cannot teach anything that they are not in. They cannot repeat to you something that they are not in that reality. Otherwise it would be a lie, they cannot lie. It means *ilm al-yaqeen, ayn al-yaqeen wa haqq al-yaqeen*, (Knowledge of Certainty, Vision of Certainty, and Truth of Certainty). That they are dressed from that reality and given a permission to speak  from that reality. You can't hear something that you're not from and repeat it to people. It's lying, because it's not a *haqq* (truth) at that time.

La Ilaha IllAllah in the Upper Triangle of Soul

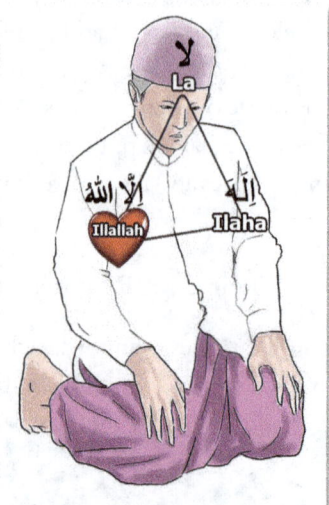

From their oceans of understanding, then we have an upper triangle and lower triangle. And our whole life is going to be based on that struggle. That you have from *la* being the reality of your soul, that the *la* that comes to your head, *ilaha* to right side of chest, *illallah* to left side of chest – the heart. So, it breaks into *La, ilaha, illallah*. And to open that reality is a power of the soul. What Allah ﷻ wants from us is to be dressed from the soul reality.

That, that *la*, when you draw upon your head means in all your *tafakkur* (contemplation), the first *zikr* (chanting) of all the *turuqs* (spiritual paths) is *La ilaha illallah* (there is no God but Allah). Why? To take you away from the worshipping of many things to the Oneness of Allah ﷻ. That is that door of reality. That what Prophet ﷺ wanted for us is that these lights and this reality, it's not going to come to your head, so that you bring the breath in, it moves to *la*, to your forehead.

The La is the Zulfiqar and Where the Two Oceans Meet

The *la* is symbolic upon the forehead that one – it has a tremendous reality because that *la* is also the *zulfiqar* (two-spiked sword). The *la* is a *zulfiqar* that has the loop and the two oceans, and these are the two oceans that Nabi Musa ﷺ wanted, 'Ya Rabbi, I won't stop until I reach where the two oceans meet.' Where they meet is the handle of realities.

وَإِذْ قَالَ مُوسَىٰ لِفَتَاهُ لَا أَبْرَحُ حَتَّىٰ أَبْلُغَ مَجْمَعَ الْبَحْرَيْنِ أَوْ أَمْضِيَ حُقُبًا ﴿٦٠﴾

18:60 – *"Wa idh qala Mosa lefatahu laa abrahu hatta ablugha majma'a albahrayni aw amdiya huquba."* (Surat Al-Kahf)

"Behold, Moses said to his attendant, I will not give up until I reach the junction of the two seas or (until) I spend years and years in travel." (The Cave, 18:60)

The *zulfiqar* was the gift of Sayyidina Muhammad ﷺ. And this is the city of all knowledges and that *zulfiqar* was given to Imam 'Ali ؑ as the one who carries the door and responsible for the door of the city of that reality.

قَالَ رَسُولَ اللَّهِ صلى الله عليه وسلم "انا مدينة العلم و علي بابها"

Qala RasulAllah ﷺ - *"Ana madinatul-ilmin wa 'Aliyun baabuha."*

"I am city of knowledge and 'Ali is the door."
(Prophet Muhammad (pbuh))

La Means Don't Use the Head for Paradise Realities

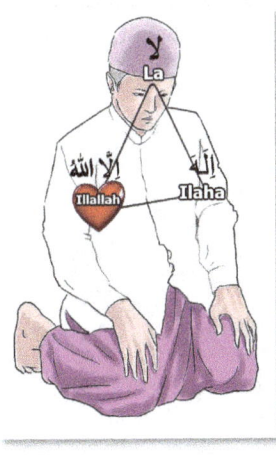

So, one when we see the *lam alif*, it is the secret of *La ilaha illallah Muhammadun RasulAllah* ﷺ (There is no deity but Allah, Prophet Muhammad (pbuh) is the messenger of Allah ﷻ) has tremendous realities. That *zulfiqar* (double-spiked sword) is a reminder for us that when the *zulfiqar* and the *lam alif* comes to your head, Prophet ﷺ taught this way of reality, don't use your head. Use your head for your business, for your *rizq*

(sustenance). But for paradise and paradise realities, don't use your head. The head will have no way of understanding.

Tawhid Means Everything is Always in Allah's ﷻ Hands

It means that our whole life is then based on this reality of *La ilaha illallah*.  And how to open the power of the soul, and that how to bring the faith and the *nur* (light) of *iman* (faith) into the heart. That, 'Ya Rabbi, there's nothing but You, Your Light into my heart.' So that to leave the fear of everything and move towards the worshipness of Allah ﷻ and to the oceans of real *tawhid* (oneness of God), where you begin to believe all your life that everything is completely in Allah's ﷻ Hands. Whether it's been written good for you, bad for you, Allah's ﷻ Hand is upon everything. When pious people truly believed and understood, it means many openings within their heart.

Muhammadun Rasul Allah ﷺ in the Lower Triangle

Now to understand the lower triangle within our body is *Muhammadun Rasul Allah* ﷺ, *Muhammadun Rasul Allah* ﷺ (Prophet Muhammad (pbuh) is the Messenger of Allah ﷻ). That Allah ﷻ, the energy of that reality is coming into the stomach to tame and to bring a discipline upon the physicality. So, *la ilaha illallah* is the power of the soul, and is the reality and the dress of the soul. What they want us to know is that you 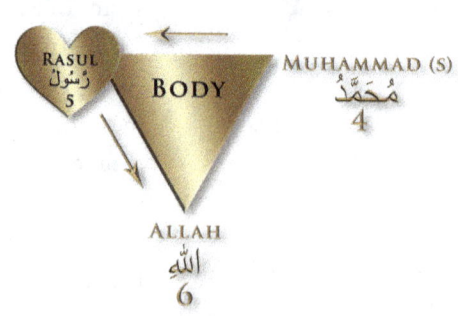 have a soul reality and you have a physical reality. Each are taking a different understanding, each have a different sustenance, that Allah ﷻ said, *"Wa ma arsalnaka rahmatan lil alamin."* (We have not sent you, [O Muhammad (pbuh)], except as a mercy to the creation).

وَمَا أَرْسَلْنَاكَ إِلَّا رَحْمَةً لِّلْعَالَمِينَ ﴿١٠٧﴾

21:107 – "Wa maa arsalnaka illa Rahmatan lil'alameen."
(Surat Al-Anbiya)

"And We have not sent you, [O Muhammad (pbuh)], except as a mercy to the worlds/creation." (The Prophets, 21:107)

All 124,000 Prophets Came to Teach to Discipline the Body

That Prophet ﷺ has been sent and that *risalat* (messingership) of Prophet ﷺ is from beginning of time is the reality of *Muhammadun RasulAllah* ﷺ. It means only one *risalat*. Every prophet is an agency within the agency of Sayyidina Muhammad ﷺ. It means that Prophet ﷺ is a creation from Allah ﷻ; the reality of *Muhammadun RasulAllah* ﷺ is to come onto this earth, that Prophet ﷺ can bring a discipline to the physicality. Therefore Allah ﷻ sent 124,000 *nabis*, prophets, and 313 *Rasuls*, messengers for all of creation. 124,000 entire prophets, and 313 of them with a message of Allah ﷻ. Why? To bring a discipline upon the physicality.

Lower Triangle of Ignorance, Anger, and Fire

It means to open the reality of the discipline of the body, it's essential to know that we are made from these two halves. That the lower triangle of our body is based on this *dunya* (material world), the lower is the fire of *dunya*. It means this *dunya* is based on ignorance, anger and fire. Ignorance on your right, right on the chest, anger that enters into the heart, and that creates the fire of the material world.

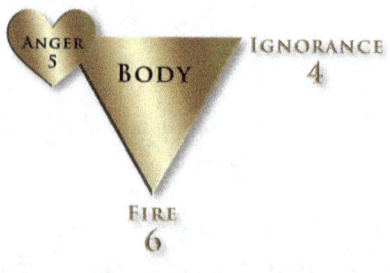

What *shaytan* (satan) and *dajjal* want is to govern *insan* (mankind) based on that understanding. As much as he can keep *insan* in ignorance, because they're *jahil* (ignorant). At the time that Prophet ﷺ came was a *jahiliya* (era of ignorance). And now on this earth is the second *jahiliya*, is a great ignorance that's moving upon the earth. So, when we understand our geometry and our physiology, we can move towards our reality. This means the lower triangle is then everything of the satanic force wants to bring the power of the lower triangle. So, to create an ignorance, a great ignorance.

Ignorance is the Door to Anger

Ignorance opens the door to anger. The anger now is on the heart. You have ignorance and then *ghadab*, anger, into the heart. That ignorance and anger makes the person very *narani*, fiery, very angry, very uncontrollable desires, very violent desires. It means everything about them is governed from the lowest level of their reality, not from the highest level of the reality that's based onto the heart.

Muhammadun RasulAllah ﷺ Comes to Destroy Ignorance and Anger

It means everything that Prophet ﷺ wanted for us is to destroy that ignorance; then who comes to destroy ignorance – Muhammadun ﷺ. Who comes to destroy the anger that's entering into the heart – the *RasulAllah* ﷺ, because you can't have the *Nur* (light) of Allah عز وجل without the light of *RasulAllah* ﷺ to bring that light, to bring that power into the heart.

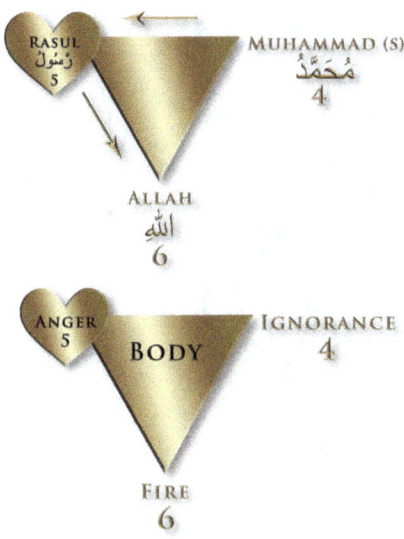

As a result of *Muhamamdun RasulAllah* ﷺ, Allah عز وجل says, 'I am with the *Nabiyeen, Siddiqeen, Shuhadahi wa Saliheen* (the Prophets, the Truthful, the Witnesses [who testify], and the Righteous ones).'

وَمَن يُطِعِ اللَّهَ وَالرَّسُولَ فَأُولَٰئِكَ مَعَ الَّذِينَ أَنْعَمَ اللَّهُ عَلَيْهِم مِّنَ النَّبِيِّينَ وَالصِّدِّيقِينَ وَالشُّهَدَاءِ وَالصَّالِحِينَ ۚ وَحَسُنَ أُولَٰئِكَ رَفِيقًا ﴿٦٩﴾

4:69 – *"Wa man yuti' Allaha war Rasula faolayeka ma'al ladheena an'ama Allahu 'alayhim minan Nabiyeena, was Siddiqeena, wash Shuhadai, was Saliheena wa hasuna olayeka rafeeqan."*
(Surat An-Nisa)

"And whoever obeys Allah and the Messenger (pbuh) are in the company of those on whom Allah has bestowed His Favours/Blessings - of the prophets, the sincere Truthful, the witnesses (who testify), and the Righteous, and excellent are those as companions." (The Women, 4:69)

Allah's ﷻ Support With Presence of Sayyidina Muhammad ﷺ, Extinguishes the Fire

If that *Nur* (light) of Allah ﷻ becomes and begins to dress the servant it means the *ghadab* (anger) and the fire, *"Qul ya nahru, kuni Bardan wa Salaman 'ala Ibrahim"* (O fire, be cool and peaceful upon Abraham, Holy Qur'an, 21:69). The fire of their *jahiliya* (ignorance), the fire of Nimrod that wants to burn *insan* (mankind); only by the Support of Allah ﷻ with the presence of Sayyidina Muhammad ﷺ, that light can go down, that energy, that fire begins to go down. And the dress of the soul can be dressed upon that servant.

قُلْنَا يَا نَارُ كُونِي بَرْدًا وَسَلَامًا عَلَىٰ إِبْرَاهِيمَ ﴿٦٩﴾

21:69 – *"Qulna ya Naaru, kuni Bardan wa Salaman 'ala Ibrahim."*
(Surat Al-Anbiya)

"We said, O fire, be cool and Peaceful upon Abraham."
(The Prophets, 21:69)

Excessive Anger is From Lack of Iman (Faith)

It means when we understand that reality, that everything is based on trying to make us angry, everything is based on trying to make us to be ignorant. What they (guides) want us to understand that if you're living your life by anger, it's from a lack of faith. Anybody who is excessively angry, it's from a lack of *iman* (faith), because *iman* and anger, they don't go together.

It means that our life's purpose is to destroy anger. If we don't make that attempt to destroy anger, everything about our being is on fire; and there is no *nur* (light). There is nobody who is yelling and angry and exploding in an instant and then think that they have faith and that they are *nurani* (luminous). But they're actually *narani* (fiery); they're more like the fires of *jahannam* (hell).

Make Durood Sharif to Bring the Presence of Prophet Muhammad ﷺ

What we're asking from these realities is that to bring the light of faith within your heart. It means all your spiritual practices; all of these teachings are for us to become conscious. That, '*Ya Rabbi*, don't let fire to overtake me, don't let anger to overtake me.' Then Allah ﷻ says, 'If you don't want that fire and you don't want that anger, very simple solution – bring *Muhammadun RasulAllah* ﷺ into your life.' And that's why the *mahfil*  (gatherings), the *zikrs* (associations), the *mawlids*, the *salawats* (praisings on Prophet ﷺ), the *durood sharif;* it's all for us to understand – you want to reach to be a star, this fire and *ghadab* and anger has to be destroyed.

As soon as you begin to praise upon Prophet ﷺ by making *durood sharif*, *Allahumma salli ala Sayyidina Muhammad wa ala aali Sayyidina Muhammad* ﷺ, the light of Prophet ﷺ comes to be present.

اللَّهُمَّ صَلِّ عَلَى سَيِّدِنَا مُحَمَّدٍ، وَعَلَى آلِ سَيِّدِنَا مُحَمَّدٍ وَ سَلِّمْ

Allahumma salli 'ala Sayyidina Muhammadin wa 'ala aali Sayyidina Muhammadin wa Sallim.

O Allah! Send Peace and blessings upon Muhammad and upon the Family of Muhammad (pbuh)

Nur Muhammad ﷺ Will Guide You and Destroy Ignorance

That light of Prophet ﷺ is enough to take away ignorance. Why? Because Allah ﷻ described that Prophet ﷺ is going to guide you. He is going to *zaki*, he is going to clean you.

كَمَا أَرْسَلْنَا فِيكُمْ رَسُولًا مِنكُمْ يَتْلُو عَلَيْكُمْ آيَاتِنَا وَيُزَكِّيكُمْ وَيُعَلِّمُكُمُ الْكِتَابَ وَالْحِكْمَةَ وَيُعَلِّمُكُم مَّا لَمْ تَكُونُوا تَعْلَمُونَ ﴿١٥١﴾

2:151 - "*Kama arsalna feekum Rasulam minkum yatlo 'Alaykum ayatina wa yuzakkeekum wa yu'Allimukumul kitaba walhikmata wa yu'Allimukum ma lam takono ta'Alamon.*" (Surat Al-Baqarah)

"*Just as We have sent among (within) you a messenger of your own, reciting to you Our Signs, and purifying you, and teaching you the Book/Scripture (Qur'an) and Wisdom, and teaching you New Knowledge, that which you did not know.*" (The Cow, 2:151)

It means as soon as you start making *durood* and *salawat* (praisings) upon Sayyidina Muhammad ﷺ the light of Prophet ﷺ begins to come into your life and begins to guide you so now it's taking away ignorance. When you are making *durood sharif* on Prophet ﷺ, the light of Prophet ﷺ, you keep making, throughout the day, keep making *durood sharif*, that light becomes the light within the heart.

If the light of Prophet ﷺ is entering within the heart, it begins to push down all of the anger. All of the practices that they're giving to us, that wash when you're angry.

عَنْ عَطِيَّةَ بْنِ عُرْوَةَ السَّعْدِيِّ رَضِيَ اللهُ، عَنِ النَّبِيِّ صَلَّى اللهُ عَلَيْهِ وَسَلَّمَ قَالَ

إِنَّ الْغَضَبَ مِنَ الشَّيْطَانِ وَإِنَّ الشَّيْطَانَ خُلِقَ مِنَ النَّارِ وَإِنَّمَا تُطْفَأُ النَّارُ بِالْمَاءِ فَإِذَا غَضِبَ أَحَدُكُمْ فَلْيَتَوَضَّأْ. رَوى الإمام أحمد في "المسند" **(505/29)** وأبو داود **(4784)**

'An 'Atiyat bin 'Urwatul Sa'di (ra) 'Anan Nabi (saws) Qal:

"'Annal ghadaba minash shaitani wa innash shaitana khuliqa minan 'Naar, wa innama tutfa annaaru bil Maayi fa iza ghadeba ahadakum falyatawadda." [Rawayil Imam Ahmad fil Musanad wa Abu Dawud]

Atiyah Bin Orwah Alsaadi (ra) said, that the messenger of Allah (pbuh) said: "Anger is from Satan, and Satan was created from fire, and in which fire is extinguished by water. So if one of you got angry he should make Wudu (ablution)." [Narrated by Imam Ahmad in his Musnad (29/505, and Imam Abu Dawood (4784)]

Allah ﷻ Will Love You When Love of Sayyidina Muhammad ﷺ is in Your Heart

Take away that *ghadab*, take away that anger, and bring the *durood sharif* and the *salawats* and the love of Sayyidina Muhammad ﷺ into the heart. *"Qul in kuntum tuhibbon Allaha fattabi'oni..."*. Allah ﷻ says, 'I'm not going to love you until you love what I love.'

قُلْ إِن كُنتُمْ تُحِبُّونَ اللَّهَ فَاتَّبِعُونِي يُحْبِبْكُمُ اللَّهُ وَيَغْفِرْ لَكُمْ ذُنُوبَكُمْ ۗ وَاللَّهُ غَفُورٌ رَّحِيمٌ ﴿٣١﴾

3:31 – "Qul in kuntum tuhibbon Allaha fattabi'oni, yuhbibkumullahu wa yaghfir lakum dhonobakum wallahu Ghaforur Raheem." (Surat 'Ali 'Imran)

"Say, [O Muhammad], "If you should love Allah, then follow me, [so] Allah will love you and forgive you your sins. And Allah is Forgiving and Merciful." (Family of Imran, 3:31)

So as soon as you're making praisings upon Prophet ﷺ, that light is entering into the heart. If Allah ﷻ sees the love of Sayyidina Muhammad ﷺ into the heart of the believer, Allah's ﷻ promise that, 'My Love is coming. If My Love is coming,' it means that *nur* (light) of *iman* (faith) is coming.

When the Soul and Body Triangles Lock a Star is Born

That's what they're trying to teach now is that if you can control the lower, if you can take away ignorance by seeking knowledge, if you can take away the anger by replacing with love and *muhabbat* and faith, that will begin to conquer that lower and begin to extinguish the fire of bad desires.

If those two come together, that servant is now reaching towards the reality of being a star. Because the soul will come and lock the lower reality and bring it into control, so that they govern their body through

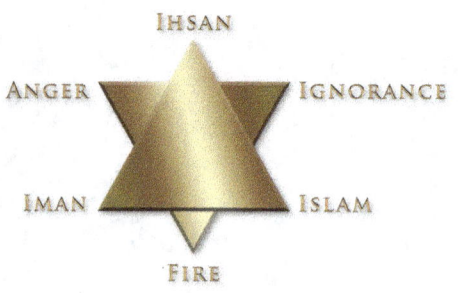

the power of their soul, because they're opening the reality of that understanding. That in that servant, the lower triangle and the upper triangle will come and begin to lock onto them so that they are reaching a *kamil* state, a perfected state, in which the reality and the power of their soul is dressing their physicality and dressing their body, controlling the body desires.

313 Awliyaullah Inherit From 313 Messengers and Represent the Realities of Sayyidina Muhammad ﷺ

If the state begins to dress upon that servant, each corner of these six points is a *lam alif* because now this enters into the opening of the six powers of the heart. You have three points up, three points down, and one *sultan* in the middle of that star. And that inherits now from the 313 messengers of Allah ﷻ, that they dressed the 313 *awliyaullah* (saints) who have permission to speak. There are 313 *awliyaullah* on earth, that they represent the *haqqaiqs* (realities) of Sayyidina Muhammad ﷺ.

All of them from the secret of seven, because you have six points and the seven is representing the *sultan* inside the centre of that heart. Where Allah ﷻ created creation in six days and then they say rested, but it's not a rest. Allah ﷻ doesn't get tired.

اللَّهُ الَّذِي خَلَقَ السَّمَاوَاتِ وَالْأَرْضَ وَمَا بَيْنَهُمَا فِي سِتَّةِ أَيَّامٍ ثُمَّ اسْتَوَىٰ عَلَى الْعَرْشِ ۖ مَا لَكُم مِّن دُونِهِ مِن وَلِيٍّ وَلَا شَفِيعٍ ۚ أَفَلَا تَتَذَكَّرُونَ ﴿٤﴾

32:4 – "Allaahul lazee khalaqas samaawaati wal arda wa maa bainahumaa fee sittati ayyaam; Thummas tawaa 'alal 'arsh; maa lakum min doonihee minw-wwaliyyinw-wala shafee'; afala tatazakkaroon" (Surat As-Sajdah)

"It is Allah Who has created the heavens and the earth, and all between them, in six Days, and is firmly established on the Throne (of Authority): ye have none, besides Him, to protect or intercede (for you): will ye not then receive admonition?" (The Prostration, 32:4)

But this has to do with the secret of creation that these are six *qudras*, and six powers, that bring creation into existence, and the seventh in the centre is the position of *Sultan an Nasira* (the Victorious King). That these are *sultans* and they take their authority from that reality which is from the realities and *haqqaiqs* of Sayyidina Muhammad ﷺ.

وَقُل رَّبِّ أَدْخِلْنِي مُدْخَلَ صِدْقٍ وَأَخْرِجْنِي مُخْرَجَ صِدْقٍ وَاجْعَل لِّي مِن لَّدُنكَ سُلْطَانًا نَّصِيرًا ﴿٨٠﴾

17:80 – *"Wa qul Rabbi adkhelni mudkhala Sidqin wa akhrejni mukhraja Sidqin waj'al li min ladunka Sultanan NaSeera."*
(Surat Al-Isra)

"Say: O my Lord! Let my entry be by the Gate of Truth and Honour, and likewise my exit by the Gate of Truth and Honour; and grant me from Your Presence a King to aid (me)." (The Night Journey, 17:80)

Knowledge of Awliya Raises the Station of Our Souls

It means that each point is a *lam alif*. If you don't understand don't worry, it will come later. That doesn't matter. So, we've seen that diagram before; this is a reminder. Every year we make the reminder because every year it's the same journey towards that light. At one point it'll click and *inshaAllah* with Mawlana's *barakah* (blessings) things begin to open; and each one at their own pace and own level. Don't despair for the *Rahmah* and Mercy of Allah ﷻ. *"...Laa taqnatoo mirrahmatil laah; innal*

laaha" (Holy Qur'an, 39:53). Whatever they want taught, the soul will be dressed by it. Every knowledge that when you sleep, once you heard, when you sleep your soul will go and ask Allah ﷻ, 'Ya Rabbi, I heard these realities.' Allah ﷻ is generous, saying 'Oh My servant, swim in that ocean. Take as much as you can take from that ocean.'

اللَّهُ يَتَوَفَّى الْأَنْفُسَ حِينَ مَوْتِهَا وَالَّتِي لَمْ تَمُتْ فِي مَنَامِهَا ۖ فَيُمْسِكُ الَّتِي قَضَىٰ عَلَيْهَا الْمَوْتَ وَيُرْسِلُ الْأُخْرَىٰ إِلَىٰ أَجَلٍ مُسَمًّى ۚ إِنَّ فِي ذَٰلِكَ لَآيَاتٍ لِقَوْمٍ يَتَفَكَّرُونَ ﴿٤٢﴾

39:42 – "Allaahu yatawaffal anfusa heena mawtihaa wallatee lam tamut fee manaamihaa fa yumsikul latee qadaa 'alaihal mawta wa yursilul ukhraaa ilaa ajalim musammaa; inna fee zaalika la Aayaatil liqawmai yatafakkarroon." (Surat Az-Zumar)

"Allah takes the souls at the time of their death, and those that do not die [He takes] during their sleep. Then He keeps those for which He has decreed death and releases the others for a specified term. Indeed in that are signs for a people who give thought." (The Troops, 39:42)

That's why their teachings can lift the soul of believers. They're not stale and dead, but these are from the *haqqaiqs* and the reality of Prophet ﷺ. Their associations have the ability to raise the *darajat* (station) of the souls of people by the *uloom* and the knowledges that they bring.

Lam Alif is the Secret of 'Qaaba Qawsayn'

That *lam alif* and the secret of that *lam alif* is the secret of *qaab al qawsayni aw adna* (a distance of two bows length or nearer [to the Divine Presence]), where the *salawat* says, *"salamun lin nuqta* (dot).*"*

فَكَانَ قَابَ قَوْسَيْنِ أَوْ أَدْنَىٰ ﴿٩﴾

53:9 – "Fakana qaaba qawsayni aw adna." (Surat An-Najm)

"And was at a distance of two bow lengths or nearer [to the Divine Presence]." (The Star, 53:9)

صَلَاةٌ   بِالسَّلَامِ الْمُبِينِ
لِنُقْطَةِ التَّعْيِيْنِ   يَاغَرَامِيْ

Salaamun bi salam mubeeni
Lin nuqtati tayeeni, Ya gharami

Blessings, and infinite peace be upon the one who is the point of origin and the source of all realities (Prophet Muhammad (pbuh)),
O Our Beloved

Creation Comes to Existence From the Nuqt of Lam Alif

Everything is coming from your *nuqt* (dot), because *"qaaba qawsayni aw adna"* is the *lam alif*, where two bow lengths or near. That when the reality of Prophet ﷺ approaches the reality of Allah ﷻ, they don't touch – aw adna, qaaba qawsayni wa adna.

فَكَانَ قَابَ قَوْسَيْنِ أَوْ أَدْنَىٰ ﴿٩﴾

53:9 – "Fakana qaaba qawsayni aw adna." (Surat An-Najm)

"And was at a distance of two bow lengths or nearer [to the Divine Presence]." (The Star, 53:9)

This means it approaches or even nearer, this reality when it approaches,

the energy is so massive that the *nuqt* (dot) appears. They don't have to touch; but that *nuqt* (dot) appears and from the *nuqt* (dot) infinite creations are continuously coming into existence. That is the secret of *bi sirr at al lam jalala*, that from every reality that *lam alif* is bringing in creation, bringing in realities. It means the servant who is reaching towards a *najm* (star), reaching towards the reality of the soul, Allah's ﷻ taking them back to their reality. That from that light everything is coming into existence. At every moment, these creations are coming into existence.

There is a Lam Alif on Each Point of the Star

There are six of those *lam alifs* on each of those points. It means when they open up their *La, ilaha, illallah*, those are three points; when they open up *Muhammadun RasulAllah* ﷺ three points. These six realities are the six powers on the heart, that when the soul begins to dress the servant, they are now entering in the oceans of Allah's ﷻ *Ikhlas*

When the *hadith* of Prophet ﷺ describes, 'When My servant finished their *fard* (obligatory) but approaches Me through voluntary worship, I become the hearing in which he hears, the seeing in which he sees, the speaking in which he speaks, the hands in which he touches, the feet in which he moves.' So much so that he becomes *rabbaniyoon* (lordly soul) and has power, "*kun faya kun*" (be and it is) because their will matches the will of Prophet ﷺ, matches the Will of Allah ﷻ. So, whatever they're asking, Allah ﷻ is asking through their heart.

...وَلَا يَزَالُ عَبْدِي يَتَقَرَّبُ إِلَيَّ بِالنَّوَافِلِ حَتَّى أُحِبَّهُ، فَإِذَا أَحْبَبْتُهُ كُنْتُ سَمْعَهُ الَّذِي يَسْمَعُ بِهِ، وَبَصَرَهُ الَّذِي يُبْصِرُ بِهِ، وَيَدَهُ الَّتِي يَبْطِشُ بِهَا، وَرِجْلَهُ الَّتِي يَمْشِي بِهَا، وَلَئِنْ سَأَلَنِي لَأُعْطِيَنَّهُ، وَلَئِنْ اسْتَعَاذَنِي لَأُعِيذَنَّهُ." [رَوَاهُ الْبُخَارِيُّ

"..., wa la yazaalu 'Abdi yataqarrabu ilayya bin nawafile hatta ahebahu, fa idha ahbabtuhu kunta Sam'ahul ladhi yasma'u behi, wa Basarahul ladhi yubsiru behi, wa Yadahul lati yabTeshu beha, wa Rejlahul lati yamshi beha, wa la in sa alani la a'Teyannahu..."

"...My servant continues to draw near to Me with voluntary acts of worship so that I shall love him. When I love him, I am his hearing with which he hears, his seeing with which he sees, his hand with which he strikes and his foot with which he walks. Were he to ask [something] of Me, I would surely give it to him..."
(Hadith Qudsi, Sahih al-Bukhari, 81:38:2)

The Six Powers of the Heart and Reality of Najm (Star)

It means then open that *najm* (star), when that *najm* (star) begins to open, those *haqqaiqs* (realities) begin to dress that servant.

1. Haqqiqat ul Juzba (Realities of Magnetism)

The *haqqaiq* of *juzba* (reality of magnetism), that through the light that Allah ﷻ is opening into their heart, there's a tremendous energy force. That energy, people are attracted to that energy, what they call magnetism.

2. Haqqiqat ul Fa'iz (Realities of Downpouring)

The *haqqaiq* of *fa'iz* (realities of downpouring), that the downpouring  and emanations. When Allah ﷻ and they're like a star that emanations from the Divinely Presence of Allah ﷻ, from Sayyidina Muhammad ﷺ and from *ulul amr* (saints) begin to dress the soul and roll out like rain, like a rain that can't be seen but can be felt. These are *tajallis* (manifestations) upon their soul that emanating out their *fa'iz* (downpouring) is reaching. It can reach anybody in the room; it can reach wherever they make their intention. Their operation is from their soul and not from their body because they discipline the dirtiness of their body. They operate from the reality of their *arwah*, from their soul.

3. Haqqiqat ul Tawajju (Realities of Focusing)

From that *fa'iz* (downpouring) begins the *haqqaiq* of *tawajju* (realities of focusing) that their training and their *tafakkur* (contemplation), that when they're contemplating, they're continuously in the presence of a holy face, where Allah's ﷻ describing everything perishes but the holy face. Whether it's the holy face of Sayyidina Muhammad ﷺ, or the holy face of their Shaykh and these *awliyaullah* (saints) who inherit from the face of Prophet ﷺ. Prophet's ﷺ face is  towards the Divinely Presence of Allah ﷻ. This is like a satellite and mirrors.

وَلَا تَدْعُ مَعَ اللَّهِ إِلَٰهًا آخَرَ ۘ لَا إِلَٰهَ إِلَّا هُوَ ۚ كُلُّ شَيْءٍ هَالِكٌ إِلَّا وَجْهَهُ ۚ لَهُ الْحُكْمُ وَإِلَيْهِ تُرْجَعُونَ ﴿٨٨﴾

28:88 – "*Wala tad'uo ma'Allahi ilahan aakhara la ilaha illa huwa kullu shayin halikun illa wajha hu la hul hukmu wa ilayhi turja'oon.*" (Surat Al-Qasas)

"*...Everything (that exists) will perish except His holy Face. To Him belongs the Command, and to Him you will be returned.*"
(The Stories, 28:88)

4. Haqqiqat ul Tawassul (Realities of Conveying)

From that *tawajju* (focus), they have the *haqqaiq* of *tawassul* (realities of  conveying). Because of that face that what they're continuously in that face, they have a dialogue that not interrupted from a humanly connection. Like old internet, you dial up on your internet at old rate. But they (saints) have no dial up. As soon as Allah ﷻ makes them to operate from their soul, like a beatific dream; everybody has a beatific dream. Why do you have a beatific dream where you see some holy people in your dream? Because your *nafs* (ego) got out of the way.

There are people who don't need to dream, that their *nafs* (ego) already Allah ﷻ brought it down, and every moment they are seeing – this is the *hadith* (Prophetic ﷺ tradition)! You cannot think that what Prophet ﷺ is giving is a joke; Prophet's ﷺ words are immensely true. That is the *hadith* that those servants, they're going to hear with Allah's ﷻ hearing, not a *dunya* hearing. They're going to see what Allah ﷻ wants them to see from a divinely power.

...وَلَا يَزَالُ عَبْدِي يَتَقَرَّبُ إِلَيَّ بِالنَّوَافِلِ حَتَّى أُحِبَّهُ، فَإِذَا أَحْبَبْتُهُ كُنْتُ سَمْعَهُ الَّذِي يَسْمَعُ بِهِ، وَبَصَرَهُ الَّذِي يُبْصِرُ بِهِ، ." [رَوَاهُ الْبُخَارِيُّ]

"..., wa la yazaalu 'Abdi yataqarrabu ilayya bin nawafile hatta ahebahu, fa idha ahbabtuhu kunta Sam'ahul ladhi yasma'u behi, wa Basarahul ladhi yubsiru behi, ..."

"...My servant continues to draw near to Me with voluntary acts of worship so that I shall love him. When I love him, I am his hearing with which he hears, his seeing with which he sees,..."
(Hadith Qudsi, Sahih al-Bukhari, 81:38:2)

When they begin to see, what they see they can convey the *du'a* (supplication) to what they're seeing. To the face in which they look, they begin to convey that *du'a*, from their soul to that light that's in front of them.

As a result, the *du'as* (supplications) are moving into that presence; it doesn't mean that all the *du'as* (supplications) are accepted, otherwise everything would be miraculous. But they are conveying the *du'a* (supplication) that needs to be conveyed based on Allah ﷻ what He wants; and Allah's ﷻ Timing is best and Allah ﷻ knows His creation best.

5. Haqqiqat ul Tayy (Realities of Scrolling – Moving Between Space and Time)

So, it means that they're opening that *fa'iz* (downpouring), opening that *tawajju* (focusing), opening that *tawassul* (conveying). From there, they begin to open the realities of the *tayy* (scrolling) and the movement with their soul – *haqqiqat al tayy* – it means that they can be sitting with you, but their soul can be many places at the same time. It's nothing hard.

This is what physics only now begins to understand the duality of light. You can see light as a particle, but you have to know it is always in a wave form. You see them in front of you, but they are many places at the same time and takes no effort and no power, because Allah's ﷻ power upon the soul.

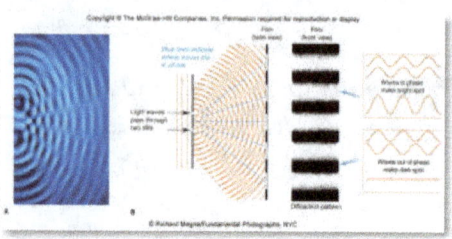

6. Haqqiqat ul Irshad (Realities of Guidance)

As a result of that, Allah ﷻ opens the last *haqqaiq* of that reality is the reality of *irshad* (guidance); that only at that time, Allah ﷻ opened from

them *irshad* and guidance, because they're guiding. They are guiding through that reality; they guide through what Allah's ﷻ dressing, they guide through what Allah's ﷻ emanations. They guide through what Allah's ﷻ granting of their visions, their *tawajju* (focusing), their *tawassul* (conveying); all of those *haqqaiq* (realities) were dressed upon them. As a result, Prophet ﷺ described his Companions, they are stars on a dark night, which means they're all *kamil* (perfected) guides. 'Any one of my Companions, I made them to be *kamil*, perfected stars. They hear, they see, they convey.'

أَصْحَابِيْ كَالنُّجُـــومْ بِأَيْهِمْ اَقْتَدَيْتِمْ اَهْتَدَيْتِمْ

"*Ashabi kan Nujoom, bi ayyihim aqta daytum ahta daytum.*"

"*My companions are like stars. Follow any one of them and you will be guided.*" (Prophet Muhammad (pbuh))

عَنْ أَنَسِ بْنِ مَالِكٍ رَضِيَ اللهُ عَنْهُ ، قَالَ : قَالَ رَسُولُ اللهِ صَلَّى اللهُ عَلَيْهِ وَسَلَّمَ : « أَنَّ مِثْلَ الْعُلَمَاءِ فِي الْأَرْضِ كَمَثَلِ النُّجُومِ ، يُهْتَدَى بِهَا فِي ظُلُمَاتِ الْبَرِّ وَالْبَحْرِ ، فَإِذَا انْطَمَسَتِ النُّجُومُ أَوْشَكَ أَنْ تَضِلَّ الْهُدَاةُ » رَوَاهُ أَحْمَدُ

'An Anasin bin Malikin (ra) Qala, Qala Rasulullahi Sallallahu 'alayhi wa sallam: "Anna mithlal 'ulamayi fil ardi kamathalan Nujomi yuhtada beha fi zulumatil barri wal bahri. Fa iza antamasati anujomi aw shaka an tadillal huda."

Narrated by Anas Bin Malik (ra) that the Messenger of Allah (pbuh) said: "The religious scholars on Earth are like the stars in the sky, they guide people through the darkness of the land and sea. When those stars fade, the guidance will be lost." [Based on Imam Ahmad]

Awliya (Saints) Confirm Hadith With Prophet ﷺ Through Their Hearts

When they (saints) close their eyes or open their eyes, they see Prophet ﷺ, they convey directly to Sayyidina Muhammad ﷺ. That's why there is no weak *hadith* (Prophetic ﷺ tradition) for them. As soon as

they mention, Prophet ﷺ will correct what he wants to be corrected. They're not taking anything from paper and something written 1,000 years ago. They merely take an understanding, an *isharat* (sign), their heart will tell them from the presence of Sayyidina Muhammad ﷺ exactly what he wants conveyed and that they know is *sahih*, because Sahih al Bukhari. Imam Bukhari said that's how he took *hadith*, that he would wash, pray, and Prophet ﷺ would come and tell him exactly what to name and where to put that *hadiths*. These are *ahlul basirah* (people of spiritual vision), the people who operate from their heart. They're not imagining; these are all the realities of the star.

The Big Battle is Between Our Soul and Ego

With all of that, then Allah is describing that why to live this earthly life and dirty life, when to open all these realities and these dresses upon the soul. We pray that Allah give us more and more understanding, that to open these *lam alif*, to open an understanding of the soul, to bring the power of the soul. But most importantly is the discipline of the body. Take away the *ghadab* (anger), take away the bad characteristics so that that light can begin to dress; the light of the soul will begin to dress the physicality. Until then,  there is a big fight. The fight from the energy of the soul to the body, and this is the big *jihad*, this is the big battle in which the lights of the soul want to come, and the ego and the bad characteristics of the body want to be dominant, and that's when they begin to struggle.

We pray that Allah open more and more understanding for us and dress us from these lights and dress us to be a star on a dark night, *inshaAllah*.

Subhana rabbika rabbal 'izzati 'amma yasifoon, wa salaamun 'alal mursaleen, walhamdulillahi rabbil 'aalameen. Bi hurmati Muhammad al-Mustafa wa bi siri Surat al-Fatiha.

How a Star is Born
Perfection Through Powers of the Heart

Always a reminder for myself, *ana abdukal ajeez, wa dayeef, wa miskin, wa zhalim, wa jahl* and by the Grace of God, I'm in existence.

We took a path of asking to be nothing, in a world that completely pushes you to be something. And that by being nothing and taking a path of nothingness, place no value on what you do. Leave Allah ﷻ to set the value, the benefit of what we do.

Prophet Muhammad ﷺ is the Sultan of Stars

Alhamdulillah, from Mawlana Shaykh's teachings that talking about the perfection of *insan* (mankind), that how to rise above animal desires and to reach to the stations above even the angels, *"Wa laqad karamna Bani Adam."*

وَلَقَدْ كَرَّمْنَا بَنِي آدَمَ...﴿٧٠﴾

17:70 – *"Wa laqad karramna bani adama…"* (Surat Al-Isra)

"And We have certainly honored the children of Adam…" (The Night Journey, 17:70)

The symbolism is a star and how we put all of these knowledges together, they want us to understand that Prophet ﷺ is the *Sultan* of all

How a Star is Born – Perfection Through Powers of the Heart

stars, that all lights are coming from the light of Sayyidina Muhammad ﷺ, and that light coming from Allah ﷻ. That Prophet ﷺ perfected his Companions, that, 'All of my Companions they are like stars on a dark night.'

أَصْحَابِيْ كَالنُّجُومْ بِأَيِّهِمْ اَقْتَدَيْتِمْ اَهْتَدَيْتِمْ

"Ashabi kan Nujoom, bi ayyihim aqta daytum ahta daytum."

"My companions are like stars. Follow any one of them and you will be guided." (Prophet Muhammad (pbuh))

It means that's now *maqam ul ihsan* (station of moral excellence), beyond what humans can achieve of what Prophet ﷺ gave to his holy Companions. But below that *darajat* (station) means to move towards that *maqam ul ihsan*, that perfection. It sets now that, 'Ya Rabbi, let me to reach, by the love of Sayyidina Muhammad ﷺ, let me to reach into that understanding of what is the *najm*? What is a star? What is the perfection of *insan* (mankind) and how to reach that perfection?'

Then they teach about the Holy Face, then they teach about the Holy Heart, and all of them begin to come together. They string the beads with the string that bring all those knowledges together for an understanding of how to achieve. We said before that they are a walking *hadith* of Prophet ﷺ.

Allah ﷻ Makes His Awliya to Be Rabaniyoon (Lordly Souls)

When Allah ﷻ is describing in *hadith qudsi* that, 'When the servant completes all his *fard*, he does everything that's obligatory, but approaches Me through voluntary worship.' This means Allah's ﷻ now describing a

state in which the servant is sincere and being dressed by Allah's ﷻ Love. 'That I become the hearing in which he hears, the seeing in which he sees, the tongue in which he speaks, the breath in which he breathes. The hands and the support, the hands in which he touches, the feet in which he moves.' It means his path, his strength, all of his faculties.

...وَلَا يَزَالُ عَبْدِي يَتَقَرَّبُ إِلَيَّ بِالنَّوَافِلِ حَتَّى أُحِبَّهُ، فَإِذَا أَحْبَبْتُهُ كُنْتَ سَمْعَهُ الَّذِي يَسْمَعُ بِهِ، وَبَصَرَهُ الَّذِي يُبْصِرُ بِهِ، وَيَدَهُ الَّتِي يَبْطِشُ بِهَا، وَرِجْلَهُ الَّتِي يَمْشِي بِهَا، وَلَئِنْ سَأَلَنِي لَأُعْطِيَنَّهُ، وَلَئِنْ اسْتَعَاذَنِي لَأُعِيذَنَّهُ." رَوَاهُ الْبُخَارِيُّ

"..., wa la yazaalu 'Abdi yataqarrabu ilayya bin nawafile hatta ahebahu, fa idha ahbabtuhu kunta Sam'ahul ladhi yasma'u behi, wa Basarahul ladhi yubsiru behi, wa Yadahul lati yabTeshu beha, wa Rejlahul lati yamshi beha, wa la in sa alani la a'Teyannahu, ..."

"...My servant continues to draw near to Me with voluntary acts of worship so that I shall love him. When I love him, I am his hearing with which he hears, his seeing with which he sees, his hand with which he strikes and his foot with which he walks. Were he to ask [something] of Me, I would surely give it to him..."
(Hadith Qudsi, Sahih al-Bukhari, 81:38:2)

Allah ﷻ is giving His Divinely Attribute upon that servant. Those are the perfected, so much so that you become *rabaniyoon* (lordly souls) and has *"kun faya kun"*, be and it shall be. This means that what manifests from their heart of their prayers, Allah ﷻ makes it to manifest because they are in *taslim* (submission), complete with Allah ﷻ. So, it's actually Allah's ﷻ Will through the will of Prophet ﷺ manifesting in their heart, because you went through the ocean of *taslim* (submission).

The Star is a Symbol of Perfection

Then they begin to pull all this together; the symbol is the star of perfection. How to perfect your soul and that reality of the soul. How to discipline the physicality, then the two will lock. It means the soul, if you give it its power, you give it its authority, it will begin with all of its energy to lock the physicality.

Then they begin to teach that your heart and the *lataifs* (subtle energy points) of the heart means all of these realities are going to begin to open within the heart of the servant. That the most important faculty upon them is their holy face, that their face is going to be dressed and their face is going to submit.

Awliya Open Spiritual Senses of Their Students

We talked last night about *itibah* (following), that it's all happening at the same time by these guides. They are perfecting their students and raising them to that *hadith* (*qudsi*) of Allah, of Prophet that, 'I want that servant to be dressed from My Hearing. I want them to be dressed by My Seeing, I want them to be dressed by My Divinely Breath, I want their hands to be upon My Hand, upon the hands of Sayyidina Muhammad. I want their *qadam* and their feet to be correct and perfected on where they come and where they go, which means their worshipness for me to be clean and purified.'

...وَلَا يَزَالُ عَبْدِي يَتَقَرَّبُ إِلَيَّ بِالنَّوَافِلِ حَتَّى أُحِبَّهُ، فَإِذَا أَحْبَبْتُهُ كُنْتُ سَمْعَهُ الَّذِي يَسْمَعُ بِهِ، وَبَصَرَهُ الَّذِي يُبْصِرُ بِهِ، وَيَدَهُ الَّتِي يَبْطِشُ بِهَا، وَرِجْلَهُ الَّتِي يَمْشِي بِهَا،". رَوَاهُ الْبُخَارِيُّ

"..., wa la yazaalu 'Abdi yataqarrabu ilayya bin nawafile hatta ahebahu, fa idha ahbabtuhu kunta Sam'ahul ladhi yasma'u behi, wa

Basarahul ladhi yubsiru behi, wa Yadahul lati yabTeshu beha, wa Rejlahul lati yamshi beha, ..."

"...My servant continues to draw near to Me with voluntary acts of worship so that I shall love him. When I love him, I am his hearing with which he hears, his seeing with which he sees, his hand with which he strikes and his foot with which he walks..."
(Hadith Qudsi, Sahih al-Bukhari, 81:38:2)

It means then their job is to make that *hadith* (Prophetic ﷺ tradition) and dress upon the servant. When they're talking about these realities, they're not only talking for the sake of talking, but they're describing this process of how a star is being made. The star is the example of perfection.

We Are a Small Version of This Galaxy

Then they begin to teach about the heart and the *lataifs* (subtle energy points) of the heart and begin to understand that through their *tafakkur* (contemplation) and all of their practices, they're going to be dressed by these realities.

We said before that when they start to understand this *najm* (star) and its power, these are six *qudras* (powers) that will be opening upon the servant. Because that star, its base and its home is the reality of the heart,

because the heart of *insan* (mankind) is the sun, is the *shams*. Your galaxy that Allah ﷻ has given to every *insan*, to every person he's given them a galaxy. 'I've given you a moon, I've given you a sun, I've given you all these organs.' All your organs like the 11 planets that are in our galaxy.

Allah ﷻ says, 'You are a small version of this big galaxy. If you can run it the way I run My Galaxy, I'm going to give you your *amanat* (trust)

How a Star is Born – Perfection Through Powers of the Heart

and your *'ahd*, your covenant because you're able to manage what I've given to you; I make you a manager in what I have created, of the greater *'izzat.*'

Lam Alif is the Secret of Creation

It means they begin then to teach then that sun within the heart is going to be opened. One is the symbol of the sun and understand, *'Ya Rabbi*, I want to reach that perfection,' then they begin to teach that each of these triangles has a point. Each point is a *lam alif*, is an *'izzat* and a power that's opening. Because everything opens by *la ilaha illallah Muhammadun RasulAllah* ﷺ and that we go into later. We have talked before on the reality of *lam alif. Lam* is *lisanul haq*, is the tongue of Prophet ﷺ, is *Muhammadun RasulAllah* ﷺ; *alif* is *'IzzatAllah*.

Bi sirra lam jalala is the secret of creation. That everything is coming with that power. This means that these six points of this triangle, this one triangle up, one triangle down, these are the six powers in which Allah ﷻ described that, 'I created creation in six days,' the seventh is a rest. There's no rest for Allah ﷻ but there's a reality in that seven.

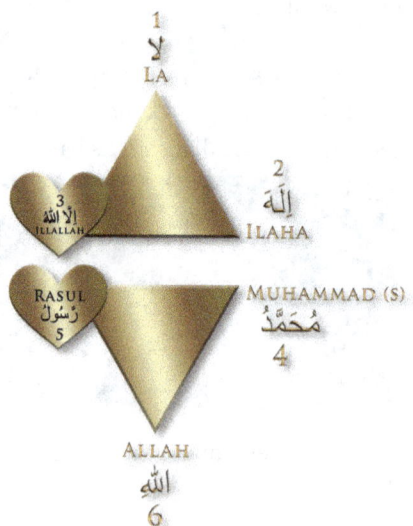

وَهُوَ الَّذِي خَلَقَ السَّمَاوَاتِ وَالْأَرْضَ فِي سِتَّةِ أَيَّامٍ وَكَانَ عَرْشُهُ عَلَى الْمَاءِ... ﴿٧﴾

11:7 – "Wa huwal ladhee khalaqas samawati wal arda fee sittati ayyamin, wa kana 'arshuhu 'alal maa ..." (Surat Hud)

"And it is He who created the heavens and the earth in six days - and His Throne had been upon water ..." (Hud, 11:7)

Star and Six Qudra (Powers) of the Heart

It means these are six *qudras* that they're going to open within the heart of the believer. As soon as the believer is taking a path of perfection, they're doing all of their *wajib* and everything that Allah ﷻ asked from them, they're entering in now the states of love and *muhabbat*. That they do extraordinary worship by coming for the love of Prophet ﷺ.

It means that first they're going to open *haqiqat ul-juzba* (reality of magnetism), because this is now the reality of a star that is coming upon them. The reality of *juzba* and attraction means that, through their practices, they are being dressed, they're being dressed, they're being dressed. The student doesn't initially know what they're being dressed by, because they have to start going into *tafakkur* (contemplation). But as you sit, it's like on a beach – the rays of the sun and the *tajallis*  (manifestations) that Allah's ﷻ sending upon them and upon all the unseen support are dressing everyone. As it dresses you, it's changing your entire being.

How a Star is Born – Perfection Through Powers of the Heart

1. Haqiqat ul-Juzba (Reality of Magnetism)
Zikr Purifies the Iron in the Blood

Juzba is magnetism; the reality of magnetism is it begins to alter all of the reality within yourself. The first reality within the self is that all the 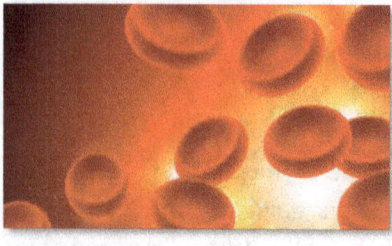 iron within your body will be purified. All the dirty iron has to be purged and taken out of the body. The light and the energy they are focusing upon the student is changing the magnetic composition of the person. They are increasing their *juzba*, their attraction. The energy and the iron within that *insan* (mankind) becomes purified, becomes cleansed.

The whole process of your *zikr* and all your chanting and all your practices is that it cleans that blood. And as that blood is being cleaned and moving, and as every breath that you bring in, it's in that worshipness and dressed by Divine *qudra* (power).

Tafakkur (Contemplation) and Zikrullah
Changes Magnetic Composition of a Person

In the *zikr* (remembrance), in your *tafakkur* (contemplation), in all your practices, are under their *nazar* (gaze). It means that every breath that you bring in of *nafas ar rahmah* (breath of mercy) is of energized and powered breath. As soon as you bring that breath upon yourself, it's cleansing your blood cells. And your blood cell carries an iron; that's what makes it to be red. It cleanses the blood and sends that blood into the heart to be stamped by *zikrullah* 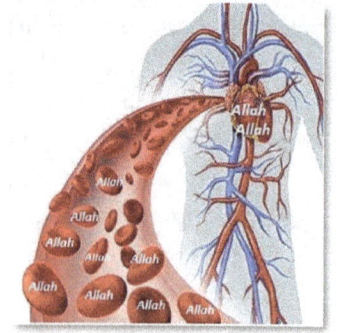 (chanting of Allah ﷻ). As a process, the heart is now energized by that support, and begins to stamp that iron within the heart of that servant with *zikrullah* (remembrance of Allah ﷻ).

As the entire reality of the servant is changing inside, they are becoming more and more magnetic. As the energy is dressing them, the *qudra* (power) and the breath is dressing them, everything inside of them is being purified specific to the heart and their focus on the heart. And in the focus of the heart is the iron that enters into the heart, the blood.

Abstain From What's Forbidden, Shaytan Runs in Our Blood

That's why Prophet ﷺ was teaching that eat *halal* (permissible), *shaytan* (satan) runs through your blood; it means don't eat *haram* (forbidden).

Zabiha (humane method of animal slaughter) is one thing and *halal* (permissible) is different thing. *Halal* and *haram* means something that is allowed or forbidden by Prophet ﷺ. To eat what is allowed by Prophet ﷺ and abstain from what's forbidden from Prophet ﷺ because *shaytan* runs in the blood.

قَالَ رَسُولُ اللَّهِ صَلَّى اللَّهُ عَلَيْهِ وَسَلَّمَ: "إِنَّ الشَّيْطَانَ يَجْرِي مِنْ ابْنِ آدَمَ مَجْرَى الدَّمِ"
[صَحِيحُ الْبُخَارِيْ، صَحِيحْ مُسْلِمْ وَ مُتَّفَقٌ عَلَيْهِ]

Qala Rasulullahi ﷺ: *"Innash shaitana yajri min ibni Adama (as) majra addami."* [*Sahih Bukhari, Sahih Muslim wa Muttafaqu 'alyhi*]

The Prophet of Allah (pbuh) said: *"Satan moves/flows in sons of Adam (as) through the blood."*
[*Sahih Bukhari, Sahih Muslim & Agreed upon by all Imams*]

So as the focus is on the blood and cleansing of the blood, focus on cleansing of the heart, it means then now the energy within the heart is beginning to change. The magnetism and the purity of their iron is becoming purified. Many people become sick by the dirty iron in their body. Many staph infections are by the iron. When the iron rots and it get contaminated with sugar, many infections inside the body begin. But this, and this understanding is this iron becomes purified.

Perfect Shaykhs Dress You With Juzba (Attraction)

In school they were teaching us with a battery how to magnetize – you can take metal and put a charge on the metal, as a result that metal becomes magnetized. Magnetized means now it has what we call *juzba*; it has the ability to attract. This means that once the servant is in, in these practices, the *haqiqat ul-juzba*, it's a continuous process, these six powers, that every association, all their practices all under that *nazar* (gaze). The Shaykh is changing them, making all of their iron to be purified. As a result of their purified iron, they have now an attraction.

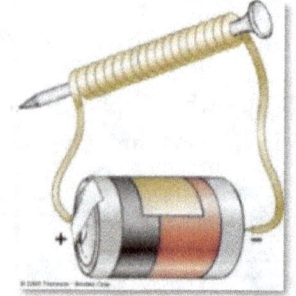

So many times, you go places and people are attracted to you. It's not because of you, but it's what you are being dressed with. It means this energy that you're not understanding at that phase, you're not understanding what's taking place; but you feel heated. You feel an energy coming on to you, you feel aggravated when you go home, because you've been cooked. As you're being cooked, your ego is becoming angry. But in the physiology of the self what they want to know is that the metal is changing: it's becoming purified. As it becomes purified, it sends out a tremendous positive charge.

True Shaykhs Emit Light and Positive Charge That Attracts People

So, the Shaykh, he represents a positive charge. Their *juzba* is such a positive charge that they can attract every negativity towards them. Because that was, *"sirat al lazhina an'amta alayhim, ghairil maghdubi alayhim, wa laddaalin."* (The path of those upon whom You have bestowed favour, not of those who have evoked [Your] anger or of those who are astray.)

صِرَاطَ الَّذِينَ أَنْعَمْتَ عَلَيْهِمْ غَيْرِ الْمَغْضُوبِ عَلَيْهِمْ وَلَا الضَّالِّينَ ﴿٧﴾

1:7 – *"Siraatal-lazeena an'amta 'alaihim ghayril-maghdoobi 'alaihim wa lad-daaalleen." (Surat Al-Fatiha)*

"The path of those upon whom You have bestowed favour, not of those who have evoked [Your] anger or of those who are astray."
(The Opener, 1:7)

All those negative charges Allah ﷻ, they made them to be positive. The Shaykhs are the positive charge and they have the ability to attract all the negative charge. They bring all the negative charge and that's called

the *juzba*. *Haqqiqat ul-juzba* is people are attracted to them and they don't even know them. Not attracted, we are not talking physical; they're talking by their soul, that there's something about you. You go to the bank, you go to the store, you go out onto the street and somebody says, 'Oh, there's something about you,' they don't know what it is.

There is a light, there is an energy emitting from that servant that people are now attracted to, because they're devoid of that energy. They are living in a world with a very negative charge. When somebody comes with a very positive charge, people are moving to them, trying to talk to them, trying to figure what is it that you're emanating that I'm feeling that energy and positivity.

RijalAllah (Men of God) Recharge People Through Their Soul (Wireless Connection)

You can even begin to change the movement and the character of people. Because anybody who is excessively negative as if their battery, its charge has been pulled. They come into the associations or they meet one of these *Rijal* (men of Allah ﷻ) and immediately their character can change. Their depression can go away in an instant, their sadness goes away in an instant, as if they've been fully recharged. It's wireless technology, they don't need a wire to charge. They're teaching you that technology, before it came! They only understand now to start charging these phones and these devices wirelessly. There's no need for a wire.

The energy then being transmitted is changing the iron of that person. As a result, the *haqqiqat ul-juzba* is being dressed upon the student; people begin to feel that attraction.

Haqqiqatul Fa'iz (Downpouring)

With *haqqiqat ul-juzba* dressing the servant, at the same time the Shaykh's work is then these lights that are transmitting from the Shaykh, and from their guides and from all the support begin to release upon  that servant the *fa'iz* (downpouring). *Fa'iz* is heavenly emanation, because you come under their sunshine. Because their souls are more powerful than the sun of this galaxy. This sun is created and Allah ﷻ says, *"Wa laqad karamna Bani Adam"* (I have honoured this creation of Adam (and Eve)). Its honour is beyond imagination. So, think of all the greatness of creation and Allah ﷻ said, 'I honoured *Bani Adam*' – Adam and Eve.

وَلَقَدْ كَرَّمْنَا بَنِي آدَمَ وَحَمَلْنَاهُمْ فِي الْبَرِّ وَالْبَحْرِ وَرَزَقْنَاهُم مِّنَ الطَّيِّبَاتِ وَفَضَّلْنَاهُمْ عَلَىٰ كَثِيرٍ مِّمَّنْ خَلَقْنَا تَفْضِيلًا ﴿٧٠﴾

17:70 – "Wa laqad karramna banee adama, wa hamalna hum filbarri wal bahri wa razaqnahum minat tayyibati wa faddalnahum 'ala katheerin mimman khalaqna tafdeela. (Surat Al-Isra)

"And We have certainly honored the children of Adam and carried them on the land and sea and provided good and pure sustenance and bestow upon them favours, and preferred them over much of what We have created, with [definite] preference." (The Night Journey, 17:70)

Real Shaykhs Have Reached Their Soul's Reality and Sent Back to Earth

These guides' sun is more powerful than this physical sun. As a result, the *haqqiqat ul-fa'iz* is that it begins raining and emanation upon their souls in every association, every *tafakkur*, every contemplation.

The soul of these guides, whom we said, they reached to *"Bismillahir Rahmanir Raheem"*, and Allah sent them back. Allah's saying, 'You want to go into your paradise and leave this world or you want to serve Me?' There's nobody who doesn't want to serve Allah, doesn't want to serve Prophet, but they have something to serve them with. It is a soul that's been ignited and energized and brought with all its realities back onto earth.

Real Shaykhs Shine Their Light and Rain Their Fa'iz on People

Then they begin the *haqqiqat al fa'iz* with emanations. As soon as these

emanations, it's like you're raising a plant; you need sunshine and water. The water of *rahmah* (mercy), the dress of *rahmah* are the emanations that are reaching the souls. When we don't understand these *haqqaiqs* (realities), they say, 'Go look outside.' Allah said, 'I'll teach you outside and I teach you inside. I show you My Signs upon the horizon.'

سَنُرِيهِمْ آيَاتِنَا فِي الْآفَاقِ وَفِي أَنفُسِهِمْ حَتَّىٰ يَتَبَيَّنَ لَهُمْ أَنَّهُ الْحَقُّ ۗ ... ﴿٥٣﴾

41:53 – "Sanureehim ayatina fil afaqi wa fee anfusihim hatta yatabayyana lahum annahu alhaqqu..." (Surat Al-Isra)

"We will show them Our signs in the horizons and within themselves until it becomes clear to them that it is the truth..."
(The Night Journey, 41:53)

The sun, they found out that all the rays and the photons of the sun penetrates everything. You are being nourished by this sun right now. It penetrates all matter; it penetrates everything, again this is an imitated sun.

The soul whom Allah honoured their soul, their souls, they rain upon everything. Anyone who loves them, more rain; anyone who doesn't love them, they get rain. Wherever they go, they emanate a *fa'iz* (downpouring). By means of that *fa'iz*, many things are taken away of difficulty, many things are dressed and blessed. Because they are taught unconditional love, not like this world. This world's love is based on how to use and abuse people with love.

Follow Those Who Do Not Ask For a Fee

Allah's love, there's no fee. What is in Surat YaSeen, 'They follow those whom ask no fee from you.'

اتَّبِعُوا مَن لَّا يَسْأَلُكُمْ أَجْرًا وَهُم مُهْتَدُونَ ﴿٢١﴾

36:21 – "Ittabi'o man la ya salukum ajran wa hum Muhtadon." (Surat YaSeen)

"Obey/Follow those who ask no reward of you (for themselves), and who have themselves received Guidance." (YaSeen, 36:21)

You can't charge for this love; you can't say this is a course in love and you have to pay before you can get it. They're teaching no, no; this love is free. And these servants are taught that whether you like them or not, they shine upon you. Whether they like you or not, they shine upon you. This is Allah's *Rahmah* (mercy), this is not something personal. This is not for them to control and to not control.

You Will Be With Whom You Love

Their *fa'iz* (downpouring) reach everywhere, that imagine those whom love them. And then you'll understand every *hadith* where Prophet is teaching, 'You'll be with whom you love.'

How a Star is Born – Perfection Through Powers of the Heart

الْمَرْءُ مَعَ مَنْ أَحَبَّ

Qala Rasulullah ﷺ: *"Almar o, ma'a man ahab."*

Prophet Muhammad (pbuh) said: *"One is with those whom he loves."*

This means that as soon as you love these pious people, your soul is moving towards them. As a result, you're directly under the fountain of their *fa'iz* (downpouring), under the waterfall of these emanations that are reaching. And with that love, you create a bond, with your light upon their light.

Awliya's Souls Are Loaded Ships, Carrying Their Students to Prophet ﷺ

Then Allah describes, and this is all from Surat YaSeen, *"Wa hamalna dhuriyatuhum fi fuluk al mashkoon."* (We have carried their atoms in the loaded ship).

وَآيَةٌ لَهُمْ أَنَّا حَمَلْنَا ذُرِّيَّتَهُمْ فِي الْفُلْكِ الْمَشْحُونِ ﴿٤١﴾

36:41 – *"Wa ayatul lahum anna hamalna dhurriyyatahum fil fulkil mashhooni."* (Surat YaSeen)

"And a sign for them is that we have carried their atoms/forefathers in the loaded ship." (YaSeen, 36:41)

Say, 'Didn't We carry you in a loaded ship,' because then you begin to think outside your physicality. Their soul fills a space that you can't imagine. As soon as you enter into their associations from here or from a distance, you've entered into their *fuluk* (ship), you've entered into their soul, not the body, we're not a people who think of the body. These are from the knowledges of *malakut* (heavenly realm) that as soon as you enter into their associations, you're in their ship of their soul.

They're in the ship of their Shaykh's soul, and the Shaykh is in their soul, all the way up into the big soul, which is Sayyidina Muhammad ﷺ.

Awliya's Spaceship Enters to Divine's Presence at Speed of Light

"Wa hamalna dhuriyatuhum fi fuluk al mashkoon; wa khalaqna mim mislahum." (We have carried their atoms in the loaded ships. And We have created for them similar [vessels] on which they ride).

وَآيَةٌ لَّهُمْ أَنَّا حَمَلْنَا ذُرِّيَّتَهُمْ فِي الْفُلْكِ الْمَشْحُونِ ﴿٤١﴾ وَخَلَقْنَا لَهُم مِّن مِّثْلِهِ مَا يَرْكَبُونَ ﴿٤٢﴾

36:41-42 – "Wa ayatul lahum anna hamalna dhurriyyatahum fil fulkil mashhooni. (41) Wa khalaqna lahum mim mithlihi ma yarkabon. (42)" (Surat YaSeen)

"And a sign for them is that we have carried their atoms/forefathers in the loaded ship. (41) And We have created for them similar (vessels) on which they ride. (42)" (YaSeen, 36:41-42)

'And We created the likes of them,' which means there are small ships and big ships. But as soon as you enter into these associations, you're in their ship. You're being dressed by their *fa'iz* (downpouring), by the

rains of these emanations dressing upon you. That's why we said these associations are loaded associations. As soon as they make their *zikr* (remembrance), their prayer, their food, whatever they're doing, these ships are launching. They are like you would see like a spaceship, beyond the speed of the blink of an eye, faster than what Sayyidina Sulayman ؑ from the one who had knowledge of the book. The *jinn* (unseen beings) said, 'I'll take some time to lift the throne.' The one who had knowledge of the book said, 'Before your eye blinks, it's going to be right in front of you.'

قَالَ الَّذِي عِندَهُ عِلْمٌ مِّنَ الْكِتَابِ أَنَا آتِيكَ بِهِ قَبْلَ أَن يَرْتَدَّ إِلَيْكَ طَرْفُكَ ۚ فَلَمَّا رَآهُ مُسْتَقِرًّا عِندَهُ قَالَ هَٰذَا مِن فَضْلِ رَبِّي لِيَبْلُوَنِي أَأَشْكُرُ أَمْ أَكْفُرُ ۖ ...﴿٤٠﴾

27:40 – *"Qala alladhee 'indahu 'ilmun minal kitabi ana ateeka bihi qabla an yartadda ilayka Tarfuka, falamma raahu mustaqirran 'indahu qala hadha min fadli rabbi..." (Surat An-Naml)*

"Said one who had knowledge of the book: "I will bring it to you within the twinkling of an eye!" Then when (Solomon) saw it placed firmly before him, he said: "This is by the Grace of my Lord!..."
(The Ant, 27:40)

How Awliya Transform Students Into Stars?

Faster than that speed, they enter into the Divinely Presence. And anyone on that ship is immediately lifted into that presence. They are dressed by the station in which Allah ﷻ is dressing that guide, by what he's being dressed by his guide, by his guide, by his guide, all the way to Sayyidina Muhammad ﷺ. And *alhamdulillah* that Allah ﷻ granted us an immense gift that we are from the people of the chairmen of the board; all our Shaykhs are *Sultan al Awliya*. This is our belief, from Sultan al Awliya Mawlana Shaykh Muhammad Nazim Haqqani ق, that these are the chairmen of the chairmen, the highest rank of *awliyaullah*.

And Allah ﷻ gave this immense *ni'mat* (blessing) that is the *haqqiqat al-fa'iz*. From that *haqqaiq* (realities) means that this is how they're making the student into a star. Each point of that star of perfection is a reality that the Shaykhs are responsible through their soul to dress the student.

Haqqaiq Tawajju (Realities of Focusing) Opens with Tafakkur (Contemplation)

Now that next *haqqaiq* (reality) that opens is the *tawajju* (focusing). That as soon as the student takes the practices of *tafakkur* and

contemplation, that they say, 'Shaykh, now I want to reach to something more. I'm feeling an energy and I want to learn how to make *tafakkur* and contemplation.' As soon as they take the practices of *tafakkur* (contemplation),

they begin to teach that all *tafakkur* is not to Allah ﷻ. Allah ﷻ doesn't want to be contemplated. It's not your station to contemplate the Creator, but you contemplate creation. Understand your place in creation.

عَنْ أَبِي جَعْفَرٍ عَلَيْهِ السَّلَامُ قَالَ: إِيَّاكُمْ وَالتَّفَكُّرَ فِي اللهِ وَلَكِنْ إِذَا أَرَدْتُمْ أَنْ تَنْظُرُوا إِلَى عَظَمَتِهِ فَانْظُرُوا إِلَى عَظِيمِ خَلْقِهِ.

'An Abi Ja'far (as) qala: "Iyakum wat tafakkaru fillahi wa lakin idha aradtum an tunzaro ila 'azamatihi fanzaro ila 'azimi khalqihi."

Abu Ja'far said, "Beware of tafakkur in God. But if you wish to view His grandeur, observe the great of His creations."

Keep the Love of Prophet Muhammad ﷺ

Then Allah ﷻ describes and says, 'The best of creation is Sayyidina Muhammad ﷺ.' Say, 'Ya Rabbi, then I want to contemplate the greatness of Prophet ﷺ.' Then they come and inspire within your heart that is a very high station, better you keep your love for Prophet ﷺ, keep

your practices for Prophet ﷺ, perfect your manners and your character for Prophet ﷺ. But focus now on what Allah ﷻ describes as the Holy Face. Everything perishes but the Holy Face. And these are the faces of *rijal Allah* (men of God).

﴿كُلُّ شَيْءٍ هَالِكٌ إِلَّا وَجْهَهُ ۚ ﴾ ۸۸

28:88 – "...*kullu shayin halikun illa wajha*" (Surat Al-Qasas)

"...*Everything (that exists) will perish except His holy Face...*" (The Stories, 28:88)

Keep the Company of the Sadiqeen Physically and Spiritually

As soon as you're making your *tafakkur* (contemplation) and asking, 'Ya Rabbi, I want to be nothing, I want to be nothing, I want to be nothing. I'm coming to the love of Sayyidina Muhammad ﷺ, I'm coming to the love of Prophet ﷺ, Ya Rabbi, dress me from those whom you're pleased with. Dress me and make my Islam to be real, my Qur'an to be real'. And Allah ﷻ says, "*Ittaqullah*,

wa kono ma'as sadiqeen." 'Have *taqwa*, have *taqwa*, My servant, and keep the company of the *sadiqeen*.'

يَا أَيُّهَا الَّذِينَ آمَنُوا اتَّقُوا اللهَ وَكُونُوا مَعَ الصَّادِقِينَ ﴿١١٩﴾

9:119 – "Ya ayyuhal ladheena amanoo ittaqollaha wa kono ma'as sadiqeen." (Surat At-Tawbah)

"*O you who have believed, have consciousness of Allah and be with those who are truthful/ Pious / sincere (in words and deed)."*
(The Repentance, 9:119)

Did Allah clarify that you had to be physically? No, because Allah is not a limited talk. Allah's Words are eternal. So, the order from Allah is, 'Keep the company of My truthful servants, who are truthful in character and in deed.' As soon as you want to keep their company, you're asking, '*Ya Rabbi*, let me to be in their company.'

Focus on the Holy Face of RijalAllah (Men of God)

Allah said then everything that perishes except their holy face (Holy Qur'an, 28:88) Then, '*Ya Rabbi*, let me to be dressed by their holy face.' That's why we said before then there are seven realities on the holy face. "*Wa laqad karamna Bani Adam,*" that Allah describes that, 'This honour I've given to Bani Adam, it's a dress  upon his face. And in warfare, you cannot strike the face of somebody. Why? Because I created creation in My Image.'

How a Star is Born — Perfection Through Powers of the Heart

وَلَقَدْ كَرَّمْنَا بَنِي آدَمَ... ﴿٧٠﴾

17:70 – *"Wa laqad karramna bani adama…"* (Surat Al-Isra)

"And We have certainly honored the children of Adam…"
(The Night Journey, 17:70)

عَنْ أَبِي هُرَيْرَةَ، قَالَ: عَنِ النَّبِيّ صَلَّى اللهُ عَلَيْهِ وَسَلَّمَ قَالَ: "إِذَا قَاتَلَ أَحَدُكُمْ أَخَاهُ، فَلْيَجْتَنِبِ الْوَجْهَ. فَإِنَّ اللهَ خَلَقَ آدَمَ عَلَىٰ صُورَتِهِ". رواه مسلم

'An Abi Hurayrah (ra) 'anin Nabi (saws) Qala: "Iza qatala ahadukum akhahu, fal yajtanebil wajha. FainAllaha khalaqa Adama 'ala Soratihi." [Rawahi Muslim]

Abu Hurayrah (as) said that the Messenger of Allah (peace and blessings of Allah be upon him) said: "When anyone fights his brother, let him avoid the face, for Allah created Adam in His image." [Muslim (2612)]

Seven Eternal Flames and Emerald Throne

'I created creation in My Image.' What does that mean is that divine attributes – there are seven divine attributes that are dressing the holy face. And in the Book of Revelation, John went up and said, 'I saw the emerald throne,' like the turban you have. He saw the emerald throne and seven eternal flames. Every book has that reality, that everything perishes but the holy face.

Divine Attributes on the Holy Face of Awliya

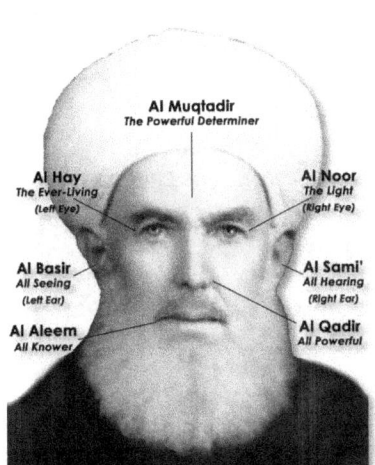

Allah ﷻ says, 'Everything perishes but the holy face' (Holy Qur'an, 28:88). Why? Because there are seven divinely essences that dress the seven openings of the servant's face. These *shuyukh* and these *awliyaullah* (saints), they are completely in that dress of that reality. Their ears are dressed by divine attribute, one attribute on the right ear, and one attribute on the left ear. The breath is dressed by a divine attribute, the speech is a divine attribute. The right eye and left eye are divine attributes, and upon the forehead is a divine attribute. It means that seven divine essences are dressing the servant.

﴿٨٨﴾ ...كُلُّ شَيْءٍ هَالِكٌ إِلَّا وَجْهَهُ ۚ لَهُ الْحُكْمُ وَإِلَيْهِ تُرْجَعُونَ

28:88 – "...*kullu shayin halikun illa wajha*" (Surat Al-Qasas)

"...*Everything (that exists) will perish except His holy Face.*"
(The Stories, 28:88)

Allah ﷻ is dressing the face of these servants with these seven divinely attributes. As soon as they begin their *tafakkur* and they've taken a way in a *turuq*, (spiritual path) then Allah ﷻ with '*Izzatullah* and Allah's ﷻ Permission begin to allow that servant a glimpse of the face of these *awliyaullah*, which is very difficult to achieve. It's not something so simple; but Allah ﷻ has to give a permission that in your *tafakkur* (contemplation), when you're consistent and you're sincere, and you're asking to be nothing and you're asking for the love of Prophet ﷺ, and, 'I'm following my guide; *ya Rabbi*, let me to be in the presence of that face that You blessed and You dressed and You made it to be honourable.'

Haqqiqatut Tawajju (Focusing)
Shaykh Opens the Hearing and Seeing of the Student

As soon as the servant is making *tafakkur*, then Allah ﷻ begins to open, 'I'm going to let that servant have from My Hearing and from My seeing.'

...وَلَا يَزَالُ عَبْدِي يَتَقَرَّبُ إِلَيَّ بِالنَّوَافِلِ حَتَّى أُحِبَّهُ، فَإِذَا أَحْبَبْتُهُ كُنْت سَمْعَهُ الَّذِي يَسْمَعُ بِهِ، وَبَصَرَهُ الَّذِي يُبْصِرُ بِهِ،. "رَوَاهُ الْبُخَارِيُّ...

"..., wa la yazaalu 'Abdi yataqarrabu ilayya bin nawafile hatta ahebahu, fa idha ahbabtuhu kunta Sam'ahul ladhi yasma'u behi, wa Basarahul ladhi yubsiru behi..."

"...My servant continues to draw near to Me with voluntary acts of worship so that I shall love him. When I love him, I am his hearing with which he hears, his seeing with which he sees..."
(Hadith Qudsi, Sahih al-Bukhari, 81:38:2)

He's going to start seeing from his heart the *tawajju* (focusing). The *tawajju* means he's going to begin to witness the face of the Shaykh. And his relationship will not only be physically with the Shaykh, but more important and much more powerful, is spiritually he is with the Shaykh, because in all his *tawajju* (focusing) is in his presence.

That is a phone from Allah ﷻ given to the guides. That you're not the people who have to make a physical phone call. Your call is a spiritual call, because they're going now into the reality of their heart, where Allah ﷻ is saying that,

'I'm in the heart of My believer. You're coming into My Kingdom in your heart. In My Kingdom, we don't use an external mobile phone, we use the internal satellite phone.'

مَا وَسِعَنِيْ لَا سَمَائِيْ ولا أَرْضِيْ وَلَكِنْ وَسِعَنِيْ قَلْبِ عَبْدِيْ اَلْمُؤْمِنْ

"Maa wasi'anee laa Samayee, wa la ardee, laakin wasi'anee qalbi 'Abdee al Mu'min."

"Neither My Heavens nor My Earth can contain Me, but the heart of my Believing Servant."

As soon as you close your eyes, the Shaykh's face is right there. That *tawajju* (focusing) means he is making his contact; he's being dressed by these seven attributes at all time upon his soul, upon his face, making his face to be noble as the nobility of his Shaykh's face. Because they're all in the face of Sayyidina Muhammad ﷺ; they're all being dressed by *nur al anwar wa sirat al asrar* (light of every secret and the secret of every light).

Haqqiqat al Tawassul (Reality of Conveying) from Soul to Soul

As a result of the *haqqiqat al tawajju*, you're now been given an ability slowly, slowly, for *haqqiqat al tawassul*. *Tawassul* is to convey. When you're able to log on with your soul's face, with your soul to their connection, it means then everything you ask them is a *tawassul*. You are able to convey what needs to be conveyed from your soul to your soul's connection, the connection which Allah ﷻ gave.

Allah's ﷻ *Azimat* (Greatness) is beyond the Apple phone. Allah ﷻ doesn't need anything from this physical world, nor does He want us to rely upon it. He said, 'I gave you all the technology within your heart. If you open your heart and approach with sincerity, then that Shaykh will

How a Star is Born – Perfection Through Powers of the Heart

begin to open the *haqqaiq* of *tawajju*, *haqqaiq* of *tawassul*. As soon as they have that power of *tawassul*, this means then they're beginning now to convey. In their *tafakkur* (contemplation), whatever needs to be conveyed.

As soon as you ask them for *du'a* (supplication), they are conveying that *du'a* into that association, and they take that *du'a* (supplication) to Prophet ﷺ, Prophet ﷺ immediately takes to Allah ﷻ; that's in their hands. The *tawassul* is a means just to convey. The result is always from Allah ﷻ.

It means these realities that they're opening upon the heart and upon the soul, these are the realities of a star; on how to reach that perfection, how to be dressed and blessed by that perfection.

We pray that Allah ﷻ grant us a long life to see the holy month of Rajab, the holy month of Shaban, the holy month of Ramadan, to be dressed by these realities and for the heart to have more and more understandings to approach these realities.

Subhana rabbika rabbal 'izzati 'amma yasifoon, wa salaamun 'alal mursaleen, walhamdulillahi rabbil 'aalameen. Bi hurmati Muhammad al-Mustafa wa bi siri Surat al-Fatiha.

Two Faces of the Moon and the Sun of Creation Reality of Hijrah and The Cave

Hijrah (Migration) to City of Light – Muhammadan Kingdom

Alhamdulillah, as a reminder for myself that this, the holy month of Muharram, has so many realities, so much importance, every moment is an immense blessing. That its power and its significance, that even the *Hijrah* of Prophet ﷺ, means the migration of Prophet ﷺ, is marked by the holy month of Muharram. When Prophet ﷺ was  given permission to begin the Nation of Islam and to move from oppression and to establish the City of Light, *Madina tul Munawwarah*. This means that everything, remember from a physical but more important for us is from *malakut* (heavenly realm), that which is eternal. That every movement of Prophet ﷺ is moving the entire Nation and Creation towards the Muhammadan Reality in Paradise.

'Thy Kingdom Come Thy Will be done on Earth as it is in Heaven.' The Kingdom of Allah ﷻ is the Kingdom of Sayyidina Muhammad ﷺ. As Prophet ﷺ is the 'King of all Created Universes', then every movement on *dunya* (material world) must be a reflection of that reality, of *akhirah* (afterlife), like a shadowing and mirroring. That when Prophet ﷺ is going to establish now the City of Light. It means open for the Kingdom of Lights and the reality of Lights to be on this *dunya* (material world), where Allah (swt) says, *"wa ma arsalnaka illa rahmatan lil 'alameen,"* (I would not have sent him except as the *Rahmah* of *'Aalameen* of all Creation), these steps are necessary for Creation. No Creation, no Prophet, no angel can reach its reality until the physicality of Prophet ﷺ comes and moves first.

وَمَا أَرْسَلْنَاكَ إِلَّا رَحْمَةً لِّلْعَالَمِينَ ﴿١٠٧﴾

21:107 – *"Wa maa arsalnaka illa Rahmatan lil'alameen."*
(Surat Al-Anbiya)

"And We have not sent you, [O Muhammad], except as a mercy to the worlds." (The Prophets, 21:107)

Allah (swt) Shows His Signs Upon the Horizon – The Sun and the Moon

Then *alhamdulillah*, *awliyaullah* (saints) are inspiring within our hearts that all of Holy Qur'an is describing, 'I will show you the Signs upon the horizon and I show you within your self.'

سَنُرِيهِمْ آيَاتِنَا فِي الْآفَاقِ وَفِي أَنفُسِهِمْ حَتَّىٰ يَتَبَيَّنَ لَهُمْ أَنَّهُ الْحَقُّ ۗ ... ﴿٥٣﴾

41:53 – *"Sanureehim ayatina fil afaqi wa fee anfusihim hatta yatabayyana lahum annahu alhaqqu..."* (Surat Al-Isra)

"We will show them Our signs in the horizons and within themselves until it becomes clear to them that it is the truth..."
(The Night Journey, 41:53)

Within the self is the most difficult to know oneself. The sign upon the horizon is Allah ﷻ saying, *Shamsi wal qamar, Shamsi wal qamar, Shamsi wal qamar. Alhamdulillah,* from Surat YaSeen, which is the heart of this reality, the heart of all realities, is the heart of Holy Qur'an. Allah ﷻ describes the 'Sun and the Moon', that the Sun is always represented by masculine as a source of Light and *Nur,* and the Moon is the reflection of that light.

وَالشَّمْسُ تَجْرِي لِمُسْتَقَرٍّ لَّهَا ۚ ذَٰلِكَ تَقْدِيرُ الْعَزِيزِ الْعَلِيمِ ﴿٣٨﴾ وَالْقَمَرَ قَدَّرْنَاهُ مَنَازِلَ حَتَّىٰ عَادَ كَالْعُرْجُونِ الْقَدِيمِ ﴿٣٩﴾

36:38-39 – "Wash Shamsu tajree li mustaqarrin laha, Dhalika taqdeerul 'Azizil 'Aleem. (38) Wal Qamara qaddarnahu manazila hatta 'ada kal 'urjoonil qadeem. (39)" (Surat YaSeen)

"And the sun runs his course for a period determined for him: that is the decree of (Him), the Exalted in Might, the All-Knowing. (38) And the Moon, We have measured for her mansions (to traverse) till she returns like the Ancient (and withered) lower part of a date-stalk. (39)" (YaSeen, 36:38-39)

The Sun is the Source of Fire (Diya), The Moon Reflects that Light (Nur)

Allah ﷻ says in Qur'an, *"Ash Shamsi wad diyaa, wal Qamari wan Noor."* (Holy Qur'an, 10:5). It means the *Shams,* the Sun is a *diya,* is a fire. In daytime we call it *nahar,* which means the fire. The *qamar,* the moon is a *nur,* it is not a source of light but merely a reflection.

هُوَ الَّذِي جَعَلَ الشَّمْسَ ضِيَاءً وَالْقَمَرَ نُورًا وَقَدَّرَهُ مَنَازِلَ لِتَعْلَمُوا عَدَدَ السِّنِينَ وَالْحِسَابَ ۚ مَا خَلَقَ اللَّـهُ ذَٰلِكَ إِلَّا بِالْحَقِّ ۚ يُفَصِّلُ الْآيَاتِ لِقَوْمٍ يَعْلَمُونَ ﴿٥﴾

Two Faces of the Moon and the Sun of Creation
Reality of Hijrah and The Cave

10:5 – *"Huwal ladhee ja'alash shamsa Diya an wal qamara Nooran wa qaddarahu manazila lita'lamo 'adadas sineena wal hisaba, ma khalaqa Allahu dhalika illa bilhaqqi, yufassilul ayati liqawmin ya'lamoon." (Surat Yunus)*

"It is He who made the Sun a Source Like Fire and the Moon a Reflected light and determined for it phases - that you may know the number of years and account [of time]. Allah has not created this except in truth. He details the signs for a people who know." (Jonah, 10:5)

The Sun and the Moon Don't Overtake Each Other

That begins to open the understanding of the relationship of Sun and Moon, which Allah ﷻ says, 'They don't overtake each other, they know their place.'

لَا الشَّمْسُ يَنبَغِي لَهَا أَن تُدْرِكَ الْقَمَرَ وَلَا اللَّيْلُ سَابِقُ النَّهَارِ ۚ وَكُلٌّ فِي فَلَكٍ يَسْبَحُونَ ﴿٤٠﴾

36:40 – *"La ash Shamsu yanbaghee laha an tudrikal Qamara wa lal laylu sabiqu annahari, wa kullun fee falakin yasbahon." (Surat YaSeen)*

"It is not permitted to the Sun to catch up the Moon, nor can the Night outstrip the Day: Each (just) Ship Sailing along in (its own) orbit (according to Law)." (YaSeen, 36:40)

It means then it is an important *isharat* (sign) to try to understand and study the importance of the Sun, the importance of the Moon. That the Moon is always following the Sun and perfecting itself as a 'source of reflection' from that reality.

وَالشَّمْسِ وَضُحَاهَا ﴿١﴾ وَالْقَمَرِ إِذَا تَلَاهَا ﴿٢﴾ وَالنَّهَارِ إِذَا جَلَّاهَا ﴿٣﴾ وَاللَّيْلِ إِذَا يَغْشَاهَا ﴿٤﴾

91:1-4 – "Wash Shamsi wa duhaha. (1) Wal Qamari idha talaha. (2) Wan nahari idha jallaha. (3) Wal layli idha yaghshaha. (4)" (Surat Ash-Shams)

"By the Sun and his (glorious) Brightness; (1) By the Moon as she follows him; (2) By the Day as it shows up (the Sun's) glory; (3) By the Night as it conceals it. (4)" (The Sun, 91:1-4)

Sayyidina Muhammad ﷺ is the Sun of Creation and His Companions Are the Moons

Then the *hijrah* (migration) has an importance and the reality of the *hijrah* when Prophet ﷺ wants to establish the importance of light. Because the 'Moon' are the Companions and Sayyidina Muhammad ﷺ is 'the Sun'. Sayyidina Muhammad ﷺ is "Sirajan Munira."

يَا أَيُّهَا النَّبِيُّ إِنَّا أَرْسَلْنَاكَ شَاهِدًا وَمُبَشِّرًا وَنَذِيرًا ﴿٤٥﴾ وَدَاعِيًا إِلَى اللَّـهِ بِإِذْنِهِ وَسِرَاجًا مُنِيرًا ﴿٤٦﴾

33:45-46 – "Ya ayyuhan Nabiyu inna arsalnaka shahidan wa mubashshiran wa nadheera. (45) Wa daiyan ila Allahi'bi-idhnihi wa Sirajan Muneera. (46)" (Surat Al-Azhab)

"O Prophet, indeed We have sent you as a witness and a bringer of good tidings and a warner. (45) And one who invites to Allah, by His permission, and an illuminating lamp (that gives light)." (The Combined Forces, 33:45-46)

Where Allah ﷻ says throughout Holy Qur'an, *'Huda*, a Light of Guidance.' Everything related to the reality of Prophet ﷺ is based on

Two Faces of the Moon and the Sun of Creation
Reality of Hijrah and The Cave

light. It means that the reality of Prophet ﷺ is representing the 'Sun' of our lives, the Sun of Creation, and the 'Sun' of all the Companions.

اللَّـهُ نُورُ السَّمَاوَاتِ وَالْأَرْضِ ۚ مَثَلُ نُورِهِ كَمِشْكَاةٍ فِيهَا مِصْبَاحٌ ۖ الْمِصْبَاحُ فِي زُجَاجَةٍ ۖ الزُّجَاجَةُ كَأَنَّهَا كَوْكَبٌ دُرِّيٌّ ... نُورٌ عَلَىٰ نُورٍ ۗ يَهْدِي اللَّـهُ لِنُورِهِ مَن يَشَاءُ ۚ وَيَضْرِبُ اللَّـهُ الْأَمْثَالَ لِلنَّاسِ ۗ وَاللَّـهُ بِكُلِّ شَيْءٍ عَلِيمٌ ٣٥

24:35 – "Allahu noorus samawati wal ardi. mathalu noorehi kamishkatin feeha misbahun, almisbahu fee zujajatin, azzujajatu kaannaha kawkabun durriyyun ... noorun 'ala noorin. yahdellahu linoorihi man yashao. Wa yadribullah ul amthala linnasi, wallahu bikulli shayin 'Aleem." (Surat An-Nur)

"Allah is the Light of the heavens and the earth. The Parable of His Light is as if there were a Niche and within it a Lamp: the Lamp enclosed in Glass: the glass as it were a brilliant star: ...Light upon Light! Allah guides whom He will to His Light: Allah present examples for the people: and Allah knows all things." (The Light, 24:35)

Family of Prophet ﷺ Are the Full Moons

We say in the *Salawats* (praisings upon Prophet ﷺ), *"Tala 'al badru 'alayna, wa ahlil badr"* (O' the full moon rose above us), *"wa Ahlul Badr"* (people of the full moon.)

طَلَعَ الْبَدْرُ عَلَيْنَا   مِنْ ثَنِيَّاتِ الْوَدَاع
وَجَبَ الشُّكْرُ عَلَيْنَا   مَا دَعَا لِلهِ دَاع

Tala'al badru 'alayna   *Min thaniyatil wada'a*
Wa jabash shukuru 'alayna   *Ma da'aa lillahi da'a*

O' the full moon rose above us, From the valley of Wada'
Gratitude is our obligation, as long as any caller calls to Allah

And

وَ بِالْهَادِى رَسُولِ اللهِ   تَوَسَّلْنَا بِبِسْمِ الله
بِأَهْلِ الْبَدْرِ يَا الله   وَ كُلِّ الْمُجَاهِدِينَ لِلَّه

Tawassalna bi bismillah   Wa bil Hadi Rasulillah
Wa kulli mujahidin lillah   Bi ahlil badri ya Allah

We sought by means of bismillah,
And by the Guide, Messenger of Allah.
And everyone striving in God's Way,
By means of the family of the full moon.

This means all of that was about the 'Moon and the *Ahlul Badr*' which they translate as the 'Family of Prophet ﷺ', meaning all the *ashiqeen* (lovers). *"Qul in kuntum tuhibbonallaha fattabioonee"* (Say, [O Muhammad], 'If you should love Allah, then follow me...'). Allah ﷻ says, 'as My Moons follow the Sun' because that is an imitated light, and that is an imitated Creation. That which is real is *Nurul Muhammadi* ﷺ (Light of Prophet ﷺ. That which is eternal, is *Nurul Muhammadi* ﷺ.

قُلْ إِن كُنتُمْ تُحِبُّونَ اللَّهَ فَاتَّبِعُونِي يُحْبِبْكُمُ اللَّهُ وَيَغْفِرْ لَكُمْ ذُنُوبَكُمْ ۗ وَاللَّهُ غَفُورٌ رَّحِيمٌ ﴿٣١﴾

3:31 – *"Qul in kuntum tuhibbon Allaha fattabi'onee, yuhbibkumUllahu wa yaghfir lakum dhunobakum wallahu Ghaforur Raheem."* (Surat 'Ali 'Imran)

Two Faces of the Moon and the Sun of Creation
Reality of Hijrah and The Cave

"*Say, [O Muhammad], 'If you should love Allah, then follow me, [so] Allah will love you and forgive you your sins. And Allah is Forgiving and Merciful'.*" (Family of Imran, 3:31)

Be Like the Moon –
Follow the Sun of Sayyidina Muhammad ﷺ

Allah ﷻ is showing, 'Look to the best of examples on what your life should be, be like the moon, like the Companions and all the *Sahabah*.' That is why we sing these *nasheeds*, they are not songs, they are praisings and Divine Realities. When we are reciting them, they are like 'seeds' on the soul that begin to dress the soul of its realities. We say, "*Tala 'al badru 'alayna*", "*wa ahlil badr, wa ahlil badr, wa ahlil badr*" (family of the Full moon – Prophet Muhammad ﷺ).

فَكَمْ مِنْ رَحْمَةٍ حَصَلَتْ
وَ كَمْ مِنْ نِعْمَةٍ وَصَلَتْ
وَكَمْ مِنْ ذِلَّةٍ فَصَلَتْ
بِأَهْلِ الْبَدْرِ يَا الله

Fakam min rahmatin hasalat   *Wa kam min dhillatin fasalat*
Wa kam min ni'matin wasalat   *Bi ahlil badri ya Allah*

How many mercies have occurred! And how many humiliations were lifted! How many favours have been granted! By means of the family of the full moon (Prophet Muhammad ﷺ), O Allah ﷻ.

It is a sign for us; 'Be from the people of the Moon', that make your whole life focus on the Sun. 'I am following the Sun, I am following the *Nur* (Light).' Within the source and the power of that *Nur* is Allah ﷻ, no doubt! The power of that Light is the Divinely Essence. But like the Moon, follow it. Follow the moon and never overtake your *Imam*

(Leader). Where Allah ﷻ describes the Moon never overtakes the place of the Sun.

لَا الشَّمْسُ يَنبَغِي لَهَا أَن تُدْرِكَ الْقَمَرَ وَلَا اللَّيْلُ سَابِقُ النَّهَارِ ۚ وَكُلٌّ فِي فَلَكٍ يَسْبَحُونَ ﴿٤٠﴾

36:40 – *"La ash Shamsu yanbaghee laha an tudrikal Qamara wa lal laylu sabiqu annahari, wa kullun fee falakin yasbahon."* (Surat YaSeen)

"It is not permitted to the Sun to catch up the Moon, nor can the Night outstrip the Day: Each (just) Ship Sailing along in (its own) orbit (according to Law)." (YaSeen, 36:40)

Sun and Moon Are Like Ships Swimming in Their Own Orbit

They both move and they swim in an orbit (Holy Qur'an, 36:40). And Allah ﷻ uses the word *"fulk"*. *Fulk* is a ship, that the Moons are a 'ship', and they go directly on a path because these *fulk*, [Shaykh points to the *Shams al Arifeen* diagram] they are moving as a ship on an orbit.

... وَكُلٌّ فِي فَلَكٍ يَسْبَحُونَ ﴿٤٠﴾

36:40 – *"...wa kullun fee falakin yasbahoon."* (Surat YaSeen)

"...Each (just) swims/floats along in (its own) orbit." (YaSeen, 36:40)

They have an exact path in which they are traversing the Muhammadan Reality and the next *ayat* (verse), Allah ﷻ describes the reality of that boat and ship, 'They are the loaded ships.' It means that these realities carry the realities of souls and guidance and they are moving and traversing that reality.

Two Faces of the Moon and the Sun of Creation
Reality of Hijrah and The Cave

وَآيَةٌ لَهُمْ أَنَّا حَمَلْنَا ذُرِّيَّتَهُمْ فِي الْفُلْكِ الْمَشْحُونِ ﴿٤١﴾

36:41 – *"Wa ayatul lahum anna hamalna dhurriyyatahum fil fulkil mashhooni."* (Surat YaSeen)

"And a sign for them is that We carried their forefathers in the Loaded ship." (YaSeen, 36:41)

The Two Faces of the Moon in Hijrah (Migration) of Prophet ﷺ

How we understand that in the opening of Muharram is that Prophet ﷺ wants to establish the City of Light. He is preparing now to move towards *Madinatul Munawarrah,* and two very important events take place.

1. Imam 'Ali ؑ Lay in Bed to Be Sacrificed

One is representing the reality of *Ahlul Bayt* (family of Prophet ﷺ) and Imam Ali ؑ that (he said), '*Sayyidi, ya Rasulullah* ﷺ, they are coming to kill you. Let us take our role as your Family and we lie within your bed and let us to be sacrificed.' *"Fasalli li rabbika wanhar"* (Holy Qur'an, 108:1-2), because these are *Ahlul Kawthar* means this is all Muharram.

إِنَّا أَعْطَيْنَاكَ الْكَوْثَرَ ﴿١﴾ فَصَلِّ لِرَبِّكَ وَانْحَرْ ﴿٢﴾

108:1-2 – *"Inna 'atayna kal kawthar. Fasali li rabbika wanhar."* (Surat Al-Kawthar)

"To thee (O Muhammad) we have granted the Fount (of Abundance). (1) So pray to your Lord and Sacrifice. (2)" (The Abundance, 108:1-2)

Imam Ali is coming and saying, 'We are from *Ahlul Kawthar*', *"fasalli li rabbika wanhar."* 'We prayed unto our Lord and we are ready to sacrifice ourselves and we lie within the bed. Take your place and your position, establish your kingdom on Earth, establish the City of Light which Allah wants you to establish. And take your complete *Siddiq*, your *Khalil*, your friend and Companion,' means the perfection of your character.

Then Sayyidina 'Ali is lying in bed taking the place of Sayyidina Muhammad so that Prophet can escape and move towards *Madinatul Munawwarah*. This was all in the first ten days of Muharram. Before entering into the city on *Ashura*, Prophet stayed in the Holy Cave with Sayyidina Abu Bakr as-Siddiq . It means then the importance of *Naqshbandiya til 'Aliya*, how it carries that reality. [The Naqshbandi *tariqah* is taking from Sayyidina Abu Bakr as-Siddiq].

There is No Mistake About the First Khalifa (Vicegerents) of Prophet Muhammad

Sayyidina 'Ali is representing, 'I am hidden and that is our place, the Family's place,' because these are the Moons [the Twelve Imams representing the 12 months in the *Shams al Arifeen* diagram]. This is a perfection of the moon that is happening on the first month.

Two Faces of the Moon and the Sun of Creation
Reality of Hijrah and The Cave

عَنْ جَابِرِ بْنِ سَمَرَةٍ قَالَ: قَالَ رَسُولُ اللهِ ﷺ: «لَا تُزَالُ هَذِهِ الْأُمَّةِ مُسْتَقِيمًا أَمْرَهَا ظَاهِرَةٌ عَلَى عَدُوِّهَا حَتَّى يَمْضِي اِثْنَا عَشَرَ خَلِيفَةً وَسَمِعْتُ كَلَامًا مِنَالنَّبِيِّ ﷺ لَمْ أَفْهَمْهُ، فَقُلْتُ لِأَبِي: مَايَقُولُ؟

.قَالَ: كُلُّهُمْ مِنْ قُرَيْشٍ

رَوَاهُ الْبُخَارِيُّ (رَقْمَ/ 7222) وَمُسْلِمٌ وَاللَّفْظُ لَهُ (رَقْمَ /1821

'An Jabir ibn Samaratin Qala: Qala Rasulullahi (saws): "La tuzalu hazihil ummati mustaqiman amraha zahiratu 'ala 'aduwwata hatta yamdi ithna 'ashshara Khalifatun."
Wwa sami'at kalaman minnan Nabiyi (saws) lam afhimahu. Faqultu li abiyi: Ma yaqolu? Qala: "Kulluhum min Quraysh."
[Rawahul Bukhariyu wa Muslimun wa lafzu lahu]

It was narrated that Jaabir ibn Samurah said: I entered upon the Prophet (pbuh) with my father, and I heard him say: "This matter will not end until there have been among them twelve caliphs."
Then he said something that I could not hear, and I said to my father: What did he say? He said: "All of them will be from Quraysh."
[Narrated by al-Bukhaari (no. 7222); based on the wording of Imam Muslim (no. 1821)].

In the first month is the first physical *Khalifa*. The face of the Nation are the *Khulafa ir Rashideen wal Mahdiyeen* (the Perfected Guides and Leaders). The first of them is Sayyidina Abu Bakr as-Siddiq ﷺ. There is no mistake. There is no confusion because in the beginning of Muharram, Imam 'Ali ﷺ is describing, 'No, no, I wasn't going to go and Sayyidina Abu Bakr ﷺ was supposed to stay behind.' From that time Sayyidina Abu Bakr as-Siddiq ﷺ was to go, he is the face of this reality, and he must accompany Sayyidina Muhammad ﷺ. (Imam 'Ali ﷺ is saying), 'My position is to be hidden. We sacrifice ourselves for that reality and we carry the Family secret of Sayyidina Muhammad ﷺ.'

They begin to teach there is 'no mistake'. There is 'no confusion'. Anyone who believes there was a mistake what they are coming against is Allah (AJ). Allah (AJ) wrote everything perfectly. They are all in *taslim* (submission) and they begin to show the highest level of reality. We know the reality; our position was to sacrifice. So Sayyidina 'Ali (AS), Imam 'Ali (AS), leads a life of sacrifice. As soon as he lay himself to represent Sayyidina Muhammad ﷺ when they came to kill, Allah (AJ) didn't allow even a hair of Sayyidina 'Ali (AS) to be touched. What happened? He was released and Sayyidina 'Ali (AS) went into *Madinatul Munawwarah*.

Imam 'Ali (AS) – The Hidden Face of the Moon

This means big sign of the Moon, the side of the Moon that you never see. You know there is a face of the Moon that always follows the Earth, because this is an *isharat* (sign) from the Heavens. That the Sun and the Moon are always together. They are constantly moving in a pattern; wherever the Sun goes the Moon is following. Wherever the Sun is shining, and the Sun becomes non-visible to humanity, the Moon is

shining and representing the Muhammadan Reality.

It means the Companions represent completely the reality of Prophet ﷺ always to Creation. And those who wish to follow that example what they describe as *awliyaullah* (saints), *saliheen* (righteous), and those who are *muhsin* and pious, they follow the way of the Moon. The reality of the Moon is that, 'purify yourself and direct yourself always to the light and that which is eternal.' It leaves us to understand the complete path, and the movement; that when Imam 'Ali (AS) sacrificed and moved into *Madinatul Munawwarah* and Sayyidina Abu Bakr as-Siddiq ؓ went with Prophet ﷺ to the Holy Cave.

2. Sayyidina Abu Bakr as-Siddiq ؓ and Reality of Holy Cave

Sayyidina Abu Bakr as-Siddiq ؓ accompanied Prophet ﷺ to the Holy Cave *(Thawr).*

إِلَّا تَنصُرُوهُ فَقَدْ نَصَرَهُ اللَّهُ إِذْ أَخْرَجَهُ الَّذِينَ كَفَرُوا ثَانِيَ اثْنَيْنِ إِذْ هُمَا فِي الْغَارِ إِذْ يَقُولُ لِصَاحِبِهِ لَا تَحْزَنْ إِنَّ اللَّهَ مَعَنَا ۖ ...﴿٤٠﴾

9:40 – *"Illa tansuroohu faqad nasarahullahu idh akhrajahul ladheena kafaro thaniya ithnayni idh huma fil ghari idh yaqolu lisahibihi la tahzan inna Allaha ma'ana..." (Surat At-Tawbah)*

"If you do not aid the Prophet - Allah has already aided him when those who disbelieved had driven him out [of Makkah] as one of two, when they were in the cave and he said to his companion, Do not grieve; indeed Allah is with us..." (The Repentance, 9:40)

The reality of the Holy Cave is that it is a Cave of Realities. That Sayyidina Muhammad ﷺ wants to pour something into the heart of Sayyidina Abu Bakr as-Siddiq ؓ and says, 'He excels not because of his praying and fasting but what I have poured into the heart of Sayyidina Abu Bakr as-Siddiq ؓ', it happens.

مَا صَبَّ اللهُ فِيْ صَدْرِيْ شَيْءٍ إِلَّا وَ صَبَبْتُهُ فِيْ صَدْرِي أَبِيْ بَكْرٍ اَلصِّدِّيْقْ

"Ma sabAllahu fi Sadri shay an illa wa sababtuhu fi sadri Abi Bakr as-Siddiq."

Prophet (pbuh) said: *"Whatever I received, I poured in the heart of Abu Bakr as-Siddiq."*

It means this Muharram is teaching us the perfection of the Moon. That the face of the Moon; the face that you see from Sayyidina Abu Bakr as-Siddiq ؓ and the side of the Moon that you don't see; you don't see what Sayyidina 'Ali ؓ sacrificed and what he had put on the line for the love of Sayyidina Muhammad ﷺ. Both are essential. If not for the sacrifice of Sayyidina 'Ali ؓ, then the movement would have been impossible or difficult. Allah ﷻ wanted it that way. This means it opens a tremendous secret.

Tariqat Naqshbandiya Carries Secrets of Abu Bakr as-Siddiq ؓ and Imam 'Ali ؓ

That is why they say *Naqshbandiya til 'Aliya* (the most distinguished path) because it carries the reality of Sayyidina Abu Bakr as-Siddiq ؓ and carries the inheritance of Sayyidina 'Ali ؓ. Sayyidina Abu Bakr as Siddiq ؓ and his son Sayyidina Qasim are dressing *Naqshbandiya* way. Sayyidina 'Ali's ؓ secret is dressing *Naqshbandiyya til 'Aliya* through Sayyidina  Salman al-Farsi ؓ and through Imam Jaffar as-Sadiq ؓ, carrying the reality of the *Ahlul Bayt* (Family of Prophet ﷺ), carrying the hidden side of this moon, that it is always accompanying in perfection.

Reality of the Cave and Ashab al Kahf (Seven Sleepers)

That Sayyidina Abu Bakr as-Siddiq ؓ is accompanying Prophet ﷺ. What do you see then on the next month (*Safar* – second lunar month) is the month of the Cave, the *Ashab al Kahf*. Why? Because this is the reality within the Cave, that Sayyidina Abu Bakr as-Siddiq ؓ is in that Cave. If you want to reach the City of Light, you cannot go directly into that City, you must go into the 'Cave'. And in the Cave we are going to dress you and bless you. And Allah ﷻ describes *Ashab al Kahf* (People of the Cave) that, 'You have to seek refuge from the *shayateen* (devils) and from the evil desires, the evilness that is all around us.'

وَإِذِ اعْتَزَلْتُمُوهُمْ وَمَا يَعْبُدُونَ إِلَّا اللَّـهَ فَأْوُوا إِلَى الْكَهْفِ يَنشُرْ لَكُمْ رَبُّكُم مِّن رَّحْمَتِهِ وَيُهَيِّئْ لَكُم مِّنْ أَمْرِكُم مِّرْفَقًا ﴿١٦﴾

18:16 – *"Wa idhi' tazaltumo hum wa ma ya'budoona illAllaha fawoo ilal kahfi yanshur lakum rabbukum mir rahmatihi wa yuhayyi lakum min amrikum mirfaqa." (Surat Al-Kahf)*

"When you turn away from them and the things they worship other than Allah, betake yourselves to the Cave: Your Lord will shower His mercies on you and disposes of your affair towards comfort and ease."
(The Cave, 18:16)

It means all that evilness and wickedness that they want us to follow 'it'; we have to seek refuge in Allah ﷻ, move into the Cave of Realities and to become from the *Ashab al Kahf* (People of the Cave). Then from *Ashab al Kahf* it moves within that reality and dresses us and blesses us from that reality.

Reality of Spiderweb Covering the Door of the Cave

From Sayyidina Abu Bakr as-Siddiq ؑ perfecting the form. He is saying that, 'When you come to the Cave, what that Cave is going to represent  is that it had a door upon it from a spiderweb. These are all movements into the realities of oneself.' That is held by *Naqshbandiya til 'Aliya*. If you want to move into the Cave of understanding yourself, there was a block upon the Cave, so that when they came to look for Prophet ﷺ they couldn't come in. It was from *Ankabut*, it was a spider web.

A spiderweb because this Cave, they begin to code it and begin to decipher the code. Surat 29 of Holy Qur'an is *Ankabut*. When you read that *Surat* (chapter) and about the *Ankabut* (spider), that what type of a home Allah ﷻ describes it is such a fragile home, but it is such a beautiful creation. That when you look at it you marvel, '*Ya Rabbi*, what kind of guidance this spider has?' That he is better than the best architect.

Busy Yourself to Please Your Lord, Allah ﷻ Will Send Your Sustenance

The spider makes a perfect web, a perfect belief and he waits for Allah ﷻ to send sustenance. He is not hunting like a bear all day long in the marketplace. This now begins to tell us about ourselves that if you want to be from this reality, then don't busy yourself in the marketplace, running for money. But busy yourself like the spider, make that which is beautiful to Allah ﷻ, because this is now the entrance to the Cave.

Spend now your time in making that which is beautiful to Allah. Allah will send you flies. Some big, some smaller flies.

But if the web has a hole then the fly goes through. It means then we  busy ourselves perfecting yourself, perfecting our character, perfecting our *akhlaq* (character), doing our *zikr* (remembrance) and that which Allah is pleased with. Allah says, 'If I am pleased with you imagine how I send to the fly its sustenance, can I not send to you your sustenance?' Because we keep thinking, 'Maybe Allah forgot about us.' Allah is describing, 'I am not forgetting about a spider anywhere on this Earth. It makes its web, I send it its sustenance.' It means busy yourself with developing yourself and perfecting yourself.

Reality of Numbers and Divinely Codes

As soon as we understand that *Ankabut*, Surat 29, they begin to teach us in the understanding of numbers. Not numerology to know your name and who you are going to be marrying and how tall your kids are going to be. These are the sciences and the codings of Divine Code, where Allah says 'everything is numbered.'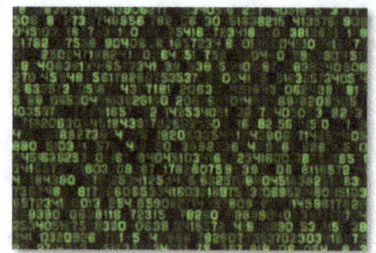

﴿٢٨﴾ ... وَأَحَاطَ بِمَا لَدَيْهِمْ وَأَحْصَىٰ كُلَّ شَيْءٍ عَدَدًا

72:28 – "...*wa ahata bima ladayhim wa ahsa kulla shay in 'adada.*" (Surat Al-Jinn)

"...and He has encompassed whatever is with them and has enumerated all things in number." (The Jinn 72:28)

Anyone who has studied software knows that everything is moving on a code. And somebody programmed it, which means the programmer is Allah ﷻ. Everything is perfectly numbered. Nothing can be random. If anything was random this whole universe would have collapsed.

92 is the Numeric Value of the Name of Sayyidina Muhammad ﷺ

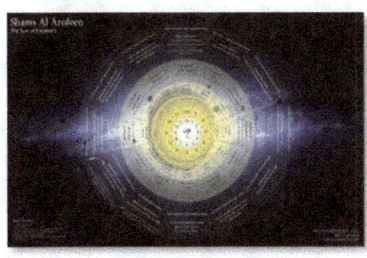

Allah ﷻ is describing that 29 is the reflection of 92 and 92 for people who understand the *huroof* (Arabic letters, numerology), that is 'Muhammad' ﷺ. They begin to teach that why the spider web because Allah ﷻ wanted us to know, 'See how this diagram looks like a spider web,' [Shaykh indicates the *Shams al Arifeen* diagram]. This was very nice. This 29 is the reflection of 92 in Paradise and to understand ourselves and what the reality of the spider is, to understand our sustenance, and how to beautify our lives. The only thing beautiful to Allah ﷻ is the *zikr* (remembrance) and *akhlaq* (good character).

محمد ﷺ			
Muhammad ﷺ			
د	م	ح	م
Daal	Meem	Haa	Meem
4	40	8	40
4+40+8+40 = 92			

Note: Please read English from right to left to coincide with Arabic.

Two Faces of the Moon and the Sun of Creation
Reality of Hijrah and The Cave

Dove With Two Eggs Represents Mulk (Created Universe) wa Malakut (Unseen Power of the Universe)

Then what you saw in the Cave was a dove with two eggs. Allah's ﷻ describing now that you enter this Cave, you are going to be the owner of these two Creations, *Mulk wa Malakut*. What is contained inside this reality is all the *Mulk* (earthly realm), all the created universes, and all the *Malakut* (heavenly realm) the unseen power of this universe, it's all going to be in the reality of this Cave.

Why Was There a Hole in the Cave?

As soon as we take our path into the Cave, we begin to read what

transpired within the Cave. That Sayyidina Abu Bakr as-Siddiq ؓ was sitting in the Cave and Sayyidina Muhammad ﷺ was with him and he put his holy head on his companion's knees and wants to rest. And there is a hole inside the Cave. And the great Siddiq ؓ of Allah ﷻ put his foot, his *qadam*, upon the hole. Because there was a snake that was coming into the Cave and the great Siddiq ؓ with his blessed *qadam* (foot) blocked the hole.

It means then our life and our understanding of life is that inside the Cave which is towards the reality of Sayyidina Muhammad ﷺ, you must be accompanied by these great *Siddiqs* (Truthful). Only their foot can block the hole of *Shaytan* (Satan) because *Shaytan* is under their dominion. *Shaytan* is asking from *'izzatullah, 'izzat ur Rasul wa 'izzaatal mu'mineen;* he has to have their permission.

﴿…وَلِلَّهِ الْعِزَّةُ وَلِرَسُولِهِ وَلِلْمُؤْمِنِينَ…﴾۸﴿

63:8 – "...Wa Lillahil 'izzatu wa li Rasooli hi wa lil Mumineen..." (Surat Al-Munafiqoon)

"...And to Allah belongs [all] honor, and to His messenger, and to the believers..." (The Hypocrites, 63:8)

Only the Qadam Siddiq (the Foot of the Truthful) Blocks Shaytan

The great Siddiq's ﷺ foot, he is teaching that, 'if you have the *qadam* and you take the path of my feet (follow on my footsteps), which was the complete love of the *Shams* (sun) of the Universe, meaning the complete love of Sayyidina Muhammad ﷺ, I am the face of the Moons. If you follow my way and your *siddiqiya* character, your truthful character, the love that you have for Sayyidina Muhammad ﷺ, I will perfect it inside and out. That if my foot is upon your foot, and my hand is upon your hand, I will block the hole of *Shaytan* and *Shaytan* has no access to you.' *Shaytan* only comes in our life when the foot begins to move. 'Oh, I am not going to listen, I am not going to follow.' As soon as you do not follow, there is this hole where *Shaytan* is coming out.

The Siddiqs Followed the Qadam ur RasulAllah (Footsteps of Prophet ﷺ)

Our whole life is to be on their *qadam*, *Qadam as-Siddiq*, the foot of the Truthful Ones and the great *Siddiq's* they are on *Qadam ar Rasul*. Mawlana Shaykh was talking and reminding us that the lives of the Prophets were so amazing that when Prophet ﷺ veiled himself from *dunya* (material world) the Companions walked completely wherever Prophet ﷺ walked. Why? Because they saw the light of Prophet ﷺ. If they went on a path they said, 'This is the way that Sayyidina Muhammad ﷺ went.' They walked exactly the same path because they saw the lights of the footsteps of Prophet ﷺ.

Now these crazy people who manage that area have destroyed all of the signs of that reality. They covered all the holy pathways and trails and put their stones and covered everything. But the Companions were seeing the steps of Prophet ﷺ. Why? Because they are teaching us that our *qadam* (feet) and steps are exactly on the steps which we saw Sayyidina Muhammad ﷺ take. On any journey that they went, they said if Prophet ﷺ went around the rock, they got off the camel and walked around the rock. Because for them, the *tabarak*, the blessings to see the light of Prophet ﷺ and step on that light meant to be dressed by that light, dressed by that *amal* (action), dressed by the reality of complete submission and following.

The Perfection of the Moon – Abu Bakr as-Siddiq ؓ and Imam 'Ali ؓ

This means that Sayyidina Abu Bakr as-Siddiq ؓ begins to teach, 'Come into this Cave of Realities. Come and understand how to activate the heart within your being, follow my example and my way.' As soon as they left the Cave they entered into the City of Light and who was waiting there for them? Sayyidina 'Ali ؓ.

أَنَا مَدِيْنَةُ الْعِلْمِ وَ عَلِيٌّ بَابُهَا

"*Ana madinatul 'ilmin wa 'Aliyyun baabuha.*"

"*I am the city of knowledge and 'Ali (as) is its door/gatekeeper.*" (Prophet Muhammad (pbuh))

It means now the completion and the perfection of that Moon; the face of the Moon from the Holy Companions and the reality of the Moon

from the Holy Family. Then there are twelve faces of the Holy Companions and twelve realities of the Holy Imams that are inheritors of Sayyidina Muhammad ﷺ. They are the perfection of that reality. From the beginning of Muharram is then the face of Sayyidina Abu Bakr as-Siddiq ؑ and the first *Imam*, the first reality of that is Imam 'Ali ؑ. That is why then the perfection of that reality.

When the Perfect Moon Split, Then the Nation Split

That is when the *Ummah*, the Nation, split. One called themselves something, another one called themselves something else. And the only one going to bring them back is then the last of the *Ahlul Bayt* (Family of Prophet ﷺ). That is the importance of Sayyidina Mahdi ؑ. Where this Nation went into two different, and they were not different.

Because Muharram represents the perfection that Sayyidina Abu Bakr as-Siddiq ؑ is the face, and the Companion, that says, 'I followed completely my Sun, my light, my guidance, the *huda, sirajan munira*.' And

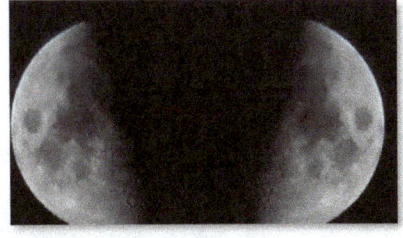

Sayyidina 'Ali ؑ says, 'I followed completely what Prophet ﷺ wanted for me as my Family inheritance, *"fasalli li rabbika wanhar"*, I sacrificed myself, I am that perfection.' The two together are the 'complete perfection'.

Two Faces of the Moon and the Sun of Creation
Reality of Hijrah and The Cave

إِنَّا أَعْطَيْنَاكَ الْكَوْثَرَ ﴿١﴾ فَصَلِّ لِرَبِّكَ وَانْحَرْ ﴿٢﴾

108:1-2 – *"Inna 'atayna kal kawthar. (1) Fasali li rabbika wanhar. (2)" (Surat Al-Kawthar)*

"To thee (O Muhammad) we have granted the Fount (of Abundance). (1) So pray to your Lord and Sacrifice. (2)" (The Abundance, 108:1-2)

This means Sayyidina 'Ali completely loved, respected, and understood Sayyidina Abu Bakr that you are the face and I am the side of the Moon that nobody sees. You will see me on the fourth Moon [Imam 'Ali was the 4th Khalifa]. There was no mistake, there was no confusion. They knew the reality and the reality transpired exactly the way Allah wanted it to transpire. It means then that anybody who comes against is actually coming against Allah, because Allah wanted it. That is the depth of that reality, the depth of what the dress of Muharram, the perfection of Muharram, the perfection of the first month of Muharram, which carries the secret and the face of Sayyidina Abu Bakr as-Siddiq, carries the secret of Imam 'Ali.

Naqshbandiya til 'Aliya (The Most Distinguished Path) is the Mahdi Tariqah

Naqshbandiya til 'Aliya is based on the two; it is the only *tariqah* (spiritual path) from Sayyidina Abu Bakr as-Siddiq and the only *tariqah* (spiritual path) that is taking the dress of Sayyidina 'Ali's Family's secret, not the Companions secrets. There are forty-two other *tariqahs* (spiritual paths) that carry the name of Imam 'Ali as a Companion but not from the realities of the Family inheritance. That secret, that inheritance, is given in *Naqshbandiya til 'Aliya* through Imam Ja'far as-Sadiq and that is why it is the *Mahdi Tariqah*.

The only *tariqah* (spiritual path) that teaches and preaches about Imam Mahdi ﷺ and that Sayyidina Mahdi ﷺ under the *tarbiya* (training) of those *awliyaullah* (saints) that was being taught by Sultan al-Awliya Mawlana Shaykh AbdAllah Faiz ad-Daghestani ق and Sultan al-Awliya Mawlana Shaykh Muhammad Nazim al-Haqqani ق and being dressed by those realities.

Imam Mahdi ﷺ Brings the Split Moon Back Together

When Imam Mahdi ﷺ appears, then it is the 'perfection of the moon' bringing these two different groups back together and teaching them this moon represents, 'We are the people who are completely in the love of the *Sunnah* of Sayyidina Muhammad ﷺ. And we are completely in the love of *Ahlul Bayt an-Nabi* ﷺ. That is the perfection of the Moon.'

If the Moon doesn't have the perfection and the love of the *Sunnah* (way of Prophet ﷺ) and the love of the *Ahlul Bayt* (Family of Prophet ﷺ), you are a split Moon. You can't do much with something split, it has to be brought back to be whole. That is why everybody is waiting for the arrival of Sayyidina Mahdi ﷺ, to bring back the moon, to bring back its authority, to bring back its reality.

عَنْ عَبْدِ اللهِ بن مسعود عَنْ النَّبِيِّ صَلَّى اللهُ عَلَيْهِ وَسَلَّمَ قَالَ : " لَا تَذْهَبُ أَوْ لَا تَنْقَضِي الدُّنْيَا حَتَّى يَمْلِكَ الْعَرَبَ رَجُلٌ مِنْ أَهْلِ بَيْتِي يُوَاطِئُ اسْمُهُ اسْمِي " مسند أحمد 199/5 ح 3573

Two Faces of the Moon and the Sun of Creation
Reality of Hijrah and The Cave

'An Abdillah bin Mas'ud, 'Anan Nabi (saws) qala:

"La tazhabu aw la tanqadid dunya hatta ymlikal 'araba rajulun min ahlil bayti yuwatiyu ismuhu ismi." (Musanad Ahmad)

AbdulAllah Ibn Masoud (ra) narrated that the messenger of Allah Prophet Muhamamd (pbuh) said: "The dunya (the material world) won't come to an end, until it's ruled by one of my grandchildren whose name is similar mine)." [Imam Ahmad's Recording]

The Sun Nourishes Us

When we understand this traversing, we begin to understand the importance of the Sun, the 'imitated Sun'. Imagine then the reality of Sayyidina Muhammad ﷺ? If you Google, what is a Sun? It is your eyesight, a light that comes from it. It is your breath from the photosynthesis and how it dresses the plants. It is your sustenance and your food; without the Sun there is  no food. And many other planets where the sun is too close, Allah's order is, 'Burn it,' and nothing can grow on that planet. It is an exact distance from the Earth, *"wa ma arsalnaka rahmatan lil 'aalameen"*, any closer the lights would have destroyed and burned everything on Earth.

وَمَا أَرْسَلْنَاكَ إِلَّا رَحْمَةً لِّلْعَالَمِينَ ﴿١٠٧﴾

21:107 – "Wa maa arsalnaka illa Rahmatan lil'alameen." (Surat Al-Anbiya)

"And We have not sent you, [O Muhammad], except as a mercy to the worlds." (The Prophets, 21:107)

Allah (AJ) is describing for us that you don't really understand. Your life on this planet is so fragile that it is unimaginable. That if that sun comes a little bit closer, you are all burned, toasted, nothing grows. The spectrum of the sun if it was a little bit off, we couldn't see because we see at a very specific spectrum of light from the sun. Everything, our breath is enough for the plants to use the carbon dioxide and produce oxygen. It means if that sun is what we need to survive, imagine (the Light of Prophet ﷺ), the 'real Sun'?

Everything Praises Sayyidina Muhammad ﷺ

Then, you read the *Dalail al-Khairat* that Allah (AJ) is to be worshipped but what Allah (AJ) gave to this light? Because the Sun is the same, there is no difference. Your worship is to Allah (AJ) but you pay your respects to the physical Sun. That is why the Earth is going around and around it. But the way of *ma'rifah* (gnosticism) is that *ya Rabbi*, when you read *Dalail al-Khairat*, you understood that for every tree and every plant is praising upon Sayyidina Muhammad ﷺ. Why? Because every flower, its *zikr* (remembrance) is the praising of Sayyidina Muhammad ﷺ. Every drop of rain...

Why? Because this is all the ocean of *"Muhammadun Rasulullah ﷺ"*. This is not *"la ilaha illAllah"*; for *la ilaha illAllah* there is no *sharik*, there is no partner. This (all of creation) Allah (AJ) is giving it all as a gift for Prophet ﷺ! When Allah (AJ) says, *innallaha wa malaikatahu yusaloona 'alan Nabi ﷺ*, it is enough there.

إِنَّ اللَّهَ وَمَلَائِكَتَهُ يُصَلُّونَ عَلَى النَّبِيِّ ۚ يَا أَيُّهَا الَّذِينَ آمَنُوا صَلُّوا عَلَيْهِ وَسَلِّمُوا تَسْلِيمًا ﴿٥٦﴾

Two Faces of the Moon and the Sun of Creation
Reality of Hijrah and The Cave

33:56 – *"Innallaha wa malaaikatahu yusalluna 'alan Nabiyi..."*
(*Surat Al-Azhab*)

"Allah and His angels send blessings on the Prophet..."
(*The Combined Forces, 33:56*)

Then for us to know that when Allah ﷻ is making that *darood*, when Allah ﷻ is making that *zikr*, when the *shakh* (shoot) of the plant comes out, it is making *zikr* (remembrance) of Prophet ﷺ. The rain when it drops, it is in the praising of Prophet ﷺ. When the flower and the leaf of a tree appears, it is in the praising of Prophet ﷺ. All are making *salawat* (praising) on the Prophet ﷺ. When you read *Dalail al-Khairat*, you are saying, 'Ya Rabbi,  as much as the rain is dropping all praising on Prophet ﷺ and all its *salawats*, I am praising again on Sayyidina Muhammad ﷺ!'

وَصَلِّ عَلَيْهِ وَعَلَى آلِهِ مِلْءَ اللَّوْحِ وَالْفَضَاءِ، وَمِثْلَ نُجُومِ السَّمَاءِ عَدَدَ الْقَطْرِ وَالْحَصَى، وَصَلِّ عَلَيْهِ وَعَلَى آلِهِ صَلَاةً لَا تُعَدُّ وَلاَ تُحْصَى.

Wa salli alaihi wa 'alaa aalihi mil allawhi wal fadhayi, wa mithla nujuumis Samaayi wa adadal-qatri wal hasa, wa salli alaihi wa 'alaa aalihi salaatan la tu'addu wa la tuhsaa.

And bless him and his family to the fullness of the Table and the cosmos and in every star in the sky and in every raindrop and in every stone, and bless him and his family with blessings innumerable and incalculable!

When we make *darood* we say, *allahumma salli 'ala Sayyidina Muhammad sallallahu alayhi wa sallam* (O Allah, send peace and blessings upon our Master Muhammad ﷺ, Peace and blessings be upon him). It means the power is so great, Allah ﷻ doesn't even give us the permission to praise upon Prophet ﷺ. You have to mention Allah's ﷻ Name to praise upon Sayyidina Muhammad ﷺ. It is such a holy reality, that you are not worthy of even dressing that reality, you ask Me again and I praise.

Then when we make *salawat* (praising) and the Companions asked how to make *salawat* upon you *ya Sayyidi ya Rasulullah*? Say,

اللَّهُمَّ صَلِّ عَلَى سَيِّدِنَا مُحَمَّدٍ، وَعَلَى آلِ سَيِّدِنَا مُحَمَّدٍ وَ سَلِّمْ

"Allahumma salli 'ala Sayyidina Muhammadin wa 'ala aali Sayyidina Muhammadin wa Sallim."

"O Allah! Send Peace and blessings upon our master Prophet Muhammad and upon the Family of our master Prophet Muhammad (Peace be Upon him)"

Even your *salawat* says *"Allahumma"* which means you have to ask Allah ﷻ again to praise upon the reality of Prophet ﷺ. That is the Sun.

Two Faces of the Moon and the Sun of Creation
Reality of Hijrah and The Cave

Muhammadan Light is the Powerful Sun in Judgment Day

Then imagine the Sun, even you look through Holy Qur'an: *Shamsi wal qamar, Shamsi wal qamar.* Then, what does the Judgment Day describe? Here comes the Sun again. On Judgment Day the Sun is going to come and cook your head. What Sun is going to come? Because it is a description.

عَنِ الْمِقْدَادِ بْنِ الْأَسْوَدِ رضي الله عنه قَالَ: "سَمِعْتُ رَسُولَ اللَّهِ صلى الله عليه وسلم يَقُولُ: «تُدْنَى الشَّمْسُ يَوْمَ الْقِيَامَةِ مِنَ الْخَلْقِ حَتَّى تَكُونَ مِنْهُمْ كَمِقْدَارِ مِيلٍ، فَيَكُونُ النَّاسُ عَلَى قَدْرِ أَعْمَالِهِمْ فِي الْعَرَقِ، فَمِنْهُمْ مَنْ يَكُونُ إِلَى كَعْبَيْهِ، وَمِنْهُمْ مَنْ يَكُونُ إِلَى رُكْبَتَيْهِ، وَمِنْهُمْ مَنْ يَكُونُ إِلَى حَقْوَيْهِ، وَمِنْهُمْ مَنْ يُلْجِمُهُ الْعَرَقُ إِلْجَامًا»، قَالَ: وَأَشَارَ رَسُولُ اللَّهِ صلى الله عليه وسل بِيَدِهِ إِلَى فِيهِ" (أَخْرَجَهُ مُسْلِمٌ).

Anil Meqdad Ibnil Aswad (ra) Qala: Sami'tu Rasulallah (saws) yaqulo: "Tudna Ash Shamsu yawmal qiyamati minal khalqi hatta takona minhum kamiqdari milin, fayakonun Nasu 'ala qadri a'malihim fil 'araqi, faminhum may yakonu ila ka'bayhi, wa minhum may yakonu ila rukbatayhi, minhum may yakonu ila haqwayhi, wa minhum man yuljimuhul 'araqu iljaman." Qala: wa 'ashara Rasulullahi (saws) bi yadihi ila fihi. [Akhrajahu Muslim]

AlMeqdad Ibn AlAswad (ra) said that I heard the Prophet Muhammad (pbuh) said: "In the judgment day, the sun is going to come down near people until it's a mile close. People will sweat as much as their deeds. Some will sweat to their heels, some will sweat to their knees, some will sweat to their waist, and some will drawn in their sweat as it reaches their mouth." [Narrated by Imam Muslim]

When Allah ﷻ begins to reveal the Light of Prophet ﷺ. That when Prophet's ﷺ light begins to unfold towards Creation. Imagine the people who didn't have that respect, who did not perfect themselves to that degree, what is going to happen to them in the presence of the Light of Prophet ﷺ? Everyone is thinking it is the physical Sun but the Light of Prophet ﷺ is ten billion times more powerful! When Prophet ﷺ appears on Judgment Day and Allah ﷻ gives permission to him, 'release your Light by *hamd* (praise) and *zikr* (remembrance), begin to make *du'as* (supplications) to My Divinely Presence.'

Those *du'as* (supplications) of the *Nurul Muhammadi* ﷺ (Light of Muhammad ﷺ) begin to melt everything, everything that is incorrect because *Haqq-Allah* (Truth of Allah) is now moving on creation. As that *Haqq* in the Light begins to unfold it burns away everything. But, not burn with a destruction, but burn with  a building. It means when that 'spectrum of Light' begins to hit, every falsehood and impurity within us melts away. That which remains is pure and brought back into the Muhammadan Light. That all creations with all prophets will be running towards that Light, all of their impurities burned away, and all of their perfections brought and dressed by that reality. That is the Sun.

وَقُلْ جَاءَ الْحَقُّ وَزَهَقَ الْبَاطِلُ ۚ إِنَّ الْبَاطِلَ كَانَ زَهُوقًا ﴿٨١﴾

17:81 – *"Wa qul jaa alhaqqu wa zahaqal baatil, innal batila kana zahooqa." (Surat Al-Isra)*

"And say, Truth has come, and falsehood has departed. Indeed is falsehood, [by nature], ever bound to depart."
(The Night Journey, 17:81)

Everything Grows With the Moonlight

Then the *qamar* (moon) and the importance of the moon in our life, then you study the moon and what is the effect of the moon on Earth? They say without the moon nothing grows; the Farmers Almanac, if no moonlight nothing grows. It means that the growth is by the moon. Then the relationship between the sun and moon is essential for life on Earth. If there is no sun and no moon, there is no life on Earth because every time the sun would vanish everything would die.

The relationship that Allah is describing for us is that the sun's light is always upon the Earth to the extent that people can carry it. When you are not seeing it, it didn't go. 'Was there ever a time that you were something not remembered?' This means the *qamar* (moon) is coming right there and watching. Their whole reality is to be dressed by the Light of Prophet whether the Light of Prophet shines upon the Earth or whether the Moons, that are always moving towards Prophet, they are shining upon the Earth.

Awliyaullah (Saints) Inherit From the Ashab an Nabi (Companions)

That is why *awliyaullah* (saints) inherit from the *Ashab an-Nabi* (Companions of Prophet), from the Companions. It means all *awliyaullah* (saints) have to be from one of the Companions. And they carry the reality from the *Ahlul Bayt* (Family of Prophet). And they are the 'full Moons' and their whole life is facing the reality of Prophet .

Allah says if not for the Sun and the Moon you have no existence on this Earth, nothing would grow on this Earth, nothing would be guided on this Earth. It would be under the hands of *shayateen* (devils). And then Allah (swt) would call the Sun to come close and begin to burn.

The Moon Affects the Oceans and Our Blood and Energy

We pray that Allah (swt) open more and more understanding for us. And everybody researches what is the Sun, what is the Moon? Our life is based on the moon. That the moon creates the tides for the water, when the moon is full what is the effect on water? If the moon can affect the ocean, imagine what it does to our blood and to the water within our body? What does it do to our psyche and to our energy?

And the 'real Moons' of Allah (swt) are *awliyaullah* (saints) who are inheriting from *Ashab an-Nabi* ﷺ (Companions of Prophet ﷺ). Their whole existence is to take that light and reflect that light out, take that light and reflect that light out. We pray that Allah (swt) opens for us from these understanding and to make our lives that are traversing the 'real Sun' of the Divinely Presence; not the 's-o-n' but the *nur* (light) and the *diya* (fire) and the 's-u-n', the Sun of all realities.

Subhana rabbika rabbal 'izzati 'amma yasifoon, wa salaamun 'alal mursaleen, walhamdulillahi rabbil 'aalameen. Bi hurmati Muhammad al-Mustafa wa bi siri Surat al-Fatiha.

REALITY of the MOON
ULUL AMR (SAINTS)

Who Are the Moons of the Nation? Rashideen, Mahdiyeen, Kamileen

A reminder for myself *ana abduka ajiz wa miskeen wa zalim wa jahl* and by the Grace of Allah ﷻ, we are still in existence. We took a path to be nothing and Allah's ﷻ *Rahmah* and Mercy to be upon us; a path in which to continuously efface, continuously to try our best to annihilate and take away bad characteristics that Allah ﷻ is not pleased with.

Sun is the Symbol of Eternity

Alhamdulillah, the way of *awliyaullah* (saints) that they inherit from the heart of Sayyidina Muhammad ﷺ. That if we have the Muhammadan Way App, or from our articles, there is a teaching of *Shams al Arifeen*, their way is the way of following the Sun. These are the suns of knowers, the suns of reality 's-u-n' not 's-o-n'; that the way of eternity, that the symbol that Allah ﷻ gave us in this *dunya* (worldly life) of eternity is the sun, and that is a tremendous *ayat al Akbar*.

Sayyidina Ibrahim عليه السلام described on his journey towards Allah ﷻ through the stars, the Moon, and arrived at the reality of the Sun, and Allah ﷻ writes in Holy Qur'an *ayat al Akbar*, the Great, Great Sign of Allah ﷻ, it is a reality of eternity. (Holy Qur'an, 6:78)

فَلَمَّا رَأَى الشَّمْسَ بَازِغَةً قَالَ هَـٰذَا رَبِّي هَـٰذَا أَكْبَرُ ۖ فَلَمَّا أَفَلَتْ قَالَ يَا قَوْمِ إِنِّي بَرِيءٌ مِّمَّا تُشْرِكُونَ ﴿٧٨﴾

6:78 – "Falamma raa ash Shamsa bazighatan qala hadha Rabbi hadha Akbaru, falamma afalat qala ya qawmi inni baree oon mimma tushrikoon." (Surat Al-An'am)

"And when he saw the sun rising, he said, 'This is my Lord; this is the greatest (of all).' But when the sun set, he said: 'O my people! I am indeed free from what you partner with Allah'." (The Cattle, 6:78)

If we have the Muhammadan Way App and you go to the *"du'as"* the section on *du'a* (supplication) then it says 'Du'a by Month'. That was Mahdi's clarification and classification, but if you go to *du'a* by month to understand the way of the *Arifeen* (knowers) and to be students of that reality.

Jumadil Thani (6th Lunar Month) Signifies the Moon
6×9 = 54

If you look at this month, it is the 6th month, Jumadil Thani. The way of the *sultan* (king), the way of the *sultanate* (kingdom) has to do with the reality of 9. They take the 9 multiply by 6 and it opens the secret of 54. This number of 54 is the *tajalli* (manifestation) of this month. There are twelve moons, twelve realities, twelve *tajallis* all based on 9 because of the *sultanate* of the number 9, that is a different talk. But in this month if you take the 9 on the 6th lunar month, it opens the reality of 54. Then this is how they decode the month and understand what is the *tajalli* of that month, how to make *du'a* (prayer)

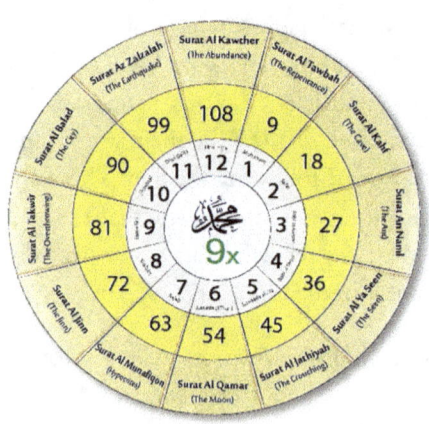

for that month, how to ask Allah (AJ), in what name to ask for that month and in what name of Prophet ﷺ.

Allah (AJ) is like the lock, Prophet ﷺ is the key. Allah (AJ) locks the heavens and Prophet ﷺ is *Miftah ur Rahman*, the key of mercy that without the key of Prophet ﷺ that lock remains locked. It means *Ismullah*, the 54th name of Allah (AJ) from *Dalail al Khairat*, *al-Mateen* (The Forceful One). The 54th name of Prophet ﷺ is *Sayyidina Siraj*, the Lamp. It means then when they begin to make their *du'as* from the reality of *Sayyidina Siraj* and asking, *ya Rabbi bi haqqi ya Mateen*, that

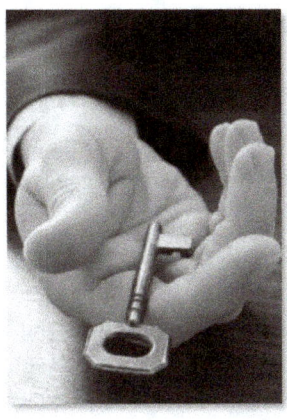

provide for us an opening and through their *tafakkur* and contemplation many different realities.

Prophet's ﷺ name is the *Siraj* and Lamp; the 54th month is Surat Al-Qamar, the Moon. In this month of *Qamar*, Allah (AJ) will open for us an understanding of this journey that we need guidance. We need to take a path that Allah (AJ) be pleased with. In Surat Al-Qamar, you read throughout all of its realities and every *surat* (chapter) of every month through their way towards reality has a secret, has a key. If we read through that *surat*, contemplate through that *surat* it has a key within that *surat* and that key will open the realities of that *surat* for that month.

We Are Dressed With the Light of Prophet Muhammad ﷺ

Every month is a *hijab* (veil) in which Allah (AJ) is eternally dressing Prophet ﷺ. So, *Nur Muhammad* ﷺ where Allah (AJ) is describing in Surat Nur, it's a Light, that Light in a *misbah*, that Light in a lantern, in a niche, and that Light is neither of east nor west means it's not from *had ad-dunya* (limited to material world). It is not from the rising of the sun and the setting of the sun. This is a Light that is a blessed Light telling us this is from *malakut* (heavenly realm). That Light of Prophet ﷺ is eternally under the *nazar* (gaze) of Allah ﷻ. Allah ﷻ has no time, Allah ﷻ is continuously gazing upon that Light of Prophet ﷺ and those are the *tajallis* (manifestations) that dress us and bless us with these twelve moons, under our galaxy and under our understanding. That these are twelve *hijabs* (veils) that are dressing all of humanity.

So *awliyaullah* (saints) are taking us on their path. The *tajalli* that Allah ﷻ is gazing upon Prophet ﷺ is the *tajalli* of Munificence, of *Haiba*, and Might and Majesty; 7,000 times in Allah's ﷻ Time, is praising upon that Light of Prophet ﷺ, the *Nazar* (gaze) dressing the Light of Prophet ﷺ, with these *tajallis*. And the *zikr* (remembrance) of that Light, *"subhana man huwal ghaniyu la yafkaru, subhana man huwal ghaniyu la yafkaru"* (Glory be to Him, He is rich and Who never grows indigent).

Each Month Has Its Own Reality

This means there is a key for every month, a reality for every month. What they want us to understand is from those teachings. And in this holy month of *Qamar*, the month of Holy Qur'an that's dressing the 54th *surat* (chapter) is that Allah ﷻ is continuously reminding, 'I will show you My Signs upon the horizon and then I show you from within yourself, but the people of *tafakkur* and contemplation are the only ones who can grasp that.' That when they want to contemplate and ask, 'Ya Rabbi, what is it You want from me?' Be like My Heavens, if you want to inherit from My Kingdom then follow My Style of management. Don't be a rogue operation on Earth doing whatever you want, then you are never going to inherit from God's Kingdom.

So then they begin to contemplate and look and they see that, 'This Sun and this Moon and Allah ﷻ throughout Holy Qur'an is giving a description of the *Shams* (sun) and *Qamar* (moon), the *Shams* and *Qamar*, the rising of the Sun and the Moon, and the setting of the Sun is the path of the Moon and

how they never go off course and the Moon its only job is to follow the Sun, it follows the Light.'

Be Like the Moon and Efface Yourself

This means then in this holy month of *Qamar* they give for us an example that, 'Keep your life to be *Qamarun*, keep your life to be like

the moon.' And the moon gives us its example to be nothing. The moon took its tremendous beatings, and the moon has so many craters upon its surface and is an example. The moon says, 'I am not like the Earth with all of its dress, and all of its allurement, that I have taken a tremendous beating.' How many craters, how many things Allah ﷻ has sent and

inflicted upon that moon for it to be what Allah ﷻ wants it to be and for Allah ﷻ to make mention of it? It means how much in its life it was tested and as a result it has nothing to show on itself; its only purpose is to follow the sun. And our life is about trying to take the example of the moon. *Ya Rabbi*, how to continuously efface ourselves, take whatever difficulties, whatever testings are coming into life and that there must be a wisdom in everything that Allah ﷻ sends. Not to be continuously trying to take them away; these inflictions and difficulties that come upon the moon is a means of its purification.

Allah ﷻ warns for us that if you want from My Heavens and you want to inherit from My Heavens then be like My Heavens. It means that the highest, highest reality of the Heavens is that the moon is following the sun and it never goes off course. Make your life in which you find a sun; you find that which is eternal and follow the light and the light is superior in our lives. They come to teach us and Allah ﷻ inspires within the heart, *Rabbil mashriq wal magharib*.

رَبُّ الْمَشْرِقَيْنِ وَرَبُّ الْمَغْرِبَيْنِ ﴿١٧﴾

55:17 – *"Rabbul mashriqayni wa Rabbul maghribayn."*
(Surat Ar-Rahman)

"[He is] Lord of the two sunrises and Lord of the two sunsets."
(The Beneficient, 55:17)

Prophets are the Suns of Creation

And *awliyaullah* (saints) come and teach, 'The Suns are the Prophets of Allah ﷻ, that Allah ﷻ gives to them a Light, they have *risalat*, they have

prophecy.' As a result, Allah ﷻ has predestined for them that they are the Suns of Allah's ﷻ Creation. That I have put a Light upon their hearts, not something they grow into, but something they have been created for. Prophets were not chosen on Earth because of good character, or by example, they are predestined and written by Allah ﷻ. When they come into their prophecy is irrelevant, but they are born as prophets of Allah ﷻ. Now when they are given permission for *risalat* (messengership) is from the age of 40 generally, but they are born in their prophecy. This means they are the Suns of Creation.

And the Moon, and Allah ﷻ makes all Creation to follow you. To follow all the prophets of Allah ﷻ is the station of belief, is the Station of *Iman*, is to believe in Allah ﷻ, believe in the holy books, believe in the prophets and believe in the angels. It means Allah ﷻ made all of Creation to follow the Suns I have created, follow the Lights, follow; they are eternal Light from My Divinely Presence. They are not a Light in which you have to try to grow into, but I have created them as a Sun; I have created them as a source of guidance. There is a secret within them like a *naar*, like a fire. All of Creation is trying to be *nurani*, trying to reach a reflection of Allah's ﷻ Light. But they are created from these Divinely Lights, they are the moving Suns upon the Earth. And their life, and our life on this Earth, was to seek out these Lights and follow them.

The Moon Shows Us to Follow the Light and Guidance

Then Allah ﷻ says, now you are taking the path of the moon, you are taking the example of the moon to be *Qamarun*. Your whole life is to follow that light, follow that light, and Allah ﷻ gave for us, *ati ullah ati ur rasul wa ulil amri minkum*. That the *ulul amr* (saints) and the people of authority, they are inheriting the Lights of Sayyidina Muhammad ﷺ upon this Earth.

﴿يَا أَيُّهَا الَّذِينَ آمَنُوا أَطِيعُوا اللَّـهَ وَأَطِيعُوا الرَّسُولَ وَأُولِي الْأَمْرِ مِنكُمْ...٥٩﴾

4:59 – "Ya ayyu hal latheena amanoo Atiullaha wa atiur Rasula wa Ulil amre minkum..." (Surat An-Nisa)

"O You who have believed, Obey Allah, Obey the Messenger, and those in authority among you..." (The Women, 4:59)

It means the *dalil* (proof) of following the guidance is everywhere. Allah ﷻ says everything is in a discipline, all My Heavens are in discipline, only this Earth with its free will is doing what it wants. Only

the inhabitants are doing what they want but for My Heavens they have a discipline. If you want to inherit from the Heavens make your life to be *Qamarun*, follow that path of realities, follow that Sun. And the Moon begins to reflect out and begins to teach as much as you take the beating, as much as you take the testing, as much as you take difficulty, the Sun is shining upon you. The Sun shines upon you with a perfect reflection that you are not claiming to be anything. But you are becoming a reflection of that Sun and as a result you become very *nurani*, you become filled with a Light, not that you are a source of Light, but you perfected a reflection of that Light.

Follow the Light of Prophet Muhammad ﷺ

So, *Qamarun* they talk only about the Sun, their focus is the love of the Sun. It means the prophets, the best of them Sayyidina Muhammad ﷺ, the one who has the most examples on this Earth, most accessible on this Earth, his beloved *Maqam* in *Madinatul Munawarrah*. Anyone whom Allah ﷻ gives a means to go fly there, and you have the most powerful Sun in all of Allah's ﷻ created universes. Allah ﷻ didn't make it difficult, so it's a *ni'mat* (blessing) for us. This life of ours is

to follow that Sun, to be dressed by that Light, to be blessed by that

Light, and then to take difficulties. That is why we were talking last night from Surat YaSeen when Allah (swt) is giving that, describing the greatness of that Sun, *YaSeen wal Quran al hakeem* (Holy Qur'an, 36:1-2).

يس ﴿١﴾ وَالْقُرْآنِ الْحَكِيمِ ﴿٢﴾

36:1-2 – "YaSeen. (1) Wal Qur'anel Hakeem. (2)" (Surat YaSeen)

"YaSeen. (1) By the Qur'an, full of Wisdom. (2)" (YaSeen, 36:1-2)

Real Guides Come to Teach Heavenly Realities

Allah (swt) testifies by the realities and every *ulama* (scholars) knows that Sayyidina YaSeen (as). YaSeen (as) is a name of Prophet (saws). And Allah's (swt) testifying by that name that all My Wisdom of Holy Qur'an, every reality of that reality, then wants for us to understand that, 'We sent companions to the city and they entered into the city to teach.' (Holy Qur'an, 36:13-14)

وَاضْرِبْ لَهُم مَّثَلًا أَصْحَابَ الْقَرْيَةِ إِذْ جَاءَهَا الْمُرْسَلُونَ ﴿١٣﴾ إِذْ أَرْسَلْنَا إِلَيْهِمُ اثْنَيْنِ فَكَذَّبُوهُمَا فَعَزَّزْنَا بِثَالِثٍ فَقَالُوا إِنَّا إِلَيْكُم مُّرْسَلُونَ ﴿١٤﴾

36:13-14 – "Wadrib lahum masalan Ashaabal Qaryatih; iz jaa'ahal mursaloon. (13) Iz arsalnaaa ilayhi musnaini fakazzaboo humaa fa'azzaznaa bisaalisin faqaaloo innaa ilaykum mursaloon. (14)" (Surat YaSeen)

"And present to them the example (story of) the Companions of the city, when the messengers came to it. (13) When We (first) sent to them two messengers, but they denied/rejected them. So We strengthened them with a third; they said, "Indeed, we have been sent to you as messengers. (14)" (YaSeen, 36:13-14)

As soon as they began to teach and this is our life lesson, in five minutes you will forget it because you will come up and start asking, 'Shaykh all the problems and difficulties, please take away this, please take away that.' But before the phase of five minutes of forgetfulness, in two minutes you forgot and exploded. It teaches you, 'I sent people with a message to the city. In the city, they got angry and they started to throw rocks at them.'

قَالُوا مَا أَنتُمْ إِلَّا بَشَرٌ مِّثْلُنَا وَمَا أَنزَلَ الرَّحْمَٰنُ مِن شَيْءٍ إِنْ أَنتُمْ إِلَّا تَكْذِبُونَ ﴿١٥﴾ قَالُوا رَبُّنَا يَعْلَمُ إِنَّا إِلَيْكُمْ لَمُرْسَلُونَ ﴿١٦﴾ وَمَا عَلَيْنَا إِلَّا الْبَلَاغُ الْمُبِينُ ﴿١٧﴾

36:15-17 – "Qaaloo maa antum illaa basharum mislunaa wa maa anzalar Rahmaanu min shay'in, in antum illaa takziboon. (15) Qaaloo Rabbunaa ya'lamu innaa ilaykum lamursaloon. (16) Wa maa 'alaynaa illal balaghul Mubeen. (17)" (Surat YaSeen)

"They said, "You are not but human beings like us, and the Most Merciful sends not sort of revelation. You are only telling lies." (15) They said, "Our Lord knows that we have been sent as messengers to you, (16) And our duty is only to proclaim the Clear Message. (17)" (YaSeen, 36:15-17)

The Moon Has Taken a Beating and Testing

Like *Ashab al Kahf* (People of the Cave) and *qitmir*, the dog of *Ashab al Kahf*, then Allah (AJ) says, look to the moon; how many times this moon, it has horrible craters, how much it took of bombing and beating. And what Allah (AJ) sent on the Moon that it looks like that? But look to the beatific Earth and how everything is so beautiful, the colors are so nice. What it took? Then Allah (AJ) says in Surat Yaseen that, 'I sent them with a Message.' (Holy Qur'an, 36:14)

Everybody has a message, you are not the Messenger, but you have the Message of Islam, of good character, the ambassador of reality. 'I sent them to the town and the town attacked them.'

قَالُوا إِنَّا تَطَيَّرْنَا بِكُمْ ۖ لَئِن لَّمْ تَنتَهُوا لَنَرْجُمَنَّكُمْ وَلَيَمَسَّنَّكُم مِّنَّا عَذَابٌ أَلِيمٌ ﴿١٨﴾ قَالُوا طَائِرُكُم مَّعَكُمْ ۚ أَئِن ذُكِّرْتُم ۚ بَلْ أَنتُمْ قَوْمٌ مُّسْرِفُونَ ﴿١٩﴾

36:18-19 – "Qaaloo inna tataiyarnaa bikum la'il-lam tantahoo lanar jumannakum wa la-yamassan nakum minnaa 'azaabun aleem. (18) Qaaloo taaa'irukum ma'akum; a'in zukkirtum; bal antum qawmum musrifoon. (19)" (Surat YaSeen)

They said, "Indeed, we consider you a bad omen. If you do not desist, we will certainly stone you, and a grievous punishment indeed will be inflicted on you by us. (18) They (messengers) said, Your omen is with yourselves. Is it because you were reminded (of Truth)? Rather, you are the people transgressing all bounds and are extreme. (19)" (YaSeen, 36:18-19)

Beware of Your Enemy Within

Any time you are going to take a step towards the truth, towards good character, towards righteous character, towards abstaining from bad things, from bad character, bad desires, Allah ﷻ is warning, they are going to attack you. Who are 'they'? Outside, inside, and from every direction, your own *nafs* (ego); your own being is going to attack you. You don't even need an outside city to attack you, you have a universe within you that is already ready for the attack. It means as soon as you give yourself, I am now going to follow that which is correct, your entire being will begin to fight you. You don't even need an outside enemy; your inside enemy is the worst. Allah ﷻ describes as soon as they began to talk, the outside began to attack. So why are you attacking? Is it that we remind you of the truth?

It means at any time we are going to give ourselves the truth or try to live a life based on this truth, live a life of truthfulness and good character. There is nothing on this Earth and within yourself that is going to accept that. This is the life you chose and why Prophet ﷺ describes, 'There is no ease in religion.'

Don't Compromise the Truth

If you compromise, you have to compromise, you have to compromise, you have to compromise until you have compromised so much that you are on the wrong side, the wrong side of that line, and you can compromise all your faith and everything you believe in. That is all what *Shaytan* (Satan) wants. Allah ﷻ is warning, 'We sent them to a village, We sent them to the town and the town told them, 'Stop talking, stop following that',' why? Is it that we remind you of the Truth? They said, 'Yes, and if you don't stop we will stone you to death.'

قَالُوا إِنَّا تَطَيَّرْنَا بِكُم ۖ لَئِن لَّمْ تَنتَهُوا لَنَرْجُمَنَّكُمْ وَلَيَمَسَّنَّكُم مِّنَّا عَذَابٌ أَلِيمٌ ﴿١٨﴾ قَالُوا طَائِرُكُم مَّعَكُمْ ۚ أَئِن ذُكِّرْتُم ۚ بَلْ أَنتُمْ قَوْمٌ مُّسْرِفُونَ ﴿١٩﴾

36:18-19 – "Qaaloo inna tataiyarnaa bikum la'il-lam tantahoo lanar jumannakum wa la-yamassan nakum minnaa 'azaabun aleem. (18) Qaaloo taaa'irukum ma'akum; a'in zukkirtum; bal antum qawmum musrifoon. (19)" (Surat YaSeen)

They said, "Indeed, we consider you a bad omen. If you do not desist, we will certainly stone you, and a grievous punishment indeed will be inflicted on you by us. (18) They (messengers) said, Your omen is with yourselves. Is it because you were reminded (of Truth)? Rather, you are the people transgressing all bounds and are extreme. (19)" (YaSeen, 36:18-19)

It means our life is about being tested. Testing is going to come, difficulty is going to come, this is not that you accepted *Islam* (submission), accepted *Iman* (faith) and now you are trying to reach to *Maqam al Ihsan* (Station of Moral Excellence) and everything is opening the doors and saying, '*Ahlan wa sahlan*, please come, come reach all the great things in life,' but everything is going to throw something.

Face the Fire of Nimrod Like Sayyidina Ibrahim

Even Sayyidina Ibrahim 🕊, the Father of *Hajj*, Father of Faith, and principles and practices of faith, that, 'As soon as I wanted to take a path of realities Nimrod tied me up and threw fire at me, cast me into a flame.'

$$\text{قَالُوا حَرِّقُوهُ وَانصُرُوا آلِهَتَكُمْ إِن كُنتُمْ فَاعِلِينَ ﴿٦٨﴾}$$

21:68 – *"Qaalo harriqoho wansuroo aalihatakum, in kuntum faa'yileen." (Surat An-Anbiya)*

"They said, "Burn him and support your gods – if you are to act." (The Prophets, 21:68)

This means every flame begins to come, not an imaginary enemy but the enemy within ourselves; every desire is pointing in a different direction, every cell of your body trying to follow its desire. You give your body the *qibla* (direction) of *haqqaiq* (realities) and say, '*Ya Rabbi*, I want to reach to the love of Sayyidina Muhammad ﷺ,' everything in you will begin to attack you and says, 'No, it's not going to happen.' Why, because they are already under the authority of the *nafs* (ego), because all your life you gave that authority to the *nafs*, we gave the authority to the *nafs*.

Our Nafs (Ego) Wants to Deny the Truth

Allah ﷻ says how is this Qur'an real and for us, it is not about storytelling? Allah ﷻ is warning, everything about you, your inside is going to throw stones at you and keep telling you, 'Don't recite, don't practice, don't do,' and you ask yourself why; is it that I remind you of the truth? And you even walk into areas and people become angered by your appearance. You have a beard and they become angry, why? Are you reminded of the truth that this is the image of the *Rijal*, this is the image of the Heavens so everything about your being doesn't want to be reminded of that? 'Don't remind me of anything from Paradise, tell me about Las Vegas.' Oh, what's in Las Vegas, slot machines, the lights are flashing everywhere, everywhere.

That's all the *nafs* (ego) wants. Allah is warning everything in you is going to throw stones at you. Then the last one Allah says, 'We strengthened them with a third,' (Holy Qur'an, 36:14)

إِذْ أَرْسَلْنَا إِلَيْهِمُ اثْنَيْنِ فَكَذَّبُوهُمَا فَعَزَّزْنَا بِثَالِثٍ فَقَالُوا إِنَّا إِلَيْكُم مُّرْسَلُونَ ﴿١٤﴾

36:14 – "Iz arsalnaaa ilayhi musnaini fakazzaboo humaa fa'azzaznaa bisaalisin faqaaloo innaa ilaykum mursaloon." (Surat YaSeen)

"When We (first) sent to them two messengers, but they denied/rejected them. So We strengthened them with a third; they said, 'Indeed, we have been sent to you as messengers'." (YaSeen, 36:14)

We Must Struggle in Allah's Way

And that *Rijal* comes running and your inner being as a warning, that if you are going to take a path, and Allah sends you to guidance, your duty as a *Rijal* is to support them, to be with them, to accompany them, and that was the character of the *Rijal* that Allah is giving.

وَجَاءَ مِنْ أَقْصَى الْمَدِينَةِ رَجُلٌ يَسْعَىٰ قَالَ يَا قَوْمِ اتَّبِعُوا الْمُرْسَلِينَ ﴿٢٠﴾ اتَّبِعُوا مَن لَّا يَسْأَلُكُمْ أَجْرًا وَهُم مُّهْتَدُونَ ﴿٢١﴾

36:20-21 – "Wa jaa'a min aqsal madinati Rajulun yas'aa, qaala yaa qawmit tabi'ul mursaleen. (20) 'Ittabi'o man la yasalukum ajran wa hum Muhtadon. (21)" (Surat YaSeen)

"And there came from the farthest end of the city a man (rijal), running. He said, 'O my people, follow the messengers. (20) Follow/obey those who ask no reward of you (for themselves), and they are rightly guided.' (21)" (YaSeen, 36:20-21)

That, 'Those whom I send, they are continuously in struggle where this is not an easy path. Everything in this *dunya* (material world) trying to come against them, to stop them from delivering that Message, stop them from supporting.' When you go out and try to do a *Mawlid an Nabi* ﷺ you think people are running [to attend]? They are continuously trying to block and block. And every time

you are trying to do something good for this world, for your community, for your family, every type of difficulty comes. You struggle through, struggle through, and [Allah ﷻ] describes that this *Rijal* who wants to reach Allah's ﷻ satisfaction, he sees the difficulty and comes running to them to be a supporter. And as he is running and asking, 'How is it that you are not supporting them when they asked no fee from you? They are trying to take you towards your reality?' And then what happens to this poor *Rijal*? *Qeelad khulil jannah*?

قِيلَ ادْخُلِ الْجَنَّةَ ۖ قَالَ يَا لَيْتَ قَوْمِي يَعْلَمُونَ ﴿٢٦﴾ بِمَا غَفَرَ لِي رَبِّي وَجَعَلَنِي مِنَ الْمُكْرَمِينَ ﴿٢٧﴾

36:26-27 – "Qeelad khulil Jannah; qaala yaa laita qawmee ya'lamoona. (26) Bimaa ghafara lee Rabbi wa ja'alanee minal mukrameen. (27)" (Surat YaSeen)

"It was said: 'Enter to paradise.' He said, 'Oh, I wish my people could know, (26) For that my Lord has granted me Forgiveness and bestowed upon me great bounty and made me from those who are held in honour!' (27)" (YaSeen, 36:26-27)

Stay Silent Through Hardship

He got stoned, was killed, and he saw his Paradise. The one who came to warn, as soon as you take a path, take a seat on this carpet, it is not about ease coming to you, and every opening coming to you, but difficulty and hardship is coming. Soon as that *Rijal* ran to them Allah's ﷻ next verse describes, 'He saw his Paradise' (YaSeen, 36:26)

It means he was finished, he got finished. Our life is about the testing, and the beauty and eloquence in which Allah ﷻ describes and *awliyaullah* (saints) inspiring within the heart, 'Don't think of it as something scary, nobody is going to kill you on this Earth, but meaning that every test that comes to you Allah ﷻ is going to give you such an amazing sweetness, if you can keep the good character of staying silent.' Because that *Rijal,* as soon as these difficulties came to him, he asked, 'I wish that my people would have seen what God is bestowing upon me. What Allah ﷻ is bestowing upon me.' We talked last night that these *Rijal* when they train to be silent, when they train to be quiet, when they took the difficulties, took the testing, being amongst people and trying to teach people, and being amongst *awliyaullah* and trying to interact with these Shaykhs, is not something easy.

Find Relief Through Tafakkur (Contemplation)

You are going to be squeezed and squeezed and squeezed, and Allah ﷻ, from heart of Qur'an, is promising that these *Rijal* are so amazed at what Allah ﷻ opens for them in their *salat* (prayer), in their *tafakkur*, in their contemplation, of what no ears have heard, no eyes have seen, that Allah ﷻ is

opening His Paradises through these difficulties, not physical death. We are talking only through spiritual, having good character, taking whatever testing is coming, remaining to be good and soft. So as soon as they send you a test, don't reply; you don't say anything, you don't lash out, but good character so that you cry on your prayer carpet. As soon as you cry on your prayer carpet, then Allah ﷻ opens. If Allah ﷻ wants to open your heart to see what no eyes have seen, what dress and what Paradise, and what Lights Allah ﷻ gives to that *Rijal*, that they feel satisfied, they feel enthusiastic, they feel a tremendous *himma*, a zeal to go again. That *Rijal* said, 'If you take me back, I will do it again.'

Sayyidina Aba Yazid al Bistami ق said the same thing after they stoned, through difficulty, '*Ya Rabbi*, if you send me back a thousand times I will come back again, I will come back again,' of what Allah ﷻ was bestowing on their practices, as soon as they close their eyes when there is difficulty, what lights Allah ﷻ will bestow on them, what characteristics Allah ﷻ will bestow upon them? But if we don't take difficulty, and we don't pass through all these characteristics, it's just a life of difficulty. These good characteristics will allow the sun to begin to shine upon the moon. If that sun begins to shine, they are so satisfied with what Allah ﷻ bestows upon them that they go again as if the next day is a new day, and they endure whatever Allah ﷻ wants to put upon them.

Our Guides Have Experienced Extreme Testing

We pray that Allah ﷻ grants us an understanding of guidance. When people become teachers, and their spouse that accompanies them, they are not of importance because of their memorizing of Qur'an and memorizing of *Hadith*; they are placed in a position of authority because of the extreme amount of testing that Allah ﷻ has put upon them. That's the importance from Allah ﷻ, "*ittaqullah wa alimukumullah*" (And Be conscious of/Fear Allah, And Allah teaches you, Holy Qur'an, 2:282)

...وَاتَّقُوا اللَّـهَ ۖ وَيُعَلِّمُكُمُ اللَّـهُ ۗ وَاللَّـهُ بِكُلِّ شَيْءٍ عَلِيمٌ ﴿٢٨٢﴾

2:282 – "...Wat taqollaha, wa yu'allimukumullahu, wallahu bi kulli shayin 'Aleem." (Surat Al-Baqarah)

"...And Be conscious of/Fear Allah, And Allah teaches you. And Allah is the All-Knower of everything." (The Cow, 2:282)

Allah ﷻ says that, 'If you have a *taqwa* and consciousness,' their lives have been through testing, they can't even talk about the level of testing, they can't even begin to explain, people will lose their faith if you hear their lives and testing that has come. But because Allah ﷻ is satisfied with their character, satisfied with how they went through their testing, how they kept their faith, kept their good characteristics, Allah ﷻ opens for them. This means they are not blind people; their hearts are open. The spouse of the Shaykh – her heart is open. If you think people can sit on this carpet and the Shaykh can open them, imagine what they have opened for that spouse.

Blessings Come to Those Who Support the Guides

And her importance is not because of her memorizing Qur'an and Hadith, it's not the *darajat* (level) for Allah ﷻ but merely she accompanied someone who was severely tested. And she took everything that he took, and she was crushed through every crushing that he went through, and that their lives are like sail boats; they go here, they go here, they go there, they go there, they go there, they go there. You deal with one problem, they sit with one problem, they sit with one known and a hundred unknown and maybe a  thousand unknown people. And those all throwing their burdens, their problems, their difficulty, their crazy characteristic upon them. Most people can't deal with one person causing them problems. Look how many you are facing right now. That's just from here, then there are hundreds or thousands through the internet. They are emailing all their problems, all their burdens. It means the life and the rank Allah ﷻ gives is what they are trying to convey in this understanding.

When Nabi Musa ﷺ wanted to reach one of Allah's ﷻ servants said we are going to send you someone who attained a *Rahmah* (mercy) and then We taught him knowledges. They are not the people who sat down and studied books and then they come and sit amongst you and say, 'Let me guide you, let me tell you about this *Hadith*, let me tell you about this *ayat al Qur'an* (verse of Holy Qur'an),' no, no, you don't need that, that is on YouTube.

Seek Advice from Real Shaykhs who Teach from Experience

But those whom Allah ﷻ tested and they were tried, and they have been certified, with that certification Allah ﷻ says, when you go to them, they are real; they don't talk from what they didn't do, they talk from what they experienced. When somebody talks from experience that is real, that is real advice. When somebody talks that has never experienced, never been crushed, never been through testing what is the value for that? It means that is the importance that these people are real. They have been tested. Based on their testing they have good characteristics. As a result, they have an immense *fa'iz* (downpouring of blessings) coming from them from the presence of Prophet ﷺ, presence of *awliyaullah*, not the knowledge but because of the good character. They became like moons, male and female, doesn't matter. Because if she is following a moon then she is a moon too, but if that life was tough and harsh, she would have said, 'I am leaving, I am gone.' This life is anything but easy. Many appearances may be in their life to show something to be easy, that is only to keep them sitting so they don't run away, but this life is very intense, this life is very, very, much about testing.

Even Sayyidina Musa ﷺ Was Tested With Sayyidina Khidr ﷺ

Look at the life of Sayyidina Khidr ﷺ and Sayyidina Musa ﷺ. He is *Kalimullah* (speaks to Allah ﷻ) and had a tough time with Sayyidina Khidr ﷺ. Imagine anybody else trying to deal with *awliyaullah*, what type of character, what type of testing they put you through, what type of difficulties, what type of shouting, what type of insult, what type of things they put you through to make you to be *Qamarun*, they don't just polish you and give you kebab. It means the life they have is through severe and extreme testing.

We pray Allah ﷻ opens for us more and more understanding to take that path, to be dressed by that reality, in the holy month of Rajab is opening, the holy month of Shaban is opening, and the holy month of Ramadan is opening. *InshaAllah*, Allah ﷻ gives us life to see those days.

Subhana rabbika rabbal 'izzati 'amma yasifoon, wa salaamun 'alal mursaleen, walhamdulillahi rabbil 'aalameen. Bi hurmati Muhammad al-Mustafa wa bi siri Surat al-Fatiha.

Full Moons – Qamarun Rashideen, Mahdiyeen, Kamileen

QAMAR

InshaAllah, always asking to be nothing, to be nothing, to be nothing, and that Allah is Great and everything. That Allah's *Rahmah* and Mercy to dress us and bless us. And the greatest blessing is the love of Sayyidina Muhammad, the love of *awliyaullah* (saints), love of all whom Allah loves, and to be distanced from all whom Allah is not pleased with.

Number 9 is the Sultan of All Numbers

Alhamdulillah, that from Mawlana Shaykh's teaching that every month has a *tajalli* (manifestation) in the way of *ma'rifah* (Gnosticism) and an understanding and a reality. And they move from the reality and the blessings of the understanding of the number 9. Nine in the understanding of numbers is a *sultan* (king). 9 is the highest single digit  number and represents complete *taslim* (submission). Its *sultanate* has a dual face. It represents the *'Azimat* (Greatness) of Allah ﷻ, the Most Powerful because everything is perfectly numbered. The numbers are higher than the *kalam* (words). With the *kalam* you can make mistakes, or you can make many different understandings from the letters; the highest program and Allah ﷻ describes that these are everything perfectly numbered. The numeric code is an understanding from angelic realities and the 9 being the highest number, the *sultan* of numbers. As a result of its *sultanate*, it represents complete *taslim* and submission. It means the 9 will take us to the *nuqt* (dot).

...وَأَحْصَىٰ كُلَّ شَيْءٍ عَدَدًا ﴿٢٨﴾

72:28 – "*… wa ahsa kulla shay in 'adada.*" (Surat Al–Jinn)

"*…and He has encompassed whatever is with them and has enumerated all things in number.*" (The Jinn, 72:28)

9th Lunar Month is Ramadan, the Sultan of the Months

The 9th lunar month is Ramadan. It is the *sultan* of the months that Allah ﷻ wants to dress us from Holy Qur'an. If we make it through Ramadan, *alhamdulillah*, with Allah's ﷻ infinite *Rahmah* and Mercy, you will be dressed from *Lailatul Qadr* and from Holy Qur'an and become *khashi'a* (dust), to be nothing. This is Allah's ﷻ *rahmah* and Mercy; and the *barakah* (blessings) of Ramadan is a fierce fire against the *nafs* (ego). Allah ﷻ grants that grant and that blessing; it's a tremendous blessing to enter into the month of Ramadan. It means Allah ﷻ is burning that *nafs* that, 'I'm going to make that *nafs* to submit and to be nothing.'

Multiplication in Spirituality is Fana (Annihilation)

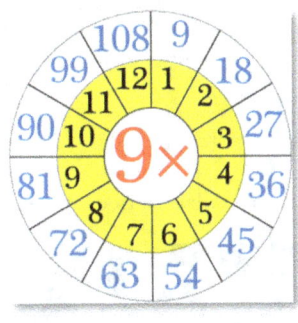

Under that understanding and many, many realities of the authority of 9, and anybody can Google 9. The power of 9 is that 9 multiplied by any number will take itself back to 9. And multiplication in spirituality is a *fana* (annihilation). Worshipness is always for Allah (swt); this has nothing to do with worshipness. This has to do with your light and the reality of light. As we sit together physically, your light also can fuse, and your light can move into another light. Just as the elements, that the hydrogen and the helium, they are separate entities and Allah (swt) allows them to make a compound and to come together. But there must be a release of an electron, there must be a release of a negative characteristic; the electrons represent negativity. If you get rid of your negativity, Allah (swt) allows a bond of 2 separate elements;

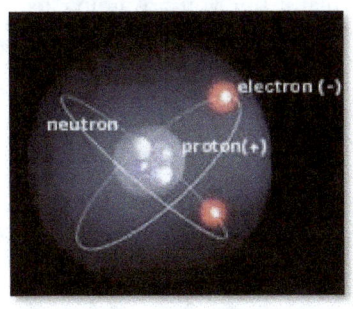

this is not *shirk* (polytheism). This has nothing to do with worshipness.

We Are Created From One Soul and to It We Shall Return

This has to do with the reality of what we see, more important of what we don't see from our atoms, our molecules, and *malakut* (heavens), and the light that encompasses and is the power of everything. It means then that, in spirituality that when you multiply your characteristic and begin to move toward the reality of that 9, it multiplies to you, annihilates you, and brings you back into being a 9 and the reality of 9; *"Wa ilaihi turja'oon."* (And to Him you will return, Holy Qur'an 36:83).

فَسُبْحَانَ الَّذِي بِيَدِهِ مَلَكُوتُ كُلِّ شَيْءٍ وَإِلَيْهِ تُرْجَعُونَ ﴿٨٣﴾

36:83 – *"Fasubhanal ladhee biyadihi Malakotu kulli shay in wa ilayhi turja'oon."* (Surat YaSeen)

"Therefore Glory be to Him in Whose hand is the [heavenly] dominion/ kingdom of all things, and to Him you will be returned."
(YaSeen, 36:83)

La sharika la (there is no partnership) – means not Allah ﷻ because we don't have *wahdatul wujud*. There's no going back to Allah ﷻ, don't make a mistake thinking you're going to Allah ﷻ. Allah's ﷻ *la sharik, la ilaha illallah* (there is no deity but Allah); but you are going back into the ocean of *Muhammadun RasulAllah* ﷺ. That, 'We created *insan* (mankind) from *nafs al-wahid*. That, 'We created *insan* from '*nafs al-wahid*', from one *nafs*, We created  all creation from one *nafs*,' *"...wa ilaihi turja'oon."* (Holy Qur'an, 36:83) and to it you are going back.

﴿مَّا خَلْقُكُمْ وَلَا بَعْثُكُمْ إِلَّا كَنَفْسٍ وَاحِدَةٍ إِنَّ اللَّهَ سَمِيعٌ بَصِيرٌ ۲۸﴾

31:28 – *"Ma khalqukum wa la ba'thukum illa kanafsin wahidatin inn Allaha Samee'un Baseer."* (Surat Al-Luqman)

"Your creation and your resurrection will not be but as that of a single soul. Indeed, Allah is Hearing and Seeing." (Luqman, 31:28)

Everyone Must Build Their Own Ship of Faith

If you make a *fana* (annihilation) and understand the way of *ma'rifah* (gnosticism) means to annihilate yourself into that reality. '*Ya Rabbi*, I want to annihilate myself into that reality.' *Awliyaullah* (saints) are *'fulukul mashhun'* – they are loaded souls, loaded ships because this is from the reality of Sayyidina Nuh ؑ.

Shaykh Nurjan Mirahmadi

وَآيَةٌ لَهُمْ أَنَّا حَمَلْنَا ذُرِّيَّتَهُمْ فِي الْفُلْكِ الْمَشْحُونِ ﴿٤١﴾

36:41 – *"Wa ayatul lahum anna hamalna dhurriyyatahum fil fulkil mashhooni."* (Surat YaSeen)

"And a sign for them is that we have carried their atoms/forefathers in the loaded ship." (YaSeen, 36:41)

Sayyidina Nuh عليه السلام is teaching that no, no, your ship; you have to build a ship too. Everybody has to build a ship and that is your soul. Your soul becomes powerful through testing and through faith. When you build your soul, it knows its way back to Allah ﷻ. It doesn't go in a different direction. The *nafs* (ego) goes in different directions. The *nafs* wants to play with *shaytan* (satan). The soul has no interest in that reality. If you build the soul with *imtihan* and with testings, with faith, and with good actions that Allah ﷻ and Prophet ﷺ have subscribed for us, the soul becomes powerful, like a *fuluk*, like a ship; and it knows its way back into its course.

Allah ﷻ Shows His Signs Upon the Horizon

Awliyaullah are the way of *ma'rifah* (gnosticism) and they follow *Shams al Arifeen* (Sun of Knowers), which is one of the names of Sayyidina Muhammad ﷺ. The sun and the light of all knowledges, again because Allah ﷻ says, 'I'm going to show you my signs upon the horizon and within yourself so that you gain clarity and faith.'

وَسَخَّرَ لَكُم مَّا فِي السَّمَاوَاتِ وَمَا فِي الْأَرْضِ جَمِيعًا مِّنْهُ إِنَّ فِي ذَٰلِكَ لَآيَاتٍ لِّقَوْمٍ يَتَفَكَّرُونَ ﴿١٣﴾

45:13 – "Wa sakhkhara lakum ma fis Samawati wa ma fil Ardi jamee'an minhu, inna fee dhalika la ayatin liqawmin yatafakkaron." (Surat Al-Jathiya)

"And He has subjected/gave the authority to you [Sayyidina Mahmood (pbuh)], as from Him, all that is in the heavens and on earth: Behold, in that are Signs indeed for those who reflect/Contemplate [Meditate]." (The Crouching, 45:13)

The sign within the self is far greater to understand. The sign upon the horizon we can see. That that sun and the power of the sun, and this sun is 1 billionth the size of the pistol star that is in the center of the entire universe, say billions of sizes bigger, is unimaginable. And what light, what energy, what realities are emanating from that pistol star.

The Piercing Star – 'At Tariq' Describes the Sun's Photons

Allah ﷻ in Holy Qur'an has so much about the heavens. How many *surats* (chapters) are related to the *buruj* (stars) and to the heavens? Surat At-Tariq is the description of *At-Tariq* (the Nightcomer)

وَالسَّمَاءِ وَالطَّارِقِ ﴿١﴾ وَمَا أَدْرَاكَ مَا الطَّارِقُ ﴿٢﴾ النَّجْمُ الثَّاقِبُ ﴿٣﴾ إِن كُلُّ نَفْسٍ لَّمَّا عَلَيْهَا حَافِظٌ ﴿٤﴾

86:1-3 – "Was Sama e wat Tariq. (1) Wa ma adraka mat tariq? (2) AnNajmu ath thaqib. (3)" (Surat At-Tariq)

"By the Sky and the Night-Visitant (therein). (1) And what will explain to thee what the Night-Visitant is? (2) (It is) the Star of piercing brightness [Pistol star]. (3)" (The Nightcomer, 86:1-3)

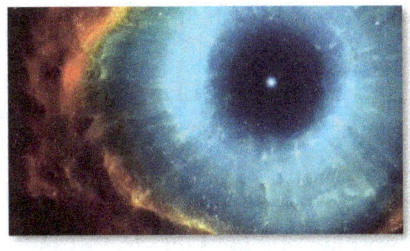

At-Tariq, that is piercing and knocking at everything, is like the description of the photons of the sun that it goes through everything. They went to the bottom of the earth and the photon, sometimes you can stare in the sky like on a nice blue day, and just look, look, look; all of a sudden you begin to see things moving. You think, wow, you reached a very strong spiritual station, you can see *malaika* (angels), but no, these are the photons. You see them, like rain coming down, that scientists went to the depth of the earth, and they say this photon goes through everything. And Allah (swt) describes that photon, *At-Tariq*, yes, it's piercing. Nothing you have can stop it, because this is Allah's (swt) *'Izzat*, Allah's (swt) Might and Magnificence that it is going to move through everything in creation. Every sun moves through every planet in its galaxy, all of them in a universe with a center. And that pierces all the universe.

The Great Star (Najm ath-Thaqib) is the Center of Everything

Then Allah (swt) describes *najm ath-thaqib*, the great star. *Najm ath-thaqib*, that is the center of everything.

وَمَا أَدْرَاكَ مَا الطَّارِقُ ﴿٢﴾ النَّجْمُ الثَّاقِبُ ﴿٣﴾ إِنْ كُلُّ نَفْسٍ لَّمَّا عَلَيْهَا حَافِظٌ ﴿٤﴾

86:2-4 – *"Wa ma adraka mat tariq? (2) AnNajmu ath thaqib. (3) In kullu nafsin lamma 'alayha hafiz. (4)" (Surat At-Tariq)*

"And what will explain to thee what the Night-Visitant is? (2) (It is) the Star of piercing brightness [Pistol star]. (3) There is no soul but has a protector over it. (4)" (The Nightcomer, 86:2-4)

Why *najm* (star)? Because it represents the light that makes your life and the center of your life to be moving towards the light. Leave that which is physical because it's perishing and by its nature it's perishing. Follow the *haq* (truth); and the *haq* is the light.

وَ قُلْ جَاءَالْحَقُّ وَزَهَقَ الْبَطِلُ، إِنَّ الْبَطِلَ كَانَ زَهُوقًا ﴿٨١﴾

17:81 – "Wa qul jaa alhaqqu wa zahaqal baatil, innal batila kana zahoqa." (Surat Al-Isra)

"And say, Truth has come, and falsehood has perished. Indeed falsehood, [by its nature], is ever perishing/ bound to perish." (The Night Journey, 17:81)

The Earth is Taking Energy From the Sun

The imitated light of what you see, when you look into the stars and look into the heavens you begin to understand Allah's ﷻ *'Izzat*, Allah's ﷻ Order, and what Allah ﷻ wants from us. That our earth, we want, we don't want, we are in *taslim* (submission) and we are submitting around the sun, taking the energy from the sun, taking our breath from that sun and what it does with the plants. All of Allah's ﷻ Might is shown in that, and that's the imitated light.

The reality and the real light is *Nurul Muhammadi* (Light of Prophet ﷺ). These are the *naats* (praisings) that we are reciting that, 'Your light gives light to the sun and the moon.' It's from the ocean of *Muhammadun RasulAllah* ﷺ.

بے نور تیرا شمس و قمر میں
تیرے لبوں کی لا لی سحر میں
خوشبو چُرا لی پھولوں نے تیری
سارے نبی تیرے در کے سوالی

Hey noor tera, shams o qamar may
Tere labo ki, Laali sahar may
Phoolo ne teri, Khushbu chura li
Saare Nabi tere dar ke sawali

Your light is in the Sun and the Moon,
the dawn has the redness of your holy lips,
All flowers have stolen your fragrance,
All prophets are at your door seeking help

Our Soul is From the Ocean of Nur Muhammadi ﷺ

This has nothing to do with worshipness. We said before you come from your mother, you're born in your mother, nobody says you worship your mother.

That's your physicality; but your soul, our soul and the light of everything around us, where does it come from? It comes from *Nurul Muhammadi* ﷺ and all of that is worshipping Allah ﷻ because the perfect servant is Sayyidina Muhammad ﷺ. All of that reality contained in the soul and the light of Prophet ﷺ.

That is the real worshipness, everything else is an imitated worshipness to the effect that Allah ﷻ makes us to move in our *salat* (daily prayer) with *alif, ha, meem, dal.* Your movement is an imitation of the *huroof* (Arabic letters) of Ahmad *(alaihis salaatus salaam): alif,* you stand, *ha* your

ruku, meem your *sajdah* and *dal* is when you are on your knees, *jalsa* reciting *attahiyat.*

It means everything we're doing is showing us the signs of that reality, and *awliya* (saints) are a ship that are moving in that ocean. That their soul moving in that reality and asking to be dressed by the lights and the reality of Prophet's ﷺ *nur al-anwar wa sirrat al-asrar* (light of every secret, and secret of every light).

Surat al-Qamar (the Moon) in the 6th Lunar Month Jumadil Thani – 6x9 = 54

In that reality of 9, that its *sultanate* is based on 9, the 6th lunar month comes and begins to open its dress for that ship. They want us to be

good passengers and enjoy the journey because as you're on their ship, you're looking out and see those ships that traverse *Shams al Arifeen,* they are in the 6th lunar month, that 6 times 9 is 54. Then they begin to talk from what they are seeing in that ocean in Surat al-Qamar (54th chapter of Holy Qur'an) because the highest is Allah's ﷻ non-created Divinely Words (Holy Qur'an).

When Allah ﷻ begins to dress their souls from that reality, they begin to speak from Surat al-Qamar; the realities of the shining moon and the reality of the moon and what it is encompassing. It is what Allah is dressing that *surat* (chapter) and dressing their realities with.

The Moon Focuses on the Sun and Makes Everything Grow

We talked before that make a life in which we are acting as a moon,  following the sun and the reality of Prophet, that we seek the light, we put our focus upon the light. That is the *nurul iman* (light of faith), to love Prophet more than you love yourself.

لاَ يُؤْمِنُ أَحَدُكُمْ حَتَّى أَكُونَ أَحَبَّ إِلَيْهِ مِنْ وَالِدِهِ وَوَلَدِهِ وَالنَّاسِ أَجْمَعِينَ.

"*La yuminu ahadukum hatta akona ahabba ilayhi min walidihi wa waladihi wan Nasi ajma'yeen.*"

"*None of you will have faith till he loves me more than his father, his children and all mankind.*" (Prophet Muhammad (pbuh))

That is the reality of the full moon; it doesn't think for itself about itself. Its only job is to focus on the sun, focus on the light. As it focuses on the light, it provides an essential service for us. You have no life on this planet if it's just the sun. If it's just the sun, there's no growth. That means what comes from the moon gives us existence on this life. Allah is saying this is all essential; if the sun is too close you burn, if it's too far you freeze, and if no moon, no growth. All the  vegetation is growing from that moon constantly giving us an energy, constantly giving us a light. It means that our whole relationship is based on that.

Siraj (Lamp) is the 54th Name of Sayyidina Muhammad ﷺ

When they traverse into the 6th month, they begin to open the understandings. The realities of the *hijab* (veil) for Jumadil Thani, the 6th month is the reality of 54. *IsmAllah*, the 54th name of Allah ﷻ *Al Matin*, The Forceful One. *Isma-Rasul* ﷺ *Siraj*, the Lamp. It means they'll ask and they'll make a request based on that name with the door of Sayyidina Muhammad ﷺ, '*Ya Rabbi, bi haqq Al-Matin, bi haq an-Nabi al-Karim ya Siraj*, open for me.' These are the names and the reality that dress that month. Surat al-Qamar being the *surat* of the month and then entering into those realities of what Allah ﷻ wants from us and wants to dress us from those realities.

Our Purpose in Life Should Be to Seek Knowledge

The highest purpose in life is to seek knowledge. The highest goal in life

is to seek knowledges; seek knowledges of the full moon, seek knowledges of the reality of light, *nurul anwar wa sirrat ul asrar* (light of every secret, and secret of every light). We said many times that if your life is not about seeking the reality of Prophet ﷺ, then we're not reaching towards eternal realities that dress the soul.

Companions of Prophet ﷺ Are the Stars of Guidance
'Rashideen al Mahdiyeen wal Kamileen'

Then they teach us that go to the *kamil*, go to the Shaykhs that are *kamil* (perfected). They are taking from the *khutbatul jumah, rashideen wal Mahdiyeen wa wuzara e kamileen mim badi. khososun minhum alla khulafahi Rasullullahi ala tahqiq, umara el mu'minin Hadarati Abu Bakr* ؓ, *Umar* ؓ, *Uthman* ؓ *wa Ali* ؓ. It means the *rashideen al-Mahdiyeen* are *kamileen*. They are *kamil* and they are the perfected ones. And all the Companions of Prophet ﷺ, but Prophet ﷺ specifically mentioned these *khulafa ar-rashideen wal Mahdiyeen*, they are *kamileen*. They are complete. 'Any one of my Companions you follow, they are like a star on a dark night and they guide you,' but these have a particular importance in your life.

أَصْحَابِي كَالنُّجُومِ بِأَيِّهِمْ اقْتَدَيْتُمْ اهْتَدَيْتُمْ

"Ashabi kan Nujoom, bi ayyihim aqta daytum ahta daytum."

"My companions are like stars. Follow any one of them and you will be guided." Prophet Muhammad (pbuh)

Now this is the battle in *dunya* (material world). These people who call themselves *salaf* and they are following the way of the Companions, they are liars and they are not following the way. There's not a single Companion who did what they are doing on this earth. They are the false moons, because everything has to have a mirror. There has to be a *haq* (truth) and there has to be a falsehood. The falsehood is like running side by side, side by side. It's *ajeeb* (strange) in this day and age that they're calling themselves with that name!

Connect to the Two Doors of the Ka'bah, Abu Bakr as-Siddiq ؓ and Imam 'Ali ؑ

What Prophet ﷺ wanted for us in every *jummah* (Friday prayer), every *jummah* we're reciting these words, be with *rashideen wal Mahdiyeen*.

They are *kamileen* (perfected ones) because *kamileen*, they are the full moons. Keep your life amongst those whom are full moons, they are *kamil*. The *Ahlul Haqqaiq* (people of realities) and the

people of the *turuqs*, all their Shaykhs trace their lineage back to Sayyidina Abu Bakr as-Siddiq ؓ or Imam Ali ؑ; the two doors of the holy covenant. This was a warning for us that Prophet ﷺ said, 'You have to be connected to these *Sahabi* (Companions).' Which one are you going to take?

Two Sides of the Full Moon – Abu Bakr as-Siddiq ؓ and Imam 'Ali ؑ

Prophet ﷺ said, for the realities and the *haqqaiq*, I gave two of my Companions special ways, and they were both related on the *hijra* (migration). Where Imam 'Ali ؑ laid into the bed and we described that

reality in Naqshbandiyya and Sayyidina Abu Bakr as-Siddiq ؓ went to the cave with Prophet ﷺ. It is the opening of the *hijra* and the holy month and the movement towards *Madinat al-Munawwarah*, the movement towards the City of Light.

Prophet ﷺ gave an example in his life because nothing is one time with Prophet ﷺ; it has to be eternal. It has to be an *isharat* (sign), that why I did what I did. Imam 'Ali

is a side of the moon that you don't see. His sacrifice to me, his reality to me is real. 42 of the *turuqs* (spiritual paths) are from that reality. And my *khalil* and my best friend, my Companion, I took to the cave. That is a completely different reality.' Going still to the same city but they carried different realities. Sayyidina Abu Bakr as-Siddiq carries a different reality. And these are the moons of guidance.

The End of Time is Near, When the Moon Split

"*Iqtarabatis Saa'atu wan shaqqal qamar*". Allah then describes that,

'The time has come and the moon has split.' (Holy Qur'an, 54:1) It is that *hijra* (migration) immediately showed that Sayyidina Ali is going to be one way because he's one side of the moon, and the face of the nation that becomes the face of *Ahlul Sunnah wal*

Jamah, Sayyidina Abu Bakr as-Siddiq is going another way. As soon as they enter into *Madinatul Munawwarah*, they completed the cycle and the reality of that moon and the moon of guidance. And deep understanding is that when Allah says, "*Iqtara batis-sati,*" (Holy Qur'an, 54:1)

Full Moons – Qamarun – Rashideen, Mahdiyeen, Kamileen

﴿١﴾ اقْتَرَبَتِ السَّاعَةُ وَانشَقَّ الْقَمَرُ

54:1 – *"Iqtarabatis Saa'atu wan shaqqal qamar."* (Surat Al-Qamar)

"The Hour (of Judgment) is near, and the moon has split [in two]."
(The Moon, 54:1)

It is that when you see the clock, the day has finished, the *zaman* (time) is finishing. Then they went literally, and they say, 'Look you make *Hajj* (pilgrimage), you see a clock!' The time can be a reference to spirituality or more literal so that Allah ﷻ said, 'Don't be confused. If you're not believing their spiritual interpretation, you go for *Hajj*, you see a clock.' Allah's ﷻ saying, 'Now the time has come.'

The moon split; *zahiri* when the moon splits the Shia and Sunnis are fighting because they are external and they are using bad characteristics. It means every sign that Prophet ﷺ brought for us are all now manifesting, that the split, the nation is split. And as a result of their split, they are fighting and killing each other, and you see a clock on *Hajj*; the world is finished for you. Prepare yourselves for the next phase of life, that your faith be strong and prepared for the difficulties that are coming upon earth. It's not a time to play and it's not a time to try to build your *dunya* (material world). Whatever you're building, build for the sake of Sayyidina Muhammad ﷺ and for the attention of Allah ﷻ.

The True Alchemy of Awliyaullah (Saints)

When they come to the people of realities they say, 'Do you people specialize in alchemy? Make this metal turn to gold for me,' because they read some books. The real alchemy is to take the trash and your five dollars that Allah (aj) is going to punish you for, and to make it to be a

house of paradise; that's the alchemy. Allah (aj) is going to question you with your *rizq* and your sustenance, that, 'What you're spending it on? Your cars, your house, your entertainment and you think you're going to get through your questioning for that?' The real alchemy of *awliyaullah* (saints) is to take what you are accountable for and take it; we have it on the wall of our Center – 'take from them', because they're not going to give it willingly, like pulling their teeth; pull their teeth. Pray for them; your prayer's going to be an ease for them.

خُذْ مِنْ أَمْوَالِهِمْ صَدَقَةً تُطَهِّرُهُمْ وَتُزَكِّيهِم بِهَا وَصَلِّ عَلَيْهِمْ ۖ إِنَّ صَلَاتَكَ سَكَنٌ لَّهُمْ ۗ وَاللَّـهُ سَمِيعٌ عَلِيمٌ ﴿١٠٣﴾

9:103 – "Khudh min amwalihim sadaqatan tutahhiruhum wa tuzakkeehim biha wa salli 'alayhim, inna salawataka sakanun lahum, wallahu samee'un 'aleem." (Surat At-Tawbah)

"Take, [O, Muhammad (pbuh)], from their wealth a charity by which you purify them and Sanctify them, and Pray on their behalf. Indeed, your Prayers are a source of Peace/security/reassurance for them. And Allah is Hearing and Knowing." (The Repentance, 9:103)

Awliya Take Your Worthless Money and Make Circles of Paradise on Earth

That's the alchemy of *haqqaiq*, is to take from people and to make for them a paradise on this *dunya* (material world) and by means of that paradise they be saved in *dunya* and in *akhirah* (hereafter).

حَدِيثُ ابْنِ عُمَرَ قَالَ: قَالَ رَسُولُ اللهِ صَلَّى اللهُ عَلَيْهِ وَسَلَّمَ: « إِذَا مَرَرْتُهُمْ بِرِيَاضِ الْجَنَّةِ فَارْتَعُوا . قَالُوا: وَمَا رِيَاضُ الْجَنَّةِ يَا رَسُولَ اللهِ ؟

قَالَ: حَلَقُ الذِّكْرِ , فَإِنَّ لِلهِ تَعَالَى سَيَّارَاتٌ مِنَ الْمَلَائِكَةِ يُطَلِّبُونَ حَلَقَ الذِّكْرِ، فَإِذَا أَتَوْا عَلَيْهُمْ حَفُّوا بِهِمْ " رَوَاهُ التِّرْمِذِيُّ

Ibn 'Umar (Radi Allahu Anhu) qala, qala Rasulullahi ﷺ:

"iza marra rathum beriyadil jannati, fa irta'o. Qalu: wa ma riyadil jannati ya Rasulillah?

Qala: Halaquz Zikri, fa inna lillahi ta'ala sayyaratun minal malayikati yutallibona halqaz zikre, fa iza ataw 'alayhum haffubihim." [Rawahu Tirmidhi]

The son of 'Umar (May Allah be pleased with him) reported that the Prophet (Peace be upon him) said: "When you pass by the gardens of Paradise, avail yourselves of them." The Companions asked: "What are the gardens of Paradise, O Messenger of Allah?"

He replied: "The circles of dhikr. There are roaming angels of Allah who go about looking for the circles of dhikr, and when they find them they surround them closely." [Narrated by Imam Tirmidhi]

What you're going to come to the table with for Sayyidina Muhammad ﷺ; that you spent more on your car than you spent on Allah ﷻ every month? How much is your car payment? Here, people are spending a good $600-$700 with insurance, spending a good $2,000 for their mortgage; you're going to sit at Prophet's ﷺ table with that?

But then they come and say the alchemy, say, 'Give me the trash, give me the things you're not going to use, give me this, give me that, give  me that,' and they make for you a paradise circle. That with that *amal*, with that action, with that reality you go before Prophet ﷺ, 'Ya Sayyidi, ya Rasulul Karim ya Habibul 'Azhim, I tried my best to do something for you, to spread your light and spread your love and make a flag and be an ambassador of love, an ambassador of your way.'

You Will Be Tested on the Path of Haq

Allah ﷻ describes, 'If you're going on *haq* (truth), your wife and your children are going to be a *fitna* (confusion) for you, because all you're going to do is keep whispering in the person's ear, 'stop what you're doing, stop what you're doing, stop what you're doing'. *Furqan* – doesn't Allah ﷻ say in Holy Qur'an that your wife and children going to be a *fitna* for you?

يَا أَيُّهَا الَّذِينَ آمَنُوا إِنَّ مِنْ أَزْوَاجِكُمْ وَأَوْلَادِكُمْ عَدُوًّا لَّكُمْ فَاحْذَرُوهُمْ ۚ وَإِن تَعْفُوا وَتَصْفَحُوا وَتَغْفِرُوا فَإِنَّ اللَّـهَ غَفُورٌ رَّحِيمٌ ﴿١٤﴾

64:14 – "Yaaa ayyuhal lazeena aamanooo inna min azwaaji kum wa awlaadikum 'aduwwal lakum fahzaroohum; wa in ta'foo wa tasfahoo wa taghfiroo fa innal laaha ghafoorur Raheem." (Surat Taghabun)

Full Moons – Qamarun – Rashideen, Mahdiyeen, Kamileen

"O ye who believe! Truly, among your wives and your children are (some that are) enemies to yourselves: so beware of them! But if ye forgive and overlook, and cover up (their faults), verily Allah is Oft-Forgiving, Most Merciful." (The Mutual Disillusion, 64:14)

He gives a warning because as soon as you move onto *haq* (truth) and your heart has love of Prophet ﷺ and that, 'I have to serve Prophet ﷺ, I have to make my house and my family to be safe, I have to make my life to be safe.' If they don't have that level of *iman* (faith), they're constantly eating your hands and feet to drop what you're doing. Then when you end up in *jahannam* (hellfire), they say 'How the heck you got us here?' They beat you anyway.

But if difficulty comes and they were right, and the love of Sayyidina Muhammad ﷺ is dressing you and blessing you, and you find yourself not like that sick, and you find yourself not like that in difficulty, and you find yourself sitting on a paradise rug and in a paradise association, then you should find yourself to be very fortunate. And that you were rightly guided, because they followed the full moon.

QAMAR

قمر		
Qamar (Moon)		
ر	م	ق
Ra	Meem	Qaf
ربانييون	محمداً	قرآن
Rabaniyoon (Lordly Souls)	Muhammadan (Muhammadan Realities)	Qur'an (Holy Qur'an)

*Note: Please read English from right to left to coincide with Arabic.

Letters of the Word Qamar – Qaf, Meem, Ra

Allah describes them, the *qamar*, they're *kamil* (perfected). *Qamar*, *qaf*, *meem*, *ra*; because *qamar* for Allah says, 'What do I care about the moon? I don't care for this *dunya*, the weight of a wing of a mosquito.' But the *qamar* is teaching us that its *qaf*, "*Qaf, wal Quranil Majeed.*" These are *Ibadur Rahman* (Servents are the Most Compassionate).

ق ۚ وَالْقُرْآنِ الْمَجِيدِ ﴿١﴾

50:1 – "*Qaf, wal Quranil Majeed.*" (Surat Qaf)

"*Qaf. By the honored Qur'an.*" (The Letter Qaf, 50:1)

These Guides are the Qamarun (Moons)

It means these guides, *qamarun, qamarun, qamarun,* they are dressed from, *"Qaf, wal Quranil Majeed." "Allamal Qur'an. Khalaqal Insaan."*

$$ عَلَّمَ الْقُرْآنَ ﴿٢﴾ خَلَقَ الْإِنسَانَ ﴿٣﴾ $$

55:2-3 – *"Allamal Qur'an (2). Khalaqal Insaan (3)."* (Surat Ar-Rahman)

"It is He Who has taught the Qur'an. (2) He has created Man. (3)" (The Beneficent, 55:2-3)

That their souls are not like your souls. Allah ﷻ created their souls, dressed them from Holy Qur'an, created their *insan* (being) and destined them for *dunya*. And they are from *Ibadur Rahman*, whom Allah ﷻ says, 'We given that light, We given that light, and We didn't give that light, there's nowhere you can get that light.' It's a *ni'mat* (blessing) and a gift from Allah ﷻ.

$$ ....مَن يَهْدِ اللَّهُ فَهُوَ الْمُهْتَدِ ۖ وَمَن يُضْلِلْ فَلَن تَجِدَ لَهُ وَلِيًّا مُّرْشِدًا ﴿١٧﴾ $$

18:17 – *"…man yahdillahu fahuwal Muhtadi, wa man yudlil falan tajida lahu waliyyan murshida."* (Surat Al-Kahf)

"… He whom Allah, guides is rightly guided; but he whom Allah leaves to stray, for him you will never find Saintly Guide to the Right Way." (The Cave, 18:17)

Then Allah ﷻ is describing, and Prophet's ﷺ describing in every *jummah* for us because what Prophet ﷺ wants is when you recite it, he's dressing it. When you recite it, Prophet ﷺ is dressing it. If you come with a sincere heart, Prophet ﷺ is going to guide you by Allah ﷻ, 'Guide them to be with my *qamars*, *ya Rabbi*, that they are from *rashideen al-Mahdiyeen*. That the *Sifat al-Rashid*, *Al-Rashid*, Allah ﷻ dresses them from the *sifat* of guidance and their souls are dressed from *Sifat al-Rashid*, they are *Abd ar-Rasheed*.

And, 'whom Allah ﷻ guides, they are the most fortunate', because Allah's ﷻ guiding them; that Allah ﷻ said, 'Those whom I guided, their consciousness I teach them,'

أُولَٰئِكَ عَلَيْهِمْ صَلَوَاتٌ مِّن رَّبِّهِمْ وَرَحْمَةٌ ۖ وَأُولَٰئِكَ هُمُ الْمُهْتَدُونَ ﴿١٥٧﴾

2:157 – "Ulaaa'ika 'alaihim salawaatun mir Rabbihim wa rahma; wa ulaaa'ika humul muhtadoon." (Surat Al-Baqarah)

"They are those on whom (Descend) blessings from Allah, and Mercy, and they are the ones that receive guidance." (The Cow, 2:157)

Allah ﷻ says, 'I teach them, no book needs to teach them.' They merely sit in *tafakkur* (contemplation) and all lights enter into their hearts. If they need from *awliyaullah* (saints), if they need from *anbiya* (prophets), if they need from whatever Allah ﷻ created, appear to them and  begin to teach their heart. These are *rashideen*, and they carry with them Allah's ﷻ *Sifat ar-Rashid*. They are *Abd ar-Rashid* whom Allah ﷻ guided.

Full Moons – *Qamarun* – Rashideen, Mahdiyeen, Kamileen

Who Are the Rashideen al-Mahdiyeen?
The Lordly Souls and Muhammadan Guides

Then Allah ﷻ is describing because this is a *ra* of *qamar*; they are *arbab*, *rabaniyoon* (lordly souls). Takes them to the *meem* and makes them to be *Mahdiyeen*. These are the *Muhammadan hadi* (guide). Allah ﷻ dressed them from *hidayat* (guidance) and the highest level of *hidayat* is from *Al Mahdiyeen*. That they carry the light of Imam Mahdi ؑ and they are *Mahdiyeen*, preparing the world for the arrival and the completion of holy *hadith* of Prophet ﷺ, that, 'One from my grandchildren will come, the world will not end until he arrives.'

قمر		
Qamar (Moon)		
ر	م	ق
Ra	Meem	Qaf
ربانييون	محمداً	قرآن
Rabaniyoon (Lordly Souls)	Muhammadan (Muhammadan Realities)	Qur'an (Holy Qur'an)
راشدين	مهديين	كاملين
Rashideen (Rightly Guided)	Mahdiyeen (Highest Muhammadan Guides)	Kamileen (Perfected Guides)

*Note: Please read English from right to left to coincide with Arabic.

عَنْ عَبْدِ اللَّهِ بْنِ مَسْعُودٍ عَنِ النَّبِيِّ صَلَّى اللَّهُ عَلَيْهِ وَسَلَّمَ قَالَ : " لاَ تَذْهَبُ أَوْ لاَ تَنْقَضِي الدُّنْيَا حَتَّى يَمْلِكَ الْعَرَبَ رَجُلٌ مِنْ أَهْلِ بَيْتِي يُوَاطِئُ اسْمُهُ اسْمِي " مسند أحمد 199/5 ح 3573

'An Abdillah bin Mas'ud, 'Anan Nabi (saws) qala: "La tazhabu aw la tanqadid dunya hatta ymlikal 'Araba rajulun min ahlil bayti yuwatiyu ismuhu ismi." (Musanad Ahmad)

AbdulAllah Ibn Masoud (ra) narrated that the messenger of Allah Prophet Muhamamd (pbuh) said:" The dunya (the material world) won't come to an end, until it's ruled by one of my grandchildren whose name is similar mine). [Imam Ahmad's Recording]

Allah ﷻ has no time; there's no clock up there Allah ﷻ says, 'Okay now, send it.' Time is *dunya*, the sun and the moon. Timeless, timeless, no time; Allah ﷻ says, 'That light of Al-Mahdi ﷺ is completely covering whom I'm giving guidance and making them to be from *mahdiyoon*,' that it's the highest Muhammadan guidance and the highest lights of Sayyidina Muhammad ﷺ begin to encompass within their being.

These Guides Take From Khulafa e Rashideen

And they are *rashideen al-Mahdiyeen*; and they are under the hands of these *khulafa*, that they take from the hand of Sayyidina Abu Bakr as-Siddiq ﷺ, they take from the hand of Imam 'Ali ﷺ, they take and they learn from Sayyidina Umar Farouq ﷺ. These are the realities and compilation of Holy Qur'an. All of these *khulafa* are encompassing the reality of the heart. That the *uloom* and the knowledges that Sayyidina Uthman ﷺ is sending of compilation of Holy Qur'an. Sayyidina

Umar ﷺ, *"Wa qul jaa alhaqqu wa zahaqal baatil..."* That, 'Come to me, I'm going to perfect. You stand for truth and you come against that which is false,' not come against by hurting people, come against in yourself. Stand for Allah's ﷻ truth within your heart and come against all these falsehoods. Then take you to Sayyidina Abu Bakr as-Siddiq ﷺ, Imam Ali ﷺ, and then into the presence of Sayyidina Muhammad ﷺ.

وَ قُلْ جَاءَالْحَقُّ وَزَهَقَ الْبَطِلُ... ﴿٨١﴾

17:81 – *"Wa qul jaa alhaqqu wa zahaqal baatil..."* (Surat Al-Isra)

"And say, Truth has come, and falsehood has perished. Indeed falsehood, [by its nature], is ever perishing/ bound to perish."
(The Night Journey, 17:81)

Holy Birth of Sayyidatina Fatima Zahra is in the 6th Lunar Month

We pray that the holy month of Jumadil Thani and that's blessed with the birth of Sayyidatina Fatima Zahra ﷺ. It means that Allah ﷻ made the birth of Sayyidatina Fatima Zahra ﷺ on this month of *qamar*, and when you call upon Sayyidatina Fatima Zahra ﷺ, say, 'Ya batul, ya batul, bi nazarkum,' that, 'gaze upon me;' she gazes from the secrets and the pure holy light of Qur'an to be dressed upon us, to be blessed upon us.

We pray that Allah ﷻ dress us from those lights, bless us from those lights and prepare us for this holy month, prepare us for the holy month of Rajab opening next, Shaban opening next and the holy month of Ramadan.

Chapters of Holy Qur'an About Stars

- 24th Chapter – Surat An Nur (The Light)
- 53rd Chapter – Surat An Najm (The Star)
- 54th chapter – Surat Al Qamar (The Moon)
- 85th Chapter – Surat Al Buruj (The Mansions of the Stars)
- 86th Chapter – Surat At Tariq (The Nightcomer Star)
- 91st Chapter- Surat Ash Shams (The Sun)

Subhana rabbika rabbal 'izzati 'amma yasifoon, wa salaamun 'alal mursaleen, walhamdulillahi rabbil 'aalameen. Bi hurmati Muhammad al-Mustafa wa bi siri Surat al-Fatiha.

Follow the Perfected Muhammadan Guides, Rashideen, Mahdiyeen, Kamileen

Nobody Understand Allah's Signs Except Those Who Tafakkur (Contemplate)

From the knowledge of Allah to the heart of Prophet, from Prophet to those whom are the lovers of Sayyidina Muhammad – *awliyaullah* (saints). That from their teachings and inspirations they teach us that when Allah said, 'I'm going to show my signs upon the horizon and I'm going to show from what's within yourself.'

سَنُرِيهِمْ آيَاتِنَا فِي الْآفَاقِ وَفِي أَنفُسِهِمْ حَتَّىٰ يَتَبَيَّنَ لَهُمْ أَنَّهُ الْحَقُّ ۗ ... ﴿٥٣﴾

41:53 – *"Sanureehim ayatina fil afaqi wa fee anfusihim hatta yatabayyana lahum annahu alhaqqu..." (Surat Al-Isra)*

"We will show them Our signs in the horizons and within themselves until it becomes clear to them that it is the truth..."
(The Night Journey, 41:53)

And no one will understand those signs except those who are in *tafakkur*, those who contemplate everything. They look and they want to know the majesty of Allah. They sit and they contemplate, take a seat on a mountain, in a park and watch the moon, the stars, the sun.

*Follow the Perfected Muhammadan Guides
Rashideen, Mahdiyeen, Kamileen*

وَسَخَّرَ لَكُم مَّا فِي السَّمَاوَاتِ وَمَا فِي الْأَرْضِ جَمِيعاً مِّنْهُ إِنَّ فِي ذَلِكَ لَآيَاتٍ لَّقَوْمٍ يَتَفَكَّرُونَ ﴿١٣﴾

45:13 – *"Wa sakhkhara lakum ma fis Samawati wa ma fil Ardi jamee'an minhu, inna fee dhalika la ayatin liqawmin yatafakkaron." (Surat Al-Jathiya)*

"And He has subjected/gave the authority to you [Sayyidina Mahmood (pbuh)], as from Him, all that is in the heavens and on earth: Behold, in that are Signs indeed for those who reflect/Contemplate [Meditate]." (The Crouching, 45:13)

Who is More Honoured, The Sun or Insan (Mankind)?

They come into our lives and remind us that who's higher in majesty and *ihtiram* (respect) for Allah ﷻ – the moon? The sun? Or *insan* (mankind)? Not the station that it represents, but that physical moon. Does the moon have more honour with Allah ﷻ or *insan* (mankind)? The sun, the physical sun, it has more honour with Allah ﷻ or *insan* (mankind)? They come into our lives and teach, No! *"Wa laqad karamna bani Adam."* (We have honored the children of Adam).

وَلَقَدْ كَرَّمْنَا بَنِي آدَمَ وَحَمَلْنَاهُمْ فِي الْبَرِّ وَالْبَحْرِ وَرَزَقْنَاهُم مِّنَ الطَّيِّبَاتِ وَفَضَّلْنَاهُمْ عَلَى كَثِيرٍ مِّمَّنْ خَلَقْنَا تَفْضِيلًا ﴿٧٠﴾

17:70 – *"Wa laqad karramna banee adama, wa hamalna hum filbarri wal bahri wa razaqnahum minat tayyibati wa faddalnahum 'ala katheerin mimman khalaqna tafdeela. (Surat Al-Isra)*

"And We have certainly honored the children of Adam and carried them on the land and sea and provided good and pure sustenance and bestow upon them favours, and preferred them over much of what We have created, with [definite] preference." (The Night Journey, 17:70)

Allah ﷻ says, 'I have honoured your creation and I blew from my realities and spirit into your being.' (Holy Qur'an, 38:72). *Wa 'Allamal Qur'an, ba'dan, Khalaqal Insaan.* I have taught you all, and dressed you from Holy Qur'an, then I made your *insan*, your form.

عَلَّمَ الْقُرْآنَ ﴿٢﴾ خَلَقَ الْإِنسَانَ ﴿٣﴾

55:2-3 – *"Allamal Qur'an (2). Khalaqal Insaan (3)."* (Surat Ar-Rahman)

"It is He Who has taught the Qur'an. (2) He has created Man. (3)" (The Beneficent, 55:2-3)

Insan (Mankind) is a Noble Creation, Angels Bow Down to Them

You're a very noble creation, where angels bow down to you. If you reach what Allah ﷻ wants of realities the angels will bow in *ihtiram* (respect). *Ibadah* and worship is only for Allah ﷻ but the angels will show their respect.

فَإِذَا سَوَّيْتُهُ وَنَفَخْتُ فِيهِ مِن رُّوحِي فَقَعُوا لَهُ سَاجِدِينَ ﴿٧٢﴾

38:72 – *"Fa idha sawwaytuhu wa nafakhtu feehi min Rohee faqa'o lahu sajideen."* (Surat As-Saad)

"So when I have proportioned him and breathed into him of My [created] soul/spirit, then fall down to him in prostration." (Saad, 38:72)

That you are noble creation and you reached your nobility, you reached what Allah ﷻ wanted for you to reach. So, it means that *insan* and people – human beings are more blessed than the moon and the sun. And that's why they (guides) come and begin to teach.

Then if you understood that and you understood how Allah ﷻ, God Almighty runs His kingdom, because we are asking to inherit from that kingdom, 'Thy kingdom come Thy will be done on earth as it is in heaven'.

"Thy kingdom come. Thy will be done, in earth as it is in heaven...;and forgive us our debts, as we forgive our debtors. And lead us not into temptation, but deliver us from evil..." (The Lord's Prayer)

This is the way of all realities and every Prophet brought the same reality; bring God's kingdom into your heart. *Qalbil mumin baytullah.*

قَلْبَ الْمُؤْمِنْ بَيْتُ الرَّبّ

"Qalb al mu'min baytur rabb."

"The heart of the believer is the House of the Lord." (Hadith Qudsi)

Bring Allah's ﷻ immense love into your heart and you'll inherit on this earth His heavenly kingdom and you'll be from the inheritors of the heavenly kingdom in *malakut* (heavenly realm).

We Are Created to Be in Need to Seek a Means to Approach Divine

They looked to the moon and they see that we have no life on this earth without that moon. So, our simple existence because we want to understand the role that Allah ﷻ shows around us. If they take the moon, you have no life on this earth.

People say, 'Oh, oh, it's just Allah ﷻ. All I need is Allah ﷻ. Don't talk to me about Shaykhs. Don't talk to me about the prophets. Don't talk to me about anything – all I need is God directly!' Allah ﷻ clarifies for us, 'Don't have that arrogance.' Everything is a *tawassul* and a means. Look at your little pity self on that earth; you're in need and I created you in need!' Allah ﷻ is the Might and Majesty of all creation but, without that moon you're not in existence.

﴿...وَخُلِقَ الْإِنسَانُ ضَعِيفًا ﴿٢٨﴾

4:28 – "...*Wa Khuliqa Al-'Insanu Da'ifaan.*" (Surat An-Nisa)

"...and mankind was created weak." (The Women, 4:28)

Allah ﷻ Placed Us On Earth to Exist, In Perfect Distance From the Sun

Without the sun you're non-existent. No life on this earth. If no sunshine, there's no breath, there's no air because there is no photosynthesis. There is no vision. There is no warmth. If you're too close to the sun, you'll burn. If you're too far from the sun, you'll freeze to death. The moon is 250 degrees in sunlight and negative 250 degrees when the sun is away – you freeze to death. You're exactly placed on an Earth in which Allah ﷻ wants you to survive. You could have been put anywhere else and immediately burn on Venus and Mars.

So, Allah ﷻ is saying there is a *tawassul*, there's a way and a means to everything. Take its understanding! Be the one who contemplates and looks, *'Ya Rabbi*, that without this sunshine twelve hours a day dressing upon me. I'm not going to grow. I'm not going to have any existence.' Actually, if the sun blocked itself, all of your bones will shatter. They become vitamin-D deficient, like in Vancouver.

Growth Comes From Precise Amounts of Sunlight and Moonlight

The sunshine, what light it sends upon you; your actual growth is from what? The moonlight. So, all the plants, all the farming, all the things that we're eating, it grows from moonlight. Allah ﷻ begins to show,

You're a creature that's in need. What light is coming from this sun, you need twelve hours of that to continuously dress your creation, it's photons to dress upon you to bless you. You are almost in more need of the moon. Because when the sun is reflecting and shining upon the moon, that moonlight is now in charge of this earth.

The Prophets Are the Suns and Their Companions Are the Moons

Because Allah ﷻ wants us to know the Prophets are the suns and the moons are those whom follow them and I am Lord of all of them; *"Rabbal Mashariq wa rabbal magharib."*

رَبُّ الْمَشْرِقَيْنِ وَرَبُّ الْمَغْرِبَيْنِ ﴿١٧﴾

55:17 – *"Rabbul mashriqayni wa Rabbul maghribayn."*
(Surat Ar-Rahman)

"[He is] Lord of the two sunrises and Lord of the two sunsets."
(The Beneficient, 55:17)

'I am the Lord of the suns, the rising suns, the sun and the plural of suns. I am the Lord of all the Prophets and I'm the Lord of all the

moons. I'm the Lord of all the companions of the prophets and those whom follow the prophets. I am the Lord over all of them.' They
have an immense reality that they dress and bless you. And the light that's sending from the prophets, humans can only take so much. Then it has to be reflected to the moonlight and the moonlight will then begin to reflect that same light back from the prophets.

The Moon is in Perfect Itibah (Obedience) to the Sun and Doesn't Go Off-Course

The moon is a perfected creation. It doesn't inject its own thought, it doesn't inject its own egoism and think that it has a light. It has been thoroughly crushed. Crushed to where it believes it has no light; it is merely the reflection and in perfect *itibah*, in perfect obedience. It follows perfectly the sun and it doesn't wander to a different sun to the left sun. It doesn't go off-course and go towards Venus, go towards

Mars, everyday making a different choice, a different direction.

وَالشَّمْسِ وَضُحَاهَا ﴿١﴾ وَالْقَمَرِ إِذَا تَلَاهَا ﴿٢﴾

91:1-2 – "Wash Shamsi wa duhaha. (1) Wal Qamari idha talaha. (2) Wan nahari idha jallaha." (Surat Ash-Shams)

Follow the Perfected Muhammadan Guides
Rashideen, Mahdiyeen, Kamileen

"By the Sun and his (glorious) Brightness. (1) By the Moon as she follows him. (2)" (The Sun, 91:1-2)

The Moon doesn't say, I'll listen to this one, I'll follow that one. Your faith become like smorgasbord or like a buffet – you take it from everywhere. The moon teaches us, No, no! Perfect *itibah* (obedience)! That this sun, I completely follow that reality and I want to be dressed by that reality.

So, they establish that we're in need. Now if you're in need of that sun and that moon, imagine then the immensity of souls. Where Prophet's ﷺ soul is more powerful that this sun. So, you're in need of the light of Prophet's ﷺ dress upon your *insan* (mankind). That's why they established this.

Do Not Ask the Shaykh to Listen to You!

So, don't come back and say, 'No, it's only Allah ﷻ.' Don't come back and say only Allah ﷻ. 'Don't be arrogant in your approach to Me! You need the sun and the moon.' More powerful than My suns and My moons is the light of Sayyidina Muhammad ﷺ, the light of all the prophets, they are suns. You need them for your perfection you need them to reach your reality, you need their *nazar* and their gaze.

That's why Allah ﷻ clarified in Qur'an, don't ask Prophet ﷺ to listen to you! Don't ask the Shaykhs to listen to you. Their ears are locked upon their Lord but ask for the *nazar* and the gaze. Why Allah ﷻ said in Qur'an when Allah ﷻ has no time? So, don't ask

Prophet ﷺ to listen to you but ask that *unzur*, that His ﷺ gaze be upon you. It means eternally. Allah (swt) has no time in Holy Qur'an, eternally! Allah (swt) is teaching us, when you address Sayyidina Muhammad ﷺ, ask for His ﷺ holy gaze to be upon you. He ﷺ is going to now reflect his lights.

﴿١٠٤﴾... يَا أَيُّهَا الَّذِينَ آمَنُوا لَا تَقُولُوا رَاعِنَا وَقُولُوا انظُرْنَا وَاسْمَعُوا

2:104 – *"Yaa ayyuhal ladheena aamano, laa taqolo ra'yina wa qolu unzurna wasma'o…"* (Surat Al-Baqarah)

"O you who believe! Do not say (to Prophet Muhammad (pbuh)) Raina, listen to us, and say Unzurna (gaze upon us) and you listen (to him (pbuh)…" (The Cow, 2:104)

Ulul Amr Are the Moons, Reflecting Lights of Prophet Muhammad ﷺ

Prophet ﷺ is going to reflect his light. The companions, *ahlul bayt*

(Family of Prophet Muhammad ﷺ) and *awliya* (saints) are from *"Atiullah atiur Rasul wa ulil amre minkum."* (Obey Allah, Obey the Messenger, and those in authority among you, Holy Qur'an, 4:59). The *ulul amr* (saints), they're inheriting from these moons. And they become moons, because they are completely reflecting the lights of Prophet ﷺ.

﴿٥٩﴾... يَاأَيُّهَا الَّذِينَ آمَنُوا أَطِيعُوا اللَّهَ وَأَطِيعُوا الرَّسُولَ وَأُولِي الْأَمْرِ مِنْكُمْ

4:59 – *"Ya ayyu hal latheena amanoo Atiullaha wa atiur Rasula wa Ulil amre minkum…"* (Surat An-Nisa)

Follow the Perfected Muhammadan Guides
Rashideen, Mahdiyeen, Kamileen

"O You who have believed, Obey Allah, Obey the Messenger, and those in authority among you..." (The Women, 4:59)

Everything is Raised by the Nazar (Gaze) of Ulul Amr (Saints)

Then Allah ﷻ is teaching, 'You're also more in need of that gaze, in this *dunya* (material world), for the gaze of these *ulul amr* (saints) because you may not be able to reach the sun directly.' If you gaze in the sun too much, it'll take away your eyesight. So, the sun, even in growth and vegetation, it merely comes for a short period to sweeten. If everything was raised in the sun, it would look like the desert. It would burn. So everything grows, everything is *rushd* and raised by the moonlight, by *ulul amr* (saints).

Because Prophet (Muhammad) ﷺ is not visible for everyone. Their level of faith is not that, that they can connect directly with Prophet ﷺ; it's their whimsical imagination. But they need, on this earth, always moons that are moving. Those moons, they reflect the reality of Prophet ﷺ. As a result, people, they grow in faith.

Real Ulul Amr (Saints) are Qamarun (Moons)!

It's all from Qur'an and *hadith* (Prophetic ﷺ traditions), but they've to be clever to understand when Allah ﷻ says, "*Ittaqullah wo kunu ma as sadiqeen.*"

يَا أَيُّهَا الَّذِينَ آمَنُوا اتَّقُوا اللَّهَ وَكُونُوا مَعَ الصَّادِقِينَ ﴿١١٩﴾

9:119 – "*Ya ayyuhal ladheena amanoo ittaqollaha wa kono ma'as sadiqeen.*" (Surat At-Tawbah)

"O you who have believed, have consciousness of Allah and be with those who are truthful/ Pious / sincere (in words and deed)."
(The Repentance, 9:119)

Allah ﷻ is telling us have a consciousness and keep the company of the *sadiqeen* (truthful ones). Later you'll understand they're like moons – they are *qamarun!* And, as a result they're reflecting the lights of Prophet ﷺ but you haven't eyes to see. You say he looks like a person, *"basharun mithluna"* (Holy Qur'an, 36:15); he's looked like a human like me, because your *nafs* and ego begin to enter. And they say throughout Holy Qur'an, they spoke the same way about Prophet ﷺ, and the companions of Prophet ﷺ.

قَالُوا مَا أَنتُمْ إِلَّا بَشَرٌ مِّثْلُنَا وَمَا أَنزَلَ الرَّحْمَـٰنُ مِن شَيْءٍ إِنْ أَنتُمْ إِلَّا تَكْذِبُونَ ﴿١٥﴾

36:15 – "Qaaloo maa antum illaa basharum mislunaa wa maa anzalar Rahmaanu min shay'in, in antum illaa takziboon." (Surat YaSeen)

"They said, You are not but human beings like us, and the Most Merciful sends not sort of revelation. You are only telling lies."
(YaSeen, 36:15)

This is not about the physical eyes. But what Allah is ﷻ describing, 'You're in need. You're in need of the light and the gaze of Prophet ﷺ.' That we're in need of the light and the gaze of these *ulul amr* (saints), who are *qamarun*. They are moons and they begin to reflect.

*Follow the Perfected Muhammadan Guides
Rashideen, Mahdiyeen, Kamileen*

Khutbatul Jumah – Awliya Dress Our Soul With Their Haqqaiqs (Realities)

Alhamdulillah, Allah ﷻ gave us to be from the flag of Sultan al-Awliya Mawlana Abdullah Faiz Dagestani ق and Sultan al-Awliya Mawlana Shaykh Nazim Haqqani ق.

In every *jumah* they (saints) are teaching us with their

words all of these *haqqaiqs* (realities). If only we repeat what they teach us, we would be completely dressing our souls. So, in the words of the *jumah* when they're going over the *jumah khutba* (sermon), *"Salla Allahu ta'ala 'alayhi wa 'ala Alihee, wa awlaadihee, wa azwaajihee, wa Ashabihee, wa ba'di min khulafayeh Rashideen al Mahdiyeen mim ba'dihee, wa wuzarai kaamileen."* So Rashideen, Mahdiyeen, wa Kamileen. *"Fi 'ahde, Khususon minhum 'ala immati khulafai Rasulallahi 'ala atahqeq umara e mu'mineen, hadarati Abi bakrin, wa 'Umarin, wa 'Uthmanin, wa 'Ali, Imam Hassan, wa Imam Hussain, wa dhawil Qadril Jaleel. Wa 'ala baqiati asSahabati wat tabi'yeen, ridwanullaahi ta'ala 'alayhim ajma'yeen."*

They gave the formula of the *qamar* (moon). Because people come back and say, 'This is the English of those words. Peace and blessings of Almighty Allah ﷻ be upon Sayyidina Muhammad ﷺ, His Holy family, His children, His wives, His Holy companions, His true followers who followed him in righteousness, kept the way of Sayyidina Muhammad ﷺ.

Upon the rightly guided and most perfected Muhammadan guides.' *Mahdiyeen* means Muhammadan guides. 'Who came after, and the perfected ministers, *wuzaraa*, and who reached immense states of moral excellence and completed their covenant with their Lord.

Special peace and blessings of Allah ﷻ be upon the *Imams* of this nation; the *khulafa*, the representatives of Sayyidina Muhammad ﷺ, the messenger of Allah ﷻ. And who achieved the immense stations of proximity to Allah ﷻ, the leader of believers Sayyidina Abu Bakr ؓ *as-Siddiq-al-Mutlaq* – perfected and being truthful, Sayyidina Umar Farooq ؓ – distinguished truth from falsehood, Sayyidina Uthman Ghani ؓ – *Jami al-Quran al-Majeed*, the compiler, the honoured compiler of the Holy Qur'an, the rich and prosperous, Sayyidina Imam Ali ؓ – *AssadAllah al-Ghalib* – the victorious lion of Allah ﷻ, Imam al-Hassan ؓ – *al-Mujtaba wal* Imam al-Hussein ؓ – *Sayed al-Shuhada;* peace and blessings be upon all their souls. And their souls have immense proximity to Allah's ﷻ divinely presence, and dress from Allah's ﷻ Divinely Oceans of Majestic Might and Majestic Beauty.'

The Formula to Become a Qamar (Moon)

It means they gave us the instructions of *qamarun*. Because people come back and say, 'Oh, I don't need to follow anyone. I can follow Prophet ﷺ directly.' You're incorrect! Because the *awliya* (saints) are teaching us, 'No! The *Rashideen, al-Mahdiyeen wa Kamileen* – the *Kamileen* is going to describe that they're *kamil* (perfected) and they inherit from *Qaf wal Quran al-Majeed* (Holy Qur'an, 50:1).' Because we said in the beginning, they're the people whom Allah ﷻ, '*Allamal Qur'an, Allamal Qur'an,* (taught the Qur'an), Holy Qur'an, 55:2); they reached to their realities.

Follow the Perfected Muhammadan Guides
Rashideen, Mahdiyeen, Kamileen

عَلَّمَ الْقُرْآنَ ﴿٢﴾

55:2 – *"Allamal Qur'an."* (Surat Ar-Rahman)

"It is He Who has taught the Qur'an." (The Beneficent, 55:2)

Letters of Qamar (Moon) Describe the Formula Qaf, Meem, Ra

QAMAR

	قمر	
	Qamar (Moon)	
ر	م	ق
Ra	**Meem**	**Qaf**
ربانيىون	محمداً	قرآن
Rabaniyoon (Lordly Souls)	Muhammadan (Muhammadan Realities)	Qur'an (Holy Qur'an)
راشدين	مهديين	كاملين
Rashideen (Rightly Guided)	Mahdiyeen (Highest Muhammadan Guides)	Kamileen (Perfected Guides)

Note: Please read English from right to left to coincide with Arabic.

Qamar – *Qaf, Meem, Ra*; you can't get to the *Qaf* without going through the *Ra*. The bull's-eye, the goal is to reach to that *Qaf, wal Quranil Majeed."* (Holy Qur'an, 50:1)

Shaykh Nurjan Mirahmadi

$$\text{ق ۚ وَالْقُرْآنِ الْمَجِيدِ ﴿١﴾}$$

50:1 – *"Qaf, wal Quranil Majeed." (Surat Qaf)*

"Qaf. By the honored Qur'an." (The Letter Qaf, 50:1)

So, our life is about understanding. When we're saying *qamarun, qamarun, qamarun,* (moon). They (saints) come back with the *huroof* (Arabic letters) and begin to teach that there's a formula in which Allah ﷻ wanted for us. That follow the *Rashideen* and *Mahdiyeen*, they are *kamileen*, they are *kamil* (perfected). This is going to be a description of them.

You Can't Achieve Any Stations Without a Guide

It means *Rashideen*, they are *Abdul Rasheed* (Servant of The Guide) and they are guided souls, whom Allah ﷻ inspired them to follow a Shaykh,

follow a moon. What I want to dress you with, you will never achieve if you don't take that path! You'll not achieve it by yourself. You will not make a connection to Prophet ﷺ by yourself. You'll not achieve any of those ranks that Allah ﷻ wants. But you cannot do it too! It doesn't matter, doesn't mean, not everybody graduates with a PhD and becomes a doctor. Some don't do anything. They don't go to any school. That's free for you, too. They're talking about a very high level of perfection. You say, 'Shaykh, I don't have to do it.' Absolutely correct! You don't have to do any of it!

Do Not Let Your Nafs (Ego) Represent You!

But if you're claiming that you're going to reach to be *kamil* (perfected), you need a guide. Whomever is not represented by a guide and whomever is not represented by a lawyer, a fool is his lawyer. It means his *shaytan* (satan) is his *wakeel* (representative). Even in the court system, they tell you only a fool represents himself. You have no understanding of any law, of any understanding of any type of defense and you want to defend yourself against Allah ﷻ, enter into His Divinely Court? And you want to follow your *nafs* (ego) and your own desires. This is impossible to reach these realities.

Rashideen (Rightly Guided)
Have License and Written Permission to Guide

In the Arabic letters, it will begin to define exactly these realities. So you must find those servants who are *Rashideen*. As a result of being *Abdul Rasheed* (Servant of the Guide), Allah ﷻ inspired them that, 'Follow the people of guidance! And those whom we granted guidance, they have an authorization of *irshad*, because they're *Abdul Rasheed*.'

Irshad means permission, written authorization to guide people; they're like licensed doctors. There are many clinics, no offense to Mexico and Tijuana – you can go across the border and you'll find many clinics. I heard there are even people doing plastic surgery and nobody even knows if he was a plumber or an electrician. There's somebody who injects his arm with motor oil and makes it to be big. This doesn't mean that that person is licensed. Anyone can claim anything they want.

But those whom Allah ﷻ made them to be *Rashideen* that they were guided, they followed a guide, they went through all what we're going to explain of that guidance. As a result, that guide signs that you are *Rashideen*. We're going to grant you *irshad*. That order is coming from Allah ﷻ, from *atiullah* given to the heart of Prophet's ﷺ soul, *atiur Rasul*, and then order comes to *ulul amr* (saints); grant that one the permission for *Irshad* (to guide)! And they sign the permission and they're *Rashideen* (rightly guided).

$$...يَاأَيُّهَا الَّذِينَ آمَنُوا أَطِيعُواللَّهَ وَأَطِيعُواْالرَّسُولَ وَأُولِي الْأَمْرِ مِنْكُمْ...﴿٥٩﴾$$

4:59 – "...*Ya ayyu hal latheena amanoo Atiullaha wa atiur Rasula wa Ulil amre minkum...*" *(Surat An-Nisa)*

"...*O You who have believed, Obey Allah, Obey the Messenger, and those in authority among you...*" *(The Women, 4:59)*

Character of Rashideen Always Remains Sweet

You see their character outside and their character inside matching; that their character is correct. Their character is filled with love. Their character is filled with compassion. Their character is the way of love. They don't scream, they don't shout, they don't attack. They are attacked and they remain sweet. They're insulted and they remain sweet. They're never salty but always sweet. Majority of people, they claim themselves to be nice, you squeeze them, you come out with words you could never have imagined from that servant. Because they claim to be sweet. Nobody is sweet until Allah ﷻ squeezes you, squeezes you, squeezes you and see how much sour is coming, how much sour is coming.

This means they've been tested. We talk from *Ashab al-Kahf* (People of the Cave), they've had rocks thrown at them, they've had difficulty thrown upon them. If they tell you clean the bathroom, you're on your knees and scrubbing. Otherwise you show, 'Oh my God, I have such a sickness. How dare you talk to me like that!' It means then you have years of cleaning ahead of you.

Follow the Perfected Muhammadan Guides
Rashideen, Mahdiyeen, Kamileen

Mahdiyeen Are Muhammadan Guides, Dressed From Sayyidina Mahdi ﷺ

So *Rashideen*, they have been brought down. They accompanied the guides. As a result, Allah ﷻ grant them *irshad* (permission). When granting of *irshad*, it means then the Shaykh at that level is also teaching, I'm going to make you *Mahdiyoon*. That you're going to come and you're going to be a *hadi* (guide) of Allah ﷻ. Because you have a *sifat* (attribute), you have *irshad* (guidance). It means now you have to be *hadi* and a guide; but you have to be a Muhammadan guide! And Allah ﷻ would begin to open the realities. Nobody can call themselves a *murshid* (authorized spiritual guide). It's just the title in the subcontinent. Everybody is a *mawlana* (master), everybody is a *murshid* (authorized spiritual guide). Everybody is everything. But what they're talking of these realities, these are very difficult to achieve.

The *Mahdiyeen* means they're the Muhammadan *hadis* (guides), that they're dressed from the realities of Sayyidina Mahdi ﷺ. We said before that Sayyidina Mahdi ﷺ is not only a timed event. We say, 'Okay, when is there the end of world coming and Sayyidina Mahdi ﷺ is coming!'

عَنْ عَبْدِ اللَّهِ بِنْ مسعود عَنِ النَّبِيِّ صَلَّى اللهُ عَلَيْهِ وَسَلَّمَ قَالَ : " لَا تَذْهَبُ أَوْ لَا تَنْقَضِي الدُّنْيَا حَتَّى يَمْلِكَ الْعَرَبَ رَجُلٌ مِنْ أَهْلِ بَيْتِي يُوَاطِئُ اسْمُهُ اسْمِي " مسند أحمد 199/5 ح 3573

'An Abdillah bin Mas'ud, 'Anan Nabi (saws) qala:
"La tazhabu aw la tanqadid dunya hatta ymlikal 'Araba rajulun min ahlil bayti yuwatiyu ismuhu ismi." (Musanad Ahmad)

AbdulAllah Ibn Masoud (ra) narrated that the messenger of Allah Prophet Muhamamd (pbuh) said: "The dunya (the material world) won't come to an end, until it's ruled by one of my grandchildren whose name is similar mine)." [Imam Ahmad's Recording]

Mahdiyeen is the Highest Level of Guidance

Mahdiyeen means there's no time. It's the highest level of guidance. The highest levels of perfection that Allah ﷻ is taking that servant. It doesn't mean that they're perfected, but continuously raising them, raising them, raising them under the *nazar* (gaze) of the soul of Sayyidina Mahdi ؑ. And it doesn't need physical appearance. But this is an eternal dress that Allah ﷻ gave to that reality that's going to make you a Muhammadan guide, a *hadi*. Allah ﷻ is going to train you.

That's the *hadith* that they came through voluntary worship and they

approached through their *nawafil*, they approached through voluntary. They did all the *fard* (obligatory worship) they came with voluntary. I became their ears in which they hear I became the eyes in which they see. Everyone knows that *hadith* here.

عَنْ أَبِي هُرَيْرَةَ رَضِيَ اللهُ عَنْهُ قَالَ: قَالَ رَسُولُ اللهِ صلى الله عليه و سلم إِنَّ اللهَ تَعَالَى قَالَ" :مَنْ عَادَى لِي وَلِيًّا فَقَدْ آذَنْتُهُ بِالْحَرْبِ، وَمَا تَقَرَّبَ إِلَيَّ عَبْدِي بِشَيْءٍ أَحَبَّ إِلَيَّ مِمَّا افْتَرَضْتُ عَلَيْهِ، وَلَا يَزَالُ عَبْدِي يَتَقَرَّبُ إِلَيَّ بِالنَّوَافِلِ حَتَّى أُحِبَّهُ، فَإِذَا أَحْبَبْتُهُ كُنْت سَمْعَهُ الَّذِي يَسْمَعُ بِهِ، وَبَصَرَهُ الَّذِي يُبْصِرُ بِهِ، وَيَدَهُ الَّتِي يَبْطِشُ بِهَا، وَرِجْلَهُ الَّتِي يَمْشِي بِهَا، وَلَئِنْ سَأَلَنِي لَأُعْطِيَنَّهُ،..." [رَوَاهُ الْبُخَارِيُّ

"Man 'ada li waliyan faqda adhantahu bilharbe, wa ma taqarraba ilayya 'Abdi bi shayin ahabba ilayya mimma aftaradtu 'alayhi,, wa la yazaalu 'Abdi yataqarrabu ilayya bin nawafile hatta ahebahu, fa idha ahbabtuhu kunta Sam'ahul ladhi yasma'u behi, wa Basarahul ladhi yubsiru behi, wa Yadahul lati yabTeshu beha, wa Rejlahul lati yamshi beha, wa la in sa alani la a'Teyannahu, ... "

Hadith qudsi narrated by Abu Hurayra, that Prophet Muhammad (pbuh) said that "Allah (AJ) said, 'I will declare war against him who shows hostility to a waliy (saint) of Mine. My servant continues to draw near to Me with voluntary acts of worship so that I shall love him. When I love him, I am his hearing with which he hears, his seeing with which he sees, his hand with which he strikes and his foot with which he walks. Were he to ask [something] of Me, I would surely give it to him..." (Hadith Qudsi, Sahih al-Bukhari, 81:38:2)

Rashideen Granted the 'Ra' and Are Rabaniyoon (Lordly Souls)

That's the *hadith* that Allah ﷻ is describing, when I'm going to open for this *hadith* that Prophet ﷺ describes. So much so that you become *rabaniyoon* (lordly soul); because you're all from the people of *irshad* (guidance), you were granted the *Ra*. You're not a normal soul, you're a lofty soul. You're *rabbaniyoon* (lordly soul) and so much so that you have power of *"kun faya kun"* (be and it is)

إِنَّمَا أَمْرُهُ إِذَا أَرَادَ شَيْئًا أَن يَقُولَ لَهُ كُن فَيَكُونُ ﴿٨٢﴾

36:82 – "Innama AmruHu idha Arada shay an, an yaqola lahu kun faya koon." (Surat YaSeen)

"His Command is when He Wills/Intends a thing, He says to it, "Be," and it is!" (YaSeen, 36:82)

That merely your heart begins to pray and Allah ﷻ begins to grant. Why? Because you've been smashed and pounded that your will is matching Prophet's ﷺ will. Prophet's ﷺ will is matching Allah's ﷻ Will. It's actually Allah's ﷻ Will that is pushing your heart to make that *du'a* and Allah ﷻ grant what Allah ﷻ wanted in the beginning.

Muhammadan Guides Don't Try to Change Allah's ﷻ Will

They never can pray against what Allah ﷻ wants. They don't change what Allah ﷻ brought. If somebody is sick, they don't make them to be good. Allah ﷻ wanted that person sick. They just advise, 'Maybe you should do some good things so that your Lord be happy with you.' They're not opening a competing store with the Divinely Presence. Allah ﷻ take away something and they put it back?

These guides, they know exactly Allah ﷻ wants something from that servant. Their responsibility is to say, Your Lord wants something from you, perfect yourself, perfect your character!

Mahdiyeen Inherit from the Tongue of Truth (Lisanul Haq wa Lisanul Siddiq ul Aliya)

Their ears will be perfected, their eyes will be perfected. Their breath will be full of *qudra* (power). As a result, they speak through that Holy Tongue, *lisanul Haq wa lisan al-Siddiq ul-Aliya* (the Tongue of Truth and the Tongue of Highest Truthful). That they inherit from a tongue of truth and from the tongue of the holy companions and they speak from that reality.

وَوَهَبْنَا لَهُم مِّن رَّحْمَتِنَا وَجَعَلْنَا لَهُمْ لِسَانَ صِدْقٍ عَلِيًّا ﴿٥٠﴾

19:50 – *"Wa wahabna lahum min rahmatina wa ja'alna lahum lisana Sidqin 'Aliya." (Surat Maryam)*

"And We bestowed of Our Mercy on them, and We granted them lofty honour from/on the tongue of truth." (Mary, 19:50)

It means they're being dressed by the Divinely Face. Their ears are dressed, their eyes are dressed, their breath is dressed. As a result, they can speak the truth, and these are *Mahdiyeen*. At that time, Allah ﷻ brings their soul and says, 'You are now *Qamarun* that look to where you're supposed to look! This sun will continuously be shining upon your face and your face be dressed by those realities.'

*Follow the Perfected Muhammadan Guides
Rashideen, Mahdiyeen, Kamileen*

Be Loyal to One Guide, Don't Go to Ten People For Guidance

We pray that Allah ﷻ guide us and give us understanding. People whom come out and keep saying that I don't need to follow a guide. No, you don't need to do anything! You can sit in Taco Bell all day long, but you're not going to reach Allah's ﷻ Divinely Realities that he wanted to bestow upon you. You have to be tested. You have to be tried. You have to be taught that, 'Don't look left and don't look right, don't go to ten different people.' This is about loyalty!  You keep one focus and that's your focus until you're in the grave. You don't choose left and right. And they begin to teach that loyalty that understanding; you're locked on! As soon you're locked on, their *nazar* (gaze) be upon you and dress you.

We pray that Allah ﷻ dress us from these lights of these holy months. This is the month of *al-Qamar* (moon) (Jumadil Thani, 6th Lunar month), opening for the holy months of Rajab, Shaban and Ramadan, *inshaAllah*.

Subhana rabbika rabbal 'izzati 'amma yasifoon, wa salaamun 'alal mursaleen, walhamdulillahi rabbil 'aalameen. Bi hurmati Muhammad al-Mustafa wa bi siri Surat al-Fatiha.

The Light of the Sun Burns All Impurities

In such simple understanding that you kind of think, 'I knew that.' It doesn't have to be in complicated language and complicated references that it is meant to go from heart to heart. They teach us from the signs outside to understand the reality inside. From the understandings of the Circles of Association, Circles of Remembrance, and the way of purification, as a reminder for ourselves, what I am trying to accomplish by being inspired by the Divine to sit in the Circles of Remembrance. That I am asking my Lord, let me to reach to Your Light, let me to reach to Your Satisfaction, I am begging Your forgiveness at every moment and seeking Your Divinely satisfaction, *"Ilahi anta maqsudi wa ridaka matlub"*.

إِلَهِى أَنْتَ مَقْصُوْدِيْ وَرِضَاكَ مَطْلُوْبِيْ

"Ilahi anta maqsudi wa radhaaka matloob."

"My God, You are my aim, and Your Satisfaction is what I seek."

Mawlana Jalaluddin Rumi ق Met the Sun, Shams ق

Then the understanding of the World of Light, to keep the company of enlightened people so that we may reach a state of enlightenment. A very simple understanding that even from traditional Sufi teachings Sayyidina Jalaluddin Rumi ق, with a lot of scholastic knowledge and exterior knowledge was lacking, in a sense

The Light of the Sun Burns All Impurities

of the fruit and the essence of the reality. He came across a master in his life, a teacher called Shams Tabriz ق. Again, for us to make it very simple, *shams* is the sun and what we have to pull from that understanding is that the sun is a light, an eternal source of light.

هُوَ الَّذِي جَعَلَ الشَّمْسَ ضِيَاءً ... ﴿٥﴾

10:5 – *"Huwal ladhee ja'alash shamsa Diya an ..." (Surat Yunus)*

"It is He who made the Sun a shining light ..." (Jonah, 10:5)

When we say 'light' are we talking of a fluorescent light? The Divine is saying, 'No, look outside in your creation, do you see that sun?' It is eternal. The Sun is in constant fusion, a very clean energy and eternal, no source of energy that we understand. The Divine has its reality, but it is taking from elements and bringing them in and creating a fire, a tremendous fire. As a result of that fire, it is emitting a tremendous light.

We Can't Exist Without the Eternal light of the Sun (Guide)

That light, when we begin to understand and study the sun, it is a source of our breath, a source of our food, a source of our sight; it is a source of our life on this planet. No doubt the originator of the entire source is the Divine, but the Divine is teaching that through means of creation, you are existing. So, one sign of your existence is that sun. Without that eternal light you cannot exist, you cannot breathe, you can't eat, you cannot see. This means for us we are asking to open the reality of that sun. Then the *tariqahs* (spiritual paths) come and begin to teach the sun and the understanding of the sun is the reality of the heart, and how to open the reality of the heart.

One reality is the understanding of the masters, and then the most important reality is the understanding of ourselves. Masters, their hearts are suns. Now how they became a sun is in the understanding of the student. We are trying to sit in the presence of a fire, and that fire is not like a regular fire, but is coming with an eternal Divinely flame. So, then the circles of *zikr* (remembrance), the real circles, with real servants of the Divine whose hearts are open, they have either a tremendous open heart or they have merely a pilot light within their heart, and immediately can be ignited and begin to emit a flame.

We Come to Spiritual Paths as Wet Logs

The importance of that understanding is to understand that we come like a wet log. These are the phases of the *zikr* (remembrance), always teaching by analogy, because people don't understand themselves. So, when you speak from analogy you get more of an understanding. When you come into the presence of a fire and you sit at the fire, the initial stage is that many come as a wet log; they have so much on themselves, so many burdens on themselves, so many distractions within their being. It is like a wet log and when you put the wet log in a fire, it feels nothing. So many come and say, 'I didn't feel anything.' They want us to understand that who knows himself will

begin to know his Lord, will begin to know his path, will begin to know what they are trying to achieve.

مَنْ عَرَفَ نَفْسَهُ فَقَدْ عَرَفَ رَبَّهُ

"Man 'arafa nafsahu faqad 'arafa Rabbahu"

"Who knows himself, knows his Lord." (Prophet Muhammad (pbuh))

If I am not feeling anything, I am like a wet log. I have lots of burdens, lots of difficulties, again by analogy, I've lots of things that are making me in a state of moisture, of wetness, I am distracted. I sit and I don't feel anything but it doesn't mean that nothing is happening. That fire is still burning, it is still trying to cook that log but it is going through so many layers of moisture and moisture, and burdens and difficulties, the log doesn't yet feel it is being cooked.

Be Like the Moth and Go to the Fire of Love

So, what they want for us at that stage is to be persistent. Keep coming, keep coming, but we have to know the objective. I am asking my Lord, I am asking to burn in Your Divinely Flame. When you read all the poetry they begin to put all the pieces together, the poetry of the moth, how the moth is attracted to the fire and they want us to be attracted to the Divinely Fire.

حیلت رها کن عاشقا دیوانه شو دیوانه شو
و اندر دل آتش درآ پروانه شو پروانه شو

*Heelat reha kun 'Ashiqa, dewana shaw,
dewana shaw
Wandar dil Atash dara, parwana shaw,
parwana shaw*

*Put aside your clever schemes!
O Lover, be mindless! Become mad!
Dive into the heart of the flame,
Become fearless, Become a moth*

– Mawlana Jalaluddin Muhammad (Rumi)

The moth doesn't think, it just sees a fire and its instinct, Divine instinct is to be lost. When you see little flies and moths back home, they go straight into the fire. The Divine is saying with that *ishq*, with that love, you must approach Me.

Allah ﷻ Has Honoured Human Being More Than the Sun and the Moon

If the outside sun you are in need of, I have *"walaqad karamna bani Adam"* (Holy Qur'an, 17:70), I have honoured Mankind beyond the sun and the moon, I have honoured the creation of Adam and Eve, I have blown of My Spirit into them. They are more powerful than suns.

وَلَقَدْ كَرَّمْنَا بَنِي آدَمَ وَ... وَفَضَّلْنَاهُمْ عَلَىٰ كَثِيرٍ مِّمَّنْ خَلَقْنَا تَفْضِيلًا ﴿٧٠﴾

17:70 – *"Wa laqad karramna banee adama, …wa faddalnahum 'ala katheerin mimman khalaqna tafdeela. (Surat Al-Isra)*

"And We have certainly honored the children of Adam and…bestow upon them favours, and preferred them over much of what We have created, with [definite] preference." (The Night Journey, 17:70)

And

$$\text{فَإِذَا سَوَّيْتُهُ وَنَفَخْتُ فِيهِ مِن رُّوحِي فَقَعُوا لَهُ سَاجِدِينَ ﴿٢٩﴾}$$

15:29 – "Fa idha sawwaytuhu wa nafakhtu feehi min Rohee faqa'o lahu sajideen." (Surat Al-Hijr)

"So when I have proportioned him and breathed into him of My [created] soul/spirit, then fall down to him in prostration."
(The Rocky Tract, 15:29)

Then they teach us by analogy to read about the sun. It is a source of fire, that many things are relying upon that sun and the Divine is saying that you are more honoured to Me than the sun, the moon and all the Heavens. This means that the potential you have within yourselves is unimaginable. So, then I am sitting and asking, let me to burn, let the badness to burn, let all that is distracting me from Your Divinely Presence to perish.

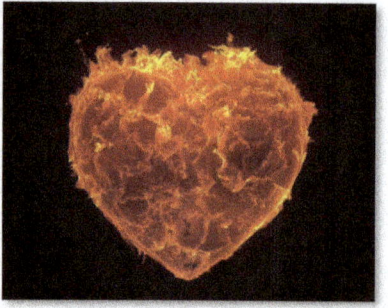

Everyone Must Face the Fire Here or in Sirat ul Mustaqeem

Many poetries from Sayyidina Jalaluddin Rumi ق is about fire; dance in the fire, seek the fire, let the fire burn all that is other than the fire.

$$\text{آتشی از عشق در جان برفروز}$$
$$\text{سر به سر فکر و عبارت را بسوز}$$

Atashi az ishq dar jan bar feroz
Sar ba sar fekro ebarat ra besoz

"Kindle in thy heart the fire of love,
and burn all your utterly thoughts and fine expressions."
– Mawlana Jalaluddin Muhammad (Rumi)

"Set your life on fire. Seek those who fan your flames."
– Mawlana Jalaluddin Muhammad (Rumi)

It means it burns your possessions away, it burns your desires away; it burns your bad characters away until you feel yourself one with the flame. This is the description of the Divine ecstasy. What is burning is all that is other than the flame.

The concept of *jahannum* (hellfire) is that everybody has to go through the flame. So, Allah ﷻ describes there is a very straight and narrow path. You have to walk on this at some day, either while you are alive and you face the fire or I catch you in the grave because the fire is My Divinely Love. You have to pass through that fire. If you are carrying anything from character, from *dunya* (material world) from all that is other than love, it is going to be burned in that *Sirat al-Mustaqeem* (Straight Path).

Like anything else if we are a light and we are a flame, we go into the flame and pass as if nothing because everything is burned already in the material world. All the desires are burned, all the bad character is burned. And it is continuously burning because these desires keep coming but *ashiqeen* and the lovers of the reality, their flame is so strong it immediately burns away again. The desires come and the flames burn, the possessions come and the flames burn. The Divine is teaching if we don't do that there is a *Sirat al-Mustaqeem* (Straight Path) and every tradition has it that you are going to pass through that fire and burns everything other than Divine Love.

People of Nabi Musa ﷺ Took Their Gold Even to the Promised Land

People of Nabi Musa ﷺ were seeking the promised land and they wouldn't let go of their gold. For forty years he was teaching them,

The Light of the Sun Burns All Impurities

'Leave the gold, leave the desires; God will open for us a promised land.' They said no, no, no.

Forty years of teaching and finally Nabi Musa ﷺ said, 'Let's go,' and they ran with so much gold they couldn't even move. That is why they couldn't escape *Fir'aun* (Pharaoh). They came with all their gold and all their possessions seeking the promised land until *Fir'aun* (Pharaoh) came upon them and tried to capture them by the water and the ocean parted and Allah ﷻ saved them on the shores of mercy.

فَأَوْحَيْنَا إِلَىٰ مُوسَىٰ أَنِ اضْرِب بِّعَصَاكَ الْبَحْرَ ۖ فَانفَلَقَ فَكَانَ كُلُّ فِرْقٍ كَالطَّوْدِ الْعَظِيمِ ﴿٦٣﴾

26:63 – "Fa awhayna ila Mosa anidrib bi'asaka albahra, fanfalaqa fakana kullu firqin kattawdil 'aZheem. (Surat Ash-Shu'ara)

"Then We inspired to Moses, 'Strike with your staff the sea,' and it parted, and each portion was like a great towering mountain."
(The Poets, 26:63)

But Allah ﷻ had a plan, He told Nabi Musa ﷺ you go up and seclude yourself with Me. I am going to inspire them to take the gold and make a cow and then I will burn it. So, He collected all their gold and manifested their desires that this is what you like. He took all the gold that they wouldn't part with for forty years, the desires of the material possessions, and Allah ﷻ inspired them to make the cow, that is really what you want.

Nabi Musa ﷺ Saw His Lord as a Burning Fire

It is a deep reality from Nabi Musa ﷺ because they are all about the same reality, because he saw his Lord as a burning fire.

لَمَّا أَتَاهَا نُودِيَ مِن شَاطِئِ الْوَادِ الْأَيْمَنِ فِي الْبُقْعَةِ الْمُبَارَكَةِ مِنَ الشَّجَرَةِ أَن يَا مُوسَىٰ إِنِّي أَنَا اللَّـهُ رَبُّ الْعَالَمِينَ ﴿٣٠﴾

28:30 – *"Falammaaa ataahaa noodiya min shaati'il waadil aimani fil buq'atil muubaarakati minash shajarati ai yaa Musa ineee Anal laahu Rabbul 'aalameen." (Surat Al-Qasas)*

"But when he came to it (fire), he was called from the right side of the valley in a blessed spot – from the tree, "O Moses, indeed I am Allah, Lord of the worlds." (The Stories, 28:30)

That is the fire that they are telling us to sit at, the *diya* of Allah ﷻ, the Divinely Fire of Allah ﷻ that we are asking, '*Ya Rabbi*, let me to sit at that fire and to sit with those whom You have put Your fire within their hearts.'

هُوَ الَّذِي جَعَلَ الشَّمْسَ ضِيَاءً ... ﴿٥﴾

10:5 – *"Huwal ladhee ja'alash shamsa Diya an ..." (Surat Yunus)*

"It is He who made the sun a shining glory ..." (Jonah, 10:5)

When the Log Becomes Dry, It Feels the Burning and Trials

Then we have to understand our stages. If I am a wet log, I don't feel anything and they are still burning, they are still cleaning until the wet becomes a bit dry. After it becomes dry, it begins to feel that when I go into the associations, into the *zikr* (remembrance) and I am living this life, I feel a burning. I feel difficulty and testing. I feel trials and tribulations. It means that log is now burning. It burns a lot

faster the more you come, because you are near a source of flame. That flame is attracted to that wood, it begins to burn, begins to burn and begins to burn it until the wood begins to catch. The wood burns and burns, at that point many people will run.

Don't Run Away From Burning and Purification

So, you see them come and you see them go because the burning and the parting from their material desires, and from their characteristics, whatever is on that wood. Again, this is an analogy, whatever is there that they thought they wanted to be burnt away, when the real fire comes, and the real fire begins, many say, 'O it's a bit too hot, I am taking off.' They may even talk bad about the fire on their way when departing. It doesn't matter. They will be caught in the grave and the burning will begin in the *qabr* (grave). It is much easier to go through it while alive, much easier to do it in a state of love. That to understand my path and I am asking, *ya Rabbi,* let me to sit in those associations, let me to take a life in which these desires begin to burn and begin to burn.

Different Levels of the Sun and Stations of the Heart

Then they remind us that in science you have three states of matter. When you come across these suns and we study the suns and the suns have degrees of what suns are. These are again like the Levels of the Heart. You have a Yellow Sun, you have a Red Sun, then you have a White Sun which they call the 'dwarf sun' and then they have a pulsar sun and then you have a 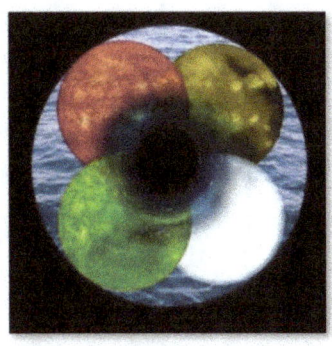 Black Hole in the center of the *lataif* (subtle energy points).

It means the degrees in which the sun and each one billion times stronger than the other one. So even among the suns these are *darajats* (stations) of suns. The most basic is the sun of our galaxy because the galaxy is our body. Our planets are our organs, our *qalb* (heart) is where the *shams* (sun) should be and the Divine is asking, ignite your heart so it becomes the sun. This is the galaxy I gave you. As you see the galaxy outside you have a galaxy within you. If you cannot manage your galaxy, how can I open My Heavenly Galaxy to you? How can I open the understanding of the heavenly universe if you can't manage your universe?

The Process of Burning at Three States of Matter

1. First State is Solid, Hard to Ignite – Student is Very Opinionated

Then they begin to teach, sit amongst them who are open-hearted and they begin the burning process.

يَا أَيُّهَا الَّذِينَ آمَنُوا اتَّقُوا اللَّهَ وَكُونُوا مَعَ الصَّادِقِينَ ﴿١١٩﴾

9:119 – *"Ya ayyuhal ladheena amanoo ittaqollaha wa kono ma'as sadiqeen." (Surat At-Tawbah)*

"O you who have believed, have consciousness of Allah and be with those who are truthful/ Pious / sincere (in words and deed)."
(The Repentance, 9:119)

By burning, burning, burning that wood becomes like hay. From a sense of hay, it becomes almost like a liquid because it has burned so much.

The guides begin to teach us that these are the states of matter. That we are at a solid state when we first come, very opinionated, very much into our desires of what we want and what we wish and what we think and what we know and what we have. That has to be burned and they teach us in very basic science, I think in 8th grade science, that if this matter is going to transform you have to leave your solid state.

So, then you sit, sit, sit, sit until you find your log is becoming like liquid, it burned, it has been tested. It sits in the flame, literally you go home heating up like you are on fire with fevers and colds and sicknesses over a lifetime, over a period of time not just in one day. Constantly, this is not only spiritual but physical testing in life, difficulties in life. Then you begin to understand that this is the life of cleansing. Better to be cleansed now than again in the grave. And that matter becomes like a liquid.

2. Second State is Liquid, Easier to Ignite – Student Becomes Flexible

Then they taught us in science that liquid is much easier to ignite than solid, so the hard part is done. So, it means as the student is moving closer to that reality their state is liquid, their state is more easily ignitable to the next state which is gaseous. To make a solid into a gas is very difficult. Solid has to be burned down, has to attend, has to do the *zikr* (remembrance), has to do the chanting, has to accompany those lights and these suns. When it accompanies, it begins to burn, begins to burn, it finds its character becoming more liquid. Hence lucid, flowing, and less objection, you see the character change. Water, anything you pour it into, okay, there is little bit of a struggle but it goes in, until more fire, more fire, and more fire.

This means as we are approaching the Divine Light, it is the light that Nabi Musa ﷺ was teaching us. That when you are in a state of love and you are asking to meet your Lord, it comes to you with a flame; this is a flame of Divinely Presence, of Divinely Light and it burns away everything other than that love and you find yourself becoming liquid.

لَمَّا أَتَاهَا نُودِيَ مِن شَاطِئِ الْوَادِ الْأَيْمَنِ فِي الْبُقْعَةِ الْمُبَارَكَةِ مِنَ الشَّجَرَةِ أَن يَا مُوسَىٰ إِنِّي أَنَا اللَّـهُ رَبُّ الْعَالَمِينَ ﴿٣٠﴾

28:30 – "Falammaaa ataahaa noodiya min shaati'il waadil aimani fil buq'atil muubaarakati minash shajarati ai yaa Moosaaa ineee Anal laahu Rabbul 'aalameen." (Surat Al-Qasas)

"But when he came to it (fire), he was called from the right side of the valley in a blessed spot – from the tree, "O Moses, indeed I am Allah, Lord of the worlds." (The Stories, 28:30)

3. Third State is Gas – Ethereal State – Student Becomes Subtle to Energies

Then turning from liquid to gas is very fast. At that state, when the student is reaching a liquid state it means their entire being can quickly ignite. They become very sensitive to the energy all around them. They begin to look at the signs in the universe. One sign is that they begin to look at the signs within the universe, you look at the physical sun and see the eruptions on the sun and you begin to understand you are heating up every time you see the sun erupting, that your body changes

based on what is happening on this *dunya* (material world) because Allah ﷻ is saying you are just a piece of this entire fabric; whatever is happening outside is a reflection of what is happening inside.

سَنُرِيهِمْ آيَاتِنَا فِي الْآفَاقِ وَفِي أَنفُسِهِمْ حَتَّىٰ يَتَبَيَّنَ لَهُمْ أَنَّهُ الْحَقُّ... ﴿٥٣﴾

41:53 – "Sanureehim ayatina fil afaqi wa fee anfusihim hatta yatabayyana lahum annahu alhaqqu..." (Surat Al-Isra)

"We will show them Our signs in the horizons and within themselves until it becomes clear to them that it is the truth..."
(The Night Journey, 41:53)

You begin to understand your subtle nature, you are moving from a physical hard nature to a subtle *lateef*, nature. Subtle nature is like gas, immediately the liquid state ignites to an ethereal angelic state, just a little bit of that light and the soul is moving freely.

They teach that these are the states we are trying to reach. This is us. When the Shaykh sees that and sees that you are reaching the ethereal state, that you are liquid, it means your *tarbiyya* (manners) and your *taslim* (submission) is very strong because you are like liquid; whatever he puts you through you endure. You keep coming, keep coming and become like a gas that immediately you are able to leave  your physical confines and you are moving with the power of your soul and at that time they give permission to ignite you.

When Ignited, an Eternal Flame is Given to the Heart of Student

When the student is ignited it means his eternal flame has been given by permission of Allah ﷻ, permission of Prophet ﷺ and permission from *awliyaullah* (saints) that the flame lit into the heart. That is an eternal gift given by Allah ﷻ that cannot be taken away. Nobody can say, 'Maybe they made a mistake, maybe they didn't know what they were doing.' They go through so much difficulty for Allah ﷻ to give that 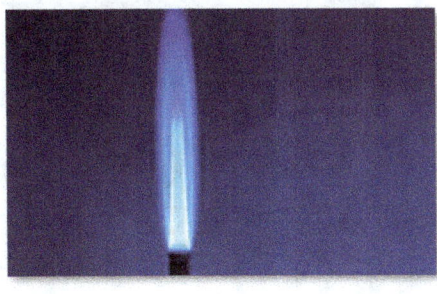 state. And what Allah ﷻ gives, He never takes back because He never made a mistake in the first place. We make mistakes. Allah ﷻ doesn't make mistakes. It means the state of 'being lit' the Shaykh at that time says, 'You are at a gaseous state and you have endured all the understanding of these testing and trials. Your pilot is lit.'

The specialty of Naqshbandiya is that when their pilot is lit and their lights are on, they have the ability to shut 'on and off' instantly. You

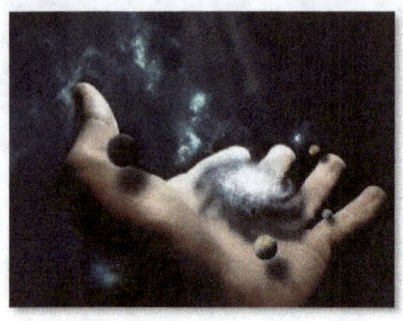

may see them as very normal people interacting in many different things but when Allah ﷻ wants them on, Prophet ﷺ wants them on, Mawlana Shaykh wants them on, immediately just their *zikr* (remembrance), their state of *haal* (spiritual state) ignites their entire being. They just pass their being through that fire and can ignite their entire soul. Their soul and the size of their soul is beyond understanding, beyond the size of this Earth. The Earth fits within the hand of their soul.

When Heart is Lit, the Process of Burning is From Within

This means that ability in which to ignite the soul, once the student is lit, it means their heart is lit. Once the heart is lit, Allah ﷻ keeps sending the fire to make sure it continues to be cleaned. This means they can be cleaned by just sitting in bed and sleeping, because Allah ﷻ sends a *tajalli* (manifestation) to a lit heart. It means the pilot is lit. All the work was to get the pilot light lit. Once it is lit, the Divine sends any type of ignition into that heart and immediately it goes into a state. It can go into a state while sleeping, while sitting, while watching TV, or eating dinner. Then immediately an energy comes

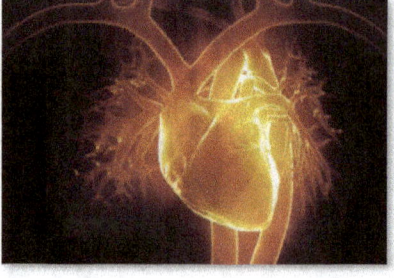

and the Divine begins the process of burning from within and begins to burn everything on the outside and constantly keeping those whom are lit to be purified and clean. These are the ones who are *mahfuz* (safeguarded), they are guarded by the Divine, because when He gives, He guards, He safeguards them. If He finds too much calcification or incorrect growing upon them, He merely ignites their heart and they go into a state of burning and again all the burning and badness will begin to burn away because they have been reached, and their internal being has been reached.

The Process of the Sun Formation and Levels of the Heart

From the level of the sun then they begin to open not regular sun, they move into the understanding of the red giant. The red when we begin

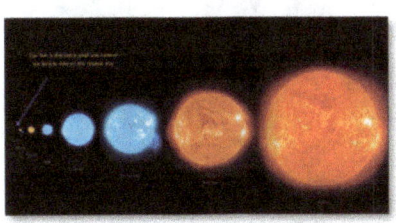

to understand, these are huge giant suns. They even have a factory within themselves of what is happening and again the degrees of *awliyaullah* (saints) are unimaginable. There is not just one level. Just for us to understand that when Mawlana Shaykh lights the heart or given permission for the heart to be lit, it is tremendous reality. And because of that reality they are capable of emitting a tremendous light.

Then from the Levels of the Heart you begin to understand the levels of the suns. Just by studying the external knowledge of the suns, the size difference, what is happening within these suns, from our little yellow sun to the big red giant suns? From the pulsar which is such a powerful massive sun that it even loses its mass and collapses within itself. This was the state in which

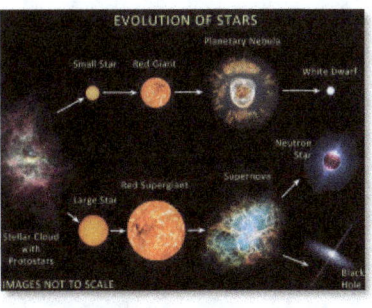

Sayyidina 'Ali was saying, 'My annihilation within my annihilation.'

It means the sun is already in a state of annihilation, it has lost its physicality and annihilated itself in Divine Reality, as a result of losing its mass it is now just energy. What Einstein was trying to understand was that formula of how to reach energy.

$E = MC^2$

Energy = Mass x Light^2

When they begin to lose the importance of their mass, then their energy is two lights; the two lights squared within them. Then as the degree of their sainthood is elevating, elevating, elevating, then you begin to study these white dwarfs and pulsars they actually collapse within their reality. Then they become so dense and so powerful that it is unimaginable until the black and the black which is the state of complete annihilation, is the black hole. The black hole means it collapses upon itself but not only it collapses upon itself but anything it approaches, it annihilates it. These are the big saints, their duty is merely to bring everybody into that annihilation and throw them from *fana* (annihilation) back into *baqa* because once you are annihilated and destroyed in that presence, you will be resurrected in the Divinely Presence. These are the stations of *awliya* (saints).

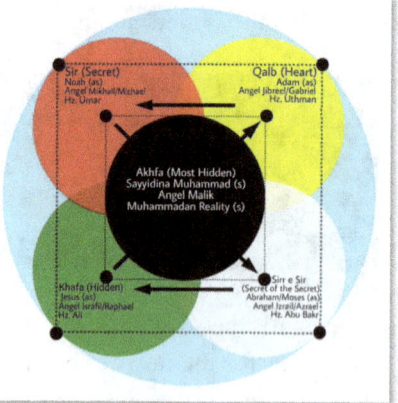

Can You Take the Heat or Run Away?

This is the chain and the understanding of these saints. Each one above is much more powerful, each one above with a completely different understanding and duty. To reach to these *awliya* (saints) and to understand that I am asking to sit in their associations I am asking to burn. Then let the burning begin. Many people as soon as the burning begins, they run because they can't take the heat. They say if you can't take the heat, get out of the kitchen. That is the cooking because they want to take us to a station of light.

If your knowledge of fire
has been turned to certainty by Words alone,
Then Seek to be cooked by the fire itself.
Don't abide in borrowed certainty
There is no real certainty until you burn;
If you wish for this, sit down in the fire"

– Mawlana Jalaluddin Balkhi (Rumi)

InshaAllah. with more understanding that Mawlana Shaykh opens for us and that Allah (ﷻ) grants us, an understanding Prophet (ﷺ) grants us, an understanding of the magnificence and the munificence of the Divinely gift, *walaqad karamna bani adam.*

وَلَقَدْ كَرَّمْنَا بَنِي آدَمَ...﴿٧٠﴾

17:70 – *"Wa laqad karramna bani adama…"* (Surat Al-Isra)

"And We have certainly honored the children of Adam…"
(The Night Journey, 17:70)

We Believe More in Our Phones Than the Power of Our Soul

The state of light and the understanding of light is beyond imagination. It is beyond what we can even understand of what Allah (ﷻ), the Divine wanted to give to us, but in exchange what we are actually choosing. We are choosing the worst and the lowest of this Creation. We are not seeking the Light but seeking everything of the material world and losing our state of light, and our

The Light of the Sun Burns All Impurities

understanding of light. Every technology we have around us is based on energy and light. We rely more on that technology than developing it for ourselves. That is what *shaytan* (satan) wants. The bad ego wants that you just play with the phone, to believe in the phone but don't ever think that you are more powerful than that phone, that your heart can move from here to the universe, to the seven heavens in the blink of an eye, it can send videos, can send signals, can send audio. We pray that the understanding begins to open more and more within our heart, *inshaAllah*.

يَا مَعْشَرَ الْجِنِّ وَالْإِنسِ إِنِ اسْتَطَعْتُمْ أَن تَنفُذُوا مِنْ أَقْطَارِ السَّمَاوَاتِ وَالْأَرْضِ فَانفُذُوا ۚ لَا تَنفُذُونَ إِلَّا بِسُلْطَانٍ ﴿٣٣﴾

55:33 – "Ya ma'ashara al jinni wal insi inistata'tum an tanfudho min aqtari asSamawati wal Ardi fanfudho, La tanfudhona illa bi Sultan." (Surat Ar-Rahman)

"O gathering/ assembly of jin and mankind, if you are able to penetrate through the atmosphere and pass beyond the zones of the Heavens and Earth, then Penetrate. You will never be able to pass, Except with a King, you need a sultan." (The Beneficient, 55:33)

Subhana rabbika rabbal 'izzati 'amma yasifoon, wa salaamun 'alal mursaleen, walhamdulillahi rabbil 'aalameen. Bi hurmati Muhammad al-Mustafa wa bi siri Surat al-Fatiha.

The Face of the Shaykh Has Authority and Power

Everything is Based on Obedience to Allah, RasulAllah, and Those in Authority

Alhamdulillah, for Mawlana Shaykh's teaching as a reminder that everything is in that reality of, *"Ati ullah ati ar rasul wa ulil amri minkum"* (Obey Allah, Obey the Messenger, and those in authority among you).

﴿يَاأَيُّهَا الَّذِينَ آمَنُوا أَطِيعُوااللَّهَ وَأَطِيعُواالرَّسُولَ وَأُولِي الْأَمْرِ مِنْكُمْ...٥٩﴾

4:59 – *"Ya ayyu hal latheena amanoo Atiullaha wa atiur Rasula wa Ulil amre minkum..."* (Surat An-Nisa)

"O You who have believed, Obey Allah, Obey the Messenger, and those in authority among you..." (The Women, 4:59)

Everything is based on obedience to Allah, obedience to the Prophetic Reality, and to follow the way of the *ulul amr* (saints). It means there is a secret in that three. So, it means to base our life off that reality that there is always going to be a secret in this number three.

Obedience to Allah is the Secret of the Essence

That obedience to Allah is like the secret of the Essence; the ultimate goal of the reality of the seeker is to reach to the obedience of Allah. For us to visualize like an Essence, like the innermost secret of a room. Allah knows that that is going to be difficult for us, just to hit right into that bullseye, so He gives for us that *ati ar rasul*.

Obey Sayyidina Muhammad; make your life to follow the way of Prophet, the way of love, patience, tolerance, and *khuluq ul azheem*, the best of character.

وَإِنَّكَ لَعَلَىٰ خُلُقٍ عَظِيمٍ ﴿٤﴾

68:4 – *"Wa innaka la'ala khuluqin 'azheem."* (Surat Al-Qalam)

"Truly, You (O Muhammad (pbuh)!) are of a magnificent character." (The Pen, 68:4)

Learn Knowledge From Shaykhs With the Best of Character

That is the litmus test because now we are bombarded with internet Shaykhs, they are everywhere. Where before you had to travel long distance, now you just sit on your laptop and you can go to one hundred Shaykhs in one day, watch all these different videos. *Awliyaullah* (saints) come into our life and teach that the most important character is *khuluq*. That they are inheriting from the 'best of character'. If whatever knowledge is coming is not based on character, run from it. It doesn't mean anything. It means you are being fed something in a dangerous cup. The *uloom* (knowledge) can be amazing, the *qira'at* (recitation) can be astonishing. So, it means then they want us to understand any knowledge, if not based on good character, it means we observe with our heart. When we see the character is good, the *akhlaq* (character) is good, the understanding, the *muhabbat* (love) is good, then that is a fountain to drink from.

Obedience to Prophet Muhammad ﷺ is Like a Room

So *ati ar rasul* ﷺ (obedience to Messenger) becomes now like a room for us; that we want to be in that room and we want to find the secret that Allah ﷻ has for us. That is our goal. 'I want the room of Prophet ﷺ.' Inside that room, like a video game that you are so familiar with, it is the same concept. When they make the video game they make just a room, and just change the scenario, you are still in the same place. That is why someday you will wake up and realize, wow that was

really crazy to play this game for so long. You never left the room! It is just one picture of a room and you are running around thinking you are going to different levels, it is still the same room just painted with different scenarios. Allah ﷻ says, the real game you should be playing is to reach to this reality. Find a room in which Prophet ﷺ is there.

Find the association in which Prophet ﷺ is there. In that association, there is going to be a secret Essence of Allah ﷻ. If they are from the *Ahbab an Nabi* ﷺ, the lovers of Prophet ﷺ, that through their character known and unknown, is based on the love of Prophet ﷺ. This means they mention Prophet ﷺ often, they praise upon Prophet ﷺ often, they talk about Prophet ﷺ in everything, they don't talk on behalf of Allah ﷻ.

The Nafs (Ego) Doesn't Accept Authority, So Bring the Ego Down

There is a bad character that always wants to go over you. We said before somebody would sit with us and say, 'Mawlana, when I am sitting and closing my eyes…' How is he talking in Mawlana's presence? 'Oh Mawlana, how am I going to connect my heart to Sayyidina Mahdi ؏?' You think, O my God, how did this person ask that in front of Mawlana? Mawlana looked at that person… 'Hmm, connect to Sayyidina Mahdi ؏? So why you have to do that? Why don't you go straight to Prophet ﷺ?' And then he thought a little bit longer, 'Why do you even have to do that? Why don't you go just directly to Allah ﷻ? You don't need to ask us, we are small people, just you go directly to Allah ﷻ.'

398

It means this character of thinking oneself high and, 'I deal with the boss' this was the character of *Shaytan* (Satan). When Allah ﷻ said, 'Make *sujood* (prostration).' This means accept the *Khalifah* (Vicegerent), accept Sayyidina Adam ؑ; he is My *Khalifa*, bow down, pay your *ihtiram* and your respect.'

وَإِذْ قَالَ رَبُّكَ لِلْمَلَائِكَةِ إِنِّي جَاعِلٌ فِي الْأَرْضِ خَلِيفَةً قَالُوا أَتَجْعَلُ فِيهَا مَن يُفْسِدُ فِيهَا وَيَسْفِكُ الدِّمَاءَ وَنَحْنُ نُسَبِّحُ بِحَمْدِكَ وَنُقَدِّسُ لَكَ قَالَ إِنِّي أَعْلَمُ مَا لَا تَعْلَمُونَ ﴿٣٠﴾

2:30 – *"Wa idh qala rabbuka lil Malayikati innee ja'ilun fil ardi khaleefatan, qaloo ataj'alu feeha man yufsidu feeha wa yasfikud dima a wa nahnu nusabbihu bihamdika wa nuqaddisu laka, Qala innee a'lamu ma la ta'lamon." (Surat Al-Baqarah)*

"And [mention, O Muhammad], when your Lord said to the angels, "Indeed, I will make upon the earth a Deputy/Representative." They [angels] said, "Will You place upon it one who causes corruption/mischief therein and shed blood, while we praise and glorify You?" Allah said, "Indeed, I know that which you do not know." (The Cow, 2:30)

وَإِذْ قُلْنَا لِلْمَلَائِكَةِ اسْجُدُوا لِآدَمَ فَسَجَدُوا إِلَّا إِبْلِيسَ ﴿٣٤﴾

2:34 – *"Wa idh qulna lil malayikati osjudo li Adama fasajado illa ibleesa..." (Surat Al-Baqarah)*

"And [mention] when We said to the angels, 'Bow Down to Adam'; so they prostrated, except for Iblis..." (The Cow, 2:34)

The character of *Shaytan* said, 'No way, there is no way I am going to accept him between me and You.' So, it means there is always an egoism in the character that never wants to accept an authority, especially an authority that is in the presence of that authority. It is easier to say, 'No, no, I don't care for your authority, I am going to make my authority with that one 4,000 miles away.' The trick that you play with yourself is that the one 4,000 miles away is not going to test you everyday. It means you are telling yourself, 'I don't have to listen to anyone, I don't have to follow anyone.'

Prophet ﷺ is Amongst You With His Awliya in 124,000 Rooms

But why Allah ﷻ has 124,000 rooms on this Earth. 124,000 *awliyaullah* (saints) between men and women? They are rooms of Prophet ﷺ where Allah ﷻ describes in Holy Qur'an that, '*Feekum*, Prophet ﷺ is amongst you.'

كَمَا أَرْسَلْنَا فِيكُمْ رَسُولًا مِّنكُمْ يَتْلُو عَلَيْكُمْ آيَاتِنَا وَيُزَكِّيكُمْ وَيُعَلِّمُكُمُ الْكِتَابَ وَالْحِكْمَةَ وَيُعَلِّمُكُم مَّا لَمْ تَكُونُوا تَعْلَمُونَ ﴿١٥١﴾

2:151 – "Kama arsalna feekum Rasulam minkum yatlo 'Alaykum ayatina wa yuzakkeekum wa yu'Allimukumul kitaba walhikmata wa yu'Allimukum ma lam takono ta'Alamon." (Surat Al-Baqarah)

"Just as We have sent among (within) you a messenger of your own, reciting to you Our Signs, and purifying you, and teaching you the Book/Scripture (Qur'an) and Wisdom, and teaching you New Knowledge, that which you did not know." (The Cow, 2:151)

Look from the World of Light. When Allah ﷻ, with no time, is saying that, 'Prophet ﷺ is amongst you.' Then He must not be talking about the form because Allah ﷻ has no time and Allah ﷻ, God forbid, makes no understandings of mistakes. So, When Allah ﷻ says, 'Prophet ﷺ is amongst you,' why are they reading Qur'an as if it was a story from something

old? Qur'an is beyond alive, it is not even created. But it must be relevant at every second, at every moment. Then Allah ﷻ is giving us an *isharat* (sign) that Prophet's ﷺ Light is all around you and those *Ahbab*, lovers, and *ashiqeen* are overflowing fountains of love of Sayyidina Muhammad ﷺ, and wherever they are, is the Light of Prophet ﷺ. There are 124,000 of those rooms on this Earth. They carry the love of Prophet ﷺ. As a result, there is a secret within their heart from the Essence of Allah ﷻ.

Each Room has a Face that Attracts you

Then for the understanding, to reach that room there is the *surat*, there is a face. There is a face that attracts you to that room otherwise how

would you find that room? Just by random chance? That you say, *ya Rabbi*, guide me and I am going to walk down that street and find that room? No, Allah ﷻ says, I will make it very easy *"ati ullah"* is a secret within their heart, *"wa 'ati ar rasul"* is whom they are, *"wa ulil amri minkum"* search these *ulul amr*. Make a life in which you are looking for these 'Men of Authority'. Men as in masculine, it can be women; men whom Allah ﷻ gives their *isharat*, gives their guidance, they are the 'People of Authority'.

...أَطِيعُوا اللَّهَ وَأَطِيعُوا الرَّسُولَ وَأُوْلِي الْأَمْرِ مِنْكُمْ... ﴿٥٩﴾

4:59 – "...*Atiullaha wa atiur Rasula wa Ulil amre minkum...*" (*Surat An-Nisa*)

"··· *Obey Allah, Obey the Messenger, and those in authority among you...*" (*The Women, 4:59*)

Muhammadan Rooms Have Permission to Show their Face

Our life was to find these *ulul amr* (saints). And their characteristic of the room that they carry, is the characteristic and the love of Sayyidina Muhammad ﷺ. This means then Allah ﷻ makes for them, propagate your face, put your face out. They have been given permission by Prophet ﷺ. If you don't have permission from Prophet ﷺ and you put your face out, you become dead and sick, because if people look at your face too much calamity will visit you, hardship will visit you, disease will be upon you. Because that face is going to attract that Light.

It means some of these 124,000 have an authority that propagate your face. As soon as your face goes out, it will attract; it will attract those people to that reality. If they come to that face and they come to that presence, they become aware of that presence. Allah ﷻ dresses their being to enter into that room. So, by the face we were attracted, it means we found them. The face is a symbol for finding, and Allah ﷻ gives an honour and majesty that, 'Everything perishes but the holy face, WajhAllah Karim.'

... كُلُّ شَيْءٍ هَالِكٌ إِلَّا وَجْهَهُ لَهُ الْحُكْمُ وَإِلَيْهِ تُرْجَعُونَ ﴿٨٨﴾

28:88 – "...*kullu shayin halikun illa wajha hu la hul hukmu wa ilayhi turja'oon.*" (Surat Al-Qasas)

"...Everything (that exists) will perish except His holy Face. To Him belongs the Command, and to Him you will be returned."
(The Stories, 28:88)

Shaykh is Given Authority and Permission to Teach

It means that when Allah (swt) gives an order to them, 'Propagate your face,' because this is an *isharat*. What is the purpose of giving somebody *isharat* if he sits by himself next to a tree? He has been given permission, he has been given that, 'You have been raised by us, you know how to be independent.' You are not going to go out and start something and everyday come back to the Shaykh and say, 'Give me five dollars, can I have ten dollars now, can I  have this now, can I have that now?' They say, 'Wait, that is what the kids did.' Kids have to keep going back to *baba* (father).

The man whom the Shaykh raised, they say to him, 'You are now ready, you go and propagate your face and whomever sees your face will come to that guidance. You have your own phone number, you have your own website, you have all your own, be independent,' and you will be given by Prophet ﷺ a means in which to reach to people. And that is the *Rahmah* of Allah (swt). Why the different *madhabs* (schools of thought)? Based on where they were, it was a mercy from Allah (swt). If everybody had to have the *madhab* of Egypt but they may be in the subcontinent and things were not relevant to them.

Authorized Shaykh Works Independently and Has His Own Mission

This means it is a *Rahmah* (mercy) when Allah has these different flavours of an approach to Prophet. One of those rooms may speak in a way that is relevant to your life and to your culture. Maybe they are serving in a certain way which is attracted to you, and that brings you into that reality. So, it's not one way. It is not all vanilla. That is why the mind doesn't understand, 'Why is he operating differently? Why is everything different?' All of it is a *rahmah* from Prophet. That that room that you operate, it has

its own phone number, has its own websites, has its own responsibility, has its own mission from Prophet that, 'You are to do and establish this.' And the Shaykhs guided them, 'Establish that,' and as a result you're like the face that will bring people to that room. Which room? The love of Sayyidina Muhammad!

7 Divinely Attributes Dress the Seven Openings of the Holy Face

As Sami' (All-Hearing) Al Basir (All-Seeing) Dress the Ears

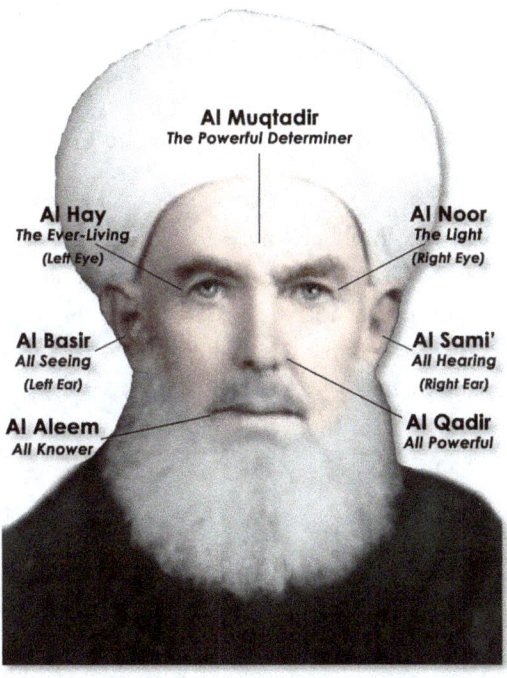

Why Allah ﷻ put an emphasis on the face? It means the face of these servants is from the Oceans of *Hayat* (Ever-Living). We described before they inherit, they inherit from the two openings of the ears, *As-Sami* (All-Hearing) *Al Basir* (All-Seeing). Allah's ﷻ Essences dress the face, because the face they look at is a reflection of the face that they look at, is a reflection to the face they look at, all the way to the *Sultan* who looks directly into the real face of Sayyidina Muhammad ﷺ. From that face of Prophet ﷺ looks to the reality of Allah ﷻ, *wajhAllah*. That face of Prophet ﷺ is *Sami al Basir*, it takes from the hearing and from the seeing. So, all the reality of hearing and seeing is being dressed upon that reality of Prophet ﷺ.

The Face of the Shaykh Has Authority and Power

$$\text{كُلُّ مَنْ عَلَيْهَا فَانٍ ﴿٢٦﴾ وَيَبْقَىٰ وَجْهُ رَبِّكَ ذُو الْجَلَالِ وَالْإِكْرَامِ ﴿٢٧﴾}$$

55:26-27 – "*Kullu man 'alayha fanin.(26) Wa yabqa wajhu Rabbika dhul jalali wal ikram. (27)*" (Surat Ar-Rahman)

"*All that is on earth will perish: (26) And there will remain (for ever) the holy Face of your Lord, Owner of Majesty, Bounty and Honor.*" (The Beneficent, 55:26-27)

Al 'Aleem (The All Knower) is Dressing the Holy Tongue

From the tongue, *Sifat al 'Aleem* (Attribute of All Knowing). So, when that face is looking to that face, these are Lights and *Sifat* of Allah ﷻ dressing upon their face. This is a description; these rooms are not random rooms, these are not something small. Most people can't even explain that reality. When they want to explain the reality, they want you to understand that face in there is an activated face, and by order of Prophet ﷺ it is operating the way it has to operate,

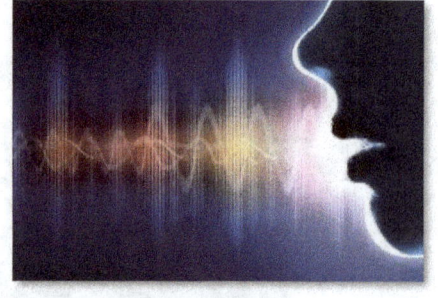

independent. It has its own phone number, it has its own website, it has its own books, has its own knowledges all from his *Sultan*, from his Shaykh. It has from *al Alim al Qadir*. This means from the *Sifat* of Allah's ﷻ Ancient Knowledges, *Aleem*. Al 'Aleem is dressing their tongue.

Sifat al Qadir (All Powerful) Dresses the Breath

Allah ﷻ is dressing upon their breath *Sifat al Qadir*. Their breath is

Allah's ﷻ *Qudra* (Power), they breathe with power upon their soul. We said many times before, that they can't even describe. In their breath they can breathe all the souls of everyone in their association. Because you think from the World of Form. Think from the World of Light. Let's say there is a Light here; in one instant that Light can pull everybody's light into it with its *nafas*, in its breath; it will clean all the imperfections, dress from whatever Allah ﷻ is dressing, Prophet ﷺ is dressing, and *awliyaullah* (saints) are dressing upon their soul and breathe it back out within an instant, in a fraction of a second. Because we think physical, we think, 'O what is happening in these associations?' The power that Allah ﷻ gives the tongue is dressed from the power of Allah's ﷻ Ancient Knowledge. Their breath from Allah's ﷻ *Qudra* and Power. That they have power within their breath and a might that moves around and it doesn't have to be locked into this room; whoever is looking to their face, they are being dressed by that reality.

Ar Rahman – Nur (Light) Dresses the Right Eye

So *Aleem al Qadir, wan Nur al Hayy*. *Nur al Hayy*, the right eye is *Nur* (light) and the left eye is *Hayy* (ever-living). From their right eye comes a *Nur*, from their left eye comes *Bahrul Hayat* (ocean of ever-living). Anyone deficient in Light

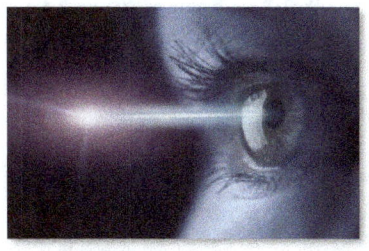

that sits with them, from their right eye comes a light from the *Nur*. That *Nur* is from *Sifat ar Rahman*. In other talks we described Allah ﷻ dressed them with *Bismillah ir Rahman ar Rahim*. In *Sifat ar Rahman*

 because *Rahman* ends with the *noon*. This *Rahim*? *Noon* means this is the secret of the whole World of Form and Light. From their right eye, a *Nur* comes out. Anyone deficient in their Light because of their *hub dunya* (love of material world), will be revitalized with that Light.

Dajjal Wants to Take Away the Light of Believers

That is why the *Dajjal* has an eye poked out. The Antichrist – we don't believe in the Anti-Christ – we believe in the person of deception, because it is not about Christ only. That every *Dajjal* that comes, his eye is missing. Every show shows his eye is missing and every television has his eye, every satellite has his eye, every eye is everywhere. Why is it 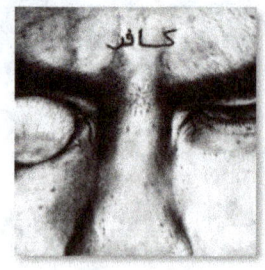 missing? To show that, 'I have no light for *akhirah* (hereafter), I am only the one who brings *hayat ad dunya* (life of material world). I have nothing to do, I am cut from *akhirah*. The whole responsibility of *Dajjal* is to take the lights and hope of *akhirah* away and fill them with the love of *dunya*.'

Followers of Dajjal Take Bayah (Initiation)

That is why all of *Dajjal's ulama* (scholars), the singers, the movie stars, the actresses, those are his scholars, they go and propagate, 'There is  nothing in the Heavens for you, live life to your fullest.' As we know that *Dajjal* is active, you don't think Allah is caring for *Ummat an Nabi* (Nation of Prophet)? Must be. But his (*Dajjal's*) activity seems to be much more powerful. He puts concerts with hundreds of thousands of people – we were talking the other night – hundreds of thousands come to their concerts and one of their *ulama* gets up and starts singing. Singing songs that dress them and possess them, and then keep putting their hand up in the middle of the event to take *bayah* (pledge

allegiance). This is an initiation. When they are putting their hand up and the other one puts his hand up, he is agreeing to take their hand. So, we sit back and we watch and say, 'Look what the *Shaytans* are doing? They are having initiations, they are giving *bayah* to everybody.' *Astaghfirullah*, they are all over, every television show in the millions.

The People of Light, they are sitting with ten people, fifty people, hundred people; the few that will represent the many, but Allah didn't leave this Nation to be empty without anything. So then they are describing that, 'This face, with this *Nur*, their Light, comes from the right eye is a *Nur* that dresses anything that sees it, and from their left eye *bahrul hayat*.'

Ar Raheem – Hay (The Ever-Living) Dresses the Left Eye True Shaykhs Revive the Hearts

From their left eyes comes *Al Hay*, *bahrul Hayat* (ocean of ever-living) which means they can *Muhyil qulubi*, revive the hearts as these *salawats* that we are reciting, because *feekum* (within you). Why are they teaching about Prophet ﷺ? Because they are the inheritors of Prophet ﷺ. If you don't know the reality of Sayyidina Muhammad ﷺ, you are definitely not going to know the reality of who *awliya* (saints) are. So, when they teach you that Prophet ﷺ, in the *salawats*

(praisings) every single one of these *ulama* (scholars) are writing these *salawats*, they are *'muhyil qulub wa mahidh dhunubi'* (The reviver of the hearts and the destroyer of sins).

يَا مُحْيِي الْقُلُوْبِ، سَلَّامْ عَلَيك ، يَا مَاحِي الذُّنُوْبِ ، سَلَّامْ عَلَيك

Ya Muhyil qulubi, Salaam 'Alayk,
Ya Mahidh dhunubi, Salaam 'Alayk

O the reviver of the hearts, O the eraser of the sins, Peace be upon you

From their left eye, a Light goes out and hits everybody and they can revive a dead heart. A heart that feels that it has no hope, has no purpose, has no understanding. In one association they can revitalize all the Light, recharge all the souls, recharge and repump the heart, recalibrate the heart back into the love of Allah ﷻ, and the love of Sayyidina Muhammad ﷺ. And from

that face and those seven points, they are taking from their Shaykhs.

The Shaykh is a Reflection of the Muhammadan Reality

So, what they take from their Shaykh is not comparable with what you think you are taking from their Shaykh. That's why they say, 'Lower yourself and your pride and sit with them.'

يَا أَيُّهَا الَّذِينَ آمَنُوا اتَّقُوا اللهَ وَكُونُوا مَعَ الصَّادِقِينَ ﴿١١٩﴾

9:119 – *"Ya ayyuhal ladheena amanoo ittaqollaha wa kono ma'as sadiqeen." (Surat At-Tawbah)*

"O you who have believed, have consciousness of Allah and be with those who are truthful/ Pious / sincere (in words and deed)."
(The Repentance, 9:119)

They will train you and teach you. But you think you are going to take

from my Shaykh what I am taking from my shaykh? *Shaytan* is fooling you and playing with you. And why hasn't your character changed? But when the Shaykh's face is dressing, he is blessing and changing the entire being of that person. It means their entire being, their energy, everything around them has been changed, because they stare into that Sun and they see the Sun with its realities, not as a reflection.

Some people may say, 'O I see too.' No, you see through a reflection. If I take the sunshine and take a mirror and point it to you, you say, 'O my gosh I am seeing the Sun.' No, incorrect, you only saw a reflection of the Sun. If you truly saw the Sun, it would begin to burn everything onto

you. If you really went out and looked to the Sun what would happen? You feel the pain coming through your eyes. What then if you were truly looking at the face of the Shaykh? Or you think you are even looking at Prophet ﷺ? You are looking at a reflection 1,000 times lower than it is, because the Shaykh also has a Muhammadan reflection. That when you see the image of Sayyidina Muhammad ﷺ you are seeing the Shaykh's reflection of his Muhammadan Reality. You are not seeing what his Shaykh sees. You are not seeing what the Shaykh above him sees and you are definitely not seeing what the *Sultan al Awliya* sees.

With Love Come Into the Hudur (Presence) of the Shaykh

These are just mirrors, that is why all of *tariqah* (spiritual path) was to come and break the mirror. Break your ego, break your bad characteristics, break all your desires. Break all these mirrors, be nothing, be nothing so they can begin to dress you. Come just as a student to be nothing. If you can come into that meditation, into that *tafakkur*, it means you become into their *hudur*, into their presence. When you truly accompany the one you are with and come into their presence then at that time they can  begin to train you. They train you and their *nazar* (gaze) will be upon you. Their *nazar* will dress you and bless you and take away all the bad characteristics. From that reality they go deeper into that person and teach them about *muhabbat* (love). That *nazar* and *muhabbat* should be changing their character, change their *ghadab*, their anger, and change all of the badness of their character.

The Spiritual Practices Should Change Your Bad Character

There are people who can get angry in an instant. What was the purpose of all your practices? We are not talking about anger when Allah ﷻ is  angry. There are certain things in life if you go out of your Islamic understanding, you anger Allah ﷻ. You are going to anger them too because they cannot tolerate a falsehood and something against their Islamic belief. But we are talking about just general characteristics. If your characteristics are not changing, your anger is not changing, your bad desires and bad characteristics are not changing; this means your *salat* (prayer) is not changing you, your *zakat* (charity) is not changing you, your fasting is not changing you. It means something is being done wrong. Because if you do it right Allah (swt) is going to change (you).

إِنَّ اللَّـهَ لَا يُغَيِّرُ مَا بِقَوْمٍ حَتَّىٰ يُغَيِّرُوا مَا بِأَنفُسِهِمْ ۗ وَإِذَا أَرَادَ اللَّـهُ بِقَوْمٍ سُوءًا فَلَا مَرَدَّ لَهُ ۚ وَمَا لَهُم مِّن دُونِهِ مِن وَالٍ ﴿١١﴾

13:11 – "…InnAllaha la yughayyiru ma biqawmin hatta yughayyiro ma bi anfusihim, wa idha arada Allahu biqawmin soo an fala maradda lahu wa ma lahum min doonihi min wal." (Surat Ar-Ra'd)

"…Indeed Allah will not change the condition of a people until they change what is in themselves. And when Allah intends for a people ill, there is no repelling it. And there is not for them besides Him anyone to protect/patron." (The Thunder, 13:11)

If you are doing your *tafakkur*, doing your contemplation, coming and asking to be dressed that, 'I am nothing, I am nothing, I am nothing,' and they would come to us and teach us. One of the bigger Shaykhs, the brother of my Shaykh, would come and say, 'Who is your Shaykh?' to continually agitate. He would say, 'Who is your Shaykh?' I'd say, 'My Shaykh? I am a *ghulam* (servant) of the one whom Allah (swt) put me in his presence. Shaykh is for the big guys, I am just a *ghulam*.' Because he wanted to come and confront. This way is about being nothing and  continuously crushing, continuous crushing, so that Allah (swt) can bring the sweetness of the reality. At that time they take you, they dress you, they bless you. When that face begins to dress you, all your characteristics change and you become a loving character, a sweet character, where people find pleasure and enjoyment in being around you.

We pray that Allah ﷻ dress us from those realities and bless us from those realities. Islam is a loaded, loaded reality. It is not something that is dry. It is coming from the Oceans of Heavens, of Paradise, filled with immense realities. We pray that Allah ﷻ dress us from those Lights and blesses us from those Lights.

Subhana rabbika rabbal 'izzati 'amma yasifoon, wa salaamun 'alal mursaleen, walhamdulillahi rabbil 'aalameen. Bi hurmati Muhammad al-Mustafa wa bi siri Surat al-Fatiha.

The Moon Doesn't Overtake the Sun (YaSeen 36:40)

We Take a Path of Humbleness

﴿٥٩﴾ ...أَطِيعُواللَّهَ وَأَطِيعُواْ الرَّسُولَ وَأُوْلِي الْأَمْرِ مِنْكُمْ...

4:59 – "...*Ateeullah wa atee ar-rasul wa ulul amrin minkum...*" (*Surat An-Nisa*)

"... *Obey Allah, Obey the Messenger, and those in authority among you...*" (*The Women, 4:59*)

Always a reminder for myself, *ana abda kul ajiz wa da'if wa miskin wa zhalim wa jahl*. That by the grace of Allah that we are still in existence.

The Shams (Sun) and Qamar (Moon) Are Symbols of Guidance

Alhamdulillah, from the heart of Sayyidina Muhammad, Mawlana Shaykh is teaching and teaching us the way of the *Arifeen* (Knowers), the way of the Heavens. That Allah wants us to look at the horizon and then look within ourself to understand the reality within ourselves. The reality of the *Shams wal Qamar*, the Sun and the Moon, to understand guidance, and a path of guidance; this has been the subject that they keep teaching here.

﴿٥٣﴾ ...سَنُرِيهِمْ آيَاتِنَا فِي الْآفَاقِ وَفِي أَنفُسِهِمْ حَتَّىٰ يَتَبَيَّنَ لَهُمْ أَنَّهُ الْحَقُّ...

The Moon Doesn't Overtake the Sun (YaSeen 36:40)

41:53 – "Sanureehim ayatina fil afaqi wa fee anfusihim hatta yatabayyana lahum annahu alhaqqu…" (Surat Fussilat)

"We will show them Our signs in the horizons and within themselves until it becomes clear to them that it is the truth…"
(Explained in Detail, 41:53)

That everyone has an understanding of what guidance will be. And  Allah ﷻ has the best of teaching for us that guidance and the way of *itibah* (obedience), the way of following, the way of realities is to look to My Heavens. That you see the Sun and you studied then the reality of the Sun, what the sun represents, the light, the reality of eternity, and how everything is nourished and blessed by that sun. Then Allah ﷻ says, that light is supreme and I made all of these planets circumambulate that sun.

Reality of the Moon and Maqam al Fardani that is held by the Ghawth

For you, your example in life of guidance is the *qamar* (moon). The way of the moon which takes a path in which to follow the sun. Everything else in this life will come as a distraction; everything will distract us to go right and to go left. The moon has a tremendous teaching, there are *awliya* (saints) who are in charge of that station. As soon as we begin to focus on that reality, that *"maqam al fardani"* that *ghawth*, the *sultans* they begin to  inspire. Are you thinking of my *maqam* (station)? You are looking at my *maqam* (station)? I am going to begin to teach you. Anything that you focus on and you read and understand, it focuses on you.

The *maqam al fardani*, the *ghawth* begins to teach. That there are stars and these are *awliya* (saints). There is the moon, which is *"maqam al fardani"* which is the *ghawth*, which is the *sultan* of the *awliya* (saints). That *sultan* (king) takes from the *shams* (sun). That *sultan* that takes from the *shams* is in charge of the inhabitants of this Earth. How the moonlight is coming and blessing everything on Earth? Don't you say Allah ﷻ! Allah ﷻ by cause and effect. Allah ﷻ says I know I own everything, but that is kindergarten. Come to the way of *arifeen* (knowers), come the way of *haqqaiqs* (realities), Allah ﷻ will explain. It is by cause and effect, everything is nourished by this sunshine, everything nourished by this moonlight and the moonlight is only capable of nourishing because it took a path in which to reflect the sunlight. Then Allah ﷻ describes their relationship.

لَا الشَّمْسُ يَنبَغِي لَهَا أَن تُدْرِكَ الْقَمَرَ وَلَا اللَّيْلُ سَابِقُ النَّهَارِ ۚ وَكُلٌّ فِي فَلَكٍ يَسْبَحُونَ ﴿٤٠﴾

36:40 – *"Lash shamsu yambaghee lahaaa an tudrikal qamara wa lal lailu saabiqun nahaar; wa kullun fee falaki yasbahoon."*
(Surat YaSeen)

"It is not permitted to the Sun to catch up the Moon, nor can the Night outstrip the Day: Each (just) swims along in (its own) orbit (according to Law)." (YaSeen, 36:40)

The Moon Doesn't Overtake the Sun (YaSeen 36:40)

Ghawth is the Highest Position of Awliya in the Muhammadan Government

So, for us to understand if we want to be from the moon, which are *awliyaullah* (saints). Our Shaykhs, Mawlana Sultanul Awliya Shaykh AbdAllah Faiz ad-Daghestani ق and Sultanul Awliya Shaykh Muhammad Nazim al Haqqani ق; these are huge *awliya* (saints). We say *fardani* but they are even beyond that understanding. But for us to understand, they say the *Ghawth* and the *Ghawth* was only one. No, you are incorrect, you don't understand anything. The *Ghawth* is the one who is in charge. *Awliyaullah* and the stations of *awliyaullah* is not a person. You don't say one shaykh is the *Ghawth* and that is the only shaykh that was the *Ghawth*. No, you don't understand. So when kindergarten people try to explain the *haqqaiqs* (realities) of *awliya* (saints), it doesn't sound right. Use your *aql* (brain).

It is a chair, it is a position, it is a Muhammadan Government. There is a *sultanate*, there is a House of Commons, there is a House of Lords, and there is a speaker of the House. Every government you have on Earth is a reflection of Allah's Government. Why you think Allah ﷻ says, 'O in Heavens we are not organized but you people on Earth, why don't you show us how to organize?' That was a joke. Right? Because people on Earth are crazy, they don't know how to organize anything. Even in their elections when they don't accept, they beat each other up in Parliament. Did you see it on Facebook when they vote and they don't like each other's vote, they start beating each other up in Parliament.

The Supreme Sultan of Creation is Sayyidina Muhammad ﷺ

Allah's ﷻ Government is supreme. The supreme *Sultan* for all of Creation, Sayyidina Muhammad ﷺ. Mawlana Shaykh describes it like a pyramid, that that *Ghawth* and that position of *Ghawth* is a chair, is a position of authority. When one sits upon that authority and they reach to that level of reality, they are taking from what Allah ﷻ gave. They take from the *surat*. They take from the face that never perishes. *Awliyaullah* (saints) come into our lives and describe this is the face and the eternal reality of Sayyidina Muhammad ﷺ.

كُلُّ شَيْءٍ هَالِكٌ إِلَّا وَجْهَهُ لَهُ الْحُكْمُ وَإِلَيْهِ تُرْجَعُونَ ﴿٨٨﴾

28:88 – *"...kullu shayin halikun illa wajha hu la hul hukmu wa ilayhi turja'oon." (Surat Al-Qasas)*

"...Everything (that exists) will perish except His Face. To Him belongs the Command, and to Him you will be returned." (The Stories, 28:88)

Sayyidina Muhammad ﷺ is the Walking Qur'an

What we said in these *nasheeds* (praisings), your *surat* and your *ayat*; in Holy Qur'an what do they say? Prophet ﷺ is the walking Qur'an.

قَسَمًا بِالنَّجْمِ حِينَ هَوَى   مَا الْمُعَافَى وَالسَّقِيْمُ سِوَى
فَاخْلَعِ الْكَوْنَيْنِ عَنْكَ سِوَى   حُبُّ مَوْلَى الْعُرْبِ وَالْعَجَمِ

Ghawthu ahlil badwi wal hadari   *Sayyidus sadati min mudari*
Manba'ul ahkami wal hikami   *Sahibul aayati wassuwari*

The Moon Doesn't Overtake the Sun (YaSeen 36:40)

O Master of the masters of people of Mudar, You are the Saviour of people of the desert and the cities, You are the Owner of the verses and chapters of holy Quran, and the Source of laws, regulations and wisdom

وَمَا عَلَّمْنَاهُ الشِّعْرَ وَمَا يَنبَغِي لَهُ إِنْ هُوَ إِلَّا ذِكْرٌ وَقُرْآنٌ مُبِينٌ ﴿٦٩﴾

36:69 – *"Wa ma'allamnahush shi'ra wa ma yambaghee lahu, in huwa illa dhikrun wa Quranun Mubeen."* (Surat YaSeen)

"We have not taught him (Prophet Muhammad (pbuh)) poetry, nor it is befitting for him. He (Prophet Muhammad (pbuh)) is not but Zikr (Remembrance/Praise) and the Qur'an making things clear." (YaSeen, 36:69)

Every Surat (Face) and Ayat (Sign) Describes His Realities

It just so happens that the chapters are called what? '*Surat*'. Every beatific chapter is a face of the reality of Prophet ﷺ. Every *ayat* (sign) '*ayat minAllah*', every Sign is the greatest of signs of Sayyidina Muhammad ﷺ. That is why the Companions described Prophet ﷺ is walking Qur'an.

قَالَتْ السَّيِّدَةُ عَائِشَةَ رَضِيَ اللهُ عَنْهَا: كَانَ قُرْآنًا يَمْشِي عَلَى الْأَرْضِ

Qalat as Sayyidatu 'Aisha: "Kana Quranan yamshi 'alal Ard."

The beloved Sayyidatina Aisha (wife of Prophet Muhammad (pbuh)) said: *"He (Prophet Muhammad (pbuh)) was a walking Qur'an on earth."*

From its names Allah ﷻ is calling a *surat* what, face? It is the face of Allah's ﷻ Most Beloved. It is a *tajalli* (manifestation), a dress, it is a reality. Every *ayat*, *ayat* means 'sign'. The greatest of Allah's ﷻ Signs is Sayyidina Muhammad ﷺ.

This means then that holy face looks to that position of authority, and from that light everything is transmitted down like a waterfall to who is the *imam* (leader) of the right and who is the *imam* of the left. Those are chairs, not people, authorities.

Awliya (Saints) are Given Couches and Thrones in Heavens

Allah ﷻ describes them on the *yawm al mahshar* (day of gathering) that 'they have couches and thrones. Who? These *sultans* because when the *sultan* retires means he passed away, he doesn't lose his couch, he didn't lose his *arsh* (throne), he didn't lose his *kursi* (chair). Allah ﷻ sets it aside for him but now your job on this physical someone else is coming, because you have been raised now into the Heavens. Then Allah ﷻ sets aside for them a *kursi* (chair), sets for them an *arsh* (throne), sets for them their chairs and couches reclining.

أُولَٰئِكَ لَهُمْ جَنَّاتُ عَدْنٍ تَجْرِي مِن تَحْتِهِمُ الْأَنْهَارُ يُحَلَّوْنَ فِيهَا مِنْ أَسَاوِرَ مِن ذَهَبٍ وَيَلْبَسُونَ ثِيَابًا خُضْرًا مِّن سُندُسٍ وَإِسْتَبْرَقٍ مُّتَّكِئِينَ فِيهَا عَلَى الْأَرَائِكِ ۚ نِعْمَ الثَّوَابُ وَحَسُنَتْ مُرْتَفَقًا ﴿٣١﴾

18:31 – "*Ulaaa'ika lahum Jannaatu 'Adnin tajree min tahtihimul anhaaru yuhallawna feehaa min asaawira min zahabinw wa yalbasoona siyaaban khudram min sundusinw wa istabraqim muttaki'eena feehaa*

'alal araaa'ik; ni'mas sawaab; wa hasunat murtafaqaa."
(Surat Al-Kahf)

"For them will be Gardens of Eternity; beneath them rivers will flow; they will be adorned therein with bracelets of gold, and they will wear green garments of fine silk and heavy brocade: They will recline therein on raised thrones. How good the recompense! How beautiful a couch to recline on!" (The Cave, 18:31)

Awliya are Trained to Move Up in Their Stations to Replace the Shaykh That Passes

But as soon as that *Ghawth* passes away, from among the living *awliyaullah* (saints), there must be somebody sitting on the chair. There is no chair empty in this Muhammadan Government. When the physicality passed immediately the next one in this line who has been trained all their lives, they are moving up. When they are at this level at the base of the pyramid, they are being trained by their soul with responsibilities. When they move up they are being trained by their responsibility. The *imam* of the right and the *imam* of the left, they have  been given all those responsibilities. There is not somebody who comes up from the bottom and shoots up and there is not somebody who passes away and the chair is left empty.

This has nothing to do with *tariqah* (spiritual path). This has nothing to do with the names of *tariqahs*. There are *awliyaullah* (saints) whom you don't know them in any *tariqah*. They may be just sitting at the end of the *masjid* (mosque) doing what Allah ﷻ wanted them to do. The *turuq* (spiritual paths) and *tariqah* are finishing schools. They train these potential candidates whom Allah ﷻ has destined, 'Have good manners, and have good character and supreme above all, love Allah ﷻ and love Sayyidina Muhammad ﷺ.' They become trained from childhood, adulthood, or from middle age. Whenever Allah ﷻ inspiring that this one of My *Awliya* (saints) is going to be coming and send them now

into that training school. Those who achieve what Allah ﷻ wanted them to achieve, they come from amongst those schools. But they are not to be confused the same as the government. It's a finishing school. Some come from Shadaliya, some come from Rifayi some come from Qadiri, some come from Naqshbandi. But the Muhammadan Government is the Muhammadan Government. That chair is never empty.

All Awliya (Saints) Take From Ghawth and He Takes From Prophet Muhammad ﷺ

Some people were asking when Sayyidina Abdul Qadir Jilani ق was describing 'my foot on the neck of *awliyaullah*.' Mawlana Shaykh described many times, that is a station.

Sayyidi Shaikh Khalifatul Akbar (Radiallahu Ta'ala Anh) states,

"I saw the Beloved Rasool (Sallallahu Alaihi Wasallam) in my dream and I asked him about the statement of Huzoor Ghaus-e-Azam (Radiallahu Ta'ala Anh) i.e. "My foot is on the neck of all the Saints." The Beloved Rasool (Sallallahu Alaihi Wasallam) said, "Abdul Qadir Jilani (Radiallahu Ta'ala Anh) has spoken the truth and why should he not say this when he is the Qutb, and I am his Guardian."

That is not a position only for his personality. But this station of *Ghawth* and that station of *sultanate*, all *awliyaullah* (saints) are under the authority of that king. That king takes his *isharat* (sign) from Prophet ﷺ directly. That is why Mawlana Shaykh put the footprint on our turbans, the

badge of Sandal of Sayyidina Muhammad ﷺ. And they don't know and they go and spread *fitna* (confusion). They don't know anything about *tariqah* (spiritual way).

Beware of Those Who Come Against Pious People

Prophet ﷺ warned that, 'Don't take the ignorant as your guides and guidance. They are like making war in front of Allah ﷻ,' because they come and say horrible things against pious people. Stay away from those whom Allah ﷻ is going to make war against them.

خُذِ الْعَفْوَ وَأْمُرْ بِالْعُرْفِ وَأَعْرِضْ عَنِ الْجَاهِلِينَ ﴿١٩٩﴾

7:199 – "Khuzil 'afwa waamur bil'urfi waa'rid 'anil jaahileen." (Surat Al-A'raf)

"Hold to forgiveness; command what is right; But turn away from the ignorant." (The Heights, 7:199)

and

عَنْ أَبِي هُرَيْرَةَ رَضِيَ اللهُ عَنْهُ قَالَ: قَالَ رَسُولُ اللهِ صلى الله عليه و سلم إِنَّ اللهَ تَعَالَى قَالَ:

"مَنْ عَادَى لِي وَلِيًّا فَقَدْ آذَنْتُهُ بِالْحَرْبِ" – رَوَاهُ الْبُخَارِيُّ

"Man 'ada li waliyan faqda adhantahu bilharbe,…" (Rawa e Bukhari)

Narrated by Abu Hurayra, that Prophet Muhammad (pbuh) said that "Allah (AJ) said, "I will declare war against him who shows hostility to a waliy (saint) of Mine…" (Hadith Qudsi [Bukhari])

They talk nonsense and they come against teachings, they come against pious people. Even those who love *awliyaullah* (saints), they are loved by Allah (AJ), even their donkey, because nobody can call themselves a *wali* (pious servant). We are donkey of big *awliyaullah* (saints). Even Allah (AJ) has a respect and *ihtiram* for the donkey of the *awliya*. Didn't they have a respect for the donkey of Sayyidina Isa (Jesus) (AS)? How much they took care of that? Even the donkeys of *walis* (pious servants) are respected by Allah (AJ). So, then they teach, 'Be careful what to say.'

The Green Dome of Madina and Prophet Muhammad's ﷺ Turban

You don't even know what the *Sultan al Awliya* was bringing. When we were singing and reciting, 'The Green Dome of Madina, the Green Dome of Madina, the Green Dome that all light vanishes in that light; why do you think then *Sultan al Awliya* made the Green Dome? The *Gumbad khazra*, these green turbans.

جیسے ہی سبز گنبد نظر آۓ گا
بندگی کا قرینہ بدل جاۓ گا

*Jaise hee sabz Gunbad nazar ayega,
Bandagi ka qareena badal jayega*

*The moment the Green Dome becomes visible,
the nature of Servanthood will change.
When the green dome of Madina comes into my sight
The whole of dunya is buried in its light*

You don't see it? Are you reciting something that you just don't understand? When we walk into a room and the *jama* walk into this

room you don't see a green dome? You must have missed also the green dome in Madina! Same thing, it is the turban of Prophet ﷺ. And it was the exact style where Prophet ﷺ had the hat and then the turban cloth that went around. This is the *urs mubarak* of Sultan al Awliya Mawlana Shaykh Nazim ق at least know what he left for us, what he gave to us. Mawlana Shaykh said, 'My love is so much for Sayyidina Muhammad ﷺ that everywhere you go, keep this green dome on your head.'

Wear the Turban, it is the Crown of the Believer

In every *salah* (prayer) that you make with a turban, there are seventy-two times blessing and it has the *ajr* (reward) of a martyr, the reward of

those who passed away and became *shaheed*. You get the reward of that because the *sunnah* (way of Prophet ﷺ) is so powerful, it is the crown of the believers. And that this is a *hadith* of Sayyidina Ali ؓ, that the turban is the crown for the believer. Then they make artificial pictures with no turban on Sayyidina Ali ؓ. Don't they

understand what he brought for *hadith*? He is the master of the crowns.

We Must Keep Our Head at the Feet of Sayyidina Muhammad ﷺ

Mawlana Shaykh brought for us what? This is a *taj* (crown), the hat we wear underneath the turban cloth. This is a Muhammadan Taj that Allah ﷻ gave to Prophet ﷺ, that all My Prophets are kings but you are a *sultan* of all of them. You are the *sultan* of *sultans*. Mawlana Shaykh Nazim ق wanted for us, that keep it on your head, like when you walk with the Holy Hair (of Prophet Muhammad ﷺ) you keep it upon your head, to say what? *Ya Rasul, ya Kareem,* keep my head at your feet. Never in my life let my head to rise above your feet. Not to bite your feet, never to come against you. And to take away in which you are the *sultan*, you are *Shams al Arifeen* (Sun of the Knowers), you are *Shams al Iman* (Sun of Faith), *Shams al Islam* (Sun of Submission), you are the light of all our light, keep me at your feet.

Sultan al Awliya brought this, see that foot, the *Nalain*? The Holy Footstep, as a reminder for us keep your whole life at the feet of Sayyidina Muhammad ﷺ. Be an inheritor of *Qadam al Haqq* and his Companions *Qadam as-Siddiq*. Make your life to be *muqaddam*, those who walk on that path. And we walk with that on our head everywhere, with his dome. These are *ashiqeen* (lovers of Prophet ﷺ). This turban was a symbol of that love. It means they brought everything for us and these positions and these authorities are beyond imagination. When one passes, the next will

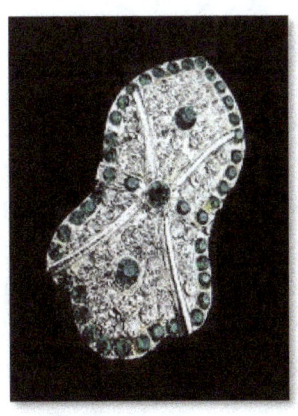

The Moon Doesn't Overtake the Sun (YaSeen 36:40)

inherit. And they come to the *turuq* (spiritual way) to understand good character, good manners.

The Moon Never Overtakes the Sun – Stay At Your Had (Limit)

From Surat YaSeen, the heart of Holy Qur'an, the heart of Sayyidina Muhammad ﷺ. Surat YaSeen Chapter 36 verse 40.

لَا الشَّمْسُ يَنبَغِي لَهَا أَن تُدْرِكَ الْقَمَرَ وَلَا اللَّيْلُ سَابِقُ النَّهَارِ ۚ وَكُلٌّ فِي فَلَكٍ يَسْبَحُونَ ﴿٤٠﴾

36:40 – *"Lash shamsu yambaghee lahaaa an tudrikal qamara wa lal lailu saabiqun nahaar; wa kullun fee falaki yasbahoon."*
(Surat YaSeen)

"It is not permitted to the Sun to catch up the Moon, nor can the Night outstrip the Day: Each (just) swims along in (its own) orbit (according to Law)." (YaSeen, 36:40)

Sadaqallah azheem wa balaghta rasul al karim. Bismillahir Rahmanir Rahim, 'It is not for the sun to overtake the moon nor does the night outstrip the day,' means nor does the moon overtake the sun, 'each of

them float in their own orbit but the *fuluk* is a ship,' *yasbahun*, like orbits like tracks, 'that they are ships, the ship is moving on a track,' and teaching that their whole life is to never overtake. This means that the moon and those who are training to be a moon their whole life will be a training that don't overtake the sun, don't overtake your position, stay at your *had* (limit).

The moon should never in its thought, and the students who are trying to be moons, should never think that they are going to outtake their Shaykh, that they are not going to shine more than their Shaykh. They are not trying to overtake. The moon is continuously reminding that this light that people see from you, the moon, the *awliya* (saints) of

that moon are teaching that this light that is reflecting from you is not yours. It is not a station that you praise yourself, this is not the work world. In the business world and work world, you try to get ahead and be recognized and show yourself in everything. That is *dunya* (material world).

The Moon Reminds Us to Be Humble

In *akhirah* (afterlife), you don't show yourself as anything, and you

never try to outrank your Shaykh or even give the appearance of that or give even the impression of that, that you are something special. The moon comes to remind us be nothing, be nothing. Don't show yourself as anything. If whatever he bestowed upon you there is a time and a place for everything but don't outshine. Don't try to make yourself more than what you are, keep yourself at your *had* (limit). If people become confused then it is your responsibility to put yourself back in your place. It means don't go out and represent yourself as something independent. Don't represent yourself as a sun. Don't do things that make it to be arrogance.

Then the *turuq* (spiritual way) come and teach everything about character. Why is this happening, why are these things happening in life? Because everything around us is pushing, even your family is *fitna* (confusion) for you because they keep pushing that it is you, it is you, it is you. You apply that into the *dunya* world that is one thing, but you apply it into the spiritual world then you are going to be crushed, you are going to be crushed. Where Allah ﷻ is warning, stay within your orbit, stay at your *had* (limit) and understand your testing. That is why the moon has many beatings upon it.

يَا أَيُّهَا الَّذِينَ آمَنُوا إِنَّ مِنْ أَزْوَاجِكُمْ وَأَوْلَادِكُمْ عَدُوًّا لَكُمْ فَاحْذَرُوهُمْ ۚ وَإِن تَعْفُوا وَتَصْفَحُوا وَتَغْفِرُوا فَإِنَّ اللَّهَ غَفُورٌ رَّحِيمٌ ﴿١٤﴾

64:14 – "Yaaa ayyuhal lazeena aamanooo inna min azwaaji kum wa awlaadikum 'aduwwal lakum fahzaroohum; wa in ta'foo wa tasfahoo wa taghfiroo fa innal laaha ghafoorur Raheem." (Surat Al-Taghabun)

"O ye who believe! Truly, among your wives and your children are (some that are) enemies to yourselves: so beware of them! But if ye forgive and overlook, and cover up (their faults), verily Allah is Oft-Forgiving, Most Merciful." (The Mutual Disillusion, 64:14)

The moon is continuously bombarded, continuously bombarded, so at any moment something tries to grow on it, something tries to inhabit it and to make the moon to deviate, Allah ﷻ sends the pelting, and the pelting and smashing. This way is a school for *qamarun*, this way is a school to be nothing, continuously to efface ourselves to be nothing. That, to efface ourselves and understand our characteristics.

Pride and Arrogance Stop Us From Growth

That the worst and the most difficult of characteristics is pride and arrogance. That, if pride and arrogance should enter into the heart it begins to make the servant to be angry.

لَا جَرَمَ أَنَّ اللَّـهَ يَعْلَمُ مَا يُسِرُّونَ وَمَا يُعْلِنُونَ ۚ إِنَّهُ لَا يُحِبُّ الْمُسْتَكْبِرِينَ ﴿٢٣﴾

16:23 – "Laa jarama annal laaha ya'lamu maa yusirrona wa ma yu'linoon; innahoo laa yuhibbul mustakbireen" (Surat An-Nahl)

"Undoubtedly Allah knows what they conceal, and what they reveal: verily He love not the arrogant." (The Bee, 16:23)

and

"He who has in his heart the weight of a mustard seed of pride shall not enter Paradise" – Prophet Muhammad (pbuh)
[Sahih Muslim, Hadith 91]

That is why we all reflect that, 'I don't know what the Shaykh is talking about,' but the teaching is to reflect upon ourselves. Why do we become angry? Why do we become confused on holy nights? And that has to do with pride and arrogance. Why is it that I don't want to listen to anyone? Pride and arrogance.

Why does the moon giving *isharat*, why does the moon think it is something special? You took a path in which to be bombarded so that you can shine as a reflection of that reality, but not to be the reality, you are nothing. Then everything in our life comes to teach, why do I get upset at the Center, why is it that something happens at the Center and I become angry? Why? Because of pride and arrogance. And the moon is reminding don't be anything, listen to people and come to serve. Don't show people that you achieved a *maqam* or station and you don't want to do anything. It means now then that arrogance is coming in and the moon is reminding from the highest level to the lowest level, we took a path to be nothing. If people should begin to feel you are something, you are in trouble with the sun and then the pelting and the attacks begin until the moon retreats and stands at its level and its *had* (limit) that we took a path in our life not to be anything, not to give the appearance of anything, not to make people think that we are something.

Walk On the Path of Thorns to Reach the Rose of Love

A reminder on these holy nights, these are the nights in which Allah ﷻ is bestowing immense light, immense blessings that we took a path in which to love Sayyidina Muhammad ﷺ and whatever sourness and

testing we go through in our life, that those are like rocks of love. As much as the person becomes bombarded in life, as much as they draw closer to Prophet ﷺ. All came to teach, Sayyidina Bilal al Habashi ؓ came – this is why our teaching, but I don't know how many people actually listen until something happens in their life. The Companions were tortured for

the love of Prophet ﷺ, not for Allah ﷻ. You can love Allah ﷻ and nobody knows it. You keep it in your heart and ride on the bus. As soon as you put that turban and walk with that beard and show yourself as Muhammadiyun everybody is going to bother you, everybody is going to attack you. Then if you are within the *turuq* (spiritual way) and everybody becomes jealous of you and everybody begins to bombard you.

You say, '*Ya Rabbi,* what is this? How come this is not a path of love?' He says no, this is a different type of love. You come up the thorns until one day you can be dressed by the fragrance of the rose. But this path of ours is a path of thorns and every time we have a *mushkilat* and difficulty and every time we are becoming angry and every time we are becoming overwhelmed, then every time we are saying, 'That's it, I am not doing it again!' It is very easy, just sit where you are and don't do anything again.

Then they remind you, 'Didn't you want to reach to Prophet ﷺ? Walk on the thorns, walk on them, don't worry about the pain it is causing, don't worry about the difficult it is causing. Don't worry about the insult that it is causing, don't worry about the shame it is causing. Just walk the thorns and keep moving because Prophet ﷺ is happy.'

از بهر وصال ماه از شب مگریز
وزبهر گل و گلاب با خار بساز

Az bahre wisale Maah, az shab maguriz
waz bahr gul o gulab, ba khaar besaz

"If you want to reach the moon, do not hide form the night
If you want the rose, don't run away from the thorns

– Mawlana Jalaladdin Rumi

Even Sayyidina Musa ﷺ Was Humiliated for Love

Sayyidina Musa ﷺ *kalimullah*, Prophet Moses ﷺ was humiliated by Sayyidina Khidr ﷺ. He speaks to Allah ﷻ and the first thing the Muhammadan Guide tells Sayyidina Musa ﷺ, 'We are not going to make it with each other, how can you have patience with something you have little knowledge of?'

$$\text{وَكَيْفَ تَصْبِرُ عَلَىٰ مَا لَمْ تُحِطْ بِهِ خُبْرًا ﴿٦٨﴾}$$

18:68 – *"Wa kayfa tasbiru 'ala ma lam tuhit bihi khubra."* (Surat Al-Kahf)

"And how can you have patience for what you do not encompass in knowledge?" (The Cave, 18:68)

He insulted his knowledge. He did that why? To be with Prophet ﷺ, 'I want to reach where these two rivers: *la ilaha illAllah Muhammadun Rasulullah* ﷺ.' (There is no deity but Allah, Muhammad ﷺ is the Messenger of Allah). He said, *'Ya Rabbi,* I want to see you.' (Holy Qur'an, 7:143) From what he saw of the lights of Prophet ﷺ, he said, 'That's it, I am willing to be humiliated and in difficulty for your love.'

$$\text{وَلَمَّا جَاءَ مُوسَىٰ لِمِيقَاتِنَا وَكَلَّمَهُ رَبُّهُ قَالَ رَبِّ أَرِنِي أَنظُرْ إِلَيْكَ ۚ قَالَ لَن تَرَانِي وَلَٰكِنِ انظُرْ إِلَى الْجَبَلِ فَإِنِ اسْتَقَرَّ مَكَانَهُ فَسَوْفَ تَرَانِي ۚ فَلَمَّا تَجَلَّىٰ رَبُّهُ لِلْجَبَلِ جَعَلَهُ دَكًّا وَخَرَّ مُوسَىٰ صَعِقًا ۚ فَلَمَّا أَفَاقَ قَالَ سُبْحَانَكَ تُبْتُ إِلَيْكَ وَأَنَا أَوَّلُ الْمُؤْمِنِينَ ﴿١٤٣﴾}$$

7:143 – *"Wa lamma jaa Musa limeeqatina wa kallamahu Rabbuhu, qala rabbi arinee anzhur ilayka, Qala lan taranee wa lakini onzhur ilal jabali fa inistaqarra makanahu, fasawfa taranee, falamma tajalla Rabbuhu lil jabali ja`alahu, dakkan wa kharra Musa sa`iqan, falamma afaqa qala subhanaka tubtu ilayka wa ana awwalul Mumineen."* (Surat Al-A'raf)

"And when Moses arrived at Our appointed time and his Lord spoke to him, he said, "My Lord, show me [Yourself] that I may look at You." [Allah] said, "you will not see Me, but look at the mountain; if it should remain in its place, then you will see Me." But when his Lord manifested His glory on the mountain, He made it as dust, and Moses fell unconscious. And when he awoke/ recovered his senses, he said, "Glory be to You! to You I turn in repentance, and I am the first of the believers." (The Heights. 7:143)

You Can't Run Away From Problems

When people come and say, 'Shaykh, I want to run away into a place in a different dimension where there is no difficulty,' how will you achieve any nearness to Prophet ﷺ? Let's find an island where there is nobody and I will sit there by myself. You will be alone, even Prophet ﷺ won't be with you. It wasn't about finding something easy. So I say, 'Go talk to your parents.' And you say, 'I don't want to talk to them, they cause a lot of problems.' Okay, who cares. What problem do you want? Do you want our problem? In our problem, you will pass out and die the next day. What  you can imagine of problems coming to you, you can't imagine their problems. You have one problem with your spouse, they have hundreds of problems of people and everyday they say, 'That's it I am quitting, I am firing.'

How many times Mawlana said, 'that is it, I am quitting', and I said, 'I am quitting, that is it, I am quitting.' There is no quitting because the next day they tell you, 'Where are you going? Walk the thorns,' and you say, 'but these thorns hurt, my feet are cut up, I am tired.' They say, 'You have to keep going until you can take your last breath.' By the end they are tired and they are ready to go, they are ready to go. But if you are looking for ease, then you have to look for something else.

With Every Difficulty Comes Ease

Allah ﷻ says, 'With difficulty comes ease, with difficulty comes ease.' (94:4-5) Surat Inshirah (Chapter 94 of Holy Qur'an) is for our heart. The heart to open, there has to be difficulty and ease, difficulty and ease; the womb of a woman is in contraction and expansion; the earth is continuously in earthquakes and expanding, earthquakes and expanding; our whole life is about that reality.

The Moon Doesn't Overtake the Sun (YaSeen 36:40)

أَلَمْ نَشْرَحْ لَكَ صَدْرَكَ ﴿١﴾ وَوَضَعْنَا عَنكَ وِزْرَكَ ﴿٢﴾ الَّذِي أَنقَضَ ظَهْرَكَ ﴿٣﴾ وَرَفَعْنَا لَكَ ذِكْرَكَ ﴿٤﴾ فَإِنَّ مَعَ الْعُسْرِ يُسْرًا ﴿٥﴾ إِنَّ مَعَ الْعُسْرِ يُسْرًا ﴿٦﴾ فَإِذَا فَرَغْتَ فَانصَبْ ﴿٧﴾ وَإِلَىٰ رَبِّكَ فَارْغَب ﴿٨﴾

94:1-8 – *"Alam nashrah laka sadrak. (1) Wa wada'na 'anka wizrak. (2) Alladhee anqada zhahrak. (3) Wa rafa'na laka dhikrak. (4) Fainna ma'al 'usri yusran. (5) Inna ma'al 'usri yusra. (6) Fa idha faraghta fainsab. (7) Wa ila rabbika farghab. (8)" (Surat Ash-Sharh)*

"Did We not expand for you, [O Muhammad], your Chest? (1) And We removed from you your burden. (2) Which had weighed upon your back. (3) And raised high for you your repute. (4) For indeed, with hardship [will be] ease. (5) Indeed, with hardship [will be] ease. (6) So when you have finished [your duties], then stand up [for worship]. (7) And to your Lord direct [your] longing. (8)" (The Relief, 94:1-8)

Each Difficulty Raises You Higher

Every time a Shaykh, a student, somebody is bombarded by difficulty, Allah ﷻ is crushing them to raise them. Every difficulty in life from your spouse and your children, from everything that you are seeing and witnessing, and you are becoming fed up, Allah ﷻ is crushing and squeezing to raise that servant and at any moment Allah ﷻ can change the condition. *Wa ufawwidu…*that is why we keep making the same prayers at the end of *salah*, *"wa ufawwidu amri illAllah innallaha basirun bil 'ibad."* 'I give all my affair to Allah. Allah sees His servants.'

وَأَفَوِّضُ أَمْرِيْ إِلَى اللهِ. إِنَّ اللهَ بَصِيْرٌ بِالْعِبَادِ

"Wa ufawwidu amri illAllah, innAllaha basirun bil 'ibad."

"I entrust my affair unto Allah. Truly, Allah Sees and is aware of His servants."

"Ya wahab ya wahab ya wahab, ya musabibal asbab, ya mufatihal abwab ya muqallibal quloob wal absar, ya dalil al mutahireen". Dalil al mutahireen because I am quitting, it is enough for me. That *dua* (supplication) is that everything is coming in every direction, 'I am tired, ya Rabbi.' That, *"ufawwidu amri illAllah innallaha basirun bil ibad"* that Allah ﷻ sees your condition, He will send a relief, after difficulty will come ease, after difficulty will come ease, this is the way of Prophet ﷺ.

يَا وَهَّابُ يَا وَهَّابُ يَا وَهَّابُ، يَا مُسَبِّبَ الْأَسْبَابِ، يَا مُفَتِّحَ الْأَبْوَابِ، يَا مُقَلِّبَ الْقُلُوْبِ وَالْأَبْصَارِ

يَا دَلِيْلَ الْمُتَحَيِّرِيْنَ يَا غِيَاثَ الْمُسْتَغِيْثِيْنَ، يَا حَيُّ يَا قَيُّوْمُ، يَا ذَا الْجَلَالِ وَالْإِكْرَامِ. وَأَفَوِّضُ أَمْرِيْ إِلَى اللهِ. إِنَّ اللهَ بَصِيْرٌ بِالْعِبَادِ

"Ya Wahhab. Ya Wahhab. Ya Wahhab. Ya musabbibal asbab, ya mufattihul abwab, ya muqallibul qulubi wal absar. Ya Dalilal mutahayyirin, ya Ghiyathal mustaghithin, ya Hayyu ya Qayyum, ya dhalJalali wal Ikram. Wa ufawwidu amri illAllah, innAllaha basirun bil 'ibad.

"O Bestower! O Bestower! O Bestower! O Originator of causes! O Opener of doors! O Tuner (Changer) of hearts and eyes!

O Guide of the perplexed! O Succour for those who seek Your aid! O Living! O Self-Subsisting One! O (You who are) possessed of Majesty and Bounty! I entrust my affair unto Allah. Truly, Allah is aware of His servants."

All Prophets and Sahabi (Companions) Suffered For the Love of Prophet Muhammad ﷺ

How much the Companions suffered for the love of Sayyidina Muhammad ﷺ? How much did all the prophets suffer for their love of Prophet ﷺ?

أَحَسِبَ النَّاسُ أَن يُتْرَكُوا أَن يَقُولُوا آمَنَّا وَهُمْ لَا يُفْتَنُونَ ﴿٢﴾ وَلَقَدْ فَتَنَّا الَّذِينَ مِن قَبْلِهِمْ ۖ فَلَيَعْلَمَنَّ اللَّهُ الَّذِينَ صَدَقُوا وَلَيَعْلَمَنَّ الْكَاذِبِينَ ﴿٣﴾

29:2-3 – "Ahasiba annasu an yutrako an yaqoolo amanna wa hum la yuftanon. (2) Wa laqad fatanna alladheena min qablihim falaya'lamanna Allahu alladheena sadaqo wa laya'lamanna alkadhibeen. (3)" (Surat Al-Ankabut)

"Do the people think that they will be left to say, "We believe" and they will not be tried? (2) But We have certainly tried those before them, and Allah will surely make evident those who are truthful, and He will surely make evident the liars." (The Spider, 29:2-3)

Sayyidina Isa عليه السلام said, 'I want to be raised to see Sayyidina Muhammad ﷺ and not die.' And he walks upon this Earth till today so that he can give his hand to Sayyidina Muhammad ﷺ in the Last Days. Nabi Musa عليه السلام wanted to be with Prophet ﷺ. Sayyidina Bilal Habashi عليه السلام wanted to be with Prophet ﷺ and suffered for Prophet ﷺ. Sayyidina Salman al Farsi ق sold himself to be *asiran* and a captive, a slave, to enter into *Madina al Munawwarah*, not with assets, not with pride, not with anything other than, 'I want to enter into your kingdom as a slave.' And he came as an *asiran* (captive), no fighting, no praying, no *zakat*, no nothing, and Prophet ﷺ's first words were, 'This is my family, this is my *Ahlul Bayt*.'

Endure Difficulties and Testing to be Closer to Prophet ﷺ

So how to make Prophet ﷺ happy is to endure through difficulty, through humiliating, and through testing, with good character, with love. And those that harm, *ya Rabbi*, forgive them for they don't know what they are doing, but by means of them Allah ﷻ is raising you. So Allah ﷻ says, pray for them that Allah ﷻ forgives them and raises them too.

وَلَمَن صَبَرَ وَغَفَرَ إِنَّ ذَٰلِكَ لَمِنْ عَزْمِ الْأُمُورِ ﴿٤٣﴾

42:43 – *"Wa laman sabara wa ghafara inna zaalika lamin 'azmil umoor (43)" (Surat Ash-Shura)*

"But indeed if any show patience and forgive [the oppressor], that would truly be an exercise of courageous will and resolution in the conduct of affairs." (The Consultation, 42:43)

Subhana rabbika rabbal 'izzati 'amma yasifoon, wa salaamun 'alal mursaleen, walhamdulillahi rabbil 'aalameen. Bi hurmati Muhammad al-Mustafa wa bi siri Surat al-Fatiha.

Illuminate the Eternal Light Within the Heart, Not the Light of the Brain (YaSeen 36:68 & 16:70)

وَاللَّـهُ خَلَقَكُمْ ثُمَّ يَتَوَفَّاكُمْ ۚ وَمِنكُم مَّن يُرَدُّ إِلَىٰ أَرْذَلِ الْعُمُرِ لِكَيْ لَا يَعْلَمَ بَعْدَ عِلْمٍ شَيْئًا ۚ إِنَّ اللَّـهَ عَلِيمٌ قَدِيرٌ ﴿٧٠﴾

16:70 – *"Wallahu khalaqakum thumma yatawaffaakum, wa minkum man yuraddu ila ardhalil 'umuri likay, la ya'lama bada 'ilmin shayan, innAllaha 'Alimun Qadeer." (Surat An-Nahl)*

"And Allah created you; then He will take your souls at death. And among you there are some who are sent back to most abject and a feeble age, so that they know nothing after having known (so much): for Allah is All-Knowing, All-Powerful." (The Bee, 16:70)

Alhamdulillahi rabbil alameen as salatu was salamu ala ashraf al mursaleen Sayyidina wa Mawlana Muhammad al Mustafa sallallahu alayhi wa sallam. Madad ya Sayyidi ya Sultan al-Awliya, Mawlana Shaykh Abdullah Faiz al-Daghestani. Madad ya Sayyidi ya Sultan al Awliya Mawlana Shaykh Muhammad Nazim Adil al Haqqani, madad ya Sayyidi ya Sultan al Qulubina, Mawlana Shaykh Hisham Kabbani, wa Shaykh Adnan Kabbani, wa Shaykh Muhammad Adil. Unzur halana wa isfalana abiduna bi madadakum wa nazarakum. Madad al haqq, ya hujjatallah al mukhlis.

Illuminate the Eternal Light within the Heart, Not the Light of the Brain (YaSeen 36:68 & 16:70)

A'udhu Billahi Minash Shaitanir Rajeem, Bismillahir Rahmanir Raheem, *"Atiullah wa ati ar rasul wa ulil amri minkum."* (Holy Qur'an, 4:59) Always a reminder for myself *ana abda kul ajee wa da'eef wa miskin wa dhalim wa jahl*, but for the grace of Allah's ﷻ *Rahmah* (mercy) be upon us all and to save us from difficulty. May Allah's ﷻ *Rahmah* to forgive us and, *inshaAllah*, continually bless us for the sake of the love of Sayyidina Muhammad ﷺ and for the Nation of Sayyidina Muhammad ﷺ.

We Go Back to Weakness After Strength at Old Age

InshaAllah, we start from Surat YaSeen, verse 68, *"Wa man nu 'amirhu nunakishu fil khalqi..."* (And he to whom We grant long life and bring onto old age...) Allah ﷻ, from this holy month, Rabbi al Thani (6th lunar month), which is the month of the *qamar*, the month of Surat Al-Qamar (54th chapter of Holy Qur'an), the moon. From the teaching of *awliyaullah* (saints) and the realities to open the heart of the seeker. That from the secret of Surat YaSeen, the heart of Holy Qur'an, Allah ﷻ is describing in this *ayat al karim* (68th), 'To whom We bring onto old age, We reverse him in creation making him to go back to weakness after We gave him strength. Have they then no sense?' It's a warning from Allah ﷻ, this life that has been given to you is temporary, there is an accounting and a *hisaab*.

وَمَن نُّعَمِّرْهُ نُنَكِّسْهُ فِي الْخَلْقِ ۖ أَفَلَا يَعْقِلُونَ ﴿٦٨﴾

36:68 – *"Wa man nu'ammirHu nunakkis-hu fil khalqi, afala ya'qiloon." (Surat YaSeen)*

"And he to whom We grant long life and bring onto old age, We reverse him in nature (to an abject state, making him to go back to weakness after strength): do they not have mind to understand?" (YaSeen, 36:68)

Some People Are Sent Back to Feeble Age

This next *ayat* (verse) further explained with the 16th *surat*, verse 70. "...*wa minkum man yuraddu ila ardhalil 'umuri likay...*" (And among you there are some who are sent back to most abject and a feeble age).

وَاللَّـهُ خَلَقَكُمْ ثُمَّ يَتَوَفَّاكُمْ ۚ وَمِنكُم مَّن يُرَدُّ إِلَىٰ أَرْذَلِ الْعُمُرِ لِكَيْ لَا يَعْلَمَ بَعْدَ عِلْمٍ شَيْئًا ۚ إِنَّ اللَّـهَ عَلِيمٌ قَدِيرٌ ﴿٧٠﴾

16:70 – *"Wallahu khalaqakum thumma yatawaffaakum, wa minkum man yuraddu ila ardhalil 'umuri likay, la ya'lama bada 'ilmin shayan, innAllaha 'Alimun Qadeer." (Surat An-Nahl)*

"And Allah created you; then He will take your souls at death. And among you there are some who are sent back to most abject and a feeble age, so that they know nothing after having known (so much): for Allah is All-Knowing, All-Powerful." (The Bee, 16:70)

Allah ﷻ is giving more understanding from the realities of Surat YaSeen in this *ayat al karim*, 'Allah ﷻ created you and caused you to die.' So, we have a death, an ending of this life. 'And amongst you is he who is brought back,' which means that Allah ﷻ didn't grant that one death but gave them long life onto this *dunya* (material world). 'Brought back but in the most abject stage of life, so that you know nothing after He hath given you knowledge and Allah ﷻ is Knower and Powerful.'

Illuminate the Eternal Light within the Heart, Not the Light of the Brain (YaSeen 36:68 & 16:70)

Don't Be Astonished By Knowledge of the Head

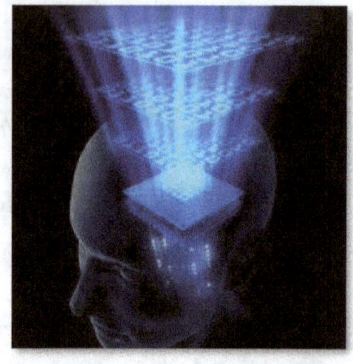

This means for our lives and what *awliyaullah* (saints) come into our life and say, 'Don't be astonished by the knowledge of the head but seek a path in which your knowledge is from the heart.' Knowledge of the head is very temporary. They illuminate only the brain. They memorize or they have strong memory, and they read and translate and keep talking from their head. These are scientists. These are professors at school. These are lawyers. These are doctors. These are all whom in this *dunya* (material world) they say, '*MashaAllah*, what a powerful mind you have, what a powerful mind that was.' A famous scientist, a famous doctor, even famous scholar, *zahiri*, we are not talking about *ahlut tariqah* (people of spiritual paths) and the students of *ahlut tariqah*, this is different.

This is whom they take their *uloom* (knowledge) in memorizing books and reciting from books. Everywhere they go, they put many books, and they have to keep reading from them. They are like libraries, huge, some events have many books. Allah is warning for external people that you may reach a height of knowledge in which We gave you a strength and knowledge, but we are going to pull it, if it is only from your head.

Shaykh Nurjan Mirahmadi

Having Knowledge of the Head is Like a Donkey Carrying Books

So, as they begin to memorize, they keep getting worried about their memory. And so they have to take more books with them everywhere they go. That knowledge that they have is by reading, reciting, reading, reciting. They keep forgetting and they bring more books, more books. Then Allah ﷻ

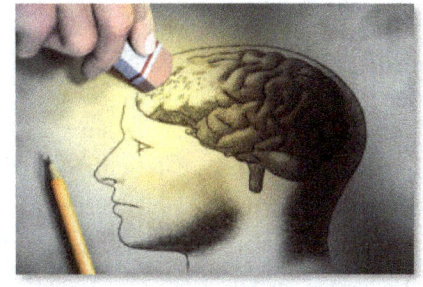

described from our cousins in Holy Qur'an (62:5) that, 'This knowledge you have, you carry it with you like a donkey carrying books.'

مَثَلُ الَّذِينَ حُمِّلُوا التَّوْرَاةَ ثُمَّ لَمْ يَحْمِلُوهَا كَمَثَلِ الْحِمَارِ يَحْمِلُ أَسْفَارًا ۚ بِئْسَ مَثَلُ الْقَوْمِ الَّذِينَ كَذَّبُوا بِآيَاتِ اللَّهِ ۚ وَاللَّهُ لَا يَهْدِي الْقَوْمَ الظَّالِمِينَ ﴿٥﴾

62:5 – *"Masalul lazeena hummilut Tawraata summa lam yahmilohaa kamasalil himaari yahmilu asfaaraa; bi'sa masalul qawmil lazeena*

kaazzaboo bi aayaatillah; wallaahu laa yahdil qawmaz zaalimeen." (Surat Al-Jum'a)

"The example of those who were entrusted with the Torah and then did not apply it on is like that of a donkey who carries volumes of books. Wretched is the example of the people who deny/falsify the signs/revelations of Allah. And Allah does not guide the wrongdoing people."

(The Congregation/Friday, 62:5)

This knowledge that you are carrying with you is like a donkey carrying books. Allah ﷻ then doesn't hold that knowledge in too much esteem. It's considered like a donkey carrying books. You are bringing this

Illuminate the Eternal Light within the Heart, Not the Light of the Brain (YaSeen 36:68 & 16:70)

---

everywhere with you. This is not a knowledge that they are talking about. Because there are many who speak and give out their knowledge from again, scientists, professors, think of all the people in our lives that Allah ﷻ is describing for us. Their knowledge didn't benefit them but they have lots of it. And they dispense it everywhere, and they reach a stage in this *dunya* (material world) of power and strength.

Then Allah ﷻ begins to shut the power off and you find them unfortunate in hospitals with Alzheimer's and dementia. They don't remember anything. They were not nobody; these were big professors, big scientists, big doctors, big people of *dunya* (material world). And Allah ﷻ is saying, 'Take a warning from that. Don't be under the illusion of a temporary *dunya* (material world).' The *uloom* (knowledges) in which they talk is very temporary, it is not illuminating the heart.

Mawlana Jalaluddin Rumi ق Met the Sun (Shams) and He Threw Out Rumi's Books

Then from Tazkiyyat ul Awliya ق and for us to understand the way of *awliyaullah* (saints) is from Sayyidina Jalaluddin Rumi ق. For us to understand, he is a big *alim* (scholar), but from the *alim* of the books; that was carrying around books and books and wanting to recite from books. He came across one of Allah's ﷻ *awliyaullah* (saints) by the name of Shams Tabriz. That should be enough of an understanding; he met the sun!

He met a *shams*. He met one of whom their hearts are illuminated. As a result of the illumination of their heart, they are reflecting these realities.

They came into contact with each other – we give a short version of the story. Shams got his books and threw them into the water. So Mawlana Rumi a big *alim* (scholar) walking with books, he came across the path of a *wali* (saint) and the *wali* took his books and threw them into the water. He didn't insult him, because there is a *haqqaiq* (realities) in every step of what is happening. Threw it into the water, didn't throw it into the mud, didn't throw into dirt, that is a respect for it. He threw it into *ma'i* (water). One, I am now going to teach you a secret from that. So Sayyidina Jalaluddin ق got very upset.

He said, 'Why did you throw my books?' He said, 'Now pick up your books.' When he picked up his books, they were not wet.

The Danger of Teaching What You Don't Practice

He said, 'This is what you need to seek. You need to seek realities. Not that which you are carrying with you and memorizing and talking. The danger of going and saying, 'I have these ten-thousand books or two-thousand books, that I have read and I will talk to you about.' Allah ﷻ will ask you, 'How many of those did you put into practice?' Thousands of *ayats* (verses) of Qur'an you want to recite to people, and not one of them you lived by? He is going to ask, these books that you are talking about and talked about all your life, you read them all? Did you practice and live by them? Or it was just you regurgitate and give to people whatever they can take?

Illuminate the Eternal Light within the Heart, Not the Light of the Brain (YaSeen 36:68 & 16:70)

And *awliyaullah* (saints) come into our life and say, 'No, no, when he threw that into the water, that knowledge was dressed by the ocean of *al hayat* (ever-living).' When he returned the books to him, pure and purified. He is teaching him now, this knowledge we are going to pull from you, what you think you know, because you are coming to us with  your cup full. We are going to pull it, not disgrace it. We are going to clean it. We are going to dress it from oceans of *al hayat* (ever-living) and give it back to you real. It means give it back to you real.

The Knowledge That Didn't Illuminate You Will Be Lost at Old Age

So now when people are so concerned in their lives that whatever they are doing, their knowledges, their books, their accreditations, their certificates, all that they have, and then this fear that I am going to get old and forget all of them. *Awliya* (saints) are coming and teaching, 'Because this knowledge you have, it did not illuminate you, and as a result now the time is in a descent.' Surat al-Asr where Allah ﷻ describes, *insan* (mankind) is in a losing state.

وَالْعَصْرِ ﴿١﴾ إِنَّ الْإِنسَانَ لَفِي خُسْرٍ ﴿٢﴾ إِلَّا الَّذِينَ آمَنُوا وَعَمِلُوا الصَّالِحَاتِ وَتَوَاصَوْا بِالْحَقِّ وَتَوَاصَوْا بِالصَّبْرِ ﴿٣﴾

103:1-3 – "*Wal 'Asr. (1) Innal insaana lafee khusr. (2) Illal ladheena aamano wa 'amilos saalihaati, wa tawasaw bil haqqi wa tawasaw bis Sabr. (3)*" *(Surat Al-'Asr)*

"By '*Asr* (the time)! (1) Verily, Mankind is in loss. (2) Except for those who have believed and done righteous deeds and advised each other to truth and advised each other to patience. (3)"
(The Declining Day, 103:1-3)

It means you have a highlight, you have a pinnacle, you have a summer of your life. You reach to that point where you think you are on top of the world. And then you are in a descent [indicates downward motion]. This point at the top is where they say you should worry. If at this point you are on the path with *awliyaullah* (saints), they will describe. But if

you are with people of this *dunya* (material world), when this point reaches and you begin your descent, it means all, everything is lost; your ability to think is lost. The knowledges that you were thinking and talking to people about are lost from your head. Even the things that you specialized in life of your law, your sciences, your architecture, everything will be lost from your head. And this becomes what Allah ﷻ describes, 'Like a feeble state', like a child, they don't know even how to take care of themselves, God forbid. They did not reach the oceans of *al hayat* and they did not accomplish what God wanted for them, what Allah ﷻ wanted for them.

The Shams (Sun) Comes to Illuminate the Heart, Not the Head

So, then *Ahlul Hayat* (people of the Ever-living), the *shams*, why Shams

Tabriz? Because they are the sun. The sun is the *najm* (star). Prophet ﷺ described, 'All my Companions are like stars', they are all *najm*. They are all stars. They are all eternal in their reality.

أَصْحَابِيْ كَالنُّجُـومْ بِأَيْهِمْ اَقْتَدَيْتِمْ اَهْتَدَيْتِمْ

"*Ashabi kan Nujoom, bi ayyihim aqta daytum ahta daytum.*"

Illuminate the Eternal Light within the Heart, Not the Light of the Brain (YaSeen 36:68 & 16:70)

"My companions are like stars. Follow any one of them and you will be rightly guided." (Prophet Muhammad (pbuh))

Awliyaullah (saints) inherit from *Ashab al Kiram*, (Noble Companions) from *Ahlul Baytul Kiram* (Noble Family of Prophet Muhammad ﷺ) and they inherit from that reality that they are a sun. When they come into your life, they are coming to illuminate your heart and say, 'Don't focus on the faculty of your head. Your head, when the circuits become old and the energy is gone, that head will be worthless to you.' Many in *dunya* (material world), already their head is worthless to them. Imagine as they get older! But, illuminate the heart. *Ahlul Hayat* (People of the Ever-living) if they come and begin to teach that illuminate your heart. If your heart is illuminated from ocean of *al hayat*, your entire being will be powered from that illumination.

أَلا وَإِنَّ فِى الْجَسَدِ مُضْغَةً إِذَا صَلَحَتْ صَلَحَ الْجَسَدُ كُلُّهُ، وَإِذَا فَسَدَتْ فَسَدَ الْجَسَدُ كُلُّهُ، أَلا وَهِىَ الْقَلْبُ

"Ala wa inna fil Jasadi mudghatan idha salahat salahal jasadu kulluho, wa idha fasadat fasadal jasadu kulluho, ala wa heyal Qalb."

"There is a piece of flesh in the body, if it becomes good (reformed) the whole body becomes good but if it gets spoiled the whole body gets spoiled and that is the heart." (Prophet Muhammad (pbuh))

The Ones Whose Hearts Are Open Have Internal Generator in Their Heart

It is hard to describe a visual. Many things can't be put into words. You are living a temporary life and the people of *dunya* (material world), there is like an energy that supports them in *had ad-dunya* (limit of material world). When the time for that energy is finished, it is like Allah ﷻ cut the power. When the power is gone, the circuits don't work - it's finished. That time is finished for that *insan* (mankind). Those whom their hearts are illuminated, Allah ﷻ is giving them an internal generator. Does it make sense? You are working on and this is only by example, they will say, 'Where is this in the Qur'an, Shaykh?' I just described the whole of Qur'an in that. You are taking from the outside power. What Allah ﷻ wanted for us, no, no, no, your heart should be alive!

وَرَبَطْنَا عَلَىٰ قُلُوبِهِمْ إِذْ قَامُوا فَقَالُوا رَبُّنَا رَبُّ السَّمَاوَاتِ وَالْأَرْضِ ... ﴿١٤﴾

18:14 – "Wa rabatnaa 'alaa quloo bihim iz qaamoo faqaaloo Rabbunaa Rabbus samaawaati wal ardi..." (Surat Al-Kahf)

"We gave strength to their hearts: Behold, they stood up and said: 'Our Lord is the Lord of the heavens and of the earth'..." (The Cave, 18:14)

Muhammadan Light is From Malakut (Heavens)

When we are reciting *salawat* (praising) that Prophet ﷺ is *Muhyi ul Qulub*. Prophet ﷺ is *Muhyi ul Qulub*.

يَا مُحْيِي الْقُلُوبِ،
يَا مَاحِي الذُّنُوبِي ، سَلَامٌ عَلَيْك

Ya Muhyil qulubi
Ya Mahidh dhunubi Salaam 'Alayk

O the reviver of the hearts, O the eraser of the sins, Peace be upon you

If your heart is with the love of Sayyidina Muhammad ﷺ, Prophet ﷺ will begin to plant into your heart the Oceans of *al Hayat* (ever-living). It means he is going to make his love like a drop, where Allah ﷻ describes Prophet ﷺ in Surat Nur, 24th *surat*, 35th verse. 'This light is not from the East or West;' we don't have an east and west, it is not from the rising of the sun and not from setting of the sun. The rising of the sun and

Illuminate the Eternal Light within the Heart, Not the Light of the Brain (YaSeen 36:68 & 16:70)

setting of sun is only from *dunya* (material world), there is no sun and moon in Paradise.

Nur Muhammad ﷺ is an Eternally Lit Brilliant Star - 'Kawkabun Durriyu'

So, when Allah ﷻ says, 'This is not from *mashariq wal magharib*,' this is not from rising or setting. It means it's not from your *dunya* (material world), this is from *malakut* (heavens), this Light.

اللَّهُ نُورُ السَّمَاوَاتِ وَالْأَرْضِ ۚ مَثَلُ نُورِهِ كَمِشْكَاةٍ فِيهَا مِصْبَاحٌ ۖ الْمِصْبَاحُ فِي زُجَاجَةٍ ۖ الزُّجَاجَةُ كَأَنَّهَا كَوْكَبٌ دُرِّيٌّ يُوقَدُ مِن شَجَرَةٍ مُّبَارَكَةٍ زَيْتُونَةٍ لَّا شَرْقِيَّةٍ وَلَا غَرْبِيَّةٍ يَكَادُ زَيْتُهَا يُضِيءُ وَلَوْ لَمْ تَمْسَسْهُ نَارٌ ۚ نُّورٌ عَلَىٰ نُورٍ ۗ يَهْدِي اللَّهُ لِنُورِهِ مَن يَشَاءُ ۚ وَيَضْرِبُ اللَّهُ الْأَمْثَالَ لِلنَّاسِ ۗ وَاللَّهُ بِكُلِّ شَيْءٍ عَلِيمٌ ﴿٣٥﴾

24:35 – "*Allahu noorus samawati wal ardi. mathalu noorehi kamishkatin feeha misbahun, almisbahu fee zujajatin, azzujajatu kaannaha kawkabun durriyyun yoqadu min shajaratim mubarakatin zaytoonatil la sharqiyyatin wa la gharbiyyatin yakadu zaytuha yudeeo wa law lam tamsashu narun. Noorun 'ala noorin. yahdellahu linoorihi man yashao. Wa yadribullah ul amthala linnasi, wallahu bikulli shayin 'Aleem.*" (Surat An-Nur)

"Allah is the Light of the heavens and the earth. The Parable of His Light is as if there were a Niche and within it a Lamp: the Lamp enclosed in Glass: the glass as it were a brilliant star: Lit from a blessed Tree an Olive, neither of the east nor of the west, whose oil is well-nigh luminous, though fire scarce touched it: Light upon Light! Allah guides whom He will to His Light: Allah present examples for the people: and Allah knows all things." (The Light, 24:35)

We go just to the center of this *ayat*, 'It is a Light like in a niche,' this Light that Allah ﷻ wants us to achieve, 'it is in a *misbah*,' its like in a lantern. These are from *haqiqat ul Muhammadiya* ﷺ (Muhammadan realities) of where Allah ﷻ placed the Light of Prophet ﷺ. 'It is like in a glass, like a brilliant star, it is lit from a blessed tree.' This is not the *had* (limit) of *dunya* (material world) tree, this is the Tree of Life, *Sidratul Muntaha* (Holy Qur'an, 53:14). Why Allah ﷻ is clarifying, 'not from the rising and setting'? It means it is not from the *had* (limit) of *dunya* (material world). Your Earth has rising and setting, My Heavens have no sun and moon. This is from the Oceans of *malakut* (heavens) and eternal realities. 'Like an olive tree, blessed, luminous, Light upon Light.'

عِندَ سِدْرَةِ الْمُنتَهَىٰ ﴿١٤﴾

53:14 – "Inda sidratel Muntaha." (Surat An-Najm)

"At the Lote Tree of the Utmost Boundary." (The Star, 53:14)

Prophet ﷺ Makes Heart of Awliya (Saints) Like a Bright Lantern

It means seek that Light, seek that reality. *Awliyaullah* (saints) carry that Light as an inheritance from *Sirajun Munira* (illuminating Lamp), that Prophet ﷺ gives to them in their heart. Because if you dive into that ocean, dive into that ocean, and you reach the *Maqam al Iman* (Station of Faith), in which you love Prophet ﷺ more than you love  yourself, and you become from *Ahbab un Nabi* ﷺ, the lovers of Sayyidina Muhammad ﷺ, Prophet ﷺ makes your heart to be like a lantern.

Illuminate the Eternal Light within the Heart, Not the Light of the Brain (YaSeen 36:68 & 16:70)

يَا أَيُّهَا النَّبِيُّ إِنَّا أَرْسَلْنَاكَ شَاهِدًا وَمُبَشِّرًا وَنَذِيرًا ﴿٤٥﴾ وَدَاعِيًا إِلَى اللَّـهِ بِإِذْنِهِ وَسِرَاجًا مُنِيرًا ﴿٤٦﴾

33:45-46 – "Ya ayyuhan Nabiyu inna arsalnaka shahidan wa mubashshiran wa nadheera. (45) Wa daiyan ila Allahi `bi-idhnihi wa Sirajan Muneera. (46)" (Surat Al-Ahzab)

"O Prophet, indeed We have sent you as a witness and a bringer of good tidings and a warner. (45) And one who invites to Allah, by His permission, and an illuminating lamp."
(The Combined Forces, 33:45-46)

and

لاَ يُؤْمِنُ أَحَدُكُمْ حَتَّى أَكُونَ أَحَبَّ إِلَيْهِ مِنْ وَالِدِهِ وَوَلَدِهِ وَالنَّاسِ أَجْمَعِينَ

"La yuminu ahadukum hatta akona ahabba ilayhi min walidihi wa waladihi wan Nasi ajma'yeen."

"None of you will have faith till he loves me more than his father, his children and all mankind." (Prophet Muhammad (pbuh))

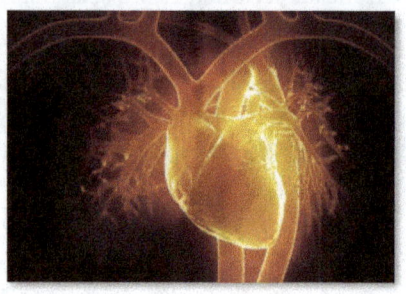

When you love Prophet ﷺ more than you love yourself, then what's in your heart if it's not yourself? Prophet ﷺ. Because he said, 'Love me more than you love yourself.' If you achieved that, it means your self is no longer in your heart. What is in your heart? It is Prophet ﷺ. He says, 'I make for your being like a lamp. Where you go, you are giving a luminous light to everything.' If they accompany you, you will revive the dead heart. If that Light enters into the heart of the believer and makes them to be illuminated by Allah's ﷻ Grace and Might, it means they begin to power all their being.

Dude (Worms) Don't Eat Ahlul Wadud (Lovers) of Prophet ﷺ in Grave

Even as they are growing old, many *awliyaullah* (saints), and there are many proofs in this *dunya* (material world), they bury them when they passed away. They've opened the grave to move it because of construction, they are fresh in their grave as if you saw them yesterday. How? When you don't have energy and you don't have anything in your heart, what's going to come if you don't have *wadud* (love)? *Dude* is coming for you. What is *dude*? Everyone calls everybody *dude*, but *dude* means 'worm' in Arabic. If you are not *Ahlul Wadud* (people of love), because *Ahlul Wadud* are filled with love. *"Qul in kuntum tuhibbunallah fattabiouni yuhbibkumullah."* (Holy Qur'an, 3:31)

قُلْ إِنْ كُنْتُمْ تُحِبُّونَ اللَّهَ فَاتَّبِعُونِيْ يُحْبِبْكُمُ اللَّهُ وَيَغْفِرْ لَكُمْ ذُنُوبَكُمْ ۗ وَاللَّهُ غَفُورٌ رَحِيمٌ ﴿٣١﴾

3:31 – "Qul in kuntum tuhibbon Allaha fattabi'oni, yuhbibkumullahu wa yaghfir lakum dhunobakum wallahu Ghaforur Raheem." (Surat Ali-'Imran)

"Say, [O Muhammad], "If you should love Allah, then follow me, [so] Allah will love you and forgive you your sins. And Allah is Forgiving and Merciful." (Family of Imran, 3:31)

If Allah ﷻ loves you and you are *Ahlul Wudud*, nothing on this earth can eat from you. They can't bite you, and they can't make your their *ta'am*, their food. They are fresh. They have an energy source within their heart and their soul, still sparking and powering their body that is parked in their grave. Their force of energy is not out, but inside, coming from *malakut* 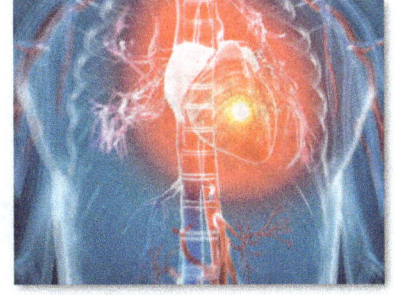 (heavens), where Allah ﷻ describes that Power, *'Kulli shay* (everything),

Illuminate the Eternal Light within the Heart, Not the Light of the Brain (YaSeen 36:68 & 16:70)

it is the Power of everything this *malakut*.' (Holy Qur'an, 36:83) If they reached to that, their hearts are lit, their body is secured by energy.

فَسُبْحَانَ الَّذِي بِيَدِهِ مَلَكُوتُ كُلِّ شَيْءٍ وَإِلَيْهِ تُرْجَعُونَ ﴿٨٣﴾

36:83 – *"Fasubhanal ladhee biyadihi Malakotu kulli shay in wa ilayhi turja'oon." (Surat YaSeen)*

"Therefore Glory be to Him in Whose hand is the dominion/ kingdom over everything in heavens, and to Him you will be returned."
(YaSeen, 36:83)

There is no *dude* (worm) eating them. Ironic how this *dunya* (material world) people call each other 'dude'. Do you think Allah ﷻ brought a program so that we would understand? So why do people go around calling each other 'worm'? So that we would understand. Allah ﷻ is giving hints in the program, it has been written. Whatever Prophet ﷺ brought for us, we see the signs everywhere.

Awliya (Saints) Are More Powerful and Knowledgeable at Their Old Age

So, illuminate the heart, bring the light within the heart. That illumination will illuminate everything and they don't become feeble. *Awliyaullah* (saints) in their old age become much more powerful, much

more knowledgeable, much more with *yaqeen* (certainty). Not becoming senile and losing of the mind because all their life was just on their *dunya* (material world). But *awliyaullah* (saints) come and teach, 'No, open the realities of the heart. Bring the light of this heart. Bring the realities of the heart.'

Tafakkur (Contemplation) and Learn Good Manners to Attain Mercy

Make *tafakkur*, contemplate and learn good manners. That is why Shams Tabriz began to teach that this knowledge of the books is of no value to you. Allah ﷻ describes one of Allah's ﷻ students, that Nabi Musa ﷺ wanted to meet, that, 'he attained the *rahmah* (mercy) and We taught him the Knowledge of Heavens.'

فَوَجَدَا عَبْدًا مِّنْ عِبَادِنَا آتَيْنَاهُ رَحْمَةً مِّنْ عِندِنَا وَعَلَّمْنَاهُ مِن لَّدُنَّا عِلْمًا ﴿٦٥﴾

18:65 – "Fawajada 'abdan min 'ibadinaa ataynahu rahmatan min 'indina wa 'allamnahu mil ladunna 'ilma." (Surat Al-Kahf)

"So they found one of Our servant from among Our servants, on whom We had bestowed Mercy from Ourselves and whom We had taught [unseen/heavenly] knowledge from Our own Presence..."
(The Cave, 18:65)

So, it means attain a *rahmah* (mercy) is through the *adab* (manners), through the *tariqah* (spiritual path); it means the good character. All of those qualities that the *turuq* (spiritual paths) have. Come to learn manners. Come to learn good character. Come to take away badness. And do *muhasaba* and accounting at night.

Illuminate the Eternal Light within the Heart, Not the Light of the Brain (YaSeen 36:68 & 16:70)

Love of Prophet ﷺ Revives the Heart and Washes Away the Sins

Do *tafakkur* (contemplation) and *muraqaba* (meditation) and bring Allah's eternal lights within the heart. This means bring the love of Sayyidina Muhammad ﷺ into the hearts. Sayyidina Muhammad ﷺ becomes *Muhyil Qulub*.

يَا مُحْيِي الْقُلُوْبِ، يَا مَاحِي الذُّنُوْبِيْ ، سَلَامٌ عَلَيك

Ya Muhyil qulubi Ya Mahidh dhunubi Salaam 'Alayk

O the reviver of the hearts, O the eraser of the sins, Peace be upon you.

And the *salawat* we were reciting says *"Mahidh Dhunubi"* not only will Prophet ﷺ revive the heart, that he will wash and clean away the sins because if the light of Prophet ﷺ. 'If you love me more than you love yourself'

لاَ يُؤْمِنُ أَحَدُكُمْ حَتَّى أَكُونَ أَحَبَّ إِلَيْهِ مِنْ وَالِدِهِ وَوَلَدِهِ وَالنَّاسِ أَجْمَعِينَ

"La yuminu ahadukum hatta akona ahabba ilayhi min walidihi wa waladihi wan Nasi ajma'yeen."

"None of you will have faith till he loves me more than his father, his children and all mankind." (Prophet Muhammad (pbuh))

Light of Sayyidina Muhammad ﷺ Cleanses Your Heart of Falsehood

Prophet ﷺ is teaching that, 'if my Light begins to enter into your heart,' do you think *"Qul ja al haqq wa zahaqal batil"*, that every falsehood in you, Prophet's ﷺ Light is going to be sitting with that?

وَ قُلْ جَاءَالْحَقُّ وَزَهَقَ الْبَطِلُ، إِنَّ الْبَطِلَ كَانَ زَهُوقًا ﴿٨١﴾

17:81 – *"Wa qul jaa alhaqqu wa zahaqal baatil, innal batila kana zahoqa." (Surat Al-Isra)*

"And say, Truth has come, and falsehood has perished. Indeed falsehood, [by its nature], is ever perishing/ bound to perish."
(The Night Journey, 17:81)

If this Light begins to come into the heart, the Light of Prophet ﷺ will destroy all falsehood. No falsehood stands in the presence of Prophet ﷺ. That is why these people can't clean themselves, and they don't leave their sins and they don't leave their bad actions. *Ahbab un Nabi* ﷺ, lovers of Prophet ﷺ, they don't need to clean themselves. Prophet ﷺ is cleaning them because the love of Prophet ﷺ is all in their heart. And when that Light is coming, its cleansing and cleaning everything with *'Izzatullah* (Allah's ﷻ Might and Magnificence).

كَمَا أَرْسَلْنَا فِيكُمْ رَسُولًا مِّنكُمْ يَتْلُو عَلَيْكُمْ آيَاتِنَا وَيُزَكِّيكُمْ وَيُعَلِّمُكُمُ الْكِتَابَ وَالْحِكْمَةَ وَيُعَلِّمُكُم مَّا لَمْ تَكُونُوا تَعْلَمُونَ ﴿١٥١﴾

2:151 – *"Kama arsalna feekum Rasulam minkum yatlo 'Alaykum ayatina wa yuzakkeekum wa yu'Allimukumul kitaba walhikmata wa yu'Allimukum ma lam takono ta'Alamon." (Surat Al-Baqarah)*

Illuminate the Eternal Light within the Heart, Not the Light of the Brain (YaSeen 36:68 & 16:70)

"Just as We have sent among (within) you a messenger of your own, reciting to you Our Signs, and purifying you, and teaching you the Book/Scripture (Quran) and Wisdom, and teaching you New Knowledge, that which you did not know." (The Cow, 2:151)

We pray that Allah ﷻ grant more and more understanding in this month from the *barakah* (blessings) of Sayyidatina Fatima Zahra ؏ that dress us, bless us, become *qamarun* and prepare for us the holy month of Rajab, Shaban and Ramadan, *inshaAllah*.

Subhana rabbika rabbal 'izzati 'amma yasifoon, wa salaamun 'alal mursaleen, walhamdulillahi rabbil 'aalameen. Bi hurmati Muhammad al-Mustafa wa bi siri Surat al-Fatiha.

Be the Moon and Follow the Sun – Even If You Are Nabi Musa ﷺ

Follow "A Servant Whom Has Attained A Mercy From Allah"

وَالشَّمْسِ وَضُحَاهَا ﴿١﴾ وَالْقَمَرِ إِذَا تَلَاهَا ﴿٢﴾

91:1-4 – "Wash Shamsi wa duhaha. (1) Wal Qamari idha talaha. (2)" (Surat Ash-Shams)

"By the Sun and his (glorious) Brightness; (1) By the Moon as she follows him; (2)" (The Sun, 91:1-4)

The Sun is Superior and the Light is Eternal

Alhamdulillah, Allah ﷻ always shows the perfection outside of us, the perfection within nature, that everything is in complete *taslim* (submission). Then to take an advice and to take an example from nature and our surroundings is to understand ourselves and our greater reality.

Alhamdulillah, "Shamsi wa al Qamar, Shamsi wa al Qamar, Shamsi wa al Qamar," (the Sun and the Moon). That throughout Holy Qur'an, Allah ﷻ is directing us that the *shams* (sun) is superior and the light that is eternal. That the light is a masculine and leadership and is the leader reality. Allah describes that that sun is always moving on its course and that the *qamar*, and the moon, its duty is only to follow. The relationship in that following, that Allah describes, is that one doesn't overtake the other.

لَا الشَّمْسُ يَنْبَغِي لَهَا أَن تُدْرِكَ الْقَمَرَ وَلَا اللَّيْلُ سَابِقُ النَّهَارِ ۚ وَكُلٌّ فِي فَلَكٍ يَسْبَحُونَ ﴿٤٠﴾

36:40 – "La ash Shamsu yanbaghee laha an tudrikal Qamara wa lal laylu sabiqu annahari, wa kullun fee falakin yasbahon."
(Surat YaSeen)

"It is not permitted to the Sun to catch up the Moon, nor can the Night outstrip the Day: Each (just) Ship Sailing along in (its own) orbit (according to Law)." (YaSeen, 36:40)

It means they don't try to confuse each other's roles. It is so important because when you look at the moon, at times you feel like it's a sun light. Full moon means the moon of perfection – it shines so much light and illuminates everywhere that, for a moment you begin to think, 'Maybe it's the sun,' because of the amount of light that it's reflecting.

The Full Moon Knows That Its Light is From the Sun

It means everything about our spiritual path and the ways towards the heavens is teaching us, where Allah is reminding that, 'If your ego overtakes you, you begin to think that you are something. That maybe you are the sun and the light that's coming through you is because of you.'

Then they remind us that, 'No, look at the role of the *qamar* (moon), that it busies itself cleansing itself. It has no *dunya* (material world) on it. There is nothing built upon the moon. It's completely bare and empty, from what we can see.' That is the example of our life, that empty yourself, cleanse yourself, bear yourself of yourself. Get rid of yourself and you just follow the sun; follow the sun and make your whole direction towards the reality of the sun.

Nur Muhammad ﷺ is the Source of the Sun's Power

We are not following the external sun. But it has an example where Allah ﷻ says, 'I'm showing you an example,' outside for us to understand the example inside.

سَنُرِيهِمْ آيَاتِنَا فِي الْآفَاقِ وَفِي أَنفُسِهِمْ حَتَّىٰ يَتَبَيَّنَ لَهُمْ أَنَّهُ الْحَقُّ ۗ ... ﴿٥٣﴾

41:53 – "Sanureehim ayatina fil afaqi wa fee anfusihim hatta yatabayyana lahum annahu alhaqqu…" (Surat Al-Isra)

"We will show them Our signs in the horizons and within themselves until it becomes clear to them that it is the truth…"
(The Night Journey, 41:53)

That which is more majestic and all that we take from the sun, imagine then the light of Prophet ﷺ, where Allah ﷻ is saying that because you can substitute to understand the two. 'You breathe from that sun, you see from the light of the sun. You have food and vegetation from the light of the sun. Imagine then the light of Sayyidina Muhammad ﷺ,' Allah's ﷻ describing and Allah ﷻ is upon the heart of that light.

Allah ﷻ wants us to understand cause and effect and wants us to understand our surrounding. As you are breathing and eating from that light, the real source of that power, that's why in the *naat* and the

Be the Moon and Follow the Sun – Even If You Are Nabi Musa ﷺ

nasheeds (praisings) and all of that describes, 'Your light outdoes the sun'. The Green Dome of Madina, when it shines, it outshines the sun. It outshines the moon.

*When the Green Dome of Madina comes in to Sight
The whole of Dunya is buried in its light*

And

أَنْتَ شَمْسٌ أَنْتَ بَدْرٌ أَنْتَ نُورٌ فَوْقَ نُورِ
أَنْتَ إِكْسِيْرٌ وَغَالِي أَنْتَ مِصْبَاحُ الصُّدُورِ

*Anta shamsun, anta badrun   Anta Nurun fawqa Nuri
Anta iksirul wa judi   Anta misbah ul sudoori*

*You are the Sun of universes, You are the perfect moon,
You are light upon lights,
You are the true alchemist that purifies and illuminates our souls,
You are the divinely light in our hearts*

Nur Muhammad ﷺ, it is the source of the light of the sun and there are billions of suns within our entire universe besides our galaxy. It is the source of all the light and Allah ﷻ is the Power upon the heart of that reality. It means nothing in *La ilaha illallah* (there is no God but Allah); but *La ilaha illallah* is the power of *Muhammadun RasulAllah* ﷺ.

لَا إِلَهَ إِلاَّ اللهُ مُحَمَّدًا رَسُولُ الله

"La ilaha illallahu Muhammadun Rasulallah."

"There is no deity but Allah, Prophet Muhammad is the messenger of Allah."

The Only Duty of the Moon is to Follow the Sun

It means then that relationship is the *qamar*. Its only duty is to follow the sun, follow the light; follow that which is eternal.

وَالشَّمْسِ وَضُحَاهَا ﴿١﴾ وَالْقَمَرِ إِذَا تَلَاهَا ﴿٢﴾ وَالنَّهَارِ إِذَا جَلَّاهَا ﴿٣﴾ وَاللَّيْلِ إِذَا يَغْشَاهَا ﴿٤﴾

91:1-4 – *"Wash Shamsi wa duhaha. (1) Wal Qamari idha talaha. (2) Wan nahari idha jallaha. (3) Wal layli idha yaghshaha. (4)"* (Surat Ash-Shams)

"By the Sun and his (glorious) Brightness; (1) By the Moon as she follows him; (2) By the Day as it shows up (the Sun's) glory; (3) By the Night as it conceals it. (4) (The Sun, 91:1-4)

Then it teaches us its *adab* (manners). So when we are confused about our *adab* (manners) in *dunya* (material world), Allah ﷻ says, 'Don't be confused. Look at the nature, how its *adab* is.' It means the moon doesn't overtake the sun. It knows its

Be the Moon and Follow the Sun – Even If You Are Nabi Musa ﷺ

position. It knows its distance, it knows its course; it knows its purpose.

$$مَنْ عَرَفَ نَفْسَهُ فَقَدْ عَرَفَ رَبَّهُ$$

"Man 'arafa nafsahu faqad 'arafa Rabbahu."

"Who knows himself, knows his Lord." (Prophet Muhammad (pbuh))

It means what is the light that is governing us? So then we took a path of trying to know our self. In the process of knowing our self, they begin to teach then make your life like *qamar* (moon), make your life like the moon in which your whole love is to follow the love of Sayyidina Muhammad ﷺ and follow the *Nur Muhammadi* ﷺ (Light of Prophet Muhammad ﷺ) so that we can gain Allah's ﷻ Love and Allah's ﷻ Satisfaction.

Learn the Manners of Following From the Moon

Then the whole *adab* (manners) begins to open. That the moon never questions the sun; doesn't argue and debate with the sun, because Allah ﷻ is describing, 'They follow a course.' The moon never comes and says, 'Are you sure you're on the right course? Maybe I should be going a little bit this way, and I catch up with you later that way.' It means every example in our understanding we can find in that nature. Where Allah ﷻ says, 'Its course is so precise,' and based on its course we have life on this *dunya* (material world).

$$الشَّمْسُ وَالْقَمَرُ بِحُسْبَانٍ ﴿٥﴾$$

55:5 – "Ash Shamsu wal Qamaru bihusban." (Surat Ar-Rahman)

"The sun and the moon [move] on their fixed courses by precise calculation." (The Beneficent, 55:5)

All Ahlul Bayt, Ashab Nabi ﷺ, and Awliya Are the Moons

Now imagine the relationship between Prophet ﷺ and *Ashab un Nabi* ﷺ – they are all moons. Prophet ﷺ and *Ahlul Bayt un Nabi* ﷺ, they are all full moons. Imagine Prophet ﷺ and the relationship with *Awliyaullah* (saints), who are the inheritors and moons.

أَصْحَابِيْ كَالنُّجُـومْ بِأَيِّهِمْ اَقْتَدَيْتِمْ اَهْتَدَيْتِمْ

"Ashabi kan Nujoom, bi ayyihim aqta daytum ahta daytum."

"My companions are like stars. Follow any one of them and you will be guided." (Prophet Muhammad (pbuh))

This *dunya* (material world) doesn't exist without the sun and the moon – no *dunya*. No light, no warmth, no food, no breath and no air; it's all from Allah ﷻ. If Allah ﷻ doesn't provide a sun and a moon, there's no life on that planet. It means our life is based on this relationship. It's based on the *barakah* and the blessings and the *nur* (light) that Allah ﷻ is sending through the soul of Sayyidina Muhammad ﷺ. Prophet's ﷺ light is enough that doesn't burn the creation but merely blesses it, *"Wa ma arsalnaka illa rahmatan lil 'aalameen."*

وَمَا أَرْسَلْنَاكَ إِلَّا رَحْمَةً لِّلْعَالَمِينَ ﴿١٠٧﴾

21:107 – *"Wa maa arsalnaka illa Rahmatan lil'alameen."* (Surat Al-Anbiya)

"And We have not sent you, [O Muhammad], except as a mercy to the worlds." (The Prophets, 21:107)

Allah's Mercy, Nur Muhammad ﷺ Can Cool Down the Fire

That Allah ﷻ is sending these *rahmah* (mercy). It's only for the sake of the *rahmah*: *"Qulna ya naru ku ni bardan wa salaaman ala Ibrahim."* (O fire, be cool and Peaceful upon Abraham).

قُلْنَا يَا نَارُ كُونِي بَرْدًا وَسَلَامًا عَلَىٰ إِبْرَاهِيمَ ﴿٦٩﴾

21:69 – *"Qulna ya Naaru, kuni Bardan wa Salaman 'ala Ibrahim."* (Surat Al-Anbiya)

"We said, "O fire, be cool and Peaceful upon Abraham."
(The Prophets, 21:69)

If for Sayyidina Ibrahim ﷺ imagine coolness, imagine Allah ﷻ sending Sayyidina Muhammad ﷺ. It means that light that's emanating, *"Qulna ya naru,"* is the power that emanates from Allah's ﷻ Divinely Presence and can be nowhere and be located nowhere except the *qalb al Muhammadi* ﷺ. It has to always be from one location; this is the *tawhid* (oneness).

If Not For Nur Muhammad ﷺ, the Divinely Power Would Burn the Earth

That, *"Qul ya naru,"* is Allah's ﷻ Divinely Speech of *Qul*. Allah ﷻ says, 'Nothing can contain My *Qul*, no planets, no mountain, nothing but the heart of Sayyidina Muhammad ﷺ.'

مَا وَسِعَنِيْ سَمَائِيْ وَلَا أَرْضِيْ وَلَكِنْ وَسِعَنِيْ قَلْبِ عَبْدِيْ الْمُؤْمِنْ

"Maa wasi'anee Samayee, wa la ardee, laakin wasi'anee qalbi 'Abdee al Mu'min."

"Neither My Heavens nor My Earth can contain Me, but the heart of my Believing Servant." (Hadith Qudsi conveyed by Prophet Muhammad (pbuh))

'Qulna ya naru," means *"Qul".* 'My Divinely Speech which is a *Quwa* (power) – it is the source of all power, moving into the soul and the heart of that soul of Sayyidina Muhammad ﷺ.' And the reality of Prophet ﷺ, *"kuni bardan wa salaaman"* (be cool and peaceful). If not for *"bardan wa salaaman"* that *Nurul Muhammadi* ﷺ would have burned everything and burned it and made nothing to live upon the earth.

Allah ﷻ described, 'Even the sun comes a little bit close, everything will burn; goes a little bit far, everything will freeze from coldness [on earth].' It means the perfection of the reality of Prophet ﷺ. And our life is to be dressed by that light, be blessed by that light, move into the light.

The Manner of Following is Set by Nabi Musa (Moses) ؏ and Sayyidina Khidr ؏

Then our path is that you get rid of yourself. And spend your whole life trying to know yourself, and until you know yourself don't claim that you know Allah ﷻ. Because you talk to people and they think that because they see things or hear things and have different experiences; this is only the beginning of the way.

Be the Moon and Follow the Sun – Even If You Are Nabi Musa ﷺ

And even in Holy Qur'an, the example of Sayyidina Khidr ؏ and Nabi Musa ؏, that when Allah ﷻ wants you to learn something, even if you are Nabi Musa ؏, you have to stay quiet. Because anybody comes, you say, 'No I can see things, I have visions. I'm talking to this spiritual person, that spiritual person.'
Allah ﷻ is giving an example, if you want from one of Allah's ﷻ servants, *ilm ul laduni* (Divinely Knowledge).

فَوَجَدَا عَبْدًا مِّنْ عِبَادِنَا آتَيْنَاهُ رَحْمَةً مِّنْ عِندِنَا وَعَلَّمْنَاهُ مِن لَّدُنَّا عِلْمًا ﴿٦٥﴾

18:65 – "Fawajada 'abdan min 'ibadinaa ataynahu rahmatan min 'indina wa 'allamnahu mil ladunna 'ilma" (Surat Al-Kahf)

"And they found a servant from among Our servants to whom we had given mercy from us and had taught him from Us [Unseen/Heavenly] knowledge." (The Cave, 18:65)

That *(ilm ul laduni)* is what you wanted (if you don't want it, do your own thing, go your own way); if you want it, the whole *adab* (manner) is set by the example of Sayyidina Khidr ؏ and Nabi Musa ؏.

If You Want to Be a Moon Don't Ask Questions, Even If You Are Nabi Musa ﷺ

The whole time Sayyidina Musa ؏ is using his connection, using his spiritual ability, to question your authority. Then Allah ﷻ is reminding us, 'That's not the sun and the moon.' That, 'you merely follow, that was your job.' On this reality, if you want to be a moon, then you have to follow Sayyidina Khidr ؏. It's not your job to ask and question every step of the way because then you are being a sun, you are being a source of light.

'You (Sayyidina Musa ﷺ) were a sun for your people but under the nation of Sayyidina Muhammad ﷺ, you are a moon. And if you are going to be a moon and want to reach the realities of Sayyidina Muhammad ﷺ, stay quiet and follow *alayhis salaatus salaam.*' [This is Qur'an, this is not me. I'm nobody.]

Allah ﷻ gives in Surat Al-Kahf, *Ashab ul Kahf*, He gives the example, when Sayyidina Khidr ﷺ kept mentioning that, 'From what you want, because you came and you wanted it; then accompany me but don't ask any questions until I give you permission to ask.'

قَالَ لَهُ مُوسَىٰ هَلْ أَتَّبِعُكَ عَلَىٰ أَن تُعَلِّمَنِ مِمَّا عُلِّمْتَ رُشْدًا ﴿٦٦﴾

18:66 – *"Qala lahu mosa hal attabi'uka 'alaa an tu'allimani mimma 'ullimta rushda." (Surat Al-Kahf)*

"Moses said to him, "May I follow you on [the condition] that you teach me from what you have been taught of sound judgement?"
(The Cave, 18:66)

قَالَ فَإِنِ اتَّبَعْتَنِي فَلَا تَسْأَلْنِي عَن شَيْءٍ حَتَّىٰ أُحْدِثَ لَكَ مِنْهُ ذِكْرًا ﴿٧٠﴾

18:70 – *"Qala fa-ini ittaba'tanee fala tasalnee 'an shay-in hatta ohditha laka minhu dhikra." (Surat Al-Kahf)*

"[Khidr] He said, 'Then if you follow me, do not ask me about anything until I make to you about it mention'." (The Cave, 18:70)

The Head is Asking the Questions, Not the Heart

It means they are teaching the example of the sun and the moon. You follow your course; your destination is the light. Your destination is Allah's ﷻ *Rida* and Satisfaction. The Sun and The Moon inside us. The question is coming from the head and not from the heart. The heart is in *taslim* (submission) and the heart should enter into the reality of *taslim*.

Then Allah ﷻ gives us a sun and the moon within ourselves. Because this is many layers of reality, that look at the outside, say, 'Okay the perfection of my creation.' Why look on the outside, because Allah ﷻ, the manager, is saying, 'With My Power, My Might and My Anger, because if it moves, it will be obliterated and be taken away.' See how that moon and that sun move exactly in their course? Our time is from that relationship. By the nanosecond, its course is precise. It doesn't drift; it doesn't go this way, it doesn't go that way. You see that? Be like that.

فَالِقُ الْإِصْبَاحِ وَجَعَلَ اللَّيْلَ سَكَنًا وَالشَّمْسَ وَالْقَمَرَ حُسْبَانًا ۚ ذَٰلِكَ تَقْدِيرُ الْعَزِيزِ الْعَلِيمِ ﴿٩٦﴾

6:96 – "Faliqul isbahi wa ja'ala al layla sakanan wash Shamsa wal Qamara husbanan, Dhalika taqdeerul 'Azeezil 'Aleem."
(Surat Al-Anam)

"[He is] the cleaver of daybreak and has made the night for rest and the sun and moon for calculation. That is the determination of the Exalted in Might, the Knowing." (The Cattle, 6:96)

Be Nothing so the Sun Dresses You With Light and Makes You a Moon

Then we took a path of trying to submit, 'Even I know, in the presence of the sun I know nothing. Even I see, in the presence of that sun, I see nothing. Even I have whatever I think I have; in the presence of the sun, I have nothing.' Be nothing, be nothing, be nothing, and the sun begins to illuminate its light and shine upon you. And then you become a moon for creation. Wherever you go, that light is being dressed and blessed, not being mixed by yourself, because you train yourself to be nothing.

The Way to Open the Spiritual Senses is Love

When You Become Nothing, the Guides Will Take Over Your Senses

When you become nothing, it means then their light can come through you. And that's the holy *hadith* (Prophetic Tradition) that, 'If you come with voluntary love, I will be the ears in which you hear,' because you trained yourself to go.

... وَلَا يَزَالُ عَبْدِي يَتَقَرَّبُ إِلَيَّ بِالنَّوَافِلِ حَتَّى أُحِبَّهُ، فَإِذَا أَحْبَبْتُهُ كُنْتُ سَمْعَهُ الَّذِي يَسْمَعُ بِهِ، وَبَصَرَهُ الَّذِي يُبْصِرُ بِهِ، وَيَدَهُ الَّتِي يَبْطِشُ بِهَا، وَرِجْلَهُ الَّتِي يَمْشِي بِهَا، وَلَئِنْ سَأَلَنِي لَأُعْطِيَنَّهُ، وَلَئِنْ اسْتَعَاذَنِي لَأُعِيذَنَّهُ." [رَوَاهُ الْبُخَارِيُّ.]

"..., wa la yazaalu 'Abdi yataqarrabu ilayya bin nawafile hatta ahebahu, fa idha ahbabtuhu kunta Sam'ahul ladhi yasma'u behi, wa Basarahul ladhi yubsiru behi, wa Yadahul lati yabTeshu beha, wa Rejlahul lati yamshi beha, wa la in sa alani la a'Teyannahu, ..."

Be the Moon and Follow the Sun – Even If You Are Nabi Musa ﷺ

"...My servant continues to draw near to Me with voluntary acts of worship so that I shall love him. When I love him, I am his hearing with which he hears, his seeing with which he sees, his hand with which he strikes and his foot with which he walks. Were he to ask [something] of Me, I would surely give it to him..." (Hadith Qudsi)

When you train yourself, 'I'm nothing', then Allah ﷻ says, 'Then We are taking over your hearing.' You train yourself to be nothing, 'We are seeing through your eyes. We are breathing through your breath. We are speaking on your tongue.' As much as you're training, you train yourself to be quiet – why? So that they can open the tongue. These are all the different attributes that Allah's ﷻ going to dress.

Stop Hearing Waswas, Stop Seeing the Dirtiness of Dunya

That, 'Your voluntary love, I'm going to begin to dress you.' The sun is

going to dress you. The *hadith* of Prophet ﷺ is going to dress you, that he's going to take over your hearing when you stop hearing your *waswas* (whispering). Stop hearing what's coming as a voice into your head. That's not a true voice. You shut it off and it's nothing, it's nothing, it's nothing; then they begin to open a Divinely hearing. You hear from your reality what Allah ﷻ wants you to hear.

You see what Allah ﷻ wants you to see when you stop seeing through these eyes but see through the eyes of your heart. These eyes have nothing to show us, just the dirtiness of *dunya* (material world).

Purify Your Breath and Sanctify Your Tongue

When you sanctify your breath and purify your breath, Allah ﷻ, said, 'I become the breath in which you are breathing from My Divinely *Qudra* (power).'

Purify and sanctify your tongue means don't lie, don't backbite, and don't talk when you're not supposed to talk. The tongue can be worse than the pen because once it says something, you cannot take it back. And the tongue has the ability to show the dirtiness of what's hidden within the heart. Imagine if somebody's tongue is bad, how bad their heart must be. That's why Allah ﷻ says in Holy Qur'an, 'They are saying bad things but what's in their heart is far worse.'

...وَدُّوا مَا عَنِتُّمْ قَدْ بَدَتِ الْبَغْضَاءُ مِنْ أَفْوَاهِهِمْ وَمَا تُخْفِي صُدُورُهُمْ أَكْبَرُ...﴿١١٨﴾

3:118 – "...wad doo ma 'anittum qad badatial baghdao min afwahihim wa ma tukhfee Sudooruhum Akbaru..." (Surat 'Ali 'Imran)

"...Hatred has already appeared from their mouths, and what their breasts conceal is greater..." (Family of Imran, 3:118)

So then the path was a path of controlling your tongue. You even have

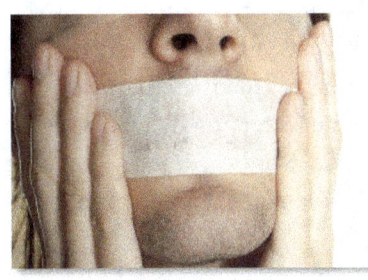

to put a rock; in *Naqshbandiya*, we are inheriting from Sayyidina Abu Bakr as-Siddiq ﷜. Put a rock in your mouth for eight years and don't talk, because the rock in the mouth means you have to take it out, 'Oh! I wasn't supposed to talk,' put it back in. So then in case you fall and trip, 'Oh I forgot, he asked me a question. I said something again.'

Reality of Hands and Importance of Taking Bayah (Pledge of Allegiance)

Hands is to purify your *rizq* and sustenance so that *Yad-Allah*, Allah's ﷻ Hand be upon your hand, *"Innal ladheena yubayi'onaka innama yubayi'onAllah."*

Be the Moon and Follow the Sun – Even If You Are Nabi Musa ﷺ

The *bayah* is a pledge that we made to Allah ﷻ when we came onto this earth.

إِنَّ الَّذِينَ يُبَايِعُونَكَ إِنَّمَا يُبَايِعُونَ اللَّهَ يَدُ اللَّهِ فَوْقَ أَيْدِيهِمْ ۚ فَمَن نَّكَثَ فَإِنَّمَا يَنكُثُ عَلَىٰ نَفْسِهِ ۖ وَمَنْ أَوْفَىٰ بِمَا عَاهَدَ عَلَيْهُ اللَّهَ فَسَيُؤْتِيهِ أَجْرًا عَظِيمًا ﴿١٠﴾

48:10 – "*Innal ladheena yubayi'oonaka innama yubayi'on Allaha yadullahi fawqa aydeehim, faman nakatha fa innama yankuthu 'ala nafsihi, wa man awfa bima 'ahada 'alayhu Allaha fasayu teehi ajran 'azheema.*" (Surat Al-Fath)

"Indeed, those who give Baya (pledge allegiance) to you, [O Muhammad] – they are actually giving Baya (pledge allegiance) to Allah. The hand of Allah is over their hands. So he who breaks his pledge/word only breaks it to the detriment/Harm of himself. And he whoever fulfills (their Bayah) that which he has promised Allah – He will grant him a great reward." (The Victory, 48:10)

Then Allah ﷻ describes in Surat At-Tawbah that, 'We took from you your *dunya* (material world) and We gave to you *akhirah* (afterlife) in exchange, and you fulfilled your *ahd*, your covenant and your pledge, your *bayah* that you made.' Now the people who translate Holy Qur'an, they want to hide that. So they don't put the word *bayah*; they put like a deal you made, like it's a *bazaar* and you made a deal. And Surat At-Tawbah (9, verse 111):

إِنَّ اللَّهَ اشْتَرَىٰ مِنَ الْمُؤْمِنِينَ أَنفُسَهُمْ وَأَمْوَالَهُم بِأَنَّ لَهُمُ الْجَنَّةَ ۚ يُقَاتِلُونَ فِي سَبِيلِ اللَّهِ فَيَقْتُلُونَ وَيُقْتَلُونَ ۖ وَعْدًا عَلَيْهِ حَقًّا فِي التَّوْرَاةِ وَالْإِنجِيلِ وَالْقُرْآنِ ۚ وَمَنْ أَوْفَىٰ بِعَهْدِهِ مِنَ اللَّهِ ۚ فَاسْتَبْشِرُوا بِبَيْعِكُمُ الَّذِي بَايَعْتُم بِهِ ۚ وَذَٰلِكَ هُوَ الْفَوْزُ الْعَظِيمُ ﴿١١١﴾

9:111 – "*Inna Allaha Ashtara Minal Mu'umineena 'Anfusahum Wa 'Amwalahum Bi anna Lahum AlJannata, ...Wa'dan 'Alayhi Haqqan fit Tawrati wal Injeeli wal Qur'ani, Wa Man Awfa Bi 'ahdihi Mina Allahi, Fastabshiro Bi bay'ikum Al Ladhi Baaya'tum Bihi, Wa Dhalika Huwal Fawzul 'Azeem.*" (Surat At-Tawbah)

"Indeed, Allah has purchased from the believers their lives and their properties [in exchange] for that they will have Paradise...[It is] a true promise [binding] upon Him in the Torah and the Gospel and the Qur'an. And who is more faithful to his covenant than Allah? Then rejoice in your Bayah which you have contracted. And it is that which is the great achievement." (The Repentance, 9:111)

Complete Your Ahd (Covenant) and Contract With Allah ﷻ

This is *ahd* (covenant) and the *bayah* (pledge of allegiance) that Allah ﷻ describes. *Tawbah* (repentance), because we are from the people of the *Baab at-Tawbah*, and Allah ﷻ is confirming that, 'We took your *dunya* (material world) and We'll give you an *akhirah* (hereafter) in exchange. And that you had a covenant and contract with Us.' That, 'before we sent you onto this earth, you had a contract with Us. Did you complete your contract before you meet Me?' Most people say No, but *Rijalullah* (men of Allah ﷻ), they reached to their contract with Allah ﷻ. Allah ﷻ says, 'Your contract is in the process of being completed and your *bayah* (allegiance) is a real *bayah*.' It means you have completed and took the hand that Allah ﷻ wanted you to take.

If they would really say the word *"bayah"* (allegiance) because of the ones who know Arabic, they know it. But when they translate it and they don't use *"bayah"* (allegiance), then nobody's looking to take *bayah*  (allegiance). If they knew that they had to have *bayah* (allegiance), they had to complete their *bayah* (allegiance), and complete their covenant before they meet Allah ﷻ. And that becomes the whole reality of the moon that follows the light, follows the sun.

The Universe Within:
The Sun (Heart), the Moon (Head), and 11 Stars (Organs)

Then Allah ﷻ gives us an example then within ourselves, 'Do you see how I manage this universe? I gave you a universe within yourself, that you have infinite amounts of creation.' Every cell, they say you have 3 to 4 trillion cells within your body, entire universe. 'I gave you a *shams* (sun) which is your heart. I gave you a *qamar* (moon) which is your head, and I gave you eleven organs just like this galaxy. Each organ that is nourished and sustained by your heart.' Then we understand that we are a walking galaxy.

إِذْ قَالَ يُوسُفُ لِأَبِيهِ يَا أَبَتِ إِنِّي رَأَيْتُ أَحَدَ عَشَرَ كَوْكَبًا وَالشَّمْسَ وَالْقَمَرَ رَأَيْتُهُمْ لِي سَاجِدِينَ ﴿٤﴾

12:4 – *"Idh qala Yosufu li abeehi ya abati innee raaytu ahada Ashara kawkaban wash Shamsa wal Qamara raaytuhum le sajideen."*
(Surat Yusuf)

"[Of these stories mention] when Joseph said to his father, 'O my father, indeed I have seen [in a dream] eleven stars and the sun and the moon; I saw them prostrating to me'." *(Joseph, 12:4)*

Shaykh is the Custodian of the Divinely Light

Allah then says, 'If you can follow like a *qamar* and you can follow like a moon, the way of *tafakkur* (contemplation),' because the way of

tafakkur is you annihilate, you annihilate, you annihilate; take the dress of the Shaykh. It's not about you. It's about taking the dress of the Shaykh. If the Shaykh is dressing you with that light so much, what happens? The heart begins to open because it's Allah's light. They are the custodians of Allah's Light. If Allah sends too much of that light and that person is not ready, they may be dead. *"Qulna ya naru kuni bardan wa salaaman."* If Allah says, 'Okay, I'm going to give you directly into your heart,' you would be dead, *khashi'a* (dust).

قُلْنَا يَا نَارُ كُونِي بَرْدًا وَسَلَامًا عَلَىٰ إِبْرَاهِيمَ ﴿٦٩﴾

21:69 – *"Qulna ya Naaru, kuni Bardan wa Salaman 'ala Ibrahim."*
(Surat Al-Anbiya)

"We said, O fire, be cool and Peaceful upon Abraham."
(The Prophets, 21:69)

Sayyidina Musa Wanted to Go Directly to Allah

That's why Nabi Musa asked in Qur'an, *'Ya Rabbi*, let me see you. I don't need to have any intermediary, no *bardan wa salaaman* for me. Let me see you directly, *ya Rabbi*!' Allah said, 'Okay you want to see Me here, I'm going to show you something but it's not going to be Me. I'm going to show you *Nur ul Muhammadi*. I'm going to show you My Glory.' What is Allah's Glory? The light of Prophet.

Be the Moon and Follow the Sun – Even If You Are Nabi Musa ﷺ

وَلَمَّا جَاءَ مُوسَىٰ لِمِيقَاتِنَا وَكَلَّمَهُ رَبُّهُ قَالَ رَبِّ أَرِنِي أَنظُرْ إِلَيْكَ ۚ قَالَ لَن تَرَانِي وَلَٰكِنِ انظُرْ إِلَى الْجَبَلِ فَإِنِ اسْتَقَرَّ مَكَانَهُ فَسَوْفَ تَرَانِي ۚ فَلَمَّا تَجَلَّىٰ رَبُّهُ لِلْجَبَلِ جَعَلَهُ دَكًّا وَخَرَّ مُوسَىٰ صَعِقًا ۚ فَلَمَّا أَفَاقَ قَالَ سُبْحَانَكَ تُبْتُ إِلَيْكَ وَأَنَا أَوَّلُ الْمُؤْمِنِينَ ﴿١٤٣﴾

7:143 – *"Wa lamma jaa Musa limeeqatina wa kallamahu Rabbuhu, qala rabbi arinee anzhur ilayka, Qala lan taranee wa lakini onzhur ilal jabali fa inistaqarra makanahu, fasawfa taranee, falamma tajalla Rabbuhu lil jabali ja`alahu, dakkan wa kharra Musa sa`iqan, falamma afaqa qala subhanaka tubtu ilayka wa ana awwalul Mumineen."* (Surat Al-A'raf)

"When Moses came to the place appointed by Us, and his Lord addressed him, He said: "O my Lord! show (Thyself) to me, that I may look upon thee." Allah said: "By no means can you see Me (direct); But look upon the mountain; if it remain in its place, then you will see Me." When his Lord manifested His glory on the Mount, He made it as dust. And Moses fell down unconcious. When he recovered his senses he said: "Glory be to Thee! To Thee I turn in repentance, and I am the first to believe (of believers)."
(The Heights, 7:143)

The light shone and Nabi Musa ﷺ was out. This is the example for us, where Allah ﷻ says, 'If Nabi Musa ﷺ, *Kalimullah*, is going to pass out like a state of death and then be revived,' we stand no chance.

The Heart is Lit by Awliyaullah's (Saints') Light

So we need the reflection from *awliyaullah* (saints): *ateeullah atee ur Rasul wa ulil amrin minkum.*

يَا أَيُّهَا الَّذِينَ آمَنُوا أَطِيعُوا اللَّهَ وَأَطِيعُوا الرَّسُولَ وَأُولِي الْأَمْرِ مِنكُمْ... ﴿٥٩﴾

4:59 – Ya ayyu hal ladheena amanoo Atiu Allaha wa atiur Rasula wa Ulil amre minkum..." (Surat An-Nisa)

"O You who have believed, Obey Allah, obey the Messenger, and those in authority among you..." (The Women, 4:59)

We need the reflection of *awliyaullah* (saints) because they are *bardan wa salaaman* (cool and peaceful). They send a cool and peaceful light as you are able to approach. As your ability is improving, your *ibadah* (worship) is improving, your worshipness is improving, you follow in *istiqam* (steadfastness), you keep firm in following, they begin to send, they begin to send, and they begin to send until the heart can become lit.

That enough of that light is coming into the heart, staying in the heart and the heart becomes lit with the light, like a pilot light that goes off. That light, if Allah ﷻ gives a permission within the heart of the believer to be lit, it is eternally lit and there's no way to un-light that light. Even the sins like a mountain, Allah ﷻ keeps that *amanat* and that trust that was given. What Allah ﷻ gives can never be taken away. And Allah ﷻ will clean that servant either in *dunya* (material world) or in the grave to reach what they achieve.

But if that one didn't destroy that, that pilot light is lit within the heart

and that becomes the source of *shams* (sun). That becomes the *shams* (sun) within the heart of the believer, that as soon as they make a *zikr* (chanting), it's like a fragrance that hits that light and begins to burn with a fragrance, with an energy that fills the room. People can feel it and pious people can smell it, the fragrance that's coming from that heart. It's lit and the *zikr* (remembrance) of Allah ﷻ, like the ethereal gases of the heavens, it merely begins to descend and lights the entire being. And their hearts are suns for their being. And Allah ﷻ says, 'Now you're inheriting from My universe. *'Wa laqad karamna bani Adam"* – I gave you an entire galaxy.'

﴿٧٠﴾...وَلَقَدْ كَرَّمْنَا بَنِي آدَمَ

17:70 – *"Wa laqad karramna bani adama..."* (Surat Al-Isra)

"We have certainly honored the children of Adam..."
(The Night Journey, 17:70)

Before you can inherit to become from the managers who are *awliyaullah* (saints), the *awliya* (saints) are the managers of the universe, Allah ﷻ says, 'Before you can become manager of the universe, manage your own galaxy.'

Until You Know Your 7 Names, Don't Talk About Allah ﷻ, Prophet ﷺ, and Awliya (Saints)

'Who knows himself will know his Lord' and if you don't know yourself, there's no way to claim you know your Lord.

مَنْ عَرَفَ نَفْسَهُ فَقَدْ عَرَفَ رَبَّهُ

"Man 'arafa nafsahu faqad 'arafa Rabbahu."

"Who knows himself, knows his Lord." (Prophet Muhammad (pbuh))

Don't speak of *awliya* (saints), don't speak of Allah ﷻ, don't speak of Prophet ﷺ – you're embarrassing everybody. If you don't know your names and your seven names in their presence, who are you to speak up for them? Say, 'How you're going to claim that you know us? You don't know your names. So don't talk about us, we get embarrassed because you said the wrong things.' There are people who go talking about

Allah ﷻ all the time on YouTube. Ask them, 'Do you know your seven names?' They say, 'No.' So how you don't know yourself and you want to know Allah ﷻ?

It means at that time, the *Sahabi* (Companions) teach us to put a rock in your mouth. Busy yourself trying to know yourself. '*Ya Rabbi*, who am I? You have sent me onto this earth, what am I, what are my names in Your Presence? What is my name on this *dunya* (material world)? What is my name in Your first paradise all the way to your seventh paradise and in Your Divinely Presence? What are my names? Who knows himself? What are the purposes of those names? What are the *tajalli* (manifestations) of that name and how are those names going to be supporting me?'

Tafakkur (Contemplation) Opens Your Heart

It means then they begin to teach, if we reach to that, all those secrets within the heart; the six powers of the heart. The reality means the heart opens and becomes a sun and all your organs will be dressed from that reality. Your blood will be dressed from that reality; your breath will be dressed from that reality – all through the *tafakkur* (contemplation) and the *muraqaba* (meditation).

It means if they follow a way and they don't make *tafakkur* (contemplation) and they don't make the *muraqaba* (meditation) to know themselves, then how is anything going to be achieved? Can you achieve anything if your heart is not opening, and the realities are not opening? And the character is not like a moon? If the character is not like a moon in which it follows, it follows exactly the course that's been written for it, and then it'll be like a *Fir'aun* (Pharaoh). As soon as something opens, it would do everything on its own and destroy everything. That would be *Fir'aun* (saying) *'anna Rabb ul a'la* (I am the Lord Most High).

$$فَقَالَ أَنَا رَبُّكُمُ الْأَعْلَى ﴿٢٤﴾$$

79:24 – "Faqala ana rabbukumu al 'Aala." (Surat An-Nazi'at)

"And Fir'aun (Pharoah) said, I am your Lord All-Highest!"
(Those Who Drag Forth, 79:24)

It means then this way is a solid and stamped way. And we pray that Allah ﷻ dress us from the lights of Sayyidina Muhammad ﷺ, the reality of the sun of the entire universe, the *Nur ul-Muhammadi* ﷺ, which is the source of all emanations and blessings; and Allah ﷻ upon the heart of Prophet ﷺ.

Subhana rabbika rabbal 'izzati 'amma yasifoon, wa salaamun 'alal mursaleen, walhamdulillahi rabbil 'aalameen. Bi hurmati Muhammad al-Mustafa wa bi siri Surat al-Fatiha.

Seek Out the Full Moons of Guidance – Secret of Juzba (Magnetism)

Allah's ﷻ Signs on the Horizon Are in Perfection

We share from their teaching and a reminder for myself that *Alhamdulillah, inshaAllah,* Allah ﷻ grant us a year of understanding the reality and the lights of Sayyidina Muhammad ﷺ. Allah ﷻ is teaching us from Holy Qur'an that, 'I'll send you the signs upon the horizon and the signs within yourself.' And these signs will lead us towards perfection.

سَنُرِيهِمْ آيَاتِنَا فِي الْآفَاقِ وَفِي أَنفُسِهِمْ حَتَّىٰ يَتَبَيَّنَ لَهُمْ أَنَّهُ الْحَقُّ ۗ ... ﴿٥٣﴾

41:53 – "Sanureehim ayatina fil afaqi wa fee anfusihim hatta yatabayyana lahum annahu alhaqqu..." (Surat Al-Fussilat)

"We will show them Our signs in the horizons and within themselves until it becomes clear to them that it is the truth..."
(Explained in Detail, 41:53)

We have said before that why Allah ﷻ says first to identify the signs on the horizon before the signs within the self. It's because the signs on the horizon – they are in Allah's ﷻ perfection. Allah ﷻ doesn't create imperfection. Allah ﷻ doesn't create *shirk* (polytheism), doesn't create

bidah (innovation), doesn't create anything that is forbidden by Allah ﷻ upon the horizon. There is something different in *dunya* (material world) and the manipulation of Allah's ﷻ creation. This means that upon the horizon are the universes. The planets and the stars and the galaxies. And Allah ﷻ asked which is more difficult to create? This creation or you, *insan* (mankind)? The heavens are far more complicated and more complex.

لَخَلْقُ السَّمَاوَاتِ وَالْأَرْضِ أَكْبَرُ مِنْ خَلْقِ النَّاسِ وَلَكِنَّ أَكْثَرَ النَّاسِ لَا يَعْلَمُونَ ﴿٥٧﴾

40:57 – "La khalqus samawati wal Ardi akbaru min khalqin nasi wa lakinna akthara annasi la ya'lamoon." (Surat Ghafir)

"The creation of the heavens and earth is greater (matter) than the creation of humans, but most of the people do not know."
(The Forgiver, 40:57)

Learn From the Moon to Focus Entirely on the Sun

Alhamdulillah, Allah ﷻ gives us for our understanding in *dunya* (material world), look at the relationship between the sun and the moon. How we take everything from the sun. Our breath is from the sun, the light from the sun, all our dress upon ourselves from the sun. And the reflection that it comes is to the moon. The way of *ma'rifah* (gnosticism) is a way of reaching towards the reality of that moon.

Allah ﷻ says why can't you be like the moon? See how the moon follows the sun and it understands its reality and it doesn't deviate from its reality. That its *nazar* (gaze), entire *nazar* is upon the sun. And it's whole existence is to focus

upon the sun. And as a result, we are taking a benefit from that reality. It reflects to us a light.

$$\text{وَالشَّمْسِ وَضُحَاهَا ﴿١﴾ وَالْقَمَرِ إِذَا تَلَاهَا ﴿٢﴾}$$

91:1-2 – *"Wash Shamsi wa duhaha. (1) Wal Qamari idha talaha. (2)"* (Surat Ash-Shams)

"By the Sun and his (glorious) Brightness. (1) By the Moon as she follows him. (2)" (The Sun, 91:1-2)

That's what we said before, when we go back and research the importance of the sun and the moon. Our existence on this *dunya* (material world) is based on that. Without the reality of the sun and the reality of the moon, we can't have an existence on this *dunya*.

Our Aim Is to Be Like a Qamar (Moon)

Then the guides teach us that be like the moon. At every instance, make our lives and recalibrate our lives that, *ya Rabbi*, we understood and I want to live our life like a *qamar* (moon). That's why all the nasheeds and all the *salawats* (praisings) are always talking about the *qamar* (moon) because it's the full light, it's the reflection.

قَمَرٌ طَابَتْ سَرِيْرَتُهُ   وَسَجَايَاهُ وَسِيْرَتُهُ
صَفْوَةُ الْبَارِيْ وَخِيْرَتُهُ   عَدْلُ أَهْلِ الْحِلِّ وَالْحِرَمِ

Qamarun Tabat sariratuHu   Wa sajayaHu wa siratuHu
Safwatul bari wa khiratuHu   Adlu ahlil hilli wal harami

Like a moon, he (Prophet Muhammad (pbuh)) is good and wholesome in his intention, his character & his way of life. He is the purest elect/ultimate choice of the Creator. He is the most trustworthy/a righteous witness for people of upright and wrongdoing

Turn Your Temporary Light to An Eternal Star

That, *ya Rabbi*, let me to be like the moon and then you identify the moon – the moon has nothing on it! It means then it begins to open a reality. That stars, they lost their mass. As soon as we die, we lose our mass and our light becomes like a star. If we nourished it, if we brought it towards its eternity and its eternal reality, instead of a temporary existence. Allah (swt) gives us a candle in *dunya* (material world).

He says you have a temporary light. Your duty in life is to make that temporary candle to become eternal, to light the reality of your soul with My *Rida* and Satisfaction. So, then we take our temporary light to become permanent lights within this universe and creation.

The Difference Between the Moon and Star is in Their Mass ($E = MC^2$)

That's why Prophet ﷺ described the companions they are the *najm* (stars). They are the stars. Any one of them you follow because a star gives light. He didn't describe them that they're planets, but they're stars – they give light!

أَصْحَابِيْ كَالنُّجُــومْ بِأَيِّهِمْ اَقْتَدَيْتِمْ اَهْتَدَيْتِمْ

"*Ashabi kan Nujoom, bi ayyihim aqta daytum ahta daytum.*"

"*My companions are like stars. Follow any one of them and you will be guided.*" (Prophet Muhammad (pbuh))

The Moon Has a Mass and Represents the Wali Who is Alive
E = MC²

The symbol of the moon is a position in which that *wali* (saint) is still alive. And he has a physical mass but his physical mass is so purified  because of his *nazar* (gaze) is constantly upon his target which is the sun of realities. It's the only mass that reflects light, versus a star because a star lost its mass. It means when you die, you lose your mass and what's left is the light² (light-squared). Your energy is the light² (light-squared). As soon as you lose the mass you become the star, if you reached eternity.

In *dunya* (material world), because the physical body of that saint and those pious people are still here, then they are referred to as the moons. So best to follow full moons. Although all *awliyaullah* (saints) are of a moon and they are in degrees of how much of the reflection of that reality they are receiving, right? So, it means if it's a little quarter of a moon, the *hilal* (crescent), it's taking from Prophet ﷺ what it can contain. But yet there is a surface that it has to be polished. That's why the *zikr* (remembrance), that's  why the *majlis*, that's why the associations.

Be of Service to Benefit the World, Like a Moon

It's that don't be like the earth filled with buildings and wants and desires and all sorts of things that are growing upon it and being built upon it  because the earth has no benefit. The earth benefits from the sun and the moon. You have time based on that sun and the moon. You have light and nourishment based on that sun and the reflection of the moon.

So they teach us be like the moon, not like the earth. As soon as you take a path of following that guidance, following Allah's ﷻ guidance of the heavens that *ya Rabbi*, let me to lose all my desires and be of service and *khidmat* to your creation. Now you're becoming like the moon. That what is reflecting through Prophet ﷺ through your being is dressing the people on earth.

Then their *darajats* (stations) of how much they're being purified are the phases of the moon until you get into the three days of the white moon. Three days; one *ghawth* and the two poles that sit to the sides. Three days of full moon. It means they are *kamil* (perfected); those *awliyaullah* (saints) are *kamil*. That they have lost all that desire. Prophet ﷺ has purified them. When we look at the surface of the moon, there's absolutely nothing there but a lot of pounding. Anybody on our  path knows that it's a difficult path. You're going to be bombarded like the moon. Test after test, after test, after test.

Be Like the Dog of Ashab al-Kahf (Companions of the Cave) and Take the Testing

We enter into the holy month of Safar (second lunar month) and the secret of *Ashab al-Kahf* (Companions/sleepers of the Cave). The best example of *Ashab al-Kahf* is the dog – the dog that they threw rocks at the dog, threw rocks at the dog. Do you want to accompany these moons? You want to accompany this reality? That don't think yourself from them. But Allah ﷻ gives us a way to approach, *ya Rabbi*, as you save the dog of *Ashab al-Kahf, ya Rabbi* save me. They said be like that dog. It took a lot of difficulty from them. They didn't want it. They didn't know that if we're going there, maybe this dog is going to eat us.

Let's throw rocks and test it. And they test it and the dog stood up. Allah ﷻ gave that dog a tongue and it says, 'Whatever you throw at me, I'm not stopping. That you'll find me to be a protection for you. You go do what Allah ﷻ wants. I'll guard the cave.' And that's why you see the moon filled with holes. It's been bombarded by asteroids, been bombarded and there's no flat surface.

It's unimaginable how much attack it has taken and it's been polished of all material desires.

Ulul Amr Are the Full Moons Reflecting Nur Muhammad ﷺ

The moon is polished and as a result, it acts like a star while its alive. It

means while it has a mass, it actually is the only thing that reflects the light of the sun for us. As a result we tell time. Why all our clocks are white like a moon and have 12 divisions? The 12 *buraj*, the 12 constellations, our phase in life, that we are constantly moving through these *hijabs*. From the first of the lunar months of Muharram and now ending and moving into Safar. The realities in which Allah ﷻ is dressing the sun and the sun is dressing the moon and the moon is dressing earth. And that's why, *"Atiullaha wa atiur Rasul wa ulil amre minkum"* (Holy Qur'an, 4:59)

...أَطِيعُواللهَ وَأَطِيعُواْ ٱلرَّسُولَ وَأُوْلِي ٱلْأَمْرِ مِنْكُمْ... ﴿٥٩﴾

4:59 – *"...Atiullaha wa atiur Rasula wa Ulil amre minkum..."* (Surat An-Nisa)

"... Obey Allah, Obey the Messenger, and those in authority among you..." (The Women, 4:59)

The real *ulul amr* (saints) that are *qamar*, that they are from the moon. They took a path in which to purify and cleanse themselves and they reflect the reality of Prophet ﷺ on earth.

Seek Out the Full Moons Who Reflect the Nur Muhammad ﷺ

Then gives us an understanding that when we are the inhabitants of earth and we want from that light, seek out the moons of Allah ﷻ! Seek out the *ahlul qamar*, *ahlul badr*. Because they reflect the light of Prophet ﷺ.

That on earth, the full moon agitates *shayateen* (devils). The *shaytans* are under big difficulty on the full moon nights. Why? Because *Nurul Muhammadi* ﷺ (Muhammadan light) is shining. When *Nurul Muhammadi* ﷺ shines, they burn and become agitated and they begin to fight and disrupt everything.

But the believers, they find peace and tranquility because they're being dressed by these lights, blessed by these lights. Then they begin to teach that with these lights and with these benefits, seek out those realities. If there's no light, it's not a moon. And if it's not a moon, it's of no benefit to you – it's a waste of your time. If you go to somebody who is not taking a path of being on a moon, not taking a path of purification, not taking a path of following that which Allah ﷻ wants us to follow.

Focus Only on the Sun of Sayyidina Muhammad ﷺ

Allah ﷻ wants us to follow Sayyidina Muhammad ﷺ. And everybody says they're following Sayyidina Muhammad ﷺ. Everyone says, *"la ilaha illAllah Muhammadan RasulAllah"* (There is no deity but Allah, Prophet Muhammad is the messenger of Allah) but why is it that their *nazar* (gaze) is not upon Prophet ﷺ? Why is it that when they talk, they're not mentioning Prophet ﷺ? When they talk, they're not mentioning the way and the mercy and the love of Sayyidina Muhammad ﷺ? Because they're not understanding where

Seek Out the Full Moons of Guidance – Secret of Juzba (Magnetism)

Allah ﷻ said, 'I'm going to show you my signs on the horizon so that you understand yourself.'

$$سَنُرِيهِمْ آيَاتِنَا فِي الْآفَاقِ وَفِي أَنفُسِهِمْ حَتَّىٰ يَتَبَيَّنَ لَهُمْ أَنَّهُ الْحَقُّ ۗ أَوَلَمْ يَكْفِ بِرَبِّكَ أَنَّهُ عَلَىٰ كُلِّ شَيْءٍ شَهِيدٌ ﴿٥٣﴾$$

41:53 – "Sanureehim Aayaatinaa fil aafaaqi wa feee anfusihim hattaa yatabaiyana lahum annahul haqq; awa lam yakfi bi Rabbika annahoo 'alaa kulli shai-in Shaheed" (Surat Al-Fussilat)

"Soon will We show them our Signs in the (furthest) regions (of the earth), and in their own souls, until it becomes manifest to them that this is the Truth. Is it not enough that thy Lord doth witness all things?" (Explained in Detail, 41:53)

The Moon is Firm in Following What Allah ﷻ Ordered

Do you look, do you see the moon focusing on a different star? No! Do you see that it takes a break and goes in a different direction? No. It means it's *istiqam*, its firmness, is its whole life, the moon follows exactly what it's been told by Allah ﷻ to follow. As a result, we take benefit.

$$وَأَن لَّوِ اسْتَقَامُوا عَلَى الطَّرِيقَةِ لَأَسْقَيْنَاهُم مَّاءً غَدَقًا ﴿١٦﴾$$

72:16 – "Wa alla wis taqaamoo 'alat tareeqati la asqaynaahum maa'an ghadaqaa." (Surat Al-Jinn)

"And [Allah revealed] that: 'If they had only remained firm on their tariqah (straight path), We would have bestowed on them Rain/water in abundance'." (The Jinn, 72:16)

Can you imagine one day the moon doesn't show up? It decides it's going in a different direction or stops. As soon as the day went, we won't have any guidance at night. Nothing will grow on this earth. It means our existence is based on their submission where Allah ﷻ describes it's a creation. The moon is a creation of Allah ﷻ. The star is a creation of Allah ﷻ.

You Cannot Deny You Are in Need of the Sun

Allah ﷻ is describing, 'I'm the power within that sun. So, understand that reality.'

اللَّهُ الَّذِي خَلَقَ السَّمَاوَاتِ وَالْأَرْضَ وَمَا بَيْنَهُمَا فِي سِتَّةِ أَيَّامٍ ثُمَّ اسْتَوَىٰ عَلَى الْعَرْشِ ۖ مَا لَكُم مِّن دُونِهِ مِن وَلِيٍّ وَلَا شَفِيعٍ ۚ أَفَلَا تَتَذَكَّرُونَ ﴿٤﴾

32:4 – *"Allaahul lazee khalaqas samaawaati wal arda wa maa bainahumaa fee sittati ayyaam; Thummas tawaa 'alal 'arsh; maa lakum min doonihee minw-wwaliyyinw-wala shafee'; afala tatazakkaroon" (Surat As-Sajdah)*

"It is Allah Who has created the heavens and the earth, and all between them, in six Days, and is firmly established on the Throne (of Authority): ye have none, besides Him, to protect or intercede (for you): will ye not then receive admonition?" (The Prostration, 32:4)

And then they come into our lives and say but you're in need of that sun. They say, 'No, no, you're only in need of Allah ﷻ.' Ok yahoo, don't be cuckoo. Everybody only needs Allah ﷻ, but cause and effect. If you don't believe, go lock yourself in a cave. Within a year of no sunlight, you'd be dead – all your bones will shatter. Allah ﷻ was there, Allah ﷻ was with you. But you're not at that *maqam* (station) to take directly from Allah ﷻ.

Allah ﷻ is cause and effect. If you're sick, go into the sunlight. If your body is not well, go into the sunlight. Go by the ocean, even the ocean is a *shifa* and a healing for you. We're not at a position because the arrogance makes us to think we're very high. Only Allah ﷻ, Allah ﷻ says, 'No, no, no, *Atiullaha wa atiur Rasul wa ulil amre minkum*" (Obey Allah, Obey the Messenger, and those in authority among you).

...يَاأَيُّهَا الَّذِينَ آمَنُوا أَطِيعُواللَّهَ وَأَطِيعُواالرَّسُولَ وَأُولِي الْأَمْرِ مِنْكُمْ... ﴿٥٩﴾

4:59 – "...*Ya ayyu hal latheena amanoo Atiullaha wa atiur Rasula wa Ulil amre minkum*..." (Surat An-Nisa)

"...O You who have believed, Obey Allah, Obey the Messenger, and those in authority among you..." (The Women, 4:59)

Take an understanding from my creation. I didn't create it as a joke! It has a tremendous reality. If you don't understand that reality, you didn't understand yourself. So what Prophet ﷺ asked us is to know yourself to know Allah ﷻ. That, *ya Rabbi*, I want to purify myself. I want to be like the moon.

مَنْ عَرَفَ نَفْسَهُ فَقَدْ عَرَفَ رَبَّهُ

"*Man 'arafa nafsahu faqad 'arafa Rabbahu.*"

"Who knows himself, knows his Lord." (Prophet Muhammad (pbuh))

The Source of Light and Iman is Nurul Muhammad ﷺ

Then follow the sun. The sun for you, the source of light for you, the source of *iman* (faith) – *iman* is *nur*, *Nurul Muhammadi* ﷺ (Muhammadan light). Follow the *nur* (light) in your life! Make the *nur* to be supreme in your life! That's all I want, *ya Rabbi*, is *nur* (light) – Nur Muhammad ﷺ (Muhammadan light) so that I can reach to *iman*, and perfect my faith.

لاَ يُؤْمِنُ أَحَدُكُمْ حَتَّى أَكُونَ أَحَبَّ إِلَيْهِ مِنْ وَالِدِهِ وَوَلَدِهِ وَالنَّاسِ أَجْمَعِينَ

"*La yuminu ahadukum hatta akona ahabba ilayhi min walidihi wa waladihi wan Nasi ajma'yeen.*"

"None of you will have faith till he loves me more than his father, his children and all mankind." (Prophet Muhammad (pbuh))

Nurul Iman Leads You to Maqamul Ihsan and Full Moons

Prophet ﷺ described if you have *nurul iman* (light of faith), then you're moving towards *maqamul ihsan* (Station of Moral Excellence)

أَنْ تَعْبُدَ اللهَ كَأَنَّكَ تَرَاهُ، فَإِنْ لَمْ تَكُنْ تَرَاهُ فَإِنَّهُ يَرَاك

"*An Ta'bud Allaha, Ka annaka tarahu, fa in lam takun tarahu fa innahu yarak.*"

"It (Ihsan – Station of Excellence) is to serve/worship Allah as though you behold [See] Him; and if you don't behold [See] him, (know that) He surely sees you." (Prophet Muhammad (pbuh))

Seek Out the Full Moons of Guidance – Secret of Juzba (Magnetism)

Maqamul ihsan describes the full moons. They pray as if they see their lord. They worship, all their worshipness is as if they see, not as if they see – they see! They see what's in front of them, they see the shining light that Allah ﷻ shines upon them. And they are the perfection of that face.

Islam is on earth. *Iman* is in the light. Islam is just *taslim* (submission) for your body, you didn't achieve. All you basically just understood, *ya Rabbi*, I want to rise above the material world. Then He says look to my heavens as an example. *Iman* (faith) is light. You see what the light is doing?

Be in a State of Nothingness, Like the Moon

That moon knows its not a sun. You're not a prophet, you're not at that stage. You're nothing. So, the moon teaches us a way of nothingness, nothing. Don't be anything. Don't claim to be anything. Take a path of scrubbing yourself to be nothing and always look to Prophet ﷺ. Always look for *nazar* (gaze) that you can't see Prophet ﷺ.

رَاعِنَا وَقُولُوا انْظُرْنَا وَاسْمَعُوا ...﴿١٠٤﴾

2:104 – "... *wa qolu unzurna wasma'o*..." (Surat Al-Baqarah)

"... and say *Unzurna* (gaze upon us) and you listen (to Prophet Muhammad (pbuh))..." (The Cow, 2:104)

Even what you see is an imagination of Prophet ﷺ. But you keep going, keep imitating, keep faking. *Ya Rabbi*, I'm coming no matter what. My whole way is in your direction and I'm facing Prophet ﷺ. I want to be dressed by Prophet ﷺ. I want to reach that light of Prophet ﷺ. They say, 'Oh, but that's *shirk* (polytheism)!' Are you crazy? We just described the moon is following the sun. If it was *shirk* (polytheism), why the moon would follow the sun? People say, 'No, I'm only following Allah ﷻ. It means what they say, we only follow Allah ﷻ. Allah ﷻ is everywhere! But Allah ﷻ teaches us by example. Don't think so high. That you have to follow *wajib al taqleed*, that you have to follow something in your life. Follow the reality of Prophet ﷺ, the light of Prophet ﷺ and be a moon and nothingness!

Empty Your Head of All Its Wants and Desires

They (guides) begin to teach us if we take that path of being nothing and following that light, to be dressed by that light, then we begin to open our understanding of ourself – what's happening upon ourself. That we have that reality within ourself, we have the sun within our heart. How to perfect the light of the sun in our heart and the face and the head becomes the moon. So then they say, empty the head. Empty the head of all its wants and desires. Don't use your head to follow those realities. Don't use your head to second guess that reality, because your head always wants to be a sun.

Our life is based on shutting down that reality of the head. That, *"la ilaha illallah, la ilaha illallah"* (there is no God but Allah). That *ya Rabbi*, I'm not going to get anywhere with this head. If the head becomes empty and becomes like a moon, it's empty. Use the head for cooking and work, accounting and business. But for Allah ﷻ and the

Seek Out the Full Moons of Guidance – Secret of Juzba (Magnetism)

heavens, empty the head, empty the head. If that light begins to shine within the heart, and the light becomes like a sun, it reflects to the head. It means the face becomes *nurani*, begins to dress from the light of what's within the heart will reflect through the head.

Allah ﷻ Gave Us Nobility and a Gift to the Soul

Through that reflection, every difficulty can be taken away. That's why they're describing for us that everything is affected by that moon. It even affects the tide on *dunya* (material world). Imagine then the walking ones whose hearts are like suns, their faces are like moons, that how much Allah ﷻ emanates through them. *"Wa laqad karramna bani Adam"* (We have certainly honored the children of Adam). It means their station is far above the planets, far above the sun and the moon.

﴾٧٠﴿... وَلَقَدْ كَرَّمْنَا بَنِي آدَمَ

17:70 – "Wa laqad karramna bani adama…" (Surat Al-Isra)

"And We have certainly honored the children of Adam…"
(The Night Journey, 17:70)

Because Allah ﷻ gave a nobility and a gift to the soul. That's what they're asking for us to rise to that reality, to understand that reality and how to perfect that reality within ourselves.

The Heart Stamps the Iron in the Blood with Zikrullah

The first level of understanding, *haqiqat ul-juzba* (reality of attraction) and how to build an attraction, how to build that light and that energy that as you breathe and understanding ourself, to understand how am I going to achieve to be a moon? They begin to teach the first step is your breath. Understand the importance of your breath that as you're breathing in, it is an energy that sustains your being. Those lungs will dress the blood.

So then immediately, the importance that Prophet ﷺ asked that safeguard for me, your mouth. One, what you eat, what you drink, what you breathe is going to affect your energy. As that breath begins to come in, it dresses the lungs, dresses the blood, blood to become purified by *zikrullah* (remembrance of Allah) and move into the heart. If the heart is based on *zikr* and *durood sharif* (praisings), it means that it's pumping "Allah, Allah", stamps the blood and that blood nourishes the

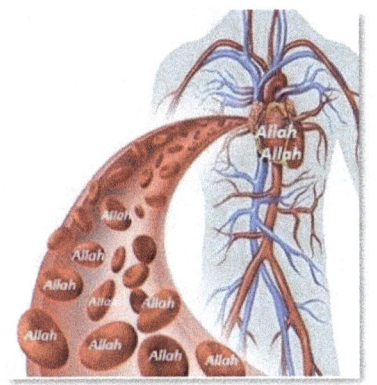

entire physiology of the body. And it stamps the blood on the iron.

Hadid (Iron) is Reality of Guidance and a Built-in GPS in All Creatures

Then the breath and the purification is based on *hadid* (iron). *Hadid* is  I think Surat 57 of Holy Qur'an. The iron is the reality of guidance. If the iron is pure, the guidance is perfected. So then all the creatures have iron within their body. The birds have iron, the whales have iron. Based on that iron, the electromagnetic frequency of the earth, they find their guidance. They have their own built-in GPS system. We lost the iron and we had to buy a box that talks to us. So the bird has iron within it. It submits, the energy of the earth, it understands. And Allah ﷻ sends it coordinates that you fly here, your sustenance is here, your home is here.

Smoking Contaminates the Iron in Your Blood and Attacks Your Heart

Then they begin to teach that the breath that you're bringing in and the *qudra* (power) and the energy that you're bringing in. All of that energy is going to be stamped on that iron. So, take a path in which you perfect and purify that iron.

So then how can you smoke and drink? That if you smoke, you are contaminating that iron, contaminating that blood, imperfecting that. Then that contamination from the lungs goes to the blood. From the blood, it attacks the heart! That's why *shaytan* wants to enter through smoking and drinking. He wants to attack the heart of the believer.

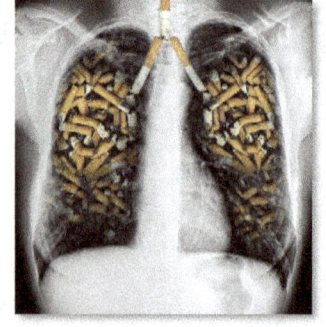

Purify Your Blood, the Beautiful Stream in Allah's ﷻ House – Your Heart

If Allah ﷻ says *qalb mumin baytullah*, then the teaching that if we want to reach to this reality and we want to reach to that perfection, that the house of the believer is the house of God Almighty.

قَلْبَ الْمُؤْمِنْ بَيْثُ الرَّبْ

"Qalb al mu'min baytur rabb."

"The heart of the believer is the House of the Lord."
(Hadith Qudsi)

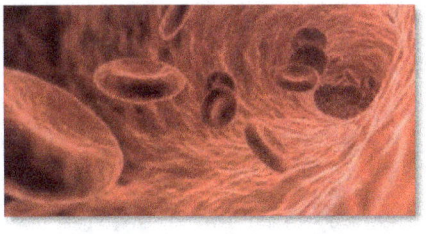

In God's house, there is a beautiful stream that passes through which is the stream of our blood. And upon that blood is every imperfection or perfection. Imperfection to attack the house, so that Allah ﷻ won't reside within that house. The Divine won't reside within a house that is contaminated by the contaminants that are running through the blood. If Allah ﷻ is not residing within that house, and the contaminants are flowing through the heart, it hits all the organs of the body and makes the body to be sick.

Your Lungs Are Your Tree of Life

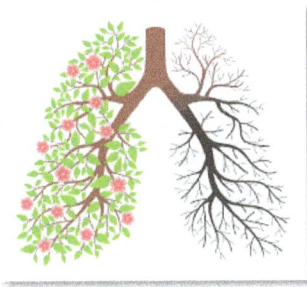

The way of perfection is Allah ﷻ teaching, 'No you can't. Perfect your breath, perfect your lungs. Your lungs are the tree of life.' (We covered this 8 years ago, but they didn't document it good and they never wrote it.) It's the tree of life that everybody is in search of. Allah ﷻ gave that tree within the lungs. So, the whole *qudra*, the whole power and all the *tafakkur* (contemplation) begins to open, it's going to open the power of the breath. That every *zikr* (chanting) *awliya* are making, they're making it with the power of their soul and their breath. And they feel it in every cell of their body – only by a purified breath. Once that's purified and cleansed, that iron is stamped and cleaned, moved into the heart. It's a beautiful stream moving into the house of Allah ﷻ. And Allah ﷻ stamps that light, stamps that energy and the *qudra* (power) upon that cell and that cell begins to radiate throughout their body. Every cell sits under a hair.

How the Moon of Awliya Begins to Shine Through Tafakkur (Contemplation)

As soon as they energize themselves for *tafakkur* (contemplation), this is how the moon begins to shine. This means they begin to make their *tafakkur* and their contemplation. As soon as they make their

contemplation and negate themselves and they flip their switch to be nothing, every cell of iron in their body becomes magnetized. From the energy that is emanating from their heart, their entire being begins to send out energy. Not through hand, but their entire being is emanating energy. Again, depending upon how much they're able to negate themselves and how much they're able to purify themselves.

There's no way to reach that with impurities and sicknesses. Nobody can damage the form and then claim to be giving Divinely and heavenly dresses and lights. These are the ways of Prophet (Muhammad) ﷺ and the ways of perfection. The guides teach us then perfect, dress.

Hijama (Cupping) Extracts Dirty Iron From the Body

Then to understand the importance of that iron; the only way to purify and cleanse that iron is through *hijama*, it's the cupping of the body. They cup the back of the shoulder because all of the dirty iron of the body goes upon the shoulder. This area of the shoulder in the back is where the body takes the dirty iron. When the iron becomes of no use to the body, it sends all that iron up onto the shoulder region.

That's the same place where the *shayateen* (devils) come and attack the believer; that the energy people begin to feel when they're under attack. They never come to a believer from the front, because the heart of the believer is a shield. These *shayateen* (devils), they come from behind and they land right onto that back with a dirty metal. And they say the cause of staph infection is from the bacteria that clings onto the metal within the blood.

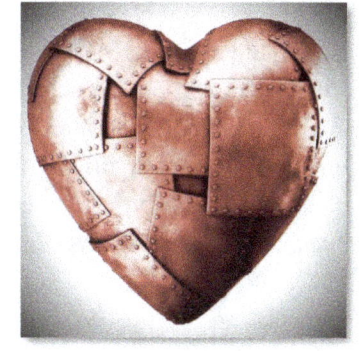

It means that everything of our physiology is teaching us about our reality. That when you do *hijama* (cupping) once or twice a year, you pull all of that negative iron. They pull and cleanse all that negative iron as if cleaning the filters of a building. Once you clean the filters of a building, it's able to flow fresh and clean again.

Purify the Iron and Build Inner Protection to Shield You From Outside

Then we are taking a path of perfecting what we eat and what we drink. Everything Prophet ﷺ brought for us was for the perfection of energy.

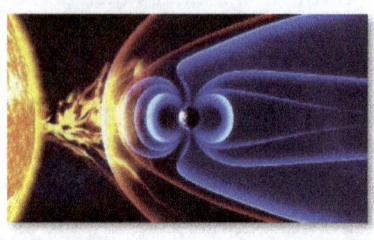

So, when people don't eat *halal* (permissible) and don't drink *halal* and don't take care of themselves, they're amazed at why their energy has dropped. If your energy drops, you are lending yourself to be attacked. The shield that you carry within yourself, is a shield of protection. And the earth has a magnetic core. The earth has an iron core. That melted core creates a *nazma* and a protection around the earth. This means nothing can penetrate the earth because of its magnetic core.

Allah ﷻ says you have the same core. You have that iron within you. If you build your inner perfection and inner protection, the inner energy will protect you on the outside of your being. But if you have nothing inside, you'll have nothing outside. It's impossible to say I have an outside energy, but inside is rotten. It means by eating *halal*, why Prophet ﷺ brought it? He didn't have any particular reasons to do that other than Allah ﷻ ordering it for the perfection of their energy. When you eat that

which is blessed, that which is nourished, you are taking away all of its negative energies and bringing Allah's ﷻ *rahmah* (mercy) and perfection. What you drink will bring in the perfection of your blood, so drink a lot of water to purify and sustain that blood.

Light Your Heart With the Divinely Presence!

It means everything that comes into that body is going to affect the blood and affect the heart. As much as we can bring of perfection, as much as that heart will be nourished.  If that heart is nourished, it's becoming more and more like a sun. Allah ﷻ begins to describe, 'That sun is eternal. When I turn that on and when I turn it off, nobody knows. If you want something to be given to you of eternity, then light the heart. Light the heart with My Divinely Presence! But my presence can't come into the heart with all these imperfections and impurities.'

Subhana rabbika rabbal 'izzati 'amma yasifoon, wa salaamun 'alal mursaleen, walhamdulillahi rabbil 'aalameen. Bi hurmati Muhammad al-Mustafa wa bi siri Surat al-Fatiha.

How to Accompany 'Ibadullah – Whom Allah ﷻ Has Taught

Etiquette of Seeking Heavenly Knowledge

How to Accompany Ibadullah – The Ones Whom Allah ﷻ Has Dressed and Taught

Alhamdulillah, that the guides are teaching of *Shamsi wal Qamar* (The Sun and the Moon), the way of following and *itibah* (obedience), the way of and reaching towards knowledges. That Allah ﷻ shows us the real way. It means to follow the *shams* (sun) and be like a *qamar* (moon), and efface yourself and be nothing, be nothing, and keep staring at that sunshine, *shamsud duha*.

لَا الشَّمْسُ يَنبَغِي لَهَا أَن تُدْرِكَ الْقَمَرَ وَلَا اللَّيْلُ سَابِقُ النَّهَارِ ۚ وَكُلٌّ فِي فَلَكٍ يَسْبَحُونَ ﴿٤٠﴾

36:40 – "*La ash shamsu yan baghee la haan tudrika al qamara wala allay lu sabiqu an nahari wa kullun fee falakin yasbahoon.*" (Surat Yaseen)

"It is not permitted to the Sun to catch up/reach the Moon, nor can the Night overtake the Day: Each (just) swims along in (its own) orbit (according to Law)." (YaSeen, 36:40)

It means all the *naats* (praises) that we are reciting, they knew that reality. It is nice to be taught the reality then recite the *naat* and begin to understand that their whole way was the way of the moon. To be a moon, to be nothing. Don't be like the Earth with all of its buildings and its structures. The way of nothingness is to be nothing and to efface.

Reality of Number 18 = 8 Holds the Throne of One King

The relationship that Allah ﷻ wants for us is based on the secret of the nine. That from the ninth chapter of Holy Qur'an, Surat At-Tawbah, the fortieth verse in which Prophet ﷺ describes that he entered into the cave with Sayyidina Abu Bakr as-Siddiq ؓ.

...ثَانِيَ اثْنَيْنِ إِذْ هُمَا فِي الْغَارِ إِذْ يَقُولُ لِصَاحِبِهِ لَا تَحْزَنْ إِنَّ اللَّهَ مَعَنَا ۖ فَأَنزَلَ اللَّـهُ سَكِينَتَهُ عَلَيْهِ وَأَيَّدَهُ بِجُنُودٍ لَّمْ تَرَوْهَا ... (٤٠)

9:40 – "...thaniya ithnayni idh huma fil ghari idh yaqolu lisahibihi la tahzan inna Allaha ma'ana, fa anzalAllahu sakeenatahu, 'alayhi wa ayyadahu, bi junodin lam tarawha ..." (Surat At-Tawbah)

"... as one of two, when they were in the cave and he said to his companion, "Do not grieve; indeed Allah is with us." And Allah sent down his tranquility upon him and supported him with angels you did not see ..." (The Repentance, 9:40)

From that 9:40 it opens for us that in the month of Safar (second Lunar month) in the power and reality of the *sultanate (kingdom)* of nine; that eight will uphold the throne and there is a *Malik* (King).

وَالْمَلَكُ عَلَىٰ أَرْجَائِهَا ۚ وَيَحْمِلُ عَرْشَ رَبِّكَ فَوْقَهُمْ يَوْمَئِذٍ ثَمَانِيَةٌ ﴿١٧﴾

69:17 – "Wal Malaku 'ala arjayeha, wa yahmilu 'Arsha Rabbika fawqahum yawmaidhin thamaniyatun." (Surat Haqqah)

"And the angels will be on its sides, and eight will, that Day, bear the Throne of thy Lord above them." (The Reality, 69:17)

That *Malik* (King), cannot be described as Allah (swt), *la sharik* (no partner), nothing can hold Allah (swt). There is no angel created to hold Allah (swt); then you will be saying the angel is more powerful than Allah (swt). So that *Malik* and the one who sits upon the seat of authority is Sayyidina Muhammad (saws).

We Are Stamped with 18 = ١٨

That eight and one ١٨ is our whole life and we are stamped with that

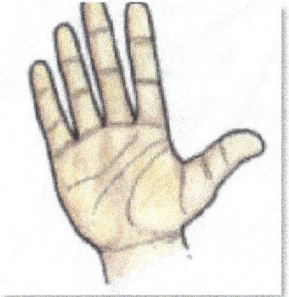

one and the eight on our hands (left palm and right palm) and Allah (swt) created perfect symmetry of that reality.

From that understanding of eighteen we look to *Ashab al Kahf* in Surat Al-Kahf (Chapter 18 of Holy Qur'an) and begin the understanding and dress of *atiullah*. Allah (swt) wants from us *atiullah, ati ur Rasul* and then how it is taught to us by *Ulul amr*.

يَاأَيُّهَا الَّذِينَ آمَنُوا أَطِيعُوا اللَّهَ وَأَطِيعُوا الرَّسُولَ وَأُوْلِي الْأَمْرِ مِنْكُمْ ... ﴿٥٩﴾

4:59 – "Ya ayyu hal ladheena amanoo Atiullaha wa atiur Rasula wa Ulil amre minkum..." (Surat An-Nisa)

"O You who have believed, Obey Allah, Obey the Messenger, and those in authority among you..." (The Women, 4:59)

What Allah (swt) wants for us is to be like My *Qamar*, be like the moon and follow the sun. Your eyes should always be upon the light of Prophet (saws), the love of Sayyidina Muhammad (saws) and that is all that should occupy your existence. Don't look left or right.

Sayyidina Musa ﷺ Wanted to Reach Where the Two Rivers Meet

The guides begin to teach from Nabi Musa (Moses) ﷺ. Why Nabi Musa ﷺ? Because he is *kalimullah*, the one who speaks to Allah ﷻ. The example is set so high, from teaching of *Shamsi wal Qamar*, Allah ﷻ begins to teach that I will show you now from the one who speaks to Me, speaks to My Divinely Presence that he is also in need of these realities. Nabi Musa ﷺ wanted from these realities. That what he had from realities had a *had*, a limit.

وَإِذْ قَالَ مُوسَىٰ لِفَتَاهُ لَا أَبْرَحُ حَتَّىٰ أَبْلُغَ مَجْمَعَ الْبَحْرَيْنِ أَوْ أَمْضِيَ حُقُبًا ﴿٦٠﴾

18:60 – *"Wa idh qala Mosa lefatahu laa abrahu hatta ablugha majma'a al bahrayni aw amdiya huquba." (Surat Al-Kahf)*

"Behold, Moses said to his attendant, 'I will not give up until I reach the junction of the two seas or (until) I spend years and years in travel'." (The Cave, 18:60)

The Two Rivers Meet at Two Bow Length or Nearer – 'Qaba Qawsayni aw Adna'

What he wanted, from what he saw when he asked to see Allah ﷻ, he saw the *ruhaniyat* (light) of Sayyidina Muhammad ﷺ. And he said this is what I want, this power, this light, this authority. Then I am going set my life to meet where the two rivers meet.

We said the two rivers meet between *la ilaha illAllah Muhammadan RasulAllah* ﷺ (there is no God but Allah and Muhammad ﷺ is his Messenger) because Allah ﷻ doesn't care for *dunya* (material world). It is not the Tigris and Euphrates. What they want is from *malakut*, the heavenly realm, from the oceans of these realities. It means where *la ilaha illAllah*, *Ha*, *Waw*, *Meem* connects and become *Muhammadun RasulAllah* ﷺ. These are Allah's ﷻ ancient realities.

لَا إِلَٰهَ إِلَّا اللهُ مُحَمَّدٌ رَّسُولُ اللهِ

"La ilaha illAllahu Muhammadu RasulAllah."

"There is no God but Allah, Muhammad is the Messenger of Allah."

It means that the secret between *Ha*, *Waw*, and *Meem*, is *Qaba Qawsayni aw Adna*. Where *la ilaha illAllah* is *la Sharik* (no partner to Allah ﷻ), nothing from that ocean of *la ilaha illAllah* but with a *Waw* and the secret of love, it brings *Muhammadun RasulAllah* ﷺ. It means *la ilaha illAllah* (on one side) and *Muhammadun RasulAllah* ﷺ (on the opposite side); this is *Qaba Qawsayni aw Adna*. "*Aw Adna*" is the *Waw*, that this Creation is the creation of love.

فَكَانَ قَابَ قَوْسَيْنِ أَوْ أَدْنَىٰ (٩)

53:9 – *"Fakana qaaba qawsayni aw adna."* (Surat An-Najm)

"And was at a distance of two bow lengths or nearer." (The Star, 53:9)

Ha is for Hidayat – Guidance That is Inside the Cave

Where the *Ha* comes with *hidayat* (guidance) directing and pointing to us that the *Ha* of *la ilaha illAllah* (there is no God but Allah ﷻ). There is a hidden *Waw* inside the *Ha*; when you make the *Ha* you put the *Waw* within and that is the cave. So, the *hidayat* (guidance) is inside the cave and inside the cave are the *Ahlul Muhabbat*, the People of Love, the people of realities that Allah ﷻ dressed them from the oceans of *hayat* (ever-living).

إِنَّ الَّذِينَ آمَنُوا وَعَمِلُوا الصَّالِحَاتِ سَيَجْعَلُ لَهُمُ الرَّحْمَٰنُ وُدًّا ﴿٩٦﴾

19:96 – "*Innal ladheena Amano wa 'amilos salihati sayaj'alu lahumur Rahmanu Wudda.*" (Surat Maryam)

"*Indeed, those who have believed and done righteous deeds - the Most Merciful will appoint/bestow/grant for them Love.*" (Mary, 19:96)

Souls Come to Life in the Presence of Ibadur Rahman

Nabi Musa ؏ wanted that reality. We said it before that he was going in search of that reality and the sign of where he reached was a dead fish that he had to eat for lunch, came to life and jumped into the water. There must be a secret of *hayat* (eternal life) and these are *Ibadur Rahman* (Servants of the Most Compassionate) that Allah ﷻ mentions, "*Alamal Qur'an. Khalaqal insaan.*" (Holy Qur'an, 55:2-3).

عَلَّمَ الْقُرْآنَ ﴿٢﴾ خَلَقَ الْإِنسَانَ ﴿٣﴾

55:2-3 – "*Allamal Qur'an. Khalaqal Insaan.*" (Surat Ar-Rahman)

"It is He Who has taught the Qur'an. He has created Mankind."
(The Beneficent 55:2-3)

They carry the lights and the realities and secrets of Holy Qur'an. They have been granted a light from Allah ﷻ that worshipness cannot achieve. It is a grant from Allah ﷻ. Allah ﷻ then describes that things come to life in their presence. The fish is  symbolic of the soul and all souls come to life in their reality and in their presence. And he said *ajaban*, the one accompanying Nabi Musa ﷺ saw a dead fish come to life and jump into the water.

قَالَ أَرَأَيْتَ إِذْ أَوَيْنَا إِلَى الصَّخْرَةِ فَإِنِّي نَسِيتُ الْحُوتَ وَمَا أَنسَانِيهُ إِلَّا الشَّيْطَانُ أَنْ أَذْكُرَهُ ۚ وَاتَّخَذَ سَبِيلَهُ فِي الْبَحْرِ عَجَبًا (٦٣)

18:63 – "Qala araayta idh awayna ilas sakhrati fa-innee naseetu alhoota wa ma ansaneehu illash Shaytanu an adhkurahu, wat takhadha sabeela hu fee al bahri 'ajaba." (Surat Al-Kahf)

"He said, Did you see when we retired to the rock? Indeed, I forgot [there] the fish. And none made me forget it except Satan – that I should mention it. And it took its course into the sea amazingly."
(The Cave, 18:63)

 It means these are the realities of the soul. That if the soul dried up and is hopeless and giving up any chance of mercy or swimming in the oceans of *ma'rifah* (gnosticism), Allah ﷻ says, 'No, no, what We have dressed of Our servants,' and that was just

one of the servants, that *tajalli* (manifestation) and that light and that dress is upon them and Nabi Musa ﷺ wanted that knowledge.

Ibadur Rahman Are Servants of Allah ﷻ Who Attained Mercy and Heavenly Knowledge

فَوَجَدَا عَبْدًا مِّنْ عِبَادِنَا آتَيْنَاهُ رَحْمَةً مِّنْ عِندِنَا وَعَلَّمْنَاهُ مِن لَّدُنَّا عِلْمًا ﴿٦٥﴾

18:65 – "Fawajada 'abdan min 'ibadinaa ataynahu rahmatan min 'indina wa 'allamnahu mil ladunna 'ilma." (Surat Al-Kahf)

"So they found one of Our servants, on whom We had bestowed Mercy from Ourselves and whom We had taught knowledge from Our own Presence." (The Cave, 18:65)

What Nabi Musa ﷺ wanted was these knowledges and realities. This is an *isharat* (sign) that wherever there is knowledge, Divinely knowledge, *ilm Ladunee wa hikmati bis Saliheen* (Divinely Knowledge and Wisdom of the Righteous). Not people who memorize books, not people who make a translation of one language to the next. They take the Arabic and give the Holy *Hadith* (traditions of Prophet ﷺ) and tell it to you in Urdu and English and people are astonished. They are astonished because these are the Holy *Hadith* of Sayyidina  Muhammad ﷺ. What the guides are talking about is the realities of these Holy *Hadith* and realities of Holy Qur'an. These Servants of Allah ﷻ attained mercy, then Allah ﷻ taught them in their hearts through their *murshids* (spiritual guides).

The Etiquette of Seeking Divinely Knowledge According to Holy Qur'an

Then Allah (AJ) begins to describe, 'If you are seeking knowledges like Nabi Musa (AS) there is an entire way to achieve that reality; it is not easy to achieve.' It means if you are seeking these knowledges and wish to sit with those who have been dressed by heavenly knowledges, there is an entire *adab* (etiquette) in their company.

1. Itibah (Follow) – Admit That You Want to Be His Follower

The first thing that Nabi Musa (AS) is teaching us is that, 'As soon as I am going, I am admitting to that teacher that I want to be from your *tabi'een* (followers).'

قَالَ لَهُ مُوسَىٰ هَلْ أَتَّبِعُكَ عَلَىٰ أَن تُعَلِّمَنِ مِمَّا عُلِّمْتَ رُشْدًا (٦٦)

18:66 – *"Qala lahu moosa hal attabi'uka 'alaa an tu'allimani mimma 'ullimta rushda." (Surat Al-Kahf)*

"Moses said to him: May I follow thee, on the footing that thou teach me something of the (Higher) Truth which thou hast been taught?"
(The Cave, 18:66)

I want to follow you means immediately I am going to take my rank off, anything that distinguishes me of any hierarchy. That in the presence of that teacher, there is no permission to show any hierarchy. This is Nabi Musa (AS); this is something that people do not make up, but this is what Allah (AJ) wants.

Above Every Knower is a Knower

Above every knower is a knower with higher/more knowledge. Even Nabi Musa (AS) was asking for The Muhammadan Reality. Allah (AJ) says, this knowledge and its *azimat* (greatness) requires certain characteristics. From the one who speaks to My Divinely Presence, how difficult it is that he immediately humbled himself and said, 'If you grant me permission to follow you, *itibah* (obedience).' That implies that he could not use his prophecy and he could not use whatever Allah (ﷻ) had given him in accompanying that one. (It means I cannot use whatever Allah (ﷻ) has given me in accompanying you.)

It means you cannot tell your dreams to the Shaykh to influence the Shaykh; you cannot tell stories, you cannot have discussions, you cannot give *suhbats* (lectures); you cannot do anything that is going to use your signal with the signal of that guide. There are many different realities in that. There are many different ways that people's egos try to control the guide and teachers. They tell them stories and events and begin to use their connection in the presence of that one. It is not allowed. It is going to block everything and makes everything difficult.

The bar that Allah (ﷻ) is setting is that My *Kalimullah*/Nabi Musa (عليه السلام) came and said, 'Let me to be your student. *InshaAllah*, you find me to be patient with you and be taught from what you know of knowledge and *adab* (manners) and characteristics.'

قَالَ لَهُ مُوسَىٰ هَلْ أَتَّبِعُكَ عَلَىٰ أَن تُعَلِّمَنِ مِمَّا عُلِّمْتَ رُشْدًا (٦٦)

18:66 – *"Qala lahu Musa hal attabi'uka 'alaa an tu'allimani mimma 'ullimta rushda." (Surat Al-Kahf)*

"Moses said to him: May I follow thee, on the footing/condition that thou teach me something of the (Higher) Truth which thou hast been taught?" (The Cave, 18:66)

2. Be Patient – Accompanying These Guides Requires Patience

Then Sayyidina Khidr (عليه السلام) clarifies for us that you are not going to be able to be patient.

قَالَ إِنَّكَ لَن تَسْتَطِيعَ مَعِيَ صَبْرًا (٦٧)

18:67 – *"Qala innaka lan tastatee'a ma'iya sabra." (Surat Al-Kahf)*

"(The Other) said, Verily you will not be able to have patience with me!"
(The Cave, 18:67)

It means then the biggest characteristic of this path, not the smallest, is *sabr* (patience). Because he knows this is a great prophet of God. Allah ﷻ is giving us an example because this is the highest level to set the standard of the character. There is another secret in why Nabi Musa عليه السلام humbled himself. Maybe he was testing Sayyidina Khidr عليه السلام?

That is for a different time, but tonight they set the standard so high that to be nothing and to approach in that ocean of nothingness that I want to be granted from the knowledges that you have, and they begin to teach that it requires a tremendous *sabr, wa ta wa saw bil haqqi wa tawa saw bi-sabr*. The way is based on *haqq*, its bricks are *sabr*, and *sabr* is patience.

وَالْعَصْرِ ﴿١﴾ إِنَّ الْإِنسَانَ لَفِي خُسْرٍ ﴿٢﴾ إِلَّا الَّذِينَ آمَنُوا وَعَمِلُوا الصَّالِحَاتِ وَتَوَاصَوْا بِالْحَقِّ وَتَوَاصَوْا بِالصَّبْرِ ﴿٣﴾

103:1-3 – *"Wal 'Asr. (1) Innal insaana lafee khusr. (2) Illal ladheena aamano wa 'amilos saalihaati, wa tawasaw bil haqqi wa tawasaw bis Sabr. (3)" (Surat Al-'Asr)*

"By Al 'Asr (the time)! (1) Verily, Mankind is in loss. (2) Except for those who have believed and done righteous deeds and advised each other to truth and advised each other to patience. (3)"
(The Declining Day, 103:1-3)

You Can't Be Patient With What You Don't Know

The next *ayat* (verse) Sayyidina Khidr ؏ tells Sayyidina Musa ؏, who is *kalimullah*.

$$\text{وَكَيْفَ تَصْبِرُ عَلَىٰ مَا لَمْ تُحِطْ بِهِ خُبْرًا ﴿٦٨﴾}$$

18:68 – *"Wa kayfa tasbiru 'ala ma lam tuhit bihi khubra."* (Surat Al-Kahf)

"And how can you have patience about things which your understanding is not complete?" (The Cave, 18:68)

For anyone who is following and trying to take a path of realities and constantly trying to hear something and make a comment; they think they saw something and make a comment. They think they had a dream and make a comment. Many different variables, everybody is at different levels. This way requires everything to be shut off in the pursuit of that knowledge. It teaches that how can you have patience with something where your knowledge is incomplete with it. It means I am going to teach you from a knowledge you don't have. If you don't have it, you are going to be impatient in trying to pursue it. So again, established that a tremendous amount of patience that is required.

3. Do Not Ask Any Questions

If you follow, no questions about anything until I myself speak to you about it.

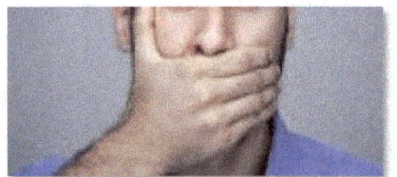

$$\text{قَالَ فَإِنِ اتَّبَعْتَنِي فَلَا تَسْأَلْنِي عَن شَيْءٍ حَتَّىٰ أُحْدِثَ لَكَ مِنْهُ ذِكْرًا ﴿٧٠﴾}$$

18:70 – *"Qala fa ini ittaba'tanee fala tasalnee 'an shay-in hatta ohditha laka minhu dhikra."* (Surat Al-Kahf)

"[Khidr] He said, Then if you follow me, do not ask me questions about anything until I myself speak to you concerning it." (The Cave, 18:70)

What you learn in college and schools today is the worst of manners. What you learn in school is to constantly ask the professor, challenge the professor, and examine the professor, which is *tark al adab* (leaving manners) and the worst of manners.

Iman (Faith) is Blind Like Love

Because faith is blind, it is like love. They make fun of this, 'Oh, blind faith, blind faith!' Yes, it is an oxymoron statement. Faith has to be blind because you are not seeing *Iman*. *Iman* (faith) is an action based on love, they don't see love either. Faith has to be and is required to be blind. It means that you believe in your heart the actions are correct, the understanding is correct and when you act on faith, Allah ﷻ grants you the *darajats* of *Iman* (Station of Faith). If you have to prove it, that is no longer your *iman*, this is now your *aql* (reasoning). That (*iman*) is involved with something in your heart which is superior and then begin the path.

4. Be Patient and Don't Be Disobedient

Sayyidina Musa ﷺ said, *InshaAllah*, you will find me to be patient with you, I will accompany you. Everybody knows the story that they came across three tests and each test Nabi Musa ﷺ had something to say.

قَالَ سَتَجِدُنِي إِن شَاءَ اللَّـهُ صَابِرًا وَلَا أَعْصِي لَكَ أَمْرًا ﴿٦٩﴾

18:69 – "Qala satajidunee in shaa Allahu sabiran wa la a'see laka amra." (Surat Al-Kahf)

"[Moses] said, You will find me, if Allah wills, (truly) patient, and I will not disobey you in [any] order." (The Cave, 18:69)

The Eternal Tests in the Pursuit of Heavenly Knowledge

1. Sayyidina Khidr ؑ Sinks the Boat – Earning Rizq (Sustenance)

They came across the boat that the fisherman had and we won't go into depth about that. But the importance is that they came across a boat and that boat symbolizes *rizq* and sustenance. It means the way in which you are going to achieve your *rizq* or sustenance, there is going to be an issue with it. Sayyidina Khidr ؑ had involvement with that sustenance to lower the boat and not to destroy it, and Nabi Musa ؑ had an issue with it. 'Why are you doing that?'

It means there is going to be an importance in that guidance that is going to deal with our *rizq*, our sustenance. It means how you interact with that teacher and guide, and the knowledges they are conveying, that they are going to be directly involved in your sustenance. They give advice on how to achieve your sustenance. How to lower the importance of that sustenance, how to take it out of your eyes because it is going to block you. Then the *ayat* (verse of Holy Qur'an) becomes clear of why that happened.

Fear of Poverty Blocks From the Pursuit of Spiritual Realities

When Nabi Musa ؑ asked, 'Why did you break the boat?' because that

boat that he was earning his income with, *Shaytan* (Satan) was after it. It means that your income and money is under the influence of *Shaytan*. It is never going to move towards *Rahman*

(Gracious), because *Shaytan* is going to keep coming to you and whispering, 'It is going to finish, it is going to finish,' and you begin to save it, save it, save it. It means that *rizq* is going to be a direct (link). That is why Allah (swt) is saying that in pursuit of these knowledges these three tests are eternal tests. It was not only for Nabi Musa (as). The pursuit of money is going to block us from the pursuit of realities and the fear of poverty is also going to block us. So already they had a difficulty at that test. 'Why did you have to break that boat?' He described later why they had to break that boat. Again he said, 'I will be patient, I will be patient, please bear with me.'

أَمَّا السَّفِينَةُ فَكَانَتْ لِمَسَاكِينَ يَعْمَلُونَ فِي الْبَحْرِ فَأَرَدتُّ أَنْ أَعِيبَهَا وَكَانَ وَرَاءَهُم مَّلِكٌ يَأْخُذُ كُلَّ سَفِينَةٍ غَصْبًا ﴿٧٩﴾

18:79 – "Amma assafeenatu fakanat limasakeena ya'maloona fee albahri faarattu an a'ebaha wa kana wa ra-ahum malikun ya khudhu kulla safeenatin ghasba." (Surat Al-Kahf)

"As for the ship, it belonged to poor people working at sea. So I intended to cause defect in it as there was after them a king who seized every [good] ship by force." (The Cave, 18:79)

2. Sayyidina Khidr (as) Made the Boy Zabiha (Sacrifice)

The next test that the people of knowledges will be involved in your life. And we saw it in our own lives and we see it every day with everything that transpires. They came across a boy and the boy was ordered by Allah (swt) to be slain. And Sayyidina Khidr (as) slayed the boy and Nabi Musa (as) said, 'That's it, why did you do an extreme injustice against such a pure *ghulam* (servant)?

فَانطَلَقَا حَتَّىٰ إِذَا لَقِيَا غُلَامًا فَقَتَلَهُ قَالَ أَقَتَلْتَ نَفْسًا زَكِيَّةً بِغَيْرِ نَفْسٍ لَّقَدْ جِئْتَ شَيْئًا نُّكْرًا ﴿٧٤﴾

18:74 – *"Fantalaqa hatta idha laqiya ghulaman faqatalahu qala aqatalta nafsan zakiyatan bighayri nafsin laqad jita shay-an nukra."*
(Surat Al-Kahf)

"So they set out, until when they met a boy, al Khidhr killed him. [Moses] said, "Have you killed a pure soul for other than [having killed] a soul? You have certainly done a deplorable thing."
(The Cave, 18:74)

It means here is a big time to *tafakkur* (contemplate) that, in this way of relates everything about us has to be destroyed, there cannot be two in that presence. What they want is everything to be brought down so that that light of Allah's 𐑘 Divine Presence, the light of Sayyidina Muhammad ﷺ to shine within us. So what is blocking is 'us'. What is blocking is my 'I-ness', my 'Me-ness', as much as 'I am there', I am distant from that reality.

Relevance of the Three Tests in Our Spiritual Path

1. Don't Run After Dunya, Build Your Iman (Faith)

First, we pursued a *rizq*, a sustenance that becomes my whole focus in life. We say like running constantly in the *bazaar* (marketplace) looking for where is the money is. We are the people of being spider, *ankabut*. You build your web, do your *zikr* (remembrance), do the things that Allah 𐑘 finds to be beautiful and Allah 𐑘 sends the sustenance. There are many who live like that as a *dalil*, as a proof. They do what Allah 𐑘 wants them to do and Allah 𐑘 sends them and can send from ways you never imagined.

2. Get Rid of Your Bad Characteristics/Ego

Then the boy, and it is *nafs al amarah*, the very bad characteristic that constantly is in a naughty condition. Then when Nabi Musa ﷺ complained but he attributed it in words of Arabic that, 'This is a very purified *Ghulam (servant)*. Why did you do that?' It means it is an *isharat* (sign) for us that everybody thinks themselves to be great, that I am very pure, I am very wonderful, why is it that I am coming under attack? Why is it that I am having testing in my life? Why am I constantly under difficulty, I am a very wonderful person.

Sayyidina Khidr ﷺ Told Nabi Musa ﷺ About the Naughty Boy

وَأَمَّا الْغُلَامُ فَكَانَ أَبَوَاهُ مُؤْمِنَيْنِ فَخَشِينَا أَن يُرْهِقَهُمَا طُغْيَانًا وَكُفْرًا ﴿٨٠﴾ فَأَرَدْنَا أَن يُبْدِلَهُمَا رَبُّهُمَا خَيْرًا مِّنْهُ زَكَاةً وَأَقْرَبَ رُحْمًا ﴿٨١﴾

18:80-81 – "Wa amma alghulamu fakana abawahu muminayni fakhasheena an yurhiqahuma tughyanan wa kufra."
"Faaradna an yubdi lahuma rabbuhuma khayram minhu zakatan wa aqraba ruhma." *(Surat Al-Kahf)*

"And as for the boy, his parents were believers, and we feared that he would overburden them by transgression and disbelief. (80) So we intended that their Lord should substitute for them one better than him in purity and nearer to mercy. (81)" *(The Cave, 18:80-81)*

The dialogue that Sayyidina Khidr ﷺ was teaching about the boy, 'No, no, that naughty one is going to be blocking. If you let it to die, Allah ﷻ will replace it with a *rahmah*, a mercy, something that will be merciful to you.' It means the new reality that is born within somebody is a pure reality that guides us and assists us in reaching towards our realities. It means now the sustenance is going to be after it. The pureness of the inner character and that we stick to it thinking it is a pure *ghulam* (servant) and they are teaching from Allah ﷻ that 'No, no, put that down and make a *zabiha* (sacrifice). That character was to be purified.'

3. Live a Life of Service and Khidmat

Then the last test was the building of the wall. The building of the wall is living the life of service, of *khidmat* and open the reality of *khidmat*. That is why you have to build the wall and you didn't charge? It means everything we do we have to get money for it, you have to live a life of money. But when you look at these *mukhlis* (sincere people), they don't live a life of money, they live a life of service. They serve Allah ﷻ and money flows from every direction possible, that is not the issue.

اتَّبِعُوا مَن لَّا يَسْأَلُكُمْ أَجْرًا وَهُم مُّهْتَدُونَ ﴿٢١﴾

36:21 – "Ittabi'o man la ya salukum ajran wa hum Muhtadon." (Surat YaSeen)

"Obey/Follow those who ask no reward of you (for themselves), and who have themselves received Guidance." (YaSeen, 36:21)

The issue that Nabi Musa ﷺ was complaining to Sayyidina Khidr ﷺ that, why we didn't charge? He said, 'That is where we are having problems now.'

فَانطَلَقَا حَتَّىٰ إِذَا أَتَيَا أَهْلَ قَرْيَةٍ اسْتَطْعَمَا أَهْلَهَا فَأَبَوْا أَن يُضَيِّفُوهُمَا فَوَجَدَا فِيهَا جِدَارًا يُرِيدُ أَن يَنقَضَّ فَأَقَامَهُ ۖ قَالَ لَوْ شِئْتَ لَاتَّخَذْتَ عَلَيْهِ أَجْرًا ﴿٧٧﴾

18:77 – *"Fantalaqa hatta idha ataya ahla qaryatin istat'ama ahlaha faabaw an yudayyifoo huma fawajada feeha jidaran yureedu an yanqadda faaqamahu, qala law sheta lat takhadhta 'alayhi ajra."*
(Surat Al-Kahf)

"So they set out, until when they came to the people of a town, they asked its people for food, but they refused to offer them hospitality. And they found therein a wall about to collapse, so al Khidhr restored it. [Moses] said, "If you wished, you could have taken for it a payment."
(The Cave, 18:77)

It means this reality of doing something for Allah (اج) and not asking anything in return for it. Live a life of *khidmat* (service) means serve Allah (اج), serve Sayyidina Muhammad (ﷺ); do what you have to do and Allah (اج) will sustain you. Allah (اج) will take care of you. And at that point Sayyidina Khidr (عليه السلام) was the first to say that, 'This is enough. I am going to free you from these responsibilities so that Allah (اج) won't be angry with you.'

قَالَ هَٰذَا فِرَاقُ بَيْنِي وَبَيْنِكَ ۚ سَأُنَبِّئُكَ بِتَأْوِيلِ مَا لَمْ تَسْتَطِع عَّلَيْهِ صَبْرًا ﴿٧٨﴾

18:78 – *"Qala hadha firaqu baynee wa baynika, saonabbioka bitaweeli ma lam tastati' 'alayhi sabra." (Surat Al-Kahf)*

"[Al-Khidhr] said, This is parting between me and you. I will inform you of the interpretation of that about which you could not have patience." (The Cave, 18:78)

We Must Go Through These Three Tests to Get Our Amanat (Trust)

Sayyidina Khidr (عليه السلام) said, 'This is where we can go no more.' They open a reality for us that why the *adab* (etiquette) is like that. It means that when we want to achieve what Allah (اج) wants to grant us of our *amanat*, it is a trust that has been set aside for ourselves. And these three tests are the way to our own *amanat* (trust) and if that relationship is built on doubt and constant questioning, it is no longer *iman* (faith).

They can give you all the answers; every time you question them and have doubt, they give you an answer, you didn't get granted anything from *iman*. You just got granted a satisfaction in your mind. Allah (swt) will still test again.

Faith Requires Patience – Know That Allah's (swt) Hand is in Everything

It means the way of *iman* (faith) is not something that is needed through the head but through *sabr* (patience). That is why it was clarified at the beginning of the relationship. That, 'Are you sure you want these realities? These are the realities of the Paradises, not the knowledges of *dunya* (material world).' The way of Paradise requires *sabr*, an extreme level of faith where whatever is done to you, be patient, because Allah (swt) knows best. Allah's (swt) hand is complete *tawhid (oneness)*.

1. Allah's (swt) hand is in everything. If He lowers your sustenance don't be distracted by it. As much as you are distracted by it is as much as your attachment to it. Once it loses its attachment from your house all the wealth of the world can be put in front of you and *Shaytan* (Satan) won't have a share in it because you do everything for the sake of Sayyidina Muhammad (saws) with it.

2. The second is if you don't allow the character to be *zabiha* (sacrificed) and cleaned then you will always have that bad characteristic, that naughty characteristic which will always be rebellious against Allah (swt), rebellious against Sayyidina Muhammad (saws) and rebellious against *Ulul amr* (saints).

3. If those two characteristics are met the third becomes perfected; they live a life of service. They do everything, they may work but they eagerly await to serve Allah ﷻ, to serve Sayyidina Muhammad ﷺ and they live a life of *khidmat* (service). So much so that for the people in *khidmat* the people outside keep coming to them asking, 'Why did you do that?

Why are you always going there? Why are you always serving there? Why are you doing like this? Who is paying you? Why are they not doing like this?' Because *dunya* (worldly) people do not understand *khidmat* (service). They only understand that you do something and you get $20 and you do this you get $20, you do this you get $20 but to be paid by Allah ﷻ, that requires a high level of faith, a level of *taslim*, and submission.

It means that is what was being conveyed and the understanding of the conveyance that when Sayyidina Khidr ؑ said, 'This is enough for us,' that (it is) the way of patience, the way of *itibah* (obedience) and following guidance and how to take away the bad characteristic of doubt. As much as there is doubt and as much as there is questioning, there is no more a relationship of these realities and that is when the student and the guide part their ways. Because any more time in that will actually be written against the student, because it is no longer faith. It is constant questioning, constant questioning; it is no longer any *iman* (faith). If there is no *iman* involved in it, then it becomes detrimental to the growth of that student and that is why at that time they part their ways. You are free to go in your direction and we go back to our direction.

We pray that Allah ﷻ open for us these understandings from this holy month of Safar; opens the holy month of Rabbi al Awwal and the full sun shining of Sayyidina Muhammad ﷺ, that Allah ﷻ grant us more and more understanding, more and more *adab* (manners), more and more love for Sayyidina Muhammad ﷺ and love for *Awliyaullah* (saints) and all of that love to be dressed with patience and *sabr, InshaAllah*.

Three Tests Reflect Nabi Musa's ؑ Life

The three tests with a trust for that reality that Nabi Musa ؑ wanted, means that when you look at the miracle of the path what they test you on is for your *amanat* (trust). It is not a test from the Shaykh. That is what Sayyidina Khidr ؑ was trying to convey to Nabi Musa ؑ that, 'This test Allah ﷻ is sending you on is so miraculous; it is a reflection of your life, not my life because:

1. You were thrown into the water in a basket so if you have a problem of throwing ships and drowning ships, your mom threw you in a basket.' You see this ship, this has to do with how your mom threw you in the water. What was the *hikmah* and the wisdom of that? That you will be saved by that basket because Allah ﷻ is great, you have nobody to fear. Allah ﷻ raised you in the hands of your enemy, who wanted and slayed many thousands of

children looking for you. Allah's ﷻ greatness is that I am going to make you feed him, clean him, wash him and raise him, because Allah ﷻ is great.

2. 'You have a problem with this boy, but weren't you the one who hit the guard with your hand to save one from your community? Allah ﷻ

wants to show you your own *ma'rifah* (gnosticism) within the way of *ma'rifah* because it is your *amanat* (trust) that you want, it is your trust, your characteristics that Allah ﷻ wants to show to you.' It is not about the Shaykh's characteristics; he is merely a guide taking you, be patient, be patient.

3. 'The wall that you were so upset about, you gave the well of Mad'een, you gave water to the ladies that you wanted a wife from one of them.' It means every test that Allah ﷻ sent was a reflection of your own life. And if we are patient to understand, patient to take the way, we will find that the *amanat* (trust) that they set aside for us is the *amanat* that was our inheritance. It means you inherit the pen of realties and then you will be tested all the way to reach towards that reality, to be dressed by that reality. And we pray that Allah ﷻ grant us from these realities and what we were promised on the Day of Promises, *InshaAllah*.

Subhana rabbika rabbal 'izzati 'amma yasifoon, wa salaamun 'alal mursaleen, walhamdulillahi rabbil 'aalameen. Bi hurmati Muhammad al-Mustafa wa bi siri Surat al-Fatiha.

Fulfill Your Trust (Amanat), Covenant ('Ahd), and Your Allegiance (Bayah)

إِنَّ اللَّهَ اشْتَرَىٰ مِنَ الْمُؤْمِنِينَ أَنفُسَهُمْ وَأَمْوَالَهُم بِأَنَّ لَهُمُ الْجَنَّةَ ... وَعْدًا عَلَيْهِ حَقًّا فِي التَّوْرَاةِ وَالْإِنجِيلِ وَالْقُرْآنِ وَمَنْ أَوْفَىٰ بِعَهْدِهِ مِنَ اللَّهِ فَاسْتَبْشِرُوا بِبَيْعِكُمُ الَّذِي بَايَعْتُم بِهِ وَذَٰلِكَ هُوَ الْفَوْزُ الْعَظِيمُ ﴿١١١﴾

9:111 – *"Inna Allaha Ashtara Minal Mu'umineena 'Anfusahum Wa 'Amwalahum Bi anna Lahumul Jannata, ...Wa'dan 'Alayhi Haqqan fit Tawrati wal Injeeli wal Qur'ani, Wa Man Awfa Bi 'Ahdihi Mina Allahi, Fastabshiro Bi bay'ikum Al Ladhi Baaya'tum Bihi, Wa Dhalika Huwal Fawzul 'azeem." (Surat At-Tawbah)*

"Indeed, Allah has purchased from the believers their lives and their properties [in exchange] for that they will have the Paradise..., a promise binding on Him in truth, in the Torah and the Gospel and the Qur'an. And who is more faithful to his 'Ahd (Covenant) than Allah? Then rejoice in your Bayah/Allegiance which you have fulfilled. And that is the great achievement." (The Repentance, 9:111)

Fulfill Your Trust (Amanat), Covenant ('Ahd), and Your Allegiance (Bayah)

The Covenant Was Offered to Creation and Ignorant Humans Accepted It

A covenant that was offered, a covenant, *'ahd*, that was offered to all of creation and all creation refused the covenant, a contract, an agreement. And the *jahul, insan* (human being), was ignorant and he accepted that covenant.

إِنَّا عَرَضْنَا الْأَمَانَةَ عَلَى السَّمَاوَاتِ وَالْأَرْضِ وَالْجِبَالِ فَأَبَيْنَ أَن يَحْمِلْنَهَا وَأَشْفَقْنَ مِنْهَا وَحَمَلَهَا الْإِنسَانُ ۖ إِنَّهُ كَانَ ظَلُومًا جَهُولًا ﴿٧٢﴾

33:72 – "*Inna a'radnal amanata 'alas Samawati wal ardi wal jibali, fa abayna an yahmilnaha wa ashfaqna minha wa hamalaha al Insanu, innahu kana zhaloman jahoola.*" (Surat Al-Ahzab)

"Indeed, we offered the Trust to the heavens and the earth and the mountains, and they declined to bear it and feared it; but man [undertook to] bear it. Indeed, he was Oppressor/unjust and ignorant." (The Combined Forces, 33:72)

Then somebody came back and asked that, 'Are you talking about the Qur'an being revealed?' And I said, 'No, no, no, *astaghfirullah*, it has nothing to do with Qur'an. Nothing can carry Holy Qur'an.' Allah ﷻ describes that his ancient word, not created word, if it goes upon the mountain, it's *khashi'a (dust).* But upon the heart of Sayyidina Muhammad ﷺ it flows;  the source of Holy Qur'an being the heart of Sayyidina Muhammad ﷺ.

لَوْ أَنزَلْنَا هَٰذَا الْقُرْآنَ عَلَىٰ جَبَلٍ لَّرَأَيْتَهُ خَاشِعًا مُّتَصَدِّعًا مِّنْ خَشْيَةِ اللَّهِ ۚ وَتِلْكَ الْأَمْثَالُ نَضْرِبُهَا لِلنَّاسِ لَعَلَّهُمْ يَتَفَكَّرُونَ ﴿٢١﴾

59:21 – "Law anzalna hadha alQurana 'ala jabalin laraaytahu, khashi'an mutasaddi'an min khashyatillahi, wa tilkal amthalu nadribuha linnasi la'allahum yatafakkaroon." (Surat Al-Hashr)

"Had We sent down this Qur'an on a mountain, verily, you would have seen it obliterated to dust (from its power) And these examples We present to the people that perhaps they will Contemplate…"
(The Exile, 59:21)

Human Being Forgot Their 'Ahd (Covenant) With Allah ﷻ

This has to do with *'ahd* and a covenant in which is mixed with our free will. The reason why Allah ﷻ gave us a free will is the secret of that *'ahd* and that covenant. Our life is to reach towards that *amanat* (trust). That when they described *jahul* (ignorant), because *insan* (human being) came and forgot. *"Alastu biRabbikum, qalo bala"* (Am I not your Lord? They said, 'Yes, we do testify!')

﴿وَإِذْ أَخَذَ رَبُّكَ مِن بَنِي آدَمَ مِن ظُهُورِهِمْ ذُرِّيَّتَهُمْ وَأَشْهَدَهُمْ عَلَىٰ أَنفُسِهِمْ أَلَسْتُ بِرَبِّكُمْ ۖ قَالُوا بَلَىٰ ۛ شَهِدْنَا ۛ أَن تَقُولُوا يَوْمَ الْقِيَامَةِ إِنَّا كُنَّا عَنْ هَٰذَا غَافِلِينَ ﴿١٧٢﴾

7:172 – "Wa idh akhadha rabbuka min banee adama min Zhuhorihim dhurriyyatahum wa ashhadahum 'ala anfusihim alastu biRabbikum qalo bala shahidna an taqolo yawmal qiyamati inna kunna 'an hadha ghafileen." (Surat Al-A'raf)

"And [mention] when your Lord took from the children of Adam from their atoms/loins – their descendants and made them testify concerning themselves, [saying to them], "Am I not your Lord?" They said, "Yes, we do testify!" [This] - lest you should say on the day of Resurrection, 'Indeed, we were of this unaware.'" (The Heights, 7:172)

We Made Three Contracts to Obey Allah ﷻ, Obey the Prophet Muhammad ﷺ, and Ulul Amr (Saints)

Allah ﷻ, in the world of light explained, that covenant, that contract and its responsibilities. When we in *tariqatun Naqshbandiya til 'Aliya*

Fulfill Your Trust (Amanat), Covenant ('Ahd), and Your Allegiance (Bayah)

(Spiritual path of Naqshbandi) take *bayah* (allegiance), say, "*Allah Hu, Allah Hu, Allah Hu Haq*". We say it three times because we made a covenant with Allah ﷻ, "*Atiullaha wa atiur Rasul wa ulil amre minkum.*" There were three contracts that were made for our obedience to Allah ﷻ, the obedience and the following of Sayyidina Muhammad ﷺ, and the obedience to the *ulul amr* (saints).

يَاأَيُّهَا الَّذِينَ آمَنُوا أَطِيعُوا اللَّهَ وَأَطِيعُوا الرَّسُولَ وَأُولِي الْأَمْرِ مِنْكُمْ...﴿٥٩﴾

4:59 – "*Ya ayyu hal latheena amanoo Atiullaha wa atiur Rasula wa Ulil amre minkum...*" (Surat An-Nisa)

"O You who have believed, Obey Allah, Obey the Messenger, and those in authority among you..." (The Women, 4:59)

Bayah (Allegiance) is Mandatory to Complete your 'Ahd (Covenant)

That's why Allah ﷻ describes in Surat At-Tawbah that they completed their *'ahd* (covenant) and fulfilled their *bayah* (allegiance).

إِنَّ اللَّهَ اشْتَرَىٰ مِنَ الْمُؤْمِنِينَ أَنفُسَهُمْ وَأَمْوَالَهُم بِأَنَّ لَهُمُ الْجَنَّةَ... وَعْدًا عَلَيْهِ حَقًّا فِي التَّوْرَاةِ وَالْإِنجِيلِ وَالْقُرْآنِ وَمَنْ أَوْفَىٰ بِعَهْدِهِ مِنَ اللَّهِ فَاسْتَبْشِرُوا بِبَيْعِكُمُ الَّذِي بَايَعْتُم بِهِ وَذَٰلِكَ هُوَ الْفَوْزُ الْعَظِيمُ ﴿١١١﴾

9:111 – "*Inna Allaha Ashtara Minal Mu'umineena 'Anfusahum Wa 'Amwalahum Bi anna Lahum AlJannata, ...Wa'dan 'Alayhi Haqqan fit Tawrati wal Injeeli wal Qur'ani, Wa Man Awfa Bi 'ahdihi Mina Allahi, Fastabshiro Bi bay'ikum Al Ladhi Baaya'tum Bihi, Wa Dhalika Huwal Fawzul 'azeem.*" (Surat At-Tawbah)

"Indeed, Allah has purchased from the believers their lives and their properties [in exchange] for that they will have Paradise...[It is] a true promise [binding] upon Him in the Torah and the Gospel and the Qur'an. And who is more faithful to his covenant than Allah? Then rejoice in your Bayah which you have contracted. And it is that which is the great achievement. (The Repentance, 9:111)

So, then *bayah* (allegiance) is mandatory to complete the *'ahd*, the covenant in which Allah (swt) gave us. That covenant cannot be reached without the *bayah* (allegiance) because the *bayah* (allegiance) is *'bi hablillah.'*

وَاعْتَصِمُوا بِحَبْلِ اللَّهِ جَمِيعًا وَلَا تَفَرَّقُوا ۚ ﴿١٠٣﴾

3:103 – *"Wa'tasimo bihab lillahi jamee'an wa la tafarraqo..."* (Surat Ali-Imran)

"And hold firmly to the rope of Allah all together and do not separate..." (Family of Imran, 3:103)

Take Bayah in the Hands of Awliya, Allah's (swt) Hand is Upon Their Hand

Allah (swt) is describing, 'hold tight to the rope of Allah (swt). Don't separate.'

وَاعْتَصِمُوا بِحَبْلِ اللَّهِ جَمِيعًا وَلَا تَفَرَّقُوا ۚ ... ﴿١٠٣﴾

3:103 – *"Wa'tasimo bihab lillahi jamee'an wa la tafarraqo..."* (Surat 'Ali 'Imran)

"And hold firmly to the rope of Allah all together and do not separate..." (Family of Imran, 3:103)

Fulfill Your Trust (Amanat), Covenant ('Ahd), and Your Allegiance (Bayah)

'Don't separate', not separate as in from people, because the only one who can bring people together is Sayyidina Muhammad ﷺ. From the minute Prophet ﷺ hid his physicality, the nation was split and fighting.

So, nobody is going to bring everybody together. This is not in reference to bringing people together and we all hold hands and sing 'kumbaya'. It means nobody is going to come together. This 'hold together' was with *awliyaullah* (saints). That keep your hand upon their hand.

إِنَّ الَّذِينَ يُبَايِعُونَكَ إِنَّمَا يُبَايِعُونَ اللَّـهَ يَدُ اللَّـهِ فَوْقَ أَيْدِيهِمْ ۚ فَمَن نَّكَثَ فَإِنَّمَا يَنكُثُ عَلَىٰ نَفْسِهِ ۖ وَمَنْ أَوْفَىٰ بِمَا عَاهَدَ عَلَيْهُ اللَّـهَ فَسَيُؤْتِيهِ أَجْرًا عَظِيمًا ﴿١٠﴾

48:10 – *"Innal ladheena yubayi'oonaka innama yubayi'on Allaha yadullahi fawqa aydeehim, faman nakatha fa innama yankuthu 'ala nafsihi, wa man awfa bima 'ahada 'alayhu Allaha fasayu teehi ajran 'azheema." (Surat Al-Fath)*

"Indeed, those who give Bayah (pledge allegiance) to you, [O Muhammad] – they are actually giving Bayah (pledge allegiance) to Allah. The hand of Allah is over their hands. So he whoever breaks his pledge/oath, only breaks it to the detriment/Harm/loss of himself. And whoever fulfills their Covenant (Bayah) that which he has promised Allah – He will grant him a great reward." (The Victory, 48:10)

Who fulfills their *bayah* (allegiance) has a supreme reward. So, it's not something small, but it is the purpose of our existence upon this earth. And of which they don't talk anymore. They talk about *bayah* (allegiance) being something that you know, you find Sufi people and take *bayah* (allegiance). But this was our whole reality. That we have to be holding the hand of *ulul amr* (saints) and the *ulul amr* (saints) who are *Ahlul Basirah* (people with spiritual vision), that their hearts are open and as a result, they see what people don't see.

...وَمَنْ أَوْفَىٰ بِعَهْدِهِ مِنَ اللَّهِ فَاسْتَبْشِرُوا بِبَيْعِكُمُ الَّذِي بَايَعْتُم بِهِ ۚ وَذَٰلِكَ هُوَ الْفَوْزُ الْعَظِيمُ ﴿١١١﴾

9:111 – *"...Wa Man Awfa Bi 'ahdihi Mina Allahi, Fastabshiro Bi bay'ikum Al Ladhi Baaya'tum Bihi, Wa Dhalika Huwal Fawzul 'azeem." (Surat At-Tawbah)*

"...And who is more faithful to his covenant than Allah? Then rejoice in your Bayah which you have contracted. And it is that which is the great achievement. (The Repentance, 9:111)

Four Corners of Ka'bah Represent Four Categories: Nabiyeen (Prophets), Siddiqeen (Truthful), Shuhada (Martyrs) and Saliheen (Righteous)

That's why the Ka'bah is a symbol from them. That if you want to be with Allah ﷻ, you have to be with *Nabiyeen* (Prophets) which is *Hajar al-Aswad* (black stone in Ka'bah); *Siddiqeen* (Truthful), the corner closest to Prophet ﷺ; *Shuhada* (Martyrs) because they see and those *Shuhada* (Martyrs), they produce *Saliheen* (Righteous). If not a *shuhada* (martyr), if not from one who sees in their association, they're never going to reach to be *saliheen* (righteous). It's just the formula which Allah ﷻ is creating that reality.

Ahlul Basira (People of Spiritual Vision) Attract Souls of People

So, by entering in and finding the groups of *saliheen* (righteous), they must have from amongst them *Ahlul Basirah* (people of spiritual vision) whom they have trained and their desires have dropped. As a result of the desires dropping, Allah ﷻ describes, 'We took the lock off their

Fulfill Your Trust (Amanat), Covenant ('Ahd), and Your Allegiance (Bayah)

---

ears. We took the lock off their eyes which is the *'ayn* of their heart, and we removed the *kiswah* and the veils that are blocking them.'

خَتَمَ اللَّـهُ عَلَىٰ قُلُوبِهِمْ وَعَلَىٰ سَمْعِهِمْ ۖ وَعَلَىٰ أَبْصَارِهِمْ غِشَاوَةٌ ۖ وَلَهُمْ عَذَابٌ عَظِيمٌ ﴿٧﴾

2:7 – "Khatama Allahu 'ala qulobihim, wa 'ala sam'ihim wa 'ala absarihim ghishawatun wa lahum 'adhabun 'azheem."
(Surat Al-Baqarah)

"Allah has set a seal upon their hearts and upon their hearing, and over their vision is a veil. And for them is a great punishment."
(The Cow, 2:7)

It means by keeping their company, their whole purpose is not the physical association, but by means of the physical, they're able to pull the souls of people. So, from *"malakut kulli shay"* (encompassing everything in heavens).

فَسُبْحَانَ الَّذِي بِيَدِهِ مَلَكُوتُ كُلِّ شَيْءٍ وَإِلَيْهِ تُرْجَعُونَ ﴿٨٣﴾

36:83 – *"Fasubhanal ladhee biyadihi Malakotu kulli shay in wa ilayhi turja'oon."* (Surat YaSeen)

"Therefore Glory be to Him in Whose hand is the [heavenly] dominion/kingdom of all things, and to Him you will be returned."
(YaSeen, 36:83)

It means that we come into a physical association and we seek out a physical association. But these *Ahlul Basirah* (people of spiritual vision), they are from the people of light. That immediately, their soul in the room and their soul is able to grab all the souls of everybody present. By grabbing them and taking them to what Allah ﷻ wants from the fulfilling of the contract.

Nabi Musa's ﷺ Ark of the Covenant Was Symbolic

In the time of Nabi Musa (Moses) ﷺ, that *'Ahd* (Covenant) was the Ark of the Covenant, because everything was an imitation for the arrival of Sayyidina Muhammad ﷺ. So, they had the Tablets and they put it in a Box and the four angels held the Box and everywhere they moved they were victorious. That was symbolic of the Divine Presence at the *maqam* (station) of Sayyidina Musa ﷺ.

Prophet Muhammad's ﷺ Heart is the Ark of Covenant

The greatness of Sayyidina Muhammad ﷺ is that he is the custodian of all realities. It means when he arrived upon Earth, the real Covenant, the real *'Ahd* of Allah ﷻ, opened upon the Earth. That is the heart of the believer. This is the Covenant that Prophet ﷺ brought. Allah ﷻ says, 'I am not in Heaven, I am not on Earth, I am not in that Box, I am not anywhere but I am in the heart of My Believer.'

مَا وَسِعَنِيْ سَمَائِيْ ولا اَرْضِيْ وَلَكِنْ وَسِعَنِي قَلْبِ عَبْدِيْ اَلْمُؤْمِنْ

"Maa wasi`anee Samayee, wa la ardee, laakin wasi'anee qalbi 'Abdee al Mu'min."

"Neither My Heavens nor My Earth can contain Me, but the heart of my Believing Servant."
(Hadith Qudsi conveyed by Prophet Muhammad (pbuh))

Allah's ﷻ only believer who arrived upon Earth is Sayyidina Muhammad ﷺ. The only believer which Allah ﷻ looks to is Sayyidina

Fulfill Your Trust (Amanat), Covenant ('Ahd), and Your Allegiance (Bayah)

Muhammad ﷺ. Sayyidina Muhammad ﷺ looks to all Creation. Allah's ﷻ *nazar* (gaze) is only upon Sayyidina Muhammad ﷺ.

It means then this heart and its *lataif* (subtle energy points) is the Covenant of Allah ﷻ for *Ummati Muhammad* ﷺ. They don't have to look for a Box; they don't need angels to carry a Box for them to be victorious in battle. Where now that is what they are looking for; they are going to try to tear apart *Masjid al-Aqsa* to get to the Covenant, to get to their Box. They believe with that Box they should be victorious. But with the arrival of Sayyidina Muhammad ﷺ that Box was negated. What is victorious is the heart of the believer!

The Archangels Guard the Heart and Levels of the Heart

That is why we study the Levels of the Heart and go into its teachings. These are the angels that are guarding the heart; Sayyidina Jibreel عليه السلام at the First Station – the Heart (*Qalb*), Sayyidina Mikhail عليه السلام at the Second Station – the Secret (*Sir*), Sayyidina Izrail عليه السلام at the Third Station – the Secret of the Secret (*Sirr e Sir*), Sayyidina Israfil عليه السلام at the Fourth Station – the Hidden (*Khafa*). Then Sayyidina Malik عليه السلام is at the Fifth Station – the Most Hidden (*Akhfa*). He is at the center and the guardian, the

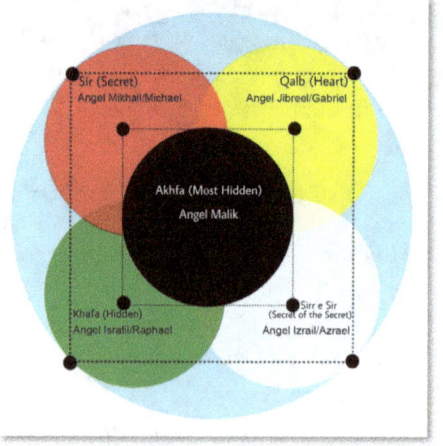

enforcer for all of the *lataif* and Levels of the Heart. For, if anything should open of this heart, the guardians of Hell, Sayyidina Malik عليه السلام should be guarding that servant. It means they use Sayyidina Malik عليه السلام

as a dragon that is upon them, as a guardian for their presence on Earth. Otherwise these realities that open upon Earth, the *shayateen* (devils) would have destroyed them.

The Heart Can Only Be Opened By Ibadur Rahman (Servants of Allah ﷻ, the Most Compassionate)

It means the Covenant, the *'Ahd* that they want for us to open is the reality of the heart; and how to focus upon the heart and how to open its realities. That can only be opened by those who are *Ahlul Basirah* (Pious People with Spiritual Vision). From among a select group of *Ahlul Basirah*, there are some from *Ibadur Rahman* (Servants of the Most Compassionate). Allah ﷻ mentions, *"Allamal Qur'an. Khalaqal insan"* (Taught the Qur'an, then created the Human Being).

الرَّحْمَٰنُ ﴿١﴾ عَلَّمَ الْقُرْآنَ ﴿٢﴾ خَلَقَ الْإِنسَانَ ﴿٣﴾

55:1-3 – "Ar Rahmaan. 'Allamal Qur'an. Khalaqal Insaan."
(Surat Ar-Rahman)

"The Most Merciful. (1) It is He Who has taught the Qur'an. (2) He has created mankind. (3)" (The Beneficent, 55:1-3)

It is a description for a reality that Allah ﷻ has been given to them, that they are the custodians of the reality of the Holy Qur'an within their

heart. We pray that Allah ﷻ keeps them amongst us. *Alhamdulillah* from *Ibadur Rahman* are Sultan al-Awliya Mawlana Shaykh AbdAllah Fa'iz ad-Daghestani ق and Sultan al-Awliya Mawlana Shaykh Muhammad Nazim Adil al-Haqqani ق. They are the custodians of that reality upon the Earth, it's far greater than any *tariqah* (spiritual path), and the names of *tariqahs*, which mean nothing anymore.

Be "Muhammadiyoon"
Sayyidina Mahdi ﷺ is Coming as Muhammadan Representative

The names of all *tariqahs* (spiritual paths) are going to vanish. All that matters is to be *"Muhammadiyoon"*. Sayyidina Mahdi's ﷺ arrival upon Earth is very close, very, very close. Many, many signs are moving very quickly upon Earth. Sayyidina  Mahdi ﷺ does not follow anyone's name and all names must follow Sayyidina Mahdi ﷺ. He is the Muhammadan representative and the Muhammadan Way. We pray that Allah ﷻ gives us life to see those days and prepares our hearts for the arrival of Sayyidina Mahdi ﷺ.

The Moon Focuses Only on the Sun

We pray for our focus to be on what is real and keep the company of those who are real. They *(awliyaullah)* are fragranced from the presence  of Sayyidina Muhammad ﷺ. They are fragranced from the lights of Sayyidina Muhammad ﷺ and their entire *nazar* (gaze) is upon Sayyidina Muhammad ﷺ.

Awliyaullah's (saints) whole *tafakkur*, contemplation, is to always be present in the presence of Sayyidina Muhammad ﷺ! If for a moment Prophet ﷺ should turn away from them, it would be better to be dead, that something must be wrong, and Prophet ﷺ must be upset.

It means then, it gives us an understanding that those types of souls only focus on the 'Sun'. If you were to talk to the Moon, the Moon doesn't talk about Saturn, and Jupiter; it only knows what Allah ﷻ wants it to

know. It means it focuses on the Sun; it focuses on the Muhammadan Reality. It focuses on the love of Sayyidina Muhammad ﷺ, on how to achieve the love of Sayyidina Muhammad ﷺ so that we can achieve Allah's ﷻ satisfaction. So to be dressed by that light, be blessed by that light and as a result of that dress and that blessings then you should be a reflection of that light because anything you focus on should be focusing on you.

It means if the focus is sincere, and the focus is towards Sayyidina Muhammad ﷺ then those beatific lights begin to dress the believer; the *Sunnah* of Prophet ﷺ begins to dress the believer and the eloquence of speech and softness of character begins to dress the believer.

Only *Tafakkur* (Contemplation) Opens the Heart

We pray that Allah ﷻ dresses us and blesses us from these holy lights

and allows us to reach that Covenant. And to take the steps necessary in which to open the heart and that is only through *tafakkur*, contemplation. Nothing in *had ad-dunya* (limit of the material world) is going to open those realities. This (opening) is from the *malakut* (heavens).

Fulfill Your Trust (Amanat), Covenant ('Ahd), and Your Allegiance (Bayah)

In days of difficulty the believers will go underground. The underground which is the reality of the Cave, is that they find no safety above on the surface of the world. The only safety they have is through their *tafakkur* (contemplation/meditation). By training on your *tafakkur*, contemplation, it becomes your life line. When you understand your life line and who is sending you support, you don't look left or right. Everything else is a distraction and many things can come into our life that will cut that life line.

It means by being from *Ahl at-Tafakkur* (People of Contemplation),

they are guarding that life line with all their being. It means they sit and contemplate, train on how to negate themselves, and by negating themselves they are asking for the *madad* (support). They are asking for the support of Mawlana, the most powerful *awliyaullah* (saint) on this Earth right now, where he carries the entire Earth beyond what we can imagine with our imagination.

The Sun, the Moon, and 11 Stars Made Sajdah (Prostration) to Sayyidina Yusuf ﷺ

We were saying with Surat Yusuf when Sayyidina Yusuf ﷺ was describing that, 'My brothers are 11 stars. I saw 11 stars bowing to me, the sun and moon bowing to me making a *sadjah* (prostration).'

إِذْ قَالَ يُوسُفُ لِأَبِيهِ يَا أَبَتِ إِنِّي رَأَيْتُ أَحَدَ عَشَرَ كَوْكَبًا وَالشَّمْسَ وَالْقَمَرَ رَأَيْتُهُمْ لِي سَاجِدِينَ ﴿٤﴾

12:4 – "Idh qala Yosufu li abeehi ya abati innee raaytu ahada Ashara kawkaban wash Shamsa wal Qamara raaytuhum le sajideen."
(Surat Yusuf)

"[Of these stories mention] when Joseph said to his father, "O my father, indeed I have seen eleven stars and the sun and the moon; I saw them prostrating to me." (Joseph, 12:4)

The *sajdatul ihtiram* (respectful prostration). But also it's a sign for us that Allah ﷻ placed under his feet the authority of that galaxy. And that was the ocean of beauty of Prophet ﷺ. All *awliyaullah* (saints) inheriting from that reality.

Awliyaullah (Saints) Have Authority Over the Sun, the Moon, and 11 Stars

When we call them *"Awliyaullah"* (saints) and we call them a *"Qutb"* and we call them *"al-Mutassarif"*, it means they inherit because Prophet ﷺ describes that, 'My *Ulama* are inheritors of the prophets of Bani Israel.'

عُلَمَاءِ وَرِثَةُ الْأَنْبِيَاءِ

"Ulama e warithatul anbiya."

"The scholars are the inheritors of the prophets."

Whatever their *maqams* (stations), the *maqams* (stations) that He (Allah ﷻ) gave from Sayyidina Muhammad ﷺ are as powerful. Under their feet are 11 stars. Under their feet is a moon. Under their feet is the sun. They control the movement of the sun. They control  the movement of the moon and they control the 11 planets and the 11 stars

Fulfill Your Trust (Amanat), Covenant ('Ahd), and Your Allegiance (Bayah)

So, it's not something small. They're not just sitting for ten people. What Allah (swt) gives of the *'ahd* and covenant, as we said before, that He wants to see how do you govern your 11 organs? Those stars are within us. How do you govern your *shams* (heart)? How do you govern your *qamar* (face)? If you're able to govern it the way Allah (swt) governs His galaxy, He begins to grant the *amanat* and the trust. If you don't light your heart and don't light the heart to be a *shams* (sun), you don't get the *amanat* (trust).

Ibadur Rahman Are Custodians of a Very Specific Light

You can light your heart only through *tafakkur* (contemplation). The heart doesn't light by the brain; the heart can only light from *Ibadur Rahman* where Allah (swt) says, 'Whom We granted a light, We granted a light, whom We didn't give light, they have no light.'

مَن يَهْدِ اللَّـهُ فَهُوَ الْمُهْتَدِ ۖ وَمَن يُضْلِلْ فَلَن تَجِدَ لَهُ وَلِيًّا مُّرْشِدًا ﴿١٧﴾

18:17 – "... *man yahdillahu fahuwal Muhtadi, wa man yudlil falan tajida lahu waliyyan murshida.*" (Surat Al-Kahf)

"...He whom Allah, guides is rightly guided; but he whom Allah leaves to stray, for him you will never find Saintly Guide to the Right Way." (The Cave, 18:17)

What He is talking from is the *Ibadur Rahman* (Servants of the Most Compassionate), that they are custodians of a very specific light. By keeping their company, and by keeping their practices, they are able to light the student through their *tafakkur*, and contemplation. They will be trained to carry the light, carry the light. If they (students) are able to keep themselves clean in that process then the permission comes from Prophet ﷺ and the heart will be lit. It means it will become the initial stage of a sun.

Allah ﷻ Does Not Take Back What He Gives

What Allah ﷻ gives, Allah ﷻ never takes away. But the process of receiving that grant from Allah ﷻ is extreme testing. There has to be a high level of testing, high level of sincerity, high level of integrity and good manners and good characteristics. Because whatever Allah ﷻ gives, He doesn't take away. If He's going to give somebody a gift like that, He's not expecting them to take it and to run.

Hence, all of the testing in *tariqah* (spiritual path). All the way of keeping their companionship. All of the testing that comes into their life is so that Allah ﷻ can see the character of that servant and sign off for that servant. Once that has been signed off upon them, that they are loyal and they are not going to take it and run. They're not going to take it and cheat. They're not going to take it and steal.

Fulfill Your Trust (Amanat), Covenant ('Ahd), and Your Allegiance (Bayah)

Awliya Transmit Light from Their Heart to Our Heart During Tafakkur (Contemplation)

Then begins the process of the transmission from their heart to the heart of that servant. A light begins to dress them, begins to dress them, begins to dress them. That's what we were reciting in the *salawats* (praisings on Prophet ﷺ). These are the *ahlul haal* (people of spiritual state of ecstasy).

حَالُ ٱلْعَارِفِيْنْ مُتَقَابِلِين   عَلَى سُرُرِ يَاسِيدِيْ، مُسْتَبْشِرِيْنَ

*Haalul 'Aarifeen, Mutaqabeleen
'Aala Sururi Ya Sayyidi Mustabshirina*

"In Gardens of Heaven",
the Gnostics "Facing each other upon Thrones of honour"
(Qur'an, 37:43-44)

Their *haal* (state) is strong enough, that comes out means you're feeling the movement of their soul. Their soul comes out and begins to dress everybody in the room to be dressed from those lights. As much as they can keep those lights and more *tafakkur* (contemplation), more *tafakkur*, more *tafakkur*.

It means then we begin to understand the power source. We begin to see them with our eyes closed as we see each other in physicality. And from their entire being, they begin to dress lights upon us.

Awliya Dress Us From Their Holy Face and the 7 Holy Attributes

Then these *awliya* dress us from their holy face. Where Allah ﷻ describes, 'Everything perishes but the holy face.'

وَلَا تَدْعُ مَعَ اللَّهِ إِلَهًا آخَرَ لَا إِلَهَ إِلَّا هُوَ كُلُّ شَيْءٍ هَالِكٌ إِلَّا وَجْهَهُ لَهُ الْحُكْمُ وَإِلَيْهِ تُرْجَعُونَ ﴿٨٨﴾

28:88 – *"Wala tad'uo ma'Allahi ilahan aakhara la ilaha illa huwa kullu shayin halikun illa wajha hu la hul hukmu wa ilayhi turja'oon."* (*Surat Al-Qasas*)

"...Everything (that exists) will perish except His holy Face. To Him belongs the Command, and to Him you will be returned." (*The Stories, 28:88*)

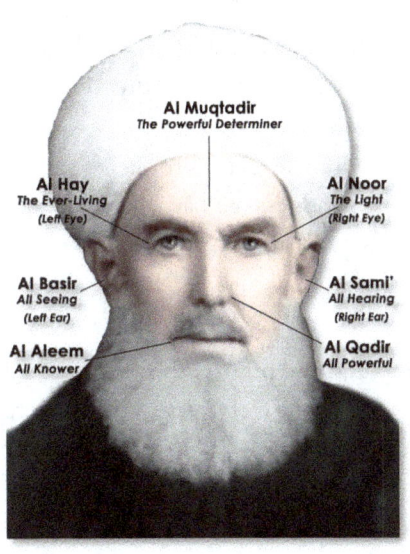

This means that all of the practicing, practicing, practicing until they begin to dress the servant. Once they being to dress the servant, then they begin to dress them from the eyes. All of the essences, the 7 essences of Allah ﷻ, will begin to dress them. And dress their 7 holy openings that are taking from the holy face of that *awliya* (saint). And that *awliya* taking from that *awliya* above them all the way from the presence of Sayyidina Muhammad ﷺ: *Al-Qadir* (All Powerful), *Al-Muqtadir* (The Powerful Determiner), *Al-Sami* (All Hearing), *Al-Basir* (All Seeing), *Al-Aleem* (All Knower), *Al-Noor* (the Light), *Al-Hayy* (the Ever-Living).

It means 7 essences that are dressing upon their face and taking from the holy face of the *awliya* (saint) in front of them. That *wali* (saint) when they look to that *wali*, they believe it to be Sayyidina Muhammad ﷺ. But their structure is a pyramid and nobody sees the face of Sayyidina Muhammad ﷺ in its complete reality except the *Ghawth* (highest station of a saint).

Fulfill Your Trust (Amanat), Covenant ('Ahd), and Your Allegiance (Bayah)

The image you see of Sayyidina Muhammad ﷺ is the *wali* (saint) of that area, in his Muhammadan dress. You begin to have many visions and sights of Prophet ﷺ, that is their Muhammadan dress because this pyramid, nobody can jump. So, what you see is from your level, you see only the *wali* (saint) above you to his feet. From that *wali* (saint) sees the *wali* (saint)  above them. So, from this pyramid all the way up to the *Ghawth* (highest station of a saint). And the *Ghawth* sees Prophet ﷺ and dressed from the holy 7 attributes that are dressing the face of Prophet ﷺ. Like a sunshine, every time they look upon the face of Prophet ﷺ, it's a sunshine that dissolves and destroys all badness, all bad characteristics and dresses the soul with all of it's lights and all of its blessings.

The Sign of Last Days Are Already Here

We pray that Allah ﷻ bless us on this Eid and prepare us for the arrival of Sayyidina Mahdi عليه السلام whose time is coming very, very quick where oppression is filling the earth and day by day *hadith* (traditions of Prophet ﷺ) are coming. We witnessed the *hadith* of Umran, the 5 years old boy, who Prophet ﷺ described and Prophet ﷺ saw the boy. And that boy, when the world saw it, brought it to attention. 'That little children, of age 5 to 7, their hair will turn grey from the difficulty of what they see.

فَكَيْفَ تَتَّقُونَ إِن كَفَرْتُمْ يَوْمًا يَجْعَلُ الْوِلْدَانَ شِيبًا ﴿١٧﴾

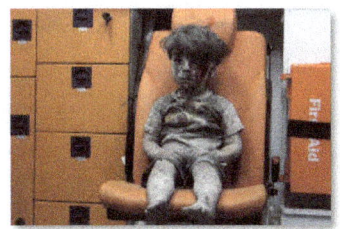

73:17 – "Fakaifa tattaqoona in kafartum yawmany yaj'alul wildaana sheeba." (Surat Al-Muzzammil)

"Then how can you fear, if you disbelieve, a Day that will make the children white-haired?" (The Enshrouded One, 73:17)

And for us, an understanding and a very basic understanding that these children are being buried alive. And they're coming out with the dust of this *azab* (hardship) upon them. Prophet ﷺ was describing that these events that are taking place means day by day the hadith are coming in. They're coming in like headlines that you see on the news for the whole world to see it and the whole world can't deny it.

We pray that Allah ﷻ prepare our hearts for these events and to keep us under the flag of Sayyidina Mahdi ﷺ, the 7 *Wazirs* (Ministers) of Sayyidina Mahdi ﷺ, the *Khulafa* (Viceroy) of Sayyidina Mahdi ﷺ, the *Nawab* (Governor) of Sayyidina Mahdi ﷺ.

Subhana rabbika rabbal 'izzati 'amma yasifoon, wa salaamun 'alal mursaleen, walhamdulillahi rabbil 'aalameen. Bi hurmati Muhammad al-Mustafa wa bi siri Surat al-Fatiha.

Empty Your Cup, "I Wish I Was a Thing Forgotten" (Holy Qur'an, 19:23)

يَاأَيُّهَا الَّذِينَ آمَنُوا أَطِيعُوا اللهَ وَأَطِيعُوا الرَّسُولَ وَأُولِي الْأَمْرِ مِنْكُمْ... ﴿٥٩﴾

4:59 – *"Ya ayyu hal ladheena amanoo Atiullaha wa atiur Rasula wa Ulil amre minkum…" (Surat An-Nisa)*

"O You who have believed, Obey Allah, Obey the Messenger, and those in authority among you…" (The Women, 4:59)

Admit That You Are *Zalim* (Oppressor) to Yourself

In their way of *haqqaiq* (realities) the guides open from the realities of Holy Qur'an. But they can't open until the student is in a state of *taslim* (submission), where you admit to yourself that you are *zalim* (oppressor). *La ilaha illa anta subhaanaka inni kuntu min az Zhalimeen* (Glory be to Allah ﷻ and for sure I am an oppressor to myself, Holy Qur'an, 21:87)

If you are *zalim*, and you believe you are *zalim* (oppressor), then we don't count anything. You pray but you don't think that it's counting. You are not proud, the *zalim* shouldn't be proud of his prayer because that was the door. If Sayyidina Yunus (Jonah) ﷺ is repeating that (prayer), that he had to go with anger. When you read the *ayat* (verse) of the Qur'an, it describes that he left angry.

Empty Your Cup, "I Wish I Was a Thing Forgotten"
(Holy Qur'an, 19:23)

وَذَا النُّونِ إِذ ذَهَبَ مُغَاضِبًا فَظَنَّ أَن لَّن نَّقْدِرَ عَلَيْهِ فَنَادَىٰ فِي الظُّلُمَاتِ أَن لَّا إِلَٰهَ إِلَّا أَنتَ سُبْحَانَكَ إِنِّي كُنتُ مِنَ الظَّالِمِينَ ﴿٨٧﴾

21:87 – *"Wa dhan Nooni idh dhahaba mughadiban fazhanna al lan naqdira 'alayhi fanada fizh zhulumati an la ilaha illa anta Subhanaka, innee kuntu minazh zhalimeen." (Surat Al-Anbiya)*

"And [mention] Zun-nun [Yunus (Jonah) (as)], when he went off in anger and thought that We had no power/decree over him! But he cried out through the depths of darkness, "There is no god/diety except You; Glory to you: Indeed I have been of the wrongdoers/Oppressor to Myself!" (The Prophets, 21:87)

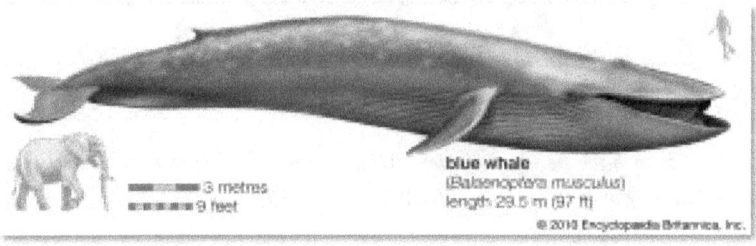

It means anyone with *ghadab* (anger) is a *zalim* (oppressor). And Allah ﷻ had to have him (Yunus ﷺ) swallowed by a whale. So Allah ﷻ is not happy with anger. Anyone who shows anger at any moment enters a state of *kufr*, or disbelief. That is what they talk about, *thumma amano thumma kafaro* (believe, then disbelieve, then believe). You can't say you are a big believer if you are getting angry; you are a *kafir* (disbeliever), in a nice and polite sense. So we are not *mukhlis* (sincere) where they don't get angry.

Don't Be Proud Performing 5 Pillars of Islam

So you admit to Allah ﷻ, '*Ya Rabbi*, I am a *zalim*, I am getting angry, I have all sorts of bad character. I know You are not counting my *salat* (daily prayer), I am coming through the Door of Your *Maghfirah* (forgiveness), *ya Rabbi*.' I am imitating what Prophet ﷺ asked me to imitate, I am praying through imitation.

If you devalue it leave it for Allah (AJ) to value it. If you value it, leave it to Allah (AJ) to devalue it. Hey, that's a nice quote. Right? Isn't it more polite to go to Allah (AJ) and say, 'Ya Rabbi, it's nothing? You asked me and all my *amal* (actions), my *Shahada* (testimony) is a lie.'

Are you witnessing anything when we say, "*Ashadu an la ilaha illAllah wa ashadu ana Muhammadan `abduhu wa habeebuhu wa rasuluhu?*"

أَشْهَدُ أَنْ لَا إِلَهَ إِلاَّ الله وَأَشْهَدُ أَنَّ مُحَمَّدًا عَبْدُهُ وَرَسُولُهُ

"*Ashhadu an la ilaha illa-lah, wa ashhadu anna Muhammadan rasulu hu.*"

"I bear witness that there is no god but Allah, and I bear witness that Muhammad is the messenger of Allah."

Did you witness anything? It means it is a lie and so you are a liar too! You are praying *salat* (daily prayer), but you are praying and thinking of all the different things, all the *waswas* (whispering) and anger. This one and that one, this beautiful person, this ugly person, this person did this, this person did that, that *salat* is not for Allah (AJ).

Empty Your Cup, "I Wish I Was a Thing Forgotten"
(Holy Qur'an, 19:23)

With the *zakat* (charity), 'Oh, I don't want to give, maybe it will come back, maybe it won't come back. I am never going to have it again, it is going to lower my account; it is not going to increase my account.' The *zakat* didn't count.

Hajj (pilgrimage), 'Oh, it's too far; it is going to be too long.' *Hajj* didn't count. *Siyam* (Fasting)? 'Oh, it was just thirty days of complaints. Oh, how long is this day? *Ya Latif*, when is it going to be *iftar* (time of breaking fast)? Why is it so long? Why is it so hard?' So fasting was all thirty days of complaints.

Be True With Allah ﷻ, Admit Your Nothingness

Then they come and teach, 'Be true with Allah ﷻ; you can't lie with Allah ﷻ, you can't make a facade with Allah ﷻ. Be truthful with Allah ﷻ, *ana 'abduka ajiz, wa daeef wa miskeen wa zalim wa jahl* (I am a servant that is weak, poor, oppressor, and ignorant). If not by Your *Rahmah* (Mercy), *ya Rabbi*, nothing is going to happen for me. My prayer doesn't count, my fasting didn't count, my *Shahada* (testimony) was a lie, my *zakat* (charity) is with trembling hands, my *Hajj* (pilgrimage) is too far; everything, *ya Rabbi*, is nothing, nothing, nothing.

They want the student to admit his nothingness. As soon as he becomes nothing, his cup becomes empty. Every spiritual way, every prophetic way, every reality was to be nothing, be nothing, be nothing in the face of your Lord, Most High.

"My Lord, I Wish I Was Nothing"

If you are truly entering a state of nothingness then Sayyidatina Maryam's ﷻ prayer, *"Nasiyam mansiyya."*

...قَالَتْ يَا لَيْتَنِي مِتُّ قَبْلَ هَذَا وَكُنتُ نَسْيًا مَّنسِيًّا...

19:23 – *"... qalat ya laytanee mittu qabla hadha wa kuntu nasyam mansiyya."* (Surat Maryam)

".... She cried (in her anguish): "Oh, I wish I had died before this! and I was a thing forgotten and out of sight!" (Maryam, 19:23)

'O my Lord, I wish I was nothing, something completely forgotten because even my name and what is going to come from my name, is going to make a *fitna* (confusion) on this Earth.' When she realized that they would call Sayyidina Isa (Jesus) ﷻ 'God', she was trembling. 'How am I going to be in the Heaven and people are going to be calling my son, the Creator? *Astagfirullah al 'Azeem*. With this destiny, I wish I was nothing, *ya Rabbi*, I wish I was non-existent, whatever the *hikmah* (wisdom) is I am still wishing to be nothing, nothing, nothing.'

If You Are an Oppressor, How Could You See Problems in Others?

So it means everything came to us, to be nothing. So *awliyaullah* (saints) come into our lives and remind, 'If you are truly accepting to be nothing, then we will come and show you.' If you are nothing, then don't see any problem in how people pray because you said you were a *zalim* (oppressor). Can a *zalim* talk about how other people pray? You have to worry about your *zulumat*. How other people pray, how other people

Empty Your Cup, "I Wish I Was a Thing Forgotten"
(Holy Qur'an, 19:23)

---

look, their appearance. You are a *zalim*, you have to hope Allah ﷻ doesn't punish you in *jahannam* (hellfire).

So why do you worry about other people? Worry only about yourself. If you worry only about yourself, you will be set in life because you will truly be humble. *Ya Rabbi*, grant me Your *Maghfirah* (Forgiveness), *ya Rabbi*, grant me Your *Maghfirah*, I am nothing, I am nothing. Only at that time you begin to negate everything that you don't look to anything. You don't look to your left or your right, I negate myself, I negate myself; I know nothing because I am only concerned about the one who is going in the grave and that is my grave. Every grave has one person. I am only interested in this person and what is going to happen in my grave.

Take the Hand of Ulul Amr, They Help You Complete Your Covenant – Bayah (Allegiance)

Then, at that level, the student is ready. When the student is ready and has negated himself, because the self is the one who is going to be fighting with the Shaykh. From *ati ullah*, to obey Allah ﷻ, *ati ar Rasul*, to obey Prophet ﷺ and the third order, *wa ulil amri minkum*, to obey those in authority.

يَاأَيُّهَا الَّذِينَ آمَنُوا أَطِيعُوا اللَّهَ وَأَطِيعُوا الرَّسُولَ وَأُولِي الْأَمْرِ مِنْكُمْ... ﴿٥٩﴾

4:59 – "*Ya ayyu hal ladheena amanoo Atiullaha wa atiur Rasula wa Ulil amre minkum...*" (Surat An-Nisa)

"O You who have believed, Obey Allah, Obey the Messenger, and those in authority among you..." (The Women, 4:59)

How are you going to obey *ulul amr* (saints) when you are obeying yourself? That is why you have to negate. When you negate yourself, I am nothing, I am nothing, I am nothing, then you put your hand into their hand and say, 'You take care of me. I am nothing and I agreed that I was nothing.' So be in the hands of the *ulul amr*. They take your hand and say, 'Come, we are going to start to train you on how to complete your covenant with Allah ﷻ.'

إِنَّ الَّذِينَ يُبَايِعُونَكَ إِنَّمَا يُبَايِعُونَ اللَّـهَ يَدُ اللَّـهِ فَوْقَ أَيْدِيهِمْ ۚ فَمَن نَّكَثَ فَإِنَّمَا يَنكُثُ عَلَىٰ نَفْسِهِ ۖ وَمَنْ أَوْفَىٰ بِمَا عَاهَدَ عَلَيْهُ اللَّـهَ فَسَيُؤْتِيهِ أَجْرًا عَظِيمًا ﴿١٠﴾

48:10 – "Innal ladheena yubayi'oonaka innama yubayi'on Allaha yadullahi fawqa aydeehim, faman nakatha fa innama yankuthu 'ala nafsihi, wa man awfa bima 'ahada 'alayhu Allaha fasayu teehi ajran 'azheema." (Surat Al-Fath)

"Indeed, those who give Bayah (pledge allegiance) to you, [O Muhammad] – they are actually giving Bayah (pledge allegiance) to Allah. The hand of Allah is over their hands. So he whoever breaks his pledge/oath, only breaks it to the detriment/Harm/loss of himself. And whoever fulfills their Covenant (Bayah) that which he has promised Allah – He will grant him a great reward." (The Victory, 48:10)

You took your *bayah* (covenant) that you would have your allegiance to Allah ﷻ, through the hand of Sayyidina Muhammad ﷺ, brought to you by the *ulul amr* (saints). *Awliyaullah* are the walking hands and feet of Prophet ﷺ on this *dunya (world)*. They are the Muhammadan guides and the Muhammadan representatives.

Empty Your Cup, "I Wish I Was a Thing Forgotten"
(Holy Qur'an, 19:23)

Keep the Company of the *Sadiqeen* (Truthful Servants of Allah ﷻ)

They begin to teach then that the Holy Qur'an has all of those realities, but you have to be nothing to begin to see it. *Ittaqulla wa konu ma'as Sadiqeen.*

يَا أَيُّهَا الَّذِينَ آمَنُوا اتَّقُوا اللَّـهَ وَكُونُوا مَعَ الصَّادِقِينَ ﴿١١٩﴾

9:119 – "*Ya ayyuhal ladheena amanoo ittaqollaha wa kono ma'as sadiqeen.*" (Surat At-Tawbah)

"*O you who have believed, be conscious of Allah and be with those who are truthful/sincere (in words and deed).*" (The Repentance, 9:119)

'Have a consciousness and accompany the *sadiqeen* (truthful).' It means then in the world of light which is their world, they are the people from

the world of light and they don't care for the material world. So their guidance and their realities of Holy Qur'an are from the *Malakut*, the Heavenly Realm which is the superior realm. This is the false and the perishing graveyard of *insan* (mankind). This *dunya* (material world) is the graveyard; the Heavens is where the reality is.

"*Wa koonu ma'as Sadiqeen, ittaqulla*" means they have such a level of consciousness, then accompany Allah's ﷻ truthful servants. So it means then you will be taught how to accompany them physically, and more importantly how to accompany them spiritually. They have a physical body which you accompany; you see and you eat and you drink and you pray with them, but they have a spiritual body which is more superior.

They have a spiritual body that you should be feeling; you should be connecting with that spiritual body. Then Allah's ﷻ Words are true, no time, no limit and Allah ﷻ does not care for *dunya* (material world). So what does Allah ﷻ mean when He ﷻ says, 'Be conscious of Me and keep the company of the *siddiqeen* (truthful) and the *sadiq*'? It means at every moment you should be training that, '*Ya Rabbi*, wherever I am, let me be in the company of those who are truthful.' If they are truthful these are the servants who are with Allah ﷻ, *Nabiyeen, Siddiqeen, Shuhada wa Saliheen*, Prophets, Truthful, Martyrs, and Righteous.

وَمَن يُطِعِ اللَّهَ وَالرَّسُولَ فَأُولَٰئِكَ مَعَ الَّذِينَ أَنْعَمَ اللَّهُ عَلَيْهِم مِّنَ النَّبِيِّينَ وَالصِّدِّيقِينَ وَالشُّهَدَاءِ وَالصَّالِحِينَ ۚ وَحَسُنَ أُولَٰئِكَ رَفِيقًا ﴿٦٩﴾

4:69 – "*Wa man yuti' Allaha war Rasula faolayeka ma'al ladheena an'ama Allahu 'alayhim minan Nabiyeena, was Siddiqeena, wash Shuhadai, was Saliheena wa hasuna olayeka rafeeqan.*"
(*Surat An-Nisa*)

"*And whoever obeys Allah and the messenger, then those are with the ones on whom Allah bestowed his softness amongst the prophets, the highly Righteous [Truthful], the Witnesses to the truth, and the Righteous. And excellent are those as companions.*" (*The Women, 4:69*)

Allah ﷻ says, 'They are with Me and those are the best of company.' I will dispatch from those who are with Me to be with you. They are *al hayyu al-qayyum* (ever-Living and self-sustaining), their souls are alive in their graves and their light is everywhere. They watch over you and you watch over them. Keep their company means you will be trained. '*Ya Rabbi*, they must be with me at all times, I want to feel their presence,' but you have to be nothing. Otherwise your ego is saying, 'No it is the boss, it knows that you don't want to be with them.'

Accompany Awliya (Saints) With Your Soul and Body

Allah ﷻ says, 'Hold tight to the rope of Allah ﷻ.'

وَاعْتَصِمُوا بِحَبْلِ اللَّهِ جَمِيعًا وَلَا تَفَرَّقُوا ﴿١٠٣﴾

Empty Your Cup, "I Wish I Was a Thing Forgotten"
(Holy Qur'an, 19:23)

3:103 – "Wa'tasimo bihab lillahi jamee'an wa la tafarraqo."
(Surat 'Ali 'Imran)

"And hold firmly to the rope of Allah all together and do not separate."
(Family of Imran, 3:103)

It means in every instant Allah ﷻ is giving that you have to be with these people from the spiritual world. The physical world is the best. If your physical world is eating with pious people, praying with pious people, drinking with pious people, *Alhamdulillah*, it is a good sign that you are probably in a good place in Paradise. But if you are with the worst of people in *dunya* (material world) and you are expecting to be with the best of people in *akhirah* (hereafter) that is not going to happen! This *dunya* is just a sign for us.

So, *Alhamdulillah*, we all eat and drink and we are following our beloved Sultan al Awliya Mawlana Shaykh Muhammad Nazim al-Haqqani ق, under the flag of Mawlana Shaykh 'AbdAllah Fa'iz ad-Daghestani ق. All *Sultan al Awliyas*, the cream of the creams, the chairmen of the board. What better company than that? But I don't want to follow them only by my body, my body is not important, I want to be with them with my soul. Allah ﷻ says, hold tight to their rope.

Souls of Pious People Are Everywhere, Connect With Them

It means then you begin to train that if you truly believe that you are nothing and every time you say, '*Ya Rabbi*, I am nothing, I am nothing, let me to be with them.' Allah ﷻ then begins to train, Prophet ﷺ begins to train, that every sense you have has a sense and a reality from your soul. It means your ears have a physical ear, but you also have a spiritual ear. So, you begin to train yourself when you close your room and make your *itikaaf* (seclusion) every day. You close your room and close everything off and spend a few minutes contemplating, making *tafakkur* (contemplation) that, 'I am nothing, let me to be with them.'

Madad ya Sayyidi, madad ya Sayyidi, what Allah ﷻ gave you of your power, your soul is *al hayy al qayyum* (ever-living and self-sustaining), it is not limited to your body. Your soul has its power everywhere. And Allah ﷻ said to be with you, to be with the *Nabiyeen* (Prophets) to be with the *Siddiqeen* (Truthful) to be with the *Shuhada wa Saliheen* (Martyrs, and Righteous). I want to be with Prophet ﷺ. I want to be with the *Saliheen*, who are *Ahlul Bayt* (Family of Prophet ﷺ) and *Ashab an-Nabi* ﷺ. I want to be with the *Shuhada*, those who martyred their desires and their hearts are open. *Ya Rabbi*, I want to be with them now when I make *salah* (daily prayer).

We Give Salaam to Ibadullahi Saliheen in Our Salah

These are Allah's ﷻ Words, this is not *shirk* (polytheism). Worship is only for Allah ﷻ. You make your *tafakkur* (contemplation) that they are there, I am saying it in my *salah* (daily prayer), I am saying *asalaamu 'alayka ayyu hanNabi* (Peace be upon you, O Prophet ﷺ), and I am not seeing Prophet ﷺ.

اَلسَّلَامُ عَلَيْكَ أَيُّهَا النَّبِيُّ وَرَحْمَةُ اللهِ و بَرَكَاتُهُ. اَلسَّلَامُ عَلَيْنَا وَعَلَي عِبَادِ اللهِ الصَّالِحِينْ.

Empty Your Cup, "I Wish I Was a Thing Forgotten"
(Holy Qur'an, 19:23)

"Assalamu alayka ayyu hanNabi wa rahmatullahi wa barakatuhu. AsSalamu alayna wa ala Ibadullahis Saliheen."

"Peace be upon You O' Prophet (Muhammad (pbuh), His Mercy and His blessings too. Peace be on us and on all righteous servants of Allah."

I have to train myself that Prophet ﷺ must be there, *ibadallah saliheen* (Righteous Servants) must be all around me. But let me start with the easiest rope because the rope that is reaching to me is my *Saliheen* and my beloved guides.

Do *Muraqabah* – Connect With Your Shaykh Spiritually

'Madad ya Sayyidi, ya Mawlana Shaykh, unzur halana wa ishafalana Sayyidi (O my master, support me, gaze upon me and intercede for me).

I know that you are with them and that you are watching over me, I want to feel your presence. I want to feel your light and your energy that you are always with me, *Sayyidi*. I am not worthy of seeing you, but I know your light is with me.'

You build a relationship with the Shaykh, just like it is physical. It's no difference for you if you are from the *malakut* (heavens); the spiritual realm is more important than the physical realm. As we are seeing the Shaykh is praying, as you are sitting down to pray, then spiritually he must be present right there in front of you. You are saying it; you are giving *salaam* (greetings) to Prophet ﷺ and *ibadillahis-saliheen* (Righteous Servants) in every prayer. These are Allah's ﷻ *Saliheen*.

So you are training yourself, '*Madad ya Sayyidi, ya* Mawlana Shaykh, let your light be with me. That from your *fa'iz* (downpouring blessings), from your light dress me, and bless me from what Allah ﷻ has given to you. What Allah ﷻ has dressed upon you, dress it upon me.' You train yourself and visualize yourself in their presence. Stay in a state of quietness and calmness and then begin to make a *hisaab* (accounting).

Then their *fa'iz* and their light begins to dress you. They begin to teach that every time you begin to do something bad you lose the *fa'iz*. Their light is coming to dress you from Prophet ﷺ. Every time you do something bad that light goes and the connection will be lost. Every time you keep yourself to be good and that becomes your *muhasabah* (taking an account of yourself).

People don't know that if you do your *muhasabah* without connecting to these lights. Without understanding the presence of these lights it's not going to open anything to you. You are not going to open anything from yourself. You are not going to be able to pull from your reality and break through all of these problems, but you need the *awliyaullah* (saints) to be present with you to begin to sign off on what you are doing.

Empty Your Cup, "I Wish I Was a Thing Forgotten"
(Holy Qur'an, 19:23)

People don't know that if you do your *muhasabah* without connecting to these lights. Without understanding the presence of these lights it's not going to open anything to you. You are not going to open anything from yourself. You are not going to be able to pull from your reality and break through all of these problems, but you need the *awliyaullah*  (saints) to be present with you to begin to sign off on what you are doing.

The Saliheen and Shaykhs Are Watching You

Allah ﷻ says in the *salah* (daily prayer), *ibadillahis-saliheen*. These *Saliheen* must be there, they are watching but there is a *hijab* that is veiling you from their presence. Of course, they accompany you everywhere you go. The angels accompany you, the *jinn* (unseen beings) are accompanying you. Why? The *Saliheen's* light has a difficult time  and doesn't find a bus to get there? Their light is everywhere! People don't think. They think they need to find a bus to find where you are. No, their light is accompanying you. Allah ﷻ is saying that in every *salah* you make, you are giving *salaam* (greetings) to them. Allah ﷻ is teaching you the best, *ya Nabi salaam 'alayka…*

يَا رَسُولْ سَلَامْ عَلَيْكَ   يَا نَبِيْ سَلَامْ عَلَيْكَ
صَلَوَاتُ الله عَلَيْكَ   يَا حَبِيبْ سَلَامْ عَلَيْكَ

Ya Nabi Salaam 'Alayka   Ya Rasul Salam 'Alayka
Ya Habib salam 'Alayka   Salawatullah 'Alayka

O' Prophet, peace be upon you, O' Messenger, peace be upon you
O' my beloved, peace be upon you, Praises of Allah be upon you

Allah ﷻ is teaching you the best of manners so give them *salaams*, they are always with you. Give *salaams* to your beloved Prophet ﷺ, he is your *imam*. Your *salah* is not even coming to Me without mentioning Sayyidina Muhammad ﷺ. And who is with Prophet ﷺ? The *Saliheen*, all *awliyaullah*, all the lovers of Sayyidina Muhammad ﷺ are accompanying Prophet ﷺ.

Every Night Do Muraqabah, Connect With Saliheen and Siddiqeen

They are there; they must be training on how to connect with the world of light. They say, 'Yes, sit, close your eyes and spend a few minutes every night when the system is off,' and Allah ﷻ says, 'We made the day as busy, business time for you but the night is quiet and peaceful.' In *Salat at-Tahajjud* Allah ﷻ describes then in *Surat Al-Isra* that there is the gate of the *Siddiq's*, 'Ya Rabbi, let me to enter from the gates of the *Siddiq's* and to exit from the gate of the *Siddiq's* and *Sultanun Naseerah*.'

وَقُل رَّبِّ أَدْخِلْنِي مُدْخَلَ صِدْقٍ وَأَخْرِجْنِي مُخْرَجَ صِدْقٍ وَاجْعَل لِّي مِن لَّدُنكَ سُلْطَانًا نَّصِيرًا ﴿٨٠﴾

17:80 – *"Wa qul Rabbi adkhelni mudkhala Sidqin wa akhrejni mukhraja Sidqin waj'al li min ladunka Sultanan NaSeera."*
(*Surat Al-Isra*)

Empty Your Cup, "I Wish I Was a Thing Forgotten" (Holy Qur'an, 19:23)

Say: "O my Lord! Let my entry be by the Gate of Truth and Honour, and likewise my exit by the Gate of Truth and Honour; and grant me from Your Presence a King to aid (me)." (The Night Journey, 17:80)

So there is a *baab* (door), there is an opening. In which at night you are meditating and contemplating, '*Ya Rabbi*, let me to be in the presence of these great *Siddiq's*. Let my soul to be in their presence, let their *fa'iz* (blessings) and their lights be dressed upon me.' And you are visualizing their presence and asking from your soul to feel them.

Then you begin to realize and they say, 'If you want to feel us then correct yourself because *haq* (truth) and falsehood can't be together.'

وَ قُلْ جَاءَالْحَقُّ وَزَهَقَ الْبَطِلُ، إِنَّ الْبَطِلَ كَانَ زَهُوقًا ﴿٨١﴾

17:81 – "Wa qul jaa alhaqqu wa zahaqal baatil, innal batila kana zahoqa." (Surat Al-Isra)

"And say, "Truth has come, and falsehood has perished. Indeed falsehood, [by its nature], is ever perishing/ bound to perish." (The Night Journey, 17:81)

You don't do crazy things and think that I am going to feel the Shaykh. No, they put an iron door and say, 'Forget it for you!' No, you do good things, good *amal* (deeds), completely listen to what they are teaching, have good actions, so that this *pardah* (veil) can be moved away. So it is all about good characteristics. Those good characteristics are going to begin to open all their *fa'iz*, their lights.

Every Night Make a Muhasabah, Take An Account of Yourself

Then they say, 'When you are doing the *muraqabah* (contemplation), do *muhasabah* (accounting).' As soon as you are sitting and contemplating late at night, put a little bit of *salawat* (prophetic praisings), so that you feel the love of Prophet ﷺ. And with the *salawat* playing they are taking away the *waswas* (whispering) that are coming into the ear, 'Oh, you have to go check your email, you have to do this, and you have to do that.'

No, knock all of that off. You are listening to *salawat* and you are sitting and contemplating that Mawlana Shaykh must be in front of me, he must be watching me, his light is all around from the *ibadillahis-saliheen*.

Who am I to connect with Prophet ﷺ? Let me first be humble and I said I was nothing, I was a *zalim* (oppressor). *InshaAllah*, this Shaykh accepts me in my *zulumat* (oppression) and that he washes me and cleanses me. As soon as you begin to connect with them, they inspire from the teaching, 'Now make a *hisaab*, an accounting, of yourself. What did you do that night? What did you do that day? What did you do throughout the day? Correct your actions.'

Our Bad Actions Create a Veil That Block Us From Our Shaykh

If the actions are incorrect, this wall is going to be solid steel. If the actions are correct and the training is correct, this wall begins to melt; the wall that separates us from them begins to melt, and every night we begin to take a *hisaab* (accounting).

Empty Your Cup, "I Wish I Was a Thing Forgotten"
(Holy Qur'an, 19:23)

Every night we connect our heart and say, '*Sayyidi*, dress me from your *fa'iz*, dress me from your light. I am not doing anything right, I know Allah ﷻ is going to be angry with me.'

Again, they inspire within us, 'Take your *hisaab*, take your *hisaab*, what are you doing wrong within that day? Did you harm anybody with your speech? Did you break anybody's heart with your actions? Those are what count for Allah ﷻ.'

And the guides continue to inspire, inspire, inspire so this *pardah* (veil) goes, this *pardah* goes, this *pardah* goes. And as the actions become correct, the *amal* (action) becomes correct, then you begin to feel their *fa'iz*. Their energy is very powerful and you begin to feel that energy. The vigilance they are talking about is that, you vigilantly meditate that dress me from your light, dress me from your light.

Empty what is in your head, empty everything about your understanding. The active mind is blocking the heart, because the mind is filled with *waswas*, (whispering of Satan), it is filled with *shak*, doubt. It has doubt in every action they do, in every understanding and every reality. That doubt will not let anything to enter in.

That is why the Prophet ﷺ said, 'Take your head off if you are coming to the Divinely Presence.' It means the *zikr* is *la ilaha illAllah*, *La* to the head; don't use your head to think, 'How is this going to be possible?' How will you reach to the Heavens with this head? It has to be through the heart.

You Must Connect to the Living Shaykh (Guide)

It has to be the living guide who has the authority and is holding to an electrical line. Because if you are not connected to the living guide it is very difficult to connect to the ones who have passed. That is not how the system works. Allah (swt) wants us to be connected to the living guide so that we have safety on Earth. That the *fa'iz* reaches us in our existence on this *dunya*. It means then we seek out the living guides.

We take a way of being nothing and begin to train every night on how to be nothing, how to be nothing, how to take that *hisaab* (accounting). And how to be dressed from their lights, blessed from their lights. As the action becomes better and better and we begin to ask, '*Ya Sayyidi*, dress me from your light, bless me from your light.' You begin to feel their light dressing. You begin to feel their energies dressing. Then they begin to teach that, you be nothing, you said you are nothing.

I am saying I am nothing, I am nothing, let me be a dot in your *jubbah* (robe), like a piece of dust. That is why when you read these *du'as* (supplications) that let me just be dust under the feet of Prophet ﷺ, then just let me be dust in your *jubbah*. I am not asking, I don't want my existence, I don't want to be around, I want to be nothing, to be nothing.

That *muhabbat*, that love, brings us to the *turooq* (spiritual paths). The Shaykh is the symbol of the Prophet ﷺ coming, this love is bringing us.

Empty Your Cup, "I Wish I Was a Thing Forgotten"
(Holy Qur'an, 19:23)

They are teaching and training that whatever you know, even you think you know, you know nothing. You empty out. You know nothing and you become empty. Through the *muraqabah* (meditation) and the practices and meditation and contemplation you are slowly trying to connect and get closer.

It is like a jet trying to connect with another jet in mid-air. You are constantly balancing, until your good character is correct. Then the love is coming, and then there is a connection. Because you have negated, you loved, you obeyed, and you gave all the teachings the way they wanted it to be taught. They said, 'Relieve yourself of the bad characteristics.' As soon as there is connection it means your love and their soul is connected.

If that soul reaches out and connects with the student through their good character, not proximity to them but through their good character, there is a bond; this light bonds. Through that bond they can bring that student to be closer and closer and closer into the reality.

As soon as the student becomes closer in the reality they are being dressed by that light, blessed by that light and that is what they call the *fana* (annihilation). It means with *muhabbat*, you came with love, you kept the *hudur*, the presence; the *hudur* is physical and spiritual. You have to keep their spiritual presence.

Be Vigilant – Whatever You Do, Shaykh is Right There

'They are with me wherever I am. If I am on the bus talking bad to people, my Shaykh is sitting right there,' If I am talking to people I should not be conversing with, my Shaykh is right there. I am cheating people; my Shaykh is right there. Whatever I am doing, I am believing that my Shaykh is right there, that light is right there. Allah سُبْحَانَهُ وَتَعَالَى sees, the angels see, the *jinn* (unseen beings) see. You don't think the light of Prophet ﷺ is seeing? They are seeing!

So then you are constantly keeping your vigil. You are vigilant that they are with me; I have to govern myself accordingly. As much as I govern myself accordingly, their light stays. If I do crazy things, their light goes, their light goes.

If You Do Wrong Things, Prophet's ﷺ Light Leaves You

The Shaykh's light is *haq* (truth). *Haq* and falsehood don't go together. If you capture a few minutes of light and go out and do false and bad things, their light leaves. It can't be together. You can't take a Muhammadan Light and go out and do crazy things. So you govern yourself.

Your whole character begins to change because at night they begin to teach in the meditation, 'No, no you can't do that. Prophet's ﷺ light is not going to stay with that.' As soon as you lose your temper that light is gone. How then are you going to capture it? You have to start all over again.

That is why it is the good character. If these people are able to keep the love of Prophet ﷺ, it is through their good character, through their love, through their humbleness, that light stays. That light stays and it begins to bless them and begins to nourish them and begins to change everything. That is what the real *taqwa* (consciousness) is.

If somebody doesn't have that light, they have no understanding of *taqwa*. They don't care, they are like being behind steel walls; it could be another seven inches of steel for all they care. But if you are feeling that light, feeling their presence, feeling their love, are you going to go do something crazy and risk all of that? No.

Empty Your Cup, "I Wish I Was a Thing Forgotten"
(Holy Qur'an, 19:23)

So then the guides have a very humble character. They have a lot of *khushiya* in their heart. They are fearful that Allah (swt) and Prophet ﷺ are going to be upset with them; *awliyaullah* will be upset with them and lose all the *fa'iz*, lose all the emanations that are coming to them. So it builds beatific characteristics. As a result, whatever comes to them they stay quiet, they have the best of character and more is being dressed upon them.

Gift From Allah (swt) – The Light of Awliya That Is From Nur Muhammad ﷺ

The light that they are sending is the light of Sayyidina Muhammad ﷺ because it is all from *Tawhid, la ilaha illAllah Muhammadun RasulAllah* ﷺ (There is no God but Allah and Muhammad ﷺ is the Messenger of Allah).

So *awliyaullah* (saints) are not a light separate for themselves. Some people say, 'No, no I follow this *wali* (saint), not this *wali*." They are all *Muhammadan Wali*, they are all Muhammadan lights, their *darajat* (level) of strengths is what is important. There are some small suns and there are some very big powerful suns.

And we need the one that is alive now that is constantly dressing, constantly blessing, because the *fa'iz* (downpouring blessings) is coming to him, Prophet's ﷺ support is coming to him. It comes to the living saints of this *dunya* (worldly life), of this *zaman* (time). Those living saints carry the authority of Prophet ﷺ on Earth.

It is Allah's (swt) Gift to Have a Saintly Guide (Waliyan Murshida)

When you connect with them and keep them into your life, it is like sunshine where you have your own sun. Allah (swt) gives you your very own sun; wherever you go this sun is shining. Who has no sun has no sun at all, no *waliyan murshida*, (Allah ﷻ says),

$$...\text{ذَٰلِكَ مِنْ آيَاتِ اللَّهِ ۗ مَن يَهْدِ اللَّهُ فَهُوَ الْمُهْتَدِ ۖ وَمَن يُضْلِلْ فَلَن تَجِدَ لَهُ وَلِيًّا مُّرْشِدًا ﴿١٧﴾}$$

18:17 – "... *Dhalika min ayati Allahi, man yahdillahu fahuwal Muhtadi, wa man yudlil falan tajida lahu waliyyan murshida.*"
(*Surat Al-Kahf*)

"...*That was from the Signs of Allah: He whom Allah, guides is rightly guided; but he whom Allah leaves to stray, for him you will never find Saintly Guide to the Right Way.*" (The Cave, 18:17)

Whom We didn't give a guide, they have no *wali murshid*, the guide who is a saint of Allah ﷻ. Whom Allah ﷻ gives is then a huge *ni'mat* (blessing).

That *wali*, the light he is sending out is the light of Prophet ﷺ. It increases your love of Sayyidina Muhammad ﷺ, it increases your consciousness of Sayyidina Muhammad ﷺ, it increases every knowledge within the heart of the love of Sayyidina Muhammad ﷺ. Why? Because he is *feekum*, he is amongst you and spreading your heart, spreading your soul, filling your soul with all the love of Prophet ﷺ. So then they become *ashiqeen*, they become the lovers of Sayyidina Muhammad ﷺ.

$$\text{كَمَا أَرْسَلْنَا فِيكُمْ رَسُولًا مِّنكُمْ يَتْلُو عَلَيْكُمْ آيَاتِنَا وَيُزَكِّيكُمْ وَيُعَلِّمُكُمُ الْكِتَابَ وَالْحِكْمَةَ وَيُعَلِّمُكُم مَّا لَمْ تَكُونُوا تَعْلَمُونَ ﴿١٥١﴾}$$

Empty Your Cup, "I Wish I Was a Thing Forgotten"
(Holy Qur'an, 19:23)

2:151 – *"'Kama arsalna feekum Rasulam minkum yatlo 'Alaykum ayatina wa yuzakkeekum wa yu'Allimukumul kitaaba walhikmata wa yu'Allimukum ma lam takono ta'Alamon." (Surat Al-Baqarah)*

"Just as We have sent among (within) you a messenger from your own, reciting to you Our Signs, and purifying you, and teaching you the Scripture/Book and Wisdom and teaching you New Knowledge, that which you did not know." (The Cow, 2:151)

We pray that Allah ﷻ grants us more and more understanding on how to truly use this body He gave us. How to keep it in its surrender and how to dress the soul with its reality. Those who think they can do it by themselves they have a very difficult path ahead of them. Those who acknowledge they are nothing and they have been defeated by their own *Shaytan* (Satan), as soon as they tap out and surrender, *Shaytan* got me in a headrest and I can't get out of it, then the *waliyan murshida* will appear; the *awliya* (saint) will appear in their lives to rescue them

Ask For Awliya's (Saint's) Support, You Can't Win This Battle With Shaytan (Satan)

Allah's ﷻ love for *Bani Adam* (Children of Adam) and this Creation in this *Nur Muhammadi* ﷺ just requires us to surrender. You know nothing and *Shaytan* (Satan) gets you in a big headlock, then Allah ﷻ sends that one who can defend us. They begin to come and teach that, 'If you think you are going to fight it, *Shaytan* is going to defeat you in an instant.'

But if you want their support, then take the way of training on how to bring their light, how to bring their *fa'iz*, how to bring their emanations upon our life. And that will change us, our families, and our whole community will be under their dress.

Now in days of difficulty it is needed more than ever. If anyone thinks they have the ability to protect themselves from what is coming upon the Earth, God help them, Allah (AJ) help them. Those who agreed they are helpless and said, *ya Rabbi*, we need *rijalAllah* (Men of God). We need to be amongst the *rijalAllah* whom, *ya Rabbi*, You have blessed and You supported. And those whom Your hand and Prophet's ﷺ hand is upon, we need that hand, *ya Rabbi*, and that we are nothing.

Subhana rabbika rabbal 'izzati 'amma yasifoon, wa salaamun 'alal mursaleen, walhamdulillahi rabbil 'aalameen. Bi hurmati Muhammad al-Mustafa wa bi siri Surat al-Fatiha.

LEVELS OF THE HEART
LATAIF AL QALB

SECRET REALITIES OF HAJJ

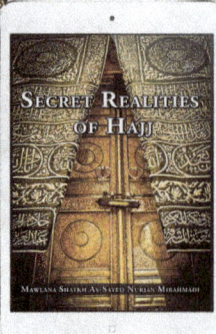

ABOUT THE BOOK

There are subtle energies and realities that are dressing the heart – these are the Levels of the Heart (Lataif al qalb). Shaykh Nurjan has composed an exceptional work on the map of the heart, intertwining the teachings of its spiritual attributes and how they affect every aspect of a seeker's path.

Filled with invaluable treasures, this unique masterpiece invites readers from all faiths to step forward and begin the process of unveiling the true spiritual realities within their own hearts.

ABOUT THE BOOK

Secret Realities of Hajj features invaluable teachings and spiritual insight into the Islamic holy pilgrimage of Hajj. From the historical references of holy prophets to the remarkable scientific explanations of the circumambulation, this book provides a deeper understanding of this important pillar of faith. The beautiful illustrations aid in explaining the concepts, allowing the reader to fully comprehend its profound realities.

FIVE-STAR REVIEWS
By Amazon Reviewers ★★★★★

"I've learned more about Islam in 6 months than in 20 years reading Shaykh Nurjan's books, reading the articles on his app and watching his YouTube channel videos. His teachings transcend the worldly divisions we've created and helps unveil our deeper spiritual and universal realities within."

"To finally have all this information in one book is simply incredible. It is an ocean of spiritual knowledge."

FIVE-STAR REVIEWS
By Amazon Reviewer ★★★★★

"Amazing! A rare jewel filled with illuminating knowledge. Highly recommended for non-Muslims and Muslims equally, as the secrets referred to are, in reality, secrets related to creation itself, and the inner reality of the human heart."

"A must-read for anyone about to make Hajj or has already gone. A must-read for people interested in the spirtitual dimensions and secrets of the Hajj. The author has intimate knowledge of the topic from a long lineage of Sufi Masters. Pick up and enjoy, I did."

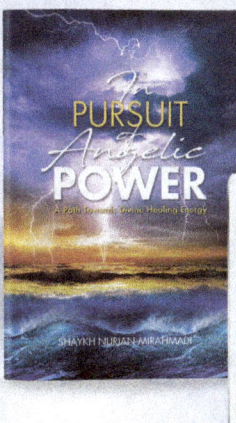

ABOUT THE BOOK

As heavenly beings, our souls are eternally in pursuit of healing energy through Divine and Angelic Power. By understanding the origins of energy through light and sound, the seeker learns to attune to the guides of heavenly knowledge and discovers essential techniques to acquire and increase positive energy within our beings.

This book examines transformational practices such as chanting, meditation, breathing, and becoming conscious of everyday habits that can elevate one's circle of protection.

FIVE-STAR REVIEWS
By Amazon Reviewers
★★★★★

"This invigorating book broadens and promotes a knowledge of the affinity and interactions between Angels and Humans."

"This incredible book is a must have for the spiritual seeker of any background, as it clearly and practically guides the reader through the process of attuning to the subtle angelic realm/quantum field. Unique & one of a kind - you will see the results!"

The Healing Power of Sufi Meditation

ABOUT THE BOOK

For those who have reached a level of understanding of the illusory nature of the world around us and seek to discern the reality that lies behind it, Sufi meditation (muraqabah) is the doorway through which we can pass from this realm of delusion into the realm of realities. Through meditation the seeker has a means to return to his or her perfected original self. Muraqabah is the fastest and most direct method for advancing in spiritual degrees. Through meditation higher states of consciousness are attained, and the connection to the seeker's true inner self is established, built-up and maintained, providing the practitioner with a lifeline to the Divine Presence.

FIVE-STAR REVIEWS
By Amazon Reviewers
★★★★★

This is a one-of-a-kind book by an actual authorized teacher of Sufi meditation. Not only it details the methods of meditation, but it also gives the practical advice regarding everything a seeker needs in order to pursue such a journey, first of which is to have a guide!"

"The book is rare gem in English language, providing the much needed instructions of Sufi meditation in a clear way. It contains some extra-ordinary illustrations, which is a huge plus for a beginner. It is for the serious minded. But every honest seeker will find some treasure in it that he/she will be able to carry throughout life. Buy a copy today and begin your journey!"

DIVINELY PRAISING UPON THE PEARL OF CREATION
HUB-E-RASUL

YASEEN
PROPHET ﷺ IS THE WALKING QURAN

Download the **FREE APP!**
MUHAMMADAN WAY

ABOUT THE BOOK

"Divinely Praising Upon the Pearl of Creation" is a distinguished collection of supplications and praisings upon the Prophet Muhammad (pbuh). By sending salutations the reciter builds a tremendous light and energy within their heart and soul while increasing love and gratitude for all Prophets and the Divine. Salawats carry an immense power and provide healing and relief from ailments and difficulties.

This compilation of invocations comes from authentic Arabic and Urdu sources which have been recited for centuries.

ABOUT THE BOOK

Prophet Muhammad ﷺ has been granted the highest of stations by Allah ﷻ (the Divine) and nowhere is it clearer than in the heart of the Holy Qur'an, Surat YaSeen. It is through Prophet Muhammad's ﷺ light that all of creation came into existence and it is through his heart that the Holy Qur'an was revealed. As the chief of all Prophets, he is the literal Walking Qur'an, conveying the sublime realities of Allah's ﷻ Holy Speech to all. The virtues of Surat YaSeen are masterfully explained including the importance of seeking guidance from those who truly love the Prophet ﷺ, as it is through remembrance and contemplation that the seeker expands their ocean of faith.

FIVE-STAR REVIEWS
By Amazon Reviewers ⭐⭐⭐⭐⭐

"A beautiful compilation of Praisings on the master of Prophets. Transliteration provides an easy way to recite for anyone. Translation gives the reader glimpse of beauty and depth of these poems and praisings. A MUST Have."

"A blessed and amazing treasury of praisings! Truly appreciate having this book available on the **Muhammadan Way** app - so easy to use from anywhere!"

FIVE-STAR REVIEWS
By Amazon Reviewer ⭐⭐⭐⭐⭐

"This is yet another amazing book from Shaykh Nurjan. His knowledge is without limit and his delivery is digestible to the well versed and the initiate. Illustrations are beautiful and fill this book from the first page to the last."

"From the very first line you can feel that every single word is its own ocean of realities. Truth and nothing else. This book moves you inside out. Forces you to contemplate and meditate. My favorite book hands down!"

"Author's heavenly knowledge touches the heart and feeds the soul. If knowledge is power, then can you imagine what heavenly knowledge is? Empower your soul and buy this book."

Available at **amazon** — Order Your Copy Today!

www.ingramcontent.com/pod-product-compliance
Lightning Source LLC
Chambersburg PA
CBHW071946070526
44583CB00015B/1091